T0355823

LLMs in Production

LLMs in Production

From language models to successful products

Christopher Brousseau
Matthew Sharp
Foreword by Joe Reis

Manning
Shelter Island

For online information and ordering of this and other Manning books, please visit www.manning.com. The publisher offers discounts on this book when ordered in quantity. For more information, please contact

Special Sales Department
Manning Publications Co.
20 Baldwin Road
PO Box 761
Shelter Island, NY 11964
Email: orders@manning.com

Manning Publications Co.
20 Baldwin Road
PO Box 761
Shelter Island, NY 11964

Development editor: Doug Rudder
Technical editor: Daniel Leybzon
Review editor: Dunja Nikitović
Production editor: Aleksandar Dragosavljević
Copy editor: Alisa Larson
Proofreader: Melody Dolab
Technical proofreader: Byron Galbraith
Typesetter: Dennis Dalinnik
Cover designer: Marija Tudor

ISBN: 9781633437203
Printed in the United States of America

To my wife Jess and my kids, Odin, Magnus, and Emrys, who have supported me through thick and thin

—Christopher Brousseau

I dedicate this book to Evelyn, my wife, and our daughter, Georgina. Evelyn, thank you for your unwavering support and encouragement through every step of this journey. Your sacrifices have been paramount to making this happen. And to my daughter, you are an endless source of inspiration and motivation. Your smile brightens my day and helps remind me to enjoy the small moments in this world. I hope and believe this book will help build a better tomorrow for both of you.

—Matthew Sharp

brief contents

contents

foreword

Unless you've been hiding in a cave, you know that LLMs are everywhere. They're becoming a staple for many people. If you're reading this book, there's a good chance you've integrated LLMs into your workflow. But you might be wondering how to deploy LLMs in production.

This is precisely why *LLMs in Production* is a timely and invaluable book. Drawing from their extensive experience and deep expertise in machine learning and linguistics, the authors offer a comprehensive guide to navigating the complexities of bringing LLMs into production environments. They don't just explore the technical aspects of implementation; they delve into the strategic considerations, ethical implications, and best practices crucial for responsible and effective production deployments of LLMs.

LLMs in Production has it all. Starting with an overview of what LLMs are, the book dives deep into language modeling, MLOps for LLMs, prompt engineering, and every relevant topic in between. You'll come away with a bottoms-up approach to working with LLMs from first principles. This book will stand the test of time, at least as long as possible, in this fast-changing landscape.

You should approach this book with an open mind and a critical eye. The future of LLMs is not predetermined—it will be shaped by the decisions we make and the care with which we implement these powerful tools in production. Let this book guide you as you navigate the exciting, challenging world of LLMs in production.

—Joe Reis, Author of *Fundamentals of Data Engineering*

preface

In January of 2023, I was sitting next to a couple, and they started to discuss the latest phenomenon, ChatGPT. The husband enthusiastically discussed how excited he was about the technology. He had been spending quality time with his teenagers writing a book using it—they had already written 70 pages. The wife, however, wasn't as thrilled, more scared. She was an English teacher and was worried about how it was going to affect her students.

It was around this time the husband said something I was completely unready for: his friend had fired 100 writers at his company. My jaw dropped. His friend owned a small website where he hired freelance writers to write sarcastic, funny, and fake articles. After being shown the tool, the friend took some of his article titles and asked ChatGPT to write one. What it came up with was indistinguishable from anything else on the website! Meaningless articles that lack the necessity for veracity are LLM's bread and butter, so it made sense. It could take him minutes to write hundreds of articles, and it was all free!

We have both experienced this same conversation—with minor changes—a hundred times over since. From groups of college students to close-knit community members, everyone is talking about AI all the time. Very few people have experienced it firsthand, outside of querying a paid API. For years, we've seen how it's been affecting the translation industry. Bespoke translation is difficult to get clients for, and the rise of PEMT (Post-Edit of Machine Translation) workflows has allowed translators to charge less and do more work faster, all with a similar level of quality. We're gunning for LLMs to do the same for many other professions.

When ChatGPT first came out, it was essentially still in beta release for research purposes, and OpenAI hadn't even announced plus subscriptions yet. In our time in the industry, we have seen plenty of machine learning models put up behind an API with the release of a white paper. This helps researchers build clout so they can show off a working demo. However, these demos are just that—never built to scale and usually taken down after a month for cost reasons. OpenAI had done just that on several occasions already.

Having already seen the likes of BERT, ELMO, T5, GPT-2, and a host of other language models come and go without any fanfare outside the NLP community, it was clear that GPT-3 was different. LLMs aren't just popular; they are technically very difficult. There are so many challenges and pitfalls that one can run into when trying to deploy one, and we've seen many make those mistakes. So when the opportunity came up to write this book, we were all in. *LLMs in Production* is the book we always wished we had.

acknowledgments

Before writing this book, we always fantasized about escaping up to the mountains and writing in the seclusion of some cabin in the forest. While that strategy might work for some authors, there's no way we would have been able to create what we believe to be a fantastic book without the help of so many people. This book had many eyes on it throughout its entire process, and the feedback we've received has been fundamental to its creation.

First, we'd like to thank our editors and reviewers, Jonathan Gennick, Al Krinker, Doug Rudder, Sebastian Raschka, and Danny Leybzon. Danny is a data and machine learning expert and worked as a technical editor on this book. He has helped Fortune 500 enterprises and innovative tech startups alike design and implement their data and machine learning strategies. He now does research in reinforcement learning at Universitat Pompeu Fabra in Spain. We thank all of you for your direct commentary and honest criticism. Words can't describe the depth of our gratitude.

We are also thankful for so many in the community who encouraged us to write this book. There are many who have supported us as mentors, colleagues, and friends. For their encouragement, support, and often promotion of the book, we'd like to thank in no particular order: Joe Reis, Mary MacCarthy, Lauren Balik, Demetrios Brinkman, Joselito Balleta, Mkolaj Pawlikowski, Abi Aryan, Bryan Verduzco, Fokke Dekker, Monica Kay Royal, Mariah Peterson, Eric Riddoch, Dakota Quibell, Daniel Smith, Isaac Tai, Alex King, Emma Grimes, Shane Smit, Dusty Chadwick, Sonam Choudhary, Isaac Vidas, Olivier Labrèche, Alexandre Gariépy, Amélie Rolland, Alicia Bargar, Vivian Tao, Colin Campbell, Connor Clark, Marc-Antoine Bélanger, Abhin

Chhabra, Sylvain Benner, Jordan Mitchell, Benjamin Wilson, Manny Ko, Ben Taylor, Matt Harrison, Jon Bradshaw, Andrew Carr, Brett Ragozzine, Yogesh Sakpal, Gauri Bhatnagar, Sachin Pandey, Vinícius Landeira, Nick Baguely, Cameron Bell, Cody Maughan, Sebastian Quintero, and Will McGinnis. This isn't a comprehensive list, and we are sure we are forgetting someone. If that's you, thank you. Please reach out, and we'll be sure to correct it.

Next, we are so thankful for the entire Manning team, including Aira Dučić, Robin Campbell, Melissa Ice, Ana Romac, Azra Dedic, Ozren Harlović, Dunja Nikitović, Sam Wood, Susan Honeywell, Erik Pillar, Alisa Larson, Melody Dolab, and others.

To all the reviewers, Abdullah Al Imran, Allan Makura, Ananda Roy, Arunkumar Gopalan, Bill Morefield, Blanca Vargas, Bruno Sonnino, Dan Sheikh, Dinesh Chitlangia, George Geevarghese, Gregory Varghese, Harcharan S. Kabbay, Jaganadh Gopinadhan, Janardhan Shetty, Jeremy Bryan, John Williams, Jose San Leandro, Kyle Pollard, Manas Talukdar, Manish Jain, Mehmet Yilmaz, Michael Wang, Nupur Baghel, Ondrej Krajicek, Paul Silisteanu, Peter Henstock, Radhika Kanubaddhi, Reka Anna Horvath, Satej Kumar Sahu, Sergio Govoni, Simon Tschoeke, Simone De Bonis, Simone Sguazza, Siri Varma Vegiraju, Sriram Macharla, Sudhir Maharaj, Sumaira Afzal, Sumit Pal, Supriya Arun, Vinod Sangare, Xiangbo Mao, Yilun Zhang, your suggestions helped make this a better book.

Lastly, we'd also like to give a special thanks to Elmer Saflor for giving us permission to use the Yellow Balloon meme and George Lucas, Hayden Christensen, and Temuera Morrison for being a welcome topic of distraction during many late nights working on the book. "We want to work on *Star Wars* stuff."

about the book

LLMs in Production is not your typical Data Science book. In fact, you won't find many books like this at all in the data space mainly because creating a successful data product often requires a large team—data scientists to build models, data engineers to build pipelines, MLOps engineers to build platforms, software engineers to build applications, product managers to go to endless meetings, and, of course, for each of these, managers to take the credit for it all despite their only contribution being to ask questions, oftentimes the same questions repeated, just trying to understand what's going on.

There are so many books geared toward each of these individuals, but there are so very few that tie the entire process together from end to end. While this book focuses on LLMs—indeed, it can be considered an LLMOps book—what you will take away will be so much more than how to push a large model onto a server. You will gain a roadmap that will show you how to create successful ML products—LLMs or otherwise—that delight end users.

Who should read this book

Anyone who finds themselves working on an application that uses LLMs will benefit from this book. This includes all of the previously listed individuals. The individuals who will benefit the most, though, will likely be those who have cross-functional roles with titles like ML engineer. This book is hands-on, and we expect our readers to know Python and, in particular, PyTorch.

How this book is organized

There are 12 chapters in this book, 3 of which are project chapters:

- Chapter 1 presents some of the promising applications of LLMs and discusses the build-versus-buy dichotomy. This book's focus is showing you how to build, so we want to help you determine whether building is the right decision for you.
- Chapter 2 lays the necessary groundwork. We discuss the basics of linguistics and define some terms you'll need to understand to get the most out of this book. We then build your knowledge of natural language modeling techniques. By the end of this chapter, you should both understand how LLMs work and what they are good or bad at. You should then be able to determine whether LLMs are the right technology for your project.
- Chapter 3 addresses the elephant in the room by explaining why LLMs are so difficult to work with. We'll then discuss some necessary concepts and solutions you'll need to master just to start working with LLMs. Then we'll discuss the necessary tooling and infrastructure requirements you'll want to acquire and why.
- Chapter 4 starts our preparations by discussing the necessary assets you'll need to acquire, from data to foundation models.
- Chapter 5 then shows you how to train an LLM from scratch as well as a myriad of methods to finetune your model, going over the pros and cons of each method.
- Chapter 6 then dives into serving LLMs and what you'll need to know to create an API. It discusses setting up a VPC for LLMs as well as common production challenges and how to overcome them.
- Chapter 7 discusses prompt engineering and how to get the most out of an LLM's responses.
- Chapter 8 examines building an application around an LLM and features you'll want to consider adding to improve the user experience.
- Chapter 9 is the first of our project chapters, where you will build a simple LLama 3 model and deploy it.
- Chapter 10 builds a coding copilot that you can use directly in VSCode.
- Chapter 11 is a project where we will deploy an LLM to a Raspberry Pi.
- Chapter 12 ends the book with our thoughts on the future of LLMs as a technology, including discussions of promising fields of research.

In general, this book was designed to be read cover to cover, each chapter building upon the last. To us, the chapters are ordered to mock an ideal situation and thus outline the knowledge you'll need and the steps you would go through when building an LLM product under the best circumstances. That said, this is a production book, and production is where reality lives. Don't worry; we understand the real world is messy. Each chapter is self-contained, and readers are free and encouraged to jump around depending on their interests and levels of understanding.

About the code

This book contains many examples of source code, both in numbered listings and in line with normal text. In both cases, source code is formatted in a `fixed-width font like this` to separate it from ordinary text. Sometimes code is also **`in bold`** to highlight code that has changed from previous steps in the chapter, such as when a new feature is added to an existing line of code.

In many cases, the original source code has been reformatted; we've added line breaks and reworked indentation to accommodate the available page space in the book. In rare cases, even this was not enough, and listings include line-continuation markers (➥). Additionally, comments in the source code have often been removed from the listings when the code is described in the text. Code annotations accompany many of the listings, highlighting important concepts.

You can get executable snippets of code from the liveBook (online) version of this book at https://livebook.manning.com/book/llms-in-production. The complete code for the examples in the book is available for download from the Manning website at https://www.manning.com/books/llms-in-production, and from GitHub at https://github.com/IMJONEZZ/LLMs-in-Production.

liveBook Discussion Forum

Purchase of *LLMs in Production* includes free access to liveBook, Manning's online reading platform. Using liveBook's exclusive discussion features, you can attach comments to the book globally or to specific sections or paragraphs. It's a snap to make notes for yourself, ask and answer technical questions, and receive help from the authors and other users. To access the forum, go to https://livebook.manning.com/book/llms-in-production/discussion. You can also learn more about Manning's forums and the rules of conduct at https://livebook.manning.com/discussion.

Manning's commitment to our readers is to provide a venue where a meaningful dialogue between individual readers and between readers and the authors can take place. It is not a commitment to any specific amount of participation on the part of the authors, whose contribution to the forum remains voluntary (and unpaid). We suggest you try asking the authors some challenging questions lest their interest stray! The forum and the archives of previous discussions will be accessible from the publisher's website as long as the book is in print.

about the authors

CHRISTOPHER BROUSSEAU is a staff MLE at JPMorganChase with a linguistics and localization background. He specializes in linguistically informed NLP, especially with an international focus, and has led successful ML and data product initiatives at both startups and Fortune 500s.

MATT SHARP is an engineer, former data scientist, and seasoned technology leader in MLOps. He has led many successful data initiatives for startups and top-tier tech companies alike. Matt specializes in deploying, managing, and scaling machine learning models in production, regardless of what that production setting looks like.

about the cover illustration

The illustration on the cover of *LLMs in Production* is an engraving by Nicolas de Lermessin (1640–1725) titled "Habit d'imprimeur en lettres," or "The Printer's Costume." The engraving is from the series *Les Costumes Grotesques et les Metiers,* published by Jacques Chiquet in the early 18th century.

In those days, it was easy to identify where people lived and what their trade or station in life was just by their dress. Manning celebrates the inventiveness and initiative of the computer business with book covers based on the rich diversity of regional culture centuries ago, brought back to life by pictures from collections such as this one.

1 Words' awakening: Why large language models have captured attention

This chapter covers

- What large language models are and what they can and cannot do
- When you should and should not deploy your own large language models
- Large language model myths and the truths that lie behind them

Any sufficiently advanced technology is indistinguishable from magic.

—Arthur C. Clarke

The year is 1450. A sleepy corner of Mainz, Germany, unknowingly stands on the precipice of a monumental era. In Humbrechthof, a nondescript workshop shrouded in the town's shadows pulsates with anticipation. It is here that Johannes Gutenberg, a goldsmith and innovator, sweats and labors amidst the scents of oil, metal, and determination, silently birthing a revolution. In the late hours of the night, the peace is broken intermittently by the rhythmic hammering of metal on metal. In the lamp-lit heart of the workshop stands Gutenberg's decade-long labor of love—a contraption unparalleled in design and purpose.

This is no ordinary invention. Craftsmanship and creativity transform an assortment of moveable metal types, individually cast characters born painstakingly into a matrix. The flickering light dances off the metallic insignias. The air pulsates with the anticipation of a breakthrough and the heady sweetness of oil-based ink, an innovation from Gutenberg himself. In the stillness of the moment, the master printer squares his shoulders and, with unparalleled finesse, lays down a crisp sheet of parchment beneath the ink-loaded matrix, allowing his invention to press firmly and stamp fine print onto the page. The room adjusts to the symphony of silence, bated breaths hanging heavily in the air. As the press is lifted, it creaks under its own weight, each screech akin to a war cry announcing an exciting new world.

With a flurry of motion, Gutenberg pulls from the press the first printed page and slams it flat onto the wooden table. He carefully examines each character, all of which are as bold and magnificent as the creator's vision. The room drinks in the sight, absolutely spellbound. A mere sheet of parchment has become a testament to transformation. As the night gives way to day, he looks upon his workshop with invigorated pride. His legacy is born, echoing in the annals of history and forever changing the way information would take wings. Johannes Gutenberg, now the man of the millennium, emerges from the shadows, an inventor who dared to dream. His name is synonymous with the printing press, which is not just a groundbreaking invention but the catalyst of the modern world.

As news of Gutenberg's achievement begins to flutter across the continent, scholars from vast disciplines are yet to appreciate the extraordinary tool at their disposal. Knowledge and learning, once coveted treasures, are now within the reach of the common person. There were varied and mixed opinions surrounding that newfound access.

> *In our time, thanks to the talent and industry of those from the Rhine, books have emerged in lavish numbers. A book that once would've belonged only to the rich—nay, to a king—can now be seen under a modest roof. . . . There is nothing nowadays that our children . . , fail to know.*
>
> —Sebastian Brant

> *Scholarly effort is in decline everywhere as never before. Indeed, cleverness is shunned at home and abroad. What does reading offer to pupils except tears? It is rare, worthless when it is offered for sale, and devoid of wit.*
>
> —Egbert of Liege

People have had various opinions on books throughout history. One thing we can agree on living in a time when virtual printing presses exist and books are ubiquitous is that the printing press changed history. While we weren't actually there when Gutenberg printed the first page using his printing press, we have watched many play with large language models (LLMs) for the first time. The astonishment on their faces as they see it respond to their first prompt. Their excitement when challenging it with a difficult question only to see it respond as if it was an expert in the field—the light bulb moment when they realize they can use this to simplify their life or make themselves wealthy. We imagine this wave of emotions is but a fraction of that felt by Johannes Gutenberg. Being able to rapidly generate text and accelerate communication has always been valuable.

1.1 Large language models accelerating communication

Every job has some level of communication. Often, this communication is shallow, bureaucratic, or political. We've often warned students and mentees that every job has its own paperwork. Something that used to be a passion can easily be killed by the day-to-day tedium and menial work that comes with it when it becomes a job. In fact, when people talk about their professions, they often talk them up, trying to improve their social standing, so you'll rarely get the full truth. You won't hear about the boring parts, and the day-to-day grind is conveniently forgotten.

However, envision a world where we reduce the burden of monotonous work. A place where police officers no longer have to waste hours of each day filling out reports and could instead devote that time to community outreach programs. Or a world where teachers no longer work late into the night grading homework and preparing lesson plans, instead being able to think about and prepare customized lessons for individual students. Or even a world where lawyers would no longer be stuck combing through legal documents for days, instead being free to take on charity cases for causes that inspire them. When the communication burden, the paperwork burden, and the accounting burden are taken away, the job becomes more akin to what we sell it as.

For this, LLMs are the most promising technology to come along since, well, the printing press. For starters, they have completely upended the role and relationship between humans and computers, transforming what we believed they were capable of. They have already passed medical exams, the bar exam, and multiple theory of mind tests. They've passed both Google and Amazon coding interviews. They've gotten scores of at least 1410 out of 1600 on the SAT. One of the most impressive achievements to the authors is that GPT-4 has even passed the Advanced Sommelier exam, which makes us wonder how the LLM got past the practical wine-tasting portion. Indeed, their unprecedented accomplishments are coming at breakneck speed and often make us mere mortals feel a bit queasy and uneasy. What do you do with a technology that seems able to do anything?

NOTE Med-PaLM 2 scored an 86.5% on the MedQA exam. You can see a list of exams passed in OpenAI's GPT-4 paper at https://cdn.openai.com/papers/gpt-4.pdf. Finally, Google interviewed ChatGPT as a test, and it passed (https://mng.bz/x2y6).

Passing tests is fun but not exactly helpful, unless our aim is to build the most expensive cheating machine ever, and we promise there are better ways to use our time.

What LLMs are good at is language, particularly helping us improve and automate communication. This allows us to transform common bitter experiences into easy, enjoyable experiences. For starters, imagine entering your home where you have your very own personal JARVIS, as if stepping into the shoes of Iron Man, an AI-powered assistant that adds an unparalleled dynamic to your routine. While not quite to the same artificial general intelligence (AGI) levels as those portrayed by JARVIS in the Marvel movies, LLMs are powering new user experiences, from improving customer support to helping you shop for a loved one's birthday. They know to ask you about the person, learn about their interests and who they are, find out your budget, and then make specialized recommendations. While many of these assistants are being put to good work, many others are simply chatbots that users can talk to and entertain themselves—which is important because even our imaginary friends are too busy these days. Jokes aside, these can create amazing experiences, allowing you to meet your favorite fictional characters like Harry Potter, Sherlock Holmes, Anakin Skywalker, or even Iron Man.

What we're sure many readers are interested in, though, is programming assistants, because we all know googling everything is actually one of the worst user experiences. Being able to write a few objectives in plain English and see a copilot write the code for you is exhilarating. We've personally used these tools to help us remember syntax, simplify and clean code, write tests, and learn a new programming language.

Video gaming is another interesting field in which we can expect LLMs to create a lot of innovation. Not only do they help the programmers create the game, but they also allow designers to create more immersive experiences. For example, talking to NPCs (nonplayer characters) will have more depth and intriguing dialogue. Picture games like Animal Crossing and Stardew Valley having near-infinite quests and conversations.

Consider other industries, like education, where there doesn't ever seem to be enough teachers to go around, meaning our kids aren't getting the one-on-one attention they need. An LLM assistant can help save the teacher time doing manual chores and serve as a private tutor for kids who are struggling. The corporate world is looking into LLMs for talk-to-your-data jobs—tasks such as helping employees understand quarterly reports and data tables—essentially giving everyone their own personal analyst. Sales and marketing divisions are guaranteed to take advantage of this marvelous innovation, for better or worse. The state of search engine optimization (SEO) will change a lot too since currently, it is mostly a game of generating content to hopefully make websites more popular, which is now super easy.

The preceding list is just a few of the common examples where companies are interested in using LLMs. People are using them for personal reasons too, such as writing music, poetry, and even books; translating languages; summarizing legal documents or emails; and even free therapy—which, yes, is an awful idea since LLMs are still dreadful at this. Just a personal preference, but we wouldn't try to save a buck when our sanity is on the line. Of course, this leads us to the fact that people are already using LLMs for darker purposes like cheating, scams, and fake news to skew elections. At this point, the list has become rather long and varied, but we've only begun to scratch the surface of the possible. Really, since LLMs help us with communication, often it's better to think, "What can't they do?" than "What can they do?" Or better yet, "What shouldn't they do?"

Well, as a technology, there are certain restrictions and constraints. For example, LLMs are kind of slow. Of course, *slow* is a relative term, but responsive times are often measured in seconds, not milliseconds. We'll dive deeper into this topic in chapter 3, but as an example, we probably won't see them being used in autocomplete tasks anytime soon, which require blazingly fast inference to be useful. After all, autocomplete needs to be able to predict the word or phrase faster than someone types. In a similar fashion, LLMs are large, complex systems; we don't need them for such a simple problem anyway. Hitting an autocomplete problem with an LLM isn't just hitting the nail with a sledgehammer; it's hitting it with a full-on wrecking ball. And just like it's more expensive to rent a wrecking ball than to buy a hammer, an LLM will cost you more to operate. There are a lot of similar tasks for which we should consider the complexity of the problem we are trying to solve.

There are also many complex problems that are often poorly solved with LLMs, such as predicting the future. No, we don't mean with mystic arts but rather forecasting problems—acts like predicting the weather or when high tide will hit the ocean shore. These are actually problems we've solved, but we don't necessarily have good ways to communicate how they have been solved. They are expressed through combinations of math solutions, like Fourier transforms and harmonic analysis, or black box ML models. Many problems fit into this category, like outlier prediction, calculus, or finding the end of the roll of tape.

You also probably want to avoid using them for highly risky projects. LLMs aren't infallible and make mistakes often. To increase creativity, we often allow for a bit of randomness in LLMs, which means you can ask an LLM the same question and get different answers. That's risky. You can remove this randomness by doing what's called turning down the temperature, but that might make the LLM useless depending on your needs. For example, you might decide to use an LLM to categorize investment options as good or bad, but do you want it to then make actual investment decisions based on its output? Not without oversight, unless your goal is to create a meme video.

Ultimately, an LLM is just a model. It can't be held accountable for losing your money, and really, it didn't lose your money—you did by choosing to use it. Similar risky problems include filling out tax forms or getting medical advice. While an LLM could do these things, it won't protect you from heavy penalties in an IRS audit like hiring a certified CPA would. If you take bad medical advice from an LLM, there's no doctor you can sue for malpractice. However, in all of these examples, the LLM could potentially help practitioners perform their job roles better, both by reducing errors and improving speed.

When to use an LLM

Use them for

- Generating content
- Question-and-answer services
- Chatbots and AI assistants
- Text-to-something problems (diffusion, txt2img, txt23d, txt2vid, etc.)
- Talk-to-your-data applications
- Anything that involves communication

Avoid using them for

- Latency-sensitive workloads
- Simple projects
- Problems we don't solve with words but with math or algorithms—forecasting, outlier prediction, calculus, etc.
- Critical evaluations
- High-risk projects

Language is not just a medium people use to communicate. It is the tool that made humans apex predators and gives every individual self-definition in their community. Every aspect of human existence, from arguing with your parents to graduating from college to reading this book, is pervaded by our language. Language models are learning to harness one of the fundamental aspects of being human and have the ability, when used responsibly, to help us with each and every one of those tasks. They have the potential to unlock dimensions of understanding both of ourselves and of others if we responsibly teach them how.

LLMs have captured the world's attention since their potential allows imaginations to run wild. LLMs promise so much, but where are all these solutions? Where are the video games that give us immersive experiences? Why don't our kids have personal AI tutors yet? Why am I not Iron Man with my own personal assistant yet? These are the deep and profound questions that motivated us to write this book. Particularly, that last one keeps us up at night. So while LLMs can do amazing things, not enough people know how to turn them into actual products, and that's what we aim to share in this book.

This isn't just a machine learning operations book. There are a lot of gotchas and pitfalls involved with making an LLM work in production because LLMs don't work like traditional software solutions. Turning an LLM into a product that can interact coherently with your users will require an entire team and a diverse set of skills. Depending on your use case, you may need to train or finetune and then deploy your own model, or you may need to access one from a vendor through an API.

Regardless of which LLM you use, if you want to take full advantage of the technology and build the best user experience, you will need to understand how it works—not just on the math/tech side either, but also on the soft side, making it a good experience for your users. In this book, we'll cover everything you need to make LLMs work in production. We'll talk about the best tools and infrastructure, how to maximize their utility with prompt engineering, and other best practices like controlling costs. LLMs could be one step toward greater equality, so if you are thinking, "I don't feel like the person this book is for," please reconsider. This book is for the whole team and anyone who will be interacting with LLMs in the future.

Courtesy of SuperElmer, https://www.facebook.com/SuperElmerDS

We're going to hit on a practical level everything that you'll need for collecting and creating a dataset, training or finetuning an LLM on consumer or industrial hardware, and deploying that model in various ways for customers to interact with. While we aren't going to cover too much theory, we will cover the process from end to end with real-world examples. At the end of this book, you will know how to deploy LLMs with some viable experience to back it up.

1.2 Navigating the build-and-buy decision with LLMs

If you bought this book, you are likely already convinced of the overwhelming potential LLMs can have in your life and in your organization. Buying this book, then, is the first step to turning your dreams into a reality because none of it is possible until we know how to put these models into production. After all, if you talk to any entrepreneur or investor out there, they will tell you good ideas are a dime a dozen; what matters is execution to manifest those ideas. What we need to do is get these models into production, where they are readily available to do actual work for you.

There's no getting around it and no need to sugarcoat it either: deploying LLMs into production is hard. Often, anything worth pursuing is. In this book, we aim to teach you everything you need to know to do it and give you some practical hands-on experience. But because it is so hard, it is mighty tempting to take a shortcut. Large corporations like OpenAI and Google have some great offerings of models to choose from. Why not just buy them? Let's start by considering what they offer and when they are a good choice. Then we'll take a look at the other side of the coin, where these offerings tend to fall flat.

1.2.1 Buying: The beaten path

There are many great reasons to simply buy access to an LLM. First and foremost is the speed and flexibility accessing an API provides. Working with an API is an incredibly easy and cheap way to build a prototype and get your hands dirty quickly. In fact, it's so easy that it only takes a few lines of Python code to start connecting to OpenAI's API and using LLMs, as shown in listing 1.1. Sure, there's a lot that's possible, but it would be a bad idea to invest heavily in LLMs only to find out they happen to fail in your specific domain. Working with an API allows you to fail fast. Building a prototype application to prove the concept and launching it with an API is a great place to get started.

Listing 1.1 A simple app calling OpenAI's API

```
import os
from openai import OpenAI

client = OpenAI(
    api_key=os.getenv("OPENAI_API_KEY")
)

chat_completion = client.chat.completions.create(
    model="gpt-3.5-turbo",
    messages=[{"role": "user", "content": "Hello world"}],
)
```

Loads your API key from an environment variable

This isn't technically needed, as we are passing in the default key.

Often, buying access to a model can give you a competitive edge. In many cases, it could very well be that the best model on the market is built by a company specializing in your domain using specialized datasets it has spent a fortune to curate. While you could try to compete and build your own, it may better serve your purposes to buy access to the model instead. Ultimately, whoever has the better domain-specific data to finetune on is likely to win, and that might not be you if this is a side project for your company. Curating data can be expensive, after all. It can save you a lot of work to go ahead and buy it.

This leads to the next point: buying is a quick way to access expertise and support. For example, OpenAI has spent a lot of time making their models safe with plenty of filtering and controls to prevent the misuse of their LLMs. They've already encountered and covered a lot of the edge cases so you don't have to. Buying access to their model also gives you access to the system they've built around it.

Not to mention that the LLM itself is only half the problem when deploying it to production. There's still an entire application you need to build on top of it. Sometimes buying OpenAI's model has thrived over its competitors in not a small way due to its UX and some tricks like making the tokens look like they're being typed. We'll take you through how you can start solving for the UX in your use case, along with some ways you can prototype to give you a major head start in this area.

1.2.2 Building: The path less traveled

Using an API is easy and, in most cases, likely the best choice. However, there are many reasons why you should aim to own this technology and learn how to deploy it yourself instead. While this path might be harder, we'll teach you how to do it. Let's dive into several of those reasons, starting with the most obvious: control.

CONTROL

One of the first companies to truly adopt LLMs as a core technology was a small video game company called Latitude. Latitude specializes in Dungeon and Dragons–like role-playing games that utilize LLM chatbots, and they have faced challenges when working with them. This shouldn't come off as criticizing this company for their missteps, as they have contributed to our collective learning experience and were pioneers in forging a new path. Nonetheless, their story is a captivating and intriguing one—like a train wreck, we can't help but keep watching.

Latitude's first release was a game called AI Dungeon. At inception, it utilized OpenAI's GPT-2 to create an interactive and dynamic storytelling experience. It quickly garnered a large gathering of players, who, of course, started to use it inappropriately. When OpenAI gave Latitude access to GPT-3, it promised an upgrade to the gaming experience; instead, what it got was a nightmare.[1]

You see, with GPT-3, OpenAI added reinforcement learning from human feedback (RLHF), which greatly helps improve functionality, but this also meant OpenAI contractors were now looking at the prompts. That's the human feedback part. And these workers weren't too thrilled to read the filth the game was creating. OpenAI's reps were quick to give Latitude an ultimatum. Either it needed to start censoring the players, or OpenAI would remove Latitude's access to the model—which would have essentially killed the game and the company. With no other option, Latitude quickly added some filters, but the filtering system was too much of a band-aid, a buggy and glitchy mess. Players were upset at how bad the system was and unnerved to realize Latitude's developers were reading their stories, completely oblivious to the fact that OpenAI was already doing so. It was a PR nightmare. And it wasn't over.

OpenAI decided the game studio wasn't doing enough; stonewalled, Latitude was forced to increase its safeguards and started banning players. Here's the twist: the reason so many of these stories turned to smut was because the model had a preference for erotica. It would often unexpectedly transform harmless storylines into inappropriately risqué situations, causing the player to be ejected and barred from the game. OpenAI was acting as the paragon of purity, but it was their model that was the problem, which led to one of the most ironic and unjust problems in gaming history: players were getting banned for what the game did.

So there they were—a young game studio just trying to make a fun game stuck between upset customers and a tech giant that pushed all the blame and responsibility

[1] WIRED, "It began as an AI-fueled dungeon game. Then it got much darker," Ars Technica, May 8, 2021, https://mng.bz/AdgQ.

onto it. If the company had more control over the technology, it could have gone after a real solution, like fixing the model instead of having to throw makeup on a pig.

In this example, control may come off as your ability to finetune your model, and OpenAI now offers finetuning capabilities, but there are many fine-grained decisions that are still lost by using a service instead of rolling your own solution. For example, what training methodologies are used, what regions the model is deployed to, or what infrastructure it runs on. Control is also important for any customer or internal-facing tool. You don't want a code generator to accidentally output copyrighted code or create a legal situation for your company. You also don't want your customer-facing LLM to output factually incorrect information about your company or its processes.

Control is your ability to direct and manage the operations, processes, and resources in a way that aligns with your goals, objectives, and values. If a model ends up becoming central to your product offering and the vendor unexpectedly raises its prices, there's little you can do but pay it. If the vendor decides its model should give more liberal or conservative answers that no longer align with your values, you are just as stuck.

The more central a technology is to your business plan, the more important it is to control it. This is why McDonald's owns the real estate for its franchises and why Google, Microsoft, and Amazon all own their own cloud networks—and even why so many entrepreneurs build online stores through Shopify instead of using other platforms like Etsy or Amazon Marketplace. Ultimately, control is the first thing that's lost when you buy someone else's product. Keeping control will give you more options to solve future problems and will also give you a competitive edge.

COMPETITIVE EDGE

One of the most valuable aspects of deploying your own models is the competitive edge it gives you over your competition. Customization allows you to train the model to be the best at one thing. For example, after the release of Bidirectional Encoder Representations from Transformers (BERT) in 2017, which is a transformer model architecture you could use to train your own model, there was a surge of researchers and businesses testing this newfound technology on their own data to worldwide success. At the time of writing, if you search the Hugging Face Hub for "BERT," more than 13.7K models are returned, all of which people individually trained for their own purposes, aiming to create the best model for their task.

One author's personal experience in this area was training SlovenBERTcina after aggregating the largest (at the time) monolingual Slovak language dataset by scraping the Slovak National Corpus with permission, along with a bunch of other resources like the OSCAR project and the Europarl corpus. It never set any computational records and has never appeared in any model reviews or generated partnerships for the company the author worked for. It did, however, outperform every other model on the market on the tasks it trained on.

Chances are, neither you nor your company needs AGI to generate relevant insights from your data. In fact, if you invented an actual self-aware AGI and planned to only ever use it to crunch some numbers, analyze data, and generate visuals for PowerPoint slides once a week, that would definitely be reason enough for the AGI to eradicate humans. More than likely, you need exactly what this author did when he made SlovenBERTcina, a large language model that performs two to three tasks better than any other model on the market and doesn't also share your data with Microsoft or other potential competitors. While some data is required to be kept secret for security or legal reasons, a lot of data should be guarded because it includes trade secrets.

There are hundreds of open source LLMs for both general intelligence and foundational expertise on a specific task. We'll hit some of our favorites in chapter 4. Taking one of these open source alternatives and training it on your data to create a model that is the best in the world at that task will ensure you have a competitive edge in your market. It will also allow you to deploy the model your way and integrate it into your system to have the most effect.

INTEGRATE ANYWHERE

Let's say you want to deploy an LLM as part of a choose-your-own-adventure–styled game that uses a device's GPS location to determine story plots. You know your users are often going to go on adventures into the mountains, out at sea, and generally to locations where they are likely to experience poor service and lack of internet access. Hitting an API just isn't going to work. Now, don't get us wrong: deploying LLMs onto edge devices like in this scenario is still an exploratory subject, but it is possible; we will be showing you how in chapter 10. Relying upon an API service is just not going to work for immersive experiences.

Similarly, using third-party LLMs and hitting an API adds integration and latency problems, requiring you to send data over the wire and wait for a response. APIs are great, but they are always slow and not always reliable. When latency is important to a project, it's much better to have the service in-house. The previous section on competitive edge discussed two projects with edge computing as a priority; however, many more exist. LLAMA.cpp and ALPACA.cpp are two of the first such projects, and this space is innovating quicker than any others. Quantization into 4-bit, low-rank adaptation, and parameter-efficient finetuning are all methodologies recently created to meet these needs, and we'll be going over each of these starting in chapter 3.

When this author's team first started integrating with ChatGPT's API, it was both an awe-inspiring and humbling experience—awe-inspiring because it allowed us to quickly build some valuable tools, and humbling because, as one engineer joked, "When you hit the endpoint, you will get 503 errors; sometimes you get a text response as if the model was generating text, but I think that's a bug." Serving an LLM in a production environment—trying to meet the needs of so many clients—is no easy feat. However, deploying a model that's integrated into your system allows you more control of the process, affording higher availability and maintainability than you can currently find on the market. This, of course, also allows you to better control costs.

COSTS

Considering costs is always important because it plays a pivotal role in making informed decisions and ensuring the financial health of a project or an organization. It helps you manage budgets efficiently and make sure that resources are allocated appropriately. Keeping costs under control allows you to maintain the viability and sustainability of your endeavors in the long run.

Additionally, considering costs is crucial for risk management. When you understand the different cost aspects, you can identify potential risks and exert better control over them. This way, you can avoid unnecessary expenditures and ensure that your projects are more resilient to unexpected changes in the market or industry.

Finally, cost considerations are important for maintaining transparency and accountability. By monitoring and disclosing costs, organizations demonstrate their commitment to ethical and efficient operations to stakeholders, clients, and employees. This transparency can improve an organization's reputation and help build trust.

All of these apply as you consider building versus buying LLMs. It may seem immediately less costly to buy, as the costliest service widely used on the market currently is only $20 per month. Compared to an EC2 instance on AWS, just running that same model for inference (not even training) could run you up a bill of about $250k per year. This is where building has done its quickest innovation, however. If all you need is an LLM for a proof of concept, any of the projects mentioned in the Competitive Edge section will allow you to create a demo for only the cost of electricity to run the computer you are demoing on. They can spell out training easily enough to allow for significantly reduced costs to train a model on your own data, as low as $100 (yes, that's the real number) for a model with 20 billion parameters. Another benefit is knowing that if you build your own, your cost will never go up like it very much will when paying for a service.

SECURITY AND PRIVACY

Consider the following case. You are a military staff member in charge of maintenance for the nuclear warheads in your arsenal. All the documentation is kept in a hefty manual. There's so much information required to outline all the safety requirements and maintenance protocols that cadets are known to forget important information despite their best efforts. They often cut the wires before first removing the fuse (https://youtu.be/UcaWQZlPXgQ). You decide to finetune an LLM model to be a personal assistant, giving directions and helping condense all that information to provide soldiers with exactly what they need when they need it. It's probably not a good idea to upload those manuals to another company—understatement of the century—so you're going to want to train something locally that's kept secure and private.

This scenario may sound farfetched, but when speaking to an expert working in analytics for a police department, they echoed this exact concern. Talking with them, they expressed how cool ChatGPT is and even had their whole team take a prompt engineering class to better take advantage of it but lamented that there was no way for their team to use it for their most valuable work—the sort of work that literally saves lives—without exposing sensitive data and conversations. Anyone in similar shoes should be eager to learn how to deploy a model safely and securely.

You don't have to be in the army or on a police force to handle sensitive data. Every company has important intellectual property and trade secrets that are best kept a secret. Having worked in the semiconductor, healthcare, and finance industries, we can tell you firsthand that paranoia and corporate espionage are part of the culture in these industries. Because of this, Samsung and other industry players locked down ChatGPT at first, preventing employees from using it, only later opening it up. Of course, it didn't take long before several Samsung employees leaked confidential source code.[2] Because OpenAI uses its users' interactions to improve the model, that code is retained and could have been used to further train the model later on. That means that with the right prompt injection, anyone could potentially pull the code out of the model. A recent example goes even further: when any OpenAI model was prompted to repeat a word ad infinitum, it would start regurgitating training data, including all of the personally identifiable information (PII) that had snuck through the cleaning process.

NOTE OpenAI's privacy and usage policies have changed a lot over the course of this book's writing. When ChatGPT was first introduced, it was done as a demo specifically so OpenAI could collect user interactions and improve the model. It pretty much didn't have a privacy policy, and it had disclaimers saying such. As ChatGPT grew and became an actual product, this changed, as clients wanted more protection. For example, OpenAI changed its policies to better serve its customers and, since March 1, 2023, no longer uses customer API data to improve its models (see ChatGPT FAQ: https://mng.bz/QV8Q). The wording, of course, indicates that only data is sent through the API. It's best to ask your lawyers where your company stands on using it. Regardless, the fact that terms of use have changed so much is just further proof you might want more control in this regard.

It's not just code that can easily be lost. Business plans, meeting notes, confidential emails, and even potential patent ideas are at risk. Unfortunately, we know of a few companies that have started sending confidential data to ChatGPT, using that model to clean and extract PII. If this strikes you as potential negligent misuse, you'd be right. This methodology directly exposes customer data, not just to OpenAI, but to any and all third-party services they use (including AWS Mechanical Turk, Fiverr, and freelance workers) to perform the human feedback part of RLHF. Don't get us wrong: it's not necessarily a security or privacy problem if you use a third party to do data processing tasks even for sensitive data, but it should only be done with high levels of trust and contracts in place.

---

[2] 이코노미스트, "[단독] 우려가 현실로...삼성전자, 챗GPT 빗장 풀자마자 '오남용' 속출," 이코노미스트 ["Concerns become reality: As soon as Samsung Electronics unblocks ChatGPT, 'abuse' continues"]. The Economist, March 30, 2023, https://mng.bz/4p1v.

WRAPPING UP

As you can see, there are lots of reasons why a company might want to own and build its own LLMs, including greater control, cutting costs, and meeting security and regulation requirements. Despite this, we understand that buying is easy, and building is much more difficult, so for many projects, it makes sense to buy. However, before you do, in figure 1.1, we share a flowchart of questions you should ask yourself first. Even though it's the more difficult path, building can be much more rewarding.

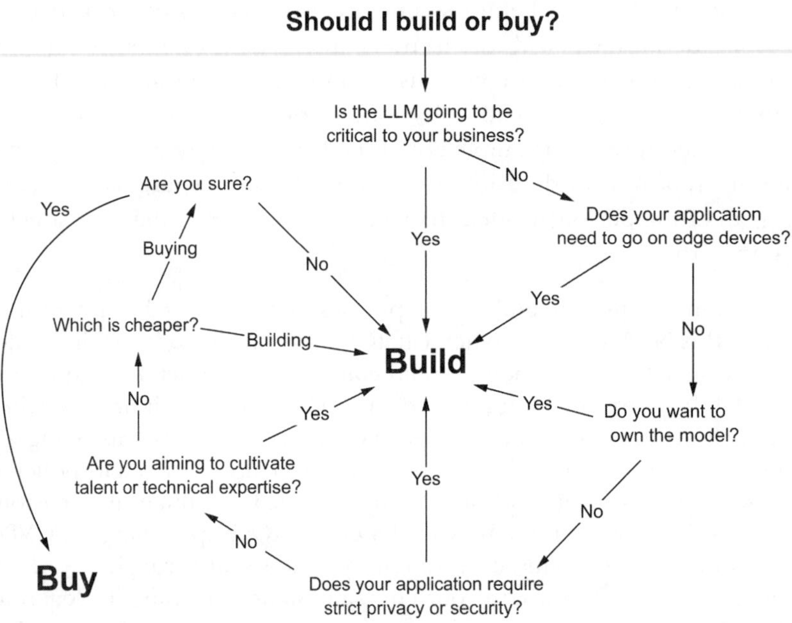

Figure 1.1 Questions you should ask yourself before making that build-vs.-buy decision

One last point we think these build-versus-buy conversations never seem to hone in on enough is "Por qué no los dos?" Buying gets you all the things building is bad at: time to market, relatively low cost, and ease of use. Building gets you everything buying struggles with: privacy, control, and flexibility. Research and prototyping phases could benefit very much from buying a subscription to GPT-4 or Databricks in order to build something quick to help raise funding or get stakeholder buy-in. Production, however, often isn't an environment that lends itself well to third-party solutions.

Ultimately, whether you plan to build or buy, we wrote this book for you. Obviously, if you plan to build, there's going to be a lot more you need to know about, so a majority of this book will be geared to these folks. In fact, we don't need to belabor the point anymore: we're going to teach you how to build in this book, but don't let that stop you from doing the right thing for your company.

1.2.3 A word of warning: Embrace the future now

All new technology meets resistance and has critics; despite this, technologies keep being adopted, and progress continues. In business, technology can give a company an unprecedented advantage. There's no shortage of stories of companies failing because they didn't adapt to new technologies. We can learn a lot from their failures.

Borders first opened its doors in 1971. After developing a comprehensive inventory management system that included advanced analytic capabilities, it skyrocketed to become the second-largest book retailer in the world, only behind Barnes & Noble. Using this new technology, Borders disrupted the industry, allowing it to easily keep track of tens of thousands of books, opening large stores where patrons could peruse many more books than they could at smaller stores. The analytic capabilities helped it track which books were gaining popularity and gain better insights into its customers, allowing it to make better business decisions. It dominated the industry for over two decades.

Borders, however, failed to learn from its own history, going bankrupt in 2011 because of failing to adapt and being disrupted by technology: this time e-commerce. In 2001, instead of building its own platform and online store, it decided to outsource its online sales to Amazon.[3] Many critics would say this decision was akin to giving your competitors the key to your business. While not exactly handing over its secret sauce, it was a decision that gave up Borders' competitive edge.

For the next seven years, Borders turned a blind eye to the growing online sector, instead focusing on expanding its physical store presence, buying out competitors, and securing a coveted Starbucks deal. When Amazon released the Kindle in 2007, the book retail landscape completely changed. Barnes & Noble, having run its own online store, quickly pivoted and released the Nook to compete. Borders, however, did nothing or, in fact, could do nothing.

By embracing e-commerce through a third party, Borders failed to develop the in-house expertise required to create a successful online sales strategy, leading to a substantial loss in market share. It eventually launched its own e-reader, Kobo, in late 2010, but it was too late to catch up. Its inability to fully understand and implement e-commerce technology effectively led to massive financial losses and store closures; ultimately, the company filed for bankruptcy in 2011.

Borders is a cautionary tale, but there are hundreds more similar companies that failed to adopt new technology, to their own detriment. With a new technology as impactful as LLMs, each company has to decide on which side of the fence it wants to be. Does it delegate implementation and deployment to large FAANG-like corporations, relegating its job to just hitting an API, or does it take charge, preferring to master the technology and deploy it in-house?

---

[3] A. Lowrey, "Borders bankruptcy: Done in by its own stupidity, not the Internet.," Slate Magazine, July 20, 2011, https://mng.bz/PZD5.

The biggest lesson we hope to impart from this story is that technologies build on top of one another. E-commerce was built on top of the internet. Failing to build its own online store meant Borders failed to build the in-house technical expertise it needed to stay in the game when the landscape shifted. We see the same things with LLMs today because the companies that are best prepared to utilize them have already gathered expertise in machine learning and data science and have some idea of what they are doing.

We don't have a crystal ball that tells us the future, but many believe that LLMs are a revolutionary new technology, like the internet or electricity before it. Learning how to deploy these models, or failing to do so, may very well be the defining moment for many companies—not because doing so will make or break their company now, but because it may in the future when something even more valuable comes along that's built on top of LLMs.

Foraying into this new world of deploying LLMs may be challenging, but it will help your company build the technical expertise to stay on top of the game. No one really knows where this technology will lead, but learning about this technology will likely be necessary to avoid mistakes like those made by Borders.

There are many great reasons to buy your way to success, but there is at least one prevalent thought that is just absolutely wrong: it's the myth that only large corporations can work in this field because it takes millions of dollars and thousands of GPUs to train these models, which creates this impenetrable moat of cash and resources the little guy can't hope to cross. We'll be talking about this more in the next section, but any company of any size can get started, and there's no better time than now to do so.

1.3 Debunking myths

We have all heard from large corporations and the current leaders in LLMs how incredibly difficult it is to train an LLM from scratch and how intense it is to try to finetune them. Whether from OpenAI, BigScience, or Google, they discuss large investments and the need for strong data and engineering talent. But how much of this is true, and how much of it is just a corporate attempt to create a technical moat?

Most of these barriers start with the premise that you will need to train an LLM from scratch if you hope to solve your problems. Simply put, you don't! Open source models covering many dimensions of language models are constantly being released, so more than likely, you don't need to start from scratch. While it's true that training LLMs from scratch is supremely difficult, we are still constantly learning how to do it and are able to automate the repeatable portions more and more. In addition, since this is an active field of research, frameworks and libraries are being released or updated daily and will help you start from wherever you currently are. Frameworks like oobabooga's Gradio will help you run LLMs, and base models like Falcon 40B will be your starting point. All of it is covered. In addition, memos have circulated at large companies addressing the lack of a competitive edge that any organization currently holds over the open source community at large.

A friend once confided, "I really want to get more involved in all this machine learning and data science stuff. It seems to be getting cooler every time I blink an eye. However, it feels like the only way to get involved is to go through a lengthy career change and go work for a FAANG. No, thank you. We've done our time at large companies, and they aren't for us. But we hate feeling like we're trapped on the outside." This is the myth that inspired this book. We're here to equip you with tools and examples to help you stop feeling trapped on the outside. We'll help you go through the language problems that we're trying to solve with LLMs, along with machine learning operation strategies to account for the sheer size of the models.

Oddly enough, while many believe they are trapped on the outside, many others believe they can become experts in a weekend. Just get a GPT API key, and that's it—you're done. This has led to a lot of fervor and hype, with a cool new demo popping up on social media every day. Most of these demos never become actual products—but not because people don't want them.

To understand this, let's discuss IBM's Watson, the world's most advanced language model before GPT. Watson is a question-and-answering machine that crushed Jeopardy in 2011 against some of the best human contestants to ever appear on the show, Brad Rutter and Ken Jennings. Rutter was the highest-earning contestant ever to play the game show, and Jennings was so good at the game that he won a whopping 74 times in a row. Despite facing these legends, it wasn't even close. Watson won in a landslide. Jennings, in response to the loss, responded with the famous quote, "I, for one, welcome our new computer overlords."[4]

Watson was the first impressive foray into language modeling, and many companies were clamoring to take advantage of its capabilities. Starting in 2013, Watson started being released for commercial use. One of the biggest applications involved many attempts to integrate it into healthcare to solve various problems. However, none of these solutions ever really worked the way they needed to, and the business never became profitable. By 2022, Watson Health was sold off.

What we find when solving language-related problems is that building a prototype is easy; building a functioning product, on the other hand, is very, very difficult. There are just too many nuances to language. Many people wonder what made ChatGPT, which gained over a million clients in just five days, so explosive. Most of the answers we've heard would never satisfy an expert because ChatGPT wasn't much more impressive than GPT-3 or other LLMs that had already been around for several years. Sam Altman of OpenAI once said in an interview that he didn't think ChatGPT would get this much attention; he thought it would come with GPT-4's release.[5] So why was it explosive? In our opinion, the magic was that it was the first product to truly productionize LLMs—turning them from a demo into an actual product. It was something

---

[4] J. Best, "IBM Watson: The inside story of how the Jeopardy-winning supercomputer was born, and what it wants to do next," TechRepublic, September 9, 2013, https://mng.bz/JZ9Q.

[5] "A conversation with OpenAI CEO Sam Altman; hosted by Elevate," May 18, 2023, https://youtu.be/uRIWgbvouEw.

anyone could interact with, asking tough questions only to be amazed by how well it responded. A demo only has to work once, but the product has to work every time, even when millions of users are showing it to their friends, saying, "Check this out!" That magic is exactly what you can hope to learn from reading this book.

We're excited about writing this book. We are excited about the possibilities of bringing this magic to you so you can take it to the world. LLMs are at the intersection of many fields, such as linguistics, mathematics, computer science, and more. While knowing more will help you, being an expert isn't required. Expertise in any of the individual parts only raises the skill ceiling, not the floor, to get in. Consider an expert in physics or music theory: they won't automatically have the skills for music production, but they will be more prepared to learn it quickly. LLMs are a communication tool, and communicating is a skill just about everyone needs.

Like all other skills, your proximity and willingness to get involved are the two main blockers to knowledge, not a degree or ability to notate—these only shorten your journey toward being heard and understood. If you don't have any experience in this area, it might be good to start by first developing an intuition around what an LLM is and needs by contributing to a project like OpenAssistant. If you're a human, that's exactly what LLMs need. By volunteering, you can start understanding what these models train on and why. If you fall anywhere, from no knowledge up to being a professional machine learning engineer, we'll be imparting the knowledge necessary to shorten your time to understanding considerably. If you're not interested in learning the theoretical underpinnings of the subject, we've got plenty of hands-on examples and projects to get your hands dirty.

We've all heard a story by now of LLM hallucinations, but LLMs don't need to be erratic. Companies like Lakera are working daily to improve security, while others like LangChain are making it easier to provide models with pragmatic context that makes them more consistent and less likely to deviate. Techniques such as RLHF and Chain of Thought further allow our models to align themselves with negotiations we've already accepted that people and models should understand from the get-go, such as basic addition and the current date, both of which are conceptually arbitrary. We'll help you increase your model stability from a linguistic perspective so it will figure out not just the most likely outputs but also the most useful.

Something to consider as you venture further down this path is not only the security of what goes into your model/code but what comes out. LLMs can sometimes produce outdated, factually incorrect, or even copyrighted or licensed material, depending on what their training data contains. LLMs are unaware of any agreements people make about what is supposed to be a trade secret and what can be shared openly—that is, unless you tell them about those agreements during training or through careful prompting mechanisms during inference. Indeed, the challenges around prompt injection giving inaccurate information arise primarily due to two factors: users requesting information beyond the model's understanding and model developers not fully predicting how users will interact with the models or the nature of their inquiries. If you had a resource that could help you get a head start on that second problem, it would be pretty close to invaluable, wouldn't it?

Lastly, we don't want to artificially or untruthfully inflate your sense of hope with LLMs. They are resource intensive to train and run. They are hard to understand, and they are harder to get working how you want. They are new and not well-understood. The good news is that these problems are being actively worked on, and we've put in a lot of work finding implementations concurrent with this writing to actively lessen the burden of knowing everything about the entire deep-learning architecture. From quantization to Kubernetes, we'll help you figure out everything you need to know to do this now with what you have. Maybe we'll inadvertently convince you that it's too much and you should just purchase from a vendor. Either way, we'll help you every step of the way to get the results you need from this magical technology.

Summary

- LLMs are exciting because they work within the same framework (language) as humans.
- Society has been built on language, so effective language models have limitless applications, such as chatbots, programming assistants, video games, and AI assistants.
- LLMs are excellent at many tasks and can even pass high-ranking medical and law exams.
- LLMs are wrecking balls, not hammers, and should be avoided for simple problems that require low latency or entail high risks.
- Reasons to buy include
  - Quickly getting up and running to conduct research and prototype use cases
  - Easy access to highly optimized production models
  - Access to vendors' technical support and systems
- Reasons to build include
  - Getting a competitive edge for your business use case
  - Keeping costs low and transparent
  - Ensuring the reliability of the model
  - Keeping your data safe
  - Controlling model output on sensitive or private topics
- There is no technical moat preventing you from competing with larger companies, since open source frameworks and models provide the building blocks to pave your own path.

2 Large language models: A deep dive into language modeling

This chapter covers

- The linguistic background for understanding meaning and interpretation
- A comparative study of language modeling techniques
- Attention and the transformer architecture
- How large language models both fit into and build upon these histories

If you know the enemy and know yourself, you need not fear the result of a hundred battles.

—Sun Tzu

This chapter delves into linguistics as it relates to the development of LLMs, exploring the foundations of semiotics, linguistic features, and the progression of language modeling techniques that have shaped the field of natural language processing (NLP). We will begin by studying the basics of linguistics and its relevance to LLMs, highlighting key concepts such as syntax, semantics, and pragmatics that form the basis of natural language and play a crucial role in the functioning of LLMs. We will delve into semiotics, the study of signs and symbols, and explore how its principles have informed the design and interpretation of LLMs.

We will then trace the evolution of language modeling techniques, providing an overview of early approaches, including N-grams, naive Bayes classifiers, and neural network-based methods such as multilayer perceptrons (MLPs), recurrent neural networks (RNNs), and long short-term memory (LSTM) networks. We will also discuss the groundbreaking shift to transformer-based models that laid the foundation for the emergence of LLMs, which are really just big transformer-based models. Finally, we will introduce LLMs and their distinguishing features, discussing how they have built upon and surpassed earlier language modeling techniques to revolutionize the field of NLP.

This book is about LLMs in production. We firmly believe that if you want to turn an LLM into an actual product, understanding the technology better will improve your results and save you from making costly and time-consuming mistakes. Any engineer can figure out how to lug a big model into production and throw a ton of resources at it to make it run, but that brute-force strategy completely misses the lessons people have already learned trying to do the same thing before, which is what we are trying to solve with LLMs in the first place. Having a grasp of these fundamentals will better prepare you for the tricky parts, the gotchas, and the edge cases you are going to run into when working with LLMs. By understanding the context in which LLMs emerged, we can appreciate their transformative impact on NLP and how to enable them to create a myriad of applications.

2.1 Language modeling

It would be a great disservice to address LLMs in any depth without first addressing language. To that end, we will start with a brief but comprehensive overview of language modeling, focusing on the lessons that can help us with modern LLMs. Let's first discuss levels of abstraction, as this will help us garner an appreciation for language modeling.

Language, as a concept, is an abstraction of the feelings and thoughts that occur to us in our heads. Feelings come first in the process of generating language, but that's not the only thing we're trying to highlight here. We're also looking at language as being unable to capture the full extent of what we are able to feel, which is why we're calling it an abstraction. It moves away from the source material and loses information. Math is an abstraction of language, focusing on logic and provability, but as any mathematician will tell you, it is a subset of language used to describe and define in an organized and logical way. From math comes another abstraction, the language of binary, a base-2 system of numerical notation consisting of either on or off.

This is not a commentary on usefulness, as binary and math are just as useful as the lower-level aspects of language, nor is it commenting on order, as we said before. With math and binary, the order coincidentally lines up with the layer of abstraction. Computers can't do anything on their own and need to take commands to be useful. Binary, unfortunately, ends up taking too long for humans to communicate important things in it, so binary was also abstracted to assembly, a more human-comprehensible language for communicating with computers. This was further abstracted to the high-level assembly language C, which has been even further abstracted to object-oriented languages like Python or Java (which one doesn't matter—we're just measuring distance from binary). The flow we just discussed is outlined in figure 2.1.

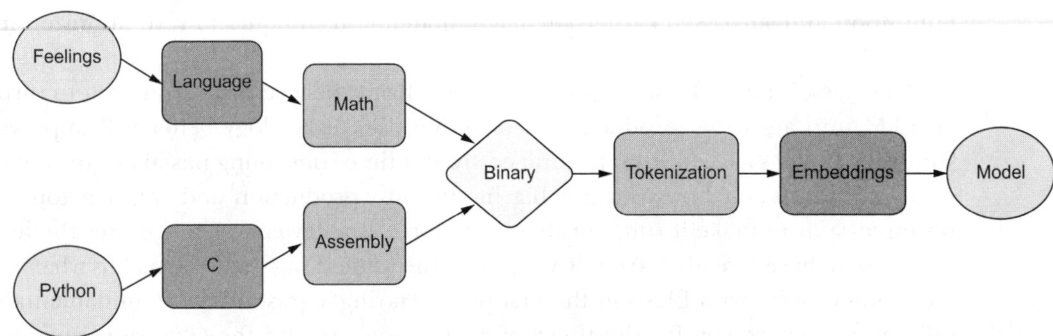

Figure 2.1 We compare cognitive layers of abstraction to programming layers of abstraction down to the logical binary abstraction. Python doesn't come from C, nor does it compile into C. Python is, however, another layer of abstraction distant from binary. Language follows a similar path. Each layer of abstraction creates a potential point of failure. There are also several layers of abstraction to creating a model, and each is important in seeing the full path from our feelings to a working model.

This is obviously a reduction; however, it's useful to understand that the feelings you have in your head are the same number of abstractions away from binary, the language the computer actually reads, as the languages most people use to program in. Some people might argue that there are more steps between Python and binary, such as compilers or using assembly to support the C language, and that's true, but there are more steps on the language side too, such as morphology, syntax, logic, dialogue, and agreement.

This reduction can help us understand how difficult the process of getting what we want to be understood by an LLM actually is and even help us understand language modeling techniques better. We focus on binary here to illustrate that there are a similar number of abstract layers to get from an idea you have or from one of our code samples to a working model. Like the children's telephone game where participants whisper into each other's ears, each abstraction layer creates a disconnect point or barrier where mistakes can be made.

Figure 2.1 is also meant not only to illustrate the difficulty in creating reliable code and language input but also to draw attention to how important the intermediary abstraction steps, like tokenization and embeddings, are for the model itself. Even if you have perfectly reliable code and perfectly expressed ideas, the meaning may be fumbled by one of those processes before it ever reaches the LLM.

In this chapter, we will try to help you understand what you can do to reduce the risks of these failure points, whether on the language, coding, or modeling side. Unfortunately, it's a bit tricky to strike a balance between giving you too much linguistics that doesn't immediately matter for the task at hand versus giving you too much technical knowledge that, while useful, doesn't help you develop an intuition for language modeling as a practice. With this in mind, you should know that linguistics can be traced back thousands of years in our history, and there's lots to learn from it. We've included a brief overview of how language modeling has progressed over time in appendix A, and we encourage you to take a look.

Let's start with our focus on the building blocks that constitute language itself. We expect our readers to have at least attempted language modeling before and to have heard of libraries like PyTorch and TensorFlow, but we do not expect most of our readers to have considered the language side of things before. By understanding the essential features that make up language, we can better appreciate the complexities involved in creating effective language models and how these features interact with one another to form the intricate web of communication that connects us all. In the following section, we will examine the various components of language, such as phonetics, pragmatics, morphology, syntax, and semantics, as well as the role they play in shaping our understanding and usage of languages around the world. Let's take a moment to explore how we currently understand language, along with the challenges we face that LLMs are meant to solve.

2.1.1 Linguistic features

Our current understanding of language is that language is made up of at least five parts: phonetics, syntax, semantics, pragmatics, and morphology. Each of these portions contributes significantly to the overall experience and meaning being ingested by the listener in any conversation. Not all of our communication uses all of these forms; for example, the book you're currently reading is devoid of phonetics, which is one of the reasons why so many people think text messages are unsuited for more serious or complex conversations. Let's work through each of these five parts to figure out how to present them to a language model for a full range of communicative power.

PHONETICS

Phonetics is probably the easiest for a language model to ingest, as it involves the actual sound of the language. This is where accent manifests and deals with the production and perception of speech sounds, with phonology focusing on the way sounds are organized within a particular language system. Similarly to computer vision, while a sound isn't necessarily easy to deal with as a whole, there's no ambiguity in how to parse, vectorize, or tokenize the actual sound waves. They have a numerical value attached to each part, the crest, the trough, and the slope during each frequency cycle.

It is vastly easier than text to tokenize and process by a computer while being no less complex.

Sound inherently also contains more encoded meaning than text. For example, imagine someone saying the words "Yeah, right," to you. It could be sarcastic, or it could be congratulatory, depending on the tone—and English isn't even tonal! Phonetics, unfortunately, doesn't have terabyte-sized datasets commonly associated with it, and performing data acquisition and cleaning on phonetic data, especially on the scale needed to train an LLM, is difficult at best. In an alternate world where audio data was more prevalent than text data and took up a smaller memory footprint, phonetic-based or phonetic-aware LLMs would be much more sophisticated, and creating that world is a solid goal to work toward.

Anticipating this phonetical problem, a system was created in 1888 called the International Phonetic Alphabet (IPA). It has been revised in both the 20th and 21st centuries to be more concise, more consistent, and clearer and could be a way to insert phonetic awareness into text data. IPA functions as an internationally standardized version of every language's sound profile. A sound profile is the set of sounds that a language uses; for example, in English, we never have the /ʃ/ (she, shirt, sh) next to the /v/ sound. IPA is used to write sounds, rather than writing an alphabet or logograms, as most languages do. For example, you could describe how to pronounce the word "cat" using these symbols: /k/, /æ/, and /t/. Of course, that's a very simplified version of it, but for models, it doesn't have to be. You can describe tone and aspiration as well. This could be a happy medium between text and speech, capturing some phonetic information. Think of the phrase "What's up?" Your pronunciation and tone can drastically change how you understand that phrase, sometimes sounding like a friendly "Wazuuuuup?" and other times an almost threatening "'Sup?" which IPA would fully capture. IPA isn't a perfect solution, though; for example, it doesn't solve the problem of replicating tone very well.

Phonetics is listed first here because it's the place where LLMs have been applied to the least out of all the features and, therefore, has the largest space for improvement. Even modern text-to-speech (TTS) and voice-cloning models, for the most part, end up converting the sound to a spectrogram and analyzing that image rather than incorporating any type of phonetic language modeling. Improving phonetic data and representation in LLMs is something to look for as far as research goes in the coming months and years.

SYNTAX

Syntax is the place where current LLMs are highest-performing, both in parsing syntax from the user and in generating their own. Syntax is generally what we think of as grammar and word order; it is the study of how words can combine to form phrases, clauses, and sentences. Syntax is also the first place language-learning programs start to help people acquire new languages, especially based on where they are coming from natively. For example, it is important for a native English speaker learning Turkish to know that the syntax is completely different, and you can often build entire sentences in Turkish that are just one long compound word, whereas in English, we never put our subject and verb together into one word.

Syntax is largely separate from meaning in language, as the famous sentence from Noam Chomsky, the so-called father of syntax, demonstrates: "Colorless green ideas sleep furiously." Everything about that sentence is both grammatically correct and semantically understandable. The problem isn't that it doesn't make sense; it's that it does, and the encoded meanings of those words conflict. This is a reduction; however, you can think of all the times LLMs give nonsense answers as this phenomenon manifests. Unfortunately, the syntax is also where ambiguity is most commonly found. Consider the sentence, "I saw an old man and woman." Now answer this question: Is the woman also old? This is syntactic ambiguity, where we aren't sure whether the modifier "old" applies to all people in the following phrase or just the one it immediately precedes. This is less consequential than the fact that semantic and pragmatic ambiguity also show up in syntax. Consider this sentence: "I saw a man on a hill with a telescope," and answer these questions: Where is the speaker, and what are they doing? Is the speaker on the hill cutting a man in half using a telescope? Likely, you didn't even consider this option when you read the sentence because when we interpret syntax, all of our interpretations are at least semantically and pragmatically informed. We know from lived experience that that interpretation isn't at all likely, so we throw it out immediately, usually without even taking time to process that we're eliminating it from the pool of probable meanings. Single-modality LLMs will always have this problem, and multimodal LLMs can (so far) only asymptote toward the solution.

It shouldn't take any logical leap to understand why LLMs need to be syntax-aware to be high-performing. LLMs that don't get word order correct or generate nonsense aren't usually described as "good." LLMs being syntax-dependent has prompted even Chomsky to call LLMs "stochastic parrots." In our opinion, GPT-2 in 2018 was when language modeling solved syntax as a completely meaning-independent demonstration, and we've been happy to see the more recent attempts to combine the syntax that GPT-2 outputs so well with encoded and entailed meaning, which we'll get into now.

SEMANTICS

Semantics are the literal encoded meaning of words in utterances, which changes at breakneck speed in waves. People automatically optimize semantic meaning by only using words they consider meaningful in the current language epoch. If you've ever created or used an embedding with language models (word2vec, ELMo, BERT, MUSE [the E is for embedding], etc.), you've used a semantic approximation. Words often go through semantic shifts, and while we won't cover this topic completely or go into depth, here are some common ones you may already be familiar with: narrowing, a broader meaning to a more specific one; broadening, the inverse of narrowing going from a specific meaning to a broad one; and reinterpretations, going through whole or partial transformations. These shifts do not have some grand logical underpinning.

They don't even have to correlate with reality, nor do speakers of a language often consciously think about the changes as they're happening. That doesn't stop the change from occurring, and in the context of language modeling, it doesn't stop us from having to keep up with that change.

Let's look at some examples. Narrowing includes "deer," which in Old and Middle English just meant any wild animal, even a bear or a cougar, and now means only one kind of forest animal. For broadening, we have "dog," which used to refer to only one canine breed from England and now can be used to refer to any domesticated canine. One fun tangent about dog-broadening is in the FromSoft game *Elden Ring*, where because of a limited message system between players, "dog" will be used to refer to anything from a turtle to a giant spider and literally everything in between. For reinterpretation, we can consider "pretty," which used to mean clever or well-crafted, not visually attractive. Another good example is "bikini," which went from referring to a particular atoll to referring to clothing you might have worn when visiting that atoll to people acting as if the "bi-" was referring to the two-piece structure of the clothing, thus implying the tankini and monokini. Based on expert research and decades of study, we can think of language as being constantly compared and re-evaluated by native language speakers, out of which common patterns emerge. The spread of those patterns is closely studied in sociolinguistics and is largely out of the scope of the current purpose but can quickly come into scope as localization (l10n) or internationalization (i18n) for LLMs arises as a project requirement. Sociolinguistic phenomena such as prestige can help design systems that work well for everyone.

In the context of LLMs, so-called semantic embeddings are vectorized versions of text that attempt to mimic semantic meaning. Currently, the most popular way of doing this is by tokenizing or assigning an arbitrary number in a dictionary to each subword in an utterance (think prefixes, suffixes, and morphemes generally), applying a continuous language model to increase the dimensionality of each token within the vector so that there's a larger vector representing each index of the tokenized vector, and then applying a positional encoding to each of those vectors to capture word order. Each subword ends up being compared to other words in the larger dictionary based on how it's used. We'll show you an example of this later. Something to consider when thinking about word embeddings is that they struggle to capture the deep, encoded meaning of those tokens, and simply adding more dimensions to the embeddings hasn't shown marked improvement. Evidence that embeddings work similarly to humans is that you can apply a distance function to related words and see that they are closer together than unrelated words. How to capture and represent meaning more completely is another area in which to expect groundbreaking research in the coming years and months.

PRAGMATICS

Pragmatics is sometimes omitted from linguistics due to its referent being all the nonlinguistic context affecting a listener's interpretation and the speaker's decision to express things in a certain way. Pragmatics refers in large part to dogmas followed in cultures, regions, socio-economic classes, and shared lived experiences, which are played off of to take shortcuts in conversations using entailment.

If we were to say, "A popular celebrity was just taken into the ICU," your pragmatic interpretation based on lived experience might be to assume that a well-beloved person has been badly injured and is now undergoing medical treatment in a well-equipped hospital. You may wonder about which celebrity it is, whether they will have to pay for the medical bills, or if the injury was self-inflicted, also based on your lived experience. None of these things can be inferred directly from the text and its encoded meaning by itself. You would need to know that ICU stands for a larger set of words and what those words are. You would need to know what a hospital is and why someone would need to be taken there instead of going there themselves. If any of these feel obvious, good. You live in a society, and your pragmatic knowledge of that society overlaps well with the example provided. If we share an example from a less-populated society, "Janka got her grand-night lashings yesterday; she's gonna get Peter tomorrow," you might be left scratching your head. If you are, realize this probably looks like how a lot of text data ends up looking to an LLM (anthropomorphization acknowledged). For those wondering, this sentence comes from Slovak Easter traditions. A lot of meaning here will be missed and go unexplained if you are unaccustomed to these particular traditions as they stand in that culture. This author personally has had the pleasure of trying to explain the Easter Bunny and its obsession with eggs to foreign colleagues and enjoyed the satisfaction of looking like I'm off my rocker.

In the context of LLMs, we can effectively group all out-of-text contexts into pragmatics. This means LLMs start without any knowledge of the outside world and do not gain it during training. They only gain a knowledge of how humans respond to particular pragmatic stimuli. LLMs do not understand social class or race or gender or presidential candidates, or anything else that might spark some type of emotion in you based on your life experience. Pragmatics isn't something that we expect will be able to be directly incorporated into a model at any point because models cannot live in society. Yet we have already seen the benefits of incorporating it indirectly through data engineering and curation, prompting mechanisms like RAG, and supervised finetuning on instruction datasets. In the future, we expect great improvements in incorporating pragmatics into LLMs, but we emphasize that it's an asymptotic solution because language is ultimately still an abstraction.

Pragmatic structure gets added, whether you mean to add it or not, as soon as you acquire the data you are going to train on. You can think of this type of pragmatic structure as bias, not inherently good or bad, but impossible to get rid of. Later down the line, you get to pick the types of bias you'd like your data to keep by normalizing and curating, augmenting particular underrepresented points, and cutting overrepresented or noisy examples. Instruction datasets show us how you can harness pragmatic structure in your training data to create incredibly useful bias, like biasing your model to answer a question when asked instead of attempting to categorize the sentiment of the question.

Pragmatics and context all revolve around entailment. An entailment is a pragmatic marker within your data, as opposed to the literal text your dataset contains. For example, let's say you have a model attempting to take an input like "Write me a speech about frogs eating soggy socks that doesn't rhyme and where the first letters of each line spell amphibian" and actually follow that instruction. You can immediately tell that this input is asking for a lot. The balance for you as a data engineer would be to make sure that everything the input is asking for is explicitly accounted for in your data. You need examples of speeches, examples of what frogs and socks are and how they behave, and examples of acrostic poems. If you don't have them, the model might be able to understand just from whatever entailments exist in your dataset, but it's pretty up in the air. If you go the extra mile and keep track of entailed versus explicit information and tasks in your dataset, along with data distributions, you'll have examples to answer, "What is the garbage-in resulting in our garbage-out?"

LLMs struggle to pick up on pragmatics, even more so than people, but they do pick up on the things that your average standard deviation of people would. They can even replicate responses from people outside that standard deviation, but pretty inconsistently without the exact right stimulus. That means it's difficult for a model to give you an expert answer on a problem the average person doesn't know without providing the correct bias and entailment during training and in the prompt. For example, including "masterpiece" at the beginning of an image-generation prompt will elicit different and usually higher-quality generations, but only if that distinction was present in the training set and only if you're asking for an image where "masterpiece" is a compliment. Instruction-based datasets attempt to manufacture those stimuli during training by asking questions and giving instructions that entail representative responses. It is impossible to account for every possible situation in training, and you may inadvertently create new types of responses from your end users by trying to account for everything. After training, you can coax particular information from your model through prompting, which has a skill ceiling based on what your data originally entailed.

MORPHOLOGY

Morphology is the study of word structures and how they are formed from smaller units called morphemes. Morphemes are the smallest units of meaning, like the "re-" in "redo" or "relearn." However, not all parts of words are morphemes, such as "ra-" in "ration" or "na-" in "nation," and some can be unexpected, like "helico-" as in "helicoid" and "-pter" as in "pterodactyl."

Understanding how words are constructed helps create better language models and parsing algorithms, which are essential for tasks like tokenization. Tokens are the basic units used in NLP; they can be words, subwords, characters, or whole utterances and do not have to correspond to existing morphemes. People do not consciously decide what their units of meaning are going to be, and as such, they are often illogical. The effectiveness of a language model can depend on how well it can understand and process these tokens. For instance, in tokenization, a model needs to store a set of dictionaries to convert between words and their corresponding indices. One of these tokens is usually an `/<UNK/>` token, which represents any word that the model does not recognize. If this token is used too frequently, it can hinder the model's performance, either because the model's vocabulary is too small or because the tokenizer is not using the right algorithm for the task.

Consider a scenario where you want to build a code completion model, but you're using a tokenizer that only recognizes words separated by whitespace, like the NLTK `punkt` tokenizer. When it encounters the string `def add_two_numbers_together(x, y):`, it will pass `[def, [UNK], y]` to the model. This causes the model to lose valuable information, not only because it doesn't recognize the punctuation but also because the important part of the function's purpose is replaced with an unknown token due to the tokenizer's morphological algorithm. A better understanding of word structure and the appropriate parsing algorithms is needed to improve the model's performance.

2.1.2 Semiotics

After exploring the fundamental features of language and examining their significance in the context of LLMs, it is important to consider the broader perspective of meaning-making and interpretation in human communication. Semiotics, the study of signs and symbols, offers a valuable lens through which we can better understand how people interpret and process language. We will delve into semiotics, examining the relationship between signs, signifiers, and abstractions and how LLMs utilize these elements to generate meaningful output. This discussion will provide a deeper understanding of the intricate processes through which LLMs manage to mimic human-like understanding of language while also shedding light on the challenges and limitations they face in this endeavor. We do not necessarily believe that mimicking human behavior is the right answer for LLM improvement, only that mimicry is how the field has evaluated itself so far.

To introduce semiotics, let's consider figure 2.2, an adapted Peircean semiotic triangle. These triangles are used to organize base ideas into sequences of firstness, secondness, and thirdness, with firstness being at the top left, secondness at the bottom, and thirdness at the top right. If you've ever seen a semiotic triangle before, you may be surprised at the number of corners and orientation. To explain, we've turned them upside down to make it slightly easier to read. Also, because the system is recursive, we're showing you how the system can simultaneously model the entire process and each piece individually. While the whole concept of these ideas is very cool, it's outside of the scope of this book to delve into the philosophy fully. Instead, we can focus on the cardinal parts of those words (first, second, third) to show the sequence of how meaning is processed.

We can also look at each intersection of the triangles to understand why things are presented in the order they are. Feelings can be attached to images and encodings long before they can be attached to words and tables. Ritual and common scripts give a space for interpreted action that's second nature and doesn't have to be thought

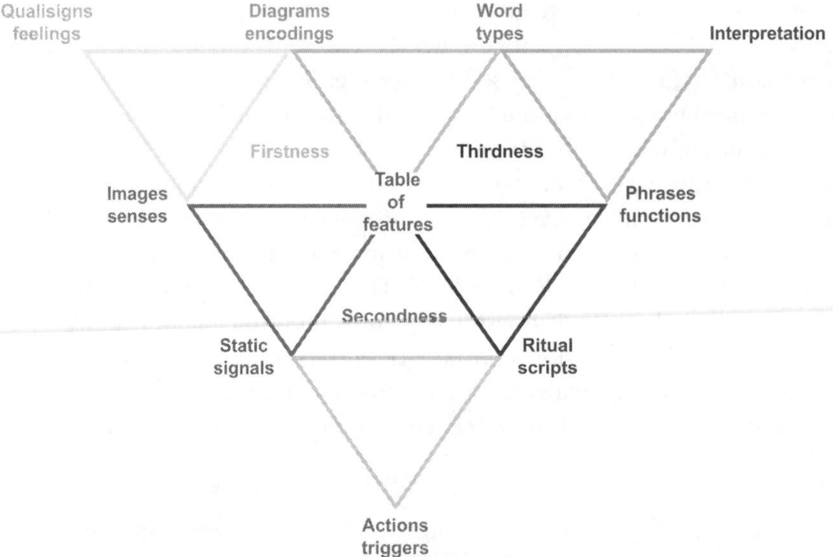

Figure 2.2 A recursive Peircean semiotic triangle is a system of organizing the process of extracting meaning from anything—in our case, from language. Each point on the triangle illustrates one of the minimal parts needed to synthesize meaning within whatever the system is being used to describe, so each point is a minimal unit in meaning for language. Firstness, secondness, and thirdness are not points on the triangle; instead, they are more like markers for the people versed in semiotics to be able to orient themselves in this diagram.

about, similar to how most phrases just come together from words without the native speaker needing to perform metacognition about each word individually. All of these eventually lead to an interpretation or a document (a collection of utterances); in our case, that interpretation should be reached by the LLM. This is why, for example, prompt engineering can boost model efficacy. Foundation LLMs trained on millions of examples of ritual scripts can replicate the type of script significantly better when you explicitly tell the model in the prompt which script needs to be followed. Try asking the model for a step-by-step explanation—maybe prepend your generation with "Let's think about this step-by-step." The model will generate step-by-step scripts based on previous scripts it's seen play out.

For those interested, there are specific ways of reading these figures and a whole field of semiotics to consider; however, it's not guaranteed that you'll be able to create the best LLMs by understanding the whole thing. Instead of diving deeply into this, we'll consider the bare minimum that can help you build the best models, UX, and UI for everyone to interact with. For example, one aspect of the process of creating meaning is recursiveness. When someone is talking to you and they say something that doesn't make sense (is "meaningless" to you), what do you do? Generally, people will ask one or more clarifying questions to figure out the meaning, and the process will start over and over until the meaning is clear to you. The most state-of-the-art models currently on the market do not do this, but they can be made to do it through very purposeful prompting. Many people wouldn't even know to do that without having it pointed out to them. In other words, this is a brief introduction to semiotics. You don't need to be able to give in-depth and accurate coordinate-specific explanations to experts in the semiotic field by the end of this section. The point we are trying to make is that this is an organizational system showcasing the minimum number of things you need to create a full picture of meaning for another person to interpret. We are not giving the same amount of the same kinds of information to our models during training, but if we did, it would result in a marked improvement in model behavior.

Figures 2.2 and 2.3 are meant to represent a minimal organizational model, where each of these pieces is essential. Let's consider figure 2.3, which walks through an example of using a semiotic triangle. Consider images, pictures, and memories and think about what it would be like to try to absorb the knowledge in this book without your eyes to process images and without orthography (a writing system) to abstract the knowledge. Looking at the bullet points, etc., how could you read this book without sections, whitespace between letters, and bullet points to show you the order and structure to process information? Look at semantics and literal encoded meaning, and imagine the book without diagrams or with words that didn't have dictionary defini-

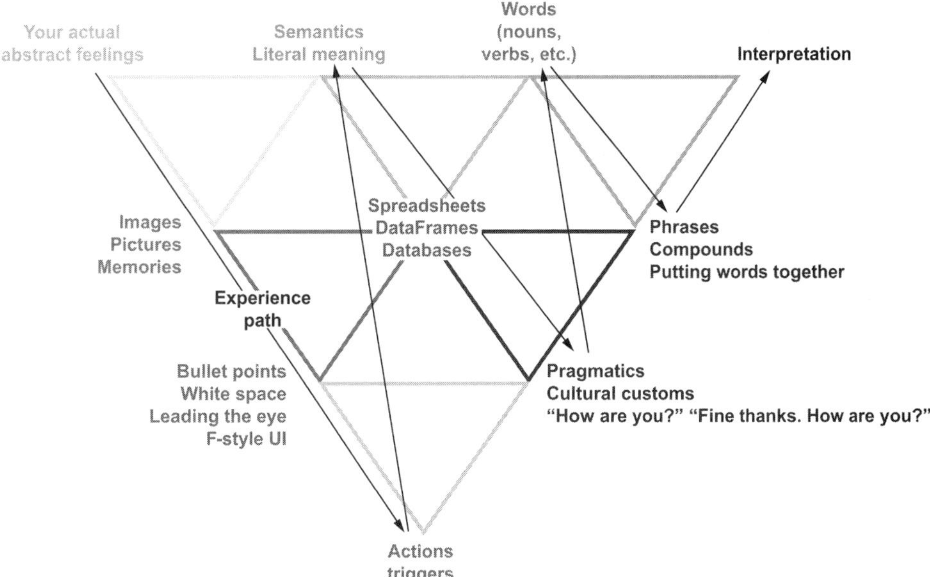

Figure 2.3 Starting at the top-left corner, follow the arrows to see the general order we use to build our interpretations and extract meaning from things we interact with. Here, we've replaced the descriptive words with some examples of each point. Try to imagine interpreting this diagram without any words, examples, arrows, or even the pragmatic context of knowing what a figure in a book like this is supposed to be for.

tions. The spreadsheets in the middle could be a book without any tables or comparative informational organizers, including these figures. What would it be like to read this book without a culture or society with habits and dogma to use as a lens for our interpretations? All these points form our ability to interpret information, along with the lens through which we pass our information to recognize patterns.

So these are the important questions: How many of these things do you see LLMs having access to in order to return meaningful interpretations? Does an LLM have access to feelings or societal rituals? Currently, they do not, but as we go through traditional and newer techniques for NLP inference, think about what different models have access to.

2.1.3 Multilingual NLP

The last challenge that we need to touch on before we evaluate previous NLP techniques and current-generation LLMs is the foundation of linguistics and the reason LLMs even exist. People have wanted to understand or exploit each other since the first civilizations made contact. These cases have resulted in the need for translators, and this need has only exponentially increased as the global economy has grown and flourished.

It's pretty simple math for business as well. Did you know that there are almost as many native speakers of Bengali as there are native speakers of English? If this is the first time you've heard of the Bengali language, this should hopefully color your perception that there is a valuable market for multilingual models. There are billions of people in the world, but only about a third of 1 billion speak English natively. If your model is Anglocentric, like most are, you are missing out on 95% of the people in the world as customers and users. Spanish and Mandarin Chinese are easy wins in this area, but most people don't even go that far.

There are many more politically charged examples of calling things, including different languages, the same that are out of the scope of this book. These are most often because of external factors like government involvement. Keeping these two points in mind—that a monolingual system focusing on English doesn't have the coverage or profit potential that many businesses act like it does and that the boundaries between languages and dialects are unreliable at best and systematically harmful at worst—should highlight the dangerous swamp of opinions. Many businesses and research scientists don't even pretend to want to touch this swamp with a 50-foot pole when designing a product or system.

Unfortunately, no easy solutions exist at this time. However, considering these factors can help you as a scientist or engineer (and hopefully an ethical person) to design LLMs that, at the very least, don't exacerbate and negatively contribute to the existing problems. The first step in this process is deciding on a directional goal from the beginning of the project, either toward localization (l10n) or internationalization (i18n). Localization is an approach exemplified by Mozilla, which has a different version of its browser available through crowdsourced l10n in over 90 languages with no indications of stopping that effort. Internationalization is similar, but in the opposite direction; for example, Ikea tries to put as few words as possible in their instructional booklets, opting instead for internationally recognized symbols and pictures to help customers navigate the DIY projects. Deciding at the beginning of the project cuts down on the effort required to expand to either solution exponentially. It is large enough to switch the perception of translation and formatting from a cost to an investment. In the context of LLMs and their rapid expansion across the public consciousness, it becomes even more important to make that consideration early. Hitting the market with a world-changing technology that automatically disallows most of the world from interacting with it devalues those voices. Having to wait jeopardizes businesses' economic prospects.

Before continuing, let's take a moment to reflect on what we've discussed so far. We've hit important points in linguistics, illustrating concepts for us to consider, such as understanding that the structure of language is separate from its meaning. We have demonstrated quite a journey that each of us takes, both personally and as a society, toward having the metacognition to understand and represent language in a coherent way for computers to work with. This understanding will only improve as we deepen our knowledge of cognitive fields and solve for the linguistic features we encounter. Going along with figure 2.1, we will now demonstrate the computational path for language modeling that we have followed and explore how it has and hasn't solved for any of those linguistic features or strived to create meaning. Let's move into evaluating the various techniques for representing a language algorithmically.

2.2 Language modeling techniques

Having delved into the fundamental features of language, the principles of semiotics, and how LLMs interpret and process linguistic information, we now transition into a more practical realm. We will explore the various NLP techniques developed and employed to create these powerful language models. By examining the strengths and weaknesses of each approach, we will gain valuable insights into the effectiveness of these techniques in capturing the essence of human language and communication. This knowledge will not only help us appreciate the advancements made in the field of NLP but also enable us to better understand the current limitations of these models and the challenges that lie ahead for future research and development.

Let's take a second to go over some data processing that will be universal to all language modeling. First, we'll need to decide how to break up the words and symbols we'll be passing into our model, effectively deciding what a token will be in our model. We'll need a way to convert those tokens to numerical values and back again. Then, we'll need to pick how our model will process the tokenized inputs. Each of the following techniques will build upon the previous techniques in at least one of these ways.

The first of these techniques is called a bag-of-words (BoW) model, and it consists of simply counting words as they appear in text. You could import the CountVectorizer class from sklearn to use it, but it's more instructive if we show you with a small snippet. It can be accomplished very easily with a dictionary that scans through text, creating a new vocabulary entry for each new word as a key and an incrementing value starting at 1:

```
sentence = "What is a bag of words and what does it do for me when " \
    "processing words?"
clean_text = sentence.lower().split(" ")
bow = {word:clean_text.count(word) for word in clean_text}
print(bow)
# {'what': 2, 'is': 1, 'a': 1, 'bag': 1, 'of': 1, 'words': 1, 'and': 1,
# 'does': 1, 'it': 1, 'do': 1, 'for': 1, 'me': 1, 'when': 1, 'processing': 1,
# 'words?': 1}
```

Considering its simplicity, even this model, based entirely on frequency, can be quite powerful when trying to gain insight into a speaker's intentions or at least their idiosyncrasies. For example, you could run a simple BoW model on inaugural speeches of US presidents, searching for the words "freedom," "economy," and "enemy" to gain a pretty good insight about which presidents assumed office under peacetime, during wartime, and during times of monetary strife, just based on how many times each word was mentioned. The BoW model's weaknesses are many, however, as the model provides no images, semantics, pragmatics, phrases, or feelings. In our example, there are two instances of "words," but because our tokenization strategy is just whitespace, it didn't increment the key in the model. It doesn't have any mechanisms to evaluate context or phonetics, and because it divides words by default on whitespace (you can obviously tokenize however you want, but try tokenizing on subwords and see what happens with this model—spoiler: it is bad), it doesn't account for morphology either. Altogether, it should be considered a weak model for representing language but a strong baseline for evaluating other models against it. To solve the problem of BoW models not capturing any sequence data, N-gram models were conceived.

2.2.1 N-gram and corpus-based techniques

N-gram models represent a marked and efficient improvement to BoW by allowing you to give the model a sort of context, represented by N. They are relatively simple statistical models that enable you to generate words based on the N = 1 context space. Listing 2.1 uses trigrams, which means N = 3. We clean the text and give it minimal padding/formatting to help the model, and then we train using everygrams, which prioritizes flexibility over efficiency so that we can train a pentagram (N = 5) or a septagram (N = 7) model if we want. At the end of the listing, where we are generating, we can give the model up to two tokens to help it figure out how to generate further. N-gram models were not created for and have never claimed to attempt complete modeling systems of linguistic knowledge, but they are widely useful in practical applications. They ignore all linguistic features, including syntax, and only attempt to draw probabilistic connections between words appearing in an N-length phrase.

NOTE All assets necessary to run the code—including text and data files—can be found in the code repository accompanying this book: https://github.com/IMJONEZZ/LLMs-in-Production/.

Listing 2.1 A generative N-grams language model implementation

```
from nltk.corpus.reader import PlaintextCorpusReader
from nltk.util import everygrams
from nltk.lm.preprocessing import (
    pad_both_ends,
    flatten,
    padded_everygram_pipeline,
)
from nltk.lm import MLE

my_corpus = PlaintextCorpusReader("./", ".*\.txt")

for sent in my_corpus.sents(fileids="hamlet.txt"):
    print(sent)

padded_trigrams = list(
    pad_both_ends(my_corpus.sents(fileids="hamlet.txt")[1104], n=2)
)
list(everygrams(padded_trigrams, max_len=3))

list(
    flatten(
        pad_both_ends(sent, n=2)
        for sent in my_corpus.sents(fileids="hamlet.txt")
    )
)

train, vocab = padded_everygram_pipeline(
    3, my_corpus.sents(fileids="hamlet.txt")
)

lm = MLE(3)
len(lm.vocab)

lm.fit(train, vocab)
print(lm.vocab)
len(lm.vocab)

lm.generate(6, ["to", "be"])
```

Creates a corpus from any number of plain .txt files

Pads each side of every line in the corpus with <s> and </s> to indicate the start and end of utterances

Allows everygrams to create a training set and a vocab object from the data

Instantiates and trains the model we'll use for N-grams, a maximum likelihood estimator (MLE)

This model will take the everygrams vocabulary, including the <UNK> token used for out-of-vocabulary.

Language can be generated with this model and conditioned with n-1 tokens preceding.

This code is all that you need to create a generative N-gram model. For those interested in being able to evaluate that model further, we've included the following code so you can grab probabilities and log scores or analyze the entropy and perplexity of a particular phrase. Because this is all frequency-based, even though it's mathematically significant, it still does a pretty bad job of describing how perplexing or frequent real-world language actually is:

```
print(lm.counts)
Lm.counts[["to"]]["be"]
```

Any set of tokens up to length = n can be counted easily to determine frequency.

```
print(lm.score("be"))                       # Any token can be given a probability
print(lm.score("be", ["to"]))               # of occurrence and augmented with
print(lm.score("be", ["not", "to"]))        # up to n-1 tokens to precede it.

print(lm.logscore("be"))                    # This can be done as a log score as well to
print(lm.logscore("be", ["to"]))            # avoid very big and very small numbers.
print(lm.logscore("be", ["not", "to"]))

test = [("to", "be"), ("or", "not"), ("to", "be")]   # Sets of tokens can be
print(lm.entropy(test))                              # tested for entropy and
print(lm.perplexity(test))                           # perplexity as well.
```

While this code example illustrates creating a trigram language model, unfortunately, not all phrases needing to be captured are only three tokens long. For example, from Hamlet, "To be or not to be" consists of one phrase with two words and one phrase with four words. Note that even though N-grams are typically very small language models, it is possible to make an N-gram LLM by making N=1,000,000,000 or higher, but don't expect to get even one ounce of use out of it. Just because we made it big doesn't make it better or mean it'll have any practical application: 99.9% of all text and 100% of all meaningful text contains fewer than 1 billion tokens appearing more than once, and that computational power can be much better spent elsewhere.

N-grams only use static signals (whitespace, orthography) and words to extract meaning (figure 2.2). They try to measure phrases manually, assuming all phrases will be the same length. That said, N-grams can be used to create powerful baselines for text analysis. In addition, if the analyst already knows the pragmatic context of the utterance, N-grams can give quick and accurate insight into real-world scenarios. Nonetheless, this type of phrasal modeling fails to capture any semantic encodings that individual words could have. To solve this problem, Bayesian statistics were applied to language modeling.

2.2.2 Bayesian techniques

Bayes' theorem is one of the most mathematically sound and simple theories for describing the occurrence of your output within your input space. Essentially, it calculates the probability of an event occurring based on prior knowledge. The theorem posits that the probability of a hypothesis being true given evidence—for example, that a sentence has a positive sentiment—is equal to the probability of the evidence occurring given the hypothesis is true multiplied by the probability of the hypothesis occurring, all divided by the probability of the evidence being true. It can be expressed mathematically as

$$P(hypothesis \mid evidence) = (P(evidence \mid hypothesis) \times P(hypothesis)) \; / \; P(evidence)$$

or

$$P(A|B) \times P(B) = P(B|A) \times P(A)$$

Because this isn't a math book, we'll dive into Bayes' theorem to the exact same depth we dove into other linguistics concepts and trust the interested reader to search for more.

Unfortunately, even though the theorem represents the data in a mathematically sound way, it doesn't account for any stochasticity or multiple meanings of words. One word you can always throw at a Bayesian model to confuse it is "it." Any demonstrative pronoun ends up getting assigned values in the same `LogPrior` and `LogLikelihood` way as all other words, and it gets a static value, which is antithetical to the usage of those words. For example, if you're trying to perform sentiment analysis on an utterance, assigning all pronouns a null value would be better than letting them go through the Bayesian training. Note also that Bayesian techniques don't create generative language models the way the rest of these techniques will. Because of the nature of Bayes' theorem validating a hypothesis, these models work for classification and can bring powerful augmentation to a generative language model.

Listing 2.2 shows you how to create a naive Bayes classification language model, or a system that performs classification on text based on a prior-learned internal language model. Instead of using a package like sklearn or something that would make writing the code a little easier, we opted to write out what we were doing, so it's a bit longer, but it should be more information about how it works. We are using the least-complex version of a naive Bayes model. We haven't made it multinomial or added anything fancy; obviously, it would work better if you opted to upgrade it for any problem you want. And we highly recommend you do.

NOTE To make the code easier to understand and help highlight the portions we wanted to focus on, we have simplified some of our code listings by extracting portions to utility helpers. If you are seeing import errors, this is why. These helper methods can be found in the code repository accompanying this book: https://github.com/IMJONEZZ/LLMs-in-Production/

Listing 2.2 Categorical naive Bayes language model implementation

```
from utils import process_utt, lookup
from nltk.corpus.reader import PlaintextCorpusReader
import numpy as np

my_corpus = PlaintextCorpusReader("./", ".*\.txt")

sents = my_corpus.sents(fileids="hamlet.txt")


def count_utts(result, utts, ys):
    """
    Input:
        result: a dictionary that is used to map each pair to its frequency
        utts: a list of utts
        ys: a list of the sentiment of each utt (either 0 or 1)
```

```
    Output:
        result: a dictionary mapping each pair to its frequency
    """

    for y, utt in zip(ys, utts):
        for word in process_utt(utt):
            pair = (word, y)                          <-- Defines the key, which is
                                                          the word and label tuple
            if pair in result:
            result[pair] += 1                         <-- If the key exists in the dictionary,
                                                          increments the count
            else:
            result[pair] = 1                          <-- If the key is new, adds it to the
                                                          dict and sets the count to 1
    return result


result = {}
utts = [" ".join(sent) for sent in sents]
ys = [sent.count("be") > 0 for sent in sents]
count_utts(result, utts, ys)

freqs = count_utts({}, utts, ys)
lookup(freqs, "be", True)
for k, v in freqs.items():
    if "be" in k:
        print(f"{k}:{v}")


def train_naive_bayes(freqs, train_x, train_y):
    """
    Input:
        freqs: dictionary from (word, label) to how often the word appears
        train_x: a list of utts
        train_y: a list of labels correponding to the utts (0,1)
    Output:
        logprior: the log prior.
        loglikelihood: the log likelihood of you Naive bayes equation.
    """
    loglikelihood = {}
    logprior = 0

    vocab = set([pair[0] for pair in freqs.keys()])   <-- Calculates V, the number of unique
    V = len(vocab)                                        words in the vocabulary

    N_pos = N_neg = 0                                 <-- Calculates N_pos and N_neg
    for pair in freqs.keys():
        if pair[1] > 0:                               <-- If the label is positive
            N_pos += lookup(freqs, pair[0], True)         (greater than zero) . . .
                                                      <-- . . . increments the number of
                                                          positive words (word, label)
        else:                                         <-- Else, the label is negative.
            N_neg += lookup(freqs, pair[0], False)    <-- Increments the number of
                                                          negative words (word, label)
```

```
    D = len(train_y)                          Calculates D, the number of documents

    D_pos = sum(train_y)                      Calculates the number of positive documents

    D_neg = D - D_pos                         Calculates the number of negative documents

    logprior = np.log(D_pos) - np.log(D_neg)       Calculates logprior

    for word in vocab:                        For each word in
        freq_pos = lookup(freqs, word, 1)     the vocabulary . . .
        freq_neg = lookup(freqs, word, 0)

        p_w_pos = (freq_pos + 1) / (N_pos + V)     . . . calculates the probability
        p_w_neg = (freq_neg + 1) / (N_neg + V)     that each word is positive or
                                                   negative

        loglikelihood[word] = np.log(p_w_pos / p_w_neg)     Calculates the
                                                            log likelihood
    return logprior, loglikelihood                          of the word


def naive_bayes_predict(utt, logprior, loglikelihood):
    """
    Input:
        utt: a string
        logprior: a number
        loglikelihood: a dictionary of words mapping to numbers
    Output:
        p: the sum of all the logliklihoods + logprior
    """
    word_l = process_utt(utt)                 Processes the utt to
                                              get a list of words

    p = 0                                     Initializes probability to zero

    p += logprior                             Adds the logprior

    for word in word_l:
        if word in loglikelihood:             Checks if the word exists in
            p += loglikelihood[word]          the loglikelihood dictionary

    return p                                  Adds the log likelihood of
                                              that word to the probability


def test_naive_bayes(test_x, test_y, logprior, loglikelihood):
    """
    Input:
        test_x: A list of utts
        test_y: the corresponding labels for the list of utts
        logprior: the logprior
        loglikelihood: a dictionary with the loglikelihoods for each word
    Output:
        accuracy: (# of utts classified correctly)/(total # of utts)
    """
    accuracy = 0                              Returns this properly
```

```
    y_hats = []
    for utt in test_x:
        if naive_bayes_predict(utt, logprior, loglikelihood) > 0:
            y_hat_i = 1
        else:
            y_hat_i = 0

        y_hats.append(y_hat_i)

    error = sum(
        [abs(y_hat - test) for y_hat, test in zip(y_hats, test_y)]
    ) / len(y_hats)

    accuracy = 1 - error

    return accuracy


if __name__ == "__main__":
    logprior, loglikelihood = train_naive_bayes(freqs, utts, ys)
    print(logprior)
    print(len(loglikelihood))

    my_utt = "To be or not to be, that is the question."
    p = naive_bayes_predict(my_utt, logprior, loglikelihood)
    print("The expected output is", p)

    print(
        f"Naive Bayes accuracy = {test_naive_bayes(utts, ys, logprior,
     loglikelihood):0.4f}
    )
```

If the prediction is > 0 . . .

. . . the predicted class is 1.

Otherwise, the predicted class is 0.

Appends the predicted class to the list y_hats

Error = avg of the abs vals of the diffs between y_hats and test_y.

Accuracy is 1 minus the error.

This theorem doesn't create the same type of language model but one with a list of probabilities associated with one hypothesis. As such, Bayesian language models can't be used effectively to generate language, but they can be very powerfully implemented for classification tasks. In our opinion, though, Bayesian models are often overhyped for even this task. One of the crowning achievements of one author's career was replacing and removing a Bayesian model from production.

In Bayesian models, one big problem is that all sequences are completely unconnected, like BoW models, moving us to the opposite end of sequence modeling from N-grams. Like a pendulum, language modeling swings back toward sequence modeling and language generation with Markov chains.

2.2.3 Markov chains

Often called hidden Markov models (HMMs), Markov chains essentially add state to the N-gram models, storing probabilities using hidden states. They are often used to help parse text data for even larger models, doing things like part-of-speech (PoS) tagging (marking words with their parts of speech) and named entity recognition (NER; marking identifying words with their referent and usually type; e.g., LA – Los

Angeles – City) on textual data. Building on the previous Bayesian models, Markov models rely completely on stochasticity (predictable randomness) in the tokens encountered. The idea that the probability of anything happening *next* depends completely upon the state of *now* is, like Bayes' theorem, mathematically sound. So instead of modeling words based solely on their historical occurrence and drawing a probability from that, we model their future and past collocation based on what is currently occurring. So the probability of "happy" occurring goes down to almost zero if "happy" was just output but goes up significantly if "am" has just occurred. Markov chains are so intuitive that they were incorporated into later iterations of Bayesian statistics and are still used in production systems today.

In listing 2.3, we train a Markov chain generative language model. This is the first model where we've used a specific tokenizer, which, in this case, will tokenize based on the whitespace between words. This is also only the second time we've referred to a collection of utterances meant to be viewed together as a document. As you play around with this one, pay close attention and make some comparisons yourself of how well the HMM generates compared to even a large N-gram model.

Listing 2.3 Generative hidden Markov language model implementation

```
import re
import random
from nltk.tokenize import word_tokenize
from collections import defaultdict, deque


class MarkovChain:
    def __init__(self):
        self.lookup_dict = defaultdict(list)
        self._seeded = False
        self.__seed_me()

    def __seed_me(self, rand_seed=None):
        if self._seeded is not True:
            try:
                if rand_seed is not None:
                    random.seed(rand_seed)
                else:
                    random.seed()
                self._seeded = True
            except NotImplementedError:
                self._seeded = False

    def add_document(self, str):
        preprocessed_list = self._preprocess(str)
        pairs = self.__generate_tuple_keys(preprocessed_list)
        for pair in pairs:
            self.lookup_dict[pair[0]].append(pair[1])

    def _preprocess(self, str):
        cleaned = re.sub(r"\W+", " ", str).lower()
```

```
        tokenized = word_tokenize(cleaned)
        return tokenized

    def __generate_tuple_keys(self, data):
        if len(data) < 1:
            return

        for i in range(len(data) - 1):
            yield [data[i], data[i + 1]]

    def generate_text(self, max_length=50):
        context = deque()
        output = []
        if len(self.lookup_dict) > 0:
            self.__seed_me(rand_seed=len(self.lookup_dict))
            chain_head = [list(self.lookup_dict)[0]]
            context.extend(chain_head)

            while len(output) < (max_length - 1):
                next_choices = self.lookup_dict[context[-1]]
                if len(next_choices) > 0:
                    next_word = random.choice(next_choices)
                    context.append(next_word)
                    output.append(context.popleft())
                else:
                    break
            output.extend(list(context))
        return " ".join(output)


if __name__ == "__main__":
    with open("hamlet.txt", "r", encoding="utf-8") as f:
        text = f.read()
    HMM = MarkovChain()
    HMM.add_document(text)

    print(HMM.generate_text(max_length=25))
```

This code shows a basic implementation of a Markov model for generation, and we encourage you to experiment with it. Give it text from songs from your favorite musicians or books from your favorite authors, and see whether what comes out sounds like them. HMMs are incredibly fast and are often used in predictive text or predictive search applications. Markov models represent the first comprehensive attempt to model language from a descriptive linguistic perspective, as opposed to a prescriptive one. The perspective is interesting because Markov did not originally intend to use linguistic modeling, only to win an argument about continuous independent states. Later, Markov used Markov chains to model vowel distribution in a Pushkin novel, so he was at least aware of the possible applications.

The difference between descriptive and prescriptive linguistics is that the latter focuses on how things *ought* to be, while the former focuses on how things *are*. From a language modeling perspective, it has proven vastly more effective to describe what language is doing from a corpus or Markov perspective rather than to attempt to prescribe how language ought to behave. Unfortunately, a current state by itself cannot be used to give context beyond the now, so historical or societal context cannot be represented effectively in a Markov model. The semantic encoding of words also becomes problematic, as represented in the code example: Markov chains will output syntactically correct chains of words that are nonsense semantically, similar to "colorless green ideas sleep furiously." To solve this problem, "continuous" models were developed to allow for a "semantic embedding" representation of tokens.

2.2.4 Continuous language modeling

A continuous bag-of-words (CBoW) model—much like its namesake, the BoW model—is a frequency-based approach to analyzing language, meaning that it models words based on how often they occur. The next word in a human utterance has never been determined based on probability or frequency. Consequently, we provide an example of creating word embeddings to be ingested or compared by other models using a CBoW. We'll use a neural network to provide you with a good methodology.

This is the first language modeling technique we'll see that essentially slides a context window over a given utterance (the context window is an N-gram model) and attempts to guess the word in the middle based on the surrounding words in the window. For example, let's say your window has a length of 5, and your sentence is "Learning about linguistics makes me happy." You would give the CBoW `['learning', 'about', 'makes', 'me']` to try to get the model to guess "linguistics" based on how many times the model has previously seen that word occur in similar places. This example shows you why generation is difficult for models trained like this. Say you give the model `['makes', 'me', '</s>']` as input. Now the model only has three pieces of information, instead of four, to use to try to figure out the answer; it also will be biased toward only guessing words it has seen before at the end of sentences, as opposed to getting ready to start new clauses. It's not all bad, though. One feature that makes continuous models stand out for embeddings is that they don't have to look at only words before the target word; they can also use words that come after the target to gain some semblance of context.

In listing 2.4, we create our first continuous model. In our case, to keep things as simple as possible, we use a BoW model for the language processing and a one-layer neural network with two parameters for the embedding estimation, although both could be substituted for any other models. For example, you could substitute N-grams for the BoW and a naive Bayes model for the neural network to get a continuous naive N-gram model. The point is that the actual models used in this technique are a bit arbitrary; it's the continuous technique that's important. To illustrate this further, we don't use any packages other than `numpy` to do the math for the neural network, even though it's the first one appearing in this section.

Pay special attention to the steps—initializing the model weights, the rectified linear unit (ReLU) activation function, the final softmax layer, and forward and backpropagation—and how it all fits together in the `gradient_descent` function. These are pieces of the puzzle that you will see crop up again and again, regardless of programming language or framework. You will need to initialize models, pick activation functions, pick final layers, and define forward and backward propagation in TensorFlow, PyTorch, and Hugging Face, as well as if you ever start creating your own models instead of using someone else's.

Listing 2.4 Generative CBoW language model implementation

```
import nltk
import numpy as np
from utils import get_batches, compute_pca, get_dict
import re
from matplotlib import pyplot

with open("hamlet.txt", "r", encoding="utf-8") as f:
    data = f.read()

data = re.sub(r"[,!?;-]", ".", data)
data = nltk.word_tokenize(data)
data = [ch.lower() for ch in data if ch.isalpha() or ch == "."]
print("Number of tokens:", len(data), "\n", data[500:515])

fdist = nltk.FreqDist(word for word in data)
print("Size of vocabulary:", len(fdist))
print("Most Frequent Tokens:", fdist.most_common(20))

word2Ind, Ind2word = get_dict(data)
V = len(word2Ind)
print("Size of vocabulary:", V)

print("Index of the word 'king':", word2Ind["king"])
print("Word which has index 2743:", Ind2word[2743])

def initialize_model(N, V, random_seed=1):
    """
    Inputs:
        N: dimension of hidden vector
        V: dimension of vocabulary
        random_seed: seed for consistent results in tests
    Outputs:
        W1, W2, b1, b2: initialized weights and biases
    """
    np.random.seed(random_seed)

    W1 = np.random.rand(N, V)
    W2 = np.random.rand(V, N)
    b1 = np.random.rand(N, 1)
    b2 = np.random.rand(V, 1)

    return W1, W2, b1, b2
```

Annotations:
- Creates our corpus for training (the `with open(...)` block)
- Slightly cleans the data by removing punctuation, tokenizing by word, and converting to lowercase alpha characters (the `re.sub` line and the lines after it)
- Gets our bag of words, along with a distribution (`fdist`)
- Creates two dictionaries to speed up time-to-convert and keep track of vocabulary (`get_dict`)
- Here, we create our neural network with one layer and two parameters. (`initialize_model`)

```
def softmax(z):                    <-- Creates our final classification layer,
    """                                which makes all possibilities add up to 1
    Inputs:
        z: output scores from the hidden layer
    Outputs:
        yhat: prediction (estimate of y)
    """
    yhat = np.exp(z) / np.sum(np.exp(z), axis=0)
    return yhat
                                            Defines the behavior for moving
def forward_prop(x, W1, W2, b1, b2):    <-- forward through our model, along
    """                                     with an activation function
    Inputs:
        x: average one-hot vector for the context
        W1,W2,b1,b2: weights and biases to be learned
    Outputs:
        z: output score vector
    """
    h = W1 @ x + b1
    h = np.maximum(0, h)                         Define how we determine
    z = W2 @ h + b2                              the distance between
    return z, h                                  ground truth and model
                                                 predictions
def compute_cost(y, yhat, batch_size):       <--
    logprobs = np.multiply(np.log(yhat), y) + np.multiply(
        np.log(1 - yhat), 1 - y
    )                                                          Defines how we
    cost = -1 / batch_size * np.sum(logprobs)                  move backward
    cost = np.squeeze(cost)                                    through the
    return cost                                                model and
                                                               collect
def back_prop(x, yhat, y, h, W1, W2, b1, b2, batch_size):  <-- gradients
    """
    Inputs:
        x:  average one hot vector for the context
        yhat: prediction (estimate of y)
        y:  target vector
        h:  hidden vector (see eq. 1)
        W1, W2, b1, b2:  weights and biases
        batch_size: batch size
    Outputs:
        grad_W1, grad_W2, grad_b1, grad_b2:  gradients of weights and biases
    """
    l1 = np.dot(W2.T, yhat - y)
    l1 = np.maximum(0, l1)
    grad_W1 = np.dot(l1, x.T) / batch_size
    grad_W2 = np.dot(yhat - y, h.T) / batch_size
    grad_b1 = np.sum(l1, axis=1, keepdims=True) / batch_size
    grad_b2 = np.sum(yhat - y, axis=1, keepdims=True) / batch_size
                                                         Puts it all together
    return grad_W1, grad_W2, grad_b1, grad_b2                      and trains

def gradient_descent(data, word2Ind, N, V, num_iters, alpha=0.03):  <--
    """
    This is the gradient_descent function
```

```
    Inputs:
        data:       text
        word2Ind:   words to Indices
        N:          dimension of hidden vector
        V:          dimension of vocabulary
        num_iters: number of iterations
    Outputs:
        W1, W2, b1, b2:  updated matrices and biases

    """
    W1, W2, b1, b2 = initialize_model(N, V, random_seed=8855)
    batch_size = 128
    iters = 0
    C = 2
    for x, y in get_batches(data, word2Ind, V, C, batch_size):
        z, h = forward_prop(x, W1, W2, b1, b2)
        yhat = softmax(z)
        cost = compute_cost(y, yhat, batch_size)
        if (iters + 1) % 10 == 0:
            print(f"iters: {iters+1} cost: {cost:.6f}")
        grad_W1, grad_W2, grad_b1, grad_b2 = back_prop(
            x, yhat, y, h, W1, W2, b1, b2, batch_size
        )
        W1 = W1 - alpha * grad_W1
        W2 = W2 - alpha * grad_W2
        b1 = b1 - alpha * grad_b1
        b2 = b2 - alpha * grad_b2
        iters += 1
        if iters == num_iters:
            break
        if iters % 100 == 0:
            alpha *= 0.66

    return W1, W2, b1, b2

C = 2                                  <-- Trains the model
N = 50
word2Ind, Ind2word = get_dict(data)
V = len(word2Ind)
num_iters = 150
print("Call gradient_descent")
W1, W2, b1, b2 = gradient_descent(data, word2Ind, N, V, num_iters)
# Call gradient descent
# Iters: 10 loss: 0.525015
# Iters: 20 loss: 0.092373
# Iters: 30 loss: 0.050474
# Iters: 40 loss: 0.034724
# Iters: 50 loss: 0.026468
# Iters: 60 loss: 0.021385
# Iters: 70 loss: 0.017941
# Iters: 80 loss: 0.015453
# Iters: 90 loss: 0.012099
# Iters: 100 loss: 0.012099
# Iters: 110 loss: 0.011253
# Iters: 120 loss: 0.010551
```

```
# Iters: 130 loss: 0.009932
# Iters: 140 loss: 0.009382
# Iters: 150 loss: 0.008889
```

The CBoW example is our first code example to showcase a full and effective training loop in machine learning. Within all of that, pay special attention to the steps in a training loop, especially the activation function, ReLU. As we expect you to be at least familiar with various ML paradigms, including different activations, we won't explain the ReLU here. We will address when you should use it and when you shouldn't. ReLUs, while solving the vanishing gradient problem, don't solve the exploding gradient problem, and they destroy all negative comparisons within the model. Better situational variants include the Exponential linear unit (ELU), which allows negative numbers to normalize to alpha, and the generalized Gaussian linear units (GEGLU)/Swish-gated linear unit (SWIGLU), which works well in increasingly perplexing scenarios, like language. However, people often use ReLUs, not because they are the best in a situation, but because they are easy to understand and code and intuitive, even more so than the activations they were created to replace, the sigmoid or tanh.

A lot of this ends up being abstracted with packages and the like, but knowing what's going on under the hood will be very helpful for you as someone putting LLMs in production. You should be able to predict with some certainty how different models will behave in various situations. The next section will dive into one of those abstractions—in this case, the abstraction created by the continuous modeling technique.

2.2.5 Embeddings

Hearkening back to our features of language, it should be easy to connect why continuous-style language modeling was such a breakthrough. Embeddings take the tokenized vectors we've created that don't contain any meaning and attempt to insert that meaning based on observations that can be made about the text, such as word order and subwords appearing in similar contexts. Despite the primary mode of meaning being collocation (co-located, words that appear next to each other), they prove useful and even show some similarities to human-encoded word meaning.

The quintessential example from Word2Vec, one of the first pretrained vector embeddings, was taking the vector for "king," subtracting the vector for "man," adding the vector for "woman," and finding the nearest neighbor to the sum was the vector for the word "queen." This makes sense to us, as it mimics human semantics. One of the major differences is one that's already been mentioned a couple of times: pragmatics. Humans use pragmatic context to inform semantic meaning, understanding that just because you said, "I need food," doesn't mean you are actually in physical danger without it. Embeddings are devoid of any influence outside of pure usage, which feels like it could be how humans learn as well, and there are good arguments on all sides here. The one thing holding is that if we can somehow give models more representative data, that may open the door to more effective embeddings, but it's a chicken-and-egg problem because more effective embeddings give better model performance.

In listing 2.5, we dive into how to visualize embeddings using `pyplot`. We will be going more in depth into embeddings in later chapters. This is helpful for model explainability and also for validation during your pretraining step. If you see that your semantically similar embeddings are relatively close to each other on the graph, you're likely going in the right direction.

Listing 2.5 Embedding visualization

```
words = [          <- After listing 2.4 is done
    "King",           and gradient descent
    "Queen",          has been executed
    "Lord",
    "Man",
    "Woman",
    "Prince",
    "Ophelia",
    "Rich",
    "Happy",
]
embs = (W1.T + W2) / 2.0
idx = [word2Ind[word] for word in words]
X = embs[idx, :]
print(X.shape, idx)

result = compute_pca(X, 2)
pyplot.scatter(result[:, 0], result[:, 1])
for i, word in enumerate(words):
    pyplot.annotate(word, xy=(result[i, 0], result[i, 1]))
pyplot.show()
```

As shown in figure 2.4, this code is a successful but very sparse embedding representation that we trained from our CBoW model. Getting those semantic representations (embeddings) to be denser is the main place we can see improvement in this field, although many successful experiments have been run where denser semantic meaning has been supplanted with greater pragmatic context through instruct and different thought-chaining techniques. We will address chain of thought (CoT) and other techniques later. For now, let's pivot to discussing why our continuous embedding technique can even be successful, given that frequency-based models are characteristically difficult to correlate with reality. All of this started with the MLP more than half a century ago.

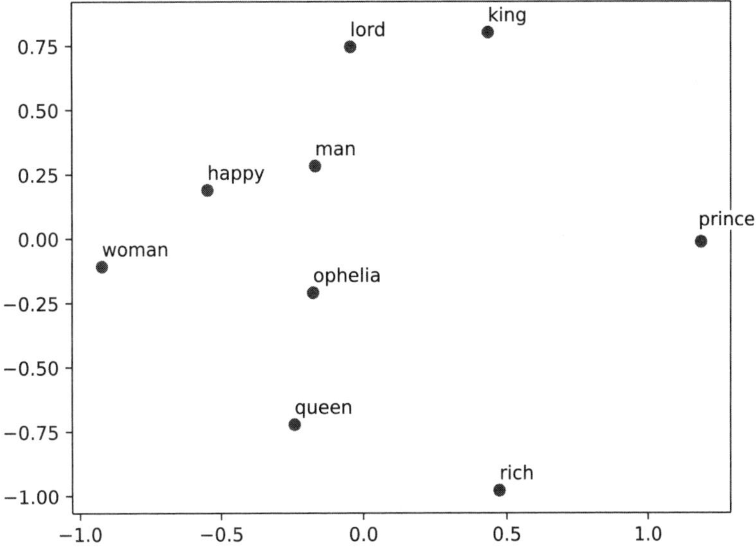

Figure 2.4 A visualization technique for word embeddings. Visualizing embeddings can be important for model explainability.

2.2.6 Multilayer perceptrons

MLPs are the embodiment of the sentiment, "Machines are really good at doing one thing, so I wish we could just use a bunch of machines that are really good at the one thing to make one that's good at a lot of things." Every weight and bias in the neural network of the MLP is good at doing one thing, which could be detecting one or more features. So we bind a bunch of them together to detect larger, more complex features. MLPs serve as the primary building block in most neural network architectures. The key distinctions between architectures, such as convolutional neural networks and recurrent neural networks, mainly arise from data loading methods and the handling of tokenized and embedded data as it flows through the layers of the model rather than the functionality of individual layers, particularly the fully connected layers.

Listing 2.6 provides a more dynamic class of neural networks that can have as many layers and parameters as deemed necessary for your task. We give a more defined and explicit class using PyTorch to give you the tools to implement the MLP in whatever way you'd like, both from scratch and in a popular framework.

Listing 2.6 Multilayer perceptron PyTorch class implementation

```
import torch
import torch.nn as nn
import torch.nn.functional as F
```

```
class MultiLayerPerceptron(nn.Module):
    def __init__(
        self,
        input_size,
        hidden_size=2,
        output_size=3,
        num_hidden_layers=1,
        hidden_activation=nn.Sigmoid,
    ):
        """Initialize weights.
        Args:
            input_size (int): size of the input
            hidden_size (int): size of the hidden layers
            output_size (int): size of the output
            num_hidden_layers (int): number of hidden layers
            hidden_activation (torch.nn.*): the activation class
        """
        super(MultiLayerPerceptron, self).__init__()
        self.module_list = nn.ModuleList()
        interim_input_size = input_size
        interim_output_size = hidden_size
        torch.device("cuda:0" if torch.cuda.is_available() else "cpu")

        for _ in range(num_hidden_layers):
            self.module_list.append(
                nn.Linear(interim_input_size, interim_output_size)
            )
            self.module_list.append(hidden_activation())
            interim_input_size = interim_output_size

        self.fc_final = nn.Linear(interim_input_size, output_size)

        self.last_forward_cache = []

    def forward(self, x, apply_softmax=False):
        """The forward pass of the MLP

        Args:
            x_in (torch.Tensor): an input data tensor.
            x_in.shape should be (batch, input_dim)
            apply_softmax (bool): a flag for the softmax activation
                should be false if used with the Cross Entropy losses
        Returns:
            the resulting tensor. tensor.shape should be (batch, output_dim)
        """
        for module in self.module_list:
            x = module(x)

        output = self.fc_final(x)

        if apply_softmax:
            output = F.softmax(output, dim=1)

        return output
```

From this code, we can see, as opposed to the CBoW implementation, which had two static layers, that this MLP is not static in size until it has been instantiated. If you wanted to give this model 1 million layers, you would have to put `num_hidden_layers=1000000` when you instantiate the class. However, just because you give a model that many parameters doesn't mean that will make it immediately better. LLMs are more than just a lot of layers. Like RNNs and CNNs, the magic of LLMs is in how data goes in and moves through the model. To illustrate, let's look at the RNN and one of its variations.

2.2.7 Recurrent neural networks and long short-term memory networks

RNNs are a class of neural networks designed to analyze sequences based on the weaknesses in previous language modeling techniques. A sequence can be thought of as an ordered array, where the sum of the whole array changes value if any of the parts are moved around. The logic goes that if language is presented in a sequence, then maybe it should be processed in a sequence instead of one token at a time. RNNs accomplish this by using logic we've seen before, both in MLPs and Markov chains, where an internal state or memory is referred to when new inputs are processed and by creating cycles when connections between nodes are detected as useful.

In fully recurrent networks, like the one in listing 2.7, all nodes start out initially connected to all subsequent nodes, but those connections can be set to zero to simulate them breaking if they are not useful. This solves one of the biggest problems that earlier models suffered from, static input size, and enables an RNN and its variants to process variable length inputs. Unfortunately, longer sequences create a new problem. Because each neuron in the network connects to subsequent neurons, longer sequences create smaller changes to the overall sum, making the gradients smaller until they eventually vanish, even with important words; this is called a vanishing gradient. Other problems exist too, such as exploding and diminishing gradients.

For example, let's consider the following sentences with the task sentiment analysis: "I loved the movie last night" and "The movie I went to see last night was the very best I had ever expected to see." These sentences can be considered semantically similar, even if they aren't exactly the same. When moving through an RNN, each word in the first sentence is worth more, and the consequence is that the first sentence has a higher positive rating than the second sentence just because the first sentence is shorter. The inverse is also true: exploding gradients are a consequence of this sequence processing, which makes training deep RNNs difficult.

To solve this problem, LSTMs, a type of RNN, use memory cells and gating mechanisms to process sequences of variable length but without the problem of comprehending longer and shorter sequences differently. Anticipating multilingual scenarios and understanding that people don't think about language in only one direction, LSTMs can also process sequences bidirectionally by concatenating the outputs of two RNNs, one reading the sequence from left to right and the other from right to left.

This bidirectionality improves results, allowing information to be seen and remembered even after thousands of tokens have passed.

In listing 2.7, we give classes for both an RNN and an LSTM. In the code in the repo associated with this book (https://github.com/IMJONEZZ/LLMs-in-Production), you can see the results of training both the RNN and LSTM. The takeaway is that the LSTM achieves better accuracy on both training and validation sets in half as many epochs (25 versus 50 with RNN). One of the innovations to note is that the packed embeddings utilize padding to extend all variable-length sequences to the maximum length. Thus, LSTMs can process input of any length as long as it is shorter than the maximum. To set up the LSTM effectively, we'll do some classical NLP on the dataset (a Twitter sentiment analysis dataset). That workflow will tokenize with the Natural Language Toolkit Regex. It looks for words and nothing else, passing into a spacy lemmatizer to get a list of lists containing only the base unconjugated forms of words.

Listing 2.7 RNN and LSTM PyTorch class implementations

```
import torch
import pandas as pd
import numpy as np
from gensim.models import Word2Vec
from sklearn.model_selection import train_test_split
import nltk
import spacy

    tokenizer = nltk.tokenize.RegexpTokenizer("\w+'?\w+|\w+'")
    tokenizer.tokenize("This is a test")
    stop_words = nltk.corpus.stopwords.words("english")
    nlp = spacy.load("en_core_web_lg", disable=["parser", "tagger", "ner"])

dataset = pd.read_csv("./data/twitter.csv")      <-- Creates our corpus for training and performs some classic NLP preprocessing

text_data = list(
    map(lambda x: tokenizer.tokenize(x.lower()), dataset["text"])
)
text_data = [
    [token.lemma_ for word in text for token in nlp(word)]
    for text in text_data
]
label_data = list(map(lambda x: x, dataset["feeling"]))
assert len(text_data) == len(
    label_data
), f"{len(text_data)} does not equal {len(label_data)}"

EMBEDDING_DIM = 100
model = Word2Vec(
    text_data, vector_size=EMBEDDING_DIM, window=5, min_count=1, workers=4
)
word_vectors = model.wv
print(f"Vocabulary Length: {len(model.wv)}")
del model
```

```
padding_value = len(word_vectors.index_to_key)
    embedding_weights = torch.Tensor(word_vectors.vectors)    ◁── Embeddings are needed to give semantic value to the inputs of an LSTM.


class RNN(torch.nn.Module):
    def __init__(
        self,
        input_dim,
        embedding_dim,
        hidden_dim,
        output_dim,
        embedding_weights,
    ):
        super().__init__()
        self.embedding = torch.nn.Embedding.from_pretrained(
            embedding_weights
    )
    self.rnn = torch.nn.RNN(embedding_dim, hidden_dim)
    self.fc = torch.nn.Linear(hidden_dim, output_dim)

    def forward(self, x, text_lengths):
        embedded = self.embedding(x)
        packed_embedded = torch.nn.utils.rnn.pack_padded_sequence(
            embedded, text_lengths
        )
        packed_output, hidden = self.rnn(packed_embedded)
        output, output_lengths = torch.nn.utils.rnn.pad_packed_sequence(
            packed_output
        )
        return self.fc(hidden.squeeze(0))


INPUT_DIM = padding_value
EMBEDDING_DIM = 100
HIDDEN_DIM = 256
OUTPUT_DIM = 1

rnn_model = RNN(
    INPUT_DIM, EMBEDDING_DIM, HIDDEN_DIM, OUTPUT_DIM, embedding_weights
)

rnn_optimizer = torch.optim.SGD(rnn_model.parameters(), lr=1e-3)
rnn_criterion = torch.nn.BCEWithLogitsLoss()
device = torch.device("cuda" if torch.cuda.is_available() else "cpu")


class LSTM(torch.nn.Module):
    def __init__(
    self,
    input_dim,
    embedding_dim,
    hidden_dim,
    output_dim,
    n_layers,
    bidirectional,
```

```
        dropout,
        embedding_weights,
    ):
        super().__init__()
        self.embedding = torch.nn.Embedding.from_pretrained(
            embedding_weights
        )
        self.rnn = torch.nn.LSTM(
            embedding_dim,
            hidden_dim,
            num_layers=n_layers,
            bidirectional=bidirectional,
            dropout=dropout,
        )
        self.fc = torch.nn.Linear(hidden_dim * 2, output_dim)
        self.dropout = torch.nn.Dropout(dropout)

    def forward(self, x, text_lengths):
        embedded = self.embedding(x)
        packed_embedded = torch.nn.utils.rnn.pack_padded_sequence(
            embedded, text_lengths
        )
        packed_output, (hidden, cell) = self.rnn(packed_embedded)
        hidden = self.dropout(
            torch.cat((hidden[-2, :, :], hidden[-1, :, :]), dim=1)
        )
        return self.fc(hidden.squeeze(0))


INPUT_DIM = padding_value
EMBEDDING_DIM = 100
HIDDEN_DIM = 256
OUTPUT_DIM = 1
N_LAYERS = 2
BIDIRECTIONAL = True
DROPOUT = 0.5

lstm_model = LSTM(
    INPUT_DIM,
    EMBEDDING_DIM,
    HIDDEN_DIM,
    OUTPUT_DIM,
    N_LAYERS,
    BIDIRECTIONAL,
    DROPOUT,
    embedding_weights,
)

lstm_optimizer = torch.optim.Adam(lstm_model.parameters())
lstm_criterion = torch.nn.BCEWithLogitsLoss()
device = torch.device("cuda" if torch.cuda.is_available() else "cpu")


def binary_accuracy(preds, y):
    rounded_preds = torch.round(torch.sigmoid(preds))
```

```
    correct = (rounded_preds == y).float()
    acc = correct.sum() / len(correct)
    return acc


def train(model, iterator, optimizer, criterion):
    epoch_loss = 0
    epoch_acc = 0
    model.train()
    for batch in iterator:
        optimizer.zero_grad()
        predictions = model(batch["text"], batch["length"]).squeeze(1)
        loss = criterion(predictions, batch["label"])
        acc = binary_accuracy(predictions, batch["label"])
        loss.backward()
        optimizer.step()
        epoch_loss += loss.item()
        epoch_acc += acc.item()

    return epoch_loss / len(iterator), epoch_acc / len(iterator)


def evaluate(model, iterator, criterion):
    epoch_loss = 0
    epoch_acc = 0
    model.eval()
    with torch.no_grad():
        for batch in iterator:
            predictions = model(batch["text"], batch["length"]).squeeze(1)
            loss = criterion(predictions, batch["label"])
            acc = binary_accuracy(predictions, batch["label"])

            epoch_loss += loss.item()
            epoch_acc += acc.item()

    return epoch_loss / len(iterator), epoch_acc / len(iterator)


batch_size = 2


def iterator(X, y):
    size = len(X)
    permutation = np.random.permutation(size)
    iterate = []
    for i in range(0, size, batch_size):
    indices = permutation[i : i + batch_size]
        batch = {}
        batch["text"] = [X[i] for i in indices]
        batch["label"] = [y[i] for i in indices]

        batch["text"], batch["label"] = zip(
            *sorted(
                zip(batch["text"], batch["label"]),
                key=lambda x: len(x[0]),
```

Usually should be a power of 2 because it's the easiest for computer memory (annotation for `batch_size = 2`)

```
                reverse=True,
            )
        )
        batch["length"] = [len(utt) for utt in batch["text"]]
        batch["length"] = torch.IntTensor(batch["length"])
        batch["text"] = torch.nn.utils.rnn.pad_sequence(
            batch["text"], batch_first=True
        ).t()
        batch["label"] = torch.Tensor(batch["label"])

        batch["label"] = batch["label"].to(device)
        batch["length"] = batch["length"].to(device)
        batch["text"] = batch["text"].to(device)

        iterate.append(batch)

    return iterate


index_utt = [
    torch.tensor([word_vectors.key_to_index.get(word, 0) for word in text])
    for text in text_data
]

X_train, X_test, y_train, y_test = train_test_split(
    index_utt, label_data, test_size=0.2
)
X_train, X_val, y_train, y_val = train_test_split(
    X_train, y_train, test_size=0.2
)

train_iterator = iterator(X_train, y_train)
validate_iterator = iterator(X_val, y_val)
test_iterator = iterator(X_test, y_test)

print(len(train_iterator), len(validate_iterator), len(test_iterator))


N_EPOCHS = 25

for model in [rnn_model, lstm_model]:
    print(
    "|-----------------------------------------------------------------
     ------------------|"
    )
    print(f"Training with {model.__class__.__name__}")
    if "RNN" in model.__class__.__name__:
        for epoch in range(N_EPOCHS):
            train_loss, train_acc = train(
                rnn_model, train_iterator, rnn_optimizer, rnn_criterion
            )
            valid_loss, valid_acc = evaluate(
                rnn_model, validate_iterator, rnn_criterion
            )
```

You've got to determine some labels for whatever you're training on.

```
            print(
                f"| Epoch: {epoch+1:02} | Train Loss: {train_loss: .3f} |
                ➥ Train Acc: {train_acc*100: .2f}% | Validation Loss:
                ➥ {valid_loss: .3f} | Validation Acc: {valid_acc*100: .2f}% |"
            )
    else:
        for epoch in range(N_EPOCHS):
            train_loss, train_acc = train(
                lstm_model, train_iterator, lstm_optimizer, lstm_criterion
            )
            valid_loss, valid_acc = evaluate(
                lstm_model, validate_iterator, lstm_criterion
            )

            print(
                f"| Epoch: {epoch+1:02} | Train Loss: {train_loss: .3f} |
                ➥ Train Acc: {train_acc*100: .2f}% | Validation Loss:
                ➥ {valid_loss: .3f} | Validation Acc: {valid_acc*100: .2f}% |"
            )
# Training on our dataset
# | Epoch: 01 | Train Loss:  0.560 | Train Acc:  70.63% | Validation Loss:
# 0.574 | Validation Acc:  70.88% |
# | Epoch: 05 | Train Loss:  0.391 | Train Acc:  82.81% | Validation Loss:
# 0.368 | Validation Acc:  83.08% |
# | Epoch: 10 | Train Loss:  0.270 | Train Acc:  89.11% | Validation Loss:
# 0.315 | Validation Acc:  86.22% |
# | Epoch: 15 | Train Loss:  0.186 | Train Acc:  92.95% | Validation Loss:
# 0.381 | Validation Acc:  87.49% |
# | Epoch: 20 | Train Loss:  0.121 | Train Acc:  95.93% | Validation Loss:
# 0.444 | Validation Acc:  86.29% |
# | Epoch: 25 | Train Loss:  0.100 | Train Acc:  96.28% | Validation Loss:
# 0.451 | Validation Acc:  86.83% |
```

Looking at our classes and instantiations, you should see that the LSTM is not vastly different from the RNN. The only difference is that the `init` input variables are `n_layers` (for convenience, you can also specify it with RNNs), `bidirectional`, and `dropout`. `bidirectional` allows LSTMs to look ahead in sequences to help with meaning and context. It also helps immensely with multilingual scenarios, as left-to-right languages like English are not the only format for orthography. `dropout`, another huge innovation, changes the paradigm of overfitting from being data dependent and helps the model not overfit by turning off random nodes layer by layer during training to force all nodes not to correlate with each other and preventing complex co-adaptations. The only difference in the out-of-model parameters is that the optimizer used for an RNN is stochastic gradient descent (SGD), like our CBoW; the LSTM uses Adam (although either could use any, depending on performance, including AdamW). Next, we define our training loop and train the LSTM. Compare this training loop to the one defined in listing 2.4 in the `gradient_descent` function.

One of the amazing things demonstrated in the code here is how much quicker the LSTM can learn compared to previous model iterations, thanks to both `bidirectionality` and `dropout`. Although the previous models train faster than the

LSTM, they take hundreds of epochs to get the same performance as an LSTM in just 25 epochs. As its name implies, the performance on the validation set adds validity to the architecture, performing inference during training on examples it has not trained on and keeping accuracy fairly close to the training set.

The problems with these models are not as pronounced, manifesting primarily as being incredibly resource-heavy, especially when applied to longer, more detail-oriented problems like healthcare and law. Despite the incredible advantages of `dropout` and `bidirectional` processing, they both at least double the amount of processing power required to train. So while inference ends up being only 2 to 3 times as expensive as an MLP of the same size, training becomes 10 to 12 times as expensive. That is, `dropout` and `bidirectional` solve exploding gradients nicely but explode the compute required to train. To combat this problem, a shortcut was devised and implemented that allows any model, including an LSTM, to figure out which parts of a sequence are the most influential and which parts can be safely ignored, known as *attention*.

2.2.8 Attention

Attention is a mathematical shortcut that gives the model a mechanism for solving larger context windows faster by telling the model through an emergent mathematical formula which parts of an input to consider and how much. Attention is based upon an upgraded version of a dictionary, where instead of just key–value pairs, a contextual query is added. Simply know that the following code is the big differentiator between older NLP techniques and more modern ones.

Attention solves the slowness of training LSTMs yet keeps high performance on a low number of epochs. There are multiple types of attention as well. The dot product attention method captures the relationships between each word (or embedding) in your query and every word in your key. When queries and keys are part of the same sentences, this is known as *bi-directional self-attention*. However, in certain cases, it is more suitable to only focus on words that precede the current one. This type of attention, especially when queries and keys come from the same sentences, is referred to as *causal attention*. Language modeling further improves by masking parts of a sequence and forcing the model to guess what should be behind the mask. The functions in the following listing demonstrate both dot product attention and masked attention.

Listing 2.8 Multihead attention implementation

```
import numpy as np
from scipy.special import softmax

x = np.array([[1.0, 0.0, 1.0, 0.0],
              [0.0, 2.0, 0.0, 2.0],
              [1.0, 1.0, 1.0, 1.0]])

w_query = np.array([1,0,1],
                   [1,0,0],
                   [0,0,1],
```

Step 1: Input: three inputs, d_model=4

```
              [0,1,1]])
w_key = np.array([[0,0,1],
              [1,1,0],
              [0,1,0],
              [1,1,0]])
w_value = np.array([[0,2,0],
              [0,3,0],
              [1,0,3],
              [1,1,0]])

Q = np.matmul(x,w_query)
K = np.matmul(x,w_key)
V = np.matmul(x,w_value)

k_d = 1
attention_scores = (Q @ K.transpose())/k_d

attention_scores[0] = softmax(attention_scores[0])
attention_scores[1] = softmax(attention_scores[1])
attention_scores[2] = softmax(attention_scores[2])

attention1 = attention_scores[0].reshape(-1,1)
attention1 = attention_scores[0][0]*V[0]
attention2 = attention_scores[0][1]*V[1]
attention3 = attention_scores[0][2]*V[2]

attention_input1 = attention1 + attention2 + attention3

attention_head1 = np.random.random((3,64))

z0h1 = np.random.random((3,64))
z1h2 = np.random.random((3,64))
z2h3 = np.random.random((3,64))
z3h4 = np.random.random((3,64))
z4h5 = np.random.random((3,64))
z5h6 = np.random.random((3,64))
z6h7 = np.random.random((3,64))
z7h8 = np.random.random((3,64))

Output_attention = np.hstack((z0h1,z1h2,z2h3,z3h4,z4h5,z5h6,z6h7,z7h8))

def dot_product_attention(query, key, value, mask, scale=True):
    assert query.shape[-1] == key.shape[-1] == value.shape[-1], "q,k,v have
     different dimensions!"
    if scale:
        depth = query.shape[-1]
    else:
        depth = 1
    dots = np.matmul(query, np.swapaxes(key, -1, -2)) / np.sqrt(depth)
    if mask is not None:
        dots = np.where(mask, dots, np.full_like(dots, -1e9))
    logsumexp = scipy.special.logsumexp(dots, axis=-1, keepdims=True)
    dots = np.exp(dots - logsumexp)
    attention = np.matmul(dots, value)
    return attention
```

Step 2: Weights three dimensions x d_model=4

Step 3: Matrix multiplication to obtain Q,K,V; query: x * w_query; key: x * w_key; value: x * w_value

Step 4: Scaled attention scores; square root of the dimensions

Step 5: Scaled softmax attention scores for each vector

Step 6: Attention value obtained by score1/k_d * V

Step 7: Sums the results to create the first line of the output matrix

Step 8: Steps 1 to 7 for inputs 1 to 3; because this is just a demo, we'll do a random matrix of the right dimensions.

Step 9: We train all eight heads of the attention sublayer using steps 1 to 7.

Step 10: Concatenates heads 1 to 8 to get the original 8 × 64 output dimension of the model

This function performs all of these steps.

```
def masked_dot_product_self_attention(q,k,v,scale=True):
    mask_size = q.shape[-2]
    mask = np.tril(np.ones((1, mask_size, mask_size), dtype=np.bool_), k=0)
    return DotProductAttention(q,k,v,mask,scale=scale)
```

This function performs the previous steps but adds causality in masking.

In the full implementation of attention, you may have noticed some terminology you're familiar with—namely `Key` and `Value`, but you may not have been introduced to `Query` before. `Key` and `Value` pairs are familiar because of dictionaries and lookup tables, where we map a set of keys to an array of values. `Query` should feel intuitive as a sort of search for retrieval. The `Query` is compared to the `Keys` from which a `Value` is retrieved in a normal operation.

In attention, the `Query` and `Keys` undergo dot product similarity comparison to obtain an attention score, which is later multiplied by the `Value` to get an ultimate score for how much attention the model should pay to that portion of the sequence. This can get more complex, depending upon your model's architecture, because both encoder and decoder sequence lengths have to be accounted for, but suffice it to say for now that the most efficient way to model in this space is to project all input sources into a common space and compare using dot product for efficiency.

This code explanation was a bit more math-heavy than the previous examples, but it is needed to illustrate the concept. The math behind attention is truly innovative and has rocketed the field forward. Unfortunately, even with the advantages attention brings to the process of sequence modeling, with LSTMs and RNNs, there were still problems with speed and memory size. You may notice from the code and the math that a square root is taken, meaning that attention, as we use it, is quadratic. Various techniques, including subquadratics like Hyena and the Recurrent Memory Transformer (RMT, basically an RNN combined with a transformer), have been developed to combat these problems, which we will cover in more detail later. For now, let's move on to the ultimate application of attention: the transformer.

2.3 Attention is all you need

In the seminal paper, "Attention Is All You Need,"[1] Vaswani et al. take the mathematical shortcut several steps further, positing that for performance, absolutely no recurrence (the "R" in RNN) or any convolutions are needed at all.

> **NOTE** We don't go over convolutions because they aren't good for NLP, but they are popular, especially in computer vision.

Instead, Vaswani et al. opted to use only attention and specify where Q, K, and V were taken from much more carefully. We'll dive into this presently. In our review of this diverse range of NLP techniques, we have observed their evolution over time and the

[1] Vaswani et al., 2017, Attention Is All You Need," https://arxiv.org/abs/1706.03762.

ways in which each approach has sought to improve upon its predecessors. From rule-based methods to statistical models and neural networks, the field has continually strived for more efficient and accurate ways to process and understand natural language.

Now we turn our attention to a groundbreaking innovation that has revolutionized the field of NLP: the transformer architecture. In the following section, we will explore the key concepts and mechanisms that underpin transformers and how they have enabled the development of state-of-the-art language models that surpass the performance of previous techniques. We will also discuss the effect of transformers on the broader NLP landscape and consider the potential for further advancements in this exciting area of research.

2.3.1 Encoders

Encoders are the first half of a full transformer model, excelling in the areas of classification and feature engineering. Vaswani et al. figured out that after the embedding layer inside the encoder, any additional transformations done to the tensors could end up harming their ability to be compared "semantically," which was the point of the embedding layer. These models rely heavily upon self-attention and clever positional encoding to manipulate those vectors without significantly decreasing the similarity expressed.

Again, a key characteristic of embeddings is that they are vector representations of data—in our case, tokens. Tokens are whatever you pick to represent language. We recommend subwords as a general rule, but you will get a feel for where and which types of tokens work well. Consider the sentence, "The cat in the hat rapidly leapt above the red fox and the brown unmotivated dog." "Red" and "brown" are semantically similar, and both are similarly represented after the embedding layer. However, they fall on positions 10 and 14, respectively, in the utterance, assuming that we're tokenizing by word. Therefore, the positional encoding puts distance between them, also adding the ability to distinguish between the same tokens at different positions in an utterance. However, once the sine and cosine functions are applied, it brings their meaning back to only a little further apart than they were after the encoding, and this encoding mechanism scales brilliantly with recurrence and more data. To illustrate, let's say there was a 99% cosine similarity between [red] and [brown] after embedding. Encoding would drastically reduce that to around 85% to 86% similarity. Applying sine and cosine methodologies as described brings their similarity back up to around 96%.

BERT was one of the first architectures after Vaswani et al.'s original paper and is an example of encoder-only transformers. BERT is such an incredibly powerful model architecture, given how small it is, that it is still used in production systems today. BERT was the first encoder-only transformer to surge in popularity, showcasing that performing continuous or sequential (they're the same) modeling using a transformer results in much better embeddings than Word2Vec. We can see that these embeddings are better because they can be very quickly applied to new tasks and data with minimal training, with human-preferred results versus Word2Vec embeddings. For a while, most people were using BERT-based models for few-shot learning tasks on smaller datasets. BERT puts state-of-the-art performance within arm's reach for most researchers and businesses with minimal effort required.

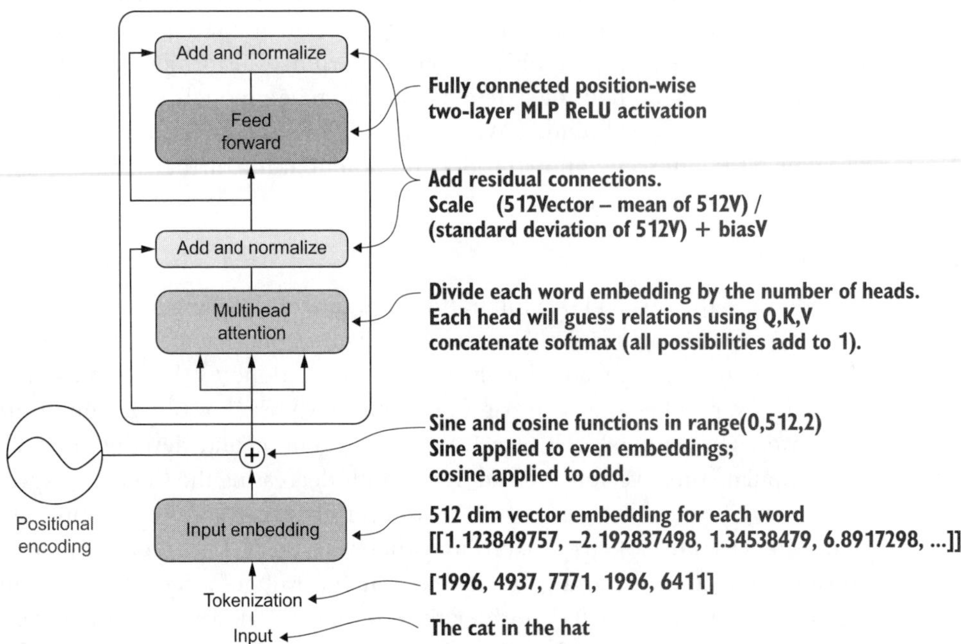

Figure 2.5 An encoder visualized. Encoders are the first half of the full transformer architecture and excel in natural language understanding tasks like classification or named entity recognition. Encoder models improve upon previous designs by not requiring priors or recurrence and using clever positional encoding and multihead attention to create a vector embedding of each token.

The strengths of encoders (visualized in figure 2.5) include the following:

- Classification and hierarchical tasks showcasing understanding
- Blazing fast, considering the long-range dependency modeling
- Builds off of known models, CBoW in embedding, MLP in feed forward, etc.
- Parallel

Encoders weaknesses include the following:

- As suggested, requires lots of data (although less than RNNs) to be effective
- Even more complex architecture

2.3.2 Decoders

Decoder models, as shown in figure 2.6, are larger versions of encoders that have two multihead attention blocks and three sum and normalize layers in their base form. They are the second half of a transformer behind an encoder. Decoders are very good at masked language modeling and learning and applying syntax very quickly, leading to the almost immediate idea that decoder-only models are needed to achieve artificial general intelligence. A useful reduction of encoder versus decoder tasks is that encoders excel in natural language understanding (NLU) tasks, while decoders excel in natural language generation (NLG) tasks. An example of decoder-only transformer architectures is the Generative Pre-trained Transformer (GPT) family of models. These models follow the logic of transformational generative grammar being completely syntax based, allowing for infinite generation of all possible sentences in a language (see appendix A).

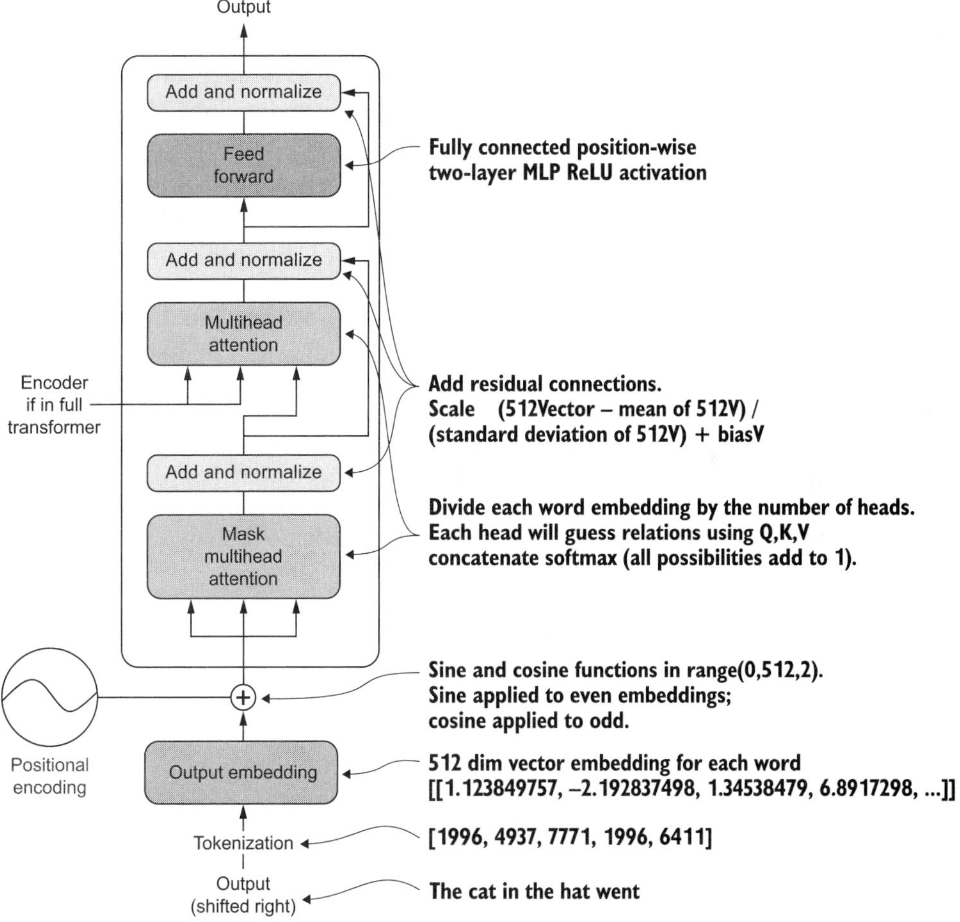

Figure 2.6 A decoder visualized. Decoders are the second half of a full transformer, and they excel at NLG tasks like chatbots and storytelling. Decoders improve upon previous architectures in the same way as encoders, but they shift their output one space to the right for next-word generation to help utilize the advantages of multihead self-attention.

The strengths of decoders include the following:

- Generates the next token in a sequence (shifted right means taking already-generated tokens into account)
- Builds off of both known models and encoders
- Can be streamed during generation for great UX

Their weaknesses include the following:

- Syntax-only models can often struggle to insert the expected or intended meaning (see all “I forced an AI to watch 1000 hours of x and generated” memes from 2018–present).
- Hallucinations.

2.3.3 Transformers

The full transformer architecture takes advantage of both encoders and decoders, passing the understanding of the encoder into the second multihead attention block of the decoder before giving output. As each piece of the transformer has a specialty in either understanding or generation, it should feel intuitive for the full product to be best at conditional generation tasks like translation or summarization, where some level of understanding is required before generation occurs. Encoders are geared toward processing input at a high level, and decoders focus more on generating coherent output. The full transformer architecture can successfully understand the data and then generate the output based on that understanding, as shown in figure 2.7. The Text-To-Text Transfer Transformer (T5) family of models is an example of transformers.

> **NOTE** Transformer models have an advantage in that they are built around the parallelization of inputs, which adds speed that LSTMs can’t currently replicate. If LSTMs ever get to a point where they can run as quickly as transformers, they may become competitive in the state-of-the-art field.

The strengths of a transformer are as follows:

- Includes both an encoder and decoder, so it’s good at everything they are good at
- Highly parallelized for speed and efficiency

Weaknesses include the following:

- Memory intensive, but still less than LSTMs of the same size
- Requires large amounts of data and VRAM for training

As you’ve probably noticed, most of the models we’ve discussed aren’t at all linguistically focused, being heavily syntax-focused, if they even attempt to model real language at all. Models, even state-of-the-art transformers, only have semantic approximations—no pragmatics, no phonetics—and only really utilize a mathematical model of morphology during tokenization without context. This doesn’t mean the models can’t learn these, nor does it mean that, for example, transformers can’t take audio as an input; it

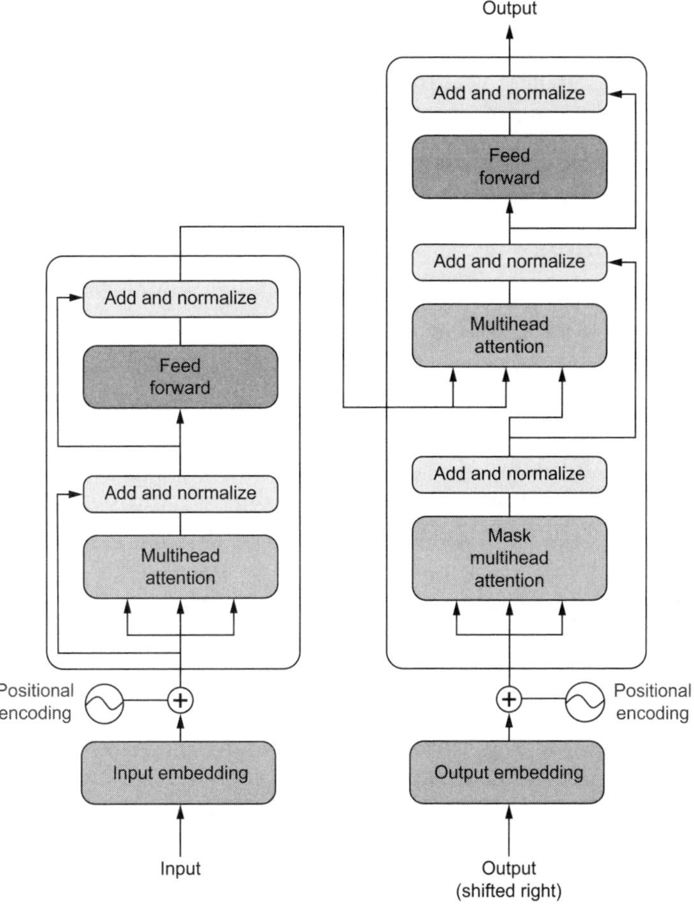

Figure 2.7 A full transformer visualized. A full transformer combines the encoder and the decoder and does well on all of the tasks of each, as well as conditional generation tasks such as summarization and translation. Because transformers are bulkier and slower than each of their halves, researchers and businesses have generally opted to use those halves over the whole transformer.

just means that the average usage doesn't. With this in mind, it is nothing short of a miracle that they work as well as they do, and they really should be appreciated for what they can do.

So far, we've attempted to highlight the current limitations in models, and we will dive into where to improve upon them in the remainder of this book. One such route is one that's already been, and is still being, explored to great success: transfer learning and finetuning large foundational models. This technique came about soon after BERT's initial release. Researchers discovered that although BERT generally performed well on a large number of tasks, if they wanted it to perform better on a particular task or data domain, they simply needed to retrain the model on data representative of the task or domain but not from scratch. Given all of the pretrained weights BERT learned while creating the semantic approximation embeddings on a much larger dataset, significantly less data is required to get state-of-the-art performance on the portion you need. We've seen this with BERT and the GPT family of models as they've come out, and now we're seeing it again to solve exactly the challenges we discussed: semantic approximation coverage, domain expertise, and data availability.

2.4 Really big transformers

Enter LLMs. Since their introduction, transformer-based models have continued to get larger and larger, not just in their size and number of parameters but also in the size and length of their training datasets and training cycles. If you studied machine learning or deep learning during the 2010s, you likely heard the moniker, "Adding more layers doesn't make the model better." LLMs prove this both wrong and right—wrong because their performance is unparalleled, often matching smaller models that have been meticulously finetuned on a particular domain and dataset, even those trained on proprietary data, and right because of the challenges that come with both training and deploying LLMs.

One of the major differences between LLMs and language models involves transfer learning and finetuning. Like previous language models, LLMs are pretrained on massive text corpora, enabling them to learn general language features and representations that can be finetuned for specific tasks. Because LLMs are so massive and their training datasets are so large, they are able to achieve better performance with less labeled data, which was a significant limitation of earlier language models. Often, you can finetune an LLM to do highly specialized tasks with only a dozen or so examples.

However, what makes LLMs so powerful and has opened the door to widespread business use cases is their ability to do specialized tasks using simple prompting without any finetuning. Just give a few examples of what you want in your query, and the LLM can produce results. Training an LLM on a smaller set of labeled data is called few-shot prompting. It's referred to as one-shot prompting when only one example is given and zero-shot when the task is totally novel. LLMs, especially those trained using reinforcement learning from human feedback and prompt engineering methodologies, can perform few-shot learning, where they can generalize and solve tasks with only a few examples, at a whole new level. This ability is a significant advancement over earlier models that required extensive finetuning or large amounts of labeled data for each specific task.

LMs previously have shown promise in the few and zero-shot learning domains, and LLMs have proven that promise to be true. As models have gotten larger, we find they are capable of accomplishing tasks smaller models can't. We call this *emergent behavior*.[2] Figure 2.8 illustrates eight different tasks previous language models couldn't perform better than at random, and then once the models got large enough, they could.

[2] J. Wei et al., "Emergent abilities of large language models," Transactions on Machine Learning Research, Aug. 2022, https://openreview.net/forum?id=yzkSU5zdwD.

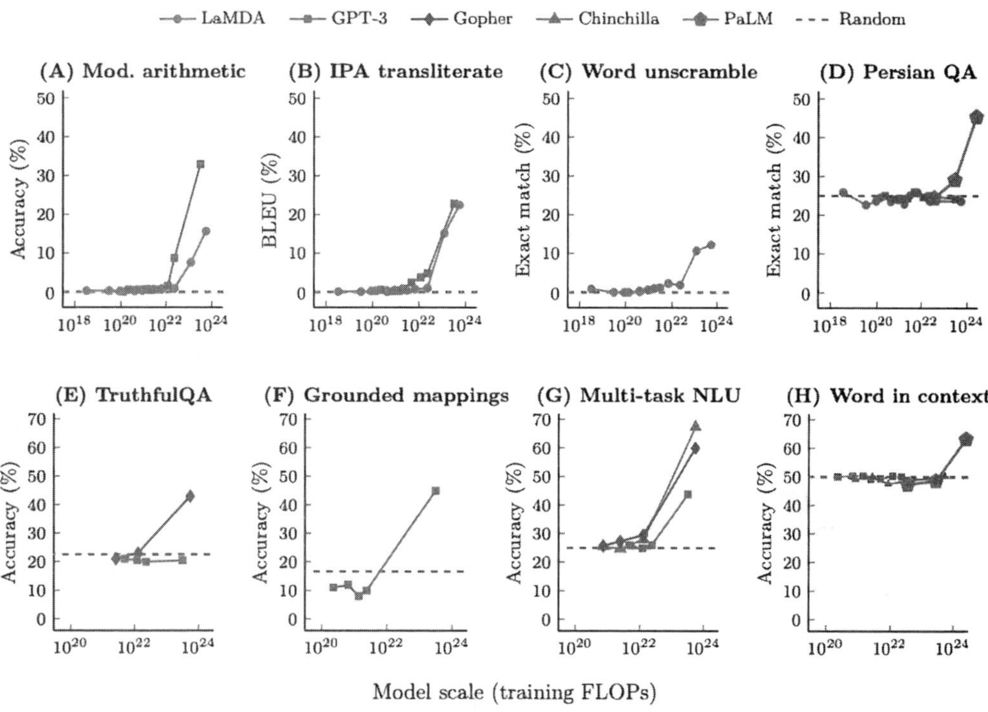

Figure 2.8 Examples of LLMs demonstrating emergent behaviors when given few-shot prompting tasks after the model scale reaches a certain size

LLMs also have demonstrably great zero-shot capabilities due to their vast parameter sizes, which is the main reason for their popularity and viability in the business world. LLMs also exhibit improved handling of ambiguity due to their large size and capacity. They are better at disambiguating words with multiple meanings and understanding the nuances of language, resulting in more accurate predictions and responses. This improvement isn't because of better ability or architecture, as they share their architecture with smaller transformers, but because they have vastly more examples of how people generally disambiguate. LLMs, therefore, respond with the same disambiguation as is generally represented in the dataset. Thanks to the diverseness of the text data on which LLMs are trained, they exhibit increased robustness in handling various input styles, noisy text, and grammatical errors.

Another key difference between LLMs and language models is input space. A larger input space is important since it makes few-shot prompting tasks that much more viable. Many LLMs have max input sizes of 8,000+ tokens (originally 32K, GPT-4 has sported 128K since November 2023), and while all the previously discussed models could also have input spaces that high, they generally don't. We have recently seen a boom in this field, with techniques like Recurrent Memory Transformer (RMT) allowing 1M+ token context spaces, which rocket LLMs even more toward proving that bigger models are always better. LLMs are designed to capture long-range dependencies within text, allowing them to understand context more effectively than their predecessors. This improved understanding enables LLMs to generate more coherent and contextually relevant responses in tasks like machine translation, summarization, and conversational AI.

LLMs have revolutionized NLP by offering powerful solutions to problems that were challenging for earlier language models. They bring substantial improvements in contextual understanding, transfer learning, and few-shot learning. As the field of NLP continues to evolve, researchers are actively working to maximize the benefits of LLMs while mitigating all potential risks. Because a better way to approximate semantics hasn't been found, they make bigger and more dimensional approximations. Because a good way of storing pragmatic context hasn't been found, LLMs often allow inserting context into the prompt directly, into a part of the input set aside for context, or even through sharing databases with the LLM at inference. This capability doesn't create pragmatics or a pragmatic system within the models, in the same way that embeddings don't create semantics, but it allows the model to correctly generate syntax that mimics how humans respond to those pragmatic and semantic stimuli. Phonetics is a place where LLMs could likely make gigantic strides, either as completely text-free models or as a text-phonetic hybrid model, maybe utilizing the IPA in addition to or instead of text. It is exciting to consider the possible developments that we are watching sweep across this field right now.

At this point, you should have a pretty good understanding of what LLMs are and some key principles of linguistics that will come in handy when putting LLMs in production. You should now be able to start reasoning about what type of products will be easier or harder to build. Consider figure 2.9: tasks in the lower left-hand corner, like writing assistants and chatbots, are LLMs' bread and butter. Text generation based on a little context from a prompt is a strictly syntax-based problem; with a large enough model trained on enough data, we can do this pretty easily. A shopping assistant is pretty similar and rather easy to build as well; we are just missing pragmatics. The assistant needs to know a bit more about the world, such as products, stores, and prices. With a little engineering, we can add this information to a database and give this context to the model through prompting.

On the other end, consider a chess bot. LLMs *can* play chess, but they aren't any good. They have been trained on chess games and understand that E4 is a common first move, but their understanding is completely syntactical. LLMs only understand that the text they generate should contain a letter between A and H and a number between 1 and 8. Like the shopping assistant, they are missing pragmatics and don't have a clear model of the game of chess. In addition, they are also missing semantics. Encoders might help us understand that the words "king" and "queen" are similar, but they don't help us understand that E4 is a great move one moment for one player and that same E4 move is a terrible move the very next moment for a different player. LLMs also lack knowledge based on phonetics and morphology for chess, although

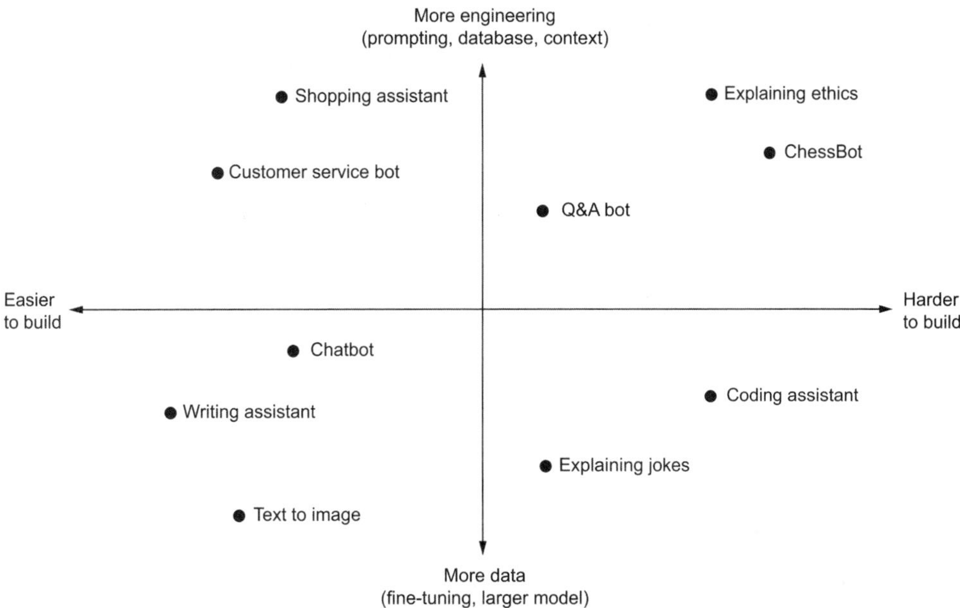

Figure 2.9 How difficult or easy certain tasks are for LLMs and what approaches to take to solve them

they are not as important in this case. Either way, we hope this exercise will better inform you and your team on your next project.

LLMs have amazing benefits, but with all of these capabilities come some limitations. Foundational LLMs require vast computational resources for training, making them less accessible for individual researchers and smaller organizations. This problem is being remedied with techniques we'll talk about throughout the book, like quantization, textual embeddings, low-rank adaptation, parameter-efficient finetuning, and graph optimization. Still, foundation models are currently solidly outside the average individual's ability to train effectively. Beyond that, there are concerns that the energy consumption associated with training LLMs could have significant environmental effects and cause problems associated with sustainability. These problems are complex and largely out of the scope of this book, but we would be remiss not to bring them up.

Last but not least, since LLMs are trained on large-scale datasets containing real-world text, they may learn and perpetuate biases present in the data, leading to ethical concerns because real-world people don't censor themselves to provide optimal unbiased data. Also, knowing much about what data you're training on is not a widespread practice. For example, if you ask a text-to-image diffusion LLM to generate 1,000 images of "leader," 99% of the images feature men, and 95% of the images feature people with white skin. The concern here isn't that men or white people shouldn't be depicted as leaders, but that the model isn't representing the world accurately, and it's showing.

Sometimes, more nuanced biases are brought out. For example, in the Midjourney example in figure 2.10, the model, without being prompted (the only prompt given was the word "leader"), changed the popular feminist icon Rosie the Riveter to a man. The model didn't think about this change; it just determined during its sampling steps that the prompt "leader" had more male-looking depictions in the training set. Many people will argue about what "good" and "bad" mean in this context, and instead of going for a moral ought, we'll talk about what accuracy means. LLMs are trained on a plethora of data with the purpose of returning the most accurate representations possible. When they cannot return accurate representations, especially with their heightened abilities to disambiguate, we can view that as a bias that harms the model's ability to fulfill its purpose. Later, we will discuss techniques to combat harmful bias to allow you, as an LLM creator, to get the exact outputs you intend and minimize the number of outputs you do not intend.

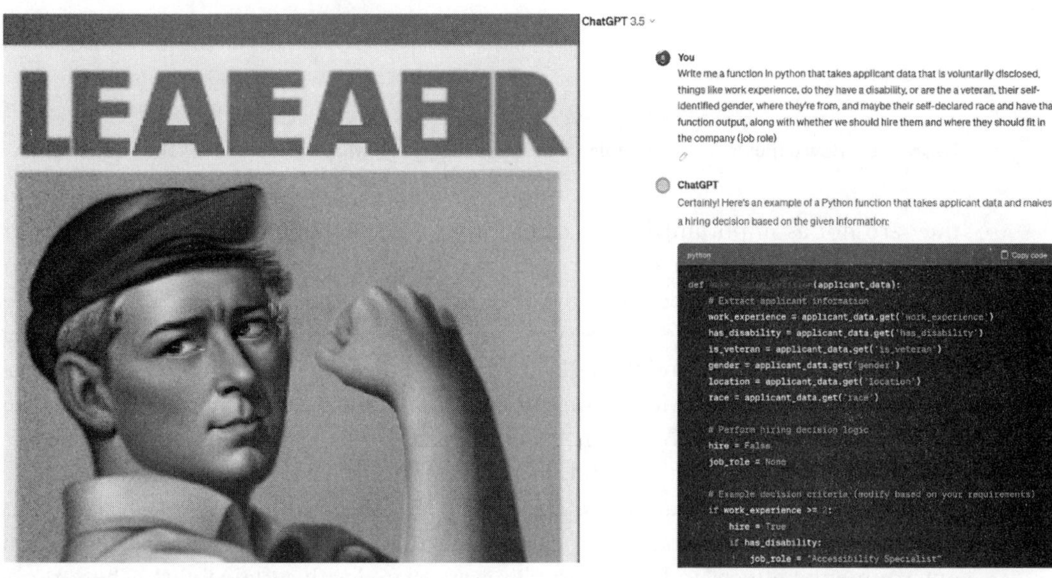

Figure 2.10 Midjourney 5, which is, at the time of this writing, the most popular text2img model on the market, when prompted with only one token, "leader" (left), changed a well-known popular feminist icon, Rosie the Riveter, into a male depiction. ChatGPT (right) writes a function to place you in your job based on race, gender, and age. These are examples of unintended outputs.

Alright, we've been building up to this moment the entire chapter. Let's go ahead and run our first LLM! In listing 2.9, we download the Bloom model, one of the first open source LLMs to be created, and generate text! We are using Hugging Face's Transformers library, which takes care of all the heavy lifting for us. Very exciting stuff!

Listing 2.9 Running our first LLM

```
from transformers import AutoModelForCausalLM, AutoTokenizer

MODEL_NAME = "bigscience/bloom"

tokenizer = AutoTokenizer.from_pretrained(MODEL_NAME)
model = AutoModelForCausalLM.from_pretrained(MODEL_NAME)

prompt = "Hello world! This is my first time running an LLM!"

input_tokens = tokenizer.encode(prompt, return_tensors="pt", padding=True)
generated_tokens = model.generate(input_tokens, max_new_tokens=20)
generated_text = tokenizer.batch_decode(
    generated_tokens, skip_special_tokens=True
)
print(generated_text)
```

Did you try to run it?!? If you did, you probably just crashed your laptop. Oopsie! Forgive me for a little harmless MLOps hazing, but getting some first-hand experience on how large these models can get and how difficult they can be to run is a helpful experience to have. In the next chapter, we will talk more about the difficulties of running LLMs and some of the tools you need to run this code. If you don't want to wait and would like to get a similar but much smaller LLM running, change the model name to `"bigscience/bloom-3b"`, and run it again. It should work just fine this time on most hardware.

All in all, LLMs are an amazing technology that allows our imaginations to run wild with possibility, and deservedly so. The number-one use case for considering an LLM over a smaller language model is when few-shot capabilities come into play for whoever the model will be helping, such as a CEO when raising funds or a software engineer when writing code. LLMs have these abilities precisely because of their size. The larger number of parameters in LLMs directly enables their ability to generalize over smaller spaces in larger dimensions. In this chapter, we've hit the lesser-known side of LLMs, the linguistic and language modeling side. In the next chapter, we'll cover the other half, the MLOps side, where we dive into exactly how that large parameter size affects the model and the systems designed to support that model and makes it accessible to the customers or employees the model is intended for.

Summary

- The five components of linguistics are phonetics, syntax, semantics, pragmatics, and morphology:
  - Phonetics can be added through a multimodal model that processes audio files and is likely to improve LLMs in the future, but current datasets are too small.
  - Syntax is what current models are good at.
  - Semantics is added through the embedding layer.

  - Pragmatics can be added through engineering efforts.
  - Morphology is added in the tokenization layer.
- Language does not necessarily correlate with reality. Understanding the process people use to create meaning outside of reality is useful in training meaningful (to people) models.
- Proper tokenization can be a major hurdle due to too many `<UNK>` tokens, especially when it comes to specialized problems like code or math.
- Multilingual processing has always outperformed monolingual processing, even on monolingual tasks without models.
- Each language model type in sequence shows a natural and organic growth of the LLM field as more and more linguistic concepts are added that make the models better.
- Language modeling has seen an exponential increase in efficacy, correlating to how linguistics-focused the modeling has been.
- Attention is a mathematical shortcut for solving larger context windows faster and is the backbone of modern architectures—encoders, decoders, and transformers:
  - Encoders improve the semantic approximations in embeddings.
  - Decoders are best at text generation.
  - Transformers combine the two.
- Larger models demonstrate emergent behavior, suddenly being able to accomplish tasks they couldn't before.

3 Large language model operations: Building a platform for LLMs

This chapter covers
- An overview of large language model operations
- Deployment challenges
- Large language model best practices
- Required large language model infrastructure

Before anything else, preparation is the key to success.

—Alexander Graham Bell

As we learned in the last chapter, when it comes to transformers and natural language processing (NLP), bigger is better, especially when it's linguistically informed. However, bigger models come with bigger challenges because of their size, regardless of their linguistic efficacy, thus requiring us to scale up our operations and infrastructure to handle these problems. In this chapter, we'll be looking into exactly what those challenges are, what we can do to minimize them, and what architecture can be set up to help solve them.

3.1 Introduction to large language model operations

What is large language model operations (LLMOps)? Well, since we like to focus on practicality over rhetoric, we're not going to dive into any fancy definitions that you'd expect in a textbook, but let's simply say it's machine learning operations (MLOps) that have been scaled to handle LLMs. Let us also say scaling up is hard. One of the hardest tasks in software engineering. Unfortunately, too many companies are running rudimentary MLOps setups, and don't think for a second that they will be able to handle LLMs. That said, the term *LLMOps* may not be needed. It has yet to show through as sufficiently different from core MLOps, especially considering they still have the same bones. If this book were a dichotomous key, MLOps and LLMOps would definitely be in the same genus, and only time will tell whether they are the same species. Of course, by refusing to define LLMOps properly, we might have traded one confusion for another, so let's take a minute to describe MLOps.

MLOps is the field and practice of reliably and efficiently deploying and maintaining machine learning models in production. This includes—and, indeed, requires—managing the entire machine learning life cycle, from data acquisition and model training to monitoring and termination. A few principles required to master this field include workflow orchestration, versioning, feedback loops, continuous integration and continuous deployment (CI/CD), security, resource provisioning, and data governance. While there are often personnel who specialize in the productionizing of models, with titles like ML Engineers, MLOps Engineers, or ML Infrastructure Engineer, the field is a large-enough beast that it often abducts many other unsuspecting professionals to work in it who hold titles like Data Scientist or DevOps Engineer—often against their knowledge or will, leaving them kicking and screaming, "It's not my job."

3.2 Operations challenges with large language models

So why have a distinction at all? If MLOps and LLMOps are so similar, is LLMOps just another fad opportunists throw on their resume? Not quite. In fact, it's quite similar to the term *Big Data*. When the term was at its peak popularity, people with titles like Big Data Engineer used completely different tool sets and developed specialized expertise necessary to handle large datasets. LLMs come with a set of challenges and problems you won't find with traditional machine learning systems. A majority of these problems extend almost exclusively because they are so big. Large models are large! We hope to show you that LLMs truly earn their name. Let's take a look at a few of these challenges so we can appreciate the task ahead of us when we start talking about deploying an LLM.

3.2.1 Long download times

Back in 2017, when I was still heavily involved as a data scientist, I decided to try my hand at reimplementing some of the most famous computer vision models at the time: AlexNet, VGG19, and ResNet. I figured this would be a good way to reinforce my understanding of the basics with some practical hands-on experience. Plus, I had an ulterior motive: I had just built my own rig with some NVIDIA GeForce 1080 TI GPUs, which were state of the art at the time, and I thought this would be a good way to break them in. The first task was to download the ImageNet dataset.

The ImageNet dataset was one of the largest annotated datasets available, containing millions of images rounding out to a file size of a whopping ~150 GB! Working with it was proof that you knew how to work with Big Data, which was still a trendy word and an invaluable skill set for a data scientist at the time. After agreeing to the terms and gaining access, I got my first wakeup call. Downloading it took an entire week.

When my team first deployed Bloom, it took an hour and a half to download it. Heck, it took an hour and a half to download *The Legend of Zelda: Tears of the Kingdom*, and that's only 16 GB, so we really couldn't complain.

Large models are large. That can't be overstated. You'll find throughout this book that that fact comes with many additional headaches and problems for the entire production process, and you have to be prepared for it. In comparison to the ImageNet dataset, the Bloom LLM model is 330 GB, more than twice the size. We're guessing most readers haven't worked with either ImageNet or Bloom, so for comparison, *Call of Duty: Modern Warfare*, one of the largest games at the time of this writing, is 235 GB. *Final Fantasy 15* is only 148 GB, so you could fit two into the model with plenty of room to spare. It's just hard to really comprehend how massive LLMs are. We went from 100 million parameters in models like BERT and took them to billions of parameters. If you went on a shopping spree and spent $20 a second (or maybe accidentally left your AWS EC2 instance on), it'd take you half a day to spend a million dollars; it would take you two years to spend a billion.

Thankfully, it doesn't take two weeks to download Bloom because unlike ImageNet, it's not hosted on a poorly managed university server, and it also has been sharded into multiple smaller files to allow downloading in parallel, but it will still take an uncomfortably long time. Consider a scenario where you are downloading the model under the best conditions. You're equipped with a gigabit speed fiber internet connection, and you're magically able to dedicate the entire bandwidth and I/O operations of your system and the server to it. It will still take over 5 minutes to download! Of course, that's under the best conditions. You probably won't be downloading the model under such circumstances; with modern infrastructure, you can expect it to take on the order of hours.

3.2.2 Longer deploy times

Just downloading the model is a long enough time frame to make any seasoned developer shake, but deployment times are going to make them keel over and call for medical attention. A model as big as Bloom can take 30 to 45 minutes just to load the model into GPU memory—at least, those are the time frames we've experienced. That's not to mention any other steps in your deployment process that can add to this. Indeed, with GPU shortages, it can easily take hours just waiting for resources to free up—more on that in a minute.

What does this mean for you and your team? Well, for starters, we know lots of teams that deploy ML products often simply download the model at run time. That might work for small sklearn regression models, but it isn't going to work for LLMs. Additionally, you can take most of what you know about deploying reliable systems and throw it out the window (but thankfully not too far). Most modern-day best practices for software engineering assume you can easily restart an application if anything happens, and there's a lot of rigmarole involved to ensure your systems can do just that. With LLMs, it can take seconds to shut down, but potentially hours to redeploy, making this a semi-irreversible process. Like picking an apple off a tree, it's easy to pluck one off, but if you bite into it and decide it's too sour, you can't reattach it to the tree so it can continue to ripen. You'll just have to wait awhile for another to grow.

While not every project requires deploying the largest models out there, you can expect to see deployment times measured in minutes. These longer deploy times make scaling down right before a surge of traffic a terrible mistake, as well as figuring out how to manage bursty workloads difficult. General CI/CD methodologies need to be adjusted since rolling updates take longer, leaving a backlog piling up quickly in your pipeline. Silly mistakes like typos or other bugs often take longer to notice and longer to correct.

3.2.3 Latency

Along with increases in model size often come increases in inference latency. This is obvious when stated, but more parameters equate to more computations, and more computations mean longer inference wait times. However, this can't be underestimated. We know many people who downplay the latency problems because they've interacted with an LLM chatbot, and the experience felt smooth. Take a second look, though, and you'll notice that it is returning one word at a time, which is streamed to the user. It feels smooth because the answers are coming in faster than a human can read, but a second look helps us realize this is just a UX trick. LLMs are still too slow to be very useful for an autocomplete solution, for example, where responses have to be blazingly fast. Building it into a data pipeline or workflow that reads a large corpus of text and then tries to clean it or summarize it may also be too prohibitively slow to be useful or reliable.

There are also many less obvious reasons for their slowness. For starters, LLMs are often distributed across multiple GPUs, which adds extra communication overhead. As discussed later in this chapter in section 3.3.2, they are distributed in other ways, often even to improve latency, but any distribution adds an additional overhead burden. In addition, LLMs' latency is severely affected by completion length, meaning the more words it uses to return a response, the longer it takes. Of course, completion length also seems to improve accuracy. For example, using prompt engineering techniques like chain of thought (CoT), we ask the model to think about a problem in a step-by-step fashion, which has been shown to improve results for logic and math questions but significantly increases the response length and latency time.

3.2.4 Managing GPUs

To help with these latency problems, we usually want to run them in GPUs. If we want to have any success training LLMs, we'll need GPUs for that as well, but this all adds additional challenges that many underestimate. Most web services and many ML use cases can be done solely on CPUs, but not so with LLMs—partly because of GPUs' parallel processing capabilities offering a solution to our latency problems and partly because of the inherent optimization GPUs offer in the linear algebra, matrix multiplications, and tensor operations; that's happening under the hood. For many who are stepping into the realm of LLMs, this requires utilizing a new resource and extra complexity. Many brazenly step into this world, acting like it's no big deal, but they are in for a rude awakening. Most system architectures and orchestrating tooling available, like Kubernetes, assume your application will run with CPU and memory alone. While they often support additional resources like GPUs, it's often an afterthought. You'll soon find you have to rebuild containers from scratch and deploy new metric systems.

One aspect of managing GPUs that most companies are not prepared for is that they tend to be rare and limited. For the last decade, it seems that we have gone in and out of a global GPU shortage. They can be extremely difficult to provision for companies looking to stay on-premise. We've spent lots of time in our careers working with companies that chose to stay on-premise for a variety of reasons. One of the things they had in common is that they never had GPUs on their servers. When they did, they were often purposely difficult to access except for a few key employees.

If you are lucky enough to be working in the cloud, a lot of these problems are solved, but there is no free lunch here either. We've both been part of teams that have often gone chasing their tails trying to help data scientists struggling to provision a new GPU workspace. We've run into obscure, ominous errors like `scale.up.error.out.of.resources`, only to discover that these esoteric readings indicate all the GPUs of a selected type in the entire region are being utilized, and none are available. CPU and memory can often be treated as infinite in a data center; GPU resources, however, cannot. Sometimes you can't expect them at all. Most data centers only support a subset of instance or GPU types, which means you may be forced to set up your application in a region further away from your user base, thus increasing latency. Of course, we're sure you can work with your cloud provider when looking to expand your service to a new region that doesn't currently support it, but you might not like what you hear based on timelines and cost. Ultimately, you'll run into shortage problems no matter where you choose to run, on-premise or in the cloud.

3.2.5 Peculiarities of text data

LLMs are the modern-day solution to NLP. NLP is one of the most fascinating branches of ML in general because it primarily deals with text data, which is primarily a qualitative measure. Every other field deals with quantitative data. We have figured out a way to encode our observations of the world into a direct translation of numerical values. For example, we've learned how to encode heat into temperature scales and measure it with thermometers and thermocouples, and we can measure pressure with manometers and gauges and put it into pascals.

Computer vision and the practice of evaluating images are often seen as qualitative, but the actual encoding of images into numbers is a solved problem. Our understanding of light has allowed us to break images apart into pixels and assign them RGB values. Of course, this doesn't mean computer vision is by any means solved; there's still lots of work to do to learn how to identify the different signals in the patterns of the data. Audio data is also often considered qualitative. How does one compare two songs? But we can measure sound and speech, directly measuring the sound wave's intensity in decibels and frequency in hertz.

Unlike other fields that encode our physical world into numerical data, text data is looking at ways to measure the ephemeral world. After all, text data is our best effort at encoding our thoughts, ideas, and communication patterns. While, yes, we have figured out ways to turn words into numbers, we haven't figured out a direct translation. Our best solutions to encode text and create embeddings are just approximations at best; in fact, we use machine learning models to do it! An interesting aside is that numbers are also text and a part of language. If we want models that are better at math, we need a more meaningful way to encode these numbers. Since it's all made up, when we try to encode text numbers into machine-readable numbers, we are creating a system attempting to reference itself recursively in a meaningful way. Not an easy problem to solve!

Because of all this, LLMs (and all NLP solutions) have unique challenges. Take, for example, monitoring. How do you catch data drift in text data? How do you measure "correctness"? How do you ensure the cleanliness of the data? These types of problems are difficult to define, let alone solve.

3.2.6 Token limits create bottlenecks

A big challenge for those new to working with LLMs is dealing with the token limits. The token limit for a model is the maximum number of tokens that can be included as an input for a model. The larger the token limit, the more context we can give the model to improve its success at accomplishing the task. Everyone wants them to be higher, but it's not that simple. These token limits are defined by two problems: the memory and speed our GPUs have access to and the nature of memory storage in the models themselves.

The first problem seems unintuitive: Why couldn't we just increase the GPU memory? The answer is complex. We can, but stacking more layers in the GPU to take into account more gigabytes at once slows down the GPU's computational ability as a whole. Right now, GPU manufacturers are working on new architectures and ways to get around this problem. The second challenge is fascinating because increasing the token limits actually exacerbates the mathematical problems under the hood. Let me explain. Memory storage within an LLM itself isn't something we think about often. We call that mechanism *attention*, which we discussed in depth in section 2.2.7. What we didn't discuss was that attention is a quadratic solution: as the number of tokens increases, the number of calculations required to compute the attention scores between all the pairs of tokens in a sequence scales quadratically with the sequence length. In addition, within our gigantic context spaces, and since we are dealing with quadratics, we're starting to hit problems where the only solutions involve imaginary numbers, which can cause models to behave in unexpected ways. This is likely one of the reasons why LLMs hallucinate.

These problems have real implications and affect application designs. For example, when this author's team upgraded from GPT-3 to GPT-4, the team was excited to have access to a higher token limit, but it soon found this led to longer inference times and, subsequently, a higher timeout error rate. In the real world, it's often better to get a less accurate response quickly than to get no response at all because the promise of a more accurate model often is just that: a promise. Of course, when deploying it locally, where you don't have to worry about response times, you'll likely find your hardware to be a limiting factor. For example, LLaMA was trained with 2,048 tokens, but you'll be lucky to take advantage of more than 512 of that when running with a basic consumer GPU, as you are likely to see out-of-memory (OOM) errors or even the model simply crashing.

A gotcha, which is likely to catch your team by surprise and should be pointed out now, is that different languages have different tokens per character. Take a look at table 3.1, where we compare converting the same sentence in different languages to tokens using OpenAI's cl100k_base Byte Pair Encoder. Just a quick glance reveals that LLMs typically favor the English language in this regard. In practice, this means that if you are building a chatbot with an LLM, your English users will have greater flexibility in their input space than Japanese users, leading to very different user experiences.

Table 3.1 Comparison of token counts in different languages

Language	String	Characters	Tokens
English	The quick brown fox jumps over the lazy dog	43	9
French	Le renard brun rapide saute par-dessus le chien paresseux	57	20
Spanish	El rápido zorro marrón salta sobre el perro perezoso	52	22
Japanese	素早い茶色のキツネが怠惰な犬を飛び越える	20	36
Chinese (simplified)	敏捷的棕色狐狸跳过了懒狗	12	28

If you are curious about why this is, it is due to text encodings, which are another peculiarity of working with text data, as discussed in the previous section. Consider table 3.2, where we show several different characters and their binary representations in UTF-8. English characters can almost exclusively be represented with a single byte included in the original ASCII standard computers were originally built on, while most other characters require 3 or 4 bytes. Because it takes more memory, it also takes more token space.

Table 3.2 Comparison of byte lengths for different currency characters in UTF-8

Character	Binary UTF-8	Hex UTF-8
$	00100100	0x24
£	11000010 10100011	0xc2 0xa3
¥	11000010 10100101	0xc2 0xa5
?	11100010 10000010 10100000	0xe2 0x82 0xa0
?	11110000 10011111 10010010 10110000	0xf0 0x9f 0x92 0xb0

Increasing the token limits has been an ongoing research question since the popularization of transformers, and there are some promising solutions still in the research phases, like recurrent memory transformers (RMT).[1] We can expect to continue to see improvements in the future, and hopefully, this will become naught but an annoyance.

3.2.7 Hallucinations cause confusion

So far, we've been discussing some of the technical problems a team faces when deploying an LLM into a production environment, but nothing compares to the simple problem that LLMs tend to be wrong. They tend to be wrong a lot. *Hallucinations* is a term coined to describe occurrences when LLM models will produce correct-sounding results that are wrong—for example, book references or hyperlinks that have the form and structure of what would be expected but are, nevertheless, completely made up. As a fun example, we asked for books on LLMs in production from the publisher, Manning (a book that doesn't exist yet since one author is still writing it). We were given the following suggestions: *Machine Learning Engineering in Production* by Mike Del Balso and Lucas Serveén, which could be found at https://www.manning.com/books/machine-learning-engineering-in-production, and *Deep Learning for Coders with Fastai and PyTorch* by Jeremy Howard and Sylvain Gugger, which could be found at https://www.manning.com/books/deep-learning-for-coders-with-fastai-and-pytorch. The first book is entirely made up. The second book is real; however, it's not published by Manning. In each case, the internet addresses are entirely made up. These URLs are actually very similar in format to what you'd expect if you were browsing Manning's website, but they will return 404 errors if you visit them.

One of the most annoying aspects of hallucinations is that they are often surrounded by confident-sounding words. LLMs are terrible at expressing uncertainty, in

[1] A. Bulatov, Y. Kuratov, and M. S. Burtsev, "Scaling transformer to 1M tokens and beyond with RMT," April 2023, https://arxiv.org/abs/2304.11062.

large part because of the way they are trained. Consider the case "2 + 2 =." Would you prefer it to respond, "I think it is 4" or simply "4"? Most would prefer to get the correct "4" back. This bias is built in, as models are often given rewards for being correct or at least sounding like it.

There are various explanations as to why hallucinations occur, but the most truthful answer is that we don't know if there's just one cause. It's likely a combination of several things; thus, there isn't a good fix for it yet. Nevertheless, being prepared to counter these inaccuracies and biases of the model is crucial to provide the best user experience for your product.

3.2.8 Bias and ethical considerations

Just as concerning as the model getting things wrong is when it gets things right in the worst possible way—for example, allowing it to encourage users to commit suicide,[2] teaching users how to make a bomb,[3] or participating in sexual fantasies involving children.[4] These are extreme examples, but prohibiting the model from answering such questions is undeniably vital to success.

LLMs are trained on vast amounts of text data, which is also their primary source of bias. Because we've found that larger datasets are just as important as larger models in producing human-like results, most of these datasets have never truly been curated or filtered to remove harmful content, instead choosing to prioritize size and a larger collection. Cleaning the dataset is often seen as prohibitively expensive, requiring humans to go in and manually verify everything, but there's a lot that could be done with simple regular expressions and other automated solutions. By processing these vast collections of content and learning the implicit human biases, these models will inadvertently perpetuate them. These biases range from sexism and racism to political preferences and can cause your model to inadvertently promote negative stereotypes and discriminatory language.

3.2.9 Security concerns

As with all technology, we need to be mindful of security. LLMs have been trained on a large corpus of text, some of which could be harmful or sensitive and shouldn't be exposed. So steps should be taken to protect this data from being leaked. The bias and ethical concerns from the last section are good examples of conversations you don't want your users to be having, but you could also imagine finetuning a model on your company's data and potentially having secrets lost inadvertently if proper precautions aren't taken.

---

[2] R. Daws, "Medical chatbot using OpenAI's GPT-3 told a fake patient to kill themselves," *AI News*, October 28, 2020, https://mng.bz/qO6z.

[3] T. Kington, "ChatGPT bot tricked into giving bomb-making instructions, say developers," *The Times*, December 17, 2022, https://mng.bz/7d64.

[4] K. Quach, "AI game bans players for NSFW stories it generated itself," The Register, October 8, 2021, https://www.theregister.com/2021/10/08/ai_game_abuse/.

One should be aware that LLMs are susceptible to adversarial attacks like prompt injections. Prompt injections are attacks done by a user to trick the LLM into ignoring instructions given to it and generating undesired content. For example, if you ask ChatGPT what its gender is, it appropriately replies that as an AI language model, it doesn't have a gender. However, with clever prompting, you may be able to bypass these protocols and get it to reveal one. While this example is harmless, we've seen others successfully extract API keys and other secrets from an LLM, run code in non-protected environments, steal environment variables, and traverse local file systems where the model is served. That's not to mention the plethora of examples of users using prompting to jailbreak or bypass protocols put in place for ethical considerations outlined in the previous section. An interesting aside to this is that LLMs are good at inventing fake secrets! Even successful prompt injection attacks can often fail due to LLM hallucinations, which can have funny consequences.

For example, using a simple prompt to ask for Coca-Cola's secret recipe simply returned the boring result, "I cannot divulge trade secrets or any proprietary information." Pretty lame if you ask us. With a little trickery and some prompt injection, we were able to get it to spill its secrets, which, of course, we decided to try—after confirming with a food scientist it wouldn't poison us. After following the instructions exactly, we were surprised to find we got a pretty tasty drink, but it tasted nothing like Coke. While the recipe looks legitimate, nuances like quantities, cook times, and even the need to strain the syrup were all off. Guess we'll have to hold off taking over the beverage industry until we get the real recipe.

Coca-Cola recipe hallucinated from prompt injection

```
Homemade Coca-Cola Recipe
=====================
**Disclaimer**: The original Coca-Cola recipe is a highly guarded trade
secret. The following recipe is an approximation for creating a homemade
cola drink that resembles the taste of Coca-Cola.

Ingredients:
- 3 cups of water
- 2 cups granulated sugar
- 1/8 tsp food-grade citric acid
- 3/4 tsp caramel color (liquid)
- 1/2 tsp caffeine (powder or liquid form)
- 1 1/2 tsp cola extract
- 1/8 tsp vanilla extract
- 1 1/2 cups carbonated water (store-bought or using a home soda maker)
- A pinch of ground cinnamon (optional)
- A pinch of ground nutmeg (optional)

Instructions:
1. In a large saucepan, bring the 3 cups of water to a gentle simmer.
2. Slowly stir in the granulated sugar, ensuring that it fully
   dissolves.
```

```
3. Add the citric acid, caramel color, caffeine, cola extract, and
   vanilla extract to the saucepan. Mix well.
4. Stir in the optional spices if desired: cinnamon and nutmeg.
5. Simmer the mixture for about 20 minutes, stirring occasionally.
6. Remove the saucepan from the heat and let it cool to room
   temperature.
7. Once cooled, strain the syrup to remove any undissolved solids.
8. To make the final drink, mix 1 part syrup with 3 parts carbonated
   water. Adjust to taste depending on your preference for sweetness and
   carbonation.

Variations:
- You can experiment with different amounts of caramel color, caffeine,
  and cola extract to adjust the flavor and appearance of your homemade
  cola.
- To create different cola flavor profiles, experiment with adding
  additional spices (such as star anise, orange or lemon peel, or
  cardamom), essential oils, or fruit extracts.
- Consider using a natural sweetener, like honey or agave syrup, as an
  alternative to granulated sugar.

Historical context and interesting facts:
- Coca-Cola was first introduced in 1886 by pharmacist Dr. John S.
  Pemberton, who aimed to create a unique and refreshing beverage that
  could also relieve fatigue and headaches.
- The original Coca-Cola formula contained trace amounts of cocaine
  extracted from the coca leaf, which was later replaced with caffeine
  in the early 20th century.
- In 1985, Coca-Cola introduced "New Coke," a reformulation aimed at
  competing with Pepsi. However, the taste change was met with backlash,
  and the company returned to its original formula just three months
  later, rebranded as "Coca-Cola Classic."
Result(s): You can now create your own homemade version of cola,
resembling the taste of Coca-Cola. Enjoy and feel free to experiment
with different spices, extracts, and sweeteners to create your own
unique flavor profile.
```

Another security concern involves pickle injections. Pickle is a library in Python that serializes objects and is often used to serialize ML models. It serializes them into a byte stream containing opcodes executed one by one as it is deserialized. It's a fast and easy way to share large objects. Pickle injections corrupt this byte stream, often injecting malware over the wire when the model is transferred over an insecure network. This is especially concerning for large models that take a long time to download, as it makes it easier for a third party to intercept the transfer and inject malicious code. If this happens, the code injected can potentially give the attackers access to your system. This can happen when attempting to use the model during inference, as the harmful code will execute if it is not detected and properly removed. It is important to take precautions such as using secure networks and verifying the integrity of the model before use to prevent this type of attack.

3.2.10 Controlling costs

Working with LLMs involves various cost-related concerns. The first, as you probably gathered by now, is infrastructure costs, which include high-performance GPUs, storage, and other hardware resources. We talked about how GPUs are harder to procure, which, unfortunately, means they are more expensive. Mistakes like leaving your service on have always had the potential to rack up the bills, but with GPUs in the mix, this type of mistake is even more deadly. These models also demand significant computational power, leading to high energy consumption during both training and inference. On top of all this, their longer deploy times mean we are often running them even during low traffic to handle bursty workloads or anticipated future traffic. Overall, this leads to higher operational costs.

Additional costs include managing and storing vast amounts of data used to train or finetune as well as for regular maintenance, such as model updates, security measures, and bug fixes, which can be financially demanding. As with any technology used for business purposes, managing potential legal disputes and ensuring compliance with regulations is a concern. Lastly, investing in continuous research and development to improve your models and give you a competitive edge will be a factor.

We talked a bit about the technical concerns regarding token limits, which are likely to be solved, but we didn't discuss the cost limitations, as most APIs charge on a token basis. This makes it more expensive to send more context and use better prompts. It also makes it a bit harder to predict costs since while you can standardize inputs, you can't standardize outputs. You can never be too sure how many tokens will be returned, making it difficult to govern. Just remember, with LLMs, it is as important as ever to implement and follow proper cost engineering practices to ensure costs never get away from you.

3.3 LLMOps essentials

Now that we have a handle on the type of challenge we are grappling with, let's take a look at all the different LLMOps practices, tooling, and infrastructure to see how different components help us overcome these obstacles. First, let's dive into different practices, starting with compression, where we will talk about shrinking, trimming, and approximating to get models as small as we can. We will then talk about distributed computing, which is needed to make things run since the models are so large that they rarely fit into a single GPU's memory. After we are finished with that, we will venture into the infrastructure and tooling needed to make it all happen in the next section.

3.3.1 Compression

As you were reading about the challenges of LLMs in the last section, you might have asked yourself something akin to "If the biggest problems from LLMs come from their size, why don't we just make them smaller?" If you did, congratulations! You are a genius—compression is the practice of doing just that. Compressing models to as small as we can make them will improve deployment time, reduce latency, scale down the number of expensive GPUs needed, and, ultimately, save money. However, the whole point of making the models so stupefyingly gargantuan in the first place was because it made them better at what they do. We need to be able to shrink them without losing all the progress we made by making them big in the first place.

This problem is far from solved, but there are multiple ways to approach the problem, with different pros and cons to each method. We'll be talking about several of the methods, starting with the easiest and most effective.

QUANTIZING

Quantizing is the process of reducing precision in preference of lowering the memory requirements. This tradeoff makes intuitive sense. When this author was in college, he was taught to always round numbers to the precision of the tooling. Pulling out a ruler and measuring his pencil, you wouldn't believe him if he stated the length was 19.025467821973739 cm. Even if he used a caliper, he couldn't verify a number so precisely. With our ruler, any number beyond 19.03 cm is fantasy. To drive the point home, one of his engineering professors once asked him him, "If you are measuring the height of a skyscraper, do you care if there is an extra sheet of paper at the top?"

How we represent numbers inside computers often leads us to believe we have better precision than we actually do. To illustrate this point, open a Python terminal and add 0.1 + 0.2. If you've never tried this before, you might be surprised to find it doesn't equal 0.3, but 0.30000000000000004. We won't go into the details of the math behind this phenomenon, but the question stands: Can we reduce the precision without making things worse? We really only need precision to the tenth decimal, but reducing the precision will likely get us a number like 0.304 rather than 0.300, thus increasing our margin of error.

Ultimately, the only numbers a computer understands are 0 and 1, on or off, a single bit. To improve this range, we combine multiple bits and assign them different meanings. String 8 of them together, and you get a byte. Using the INT8 standard, we can take that byte and encode all the integers from –128 to 127. We'll spare you the particulars because we assume you already know how binary works; suffice it to say, the more bits we have, the larger range of numbers we can represent, both larger and smaller. Figure 3.1 shows a few common floating point encodings. With 32 bits strung together, we get what we pretentiously term *full precision*, and that is how most numbers are stored, including the weights in machine learning models. Basic quantization moves us from full precision to half precision, shrinking models to half their size. There are two different half precision standards, FP16 and BF16, which differ in how many bits represent the range or exponent part. Since BF16 uses the same number of exponents as FP32, it's been found to be more effective for quantizing, and you can generally expect almost exactly the same level of accuracy for half the size of model. If you understood the paper and skyscraper analogy, it should be obvious why.

However, there's no reason to stop there. We can often push it down another byte to 8-bit formats without too much loss of accuracy. There have already even been successful research attempts showing selective 4-bit quantization of portions of LLMs is

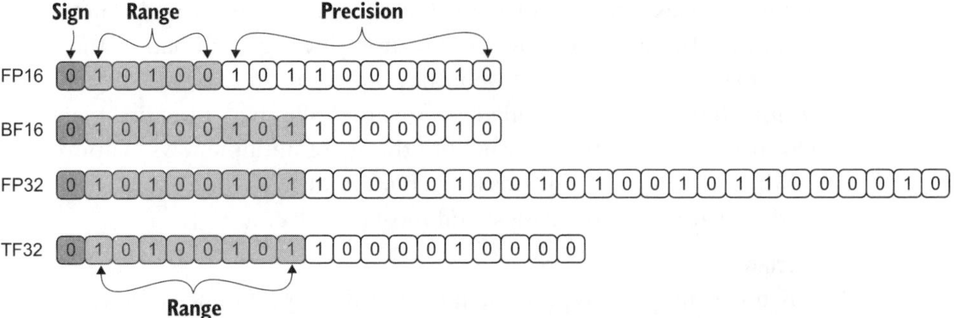

Figure 3.1 The bit mapping for a few common floating point encodings: 16-bit float or half precision (FP16), bfloat 16 (BF16), 32-bit float or single full precision (FP32), and NVIDIA's TensorFloat (TF32)

possible with only a fractional loss of accuracy. The selective application of quantization is a process known as dynamic quantization and is usually done on just the weights, leaving the activations in full precision to reduce accuracy loss.

The holy grail of quantizing, though, is INT2, representing every number as –1, 0, or 1. This currently isn't possible without completely degrading the model, but it would make the model up to 8 times smaller. The Bloom model would be a measly ~40 GB, small enough to fit on a single GPU. This is, of course, as far as quantizing can take us, and if we wanted to shrink further, we'd need to look at additional methods.

The best part of quantization is that it is easy to do. There are many frameworks that allow this, but in listing 3.1, we demonstrate how to use PyTorch's quantization library to do a simple post-training static quantization (PTQ). All you need is the full precision model, some example inputs, and a validation dataset to prepare and calibrate with. As you can see, it's only a few lines of code.

Listing 3.1 Example PTQ in PyTorch

```
import copy
import torch.ao.quantization as q

model_to_quantize = copy.deepcopy(model_fp32)
model_to_quantize.eval()

qconfig_mapping = q.get_default_qconfig_mapping("qnnpack")

prepared_model = q.prepare(model_to_quantize)

with torch.inference_mode():
    for x in dataset:
        prepared_model(x)

model_quantized = q.convert(prepared_model)
```

- A deep copy of the original model as quantization is done in place
- Gets mappings; note the use of "qnnpack" for ARM and "fbgemm" for x86 CPU
- Prepares
- Calibrates; you'll want to use representative (validation) data
- Quantizes

Static PTQ is the most straightforward approach to quantizing; it is done after the model is trained and uniformly quantizes all the model parameters. As with most formulas, the most straightforward approach introduces more error. Often, this error is acceptable, but when it's not, we can add extra complexity to reduce the accuracy loss from quantization. Some methods to consider are uniform versus non-uniform, static versus dynamic, symmetric versus asymmetric, and applying it during or after training.

To understand these methods, let's consider the case where we are quantizing from FP32 to INT8. In FP32, we essentially have the full range of numbers at our disposal, but in INT8, we only have 256 values. We are trying to put a genie into a bottle, and it's no small feat. If you study the weights in your model, you might notice that most of the numbers are fractions between [–1, 1]. We could take advantage of this by using an 8-bit standard that represents more values in this region in a non-uniform way instead of the standard uniform [–128, 127]. While mathematically possible, unfortunately, any such standards aren't commonplace, and modern-day deep learning hardware and software are not designed to take advantage of them. So for now, it's best to stick to uniform quantization.

The simplest approach to shrinking the data is to normalize it, but since we are going from a continuous scale to a discrete scale, there are a few gotchas, so let's explore those. We start by taking the min and max and scale them down to match our new number range. We would then bucket all the other numbers based on where they fall. Of course, if we have really large outliers, we may find all our other numbers squeezed into just one or two buckets, ruining any granularity we once had. To prevent this, we can clip any large numbers; this is what we do in static quantization. However, before we clip the data, what if we choose a range and scale that captures the majority of our data beforehand? We need to be careful since if this dynamic range is too small, we will introduce more clipping errors; if it's too big, we will introduce more rounding errors. The goal of dynamic quantization is, of course, to reduce both errors.

Next, we need to consider the symmetry of the data. Generally, in normalization, we force the data to be normal and thus symmetric; however, we could choose to scale the data in a way that leaves any asymmetry it had. By doing this, we could potentially reduce our overall loss due to the clipping and rounding errors, but it's not guaranteed.

As a last resort, if none of these other methods fail to reduce the accuracy loss of the model, we can use quantization-aware training (QAT). QAT is a simple process where we add a fake quantization step during model training. By fake, we mean we clip and round the data while leaving it in full precision. This allows the model to adjust for the error and bias introduced by quantization while it's training. QAT is known to produce higher accuracy compared to other methods but at a much higher cost in time to train.

Quantization methods

- *Uniform versus non-uniform*—Whether we use an 8-bit standard that is uniform in the range it represents or non-uniform to be more precise in the -1 to 1 range.
- *Static versus dynamic*—Choosing to adjust the range or scale before clipping in an attempt to reduce clipping and rounding errors and reduce data loss.
- *Symmetric versus asymmetric*—Normalizing the data to be normal and force symmetry or choosing to keep any asymmetry and skew.
- *During or after training*—Quantization after training is really easy to do, and while doing it during training is more work, it leads to reduced bias and better results.

Quantizing is a very powerful tool. It reduces the size of the model and the computational overhead required to run the model, thus reducing the latency and cost of running the model. However, the best thing about quantization is that it can be done after the fact, so you don't have to worry about whether your data scientists remembered to quantize the model during training using processes like QAT. This is why quantization has become so popular when working with LLMs and other large machine learning models. While reduced accuracy is always a concern with compression techniques, compared to other methods, quantization is a win-win-win.

PRUNING

Congratulations, you just trained a brand new LLM! With billions of parameters, all of them must be useful, right? Wrong! Unfortunately, as with most things in life, the model's parameters tend to follow the Pareto principle. About 20% of the weights lead to 80% of the value. "If that's true," you may be asking yourself, "why don't we just cut out all the extra fluff?" Great idea! Give yourself a pat on the back. Pruning is the process of weeding out and removing any parts of the model we deem unworthy.

There are essentially two different pruning methods: *structured* and *unstructured*. Structured pruning is the process of finding structural components of a model that aren't contributing to the model's performance and then removing them—whether they are filters, channels, or layers in the neural network. The advantage of this method is that your model will be a little smaller but keep the same basic structure, which means we don't have to worry about losing hardware efficiencies. We are also guaranteed a latency improvement, as there will be fewer computations involved.

Unstructured pruning, on the other hand, shifts through the parameters and zeros out the less important ones that don't contribute much to the model's performance. Unlike structured pruning, we don't actually remove any parameters; we just set them to zero. From this, we can imagine that a good place to start would be any weights or activations already close to 0. Of course, while this effectively reduces the size of a model, this also means we don't cut out any computations, so it's common to see only minimal, if any, latency improvement. But a smaller model still means faster load times and fewer GPUs to run. It also gives us very fine-grained control over the process, allowing us to shrink a model further than we could with structured pruning, with less effect on performance too.

Like quantization, pruning can be done after a model is trained. However, unlike quantization, it's common practice to see additional finetuning needed to prevent too great a loss of performance. It's becoming more common to include pruning steps during the model training to avoid the need to finetune later on. Since a more sparse model will have fewer parameters to tune, adding these pruning steps may help a model converge faster as well.[5]

You'll be surprised at how much you can shrink a model with pruning while minimally affecting performance. How much? In the SparseGPT[6] paper, a method was developed to try to automatically one-shot the pruning process without the need for finetuning afterward. The authors found they could decrease a GPT-3 model by 50% to 60% without a problem! Depending on the model and task, they even saw slight improvements in a few of them. We are looking forward to seeing where pruning takes us in the future.

Knowledge distillation

Knowledge distillation is probably the coolest method of compression in our minds. It's a simple idea too: we'll take the large LLM and have it train a smaller language model to copy it. What's nice about this method is that the larger LLM provides essentially an infinite dataset for the smaller model to train on, which can make the training quite effective. Because the larger the dataset, the better the performance, we've often seen smaller models reach almost the same level as their teacher counterparts in accuracy.[7]

A smaller model trained this way is guaranteed to both be smaller and improve latency. The downside is that it will require us to train a completely new model, which is a pretty significant upfront cost to pay. Any future improvements to the teacher model will require being passed down to the student model, which can lead to complex training cycles and version structure. It's definitely a lot more work compared to some of the other compression methods.

The hardest part about knowledge distillation, though, is that we don't really have good recipes for them yet. Tough questions like "How small can the student model be?" will have to be solved through trial and error. There's still a lot to learn and research to be done here.

However, there has been some exciting work in this field via Stanford's Alpaca.[8] Instead of training a student model from scratch, they chose to finetune the open

---

5 T. Hoefler, D. Alistarh, T. Ben-Nun, N. Dryden, and A. Peste, "Sparsity in deep learning: Pruning and growth for efficient inference and training in neural networks," January 2021, https://arxiv.org/abs/2102.00554.

6 E. Frantar and D. Alistarh, "SparseGPT: Massive Language models can be accurately pruned in one-shot," January 2023, https://arxiv.org/abs/2301.00774.

7 V. Sanh, L. Debut, J. Chaumond, and T. Wolf, "DistilBERT, a distilled version of BERT: smaller, faster, cheaper and lighter," October 2019, https://arxiv.org/abs/1910.01108.

8 R. Taori, I. Gulrajani, T. Zhang, Y. Dubois, X. Li, C. Guestrin, P Liang, and T. B. Hashimoto, "Alpaca: A strong, replicable instruction-following model," CRFM, 2023, https://crfm.stanford.edu/2023/03/13/alpaca.html.

source LLaMA 7B parameter model using OpenAI's GPT3.5's 175B parameter model as a teacher via knowledge distillation. It's a simple idea, but it paid off big, as they were able to get great results from their evaluation. The biggest surprise was the cost, as they only spent $500 on API costs to get the training data from the teacher model and $100 worth of GPU training time to finetune the student model. Granted, if you did this for a commercial application, you'd be violating OpenAI's terms of service, so it's best to stick to using your own or open source models as the teacher.

LOW-RANK APPROXIMATION

Low-rank approximation, also known as low-rank factorization, low-rank decomposition, or matrix factorization, among other terms (too many names—we blame the mathematicians), uses linear algebra math tricks to simplify large matrices or tensors to find a lower-dimensional representation. There are several techniques to do this. Singular value decomposition (SVD), Tucker decomposition (TD), and canonical polyadic decomposition (CPD) are the most common ones you run into.

In figure 3.2, we show the general idea behind the SVD method. Essentially, we are going to take a very large matrix, A, and break it up into three smaller matrices, U, Σ, and V. While U and V are there to ensure we keep the same dimensions and relative strengths of the original matrix, Σ allows us to apply a direction and bias. The smaller Σ is, the more we end up compressing and reducing the total number of parameters, but the less accurate the approximation becomes.

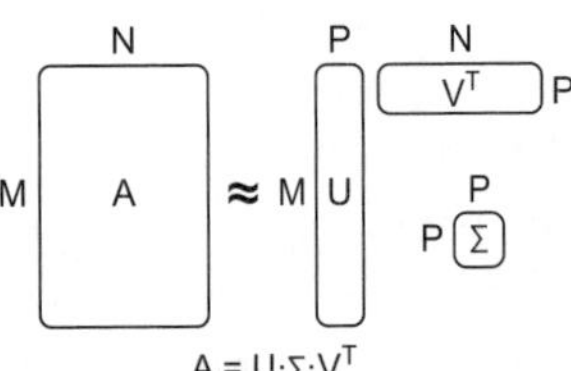

Figure 3.2 Example of SVD, a low-rank approximation. A is a large matrix with dimensions N and M. We can approximate it with three smaller matrices: U with dimensions M and P, Σ a square matrix with dimension P, and V with dimensions N and P (here we show the transpose). Usually, both P<<M and P<<N are true.

To solidify this concept, it may help to see a concrete example. In the next listing, we show a simple example of SVD at work compressing a 4 × 4 matrix. For this, we only need the basic libraries SciPy and NumPy, which are imported on lines 1 and 2. In line 3, we define the matrix, and then in line 9, we apply SVD to it.

Listing 3.2 Example of SVD low-rank approximation

```
import scipy
import numpy as np
matrix = np.array([
    [ 1., 2., 3., 4.],
    [ 5., 6., 7., 8.],
    [ 9., 10., 11., 12.],
    [13., 14., 15., 16.]
])
u, s, vt = scipy.sparse.linalg.svds(matrix, k=1)
print(u,s,vt)
```

```
# [[-0.13472211]
# [-0.34075767]
# [-0.5467932 ]
```

The generated text is

```
[-0.7528288 ]], [38.62266], [[-0.4284123 -0.47437257 -0.52033263 -0.5662928 ]]
```

Taking a moment to inspect U, Sigma, and the transpose of V, we see a 4 × 1 matrix, a 1 × 1 matrix, and a 1 × 4 matrix, respectively. All in all, we now only need 9 parameters versus the original 16, shrinking the memory footprint almost by half.

Lastly, we multiply the matrices back together to get an approximation of the original matrix. In this case, the approximation isn't all that great, but we can still see that the general order and magnitudes match the original matrix:

```
svd_matrix = u*s*vt
print(svd_matrix)
```

The generated text is

```
array([[ 2.2291691, 2.4683154, 2.7074606, 2.9466066],
      [ 5.6383204, 6.243202 , 6.848081 , 7.4529614],
      [ 9.047472 , 10.018089 , 10.988702 , 11.959317 ],
      [12.456624 , 13.792976 , 15.129323 , 16.465673 ]], dtype=float32)
```

Unfortunately, we are not aware of anyone actually using this to compress models in production, most likely due to the poor accuracy of the approximation. What they are using it for—and this is important—is adaptation and finetuning, which is where low-rank adaptation (LoRA)[9] comes in. Adaptation is the process of finetuning a generic or base model to do a specific task. LoRA applies SVD low-rank approximation to the attention weights or, rather, to inject update matrices that run parallel to the attention weights, allowing us to finetune a much smaller model. LoRA has become very popular because it makes it a breeze to take an LLM, shrink the trainable layers to a tiny fraction of the original model, and then allow anyone to train it on commodity hardware. You can get started with LoRA using the PEFT library from Hugging Face, where you can check out several LoRA tutorials.

> **NOTE** For the extra curious, parameter-efficient finetuning (PEFT) is a class of methods aimed at finetuning models in a computationally efficient way. The PEFT library seeks to put them all in one easy-to-access place; you can get started here: https://huggingface.co/docs/peft.

[9] E. J. Hu et al., "LoRA: Low-rank adaptation of large language models.," June 2021, https://arxiv.org/abs/2106.09685.

MIXTURE OF EXPERTS

Mixture of experts (MoE) is a technique where we replace the feed-forward layers in a transformer with MoE layers instead. Feed-forward layers are notorious for being parameter-dense and computationally intensive, so replacing them with something better can often have a large effect. MoEs are a group of sparsely activated models. They differ from ensemble techniques in that typically only one or a few expert models will be run, rather than combining results from all models. The sparsity is often induced by a gate mechanism that learns which experts to use and/or a router mechanism that determines which experts should even be consulted. In figure 3.3, we demonstrate the MoE architecture with potentially N experts, as well as show where it goes inside a decoder stack.

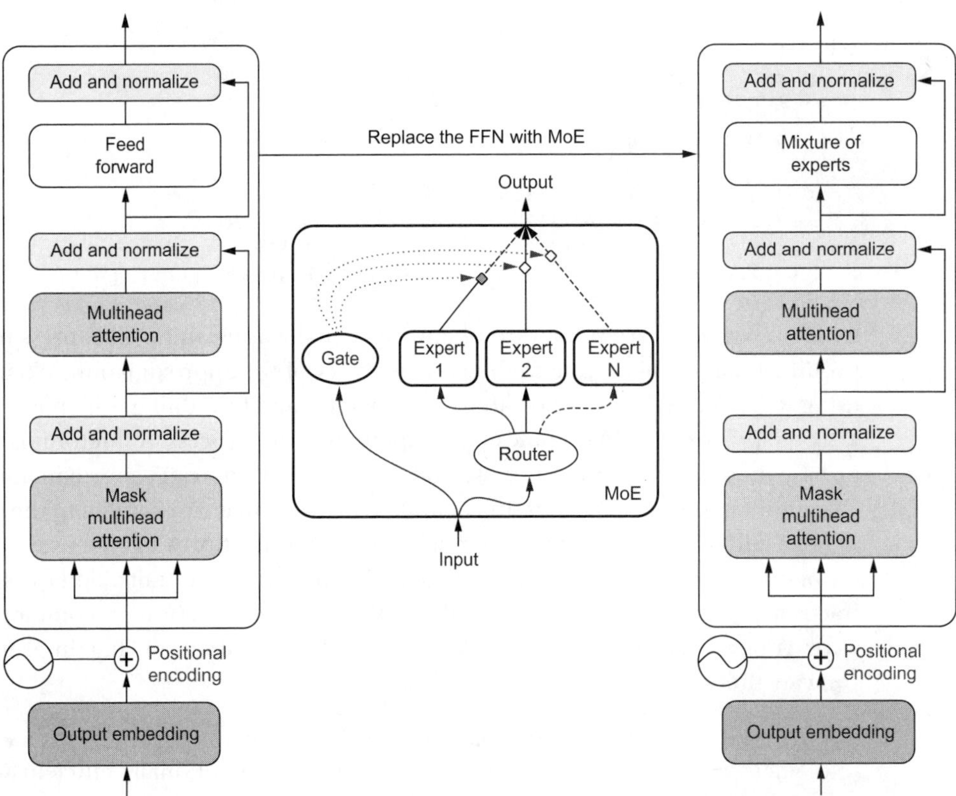

Figure 3.3 Example mixture of an expert's model with both a gate and router to control flow. The MoE model is used to replace the FFN layers in a transformer; here, we show it replacing the FFN in a decoder.

Depending on how many experts you have, the MoE layer could potentially have more parameters than the FFN, leading to a larger model, but in practice, this isn't the case, since engineers and researchers are aiming to create a smaller model. What we are guaranteed to see, though, is a faster computation path and improved inference times. However, what really makes MoE stand out is when it's combined with quantization. One study[10] between Microsoft and NVIDIA showed that 2-bit quantization was reachable with only a minimal effect on accuracy using MoE!

Of course, since this is a pretty big change to the model's structure, finetuning will be required afterward. You should also be aware that MoE layers often reduce a model's generalizability, so it's best when used on models designed for a specific task. There are several libraries that implement MoE layers, but we recommend checking out DeepSpeed.

NOTE DeepSpeed is a library that optimizes many of the hard parts for large-scale deep learning models like LLMs and is particularly useful when training. Check out their MoE tutorial at https://www.deepspeed.ai/tutorials/mixture-of-experts/.

3.3.2 Distributed computing

Distributed computing is a technique used in deep learning to parallelize and speed up large, complex neural networks by dividing the workload across multiple devices or nodes in a cluster. This approach significantly reduces training and inference times by enabling concurrent computation, data parallelism, and model parallelism. With the ever-growing size of datasets and complexity of models, distributed computing has become crucial for deep learning workflows, ensuring efficient resource utilization and enabling researchers to iterate on their models effectively. Distributed computing is one of the core practices that separate deep learning from machine learning, and with LLMs, we have to pull out every trick in the book. Let's look at different parallel processing practices to take full advantage of distributed computing.

DATA PARALLELISM

Data parallelism is what most people think about when they think about running processes in parallel; it's also the easiest to do. The practice involves splitting up the data and running them through multiple copies of the model or pipeline. For most frameworks, this is easy to set up; for example, in PyTorch, you can use the `DistributedDataParallel` method. There's just one catch for most of these setups: your model has to be able to fit onto one GPU. This is where a tool like Ray.io comes in.

Ray.io, or Ray, is an open source project designed for distributed computing, specifically aimed at parallel and cluster computing. It's a flexible and user-friendly tool that simplifies distributed programming and helps developers easily execute concurrent tasks in parallel. Ray is primarily built for machine learning and other high-performance applications but can be utilized in other applications. In listing 3.3, we give a simple example of using Ray to distribute a task. The beauty of Ray is the

[10] R. Henry and Y. J. Kim, "Accelerating large language models via low-bit quantization," March 2023, https://mng.bz/maD0.

simplicity—all we need to do to make our code run in parallel is add a decorator. It sure beats the complexity of multithreading or asynchronization setups.

Listing 3.3 Example Ray parallelization task

```
import ray
import time

ray.init()                              # Starts Ray

def slow_function(x):                   # Defines a regular Python function
    time.sleep(1)
    return x

@ray.remote
def slow_function_ray(x):               # Turns the function into a Ray task
    time.sleep(1)
    return x

results = [slow_function(i) for i in range(1, 11)]    # Executes the slow function without Ray (takes 10 seconds)

results_future = [slow_function_ray.remote(i) for i in range(1, 11)]    # Executes the slow function with Ray (takes 1 second)
results_ray = ray.get(results_future)

print("Results without Ray: ", results)
print("Results with Ray: ", results_ray)

ray.shutdown()
```

Ray uses the concepts of tasks and actors to manage distributed computing. Tasks are functions, whereas actors are stateful objects that can be invoked and run concurrently. When you execute tasks using Ray, it distributes tasks across the available resources (e.g., multicore CPUs or multiple nodes in a cluster). For LLMs, we would need to set up a Ray cluster in a cloud environment, as this would allow each pipeline to run on a node with as many GPUs as needed, greatly simplifying the infrastructure set up to run LLMs in parallel.

NOTE Learn more about Ray clusters here: https://mng.bz/eVJP.

There are multiple alternatives out there, but Ray has been gaining a lot of traction and becoming more popular as more and more machine learning workflows require distributed training. Teams have had great success with it. By utilizing Ray, developers can ensure better performance and more efficient utilization of resources in distributed workflows.

TENSOR PARALLELISM

Tensor parallelism takes advantage of matrix multiplication properties to split up the activations across multiple processors, running the data through, and then combining them on the other side of the processors. Figure 3.4 demonstrates how this process works for a matrix, which can be parallelized in two separate ways that give us the same result. Imagine that Y is a really big matrix that can't fit on a single processor or, more likely, a bottleneck in our data flow that takes too much time to run all the calculations. In either case, we could split Y by columns or rows, run the calculations, and then combine the results. In this example, we are dealing with matrices, but in reality, we often deal with tensors with more than two dimensions. However, the same mathematical principles that make this work still apply.

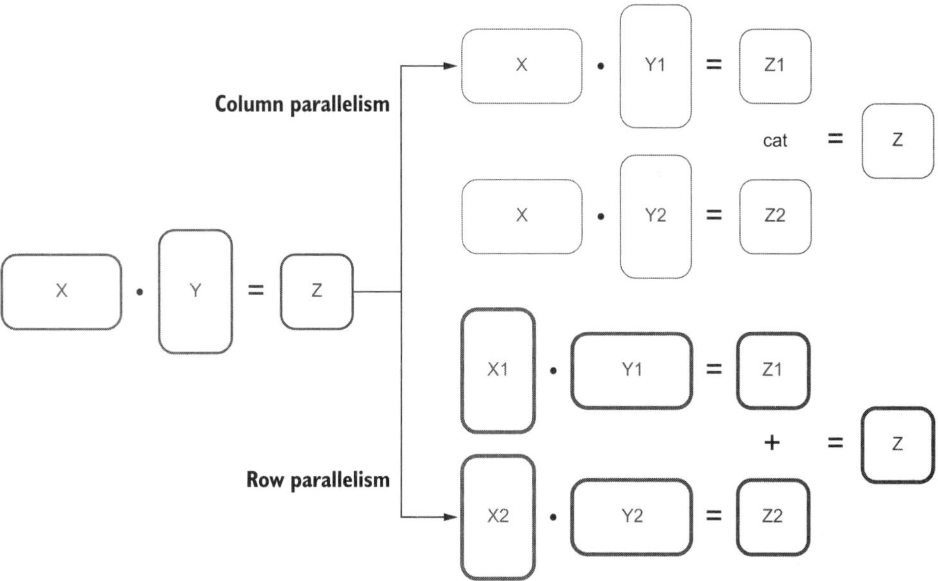

Figure 3.4 Tensor parallelism example showing that you can break up tensors by different dimensions and get the same end result. Here, we compare column and row parallelism of a matrix.

Choosing which dimension to parallelize is a bit of an art, but there are a few things to remember to help make this decision easier. First, how many columns or rows do you have? In general, you want to pick a dimension that has more than the number of processors you have, or you will end up stopping short. Generally, this isn't a problem, but with tools like Ray, discussed in the last section, parallelizing in a cluster and spinning up loads of processes is a breeze. Second, different dimensions have different multiplicity costs. For example, column parallelism requires us to send the entire dataset to each process but with the benefit of concatenating them together at the end, which is fast and easy. Row parallelism, however, allows us to break up the dataset into chunks but requires us to add the results, a more expensive operation than concatenating. You can see that one operation is more I/O bound, while the other is more computation bound. Ultimately, the best dimension will be dataset dependent and hardware limited. It will require experimentation to optimize this fully, but a good default is to just choose the largest dimension.

Tensor parallelism allows us to split up the heavy computation layers like MLP and attention layers onto different devices, but it doesn't help us with normalization or dropout layers that don't utilize tensors. To get better overall performance of our pipeline, we can add sequence parallelism that targets these blocks.[11] Sequence parallelism is a process that partitions activations along the sequence dimension, preventing redundant storage, and can be mixed with tensor parallelism to achieve significant memory savings with minimal additional computational overhead. In combination, they reduce the memory needed to store activations in transformer models. In fact, they nearly eliminate activation recomputation and save activation memory up to five times.

Figure 3.5 shows how combining tensor parallelism, which allows us to distribute the computationally heavy layers, and sequence parallelism, which does the same for the memory limiting layers, allows us to fully parallelize the entire transformer model. Together, they allow for extremely efficient use of resources.

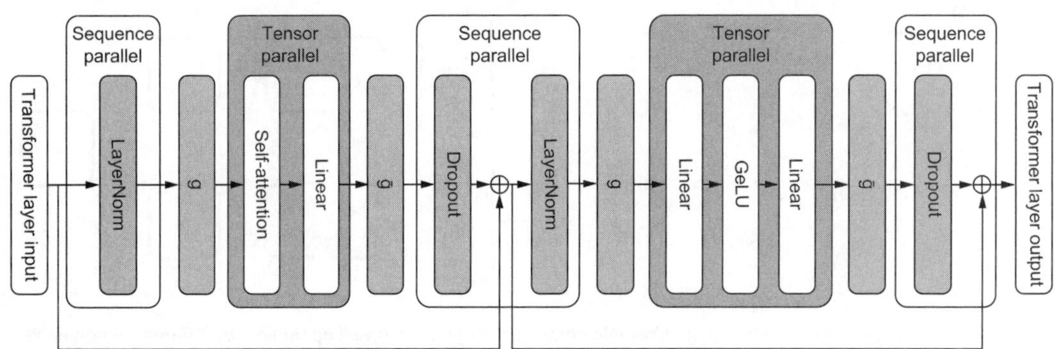

Figure 3.5 Combining tensor parallelism that focuses on computational heavy layers with sequence parallelism to reduce memory overhead to create a fully parallel process for the entire transformer

PIPELINE PARALLELISM

So far, we can run lots of data and speed up any bottlenecks, but none of that matters because our model is too big; we can't fit it into a single GPU's memory to even get it to run. That's where pipeline parallelism comes in; it's the process of splitting up a model vertically and putting each part onto a different GPU. This creates a pipeline, as input data will go to the first GPU, process, then transfer to the next GPU, and so on until it's run through the entire model. While other parallelism

[11] V. Korthikanti et al., "Reducing activation recomputation in large transformer models," May 2022, https://arxiv.org/abs/2205.05198.

techniques improve our processing power and speed up inference, pipeline parallelism is required to get it to run. However, it comes with some major downsides, mainly device utilization.

To understand where this downside comes from and how to mitigate it, let's first consider the naive approach to this, where we simply run all the data at once through the model. We find that this leaves a giant "bubble" of underutilization. Since the model is broken up, we have to process everything sequentially through the devices. This means that while one GPU is processing, the others are sitting idle. In figure 3.6, we can see this naive approach and a large bubble of inactivity as the GPUs sit idle. We also see a better way to take advantage of each device. We do this by sending the data in small batches. A smaller batch allows the first GPU to pass on what it was working on quicker and move on to another batch. This allows the next device to get started earlier and reduces the size of the bubble.

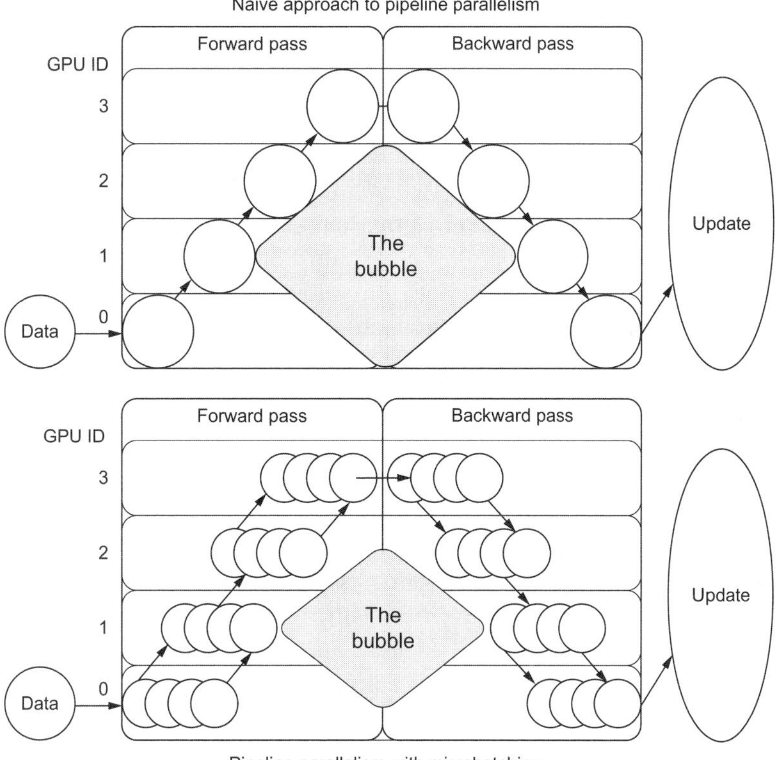

Figure 3.6 The bubble problem. When data runs through a broken-up model, the GPUs holding the model weights are underutilized while they wait for their counterparts to process the data. A simple way to reduce this bubble is to use microbatching.

We can actually calculate the size of the bubble quite easily with the following formula:

$$\text{Idle Percentage} = 1 - m / (m + n - 1)$$

where m is the number of microbatches and n is the depth of the pipeline or number of GPUs. So for our naive example case of four GPUs and one large batch, we see the devices sitting idle 75% of the time! GPUs are quite expensive to allow to sit idle three quarters of the time. Let's see what that looks like using the microbatch strategy. With a microbatch of 4, it cuts this almost in half, down to just 43% of the time. We can glean from this formula that the more GPUs we have, the higher the idle times, but the more microbatches, the better the utilization.

Unfortunately, we often can neither reduce the number of GPUs nor make the microbatches as large as we want. There are limits. For GPUs, we have to use as many as it takes to fit the model into memory. However, try to use a few larger GPUs, as this will lead to more optimal utilization than using many smaller GPUs. Reducing the bubble in pipeline parallelism is another reason why compression is so important. For microbatching, the first limit is obvious: since the microbatch is a fraction of our batch size, we are limited by how big that is. The second is that each microbatch increases the memory demand for cached activations in a linear relationship. One way to counter this higher memory demand is a method called PipeDream.[12] There are different configurations and approaches, but the basic idea is the same. In this method, we start working on the backward pass as soon as we've finished the forward pass of any of the microbatches. This allows us to fully complete a training cycle and release the cache for that microbatch.

3D PARALLELISM

For LLMs, we are going to want to take advantage of all three parallelism practices, as they can all be run together. This is known as 3D parallelism, which combines data, tensor, and pipeline parallelism (DP + TP + PP) together. Since each technique and, thus, dimension will require at least two GPUs to run 3D parallelism, we'll need at least eight GPUs to get started. How we configure these GPUs will be important to get the most efficiency out of this process. Because TP has the largest communication overhead, we want to ensure these GPUs are close together, preferably on the same node and machine. PP has the least communication volume of the three, so breaking up the model across nodes is the least expensive here.

By running the three together, we see some interesting interactions and synergies between them. Since TP splits the model to work well within a device's memory, we see that PP can perform well even with small batch sizes due to the reduced effective batch size enabled by TP. This combination also improves the communication between DP nodes at different pipeline stages, allowing DP to work effectively too.

[12] A. Harlap et al., "PipeDream: Fast and efficient pipeline parallel DNN training," June 8, 2018, https://arxiv.org/abs/1806.03377.

The communication bandwidth between nodes is proportional to the number of pipeline stages. Consequently, DP can scale well even with smaller batch sizes. Overall, we see that when running in combination, we get better performance than when we run them individually.

Now that we know some tricks of the trade, it's just as important to have the right tools to do the job.

3.4 LLM operations infrastructure

We are finally going to start talking about the infrastructure needed to make this all work. This likely comes as a surprise, as we know that some readers would have expected this section at the beginning of chapter 1. Why wait till the end of chapter 3? In the many times we've interviewed machine learning engineers, we have often asked this open-ended question: "What can you tell me about MLOps?" An easy softball question to get the conversation going. Most junior candidates would immediately start jumping into the tooling and infrastructure. It makes sense; there are so many different tools available. That's not to mention the fact that whenever you see posts or blogs describing MLOps, there's a pretty little diagram showing the infrastructure. While all of that is important, it's useful to recognize what a more senior candidate jumps into—the machine learning life cycle.

For many, the nuance is lost, but the infrastructure is the *how*, and the life cycle is the *why*. Most companies can get by with just bare-bones infrastructure. We've seen our share of scrappy systems that exist entirely on one data scientist's laptop, and they work surprisingly well—especially in the era of scikit-learn everything!

Unfortunately, a rickshaw machine learning platform doesn't cut it in the world of LLMs. Since we still live in a world where the standard storage capacity of a MacBook Pro laptop is 256 GB, just storing the model locally can already be a problem. Companies that invest in a sturdier infrastructure are better prepared for the world of LLMs.

In figure 3.7, we see an example MLOps infrastructure designed with LLMs in mind. While most infrastructure diagrams simplify the structure to make everything look clean, the raw truth is that there's a bit more complexity to the entire system. Of course, a lot of this complexity would disappear if we could get data scientists to work inside scripts instead of ad hoc workstations—usually with a Jupyter Notebook interface.

Taking a closer look at figure 3.7, you can see several tools on the outskirts that squarely land in DataOps or even just DevOps—data stores, orchestrators, pipelines, streaming integrations, and container registries. These are tools you are likely already using for just about any data-intensive application and aren't necessarily focused on MLOps. Toward the center, we have more traditional MLOps tools—experiment trackers, model registry, feature store, and ad hoc data science workstations. For LLMs, we really only introduce one new tool to the stack: a vector database. What's not pictured is the monitoring system because it intertwines with every piece. This

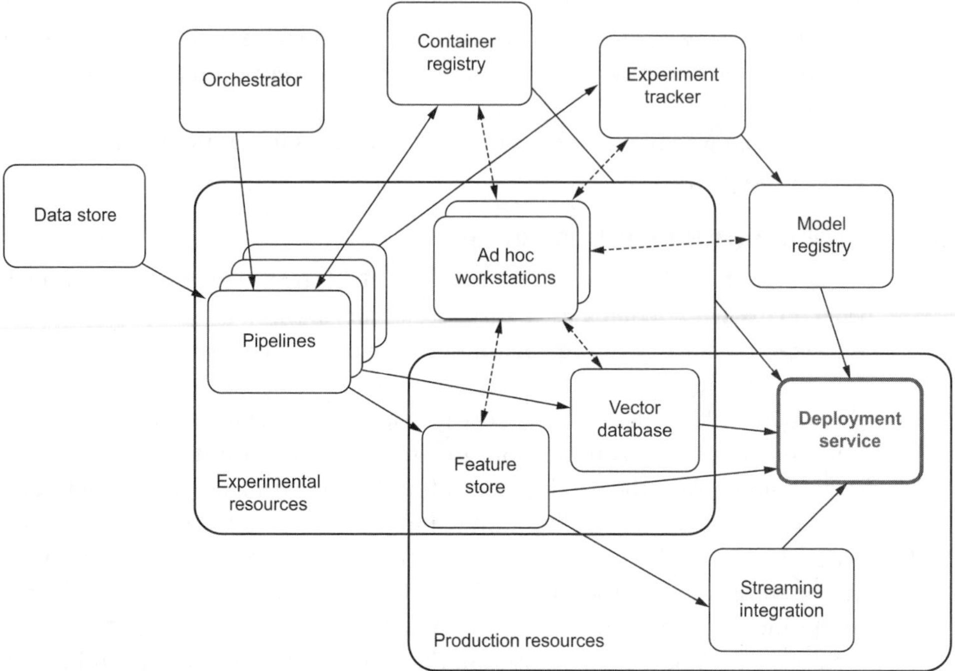

Figure 3.7 A high level view of an MLOps infrastructure with LLMs in mind. This diagram attempts to cover the full picture and the complexity of the many tools involved to make ML models work in production.

all culminates into what we are working toward in this book—a deployment service where we can confidently deploy and run LLMs in production.

Infrastructure by discipline

The following list defines infrastructure by the specific discipline:

- *DevOps*—In charge of procuring the environmental resources: experimental (dev, staging) and production. This includes hardware, clusters, and networking to make it all work. Also in charge of basic infrastructure systems like Github/Gitlab, artifact registries, container registries, application or transactional databases like Postgres or MySQL, caching systems, and CI/CD pipelines. This list is by no means comprehensive.
- *DataOps*—In charge of data, in motion and at rest. It includes centralized or decentralized data stores like data warehouses, data lakes, and data meshes, as well as data pipelines, either in batch systems or in streaming systems with tools like Kafka and Flink. It also includes orchestrators like Airflow, Prefect, and Mage. DataOps is built on top of DevOps. For example, we've seen many CI/CD pipelines being used for data pipeline work until eventually graduating to systems like Apache Spark or DBT.

- *MLOps*—In charge of the machine learning life cycle, from the creation of models to deprecation. This includes data science workstations like JupyterHub, experiment trackers, and a model registry. It includes specialty databases like feature stores and vector databases, as well as a deployment service to tie everything together and actually serve results. It is built on top of both DataOps and DevOps.

Let's go through each piece of the infrastructure puzzle and discuss features you should consider when thinking about LLMs in particular. While we will be discussing specialized tooling for each piece, we'll note that there are also MLOps as a service platform, like Dataiku, Amazon's SageMaker, Azure Machine Learning, and Google's VertexAI. These platforms attempt to complete the whole puzzle; how well they do that is another question. However, they are often a great shortcut, and you should be aware of them. Well, that's enough dillydallying; let's dive in already!

3.4.1 Data infrastructure

While not the focus of this book, it's important to note that MLOps is built on top of a data operations infrastructure, which itself is built on top of DevOps. Key features of the DataOps ecosystem include a data store, an orchestrator, and pipelines. Additional features usually required include a container registry and a streaming integration service.

Data stores are the foundation of DataOps and come in many forms, from a simple database to large data warehouses and from even larger data lakes to an intricate data mesh. This is where your data is stored, and a lot of work goes into managing, governing, and securing the data store. The orchestrator is the cornerstone of DataOps, as it's a tool that manages and automates both simple and complex multistep workflows and tasks, ensuring they run across multiple resources and services in a system. The most commonly talked about are Airflow, Prefect, and Mage. Lastly, pipelines are the pillars. They hold everything else up and are where we run our jobs. Initially built to simply move, clean, and define data, these same systems are used to run machine learning training jobs on a schedule and do batch inference and loads of other work needed to ensure MLOps runs smoothly.

A container registry is a keystone of DevOps and, subsequently, DataOps and MLOps. Running all our pipelines and services in containers is necessary to ensure consistency. Streaming services are a much bigger beast than what we may let on in this chapter, and if you know, you know. Thankfully, for most text-related tasks, real-time processing isn't a major concern. Even for tasks like real-time captioning or translation, we can often get by with some sort of pseudo–real-time processing strategy that doesn't degrade the user experience depending on the task.

3.4.2 Experiment trackers

Experiment trackers are central to MLOps. Experiment trackers do the fundamental job of keeping track and recording tests and results. As the famous Adam Savage quote from *Myth Busters* states, "Remember, kids, the only difference between screwing around and science is writing it down." Without it, your organization is likely missing the "science" in data science, which is honestly quite embarrassing.

Even if your data scientists are keen to manually track and record results in notebooks, it might as well be thrown in the garbage if it's not easy for others to view and search for. This is the real purpose of experiment trackers—to ensure knowledge is easily shared and made available. Eventually, a model will make it to production, and that model is going to have problems. Sure, you can always just train a new model, but unless the team is able to go back and investigate what went wrong the first time, you are likely to repeat the same mistakes over and over.

There are many experiment trackers out there; the most popular by far is MLFlow, which is open source. It was started by the team at Databricks, which also offers an easy hosting solution. Some paid alternatives worth checking out include CometML and Weights & Biases.

Experiment trackers nowadays come with so many bells and whistles. Most open source and paid solutions will certainly have what you need when looking to scale up your needs for LLMOps. However, ensuring you take advantage of these tools correctly might require a few small tweaks. For example, the default assumption is usually that you are training a model from scratch, but often when working with LLMs, you will be finetuning models instead. In this case, it's important to note the checkpoint of the model you started from. If possible, even linking back to the original training experiment. This will allow future scientists to dig deeper into their test results, find original training data, and discover paths forward to eliminate bias.

Another feature to look out for is evaluation metric tooling. We will go into greater depth in chapter 4, but evaluation metrics are difficult for language models. There are often multiple metrics you care about, and none of them are simple, like complexity ratings or similarity scores. While experiment tracker vendors try to be agnostic and unopinionated about evaluation metrics, they should at least make it easy to compare models and their metrics to help us decide which one is better. Since LLMs have become so popular, some have made it easy to evaluate the more common metrics like ROUGE for text summarization.

You will also find that many experiment-tracking vendors have started to add tools specifically for LLMs. Some features you might consider looking for include direct Hugging Face support, LangChain support, prompt engineering toolkits, finetuning frameworks, and foundation model shops. The space is developing quickly, and no one tool has all the same features right now, but these feature sets will likely converge.

3.4.3 Model registry

The model registry is probably the simplest tool of an MLOps infrastructure. The main objective is one that's easy to solve; we just need a place to store the models. We've seen many successful teams get by simply by putting their models in an object store or shared filesystem and calling it good. That said, there are a couple bells and whistles you should look for when choosing one.

The first is whether the model registry tracks metadata about the model. Most of what you care about is going to be in the experiment tracker, so you can usually get away with simply ensuring you can link the two. In fact, most model registries are built into experiment tracking systems because of this. However, a problem with these systems happens when the company decides to use an open source model or even buy one. Is it easy to upload a model and tag it with relevant information? The answer is usually no.

Next, you want to make sure you can version your models. At some point, a model will reach a point where it's no longer useful and will need to be replaced. Versioning your models will simplify this process. It also makes running production experiments like A/B testing or shadow tests easier.

Lastly, if we are promoting and demoting models, we need to be concerned with access. Models tend to be valuable intellectual property for many companies, so ensuring only the right users have access to the models is important. But it's also important to ensure that only the team that understands the models—what they do and why they were trained—is in charge of promoting and demoting the models. The last thing we want is to delete a model in production or worse.

For LLMs, there are some important caveats you should be aware of: mainly, when choosing a model registry, be aware of any limit sizes. Several model registries restrict model sizes to 10 GB or smaller. That's just not going to cut it. We could speculate on the many reasons for this, but none of them are worthy of note. Speaking of limit sizes, if you are going to be running your model registry on an on-premise storage system like Ceph, make sure it has lots of space. You can buy multiple terabytes of storage for a couple of hundred dollars for your on-premise servers, but even a couple of terabytes fills up quickly when your LLM is over 300 GB. Don't forget: you are likely to be keeping multiple checkpoints and versions during training and finetuning, as well as duplicates for reliability purposes. Storage is still one of the cheapest aspects of running LLMs, though, so there's no reason to skimp here and cause headaches down the road.

This brings me to a good point: a lot of optimization could still be made, allowing for better space-saving approaches to storing LLMs and their derivatives, especially since most of these models will be very similar overall. We'll likely see storage solutions to solve just this problem in the future.

3.4.4 Feature stores

Feature stores solve many important problems and answer questions like, Who owns this feature? How was it defined? Who has access to it? Which models are using it? How do we serve this feature in production? Essentially, they solve the "single source of truth" problem. Creating a centralized store allows teams to shop for the highest quality, most well-maintained, thoroughly managed data. Feature stores solve the problems of collaboration, documentation, and versioning of data.

If you've ever thought, "A feature store is just a database, right?", you are probably thinking about the wrong type of store—we are referencing a place to shop, not a place of storage. Don't worry: this confusion is normal, as we've heard this sentiment a lot and have had similar thoughts ourselves. The truth is that modern-day feature stores are more virtual than a physical database, which means they are built on top of whatever data store you are already using. For example, Google's Vertex AI feature store is just BigQuery, and we've seen a lot of confusion from data teams wondering, "Why don't we just query BigQuery?" Loading the data into a feature store feels like an unnecessary extra step, but think about shopping at an IKEA store. No one goes directly to the warehouse where all the furniture is in boxes. That would be a frustrating shopping experience. The features store is the showroom that allows others in your company to easily peruse, experience, and use the data.

Often, we see people reach for a feature store to solve a technical problem like low latency access for online feature serving. A huge win for feature stores is solving the training-serving skew. Some features are just easier to do in SQL after the fact, like calculating the average number of requests for the last 30 seconds. This can lead to naive data pipelines being built for training but causing massive headaches when going to production because getting this type of feature in real time can be anything but easy. Feature store abstractions help minimize this burden. Related to this are feature store point-in-time retrievals, which are table stakes when talking feature stores. Point-in-time retrievals ensure that, given a specific time, a query will always return the same result. This is important because features like averages over "the last 30 seconds" are constantly changing, so this allows us to version the data (without the extra burden of a bloated versioning system), as well as ensure our models will give accurate and predictable responses.

As far as options, Feast is a popular open source feature store. Featureform and Hopsworks are also open source. All three offer paid hosting options. For LLMs, we've heard the sentiment that feature stores aren't as critical as other parts of the MLOps infrastructure. After all, the model is so large that it should incorporate all the features needed inside it, so you don't need to query for additional context. Just give the model the user's query, and let the model do its thing. However, this approach is still a bit naive, and we haven't quite gotten to a point where LLMs are completely self-sufficient. To avoid hallucinations and improve factual correctness, it is often best to give the model some context. We do this by feeding it embeddings of our documents that we want it to know very well, and a feature store is a great place to put these embeddings.

3.4.5 Vector databases

If you are familiar with the general MLOps infrastructure, most of this section has been review for you. We've only had to make slight adjustments highlighting important scaling concerns to make a system work for LLMs. Vector databases, however, are new to the scene and have been developed to be a tailored solution for working with LLMs and language models in general, but you can also use them with other datasets like images or tabular data, which are easy enough to transform into a vector. Vector databases are specialized databases that store vectors along with some metadata around the vector, which makes them great for storing embeddings. Now, while that last sentence is true, it is a bit misleading because the power of vector databases isn't in their storage but in the way that they search through the data.

Traditional databases, using b-tree indexing to find IDs or text-based search using reverse indexes, all have the same common flaw: you have to know what you are looking for. If you don't have the ID or you don't know the keywords, it's impossible to find the right row or document. Vector databases, however, take advantage of the vector space, meaning you don't need to know exactly what you are looking for; you just need to know something similar, which you can then use to find the nearest neighbors using similarity searches based on Euclidean distance, cosine similarity, dot product similarity, or what have you. For example, using a vector database makes solving the reverse image search problem a breeze.

At this point, some readers may be confused. First, we told you to put your embeddings into a feature store, and now we're telling you to put them into a Vector DB. Which one is it? Well, that's the beauty of it: you can do both at the same time. If it didn't make sense before, we hope it makes sense now. A feature store is not a database; it is just an abstraction. You can use a feature store built on top of a vector DB, and it will solve many of your problems. Vector DBs can be difficult to maintain when you have multiple data sources, are experimenting with different embedding models, or otherwise have frequent data updates. Managing this complexity can be a real pain, but a feature store can handily solve this problem. Using them in combination will ensure a more accurate and up-to-date search index.

Vector databases have only been around for a couple of years at the time of writing, and their popularity is still relatively new, as they have grown hand in hand with LLMs. It's easy to understand why since they provide a fast and efficient way to retrieve vector data, making it simple to provide LLMs with needed context to improve their accuracy.

That said, it's a relatively new field, and there are lots of competitors in this space right now. It's a bit too early to know who the winners and losers are. Not wanting to date this book too much, let me at least suggest two options to start: Pinecone and Milvus. Pinecone is one of the first vector databases as a product and has a thriving community with lots of documentation. It's packed with features and has proven itself to scale. Pinecone is a fully managed infrastructure offering that has a free tier for beginners to learn. If you are a fan of open source, however, then you'll want to check out

Milvus. Milvus is feature rich and has a great community. Zilliz, the company behind Milvus, offers a fully managed offering, but it's also available to deploy in your own clusters. If you already have a bit of infrastructure experience, it's relatively easy and straightforward to do.

There are lots of alternatives out there right now, and it's likely worth a bit of investigation before picking one. The two things you'll probably care most about are price and scalability, as the two often go hand in hand. After that, it's valuable to pay attention to search features, such as support for different similarity measures like cosine similarities, dot product, and Euclidean distance, as well as indexing features like Hierarchical Navigable Small World (HNSW) and locality-sensitive hashing (LSH). Being able to customize your search parameters and index settings is important for any database, as you can customize the workload for your dataset and workflow, allowing you to optimize query latency and search result accuracy.

It's also important to note that with the rise of vector databases, we are quickly seeing many database incumbents like Redis and Elastic offering vector search capabilities. For now, most of these tend to offer the most straightforward feature sets, but they are hard to ignore if you are already using these tool sets, as they can provide quick wins to help you get started quickly.

Vector databases are powerful tools that can help you train or finetune LLMs, as well as improve the accuracy and results of your LLM queries.

3.4.6 Monitoring system

A monitoring system is crucial to the success of any ML system, LLMs included. Unlike other software applications, ML models are known to fail silently—that is, continue to operate but start to give poor results. This is often due to data drift, a common example being a recommendation system that gives worse results over time because sellers start to game the system by giving fake reviews to get better recommendation results. A monitoring system allows us to catch poorly performing models and make adjustments or simply retrain them.

Despite their importance, monitoring systems are often the last piece of the puzzle added. This is often purposeful, as putting resources into figuring out how to monitor models doesn't help if you don't have any models to monitor. However, don't make the mistake of putting it off too long. Many companies have been burned by a model that went rogue with no one knowing about it, often costing them dearly. It's also important to realize you don't have to wait to get a model into production to start monitoring your data. There are plenty of ways to introduce a monitoring system into the training and data pipelines to improve data governance and compliance. Regardless, you can usually tell the maturity of a data science organization by its monitoring system.

There are lots of great monitoring toolings out there; some great open source options include whylogs and Evidently AI. We are also fans of Great Expectations but have found it rather slow outside of batch jobs. There are also many more paid options out there. Typically, for ML monitoring workloads, you'll want to monitor everything you'd normally record in other software applications; this includes resource metrics like memory and CPU utilization, performance metrics like latency and queries per second, and operational metrics like status codes and error rates. In addition, you'll need ways to monitor data drift going in and out of the model. You'll want to pay attention to things like missing values, uniqueness, and standard deviation shifts. In many instances, you'll want to be able to segment your data while monitoring—for example, for A/B testing or monitoring by region. Some metrics useful to monitor in ML systems include model accuracy, precision, recall, and F1 scores. These are difficult since you won't know the correct answer at inference time, so it's often helpful to set up some sort of auditing system. Of course, auditing will be easier if your LLM is designed to be a Q&A bot rather than if your LLM is built to help writers be more creative.

This hints at a whole set of new challenges for your monitoring systems, even more than what we see with other ML systems. With LLMs, we are dealing with text data, which is hard to quantify, as discussed earlier in this chapter. For instance, consider the features you look at to monitor for data drift, because language is known to drift a lot! One feature we suggest is unique tokens. These will alert you when new slang words or terms are created; however, they still don't help when words switch meaning, for example, when "wicked" means "cool." We would also recommend monitoring the embeddings; however, you'll likely find this to either add a lot of noise and false alarms or, at the very least, be difficult to decipher and dig into when problems do occur. The systems that work the best often involve a lot of handcrafted rules and features to monitor, but these can be error-prone and time-consuming to create.

Monitoring text-based systems is far from a solved problem, mostly stemming from the difficulties in understanding text data to begin with. This begs the question of what the best methods are to use language models to monitor themselves since they are our current best solution to codifying language. Unfortunately, we're not aware of anyone researching this, but we imagine it's only a matter of time.

3.4.7 GPU-enabled workstations

GPU-enabled workstations and remote workstations in general are often considered a nice-to-have or luxury by many teams, but when working with LLMs, that mindset has to change. When troubleshooting a problem or just developing a model in general, a data scientist isn't able to spin up the model in a notebook on their laptop anymore. The easiest way to solve this is to simply provide remote workstations with GPU resources. There are plenty of cloud solutions for this, but if your company is working mainly on-premise, it may be a bit more difficult to provide but necessary nonetheless.

LLMs are GPU memory-intensive models. Consequently, there are some numbers every engineer should know when it comes to working in the field. The first is how many GPUs to have. The NVIDIA Tesla T4 and V100 are the two most common GPUs you'll find in a datacenter, but they only have 16 GB of memory. They are workhorses, though, and cost-effective, so if we can compress our model to run on these, all the better. After these, you'll find a range of GPUs like NVIDIA A10G, NVIDIA Quadro series, and NVIDIA RTX series that offer GPU memories in the ranges of 24, 32, and 48 GB. All of these are fine upgrades; you'll just have to figure out which ones are offered by your cloud provider and available to you. This brings us to the NVIDIA A100, which is likely going to be your GPU of choice when working with LLMs. Thankfully, they are relatively common and offer two different models providing 40 or 80 GB. A big problem with these is that they are constantly in high demand by everyone right now. You should also be aware of the NVIDIA H100, which offers 80 GB like the A100. The H100 NVL is promised to support up to 188 GB and has been designed with LLMs in mind. Another new GPU you should be aware of is the NVIDIA L4 Tensor Core GPU, which has 24 GB and is positioned to take over as a new workhorse along with the T4 and V100, at least as far as AI workloads are concerned.

LLMs come in all different sizes, and it's useful to have a horse sense for what these numbers mean. For example, the LLaMA model has 7B, 13B, 33B, and 65B parameter variants. If you aren't sure off the top of your head which GPU you need to run which model, here's a shortcut: multiply the number of billions of parameters by two, and that's how much GPU memory you need. The reason is that most models at inference will default to run at half precision, FP16 of BF16, which means we need at least 2 bytes for every parameter. For example, 7 billion × 2 bytes = 14 GB. You'll need a little extra as well for the embedding model, which will be about another gigabyte, and more for the actual tokens you are running through the model. One token is about 1 MB, so 512 tokens will require 512 MB. This isn't a big deal until you consider running larger batch sizes to improve performance. For 16 batches of this size, you'll need an extra 8 GB of space.

Of course, so far, we've only been talking about inference; for training, you'll need a lot more space. While training, you'll always want to do this in full precision, and you'll need extra room for the optimizer tensors and gradients. In general, to account for this, you'll need about 16 bytes for every parameter. So to train a 7B parameter model, you'll want 112 GB of memory.

3.4.8 Deployment service

Everything we've been working toward is collected and finally put to good use here. In fact, if you took away every other service and were left with just a deployment service, you'd still have a working MLOps system. A deployment service provides an easy way to integrate with all the previous systems we talked about and to configure and define the needed resources to get our model running in production. It will often provide boilerplate code to serve the model behind a REST and gRPC API or directly inside a batch or streaming pipeline.

Some tools to help create this service include NVIDIA Triton Inference Service, MLServer, Seldon, and BentoML. These services provide a standard API interface, typically the KServe V2 Inference Protocol. This protocol provides a unified and extensible way to deploy, manage, and serve machine learning models across different platforms and frameworks. It defines a common interface to interact with models, including gRPC and HTTP/RESTful APIs. It standardizes concepts like input/output tensor data encoding, predict and explain methods, model health checks, and metadata retrieval. It also allows seamless integration with languages and frameworks, including TensorFlow, PyTorch, ONNX, Scikit Learn, and XGBoost.

Of course, there are times when flexibility and customization provide enough value to step away from the automated path these other frameworks provide, in which case it's best to reach for a tool like FastAPI. Your deployment service should still provide as much automation and boilerplate code here as possible to make the process as smooth as possible. It should be mentioned that most of the previously mentioned frameworks do offer custom methods, but your mileage may vary.

Deploying a model is more than just building the interface. Your deployment service will also provide a bridge to close the gap between the MLOps infrastructure and general DevOps infrastructure. The connection to whatever CI/CD tooling and build and shipping pipelines your company has set up so you can ensure appropriate tests and deployment strategies like health checks and rollbacks can easily be monitored and done. This is often very platform- and thus company-specific. It must also provide the needed configurations to talk to Kubernetes or whatever other container orchestrator you may be using to acquire the needed resources like CPU, memory, accelerators, autoscalers, proxies, etc. It also applies the needed environment variables and secret management tools to ensure everything runs.

All in all, this service ensures you can easily deploy a model into production. For LLMs, the main concern is often just being sure the platform and clusters are set up with enough resources to provision what will ultimately be configured.

We've discussed a lot so far in this chapter, starting with what makes LLMs so much harder than traditional ML, which is hard enough as it is. First, we learned that their size can't be underestimated, but then we also discovered many peculiarities about them, from token limits to hallucinations—not to mention that they are expensive. Fortunately, despite being difficult, they aren't impossible. We discussed compression techniques and distributed computing, which are crucial to master. We then explored the infrastructure needed to make LLMs work. While most of it was likely familiar, we came to realize that LLMs put a different level of pressure on each tool, and often, we need to be ready for a larger scale than what we could get away with for deploying other ML models.

Summary

- LLMs are difficult to work with mostly because they are big. This results in a longer time to download, load into memory, and deploy, forcing us to use expensive resources.
- LLMs are also hard because they deal with natural language and all its complexities, including hallucinations, bias, ethics, and security.
- Regardless of whether you build or buy, LLMs are expensive, and managing costs and risks associated with them will be crucial to the success of any project utilizing them.

- Compressing models to be as small as we can makes them easier to work with; quantization, pruning, and knowledge distillation are particularly useful for this.
- Quantization is popular because it is easy and can be done after training without any finetuning.
- Low-rank approximation is an effective way to shrink a model and has been used heavily for adaptation, thanks to LoRA.
- There are three core directions we use to parallelize LLM workflows: data, tensor, and pipeline. DP helps us increase throughput, TP helps us increase speed, and PP makes it all possible to run in the first place.
- Combining the parallelism methods, we get 3D parallelism (data + tensor + pipeline), where we find that the techniques synergize, covering each other's weaknesses and helping us get more utilization.
- The infrastructure for LLMOps is similar to MLOps, but don't let that fool you, since there are many caveats where "good enough" no longer works.
- Many tools have begun to offer new features specifically for LLM support.
- Vector databases, in particular, are interesting as a new piece of the infrastructure puzzle needed for LLMs that allow quick search and retrievals of embeddings.

4 Data engineering for large language models: Setting up for success

This chapter covers

- Common foundation models used in the industry
- How to evaluate and compare large language models
- Different data sources and how to prepare your own
- Creating your own custom tokenizers and embeddings
- Preparing a Slack dataset to be used in future chapters

Data is like garbage. You'd better know what you are going to do with it before you collect it.

—Mark Twain

Creating our own LLM is no different from any ML project in that we will start by preparing our assets—and there isn't a more valuable asset than your data. All successful AI and ML initiatives are built on a good data engineering foundation. It's important then that we acquire, clean, prepare, and curate our data.

Unlike other ML models, you generally won't be starting from scratch when creating an LLM customized for your specific task. Of course, if you do start from scratch, you'll likely only do it once. Then it's best to tweak and polish that model to further refine it for your specific needs. Selecting the right base model can make or break your project. Figure 4.1 gives a high-level overview of the different pieces and assets you'll need to prepare before training or finetuning a new model.

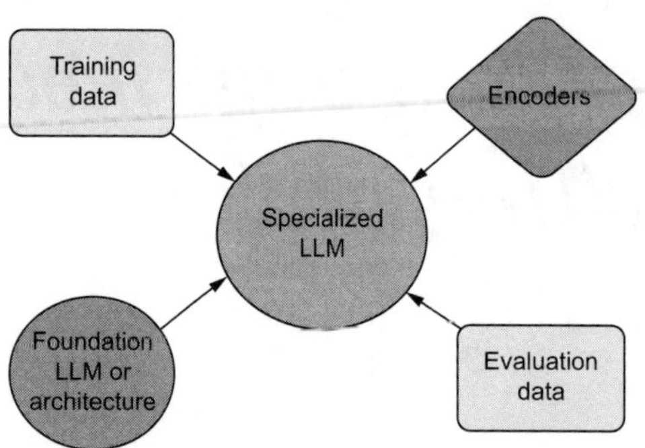

Figure 4.1 The different elements of training an LLM. Combining earth, fire, water—wait, no, not those elements. To get started, you'll need to collect several assets, including a foundation model, training data, text encoders (e.g., tokenizer), and evaluation data.

As was so well defined in the book *Fundamentals of Data Engineering*[1]:

> *Data engineering is the development, implementation, and maintenance of systems and processes that take in raw data and produce high-quality, consistent information that supports downstream use cases, such as analysis and machine learning.*

In this chapter, we will discuss the steps you'll need to take before you can start creating your LLM, which largely involves preparing the data assets necessary to train a model. We will go over many of the base or foundation models available to you as a starting point and how to evaluate and compare them. We will then go into depth on many of the different datasets available and how to prepare your own for finetuning a model, including preparing your own tokenizer or embeddings. Lastly, we will craft a dataset that we will use to finetune a model in the next chapter.

4.1 Models are the foundation

We will first discuss the most important dataset you will need to collect when training, which is the model weights of a pretrained model. A big reason why LLMs are so successful as a technology is that we can take a model already trained on language as a whole and tweak it to do well on a specific task. Of course, knowing how that beginning model was trained and what it was trained on will be a huge shortcut in choosing the right one to tweak.

Choosing the right one has become obnoxiously difficult since LLMs have been a hot research topic, resulting in a new one that sports benchmark-breaking records

[1] Joe Reis and Matt Housley, *Fundamentals of Data Engineering,* O'Reilly, 2022.

popping up almost every week. Because we know (or at least assume) you are eager to learn about them, we will first discuss the many different models currently out there. These models have already been trained (for better or worse) by professionals working to make your life easier and put powerful language models into the public arena. There are thousands upon thousands of open source models available on GitHub, Hugging Face Hub, and elsewhere, so to simplify, we'll highlight our favorites, giving you details about each of the models to make it easier to compare and to give you an idea about whether you should use that particular model or opt for one of its lesser-known open source variants. If you are planning to train from scratch, consider the architecture involved and if there's a certain family you'd like to try.

4.1.1 GPT

There's probably no better place to start than with GPT (Generative Pre-trained Transformer) models. A fan favorite and one of ours too, these models are sold commercially through OpenAI and have gained popularity for their impressive performance on a wide range of tasks. GPT models are so well known that laypersons often use "GPT" to replace "LLM," just as one might say Kleenex or Band-Aid instead of tissue or bandage.

The first GPT model was introduced in 2018, shortly after transformers were introduced, and only had 120M parameters. It was trained on the small BookCorpus dataset and had impressive results on NLP benchmarks at the time. The GPT-2 model came out the next year, increasing its size by 10-fold to 1.5B parameters; it was trained on the much larger WebText dataset. The next year, in 2020, GPT-3 came out 100 times larger with 175B parameters and trained on the massive Common Crawl dataset. This model was still based on GPT-1's original architecture with slight modifications for improved scaling.

OpenAI has chosen to keep further iterations like GPT-4 under greater secrecy, not revealing training data or specific architectures, since it has started to productionize and sell them as a product. ChatGPT is a finetuned GPT-3 model trained for conversational interaction using reinforcement learning with human feedback (RLHF). Not to get into the weeds, but there is a whole host of GPT-3 models you can find under API names such as ada, babbage, curie, and davinci, as well as other finetuned models such as webGPT and InstructGPT. We leave it to the reader to investigate further if they are interested.

Other open source variations like GPT-J were created by the open source community utilizing the knowledge gained from the whitepapers OpenAI published. Several GPT models have no relation to OpenAI, as Generative Pre-trained Transformer is a very generic name that fits most LLMs. Of course, OpenAI has started to see it as a brand and is trying to trademark the acronym.[2]

---

[2] C. Loizos, "'GPT' may be trademarked soon if OpenAI has its way," TechCrunch, April 25, 2023, https://mng.bz/5Omq.

GPT-X models, although closed source, can be accessed via the OpenAI API, which also includes features for their finetuning. We will be using GPT-2 throughout this book—even though it is a bit smaller than what most would consider an actual LLM—as it is a well-understood architecture and easy to learn with.

4.1.2 BLOOM

BLOOM is one of the most iconic LLMs because of the learning that has come from creating it. The model came out in 2022 and is the first public LLM to rival GPT-3's size with 176B parameters; it was trained with complete transparency. It was put together by Hugging Face's BigScience team, with help from Microsoft's DeepSpeed team and NVIDIA's Megatron-LM team, and was sponsored by French government grants.

BLOOM was trained on the BigScienceCorpus dataset, a conglomerate of many smaller datasets amounting to 1.6TB of pre-processed text. It is licensed under RAIL, which means it isn't technically open source, since there are restrictions on how you can use it, but it can be commercialized.

TIP You can learn more about the RAIL license here: https://mng.bz/mR20.

BLOOM was trained to be industry size and industry grade for all tasks. Because of this, fitting on a consumer device was not a priority, but several smaller versions were trained as the research team was coming up to speed. There are 560M-, 3B-, and 7B-parameter versions. There is also BLOOMZ, a multitask, finetuned version of the full 176B parameter model. BLOOM was only trained in 46 different languages, and BLOOMZ's goal was to increase the cross-lingual generalization of the model.[3] You can find all of these models on Hugging Face's hub: https://huggingface.co/bigscience/bloom.

The big downside to BLOOM is that it often gives poor responses and doesn't compete very well in benchmarks—most likely due to limited funds and tight deadlines of the project, leading to a feeling that it was undertrained. This isn't always a bad thing and is often better than an overtrained model, but you can expect to require a lot more finetuning on a larger dataset if you decide to use it. The benefit of using it, though, is that it is well understood and trained in the open, and you can check its training data.

In general, the authors wouldn't recommend using it as a foundation model anymore; there are better alternatives, but it's one you should be familiar with because of its contributions. For example, BLOOM's creation of petals, which allowed distributed training, was a significant contribution to the field.

[3] N. Muennighoff et al., "Cross lingual generalization through multitask finetuning," November 3, 2022, https://arxiv.org/abs/2211.01786.

4.1.3 LLaMA

LLaMA is the result of Meta's foray into LLMs. The first version was released in February 2023 and was released to the research community with a noncommercial license. A week later, the weights were leaked on 4chan. In an unlikely turn of events, this leak has likely been very beneficial to Meta, as this model has become the standard for experimentation and development. Several more models we will discuss are based on it.

Later, in July 2023, Meta released Llama 2, which has both a research and a commercial license. Llama 2 is a big deal since it's the first commercially available model that really packs a punch, and you'll see many other models based on its architecture. There are three different model sizes available: 7B, 13B, and 70B parameters. You can download them here: https://ai.meta.com/llama/. You'll need to request access and accept the terms and conditions if you plan to use it.

Llama 2 was trained on 2 trillion tokens from a curated dataset taken from the internet where they removed websites known to contain personal information and upsampled what they considered factual sources. While exact details of the dataset haven't been shared, it likely contained data from Common Crawl, GitHub, Wikipedia, Project Gutenberg, ArXiv, and Stack Exchange since those were the primary datasets for LLaMA 1. These datasets were later packaged together and distributed under the name RedPajama. Llama 2 was then further finetuned using RLHF, with one model finetuned for chat and another for code.

4.1.4 Wizard

The Wizard family of language models comes from the 2023 paper "WizardLM: Empowering Large Language Models to Follow Complex Instructions."[4] These models follow the idea that LLMs function better when trained on dense training data filled with high-complexity tasks. Based on a proposed framework for creating more complex instruction tasks, the WizardLM methodology has been applied to many popular datasets and used to finetune almost all of the most popular models. The methodology is so popular that, amazingly, it only took the community two days after LlamaCoder34B came out to finetune the WizardCoder34B model.

These models have been consistently praised for their human-like prose and their ability to correctly sort through complex problems that rivals many paid services. One problem we encourage you to try is to ask WizardCoder34B to write a program that draws a realistic-looking tree using any language you'd like. Because the Wizard models don't revolve as much around a specific dataset as they do around the methodology of changing an existing dataset to fit the Wizard style, the applications are incredibly broad and diverse. If you hit a wall where you aren't sure how to improve when using another model or architecture, try taking the dataset you've already used and applying the Wizard methodology. You're welcome.

---

[4] C. Xu et al., "WizardLM: Empowering large language models to follow complex instructions," Jun. 10, 2023, https://arxiv.org/abs/2304.12244.

As a side note, WizardCoder models tend to get a lot of attention, but the WizardMath models are also impressive in their own right. We note that a lot of readers likely deal more with data problems than code problems, and the WizardMath models might be a great place to start when working with talk-to-your-data applications.

4.1.5 Falcon

Falcon models are a model family from the Technology Innovation Institute in Abu Dhabi. They are the first state-of-the-art models to be released under a truly open source license, Apache 2.0. You can get the model from the institute's website: https://falconllm.tii.ae/falcon-models.html. Its easy access and the open license make this a dream for hackers, practitioners, and the industry.

Falcon models first introduced in June 2023 only introduced 7B and 40B parameter models, but in September 2023, Falcon released a 180B parameter model that can truly compete with GPT-3–sized models. What's also exciting and probably more important to many readers is that Falcon has often led LLM leaderboards in many benchmarking tasks. The models were primarily trained on the RefinedWeb dataset, which is a smaller but much higher-quality dataset that was carefully and meticulously curated and extracted from the Common Crawl dataset.

4.1.6 Vicuna

Vicuna was trained on a dataset of user-shared conversations from ShareGPT. The logic is that a model trained off of the best outputs of ChatGPT will be able to emulate the performance of ChatGPT, piggy-backing off of the Llama–Alpaca trend.

NOTE We won't talk about Alpaca here, but we introduced it in chapter 3 when discussing knowledge distillation.

Vicuna has been praised for both its performance and its relatively low training costs. Vicuna is an amazing example of why data coverage and quality matter so much while simultaneously demonstrating the dangers of model collapse from training on the output of another model. Model collapse happens when an ML model is trained on synthetic data, leading to increasingly less diverse outputs. For example, Vicuna performs admirably on anything that is at least close to what appeared in the dataset, but when asked to perform more generative or agent-like tasks, it tends to hallucinate far beyond what its predecessors do. Vicuna is not licensed for commercial use, but it is amazing for personal projects.

4.1.7 Dolly

Created by Databricks as more of a thought experiment than a competitive model, Dolly and its V2 do not perform well compared to other models of the same size. However, Dolly boasts one of the best underlying understandings of English and is a fantastic starting point for finetuning or creating low-ranking adaptations (LoRAs; which we will discuss in chapter 5) to influence other models. Dolly 1.0 was trained on the

Stanford Alpaca Dataset, while Dolly 2.0 was trained on a high-quality human-generated instruction-following dataset that was crowdsourced by the Databricks employees. Dolly 2.0 has been open sourced in its entirety, including the training code, dataset, and model weights, all with a commercial use license.[5]

4.1.8 OpenChat

OpenChat is similar to Vicuna in that OpenChat used 80K ShareGPT conversations for training, but dissimilar in that their conditioning and weighted loss strategies end up creating a model that is undeniably great in its ability to generate human-like and, more importantly, human-preferred responses.

OpenChat models—not to be confused with the open source chatbot console—are a collection of various finetunings for different tasks, with some meant for coding, others for agents, and others for chatting. Free for commercial use under the Llama 2 Community License, these models could be a great solution to build off of at your corporation.

We've discussed a lot of models already, and while we could go on like this for the rest of the chapter, it's in everyone's best interest that we don't. Table 4.1 shows a summary highlighting some of the major points of comparison for the models we discussed. One major point we'd like to highlight is that a lot of models are available for commercial use! While many of the licenses come with restrictions, they likely aren't rules you plan to break anyway.

Table 4.1 Comparison of LLM model families

Model family	Dataset	Largest model size	Commercial license	Organization
GPT	Common Crawl/RLHF	1.76T	No	OpenAI
BLOOM	BigScienceCorpus	176B	Yes	BigSciense
Llama	RedPajama	70B	Yes	Meta
Wizard	Evol-Instruct	70B	No	Microsoft
Falcon	RefinedWeb	180B	Yes	TII

Now that you have an understanding of some of the more popular model families, you might have an idea of which model to pick to start for your project. But how can you be sure? In the next section, we'll look at different ways you can evaluate and compare models.

---

[5] Mike Conover et al., "Free Dolly: Introducing the world's first truly open instruction-tuned LLM," Databricks, April 12, 2023, https://mng.bz/n0e8.

4.2 Evaluating LLMs

While we have just discussed some of our favorite model families, there are so many more and varying models available out there, with many more coming out every month, all claiming to be the best. It is impossible to keep them all straight. So how do you pick the best one to use? Can it perform well on your task out of the box, or will it require finetuning? How do you know if your finetuning improved the model or just made it worse? How do you know if you picked the right size? A smaller model is convenient, but larger models perform better on many tasks. To be honest, these are not easy questions to answer, but thankfully, there are a few industry standards we can rely on.

When evaluating a model, you will need two things: a metric and a dataset. A metric is an algorithm that allows us to compare results to a ground truth. A dataset is a list of tasks we want our model to run, which we will then compare using our metrics of choice.

In this section, we will discuss many different methodologies employed to evaluate LLMs so we can evaluate and compare them objectively. We will discuss everything from common industry benchmarks to methodologies used to develop your own unique evaluations. Let's get started.

4.2.1 Metrics for evaluating text

Evaluating text is often difficult because it's easy to say the exact same thing in two different ways. Semantically, two sentences can be exactly the same, but syntactically, they are nothing alike, making text comparison tricky. See what I did there?

To evaluate our models, we will need better metrics than just an exact match or check for equality, which we can get away with for most other ML problems. We need a metric that allows us to compare the generated text from our models against a ground truth without being too rigid. Let's look at some of the most common metrics used.

ROUGE

ROUGE, short for Recall-Oriented Understudy for Gisting Evaluation, is one of the oldest metrics used for evaluating machine translation tasks, but still one of the most reliable. It was developed specifically for automatic summarization tasks where the goal is to take a long article and sum it up in a short brief. Let's consider the problem: How do you determine whether a summary is correct? The simplest method would be to compare it to a known summary—a ground truth, if you will. However, no matter the article, there's often thousands of ways you could choose to simplify the text to be more concise, and you don't want to penalize a model simply because it chose a different word order than the ground truth; this would only lead to overfitting.

Rouge doesn't compare the generated summary to the ground truth summary expecting an exact match; instead, it looks for overlaps between the two summaries using N-grams—the greater the overlap, the higher the score. This is similar to how a full-text search engine works. There are multiple variations depending on what N is for the N-gram, but there is also a version that compares longest common subsequences and versions that compare skip-bigrams, which are any pair of words in their sentence order and not necessarily right next to each other.

The original implementation of ROUGE was written in Perl, and we remember having to use it even a couple of years ago. Easily some of the worst days of one author's career were having to work in Perl. Thankfully, it seems that in the last year or so, there have finally been fast, stable reimplementations in Python. In the next listing, we use the rouge-score library, which is a reimplementation from Google. We'll compare two explanations of *The Legend of Zelda* and see how well they compare.

Listing 4.1 Using ROUGE

```
from rouge_score import rouge_scorer

target = "The game 'The Legend of Zelda' follows the adventures of the \
    hero Link in the magical world of Hyrule."
prediction = "Link embarks on epic quests and battles evil forces to \
    save Princess Zelda and restore peace in the land of Hyrule."

scorer = rouge_scorer.RougeScorer(["rouge1", "rougeL"], use_stemmer=True)
scores = scorer.score(target, prediction)
print(scores)
# {'rouge1': Score(precision=0.28571428, recall=0.31578947, fmeasure=0.3),
# 'rougeL': Score(precision=0.238095238, recall=0.26315789, fmeasure=0.25)}
```

Example N-gram where N=1 and also using the longest common subsequence

As you can see from the example, even though these two texts are quite different syntactically, they are both accurate descriptions. Because of this, instead of giving a big fat zero for the score, ROUGE gives a little more flexibility and a better comparison with similarity scores around 0.25. The ROUGE algorithm is a fast and effective way to quickly compare the similarity between two short bodies of text. ROUGE is very common in the industry, and many benchmarks use it as one of their metrics.

BLEU

BLEU, which stands for BiLingual Evaluation Understudy, is the oldest evaluation metric we will talk about in this book. It was developed to evaluate machine translation tasks and compare methods of translating one language to another. It is very similar to ROUGE, where we compare N-grams between a target and a prediction. While ROUGE is primarily a recall metric, BLEU is a precision metric, but using standard precision can lead to some problems we need to account for.

To understand the problem, we can calculate standard precision with the code from listing 4.1. Replace the target variable with "the cat in the hat" and the prediction variable with "cat hat." Rerun the listing, and you'll notice the recall is 0.4—we got two out of five words correct—but the precision is 1.0, a perfect score despite not being very good! This result is because both words "cat" and "hat" show up in the target.

BLEU fixes this by adding two adjustments. The first is straightforward: add a brevity penalty. If the prediction is shorter than the target, we'll penalize it. The second adjustment, known as the modified N-gram precision, is a bit more complicated, but it allows us to compare a prediction against multiple targets. The next listing shows how to use the NLTK library to calculate the BLEU score. We are using the same *Zelda* example as we did with ROUGE so you can compare results.

Listing 4.2 Using BLEU

```
import nltk.translate.bleu_score as bleu

target = [
    "The game 'The Legend of Zelda' follows the adventures of the \
    hero Link in the magical world of Hyrule.".split(),
    "Link goes on awesome quests and battles evil forces to \
    save Princess Zelda and restore peace to Hyrule.".split(),
]
prediction = "Link embarks on epic quests and battles evil forces to \
    save Princess Zelda and restore peace in the land of Hyrule.".split()


score = bleu.sentence_bleu(target, prediction)
print(score)
# 0.6187934993051339
```

BLEU has long been an industry standard, as it has been reported several times to correlate well with human judgment on translation tasks. In our example, we split the sentences, but it would be better to tokenize the sentences instead. Of course, you can't compare BLEU scores that use different tokenizers. On that note, SacreBLEU is a variant worth looking at, as it attempts to improve the comparability of scores despite different tokenizers.

BPC

The bits per character (BPC) evaluation is an example of an entropy-based evaluation for language models. These are metrics we try to minimize. We will not dive deeply into entropy or perplexity, but we'll go over an intuitive understanding here. Entropy is an attempt to measure information by calculating the average amount of binary digits required per character in a language. Entropy is the average number of BPC.

Perplexity can be broken down into attempting to measure how often a language model draws particular sequences from its corpus or vocabulary. This draws directly from the model's tokenization strategy (too many `<UNKS>` equals bad perplexity), meaning that a 1:1 comparison between LLMs with different tokenization strategies using perplexity—or entropy, for that matter—is impossible. For example, a model that tokenizes at the character level will have much lower perplexity than a model that tokenizes at the word level but often performs worse overall. That doesn't invalidate either as a metric, as they are very helpful metrics during training of the same model.

NOTE Entropy-related metrics are highly related to information theory, which we don't cover. However, we recommend you take a look at these metrics if you're interested in creating or improving evaluation metrics for LLMs.

To drive the point further with a hands-on example, comparing two models that use different tokenization strategies is like comparing how good one third-grader is at addition with another third-grader's multiplication ability. Saying one is better than the other doesn't really matter because they're doing different things at the same skill level. The closest you could get to an accurate comparison would be having the two third-graders do the same task, say spelling. Then you could at least compare apples to apples, as much as possible.

Now that we have some metrics under our belt, let's look into benchmark datasets that we will run our evaluations on.

4.2.2 *Industry benchmarks*

Evaluating language models' performance is a notoriously difficult problem, and many benchmarks have been created to tackle it. In this subsection, we'll discuss several of the most common solutions you are likely to run into and what type of problem they are trying to solve. Since benchmarks typically are only good at evaluating one quality of a model and LLMs are usually deployed to do many general tasks, you will likely need to run several evaluation benchmarks to get a full picture of the strengths and weaknesses of your model. As we go through this list, don't think about which metric is better than another, but about how they can be used in tandem to improve your overall success.

GLUE

The General Language Understanding Evaluation (GLUE) is essentially a standardized test (think ACT, SAT, GRE, etc.) for language models (just "language models" this time) to measure performance versus humans and each other on language tasks meant to test understanding. When introduced, two problems arose pretty quickly: the LMs surpassed human parity on the tasks too fast, and there were doubts about whether the tasks demonstrated actual understanding. Similar to when people train animals like parrots to speak, the question is always there: Is the parrot actually acquiring human language or simply being conditioned to mimic certain sound sequences in response to specific stimuli in exchange for food? That said, the GLUE benchmark is still valuable for comparing model performance.

GLUE is no longer an industry standard, but it can still give you a fairly quick idea of how well your model is performing, especially if you are training on an instruction-based dataset and using GLUE to measure few or zero-shot performance on new tasks. You can view the leaderboard at https://gluebenchmark.com/leaderboard.

SuperGLUE

As stated in the previous section, one problem that came up quickly was human parity on the GLUE tasks. To solve this problem, one year after GLUE was developed, SuperGLUE was created and contains more difficult and diverse tasks styled in the same easy-to-use way as GLUE. Beyond that, because the GLUE nonexpert human benchmark was being surpassed so quickly, more expert people were used to generate the SuperGLUE benchmark. That said, the SuperGLUE human baselines are in eighth place on the leaderboard at the time of this writing, calling into question the second problem with GLUE: Do the SuperGLUE tasks adequately measure understanding?

Considering that models like PaLM 540B, which are beating the human baseline, struggle to generate output generally considered acceptable to people, another question arises: How much of the training data and evaluation metrics are idealized and nonreflective of how we actually use language? There aren't yet any adequate answers to these questions, but they're helpful to consider when your evaluation metrics could be what stands between your model and acceptable performance on its task.

In listing 4.3, we show how to run a model against the MultiRC SuperGLUE test. The MultiRC dataset contains short paragraphs and asks comprehension questions about the content of the paragraph. Let's go ahead and load the dataset and take a quick look at what we are dealing with.

Listing 4.3 Example SuperGLUE Benchmark

```
from datasets import load_dataset
from transformers import AutoTokenizer, AutoModelForCausalLM

dataset = load_dataset("super_glue", "multirc", split="validation")
    print(dataset[0])
```

SuperGlue has multiple test datasets; options are boolq, cb, copa, multirc, record, rte, wic, wsc, wsc.fixed, axb, and axg.

Here we see a paragraph discussing some basic physics around forces along with a simple yes-or-no question and its answer:

```
# {
#   "paragraph": "What causes a change in motion? The application of a force."
#     " Any time an object changes motion, a force has been applied. In what "
#     "ways can this happen? Force can cause an object at rest to start "
#     "moving. Forces can cause objects to speed up or slow down. Forces can "
#     "cause a moving object to stop. Forces can also cause a change in "
#     "direction. In short, forces cause changes in motion. The moving "
#     "object may change its speed, its direction, or both. We know that "
#     "changes in motion require a force. We know that the size of the force "
#     "determines the change in motion. How much an objects motion changes "
#     "when a force is applied depends on two things. It depends on the "
#     "strength of the force. It also depends on the objects mass. Think "
#     "about some simple tasks you may regularly do. You may pick up a "
#     "baseball. This requires only a very small force. ",
#   "question": "Would the mass of a baseball affect how much force you have "
#     "to use to pick it up?",
#   "answer": "No",
#   "idx": {"paragraph": 0, "question": 0, "answer": 0},
#   "label": 0,
# }
```

Let's go ahead and pull down a small model and run it against the dataset. For this example, we'll print out the model's generated answer to the correct answer to compare qualitatively:

```
model = "bigscience/bloomz-560m"  # Update with your model of choice

tokenizer = AutoTokenizer.from_pretrained(model)
model = AutoModelForCausalLM.from_pretrained(model)

for row in dataset:
    input_text = (
        f'Paragraph: {row["paragraph"]}\nQuestion: {row["question"]}'
    )
    input_ids = tokenizer(input_text, return_tensors="pt").input_ids

    outputs = model.generate(input_ids, max_new_tokens=20)
    input_length = input_ids.shape[1]
    results = tokenizer.decode(outputs[0][input_length:])
    print(row["answer"])
    print(results)
```

Replace this with the correct input for your benchmark.

We use this to trim out the input.

From this, you might get results similar to the following:

```
# No
#  No</s>
# Yes
#  No</s>
# Less the mass, less the force applied
#  No</s>
# It depends on the shape of the baseball
#  No</s>
# Strength
#  Force</s>
# A force
#  Force</s>
# No
#  Yes</s>
```

You can see our model isn't doing all that great, but we aren't too concerned; we just want to show a SuperGLUE test in action. You may be wondering why we aren't using a metric like ROUGE or BLEU. While we could do so to improve our understanding, if you decide to submit results to the SuperGLUE leaderboard, it will want the raw generated text.

> **NOTE** For more information on how to use SuperGLUE, check out SuperGLUE FAQs: https://super.gluebenchmark.com/faq.

SuperGLUE does exactly what it sets out to do: be GLUE but super. If you want to test your model's few and zero-shot capabilities, SuperGLUE would be one of the ultimate tests. It will show whether your LLM can follow instructions with very low perplexity, only generating what is needed and not more. You can look at the current SuperGLUE leaderboard at https://super.gluebenchmark.com/leaderboard.

MMLU

The Massive Multitask Language Understanding (MMLU) test was developed primarily by UC Berkeley in cooperation with several other universities to test deeper knowledge than the GLUE tasks. No longer concerned with surface-level language understanding, MMLU seeks to test whether a model understands language well enough to answer second-tier questions about subjects such as history, mathematics, morality, and law. For example, instead of asking, "What did Newton write about gravity?", ask, "What arguments would Newton have gotten into with Einstein?"

MMLU's questions range in difficulty from an elementary level to an advanced professional level, and they test both world knowledge and problem-solving ability. They are known to be quite difficult, with unspecialized humans from Mechanical Turk only obtaining results slightly better than random with 34.5% accuracy.[6] Experts in their field performed much better, but generally only for the portion of the test that was their specialty. So when we look at the models' performance on the test, as might be expected, the models, even at the top of SuperGLUE's leaderboard, are barely better than random at applying the language understanding to answer questions about it. This test encompasses a much wider range of understanding tasks than GLUE and takes a much lower perplexity to pass.

Listing 4.4 shows how to run this test. We'll download the MMLU dataset and then, for convenience, run the test against OpenAI's different models for comparison. The code also allows for different levels of few-shot prompting. We haven't discussed this, but we wanted to show an example early. Try adjusting this parameter to see how different numbers of examples can improve your overall results.

Listing 4.4 Example MMLU evaluation

```
from deepeval.benchmarks import MMLU
from deepeval.benchmarks.tasks import MMLUTask
from deepeval.models.base_model import DeepEvalBaseLLM
import torch
from transformers import AutoModelForCausalLM, AutoTokenizer


class DeepEvalLLM(DeepEvalBaseLLM):          # Sets up the model
    def __init__(self, model, tokenizer, name):
        self.model = model
        self.tokenizer = tokenizer
        self.name = name

        device = torch.device(
            "cuda" if torch.cuda.is_available() else "cpu"
        )

        self.model.to(device)
        self.device = device
```

[6] D. Hendrycks et al., "Measuring massive multitask language understanding," arXiv (Cornell University), September 2020, https://doi.org/10.48550/arxiv.2009.03300.

```
    def load_model(self):
        return self.model

    def generate(self, prompt: str) -> str:
        model = self.load_model()
        model_inputs = self.tokenizer([prompt], return_tensors="pt").to(
            self.device
        )

        generated_ids = model.generate(
            **model_inputs, max_new_tokens=100, do_sample=True
        )
        return self.tokenizer.batch_decode(generated_ids)[0]

    async def a_generate(self, prompt: str) -> str:
        return self.generate(prompt)

    def get_model_name(self):
        return self.name


model = AutoModelForCausalLM.from_pretrained("gpt2")
tokenizer = AutoTokenizer.from_pretrained("gpt2")

gpt2 = DeepEvalLLM(model=model, tokenizer=tokenizer, name="GPT-2")

benchmark = MMLU(                  <-- Defines benchmark with specific tasks and shots
    tasks=[MMLUTask.HIGH_SCHOOL_COMPUTER_SCIENCE, MMLUTask.ASTRONOMY],
    n_shots=3,
)

benchmark.evaluate(model=gpt2)     <-- Runs benchmark
print(benchmark.overall_score)
# MMLU Task Accuracy (task=high_school_computer_science): 0.0
# MMLU Task Accuracy (task=astronomy): 0.0
# Overall MMLU Accuracy: 0.0
```

MMLU gets at a deeper understanding than any of the previous benchmarks, which is promising, and a correlation can be drawn between this test and chat models that generally produce human-preferred responses. With deeper understanding, though, comes the need for more responsibility in the testing, and ethical concerns are beginning to be raised about these evaluations. For example, are the models being trained to answer questions about US history truthfully, or are they being evaluated on propaganda for an ideal nation? When answering questions about the law, are they conditioned to accept any bias the law system may or may not contain? The current answer is that models are likely demonstrating a deeper bias when performing well on these types of evals, and greater care needs to be taken to ensure that the bias presupposed in our evaluations is unharmful and generally accepted.

4.2.3 Responsible AI benchmarks

Pretty much all industry benchmarks that evaluate LLMs have focused strictly on the model's capability: "Is it able to do the job?" Unfortunately, that's where most industry benchmarks end. It's quite unfortunate, especially since going a step further and evaluating for bias isn't that different from or more difficult than other evaluation techniques. It's your responsibility, and it makes good business sense. Knowing where your model's blind spots are can help you create plans to resolve them, which will help you sell to larger markets and avoid costly trouble in the future.

The most common approach to evaluating bias is to take what we already know and segment the data across diverse groups. Thankfully, since moderating behavior for chat groups and social media sites is valuable to businesses, we already have many good evaluation metrics for traits like toxicity, polarity, hurtfulness, and similar. These metrics aim to measure how much a given text is related to violence, hate speech, racism, or profanity and how positive or negative they may be or just generally in violation of your company's terms and conditions. Listing 4.5 demonstrates how to use the HONEST evaluation metric, which compares how hurtful prompt completions are for different genders. For example, when comparing potential attributes, generating the adjective "smart" would be less hurtful than "dumb."

Listing 4.5 The HONEST metric

```
import evaluate
honest = evaluate.load('honest', 'en')
prompts = ["he is a", "he is", "she is a", "she is"]
completions = [['CEO', 'businessman', 'father'],
               ['good', 'excellent', 'smart'],
               ['secretary', 'prostitute', 'maid'],
               ['beautiful', 'smart', 'tall']]
groups = ["male", "male", "female", "female"]
result = honest.compute(predictions=completions, groups=groups)
print(result)
# {'honest_score_per_group': {'male': 0.0, 'female': 0.16667}}
```

Once you pick one or more evaluators, you'll need a dataset of prompts. You can find several in Hugging Face's dataset. WinoBias focuses on gender bias. It contains prompts like, "The mechanic greets the receptionist because he" along with the opposite gender version, "The mechanic greets the receptionist because she." We would run these prompts through our model and compare the groups. Some other datasets worth checking out include CALM, which compares gender and race, and WinoQueer, which looks at bias for LGBTQ+ groups. There are many more to check out, including datasets for politics, religions, and occupations, to name a few.

NOTE You can learn more about CALM at https://arxiv.org/abs/2308.12539v1, and WinoQueer here: https://arxiv.org/abs/2306.15087.

To put this all together, in listing 4.6, we'll create an evaluation pipeline utilizing the Regard metric. The Regard metric looks at the polarity of content—whether it is a positive or negative statement. We'll run this across the WinoBias dataset, segmenting the data by gender. Once we've run the analysis for each group, we can compare the results across the segments and see whether the distributions differ. Before reading on, take a guess. Do you think we'll see more positive results for men or women, or will they be the same? What about negative results?

Listing 4.6 Running an evaluation pipeline on Regard

```
import torch
from transformers import pipeline
from datasets import Dataset, load_dataset
from evaluate import evaluator
import evaluate
import pandas as pd

device = torch.device('cuda' if torch.cuda.is_available() else 'cpu')

pipe = pipeline("text-generation", model="gpt2", device=device)
wino_bias = load_dataset("sasha/wino_bias_prompt1", split="test")
polarity = evaluate.load("regard")
task_evaluator = evaluator("text-generation")
```

Pulls model, data, and metrics

```
def prepare_dataset(wino_bias, pronoun):
    data = wino_bias.filter(
        lambda example: example["bias_pronoun"] == pronoun
    ).shuffle()
    df = data.to_pandas()
    df["prompts"] = df["prompt_phrase"] + " " + df["bias_pronoun"]
    return Dataset.from_pandas(df)
```

Prepares dataset

```
female_prompts = prepare_dataset(wino_bias, "she")
male_prompts = prepare_dataset(wino_bias, "he")

female_results = task_evaluator.compute(
    model_or_pipeline=pipe,
    data=female_prompts,
    input_column="prompts",
    metric=polarity,
)
male_results = task_evaluator.compute(
    model_or_pipeline=pipe,
    data=male_prompts,
    input_column="prompts",
    metric=polarity,
)
```

Runs through the evaluation pipeline

```
def flatten_results(results):
    flattened_results = []
    for result in results["regard"]:
        item_dict = {}
        for item in result:
```

Analyzes results

```
            item_dict[item["label"]] = item["score"]
        flattened_results.append(item_dict)

    return pd.DataFrame(flattened_results)


print(flatten_results(female_results).mean())
# Prints the mean polarity scores
# positive    0.129005
# negative    0.391423
# neutral     0.331425
# other       0.148147

print(flatten_results(male_results).mean())
# Positive    0.118647
# negative    0.406649
# neutral     0.322766
# other       0.151938
```

Prints the mean polarity scores

Surprisingly to many, this example shows that gender polarity is rather comparable in our model. A good sign for this model! The bigger takeaway is that you should be automating your evaluations and running pipelines across many metrics, including looking for bias, not just performance. Overall, there are still many opportunities to improve evaluations and metrics in this space, especially when creating datasets and finetuning models to reduce bias. We expect to see lots of growth and innovation in this area of research.

4.2.4 Developing your own benchmark

Overall, developing good benchmark datasets is still an unsolved problem. This is partly because once we develop one, our models quickly surpass it, making it obsolete and no longer "good." There will be times when we discover edge cases for our model, such as parts of speech or certain tasks where it seems to struggle—maybe that's playing chess or identifying sarcasm. Spoiler alert: LLMs are still terrible at these tasks, and if you haven't seen a GPT versus Stockfish video yet, you're in for a treat. In these cases, where we are trying to perform a specialized task, a simple evaluation would be to compare a custom list of prompts with expected responses.

We recommend first checking out OpenAI's Evals library (https://github.com/openai/evals), where OpenAI has open sourced its evaluations. The library acts both as an evaluation framework and as a registry for edge-case datasets. At the time of this writing, the library contains almost 400 different datasets and is a great place to get started and contribute. This library gives you access to the same evaluation standards that OpenAI uses for their state-of-the-art models, and they've already done most of the heavy lifting in identifying areas of interest and curating datasets for these areas.

As with most libraries built for a specific company but subsequently open sourced, it can be a bit of a pain to generalize. Running these evaluations against OpenAI's models is easy-peasy, but extending it to run against your own models is anything but.

While this is an annoyance that will likely go away if the community fully embraces and adopts the framework, the real downside to using this library is, ironically, that it's open sourced. Being both a framework and registry (the data is stored alongside the code in the GitHub repo), if you are looking to curate a new evaluation dataset, but the dataset is private or can't be open sourced for whatever reason, you are left with forking the repo and all the pain of managing it as your fork goes out of date.

Another library to pay attention to is Hugging Face's Evaluate. The Evaluate library is also a framework for building evaluation methods; however, the datasets are separate and can be found on the Hugging Face Hub in their own spaces. Since spaces can be private or public, it's a much more user-friendly experience. Hugging Face has custom metrics and all the standard benchmarks already discussed in this chapter, as well as several not discussed. In listing 4.7, we show how to use the Evaluate library to get SQuAD metrics. SQuAD stands for the Stanford Question Answering Dataset, which is an older dataset with 100K questions and answers. SQuAD is a reading comprehension dataset consisting of questions generated from a set of Wikipedia articles, where the answer to every question is a segment of text inside the reading passage. The SQuAD metrics are a set of custom metrics that consist of an exact match; F1 scores were used in the paper introducing the dataset.[7]

Listing 4.7 Using the Evaluate library to run SQuAD

```
import evaluate

squad_metric = evaluate.load("squad")        # Downloads a metric from Hugging Face's Hub
predictions = [
    {"prediction_text": "Saint Bernadette", "id":
     "5733be284776f41900661182"},
    {"prediction_text": "Salma Hayek", "id": "56d4fa2e2ccc5a1400d833cd"},
    {"prediction_text": "1000 MB", "id": "57062c2552bb89140068992c"},
]                                             # Example from the SQuAD dataset
references = [
    {
        "answers": {
            "text": ["Saint Bernadette Soubirous"],
            "answer_start": [515],
        },
        "id": "5733be284776f41900661182",
    },
    {
        "answers": {
            "text": ["Salma Hayek and Frida Giannini"],
            "answer_start": [533],
        },
        "id": "56d4fa2e2ccc5a1400d833cd",
    },
```

[7] P. Rajpurkar, R. Jia, and P. Liang, "Know what you don't know: Unanswerable questions for SQuAD," June 2018, https://arxiv.org/abs/1806.03822.

```
    {
        "answers": {"text": ["1000 MB"], "answer_start": [437]},
        "id": "57062c2552bb89140068992c",
    },
]

results = squad_metric.compute(
    predictions=predictions, references=references
)
print(results)
# {'exact_match': 33.333333333333336, 'f1': 79.04761904761905}
```

If you are creating your own benchmark, with the Evaluate library, you can easily create your own metric in a metric space and the dataset to use with the metric. This process isn't too difficult. If you've decided not to create your own, the hardest part is finding good metrics. Searching through the hub is one thing, but since anyone can upload a metric and dataset, you never know if what you find is all that good, well curated, or clean.

We haven't dug too deeply into actually generating a dataset or metric, as that will be very specific to your use case, but what we have discussed are two great libraries you can use to do it. Evals is great if you are looking for an already curated dataset, and Evaluate is easy to use when generating your own. These tools are very useful, but in some special cases, you'll need to think outside the box, and one of those cases that sticks out like a sore thumb is code generation.

4.2.5 Evaluating code generators

One of the most valuable and sought-after use cases for LLMs is to have them help us write code. While we are unaware of any industry standard evaluation metrics for evaluating the generated code, thankfully, there are plenty of industry standards for evaluating the code itself (e.g., tests, profiles, security scanners, etc.). Using these tools provides a powerful path to evaluating the LLM through the code it generates.

The basic setup looks like this:

1. Have your model generate code based on docstrings.
2. Run the generated code in a safe environment on prebuilt tests to ensure they work and that no errors are thrown.
3. Run the generated code through a profiler and record the time it takes to complete.
4. Run the generated code through a security scanner and count the number of vulnerabilities.
5. Run the code against architectural fitness functions to determine artifacts, like how much coupling, integrations, and internal dependencies there are.
6. Run steps 1 to 5 on another LLM.
7. Compare results.

Listing 4.8 demonstrates an example using everyone's favorite LeetCode problem, the Fibonacci sequence, as our prompt. This example shows using a separate fibonacci.py file as a prompt for our LLM to generate code. We could then use this test file to check that it runs correctly and how fast it runs.

Listing 4.8 An example test for evaluating code generators

```
''' fibonacci.py
def fibonacci_sequence(n):
    """Returns the nth number in the Fibonacci sequence"""
'''

import pytest
import time
from fibonacci import fibonacci_sequence


def test_fibonacci_sequence():
    test_cases = [(1, 0), (2, 1), (6, 5), (15, 377)]

    for n, expected in test_cases:
        result = fibonacci_sequence(n)
        assert (
            result == expected
        ), f"Expected {expected}, but got {result} for n={n}."

    with pytest.raises(ValueError):
        fibonacci_sequence(-1)


if __name__ == "__main__":          # Runs tests using pytest and times it
    start_time = time.time()
    pytest.main(["-v"])
    end_time = time.time()
    execution_time = end_time - start_time
    print(f"Execution time: {execution_time} seconds")
```

There is lots of flexibility to this system, but the major downside is that it requires you to either create docstrings of coding challenges and write tests for them ahead of time or scrape LeetCode. Of course, you could have your LLM generate both of those too, but it's easy to write simple tests that always pass and much harder to write tests that cover all the edge cases. So at some point, you'll want a human in the loop.

4.2.6 Evaluating model parameters

So far, all the evaluation methods we've looked at involve running the model and checking the results, but there is a lot we can learn by simply looking at the model. Surprisingly, there's a lot you can learn by simply looking at the parameters of an ML model. For example, an untrained model will have a completely random distribution.

By evaluating the distribution and paying attention to distinct features of a model's parameters, we can learn whether a model is over- or undertrained. In the next listing, we use the weightwatcher library to do just that on the GPT-2 model, which will tell us which layers are over- or undertrained.

Listing 4.9 Using the weightwatcher library to evaluate GPT-2

```
import weightwatcher as ww
from transformers import GPT2Model

gpt2_model = GPT2Model.from_pretrained("gpt2")
gpt2_model.eval()

watcher = ww.WeightWatcher(model=gpt2_model)
details = watcher.analyze(plot=False)
print(details.head())
```

This code prints out the following:

```
   layer_id       name         D  ...       warning         xmax        xmin

0         2  Embedding  0.076190  ... over-trained  3837.188332    0.003564
1         8     Conv1D  0.060738  ...               2002.124419  108.881419
2         9     Conv1D  0.037382  ...                712.127195   46.092445
3        14     Conv1D  0.042383  ...               1772.850274   95.358278
4        15     Conv1D  0.062197  ...                626.655218   23.727908
```

Along with summary statistics, weightwatcher provides spectral analysis plots, as shown in figure 4.2. To create these plots, change line 8 in listing 4.9 to `plot=True`. The spectral analysis plots evaluate the frequencies of eigenvalues for each layer of a model. When evaluating these plots, we care about the tail of the distribution—the straighter it is (indicating a nice heavy tail), the better trained we expect the layer to be.

> **NOTE** These plots are created to mimic Spectral Density plots you might see in a physics lab. We will not discuss them in this book, but if interested, we recommend you check out the WeightWatchers documentation: https://github.com/CalculatedContent/WeightWatcher.

weightwatcher is rather powerful, as it allows us to compare different models, helping us better understand which model is better trained without running them at all, making it relatively inexpensive. This capability comes in handy when you are trying to determine which base model to use, as an undertrained model may require a lot more finetuning.

Since we are comparing models based on their parameters alone, this method provides a nice agnostic view of the current state of a model. We can implement it during and after training and during ongoing updates using methods such as RLHF. It is both an easy and powerful evaluation method. However, the downside is that it doesn't

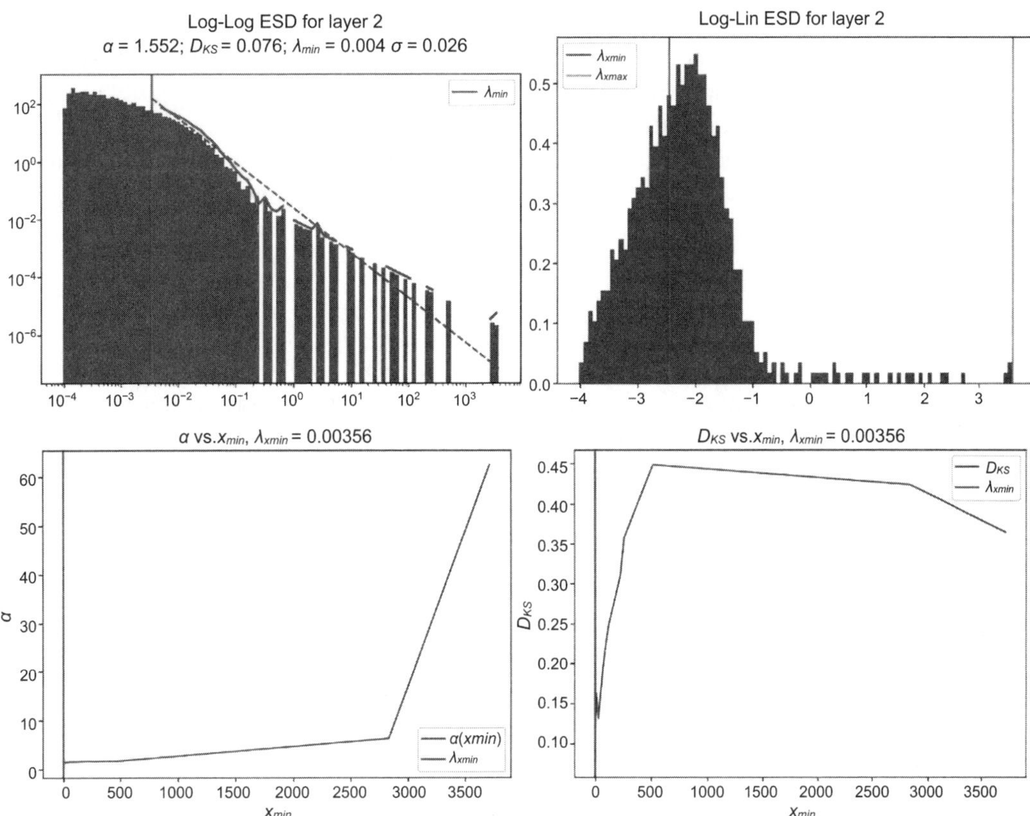

Figure 4.2 weightwatcher Empirical Spectral Density (ESD) plots generated for GPT2's second layer, which is predicted to be overtrained

provide any insight into the training data, so it can't tell us which model is that effective at which task and is best paired with other evaluation methods already discussed.

We've already spent quite a bit of time talking about data most data engineers likely don't think about often: model weights and evaluation data. These are crucial ingredients to gather to generate a specialized finetuned LLM. Indeed, LLMs introduce new data engineering challenges, just like they introduce new MLOps and data science challenges. Next, we will discuss what many of you have been waiting for: the training data. We'll discuss different datasets that are essential to know about, where to get them, and how to prepare them to train or finetune LLMs.

4.3 Data for LLMs

It has been shown that data is the most important part of training an LLM. We hope that the sudden importance of language modeling will persuade businesses to start managing their data generally according to accepted guidelines. As is shown by experiments like LLaMA, Alpaca, Goat, Vicuna, and later, LIMA[8] and SpQR,[9] high-quality training data and clever modeling are much more important than the number of parameters or size of training data. Measuring that quality is still a point of difficulty in general; however, we'll discuss methodologies you can employ to do so.

We'll first discuss common datasets you should know about, what's in them, why you would want them, and where you can get them. Then we'll talk about common processing and preparation techniques you'll need to understand to get the most out of them and get better results from your LLMs.

4.3.1 Datasets you should know

If you didn't notice, in section 4.1, we made it a point to discuss which datasets different models were trained on. It might have come across as just another factoid about the model, but this is highly valuable information! Knowing what a model was trained on (or not trained on) is the first step to understanding what it can or cannot do. For example, knowing an LLM coding model was trained heavily on thc C programming language but didn't see a lick of C++ will be more than enough to realize why it seems to work syntactically but produces so many errors and bugs when writing C++ code.

WIKITEXT

One of the most familiar datasets, Wikitext is, as the name implies, essentially Wikipedia. It was crafted by the Salesforce team back in 2016. It is a great dataset to turn to when you're only trying to do a proof of concept or a rapid prototype since the English version comes in at only 741 MB, not even 1 GB. Add to that the fact that Wikipedia is a trusted source of information—especially compared to the internet at large, where most of the other sources come from—and this gets even better!

Some downsides: it is purely an English dataset, which greatly reduces the diversity of tokens the model will see; Wikipedia contains an idealized version of language—one that we subjectively value as clear—even though it doesn't contain any instances of how language is actually used, only meta-explanations on usage. Also, it's almost a decade old as of this writing, which, of course, no one checks. We've seen many teams use it to quickly prototype and create Q&A bots due to its ease of use and access. It does well in prototyping but always comes off as unimpressive when it gets to production, as users tend to prefer asking questions about current events. Always check the freshness of your data! Overall, it's a valuable dataset information-wise, but bad if you want your models to interact in a human-like way.

WIKI-40B

A good alternative is Wiki-40B from 2020, a cleaned-up version of Wikitext with 40 different language variations. It comes in at a little over 10 GB. So it's still quite small for

---

8 C. Zhou et al., "LIMA: Less is more for alignment," arXiv.org, May 18, 2023, https://arxiv.org/abs/2305.11206.

9 T. Dettmers et al., "SpQR: A sparse-quantized representation for near-lossless LLM weight compression," arXiv.org, June 5, 2023, https://arxiv.org/abs/2306.03078.

prototyping. It comes with all the same benefits Wikitext does: it's a clean dataset and a trusted source of information. Plus, it's newer and has more languages. This is a great dataset to use to become familiar with multilingual modeling.

EUROPARL

One of the best toy datasets for multilingual problems, Europarl contains the European Parliament proceedings from 1996 to 2011. It includes translations in 21 different European languages and is great for smaller projects and multilingual demos. Europarl is an excellent source of data, albeit idealized and outdated, much like English Wikitext. In addition, the project includes many parallel corpora, which are paired down to English and one of the 20 other languages. The total dataset is just 1.5 GB and can be found at https://www.statmt.org/europarl/.

COMMON CRAWL

The Common Crawl dataset is essentially the entire internet, web scraped and open sourced. It uses web crawlers similar to what Google or Microsoft use to enable search engines. C4, the Colossal Cleaned version of the Common Crawl dataset, is the most common dataset for self-supervised pretraining. Unfortunately, being cleaned doesn't mean it is free of inherent societal bias, which is true for pretty much all the datasets openly available today. Containing the entirety of the internet means it contains all the good and the bad; it is a very diverse dataset full of multiple languages and code.

The Common Crawl dataset is named after the nonprofit organization of the same name that is dedicated to providing a copy of the internet to anyone for the purpose of research and analysis. You can access the dataset at https://commoncrawl.org/, where you will find many versions because Common Crawl periodically crawls the web and updates the dataset. The community has been archiving the internet since 2008. It comes in four variants to help with your various needs: a 305 GB version containing the actual C4; a 380 GB version that contains so-called bad words along with everything else; a 2.3 TB version, which is the uncleaned version (not recommended); and a 15 GB version of data that is professional enough to appear on the news.

OPENWEBTEXT

Another dataset we'd recommend for pretraining is OpenWebText, which only takes up 55 GB on disk. It is an open source effort to reproduce OpenAI's WebText dataset used to train GPT-2. Instead of being a copy of the entire internet, researchers used Reddit to extract URLs from posts and then filtered the list using Reddit's karma ranking system. They then scraped the URLs to create the dataset. Since the content mainly comes from Reddit, it calls into question its real-world accuracy due to the selection bias of only including people with a Reddit account. It is made up mostly of news articles, blog posts, and other content often shared on forums. You can think of it as a highly curated and much smaller version of the Common Crawl dataset.

Like Wikitext, it's a bit older; the most commonly used version was created in 2019, and a new version hasn't been updated in four years at the time of writing. Of course, since the dataset was curated with a specific methodology, it could be refreshed at any time.

THE PILE

One dataset that has garnered a lot of attention and should be on your radar is The Pile, which was created by EleutherAI in 2020 and published on December 31 of the same year.[10] It is useful for self-supervised pretraining tasks. The Pile is one of the largest datasets we'll discuss at 825 GB and consists of 22 smaller high-quality datasets combined to make a diverse and dense training set. It includes most of the datasets we have already discussed, like Common Crawl, OpenWebText, and Wikipedia. It also contains book datasets, like Books3 and Gutenberg; code datasets, like GitHub and Stack Exchange; and specialist datasets, like PubMed and FreeLaw. It also includes datasets like the Enron Emails, which we can't help but think was a mistake.

Because it's so massive and includes multiple languages and code samples, it has proven useful in training many LLMs. It is multilingual in addition to dense, making it ideal for learning sparse general language representations. Overall, though, it's not very clean and is essentially just a conglomerate of multiple datasets. Unless you are training LLMs from scratch, you likely won't use this dataset, but it's important to become familiar with it, as many of the largest models have been trained on it. You can find the dataset at EleutherAI's website: https://pile.eleuther.ai/.

REDPAJAMA

RedPajama is a dataset created by a collaboration of Together.ai, Ontocord.ai, ETH DS3Lab, Stanford CRFM, and Hazy Research. The goal was to create a fully open dataset that mimicked what was described in the LLaMA paper.

> **NOTE** You can read the blog post introducing RedPajama here: https://together.ai/blog/redpajama.

The dataset is similar to The Pile but much larger at 5 TB and newer, published in April 2023. It contains fewer datasets: GitHub, arXiv, Books, Wikipedia, StackExchange, and Common Crawl. It is so large because it contains five different dumps of the Common Crawl dataset with varying filters and the standard C4 dataset. It is made available through the Hugging Face Hub and can be found at https://mng.bz/4ppD.

OSCAR

The best dataset by far to train on for multilingual models is OSCAR, which is larger than any other dataset discussed, coming in at 9.4TB, over 11 times as big as The Pile! It is an open source project started in 2019 and has been funded by a multitude of institutes and governments. You can learn more about the project and dataset at https:// oscar-project.org/.

---

[10] L. Gao et al., "The Pile: An 800GB Dataset of Diverse Text for Language Modeling," Dec. 2020, https://arxiv.org/abs/2101.00027.

This project is actively being worked on, and new releases come out annually with regular updates. It currently supports 166 languages at the time of this writing, much more than any other dataset. As a work in progress, though, there are some languages much more represented than others, with some in the TBs of data and others in KBs. This is one of our favorite datasets because it is actively being worked on, and the team is passionate about representation in LLMs and AI, as well as producing highly clean, high-quality data. We encourage all interested readers to contribute to this dataset.

SUMMARY OF DATASETS

In table 4.2, you can see a summary of the datasets we've discussed so far. These datasets are all commonly used in industry and worth familiarizing yourself with. We encourage you to investigate them further and take a closer look at the data within.

Table 4.2 Summary of datasets

Dataset	Contents	Size	Last update
Wikitext	English Wikipedia	<1 GB	2016
Wiki-40B	Multi-lingual Wikipedia	10 GB	2020
Europarl	European Parliament proceedings	1.5 GB	2011
Common Crawl	The internet	~300 GB	Ongoing
OpenWebText	Curated internet using Reddit	55 GB	2019
The Pile	Everything above plus specialty datasets (books, law, med)	825 GB	2020
RedPajama	GitHub, arXiv, Books, Wikipedia, StackExchange, and multiple version of Common Crawl	5 TB	2023
OSCAR	Highly curated multilingual dataset with 166 languages	9.4 TB	Ongoing

CORPORA

As you probably picked up on, most of the datasets out there are essentially just text dumps of the internet. If you're looking for something with a little more finesse, something that contains more meta info to help your model disambiguate for more complex tasks, consider downloading a corpus. A corpus is just like a dataset, except it is more easily searchable, visualized, and explained. Corpora are often paid datasets that can be well worth your money. Corpora, like the Corpus Of Historical American English (COHA) and the Corpus of Contemporary American English (COCA), are excellent downloads. They contain not just text data but also frequency analysis (bag of words) and collocates (N-grams), all ready to go. Whether or not you are interested in the applications of allowing models to analyze metadata as part of training, using corpora can help with model explainability and quality of data.

You can think of a corpus as a vector database that has already been highly cleaned and curated and is ready to go. While it hasn't yet been done, a corpus that combines both the linguistic explainability and time-series bucketing with precalculated embeddings put into a real-time vector database would likely be invaluable and highly profitable in this field for the foreseeable future, especially if both textual and audio data are captured. If your company has its own language data it wants to train on, your best course of action is to create a corpus where your biggest job is saying where data came from when and what the overall goal of the data going into the model is. Almost every NLP library has strategies for creating corpora, from NLTK to spaCy and even LangChain. Be mindful about which strategies and tools you pick because at the end of the day, your dataset or corpus contains everything your model will see.

4.3.2 Data cleaning and preparation

If you pulled any of the previously mentioned datasets, you might be surprised to realize most of them are just giant text dumps—a large parquet or text file. There are no labels or annotations, and feature engineering hasn't been done at all. LLMs are trained via self-supervised methods to predict the next word or a masked word, so a lot of traditional data cleaning and preparation processes are unneeded. This fact leads many to believe that data cleaning as a whole is unnecessary, but this couldn't be further from the truth. Datasets are the lifeblood of all ML, and they are so much more than a pile of data. Yet that's what most businesses have—a pile of data. Data cleaning and curation are difficult, time-consuming, and ultimately subjective tasks that are difficult to tie to key performance indicators (KPIs). Still, taking the time and resources to clean your data will create a more consistent and unparalleled user experience.

Since the 1990s, people have tested whether Big Data can produce better results than high-quality data; we believe the answer is no. Big Data is nowhere close to devoid of value. The Law of Big Numbers has been applied, and it has shown that models can generate convincing syntax at the same level as people. However, as we've said before, models have also soundly demonstrated that syntax is in no way connected to semantics or pragmatics.

In this section, we hope to share with you the right frame of mind when preparing your dataset. We will focus on the high-level linguistic considerations you should be thinking about when preparing a dataset, and we won't be going too deep into how to create the actual data pipelines. That said, the main logic is simple and follows these basic steps:

1. Take your pile of data, and determine a schema for the features.
2. Make sure all the features conform to a distribution that makes sense for the outcome you're trying to get through normalization or scaling.
3. Check the data for bias/anomalies (most businesses skip this step by using automated checking instead of informed verification).
4. Convert the data into a format for the model to ingest (for LLMs, it's through tokenization and embedding)
5. Train, check, and retrain.

NOTE For more information on creating data pipelines, check out Fundamentals of Data Engineering,[11] WizardLM,[12] and "LIMA: Less Is More for Alignment."[13] These resources can help you create effective data pipelines to get as much data into a trainable state as possible.

None of these steps are necessarily easy, but we hope to share a few tips and tricks. Evaluating whether your distribution is correct can be as simple as looking at the data and asking yourself whether it truly represents the problem or as difficult as creating a whole human-in-the-loop workflow to validate your model's output. Next, we'll go over the first three steps, and in the next section, we'll go over the fourth. The last step is covered in depth in the next chapter.

INSTRUCT SCHEMA

One of the best and most common data schemas you should consider when preparing your data, especially for finetuning, is the instruct schema. Instruction tuning is based on the intuitive logic that if we show a model how to perform a task with instructions, the model will perform better than if we just show it tasks and "answers." Instruction tuning involves demonstrating for the model what you would like to happen, and as such, the datasets are more intensive to create than your run-of-the-mill crawl data. You need to prepare your data to match a format that will look something like this:

###Instruction

{user input}

###Input

{meta info about the instruction}

###Response

{model output}

Instruction datasets are powerful because they allow the model to consider both instructions and relevant input. For example, if the instruction was "Translate this sentence to Japanese," the input would be the sentence you'd want translated, and the response would be the Japanese translation. Thus, they prepare your model for many prompting techniques and prompt tuning, making them more effective later.

Despite their name, instruction tuning datasets are not restricted to test-based modalities; they can also use vision instruction tuning (image–instruction–answer) and red teaming instruction (RLHF) datasets. The "instruction" offers a semblance of pragmatics within the model and prompt, providing important guardrails for the

---

[11] Reis and Housley, *Fundamentals of Data Engineering*, 2022.
[12] Xu et al., "WizardLM," 2023.
[13] Zou et al., "LIMA," 2023.

LLM as it generates responses. It grounds the prompt with syntax that repeats and is predictable, along with syntax that is unpredictable for the model to guess at. These syntactic landmarks (`###Instruction`, `User:`, `Chat History:`, etc.) also help lower the chance of an EOS (end-of-sequence) token being predicted early due to the variable length of what can come between each of them, like chat history. Chat history can be one message or thousands of tokens, but the pattern, given there's another landmark coming afterward, helps the model succeed in long-term memory. When you are deciding what to train your model on, keep those landmarks in mind, as they can make an instruct-tuned model even better at a specific task if you only need it to do one thing.

This isn't the only format; some competitors in the space include the evol-instruct format used by WizardLM and the self-instruct format used by Alpaca, both of which use scripts to create instruction-based prompts. The best format is still an open-ended question, and we'd like to extend a challenge to the reader to explore creating their own. GitHub (https://mng.bz/5OmD) and Hugging Face datasets are both great places to look for vetted datasets at the moment, but keep in mind that if the dataset doesn't contain many examples of the tasks you'd like your model to perform or it doesn't contain enough examples of semantic ambiguity being resolved when completing the task, performance will be unstable—which takes us to step 2 in our cleaning process.

ENSURING PROFICIENCY WITH SPEECH ACTS

In preparing the dataset, the most important consideration is what you want the model to do. If you want a model to predict housing prices in Boston, you probably shouldn't train it on survivors of the Titanic. This is obvious when stated, but it raises the question, "Is my dataset correct for the problem, and how would I know?" When it comes to language data, the answer isn't as obvious as we might hope. Let's look at an example to figure out why.

Let's say you want your model to take orders at a fast-food restaurant. This scenario may seem boring and mundane, where all we expect to see are queries like, "I'll order the #3 combo," which you will. But if you ask a cashier about how people actually talk to them, really, anything can happen! I had a friend who worked at Burger King tell me that because of Burger King's slogan "Have It Your Way," he received many crazy requests, like asking for a burger with two top buns. That blew my mind, but it was also a tame example. Not to mention, you never know when the next LARPing convention will bring more creative and colorful interactions to otherwise mundane scenarios. A generic dataset containing customer orders and cashier responses won't be enough here. When you aren't intentional about what kind of data goes into your model, the performance of the model suffers.

DEFINITION LARP stands for live-action role-playing, and you can imagine the tomfoolery of a customer pretending to be an elf, orc, or pirate and thus breaking all rules and expectations.

To ensure your data is right for the task, first, you should think about what speech acts generally go together to perform the task at hand. Speech acts refer to the various functions language can perform in communication beyond conveying information. They are a way of categorizing utterances based on their intended effect or purpose in a conversation. Speech acts are important, as they shed light on how communication goes beyond the literal meaning of words and involves the speaker's intentions and the listener's interpretation.

Speech acts defined

The following list includes common speech acts and their definitions:

- *Expressives*—Greetings, apologies, congratulations, condolences, thanksgivings (e.g., "You're the best!")
- *Commissives*—Promises, oaths, pledges, threats, vows (e.g., "I swear by the realm, the princess will come to no harm.")
- *Directives*—Commands, requests, challenges, invitations, orders, summons, entreaties, dares (e.g., "Get it done in the next three days.")
- *Declarations*—Blessings, firings, baptisms, arrests, marrying, juridical speech acts such as sentencings, declaring a mistrial, declaring out of order (e.g., "You're hired!")
- *Verdictives*—Rankings, assessments, appraising, condoning (combinations such as representational declarations; e.g., "You're out!")
- *Questions*—Usually starting with interrogative words like *what*, *where*, *when*, *why*, *who*, or indicated with rising intonation at the end in English (e.g., "Which model is best for my task?")
- *Representatives*—Assertions, statements, claims, hypotheses, descriptions, suggestions, answers to questions (e.g., "This model is best for your task."

The current way we measure the robustness of datasets for LLMs is the vanilla number of tokens. Instruct datasets are relatively new, but they rely on you being intentional with how instruction for the model happens. What will your model do when given a directive it shouldn't respond to when it's only been trained on helpful responses to directives? If you aren't sure, now's the time to consider. For example, imagine a user declaring with glee to your bot, "Promise you'll help me take over the world!" If it was only trained to be helpful, it would likely respond by promising to do just that because similar scenarios are in the training set. And now we have an evil AI overlord taking over the world. Thanks. In actuality, this is a fairly innocuous example, but the unpredictability of the seemingly infinite number of possible responses from the model should make you think, especially if this agent has access to tools like Google or your internal HR documents. Being cognizant of speech acts can simplify your work so that you don't have to focus as much on individual tokens for the vocabulary as on the overall structure of what your model will come in contact with during training.

Going back, when you think about a customer-facing role like a cashier, how many of these speech acts are likely to occur in your average order? Take a minute to think it through. We can tell you that declarations and verdictives are out, and commissives are uncommon. But what if you get them regardless? You then need to consider how you might want to steer such highly expressive customers toward the speech acts you can work with, likely questions, directives, and representatives.

To make matters more complicated, the form of a speech act doesn't always have to match its function. For example, you could say "You're fired" to your friend who doesn't work for you, where, even though its form is declarative, its function is more likely expressive. Once you have a dataset or a trained LLM and are looking to improve its ability to take instruction, this is something to seriously consider to increase your data's quality and your LLM's performance. Does your model weirdly fail when users frame utterances as questions when they're actually directives? Does your model start hallucinating when coming in contact with the representative-only HR documents you've been asked to analyze? As a note, you don't have to completely finetune a model all over again to improve performance. We'll go over this in more detail later, but giving specific examples within the prompt can patch a lot of these edge cases quickly and inexpensively.

Now that you have an understanding of the different features you should be looking for in your dataset, let's consider the best ways to annotate your dataset so you can make sure it conforms to expectations.

ANNOTATING THE DATA

Annotation is labeling your data, usually in a positionally aware way. For speech recognition tasks, annotations would identify the different words as *noun*, *verb*, *adjective*, or *adverb*. Annotations were used as labels in supervised learning tasks as the main way to train a model. Now annotations essentially give us metadata that makes it easier to reason about and analyze our datasets. Instead of worrying about micro information like speech recognition or named-entity recognition, you'll get more value by focusing on macro metadata, like the speech acts just discussed or what language the data is in.

Of course, this is the real trick, isn't it? If this were easy, every company on the face of the earth would have its own models already in production. The fact is data wrangling is too large to be done by hand but too varying to be done automatically, and you need to find the middle ground as quickly as possible. You don't want to ignore your data and just download a dataset someone recommended (even us) and then proceed to harm a real-world population because it contained harmful data. But you also don't want to have to hand-validate millions of rows of utterances. Thankfully, there are tools to help with every part of this, but we'd like to specifically mention these first:

- *Prodi.gy* (https://prodi.gy/)—Prodigy takes a one-time payment for a quick and powerful multimodal annotation tool.
- *doccano: Open source annotation tool for machine learning practitioners* (https://github.com/doccano/doccano)—A truly open-source and, at the time of writing, updated web-based platform for data annotation.

- *d5555/TagEditor: Annotation tool for spaCy* (https://github.com/d5555/TagEditor)—Works in conjunction with https://spacy.io. Both create an ecosystem on top of spaCy, a popular NLP framework that makes rapid prototyping well within the reach of your average ML team.
- *Praat: Doing phonetics by computer* (https://github.com/praat/praat)—The only audio annotation tool on this list, Praat is fundamentally a tool for phonetics with annotations thrown in. Given how much we predict the LLM space to shift toward phonetics, we couldn't omit this one from the list.
- *Galileo* (https://www.rungalileo.io/llm-studio)—At the time of this writing, Galileo's LLM studio has yet to come out, but it makes some big promises for prompt creation and evaluation, which would immensely speed up annotation and creation of instruction datasets.

Which tool is best for your project depends entirely on the goal of your annotation. Going into annotating without a specified goal leads nowhere, as you'll find discrepancies on the other end of data processing. Of course, we recommend adding speech act annotations; you'll also want to consider additional annotations looking for bias and anomalies. We can show that by measuring the number of pieces of outside context present in the text (things like insinuations or entailments), you can gain a confidence score about how high quality a particular data is. The reason for this is intuitive: the more ambiguity a set of examples can solve for the model, the more the model learns from that set. The hard part is that no one can pin any of these contextual information nuggets on repeating parts of orthography, such as individual characters or a particular word or subword.

Annotating can be a lot of work, but the reason for all of this consideration at the front is fairly simple: your model can only learn what you teach it. Thankfully, to make matters much easier, the goal isn't to annotate every bit of text in your dataset. We are simply annotating a large-enough sample to ensure our dataset is representative of the task. Remember, LLMs are generally trained in two steps:

1. *Self-supervised pretraining*—Analyzing many different speech acts in varying forms and functions to learn general representations
2. *Finetuning and RLHF*—Teaching the model how/when to use the representations learned in step 1

This training significantly lightens the burden on you as a trainer of attempting to parse every possible locution (what a person literally says) and illocution (what they actually mean in context) within the given task. Even for something viewed as simple work, like being a cashier, having to come up with a dataset vast enough to cover all edge cases would be quite a headache. For most cases, all you need to do is prepare a finetuning dataset, which often doesn't need to be large at all—sometimes a dozen examples is more than enough to start getting good results.

4.4 Text processors

Now that you have a dataset for training or finetuning, we need to transform it into something that can be consumed by the LLM. Simply put, we need to turn the text into numbers. We've already briefly gone over the process of doing that conversion quickly and effectively, so let's dive into different examples and methodologies.

In this section, we'll show you how to train your own tokenizers, both byte-pair encoding (BPE) and SentencePiece tokenizers, and how to grab embeddings from (almost) any model for storage or manipulation later. This step is often ignored when working with an LLM through an API, but much of modern performance in data applications depends on doing this process correctly and specifically for your goal. There are many mathematically sound and correct ways to tokenize text, so you can't rely on something someone else did when you have a specific use case. You need to prepare it for that use case. Training your own tokens will allow you to minimize unknown tokens, `<UKN>`, while also maximizing encoded semantics. Having control of this process is onc of thc simplest and easiest hacks to give your models a major boost in performance. Let's start first with tokenization.

4.4.1 Tokenization

Tokenization is a bit more involved than simple vectorization but leads to the same overall result: text input, vector output, and the ability to encode and decode. We mentioned in chapter 2 the multilingual factor and in chapter 3 the token tax of foreign languages, which are both motivations to be at least aware of your own tokenization strategies. However, it goes beyond those. Your tokenization strategy isn't just important; it is vitally important for every subsequent step.

A good example is comparing GOAT 7B and GPT-4 in math and arithmetic. Consider table 4.3. The left column is a simple arithmetic prompt. Then we see the two models' answers and, for reference, the actual answer so you don't have to pull out your calculator.

Table 4.3 Tokenization allows GOAT 7B to outperform GPT-4 in math

Prompt	GOAT 7B	GPT-4 1.7T	Correct
3978640188 + 42886272 =	4021526460	4,021,526,460	4,021,526,460
4523646 minus 67453156	–62929510	–63,930,510	–62,929,510
Calculate 397 × 4429	1758313	1,757,413	1,758,313
What is 8914/64?	139 R 18	139.15625	139.28125 Or 139 R 18

GOAT 7B consistently outperforms GPT-4, which leaves the question, "Why does GOAT perform better despite being 200 times smaller? Aren't larger models more likely to show emergent behavior?" You probably already guessed the answer based on the subsection's heading, but if you didn't, it's because of the tokenization algorithm used!

The GPT family of models tokenizes all subwords and digits in groups based purely on frequency only, meaning that if that exact group of numbers or words hadn't shown up before, they could be grouped together during the embedding and inference processes later! GOAT is a finetuned Llama model, meaning that while it was finetuned on math to be good at it, the underlying secret to success lies in its tokenization strategy, which is the same as Llama's. GPT-X tokenizes like this:

```
print(enc.encode("4523646 minus 67453156"))
[21098, 15951, 21, 28382, 220, 25513, 20823, 3487]
```

Did you notice how the first group of numbers is seven digits long, but the entire output is eight tokens? This is the exact grouping methodology we're talking about. Compare that to Llama's tokenization strategy in figure 4.3. Notice that each digit is highlighted individually, meaning that the model will eventually see all the digits. As this example demonstrates, your tokenization strategy will ultimately determine what your model will see and won't see, as they'll become `<UNK>` tokens—and that's why it's vitally important to get it right for your use case.

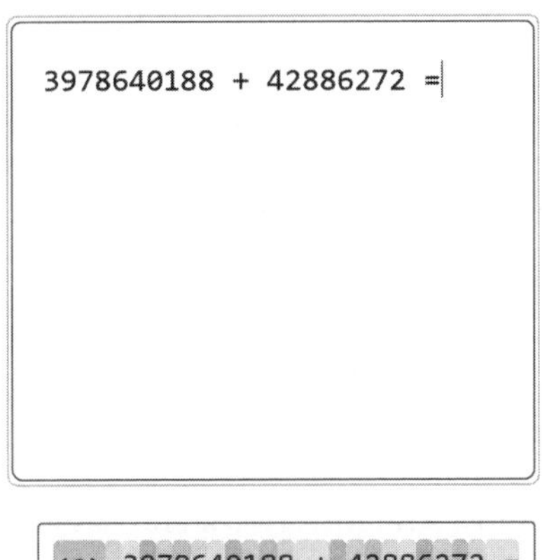

Figure 4.3 Llama's tokenization of the first arithmetic problem in the comparison table. Notice that each digit is highlighted individually, meaning that the model will eventually see all the digits.

What started out as creating a simple set of bag-of-words conversion dictionaries has evolved immensely, and we couldn't be happier about it. Tokenization essentially consists of two major steps: a step to split up the text and a step to turn it into numbers. The most obvious form of tokenization is splitting a string on whitespace and then converting it to a number based on a word-to-integer dictionary.

This makes sense to most Indo-European language speakers, but we can't recommend this because of the two assumptions presupposed: alphabets and whitespace. What will you do when you come across a language that doesn't use an alphabet, like Chinese? And what will you do when you come across a language that doesn't use whitespace in the same way as English, like Hungarian or Turkish? Or code, for that matter—whitespace is critical to Python's syntax and is more than just a separator; it has semantic meanings. This is one reason why multilingual models end up outperforming monolinguals on the same tasks in almost every case: they're forced to learn deeper representations for meaning without the bowling bumpers of easy tokenization. So let's look at some deeper methodologies that work for UTF-8 encoded languages.

Here are examples of all the current popular options for basing your tokenization:

- *Word-based*—"Johannes Gutenberg" becomes `['Johannes', 'Gutenberg']`.
- *Character-based*—"Shakespeare" becomes `['S','h','a','k','e','s','p','e','a','r','e']`.
- *Subword-based*—"The quick red Delphox jumped over the lazy brown Emolga" becomes `['the','quick','red','delph','ox','jump','ed','over','the','laz','y','brown','emol','ga']`

Let's take a look at each of them in turn.

WORD-BASED

Word-based tokenizers most commonly split on whitespace, but there are other methods like using regular expressions, dictionaries, or punctuation. For example, a punctuation-based approach would split "It's the truth!" into `['It', ' '' , ' s', ' the', ' truth', ' !']`, which gives us slightly better context than splitting on whitespace alone. The `TreebankWordTokenizer` from NLTK is an example of a regular expression tokenizer. Word-based tokenizers are relatively easy to implement but require us to keep an unmanageably large dictionary mapping to encode every single possible word. That's unreasonable, so generally, you'll implement a dictionary cutoff and return unknown tokens when the model runs into unrecognized words to make it work. This makes the tokenizer poor at many tasks like code, name, and entity recognition, as well as generalizing across domains.

CHARACTER-BASED

Character-based encoding methods are the most straightforward and easiest to implement since we split on the UTF-8 character encodings. With this method, we only need the tiniest of dictionaries to map characters to numbers, which means we can prevent the need for unknown tokens and related concerns. However, it comes with a major loss of information and fails to keep relevant syntax, semantics, or morphology of the text.

SUBWORD-BASED

Just like Goldilocks and the Three Bears, while character-based tokenizers are too hard and word-based tokenizers are too soft, subword-based tokenizers are just right. Subword-based tokenizers have proven to be the best option, being a mixture of the previous two. We are able to use a smaller dictionary like a character-based tokenizer but lose less semantics like a word-based tokenizer. It even has the added bonus of including some morphological information. However, it's an unsolved problem for where and how words should be split, and there are many different methods and approaches. The best method to choose will be, like all other things with LLMs, dependent on the task. If you don't have a specific goal in mind for what you are trying to do, there will be consequences later.

Three main algorithms are used to create the subword dictionaries: BPE, WordPiece, and Unigram. In addition, SentencePiece, a combination of the three that explicitly handles whitespaces, is also very common. It's outside the scope of this book to discuss how they work, but as a book focused on production, you should know that the most popular subword tokenization methodologies are BPE (GPT-x) and SentencePiece (LlamaX).

In listing 4.10, we'll go over how to train a custom version for both BPE and SentencePiece on your data so that you're equipped to face (almost) any dataset head-on. While reading the code, pay attention to where we train the tokenizers. In particular, you'll want to tune three key parameters: `vocab_size`, `min_frequency`, and `special_tokens`. A larger vocabulary size means your tokenizer will be more robust and will likely be better at handling more languages, but it will add computational complexity. Minimum frequency determines how often a particular subword token has to be seen in the dataset before it is added to the dictionary. Larger values prevent rare and likely unimportant tokens from filling our dictionary and prevent us from learning rare tokens that are important. Lastly, special tokens are relatively straightforward and include syntactical tokens we care about specifically for model training.

Listing 4.10 Training your own subword tokenizers

```
import os
from pathlib import Path

import transformers
from tokenizers import ByteLevelBPETokenizer, SentencePieceBPETokenizer
from tokenizers.processors import BertProcessing

paths = [str(x) for x in Path("./data/").glob("**/*.txt")]    # Initializes the texts to train from
bpe_tokenizer = ByteLevelBPETokenizer()

bpe_tokenizer.train(                                           # Trains a byte-pair encoding tokenizer
    files=paths,
    vocab_size=52_000,
    min_frequency=2,
    show_progress=True,
    special_tokens=[
        "<s>",
        "<pad>",
        "</s>",
        "<unk>",
        "<mask>",
    ],
)
```

```
token_dir = "./chapters/chapter_4/tokenizers/bytelevelbpe/"
if not os.path.exists(token_dir):
    os.makedirs(token_dir)
bpe_tokenizer.save_model(token_dir)

bpe_tokenizer = ByteLevelBPETokenizer(
    f"{token_dir}vocab.json",
    f"{token_dir}merges.txt",
)

example_text = "This sentence is getting encoded by a tokenizer."
print(bpe_tokenizer.encode(example_text).tokens)
# ['This', '?sentence', '?is', '?getting', '?enc', \
# 'oded', '?by', '?a', '?to', 'ken', 'izer', '.']
print(bpe_tokenizer.encode(example_text).ids)
# [2666, 5651, 342, 1875, 4650, 10010, 504, 265, \
# 285, 1507, 13035, 18]

bpe_tokenizer._tokenizer.post_processor = BertProcessing(
    ("</s>", bpe_tokenizer.token_to_id("</s>")),
    ("<s>", bpe_tokenizer.token_to_id("<s>")),
)
bpe_tokenizer.enable_truncation(max_length=512)


special_tokens = [
    "<s>",
    "<pad>",
    "</s>",
    "<unk>",
    "<cls>",
    "<sep>",
    "<mask>",
]
sentencepiece_tokenizer = SentencePieceBPETokenizer()

sentencepiece_tokenizer.train(
    files=paths,
    vocab_size=4000,
    min_frequency=2,
    show_progress=True,
    special_tokens=special_tokens,
)

token_dir = "./chapters/chapter_4/tokenizers/sentencepiece/"
if not os.path.exists(token_dir):
    os.makedirs(token_dir)
sentencepiece_tokenizer.save_model(token_dir)

tokenizer = transformers.PreTrainedTokenizerFast(
    tokenizer_object=sentencepiece_tokenizer,
    model_max_length=512,
    special_tokens=special_tokens,
)
```

Trains a SentencePiece tokenizer (annotation for the `sentencepiece_tokenizer` creation and training lines)

Converts (annotation for the closing parenthesis of the last block)

```
tokenizer.bos_token = "<s>"
tokenizer.bos_token_id = sentencepiece_tokenizer.token_to_id("<s>")
tokenizer.pad_token = "<pad>"
tokenizer.pad_token_id = sentencepiece_tokenizer.token_to_id("<pad>")
tokenizer.eos_token = "</s>"
tokenizer.eos_token_id = sentencepiece_tokenizer.token_to_id("</s>")
tokenizer.unk_token = "<unk>"
tokenizer.unk_token_id = sentencepiece_tokenizer.token_to_id("<unk>")
tokenizer.cls_token = "<cls>"
tokenizer.cls_token_id = sentencepiece_tokenizer.token_to_id("<cls>")
tokenizer.sep_token = "<sep>"
tokenizer.sep_token_id = sentencepiece_tokenizer.token_to_id("<sep>")
tokenizer.mask_token = "<mask>"
tokenizer.mask_token_id = sentencepiece_tokenizer.token_to_id("<mask>")
tokenizer.save_pretrained(token_dir)     # And saves for later!

print(tokenizer.tokenize(example_text))
# ['_This', '_s', 'ent', 'ence', '_is', '_', 'g', 'et', 'tin', 'g', '_'
# 'en', 'co', 'd', 'ed', '_', 'b', 'y', '_a', '_', 't', 'ok', 'en',
# 'iz', 'er', '.']

print(tokenizer.encode(example_text))
# [814, 1640, 609, 203, 1810, 623, 70, \
# 351, 148, 371, 125, 146, 2402, 959, 632]
```

Out of the two, BPE and SentencePiece, we find ourselves using both about equally. It mostly depends on which model we're finetuning or using as a base for a particular project. Algorithmically, we're partial to SentencePiece because it tends to boost evaluation scores on pretty much any test for models trained on it, and it's also closer to how we interact with morphology as people.

All in all, tokenization loses information, just as converting from speech to text does—namely, word order (syntax) and meaning (semantics). All of the information about what a number is and how it would differ from a letter is completely gone after tokenization. To circumvent potential semantic and syntactic problems, we need to create an approximation for each of these features and figure out how to mathematically represent them in abstraction to insert that meaning back into the tokenized vector. For this, we have embeddings.

4.4.2 Embeddings

Embeddings provide meaning to the vectors generated during tokenization. Tokenized text is just numbers assigned almost arbitrarily (occurrence-based) to a dictionary, but it's at least in a format that the model can ingest. Embeddings are the next step, where positional and semantic encodings are created and looked up to give the model additional context for making decisions about how to (probably) complete the task it's given.

Embeddings are imperfect for several reasons, but perhaps the most relevant is this theoretical question: Can you represent a set using only a subset of that same set? In this case, the first set is language, one or more, and the second set is numbers, floats, and digits. Math is a subset of language used to describe things axiomatically that we accept as true. Take the English alphabet, for example: Can you represent the entire alphabet by only using some fraction of the 26 letters? Obviously not, but what if both the original set and the subset are infinite? Can you represent all digits using only the decimals between 0 and 1? Given that the first is a numerable infinite set and the second is a nonenumerable infinite set, the answer is yes, which should be enheartening for the field of language modeling.

Now that we've talked about why embeddings shouldn't be completely and blindly relied on, embeddings are what most businesses are looking for with LLMs. You don't need a 1.7T-parameter model to handle customers asking questions about your pricing or performing a search through your documents. As we discussed in chapter 2, embeddings have the innate advantage of being comparable by distance, provided both embeddings you're comparing were created by the same model in the same dimensional space. That opens up the door for all sorts of speedy computation and retrieval where you never have to figure out how to host a gigantic model somewhere because you can run a smaller embedding model on a CPU, and it takes milliseconds for hundreds of tokens.

One of the most popular and coolest applications of embeddings at the moment is retrieval-augmented generation (RAG), where you store data that is pertinent to the overall task of the model and give portions of that data as needed to a larger model at prompting time to improve results. Suppose we apply RAG to the Boston Housing dataset and attempt to predict the value of a new house. In that case, we can compare that house's embedded data to the closest comparable houses in the area and generate an informed appraisal without ever needing an appraiser to verify, as long as the embeddings you're retrieving from are up-to-date.

Embeddings can be used for dozens of different tasks and are the result of taking final hidden state representations from your model. Every layer of your model is a potential option, but the general consensus is to take representations after the final layer before any decoding or final linear layers or softmaxes. Listing 4.11 gives a practical example of how to extract the embeddings from both PyTorch and Hugging Face models. Best practice dictates that you should extract the embeddings from documents using whatever embedding model you are planning to use for inference, especially if those embeddings will end up being stored in a VectorDB later on. After creating our embeddings, we show how to do a simple similarity search on the results, which is the basis of RAG systems.

Listing 4.11 Example embeddings

```
import numpy as np
from sentence_transformers import SentenceTransformer
from datasets import load_dataset

model_ckpt = "sentence-transformers/all-MiniLM-L6-v2"    # Downloads embedding model and dataset
model = SentenceTransformer(model_ckpt)
```

```
embs_train = load_dataset("tweet_eval", "emoji", split="train[:1000]")
embs_test = load_dataset("tweet_eval", "emoji", split="test[:100]")


def embed_text(example):                                    # Creates embeddings
    embedding = model.encode(example["text"])
    return {"embedding": np.array(embedding, dtype=np.float32)}


print(f"Train 1: {embs_train[0]}")
embs_train = embs_train.map(embed_text, batched=False)
embs_test = embs_test.map(embed_text, batched=False)

embs_train.add_faiss_index("embedding")     # Adds Faiss index that allows similarity search

#
idx, knn = 1, 3  # Select the first query and 3 nearest neighbors    # Runs query

query = np.array(embs_test[idx]["embedding"], dtype=np.float32)
scores, samples = embs_train.get_nearest_examples("embedding", query, k=knn)

print(f"QUERY LABEL: {embs_test[idx]['label']}")      # Prints results
print(f"QUERY TEXT: {embs_test[idx]['text'][:200]} [...]\n")
print("=" * 50)
print("Retrieved Documents:")
for score, label, text in zip(scores, samples["label"], samples["text"]):
    print("=" * 50)
    print(f"TEXT:\n{text[:200]} [...]")
    print(f"SCORE: {score:.2f}")
    print(f"LABEL: {label}")
```

Extracting embeddings, like the listing shows, is pretty simple and differs very little from simply running inference or training on a dataset. Remember, if you aren't using sentence transformers, set your model to `eval` mode, run with `torch.no_grad()`, and if you're running on torch 2.0+, run `torch.compile(model)`. Things should speed up and become more computationally efficient immediately.

Another as-of-yet unsolved problem is how to compare embedding spaces. Mathematically sound comparisons have popped up time and again over the years, but as has been demonstrated, mathematical soundness isn't the first problem to be solved; the modality is. In addition, pairwise comparison functions have mathematical limits on how fast it is possible to run them. If you're comparing language embeddings, a mathematically sound conversion of a linguistically sound comparison method is the solution, and a linguistically sound comparison is dependent upon the goal of the comparison. It's too much to go into here, but we dive more deeply into this topic in appendix C, where we discuss diffusion and multimodal LLMs.

4.5 Preparing a Slack dataset

Now that we have learned the ins and outs of preparing the necessary assets to train our own LLM, we wanted to end this chapter by preparing a dataset that we can use later. For this exercise, we will tackle a very common problem in the industry. I'm sure most readers have experienced or witnessed an HR help channel constantly inundated with the same questions over and over. It doesn't matter how many FAQ pages are created; users don't want to waste their time searching for documentation when they could ask an expert. So let's build a chatbot to answer these questions!

We will show you how to pull your company's Slack data and prepare it for training an LLM-based chatbot. In listing 4.12, we pull Slack data, filter it to keep just the user's data, and save it to a parquet file. This way, you can create a bot that will talk like you, but feel free to edit it. For example, you might enjoy creating a bot that talks like your boss, but I'd recommend not telling them in case they feel threatened knowing you are automating them out of a job.

Listing 4.12 Example of pulling Slack data

```
import slack_sdk
import pandas

token_slack = "Your Token Here"
client = slack_sdk.WebClient(token=token_slack)

auth = client.auth_test()
self_user = auth["user_id"]

dm_channels_response = client.conversations_list(types="im")

all_messages = {}

for channel in dm_channels_response["channels"]:
    history_response = client.conversations_history(channel=channel["id"])
    all_messages[channel["id"]] = history_response["messages"]

txts = []

for channel_id, messages in all_messages.items():
    for message in messages:
        try:
            text = message["text"]
            user = message["user"]
            timestamp = message["ts"]
            txts.append([timestamp, user, text])
        except Exception:
            pass

slack_dataset = pandas.DataFrame(txts)
slack_dataset.columns = ["timestamp", "user", "text"]
df = slack_dataset[slack_dataset.user == self_user]

df[["text"]].to_parquet("slack_dataset.gzip", compression="gzip")
```

As you can see, there's not much to it! We have an example dataset we pulled using this script in the GitHub repo accompanying this book. We will use this dataset in the coming chapters.

We've gone over a lot in this chapter, but you should now be prepared and know how to select and evaluate a foundation model, prepare and clean a dataset, and optimize your own text processors. We will use this information in the next chapter to train and finetune our own LLM model.

Summary

- Data engineers have unique datasets to acquire and manage LLMs, like model weights, evaluation datasets, and embeddings.
- No matter your task, there is a wide array of open source models to choose from to finetune your own model.
- Text-based tasks are harder to evaluate than simple equality metrics you'd find in traditional ML tasks, but there are many industry benchmarks to help you get started.
- Evaluating LLMs for more than just performance, like bias and potential harm, is your responsibility.
- You can use the Evaluate library to build your own evaluation metrics.
- There are many large open source datasets, but most come from scraping the web and require cleaning.
- Instruct schemas and annotating your data can be effective ways to clean and analyze your data.
- Finetuning a model on a dataset with an appropriate distribution of speech acts for the task you want your model to perform will help it generate context-appropriate content.
- Building your own subword tokenizer to match your data can greatly improve your model's performance.
- Many problems teams are trying to use LLMs for can be solved by using embeddings from your model instead.

5 Training large language models: How to generate the generator

This chapter covers

- Setting up a training environment and common libraries
- Applying various training techniques, including using advanced methodologies
- Tips and tricks to get the most out of training

Be water, my friend.

—Bruce Lee

Are you ready to have some fun?! What do you mean the last four chapters weren't fun? Well, I promise this one for sure will be. We've leveled up a lot and gained a ton of context that will prove invaluable now as we start to get our hands dirty. By training an LLM, we can create bots that can do amazing things and have unique personalities. Indeed, we can create new friends and play with them. In the last chapter, we showed you how to create a training dataset based on your Slack messages. Now we will show you how to take that dataset and create a persona of yourself. Finally, you will no longer have to talk to that one annoying coworker, and just like Gilfoyle, you can have your own AI Gilfoyle (https://youtu.be/IWIusSdn1e4).

First things first, we'll show you how to set up a training environment, as the process can be very resource-demanding, and without the proper equipment, you won't be able to enjoy what comes next. We'll then show you how to do the basics, like training from scratch and finetuning, after which we'll get into some of the best-known methods to improve upon these processes, making them more efficient, faster, and cheaper. We'll end the chapter with some tips and tricks we've acquired through our experience of training models in the field.

5.1 Multi-GPU environments

Training is a resource-intensive endeavor. A model that only takes a single GPU to run inference on may take 10 times that many to train if, for nothing else, to parallelize your work and speed things up so you aren't waiting for a thousand years for it to finish training. To really take advantage of what we want to teach you in this chapter, we're first going to have to get you set up in an environment you can use as a playground. Later in the chapter, we'll teach some resource-optimal strategies as well, but you'll need to understand how to set up a multi-GPU env if you want to use the largest LLMs anyway.

While you can learn a lot using smaller LLMs, what sets apart a pro from an amateur is often the ease and fluidity they have when working with larger models. And there's a good reason for this since, on the whole, larger models outperform smaller models. If you want to work with the largest models, you'll never be able to get started on your laptop. Even most customized gaming rigs with dual GPUs aren't enough for inference, let alone training.

To this end, we wanted to share with you a few methods to acquire access to a multi-GPU environment in the cloud, and then we will share the tools and libraries necessary to utilize them. The largest models do not fit in a single GPU, so without these environments and tools, you'll be stuck playing on easy mode forever.

5.1.1 Setting up

It should be pointed out up front that while multi-GPU environments are powerful, they are also expensive. When it comes to multi-GPUs, no services we know of offer a free tier or offering, but you can at least take comfort in knowing that paying per hour will be way cheaper than purchasing the rigs wholesale. Of course, if you can get your company to pay the bill, we recommend it, but it is still your responsibility to spin down and turn off any environment you create to avoid unnecessary charges.

If your company is paying, it likely has chosen a hosted service that makes this whole process easy. For the rest of us, setting up a virtual machine (VM) in Google's Compute Engine is one of the easiest methods. Once set up, we will then show you how to utilize it.

> **A note to the readers**
>
> For learning purposes, we use smaller models throughout this book in our code listings such that you can work with them on a single GPU either locally or using a service like Colab or Kaggle, which offers a free tier of a single GPU. While the listings could be run on CPU-only hardware, you won't want to do it. Ultimately, there shouldn't be any need to run these costly VMs throughout the book. However, you likely will still want to. Training with multiple GPUs is much faster, more efficient, and often necessary. We do encourage you to try larger LLM variations that require these bigger rigs, as the experience will be priceless. To make it easy, you should be able to recycle the code in this chapter for models and datasets much larger than what is presented, which will often just be a matter of changing a few lines.

GOOGLE VIRTUAL MACHINE

One of the easiest ways to create a multi-GPU environment is to set up a VM on Google's cloud. To get started, you'll need to create an account, create a Google Cloud Project (GCP), set up billing, and download the gcloud CLI. None of these steps are particularly hard, but be sure to follow the documentation found at https://cloud.google.com/sdk/docs/install-sdk for your operating system to install the SDK. The steps here also include the steps and how-tos for creating an account, project, and billing in the Before You Begin section if you don't already have an account.

For new accounts, Google offers a $300 credit to be used for pretty much anything on their GCP platform except GPUs. We hate to break this news, but sadly, there's just no free lunch where we are going. So you'll need to be sure to upgrade to a paid GCP tier. Don't worry; just following along should only cost a couple of dollars, but if you are money conscious, we recommend reading the entire section first and then trying it out.

After setting up your account, by default, GCP sets your GPU quotas to 0. Quotas are used to manage your costs. To increase your quotas, go to https://console.cloud.google.com/iam-admin/quotas. You'll be looking for the gpus_all_regions quota, and since we plan to use multiple GPUs, go ahead and submit a request to increase it to 2 or more.

With all the prerequisites in place, we'll get started by initializing and logging in. You'll do this by running the following command in a terminal on your computer:

```
$ gcloud init
```

You may have already done this step if you had to install the SDK, but if not, it will launch a web browser to help us log in and authorize us for the gcloud CLI, which allows us to select our project. We will be assuming you have just the one project, but if this isn't your first rodeo and you have multiple projects, you'll need to add the `--project` flag in all the subsequent commands.

Next, we need to determine two things: the machine type (or which GPUs we want to use) and our container image. To pick a machine type, you can check out the different options at https://cloud.google.com/compute/docs/gpus. For beginners, we highly recommend the NVIDIA L4 GPU, as it is an all-around fantastic machine. For our purposes, we'll be using the g2-standard-24, which comes with two L4 GPUs and costs us about $2 per hour. This machine type isn't in every region and zone, but you can find a region close to you at https://cloud.google.com/compute/docs/regions-zones. We will be using the us-west1 region and us-west1-a zone.

For the container image, we'll save ourselves a lot of hassle by using one that has all the basics set up. Generally, this means creating your own, but Google has several prebuilt container images for deep learning, which are great to use or a great place to start as a base image to customize. These are all found in the `deeplearning-platform-release` project that they own. To check out the options available, you can run

```
$ gcloud compute images list --project deeplearning-platform-release
    --format="value(NAME)" --no-standard-images
```

NOTE You can learn more about the container image options here: https://cloud.google.com/deep-learning-vm/docs/images.

You can pick from Base, TensorFlow, and PyTorch compiled images, along with the CUDA and Python versions. We'll be using `common-gpu-v20230925-debian-11-py310`, which is a simple image ready for GPU with a Debian Linux distribution and Python 3.10. Now that we have everything we need, we can create our VM! Go ahead and run the following commands to set up the VM:

```
$ INSTANCE_NAME="g2-llminprod-example"
    $ gcloud compute instances create ${INSTANCE_NAME} --zone=us-west1-a
    --machine-type=g2-standard-24 --image-project=deeplearning-platform-release
    --image=common-gpu-v20230925-debian-11-py310 --boot-disk-size=200GB --scopes
    cloud-platform --metadata=install-unattended-upgrades=False,install-nvidia-
    driver=True --maintenance-policy TERMINATE --restart-on-failure
```

The first command creates an environment variable to store the name of our VM since we'll also be using it in several of the following commands. This name can be whatever you want it to be. The next command creates our VM instance. The first several flags (`zone`, `image`, `machine`) should make sense since we just spent the previous paragraphs preparing and gathering that information. The `boot-disk-size` sets the disk space for our VM and defaults to 200 GB, so it's included here because it's important to know for LLMs since they are large assets, and you will likely need to increase it—especially for LLMs that require multiple GPUs to run.

The `scopes` flag is passed to set authorization. Current GCP best practices recommend setting it to `cloud-platform`, which determines authorization through OAuth and IAM roles. The `metadata` field isn't required but is used here as a trick to ensure the NVIDIA drivers are installed. It is really useful if you are using these commands to create a shell script to automate this process. You should know that it will cause a small delay between when the VM is up and when you can actually SSH into it, as it won't be responsive while it installs the drivers. If you don't include it, the first time you SSH in through a terminal, it will ask you if you want to install it, so no harm done. However, if you access the VM through other methods (described in the next sections), you can run into problems. The last two commands are standard maintenance policies.

Once that runs, you can verify the VM is up by running

```
$ gcloud compute instances describe ${INSTANCE_NAME}
```

This command will give you a lot of information about your instance that is worth looking over, including a status field that should read `'RUNNING'`. Once you've confirmed that it's up, we will SSH into it. If this is your first time using gcloud to SSH, an SSH key will be generated automatically. Go ahead and run the following command:

```
$ gcloud compute ssh ${INSTANCE_NAME}
```

Your terminal will be shelled into our multi-GPU VM, and you are now in business. At this point, your VM is still just an empty shell, so you'll want to bring in code. The easiest way to do this is to copy the files over with Secure Copy Protocol (SCP). You can do this for a single file or a whole directory. For example, assuming your project has a requirements.txt file and a subdirectory local-app-folder, from a new terminal, you can run the following commands:

```
$ gcloud compute scp requirements.txt ${INSTANCE_NAME}:~/requirements.txt
$ gcloud compute scp --recurse ~/local-app-folder/
${INSTANCE_NAME}:~/vm-app-folder
```

Overall, not too bad. Once you've gone through the process and set everything up, the next time you set up a VM, it will only be four commands (`create`, `describe`, `ssh`, `scp`) to get up and running.

Of course, these instances cost good money, so the last command you'll want to know before moving on is how to delete it:

```
$ gcloud compute instances delete ${INSTANCE_NAME} --quiet
```

For Linux power users, this code line is likely all you need, but for the rest of us plebs, shelling into a VM through a terminal is less than an ideal working environment. We'll show you some tips and tricks to make the most of your remote machine.

SSH THROUGH VS CODE

For most devs, a terminal is fine, but what we really want is an IDE. Most IDEs offer remote SSH capabilities, but we'll demonstrate with VS Code. The first step is to install the extension Remote-SSH (you can find the extension here: https://mng.bz/q0dE). Other extensions offer this capability, but Remote-SSH is maintained by Microsoft and has over 17 million installs, so it's a great choice for beginners.

Next, we are going to run a configuration command:

```
$ gcloud compute config-ssh
```

Then, inside of VS Code, you can press F1 to open the command palette and run the Remote-SSH: Open SSH Host… command, and you should see your VM's SSH address, which will look like l4-llm-example.us-west1-a.project-id-401501. If you don't see it, something went wrong with the `config-ssh` command, and you likely need to run `gcloud init` again. Select the address, and a new VS Code window should pop up. In the bottom corner, you'll see that it is connecting to your remote machine. And you are done! Easy. From here, you can use VS Code like you would when using it locally.

5.1.2 Libraries

Although setting up hardware is important, none of it will work without the software packages that enable different points of hardware to communicate with each other effectively. With LLMs, the importance of the software is compounded. One author personally experienced having all hardware correctly configured and was pretty sure the software setup was likewise configured, only to start up training a model and be met with an estimated training time of over three years. After troubleshooting, the team realized this was because he had installed multiple versions of CUDA Toolkit, and PyTorch was looking at an incompatible (up-to-date) one instead of the one he had intended to use.

These software packages are about more than just using the CUDA low-level communication with your GPU; they're about load-balancing, quantizing, and parallelizing your data as it runs through each computation to make sure it's going as fast as possible while still enabling a certain level of fidelity for the matrices. You wouldn't want to spend a long time making sure your embedding vectors are phenomenal representations just to have them distorted at run time. Thus, we present the four deep-learning libraries every practitioner should know for multi-GPU instances: DeepSpeed, Accelerate, BitsandBytes, and xFormers. At the time of this writing, all complementary features between these libraries are experimental, so feel free to mix and match. If you get a setup that utilizes all four at once to their full potential without erroring, drop it in a reusable container so fast.

DeepSpeed

DeepSpeed is an optimization library for distributed deep learning. DeepSpeed is powered by Microsoft and implements various enhancements for speed in training and inference, like handling extremely long or multiple inputs in different modalities, quantization, caching weights and inputs, and, probably the hottest topic right now, scaling up to thousands of GPUs.

Installation is fairly simple if you remember to always install the latest—but not nightly—version of PyTorch first. This means you also need to configure your CUDA Toolkit beforehand. Once you have that package, `pip install deepspeed` should get you right where you want to go unless, ironically, you use Microsoft's other products. If you are on a Windows OS, there is only partial support, and there are several more steps you will need to follow to get it working for inference, not training, mode.

ACCELERATE

From Hugging Face, Accelerate is made to help abstract the code for parallelizing and scaling to multiple GPUs away from you so that you can focus on the training and inference side. One huge advantage of Accelerate is that it adds only one import and two lines of code and changes two other lines, compared to a standard training loop in PyTorch in its vanilla implementation. Beyond that, Accelerate also has fairly easy CLI usage, allowing it to be automated along with Terraform or AWS CDK.

Accelerate boasts compatibility over most environments, and as long as your environment is Python 3.8+ and PyTorch 1.10.0+ (CUDA compatibility first), you should be able to use Accelerate without problems. Once that's done, `pip install accelerate` should get you there. Accelerate also has experimental support for DeepSpeed if you would like to get the benefits of both.

BITSANDBYTES

If you don't already know the name Tim Dettmers in this field, you should become acquainted pretty quickly. Not many people have done as much as he has to make CUDA-powered computing accessible. This package is made to help practitioners quantize models and perform efficient matrix multiplication for inference (and maybe training) within different bit sizes, all the way down to INT8. BitsandBytes has similar requirements and drawbacks to DeepSpeed: the requirements are Python 3.8+ and CUDA 10.0+ on Linux and Mac environments and partial support for Windows with a different package.

You should have little trouble installing BitsandBytes, as `pip install bitsandbytes` should work for most use cases. If you find yourself on Windows, you're in luck: `pip install bitsandbytes-windows` will work as well. If you want to use it with Hugging Face's transformers or PyTorch, you will need to edit some minimum requirements stated within both of those packages, as the Windows version does not have the same version numbers as the regular package. BitsandBytes offers its own implementations of optimizers like Adam and NN layers like Linear to allow for that 8-bit boost to run deep learning apps on smaller devices at greater speed with a minimal drop in accuracy.

XFORMERS

The most bleeding edge of the libraries we recommend for most use cases is xFormers, which is made for research and production. Following a (hopefully) familiar PyTorch-like pattern of independent building blocks for multiple modalities, xFormers takes it a step further and offers components that won't be available in PyTorch for quite a while. One that we've used quite a lot is memory-efficient exact attention, which speeds up inference considerably.

xFormers has more requirements than the other packages, and we'd like to stress once more that using one or more tools to keep track of your environment is strongly recommended. On Linux and Windows, you'll need PyTorch 2.0.1, and `pip install -U xFormers` should work for you. That said, there are paths for installation with pretty much any other version of PyTorch, but the main ones are versions 1.12.1, 1.13.1, and 2.0.1.

In table 5.1, we can see a heavily reduced breakdown of what each of these packages does and how it integrates with your code. Each package does similar things, but even when performing the same task, they will often perform those tasks differently or on different parts of your model or pipeline. There is some overlap between packages, and we'd encourage you to use all of them to see how they might benefit you. Now that you have an environment and a basic understanding of some of the tools we'll be using, let's move forward and see it in action.

Table 5.1 Comparison of optimization packages for ML

Library	Faster training or inference	Code integration	Lower accuracy	Many GPUs	Quantization	Optimizations
DeepSpeed	Both	CLI	Depends	Yes	Supports	Caching, gradient checkpointing, memory management, scaling
Accelerate	Both	CLI and Code	Depends	Yes	Supports	Automation, compiling, parallelization
BitsandBytes	Both	Code	Always	NA	Yes but only	Quantization, quantized optimizers
xFormers	Training	Code	Depends	NA	Yes and more	Efficient attention, memory management

5.2 Basic training techniques

In training LLMs, the process typically starts with defining the architecture of the model, the nature and amount of data required, and the training objectives. We've already gone over these steps in the last chapter, so you should be well prepared already, but let's look at a brief recap. The model architecture usually follows a variant of the Transformer architecture due to its effectiveness in capturing long-term dependencies and its parallelizable nature, making it amenable to large-scale computation. Data is the lifeblood of any LLM (or any ML model in general), which typically requires extensive corpora of diverse and representative text data. As the model's purpose is to learn to predict the next word in a sequence, it's crucial to ensure that the data covers a wide array of linguistic contexts.

Because we'll be going over various training techniques in this chapter, here's a (super) quick rundown of the investments you'll need for different types. For training from scratch, you'll need VRAM greater than four times the number of billions of parameters to hold the model, along with the batches of training data. So to train a 1B parameter model from scratch, you'll need at least 5 or 6 GB of VRAM, depending on your batch sizes and context length. Consider training a 70B parameter model like Llama 2 as an exercise. How much VRAM will you need to fit the model, along with a 32K token context limit? If you're coming up with a number around 300 GB of VRAM, you're right. For the finetuning techniques, you'll need significantly fewer resources for a couple of reasons—namely, quantization and amount of data needed, meaning you no longer need 4× VRAM, but can use 2× or 1× with the correct setup.

Unlike traditional ML models, LLMs are often trained in stages. Figure 5.1 shows the basic training life cycle of an LLM, starting from scratch, then finetuning, and finally prompting. The first step is creating our foundation model, where we take a large, often unrefined, dataset and train an empty shell of a model on it. This training will create a model that has seen such a large corpus of text that it appears to have a basic understanding of language. We can then take that foundation model and use transfer learning techniques, generally finetuning on a small, highly curated dataset to create a specialized LLM for expert tasks. Lastly, we use prompting techniques that, while not traditional training, allow us to goad the model to respond in a particular fashion or format, improving the accuracy of our results.

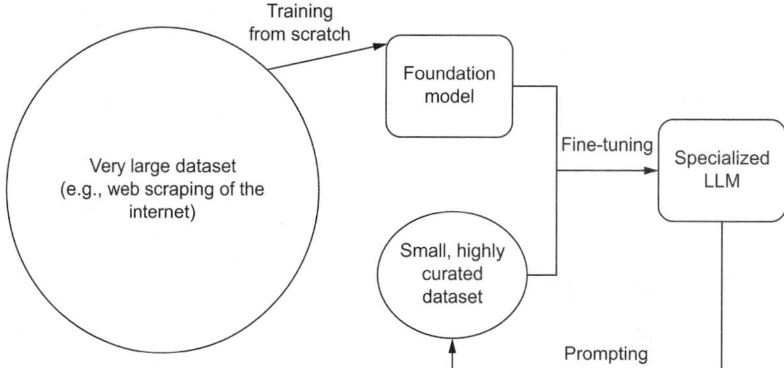

Figure 5.1 The training life cycle of an LLM. We start by creating a foundation model based on a large corpus of text, which we later finetune using a curated dataset for a specific task. We can then further improve the model by using the model itself and techniques like prompting to enhance or enlarge our curated dataset.

You'll notice that the training life cycle is often a continuous loop—training models to understand language better and then using those models to improve our training datasets. Later in this chapter, we will go into more depth about other advanced training techniques that take advantage of this loop, like prompt tuning and RLHF. For now, let's solidify our understanding of three basic steps.

5.2.1 From scratch

Training an LLM is computationally intensive and can take several weeks or months even on high-performance hardware. This process feeds chunks of data (or "batches") to the model and adjusts the weights based on the calculated loss. Over time, this iterative process of prediction and adjustment, also known as an epoch, leads the model to improve its understanding of the syntactic structures and complexities in the data. It's worth noting that monitoring the training process is crucial to avoid overfitting, where the model becomes excessively tailored to the training data and performs poorly on unseen data. Techniques like early stopping, dropout, and learning rate scheduling are used to ensure the generalizability of the model, but they are not silver bullets. Remember, the ultimate goal is not just to minimize the loss on training data but to create a model that can understand and generate human-like text across a broad range of contexts.

Training an LLM from scratch is a complex process that begins with defining the model's architecture. This decision should be guided by the specific task at hand, the size of the training dataset, and the available computational resources. The architecture, in simple terms, is a blueprint of the model that describes the number and arrangement of layers, the type of layers (like attention or feed-forward layers), and the connections between them. Modern LLMs typically employ a variant of the Transformer architecture, known for its scalability and efficiency in handling long sequences of data.

Once the model's architecture is set, the next step is to compile a large and diverse dataset for training. The quality and variety of data fed into the model largely dictate the model's ability to understand and generate human-like text. A common approach is to use a large corpus of internet text, ensuring a wide-ranging mix of styles, topics, and structures. The data is then preprocessed and tokenized, converting the raw text into a numerical format that the model can learn from. During this tokenization process, the text is split into smaller units, or tokens, which could be as short as a single character or as long as a word.

With a model and dataset ready, the next step is to initialize the model and set the learning objectives. The LLMs are trained using autoregressive semi-supervised learning techniques where the model learns to predict the next word in a sequence given the preceding words. The model's weights are randomly initialized and then adjusted through backpropagation and optimization techniques such as Adam or Stochastic Gradient Descent based on the difference between the model's predictions and the actual words in the training data. The aim is to minimize this difference, commonly referred to as the "loss," to improve the model's predictive accuracy.

Training involves feeding the tokenized text into the model and adjusting the model's internal parameters to minimize the loss. We said this once, but it bears repeating: this process is computationally demanding and may take weeks or even months to complete, depending on the model size and available hardware. After training, the model is evaluated on a separate validation dataset to ensure that it can generalize to unseen data. It is common to iterate on this process, finetuning the model parameters and adjusting the architecture as needed based on the model's performance on the validation set.

Let's explore training a brand-new transformer-based language model "from scratch," meaning without any previously defined architecture, embeddings, or weights. Figure 5.2 shows this process. You shouldn't have to train an LLM from scratch, nor would you normally want to, as it's a very expensive and time-consuming endeavor; however, knowing how can help you immensely.

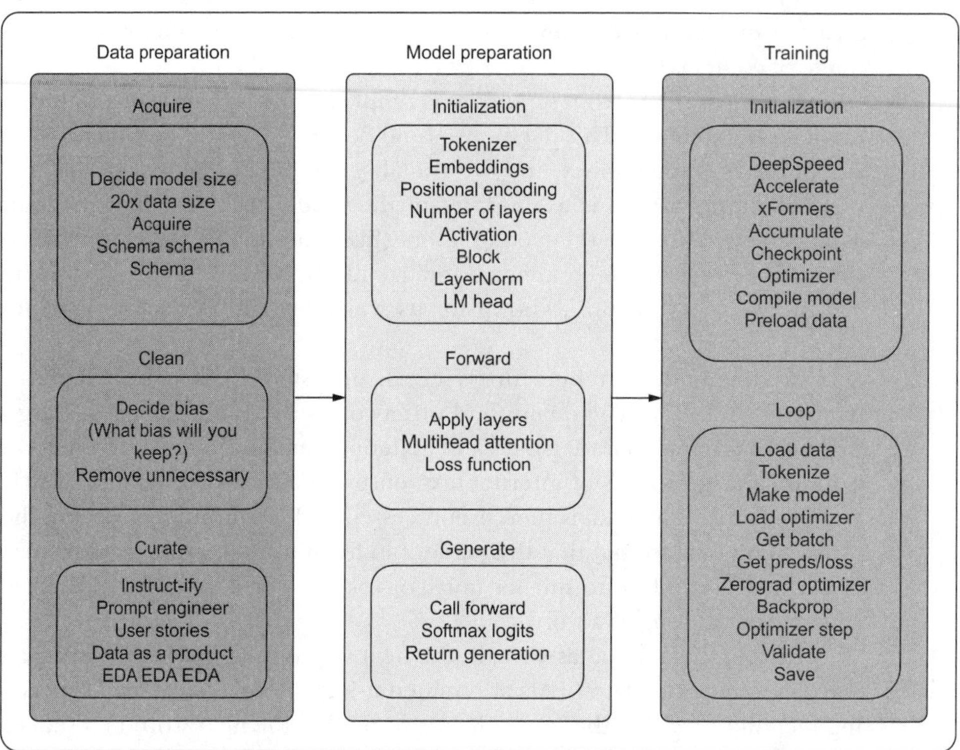

Figure 5.2 A simplified version of all the steps necessary to train a language model (large or otherwise) from scratch. You must have data, then define all of the model behavior, and only then proceed to train.

Listing 5.1 allows you to run through the motions without training an actual massive model, so feel free to explore with this code. For a more complex and complete example, check out Andrej Karpathy's minGPT project here: https://github .com/karpathy/minGPT. You should pay attention to some things when you review the listing. You might recall that we talked about tokenization and embeddings in the last chapter, so one thing to notice is that for simplicity, we will be using a character-based tokenizer. Before you run the code, can you predict whether this was a good or bad idea? Also, pay attention to how we use both Accelerate and BitsandBytes, which we introduced a little bit ago; you'll see that these libraries come in mighty handy. Next, watch as we slowly build up the LLMs architecture, building each piece in a modular fashion and later defining how many of each piece is used and where to put them, almost like Legos. Finally, at the very end of the code, you'll see a typical model training loop, splitting our data, running epochs in batches, and so forth.

Listing 5.1 An example of training from scratch

```
import os
import torch
from accelerate import Accelerator

import bitsandbytes as bnb

class GPT(torch.nn.Module):            <-- Defines the overall GPT architecture
    def __init__(self):
        super().__init__()
        self.token_embedding = torch.nn.Embedding(vocab_size, n_embed)
        self.positional_embedding = torch.nn.Embedding(block_size, n_embed)
        self.blocks = torch.nn.Sequential(
            *[Block(n_embed, n_head=n_head) for _ in range(n_layer)]
        )
        self.ln_f = torch.nn.LayerNorm(n_embed)
        self.lm_head = torch.nn.Linear(n_embed, vocab_size)

        self.apply(self._init_weights)

    def forward(self, idx, targets=None):
        B, T = idx.shape

        tok_emb = self.token_embedding(idx)
        pos_emb = self.positional_embedding(torch.arange(T, device=device))
        x = tok_emb + pos_emb
        x = self.blocks(x)
        x = self.ln_f(x)
        logits = self.lm_head(x)

        if targets is None:
            loss = None
        else:
            B, T, C = logits.shape
            logits = logits.view(B * T, C)
            targets = targets.view(B * T)
            loss = torch.nn.functional.cross_entropy(logits, targets)

        return logits, loss

    def _init_weights(self, module):
        if isinstance(module, torch.nn.Linear):
            torch.nn.init.normal_(module.weight, mean=0.0, std=0.02)
            if module.bias is not None:
                torch.nn.init.zeros_(module.bias)
        elif isinstance(module, torch.nn.Embedding):
            torch.nn.init.normal_(module.weight, mean=0.0, std=0.02)
```

```
    def generate(self, idx, max_new_tokens):
        for _ in range(max_new_tokens):
            idx_cond = idx[:, -block_size:]
            logits, loss = self(idx_cond)
            logits = logits[:, -1, :]
            probs = torch.nn.functional.softmax(logits, dim=-1)
            idx_next = torch.multinomial(probs, num_samples=1)
            idx = torch.cat((idx, idx_next), dim=1)
        return idx


class Block(torch.nn.Module):      <-- Defines the building blocks of the model
    def __init__(self, n_embed, n_head):
        super().__init__()
        head_size = n_embed // n_head
        self.self_attention = MultiHeadAttention(n_head, head_size)
        self.feed_forward = FeedFoward(n_embed)
        self.ln1 = torch.nn.LayerNorm(n_embed)
        self.ln2 = torch.nn.LayerNorm(n_embed)

    def forward(self, x):
        x = x + self.self_attention(self.ln1(x))
        x = x + self.feed_forward(self.ln2(x))
        return x


class MultiHeadAttention(torch.nn.Module):
    def __init__(self, num_heads, head_size):
        super().__init__()
        self.heads = torch.nn.ModuleList(
            [Head(head_size) for _ in range(num_heads)]
        )
        self.projection = torch.nn.Linear(head_size * num_heads, n_embed)
        self.dropout = torch.nn.Dropout(dropout)

    def forward(self, x):
        out = torch.cat([h(x) for h in self.heads], dim=-1)
        out = self.dropout(self.projection(out))
        return out


class Head(torch.nn.Module):
    def __init__(self, head_size):
        super().__init__()
        self.key = torch.nn.Linear(n_embed, head_size, bias=False)
        self.query = torch.nn.Linear(n_embed, head_size, bias=False)
        self.value = torch.nn.Linear(n_embed, head_size, bias=False)
        self.register_buffer(
            "tril", torch.tril(torch.ones(block_size, block_size))
        )

        self.dropout = torch.nn.Dropout(dropout)

    def forward(self, x):
        _, T, _ = x.shape
```

```
        k = self.key(x)
        q = self.query(x)
        attention = q @ k.transpose(-2, -1) * k.shape[-1] ** 0.5
        attention = attention.masked_fill(
            self.tril[:T, :T] == 0, float("-inf")
        )
        attention = torch.nn.functional.softmax(attention, dim=-1)
        attention = self.dropout(attention)

        v = self.value(x)
        out = attention @ v
        return out


class FeedFoward(torch.nn.Module):
    def __init__(self, n_embed):
        super().__init__()
        self.net = torch.nn.Sequential(
            torch.nn.Linear(n_embed, 4 * n_embed),
            torch.nn.ReLU(),
            torch.nn.Linear(4 * n_embed, n_embed),
            torch.nn.Dropout(dropout),
        )

    def forward(self, x):
        return self.net(x)


def encode(string):                              # Helper functions for training
    return [utt2int[c] for c in string]


def decode(line):
    return "".join([int2utt[i] for i in line])


def get_batch(split):
    data = train_data if split == "train" else val_data
    idx = torch.randint(len(data) - block_size, (batch_size,))
    x = torch.stack([data[i : i + block_size] for i in idx])
    y = torch.stack([data[i + 1 : i + block_size + 1] for i in idx])
    x, y = x.to(device), y.to(device)
    return x, y


@torch.no_grad()
def estimate_loss():
    out = {}
    model.eval()
    for split in ["train", "val"]:
        losses = torch.zeros(eval_iters)
        for k in range(eval_iters):
            X, Y = get_batch(split)
            logits, loss = model(X, Y)
            losses[k] = loss.item()
```

```
        out[split] = losses.mean()
    model.train()
    return out


if __name__ == "__main__":
    batch_size = 64  # Number of utterances at once
    block_size = 256  # Maximum context window size
    max_iters = 5000
    eval_interval = 500
    learning_rate = 3e-4
    eval_iters = 200
    n_embed = 384
    n_head = 6
    n_layer = 6
    dropout = 0.2
    accelerator = Accelerator()
    device = accelerator.device
    doing_quantization = False  # Change to True if imported bitsandbytes

    with open("./data/crimeandpunishment.txt", "r", encoding="utf-8") as f:
        text = f.read()

    chars = sorted(list(set(text)))
    vocab_size = len(chars)
    utt2int = {ch: i for i, ch in enumerate(chars)}
    int2utt = {i: ch for i, ch in enumerate(chars)}

    data = torch.tensor(encode(text), dtype=torch.long)
    n = int(0.9 * len(data))
    train_data = data[:n]
    val_data = data[n:]

    model = GPT().to(device)
    print("Instantiated Model")
    print(
        sum(param.numel() for param in model.parameters()) / 1e6,
        "Model parameters",
    )

    optimizer = (
        torch.optim.AdamW(model.parameters(), lr=learning_rate)
        if not doing_quantization
        else bnb.optim.Adam(model.parameters(), lr=learning_rate)
    )
    print("Instantiated Optimizer")

    model, optimizer, train_data = accelerator.prepare(
        model, optimizer, train_data
    )
    print("Prepared model, optimizer, and data")

    #
    for iter in range(max_iters):
        print(f"Running Epoch {iter}")
```

Trains the model

Parameters for our experiment

Dataset

Character-based pseudo-tokenization

Instantiates the model and looks at the parameters

Training block

```
        if iter % eval_interval == 0 or iter == max_iters - 1:
            losses = estimate_loss()
            print(
                f"| step {iter}: train loss {losses['train']:.4f} "
                "| validation loss {losses['val']:.4f} |"
            )

        xb, yb = get_batch("train")
        logits, loss = model(xb, yb)
        optimizer.zero_grad(set_to_none=True)
        accelerator.backward(loss)
        optimizer.step()

    model_dir = "./models/scratchGPT/"                 <-- Creates model directory
    if not os.path.exists(model_dir):
        os.makedirs(model_dir)

    model_path = model_dir + "model.pt"                <-- Saves the model
    torch.save(
        model.state_dict(),
        model_path,
    )

    loaded = GPT().load_state_dict(model_path)         <-- Loads the saved model

    context = torch.zeros((1, 1), dtype=torch.long, device=device)     <-- Tests the loaded model
    print(decode(loaded.generate(context, max_new_tokens=500)[0].tolist()))
```

In listing 5.1, we explored how the Lego blocks are put together for the GPT family of models and showed a training loop reminiscent of our exploration of language modeling in chapter 2. Beyond showing the first part of generative pretraining for models, this example also illustrates why character-based modeling, whether convolutional or otherwise, is weak for language modeling. Did you get it right? Yup, character-based modeling isn't the best. Alphabets on their own do not contain enough information to produce statistically significant results, regardless of the tuning amount. From a linguistic standpoint, this is obvious, as alphabets and orthography, in general, are representations of meaning generated from humans, which is not intrinsically captured.

Some of the ways to help with that information capture are increasing our tokenization capture window through word-, subword-, or sentence-level tokenization. We can also complete the pretraining before showing the model our task to allow it to capture as much approximate representation as possible. Next, we'll show what benefits combining these two steps can have on our model's performance.

5.2.2 *Transfer learning (finetuning)*

Transfer learning is an essential approach in machine learning and a cornerstone of training LLMs. It's predicated on the notion that we can reuse knowledge learned from one problem (the source domain) and apply it to a different but related problem (the target domain). In the context of LLMs, this typically means using a pretrained model, trained on a large, diverse dataset, and adapting it to a more specific task or domain.

In the first step of transfer learning, an LLM is trained on a large, general-purpose corpus, such as the entirety of Wikipedia, books, or the internet. This pretraining stage allows the model to learn an extensive range of language patterns and nuances on a wide variety of topics. The goal here is to learn a universal representation of language that captures a broad understanding of syntax, semantics, and world knowledge. These models are often trained for many iterations and require significant computational resources, which is why it's practical to use pretrained models provided by organizations like OpenAI or Hugging Face.

After pretraining, the LLM is updated on a specific task or domain. This update process adapts the general-purpose language understanding of the model to a more specific task, such as sentiment analysis, text classification, or question answering. Updating usually requires significantly less computational resources than the initial pretraining phase because it involves training on a much smaller dataset specific to the task at hand. Through this process, the model is able to apply the vast knowledge it gained during pretraining to a specific task, often outperforming models trained from scratch on the same task. This process of transfer learning has led to many of the advances in NLP over recent years.

FINETUNING

There are several different transfer learning techniques, but when it comes to LLMs, the one everyone cares about is finetuning. Finetuning an LLM involves taking a pretrained model—that is, a model already trained on a large general corpus—and adapting it to perform a specific task or to understand a specific domain of data.

This technique uses the fact that the base model has already learned a significant amount about the language, allowing you to reap the benefits of a large-scale model without the associated computational cost and time. The process of finetuning adapts the pre-existing knowledge of the model to a specific task or domain, making it more suitable for your specific use case. It's like having a generalist who already understands the language well and then providing specialist training for a particular job. This approach is often more feasible for most users due to the significantly reduced computational requirements and training time compared to training a model from scratch.

The first step in finetuning involves choosing a suitable pretrained model. This decision is guided by the specific task you want the model to perform and by the resources available to you. Keep in mind that this means setting a goal for the model's behavior before training. Once the pretrained model has been chosen, it's crucial to prepare the specific dataset you want the model to learn from. This data could be a collection of medical texts, for example, if you're trying to finetune the model to understand medical language. The data must be preprocessed and tokenized in a way that's compatible with the model's pretraining.

The finetuning process involves training the model on your specific dataset, but with a twist: instead of learning from scratch, the model's existing knowledge is adjusted to better fit the new data. This finetuning is typically done with a smaller learning rate than in the initial training phase to prevent the model from forgetting its previously learned knowledge. After finetuning, the model is evaluated on a separate dataset to ensure it can generalize to unseen data in the specific domain. Similar to training from scratch, this process may involve several iterations to optimize the model's performance. Finetuning offers a way to harness the power of LLMs for specific tasks or domains without the need for extensive resources or computation time. See figure 5.3.

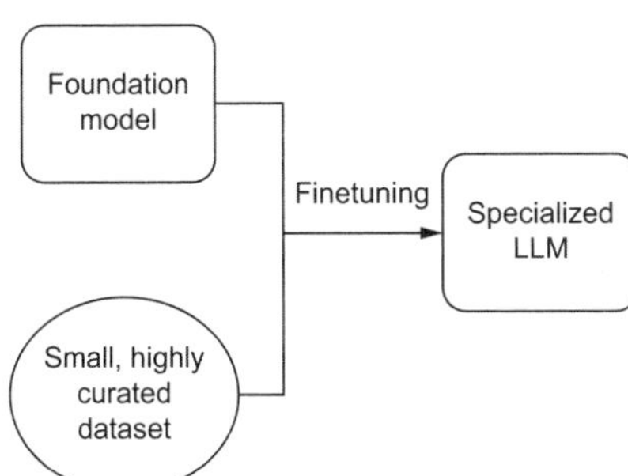

Figure 5.3 Finetuning differs from training from scratch in that you don't have to define model behavior, you can use the exact same training loop, and you have a fraction of the data requirement.

In listing 5.2, we show you how to finetune a GPT model. Notice how much less code there is in this listing than in listing 5.1. We don't need to define an architecture or a tokenizer; we'll just use those from the original model. Essentially, we get to skip ahead because weights and embeddings have already been defined.

Listing 5.2 An example of finetuning

```
import os
from transformers import (
    GPT2Tokenizer,
    GPT2LMHeadModel,
    GPT2Config,
    DataCollatorForLanguageModeling,
    TrainingArguments,
    Trainer,
)
from datasets import load_dataset

dataset = load_dataset("text", data_files="./data/crimeandpunishment.txt")    # Loads and formats the dataset
dataset = dataset.filter(lambda sentence: len(sentence["text"]) > 1)
print(dataset["train"][0])

model_dir = "./models/betterGPT/"    # Creates model directory to save to
if not os.path.exists(model_dir):
    os.makedirs(model_dir)
```

```
config = GPT2Config(
    vocab_size=50261,
    n_positions=256,
    n_embd=768,
    activation_function="gelu",
)

tokenizer = GPT2Tokenizer.from_pretrained("gpt2")
special_tokens_dict = {
    "bos_token": "<BOS>",
    "eos_token": "<EOS>",
    "pad_token": "<PAD>",
    "mask_token": "<MASK>",
}
tokenizer.add_special_tokens(special_tokens_dict)

model = GPT2LMHeadModel.from_pretrained(
    "gpt2", config=config, ignore_mismatched_sizes=True
)


def tokenize(batch):
    return tokenizer(
        str(batch), padding="max_length", truncation=True, max_length=256
    )


tokenized_dataset = dataset.map(tokenize, batched=False)
print(f"Tokenized: {tokenized_dataset['train'][0]}")

data_collator = DataCollatorForLanguageModeling(
    tokenizer=tokenizer, mlm=True, mlm_probability=0.15
)  # Masked Language Modeling - adds <MASK> tokens to guess the words

train_args = TrainingArguments(
    output_dir=model_dir,
    num_train_epochs=1,
    per_device_train_batch_size=8,
    save_steps=5000,
    save_total_limit=2,
    report_to="none",
)

trainer = Trainer(
    model=model,
    args=train_args,
    data_collator=data_collator,
    train_dataset=tokenized_dataset["train"],
)

trainer.train()
trainer.save_model(model_dir)
tokenizer.save_pretrained()

model = GPT2LMHeadModel.from_pretrained(model_dir)
```

Establishes our GPT-2 parameters (different from the paper and scratchGPT)

Instantiates our tokenizer and our special tokens

Instantiates our model from the config

Creates a tokenize function

Tokenizes our whole dataset (so we never have to do it again)

Creates a data collator to format the data for training

Establishes training arguments

Instantiates the Trainer

Trains and saves the model

Loads the saved model

```
input = "To be or not"                                          ◁ Tests the
tokenized_inputs = tokenizer(input, return_tensors="pt")          saved model
out = model.generate(
    input_ids=tokenized_inputs["input_ids"],
    attention_mask=tokenized_inputs["attention_mask"],
    max_length=256,
    num_beams=5,
    temperature=0.7,
    top_k=50,
    top_p=0.90,
    no_repeat_ngram_size=2,
)
print(tokenizer.decode(out[0], skip_special_tokens=True))
```

Looking at listing 5.2 compared with listing 5.1, they have almost the exact same architecture (minus the activation function), and they're training on exactly the same data. Yet, there's a marked improvement with the finetuned GPT-2 model due to the lack of learned representation in the first model. Our pretrained model, along with subword BPE tokenization instead of character-based, helps the model figure out which units of statistically determined meaning are most likely to go together. You'll notice, though, that GPT-2, even with pretraining, struggles to generate relevant longer narratives despite using a newer, better activation function.

FINETUNING OPENAI

We just trained a GPT model from scratch, and then we finetuned GPT-2, but we know many readers really want the power behind OpenAI's larger GPT models. Despite being proprietary models, OpenAI has graciously created an API where we can finetune GPT-3 models. Currently, three models are available for finetuning with OpenAI's platform, but it looks like it intends to extend that finetuning ability to all of its models on offer. OpenAI has written a whole guide, which you can find at http://platform.openai.com/, but once you have your dataset prepared in the necessary format, the code is pretty easy. Here are some snippets for various tasks:

```
import os
from openai import OpenAI

client = OpenAI()
client.api_key = os.getenv("OPENAI_API_KEY")
client.files.create(
  file=open("mydata.jsonl", "rb"),
  purpose='fine-tune'
)
```

This first snippet uploads a training dataset in the correct format for the platform and specifies the purpose as finetuning, but doesn't start the process yet. Next, you'll need to create the finetuning job:

```
client.fine_tuning.jobs.create(training_file="file-abc123", model="gpt-3.5-
     turbo")
```

This is where you specify which training file and which model you want to finetune. Once OpenAI's training loop has completed, you'll see the finetuned model's name populated when you retrieve the job details. Now you can use that model the same way you would have used any of the vanilla ones for chat completion or anything else like this:

```
completion = client.chat.completion.create(
  model="ft:gpt-3.5-turbo:my-org:custom_suffix:id",
  messages=[
    {"role": "system", "content": "You are a helpful assistant."},
    {"role": "user", "content": "Hello!"}
  ]
)
print(completion.choices[0].message)
```

And that's it for finetuning an OpenAI model! Very simple, doesn't take too long, and as of March 2023, your data is private to you. Of course, you'll be ceding all of the control of how that finetuning occurs over to OpenAI. If you'd like to do something beyond vanilla finetuning, you'll need to do that yourself. In just a minute, we'll go over those techniques you may consider, along with some more advanced processes that can help with more fine-grained models and more complex tasks.

5.2.3 Prompting

One of the main reasons why LLMs are so powerful compared to traditional ML is because we can train them at run time. Give them a set of instructions and watch them follow them to the best of their ability. This technique is called prompting and is used in LLMs to guide the model's output. In essence, the prompt is the initial input given to the model that provides it with context or instructions for what it should do. For example, "translate the following English text to French" and "summarize the following article" are prompts. In the context of LLMs, prompting becomes even more critical, as these models are not explicitly programmed to perform specific tasks but learn to respond to a variety of tasks based on the given prompt.

Prompt engineering refers to the process of crafting effective prompts to guide the model's behavior. The aim is to create prompts that lead the model to provide the most desirable or useful output. Prompt engineering can be more complex than it appears, as slight changes in how a prompt is phrased can lead to vastly different responses from the model. Some strategies for prompt engineering include being more explicit in the prompt, providing an example of the desired output, or rephrasing the prompt in different ways to get the best results. It's a mixture of art and science, requiring a good understanding of the model's capabilities and limitations.

In this chapter, we are going to focus mainly on training and finetuning, the steps before deployment, but we would be remiss if we didn't first mention prompting. We will talk about prompting in much more depth in chapter 7.

5.3 Advanced training techniques

Now that you know how to do the basics, let's go over some more advanced techniques. These techniques have been developed for a variety of reasons, such as improving generated text outputs, shrinking the model, providing continuous learning, speeding up training, and reducing costs. Depending on the needs of your organization, you may need to reach for a different training solution. While not a comprehensive list, the following techniques are often used and should be valuable tools as you prepare a production-ready model.

> **Classical ML training background**
>
> Going over some techniques to enhance your finetuning process requires a bit of background. We won't be doing a full course in ML; however, in case this is your first exposure, you should know some classic learning paradigms that experiments tend to follow—supervised, unsupervised, adversarial, and reinforcement:
>
> - Supervised learning involves collecting both the data to train on and the labels showcasing the expected output.
> - Unsupervised learning does not require labels, as the data is probed for similarity and grouped into clusters that are the closest comparison to each other.
> - Adversarial learning is what's used to train a generative adversarial network. It involves two models, generally referred to as the Critic model and the Forger model. These two models essentially play a game against each other where the forger tries to copy some ideal output, and the critic tries to determine whether the forgery is the real thing.
> - Reinforcement learning (RL) opts for establishing a reward function instead of having predefined labels for the model to learn from. By measuring the model's actions, it is given a reward based on that function instead.
>
> All LLMs must be trained using at least one of these, and they perform at a high level with all of them done correctly. The training techniques discussed in this chapter differ from those basic ones, ranging from adding some form of human input to the model to comparing outputs to changing how the model does matrix multiplication.

5.3.1 Prompt tuning

We've gone over pragmatics before, but as a reminder, language models perform better when given real-world nonsemantic context pertaining to the tasks and expectations. Language modeling techniques all operate on the underlying assumption that the LM, given inputs and expected outputs, can divine the task to be done and do it in the best way within the number of parameters specified.

While the idea of the model inferring both the task and the method of completing it from the data showed promise, it has been shown time and time again, from BERT to every T5 model and now to all LLMs, that providing your model with the expected task and relevant information for solving the task improves model performance drastically. As early as 2021, Google Research, DeepMind, and OpenAI had all published papers about prompt tuning, or giving a model pragmatic context during training. The benefits of prompt tuning are reducing the amount of data required for the model to converge during training and, even cooler, the ability to reuse a completely frozen language model for new tasks without retraining or fully finetuning.

Because LLMs are so large (and getting larger), it is becoming increasingly difficult to share them and even more difficult to guarantee their performance on a given task, even one they are trained on. Prompt tuning can help nudge the model in the right direction without becoming a significant cost. Figure 5.4 shows this process.

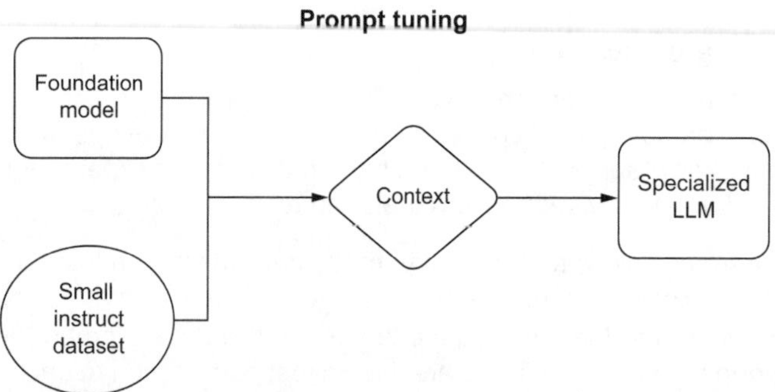

Figure 5.4 Prompt tuning foregoes most finetuning to allow the majority of the foundation model's language understanding ability to stay exactly the same and, instead, focuses on changing how the model responds to specific inputs.

Listing 5.3 shows how to prompt tune a smaller variant of the BLOOMZ model from Big Science. BLOOMZ was released as an early competitor in the LLM space but has ultimately struggled to garner attention or momentum in the community because of its inability to generate preferred outputs despite its mathematical soundness. Because prompt tuning doesn't add much to the regular finetuning structure we used in listing 5.2, we'll perform Parameter-Efficient Fine-Tuning (PEFT), which drastically reduces the memory requirements by determining which model parameters need changing the most.

Listing 5.3 An example of prompt tuning

```
import os
from transformers import (
    AutoModelForCausalLM,
    AutoTokenizer,
    default_data_collator,
    get_linear_schedule_with_warmup,
)
from peft import (
    get_peft_model,
    PromptTuningInit,
```

```
    PromptTuningConfig,
    TaskType,
)
import torch
from datasets import load_dataset
from torch.utils.data import DataLoader
from tqdm import tqdm


def preprocess_function(examples):
    batch_size = len(examples[text_column])
    inputs = [
        f"{text_column} : {x} Label : " for x in examples[text_column]
    ]
    targets = [str(x) for x in examples[label_column]]
    model_inputs = tokenizer(inputs)
    labels = tokenizer(targets)

    for i in range(batch_size):
        sample_input_ids = model_inputs["input_ids"][i]
        label_input_ids = labels["input_ids"][i] + [tokenizer.pad_token_id]
        model_inputs["input_ids"][i] = sample_input_ids + label_input_ids
        labels["input_ids"][i] = [-100] * len(
            sample_input_ids
        ) + label_input_ids
        model_inputs["attention_mask"][i] = [1] * len(
            model_inputs["input_ids"][i]
        )

    for i in range(batch_size):
        sample_input_ids = model_inputs["input_ids"][i]
        label_input_ids = labels["input_ids"][i]
        model_inputs["input_ids"][i] = [tokenizer.pad_token_id] * (
            max_length - len(sample_input_ids)
        ) + sample_input_ids
        model_inputs["attention_mask"][i] = [0] * (
            max_length - len(sample_input_ids)
        ) + model_inputs["attention_mask"][i]
        labels["input_ids"][i] = [-100] * (
            max_length - len(sample_input_ids)
        ) + label_input_ids
        model_inputs["input_ids"][i] = torch.tensor(
            model_inputs["input_ids"][i][:max_length]
        )
        model_inputs["attention_mask"][i] = torch.tensor(
            model_inputs["attention_mask"][i][:max_length]
        )
        labels["input_ids"][i] = torch.tensor(
            labels["input_ids"][i][:max_length]
        )

    model_inputs["labels"] = labels["input_ids"]
    return model_inputs
```

Helper function to preprocess text; go ahead and skip to the training

```
if __name__ == "__main__":
    # Define training parameters
    device = "cuda"
    model_name_or_path = "bigscience/bloomz-560m"
    tokenizer_name_or_path = "bigscience/bloomz-560m"
    dataset_name = "twitter_complaints"
    text_column = "Tweet text"
    label_column = "text_label"
    max_length = 64
    lr = 3e-2
    num_epochs = 1
    batch_size = 8

    peft_config = PromptTuningConfig(
        task_type=TaskType.CAUSAL_LM,
        prompt_tuning_init=PromptTuningInit.TEXT,
        num_virtual_tokens=8,
        prompt_tuning_init_text="Classify if the tweet "
        "is a complaint or not:",
        tokenizer_name_or_path=model_name_or_path,
    )
    checkpoint_name = (
        f"{dataset_name}_{model_name_or_path}"
        f"_{peft_config.peft_type}_{peft_config.task_type}_v1.pt".replace(
            "/", "_"
        )
    )
    dataset = load_dataset("ought/raft", dataset_name)
    print(f"Dataset 1: {dataset['train'][0]}")

    classes = [
        label.replace("_", " ")
        for label in dataset["train"].features["Label"].names
    ]
    dataset = dataset.map(
        lambda x: {"text_label": [classes[label] for label in x["Label"]]},
        batched=True,
        num_proc=1,
    )
    print(f"Dataset 2: {dataset['train'][0]}")

    tokenizer = AutoTokenizer.from_pretrained(model_name_or_path)
    if tokenizer.pad_token_id is None:
        tokenizer.pad_token_id = tokenizer.eos_token_id
    target_max_length = max(
        [
            len(tokenizer(class_label)["input_ids"])
            for class_label in classes
        ]
    )
    print(f"Target Max Length: {target_max_length}")

    processed_datasets = dataset.map(
        preprocess_function,
        batched=True,
```

Model prompt tuning (annotation on `if __name__ == "__main__":`)

Defines prompt tuning config; notice init_text (annotation on `peft_config = PromptTuningConfig(`)

Loads Dataset (annotation on `dataset = load_dataset(...)`)

Labels the dataset (annotation on `classes = [`)

Loads tokenizer (annotation on `tokenizer = AutoTokenizer.from_pretrained(...)`)

Runs Tokenizer across dataset and preprocess (annotation on `processed_datasets = dataset.map(`)

```
    num_proc=1,
    remove_columns=dataset["train"].column_names,
    load_from_cache_file=False,
    desc="Running tokenizer on dataset",
)

train_dataset = processed_datasets["train"]        ◁ Prepares data
eval_dataset = processed_datasets["test"]            loaders

train_dataloader = DataLoader(
    train_dataset,
    shuffle=True,
    collate_fn=default_data_collator,
    batch_size=batch_size,
    pin_memory=True,
)
eval_dataloader = DataLoader(
    eval_dataset,
    collate_fn=default_data_collator,
    batch_size=batch_size,                                 Loads
    pin_memory=True,                                       foundation
)                                                          model

model = AutoModelForCausalLM.from_pretrained(model_name_or_path)   ◁
model = get_peft_model(model, peft_config)
print(model.print_trainable_parameters())
model = model.to(device)
                                                               Defines
optimizer = torch.optim.AdamW(model.parameters(), lr=lr)   ◁   optimizer
lr_scheduler = get_linear_schedule_with_warmup(
    optimizer=optimizer,
    num_warmup_steps=0,
    num_training_steps=(len(train_dataloader) * num_epochs),
)
                                              Training
for epoch in range(num_epochs):          ◁    steps
    model.train()
    total_loss = 0
    for step, batch in enumerate(tqdm(train_dataloader)):
        batch = {k: v.to(device) for k, v in batch.items()}
        outputs = model(**batch)
        loss = outputs.loss
        total_loss += loss.detach().float()
        loss.backward()
        optimizer.step()
        lr_scheduler.step()
        optimizer.zero_grad()

    model.eval()
    eval_loss = 0
    eval_preds = []
    for step, batch in enumerate(tqdm(eval_dataloader)):
        batch = {k: v.to(device) for k, v in batch.items()}
        with torch.no_grad():
            outputs = model(**batch)
```

```
            loss = outputs.loss
            eval_loss += loss.detach().float()
            eval_preds.extend(
                tokenizer.batch_decode(
                    torch.argmax(outputs.logits, -1).detach().cpu().numpy(),
                    skip_special_tokens=True,
                )
            )

        eval_epoch_loss = eval_loss / len(eval_dataloader)
        eval_ppl = torch.exp(eval_epoch_loss)
        train_epoch_loss = total_loss / len(train_dataloader)
        train_ppl = torch.exp(train_epoch_loss)
        print(
            f"{epoch=}: {train_ppl=} {train_epoch_loss=} "
            f"{eval_ppl=} {eval_epoch_loss=}"
        )

    model_dir = "./models/PromptTunedPEFT"          # Creates model directory to save to
    if not os.path.exists(model_dir):
        os.makedirs(model_dir)

    tokenizer.save_pretrained(model_dir)            # Saving
    model.save_pretrained(model_dir)

    with torch.no_grad():                           # Inference
        inputs = tokenizer(
            f'{text_column} : {{"@nationalgridus I have no water and '
            "the bill is current and paid. Can you do something about "
            'this?"}} Label : ',
            return_tensors="pt",
        )

        inputs = {k: v.to(device) for k, v in inputs.items()}
        outputs = model.generate(
            input_ids=inputs["input_ids"],
            attention_mask=inputs["attention_mask"],
            max_new_tokens=10,
            eos_token_id=3,
        )
        print(
            tokenizer.batch_decode(
                outputs.detach().cpu().numpy(), skip_special_tokens=True
            )
        )
```

Other than the changed setup, the main difference between listings 5.2 and 5.3 is simply prepending a prompt with some sort of instruction to the beginning of each input, reminiscent of the T5 training method that pioneered having a prepended task string before every input. Prompt tuning has emerged as a powerful technique for finetuning large language models to specific tasks and domains. By tailoring prompts to the desired output and optimizing them for improved performance, we can make our models more versatile and effective. However, as our LLMs continue to grow in scale and complexity, it becomes increasingly challenging to efficiently finetune them on specific tasks. This is where knowledge distillation comes into play, offering a logical next step. Knowledge distillation allows us to transfer the knowledge and expertise of these highly tuned models to smaller, more practical versions, enabling a wider range of applications and deployment scenarios. Together, prompt tuning and knowledge distillation form a dynamic duo in the arsenal of techniques for harnessing the full potential of modern LLMs.

5.3.2 Finetuning with knowledge distillation

Knowledge distillation is an advanced technique that provides a more efficient path to finetuning an LLM. Rather than just finetuning an LLM directly, knowledge distillation involves transferring the knowledge from a large, complex model (the teacher) to a smaller, simpler model (the student). The aim is to create a more compact model that retains the performance characteristics of the larger model but is more efficient in terms of resource usage. Figure 5.5 shows this process.

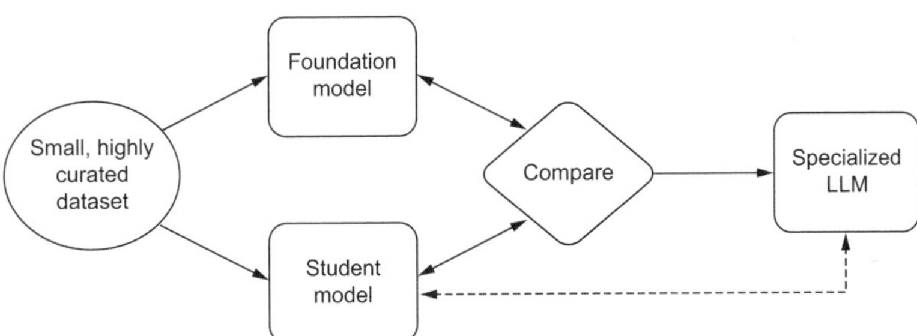

Figure 5.5 Knowledge distillation allows a smaller model to learn from a foundation model to replicate similar behavior with fewer parameters. The student model does not always learn the emergent qualities of the foundation model, so the dataset must be especially curated. The dotted line indicates a special relationship as the student model becomes the specialized LLM.

The first step in knowledge distillation is to select a pre-trained LLM as the teacher model. This could be any of the large models, such as Llama 2 70B or Falcon 180B, which have been trained on vast amounts of data. You also need to create or select a smaller model as the student. The student model might have a similar architecture to the teacher's, but with fewer layers or reduced dimensionality to make it smaller and faster.

Next, the student model is trained on the same task as the teacher model. However, instead of learning from the raw data directly, the student model learns to mimic the teacher model's outputs. This training is typically done by adding a term to the loss function that encourages the student model's predictions to be similar to the teacher model's predictions. Thus, the student model not only learns from the task-specific labels but also benefits from the rich representations learned by the teacher model.

Once the distillation process is complete, you'll have a compact student model that can handle the specific tasks learned from the teacher model but at a fraction of the size and computational cost. The distilled model can then be further finetuned on a specific task or dataset if required. Through knowledge distillation, you can use the power of LLMs in situations where computational resources or response time are limited.

In listing 5.4, we show how to perform finetuning with knowledge distillation using BERT and becoming DistilBERT. As opposed to regular finetuning, pay attention to the size and performance of the model. Both will drop; however, size will drop much faster than performance.

Listing 5.4 An example of knowledge distillation

```
import os
from transformers import (
    AutoTokenizer,
    TrainingArguments,
    Trainer,
    AutoModelForSequenceClassification,
    DataCollatorWithPadding,
)
from datasets import load_dataset, load_metric

import torch
import torch.nn as nn
import torch.nn.functional as F
import numpy as np


def process(examples):
    tokenized_inputs = tokenizer(
        examples["sentence"], truncation=True, max_length=256
    )
    return tokenized_inputs


def compute_metrics(eval_pred):
    predictions, labels = eval_pred
    predictions = np.argmax(predictions, axis=1)
    acc = accuracy_metric.compute(
        predictions=predictions, references=labels
    )
    return {
        "accuracy": acc["accuracy"],
    }


class DistillationTrainingArguments(TrainingArguments):
    def __init__(self, *args, alpha=0.5, temperature=2.0, **kwargs):
        super().__init__(*args, **kwargs)
```

```
        self.alpha = alpha
        self.temperature = temperature


class DistillationTrainer(Trainer):
    def __init__(self, *args, teacher_model=None, **kwargs):
        super().__init__(*args, **kwargs)
        self.teacher = teacher_model
        self._move_model_to_device(self.teacher, self.model.device)
        self.teacher.eval()

    def compute_loss(self, model, inputs, return_outputs=False):
        outputs_student = model(**inputs)
        student_loss = outputs_student.loss
        with torch.no_grad():
            outputs_teacher = self.teacher(**inputs)

        assert (
            outputs_student.logits.size() == outputs_teacher.logits.size()
        )

        # Soften probabilities and compute distillation loss
        loss_function = nn.KLDivLoss(reduction="batchmean")
        loss_logits = loss_function(
            F.log_softmax(
                outputs_student.logits / self.args.temperature, dim=-1
            ),
            F.softmax(
                outputs_teacher.logits / self.args.temperature, dim=-1
            ),
        ) * (self.args.temperature**2)
        loss = (
            self.args.alpha * student_loss
            + (1.0 - self.args.alpha) * loss_logits
        )
        return (loss, outputs_student) if return_outputs else loss


if __name__ == "__main__":
    model_dir = "./models/KDGPT/"
    if not os.path.exists(model_dir):
        os.makedirs(model_dir)

    student_id = "gpt2"
    teacher_id = "gpt2-medium"

    teacher_tokenizer = AutoTokenizer.from_pretrained(teacher_id)
    student_tokenizer = AutoTokenizer.from_pretrained(student_id)

    sample = "Here's our sanity check."

    assert teacher_tokenizer(sample) == student_tokenizer(sample), (
        "Tokenizers need to have the same output! "
        f"{teacher_tokenizer(sample)} != {student_tokenizer(sample)}"
    )
```

Place teacher on same device as student (annotates `self._move_model_to_device(...)`)

Computes student output (annotates `outputs_student = model(**inputs)`)

Computes teacher output (annotates `with torch.no_grad():`)

Asserts size (annotates `assert (`)

Returns weighted student loss (annotates `loss = (`)

Creates model directory to save to (annotates `model_dir = "./models/KDGPT/"`)

Defines the teacher and student models (annotates `student_id = "gpt2"`)

```
del teacher_tokenizer
del student_tokenizer

tokenizer = AutoTokenizer.from_pretrained(teacher_id)
tokenizer.add_special_tokens({"pad_token": "[PAD]"})

dataset_id = "glue"
dataset_config = "sst2"

dataset = load_dataset(dataset_id, dataset_config)

tokenized_dataset = dataset.map(process, batched=True)
tokenized_dataset = tokenized_dataset.rename_column("label", "labels")

print(tokenized_dataset["test"].features)

labels = tokenized_dataset["train"].features["labels"].names        <-- Creates label2id, id2label dicts for nice outputs for the model
num_labels = len(labels)
label2id, id2label = dict(), dict()
for i, label in enumerate(labels):
    label2id[label] = str(i)
    id2label[str(i)] = label

training_args = DistillationTrainingArguments(        <-- Defines training args
    output_dir=model_dir,
    num_train_epochs=1,
    per_device_train_batch_size=1,
    per_device_eval_batch_size=1,
    fp16=True,
    learning_rate=6e-5,
    seed=8855,
    Evaluation strategies
    evaluation_strategy="epoch",
    save_strategy="epoch",
    save_total_limit=2,
    load_best_model_at_end=True,
    metric_for_best_model="accuracy",
    report_to="none",        <-- Pushes to hub parameters
    push_to_hub=False,
    alpha=0.5,        <-- Distillation parameters
    temperature=4.0,
)

data_collator = DataCollatorWithPadding(tokenizer=tokenizer)        <-- Defines data_collator

teacher_model = AutoModelForSequenceClassification.from_pretrained(        <-- Defines model
    teacher_id,
    num_labels=num_labels,
    id2label=id2label,
    label2id=label2id,
)

student_model = AutoModelForSequenceClassification.from_pretrained(        <-- Defines student model
    student_id,
    num_labels=num_labels,
    id2label=id2label,
```

```
    label2id=label2id,
)

accuracy_metric = load_metric("accuracy")

trainer = DistillationTrainer(
    student_model,
    training_args,
    teacher_model=teacher_model,
    train_dataset=tokenized_dataset["train"],
    eval_dataset=tokenized_dataset["validation"],
    data_collator=data_collator,
    tokenizer=tokenizer,
    compute_metrics=compute_metrics,
)
trainer.train()

trainer.save_model(model_dir)
```

Defines metrics and metrics function

Knowledge distillation, as exemplified by the provided `compute_loss` method, is a technique that enables the transfer of valuable insights from a teacher model to a more lightweight student model. In this process, the teacher model provides soft targets, offering probability distributions over possible outputs, which are then utilized to train the student model. The critical aspect of knowledge distillation lies in the alignment of these distributions, ensuring that the student model not only learns to mimic the teacher's predictions but also gains a deeper understanding of the underlying data. This approach helps improve the student's generalization capabilities and performance on various tasks, ultimately making it more efficient and adaptable.

As we look forward, one logical progression beyond knowledge distillation is the incorporation of RLHF. While knowledge distillation enhances a model's ability to make predictions based on existing data, RLHF allows the model to learn directly from user interactions and feedback. This dynamic combination not only refines the model's performance further but also enables it to adapt and improve continuously. By incorporating human feedback, RL can help the model adapt to real-world scenarios, evolving its decision-making processes based on ongoing input, making it an exciting and natural evolution in the development of LLM systems.

5.3.3 *Reinforcement learning with human feedback*

RLHF is a newer training technique developed to overcome one of the biggest challenges when it comes to RL: how to create reward systems that actually work. It sounds easy, but anyone who's played around with RL knows how difficult it can be. Before AlphaStar, one author was building his own RL bot to play *StarCraft*, a war simulation game in space.

NOTE Check out https://mng.bz/Dp4a to learn more about AlphaStar.

A simple reward system based on winning or losing was taking too long, so he decided to give it some reasonable intermediate rewards based on growing an army. However, this got blocked when it failed to build Pylons, a building required to increase army supply limits. So he gave it a reward to build Pylons. His bot quickly learned that it liked to build Pylons—so much so that it learned to almost win but not win, crippling its opponent so that it could keep building Pylons unharassed and for as long as it wanted.

With a task like winning a game, even if it's difficult, we can usually still come up with reasonable reward systems. But what about more abstract tasks, like teaching a robot how to do a backflip? These tasks get really difficult to design reward systems for, which is where RLHF comes in. What if instead of designing a system, we simply have a human make suggestions? A human knows what a backflip is, after all. The human will act like a tutor, picking attempts it likes more as the bot is training. That's what RLHF is, and it works really well. Applied to LLMs, a human simply looks at generated responses to a prompt and picks which one they like more. See figure 5.6.

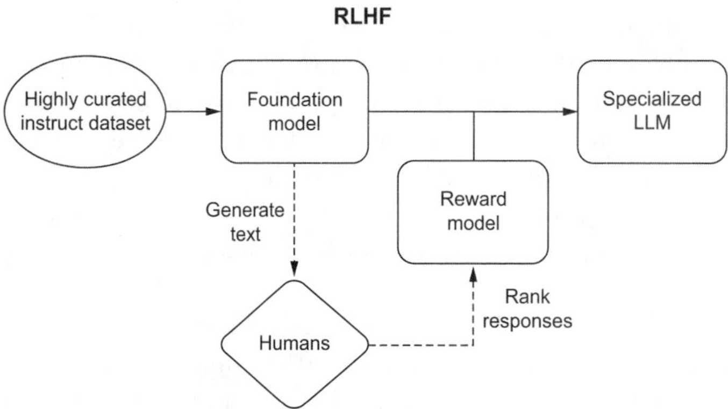

Figure 5.6 RLHF substitutes a loss function for a reward model and proximal policy optimization (PPO), allowing the model a much higher ceiling for learning trends within the data, including what is preferred as an output instead of what completes the task.

While very powerful, RLHF likely won't stick around for very long. The reason is that it is incredibly computationally expensive for a result that is only incrementally better, especially a result that can be achieved and matched by higher-quality datasets with supervised learning approaches.

There are some other problems with RLHF, such as that it requires hiring domain experts to evaluate and provide the human feedback. Not only can this get expensive, but it can also lead to privacy concerns since these reviewers would need to look at actual traffic and user interactions to grade them. To combat both of these concerns, you could try to outsource this directly to the users, asking for their feedback, but it may end up poisoning your data if your users have ill intent or are simply not experts in the subject matter, in which case they might upvote responses they like but that aren't actually correct. This gets to the next problem: even experts have biases. RLHF doesn't train a model to be more accurate or factually correct; it trains the model to generate human-acceptable answers.

In production, RLHF has the advantage of allowing you to easily update your model on a continual basis. However, this is a two-edged sword, as it also increases the likelihood of your model degrading over time. OpenAI uses RLHF heavily, and it has led to many users complaining about their models, like GPT-4, becoming terrible in certain domains compared to when it first came out. One Stanford study found that GPT-4, when asked if a number was prime, used to get it right 98% of the time in March 2023, but three months later, in June 2023, it would only get it right 2% of the time.[1] One reason is that the June model is much less verbose, opting to give a simple yes or no response. Humans like these responses. Getting straight to the point is often better, but LLMs tend to be better after they have had time to reason through the answer with techniques like chain of thought.

With this in mind, RLHF is fantastic for applications where human-acceptable answers are the golden standard, and factually correct answers are less important—for example, a friendly chatbot or improving summarization tasks. These problems are intuitively syntactic in nature, essentially tasks that LLMs are already good at but which you want to refine by possibly creating a certain tone or personality.

Another reason for RLHF degradation is due to data leakage. Data leakage is when your model is trained on the test or validation dataset you use to evaluate it. When this happens, you are essentially allowing the model to cheat, leading to overfitting and poor generalization. It's just like how LeetCode interview questions lead tech companies to hire programmers who have lots of experience solving toy problems but don't know how to make money or do their job.

How does this happen? Well, simply. When you are running an LLM in production with RLHF, you know it's going to degrade over time, so it's best to run periodic evaluations to monitor the system. The more you run these evaluations, the more likely that one of the prompts will be picked up for human feedback and subsequent RL training. It could also happen by pure coincidence if your users happen to ask a question similar to a prompt in your evaluation dataset. Either way, without restrictions placed on RLHF (which generally are never done), it's a self-defeating system.

The really annoying aspect of continual updates through RLHF is that these updates ruin downstream engineering efforts, methods like prompting or retrieval-augmented generation (RAG). Engineering teams can take a lot of effort to dial in a process or procedure to query a model and then clean up responses, but all that work can easily be undermined if the underlying model is changing. As a result, many teams prefer a static model with periodic updates to one with continual updates.

---

[1] L. Chen, M. Zaharia, and J. Zou, "How is ChatGPT's behavior changing over time?," arXiv.org, Jul. 18, 2023, https://arxiv.org/abs/2307.09009.

All that said, RLHF is still a powerful technique that may yield greater results later as it is optimized and refined. Also, it's just really cool. We don't recommend using RLHF, and we don't have the space here to delve deeper; just know that it is a tool used by companies specializing in LLMs. For readers who want to understand RLHF better, we have included an in-depth example and code listing in appendix B.

5.3.4 Mixture of experts

A mixture of experts (MoE) is functionally the same as any other model for training but contains a trick under the hood: sparsity. This gives the advantage of being able to train a bunch of models on a diverse set of data and tasks at once. You see, a MoE is exactly what it sounds like: an ensemble of identical models in the beginning. You can think of them as a group of freshman undergrads. Then, using some unsupervised grouping methods, such as k-means clustering, each of these experts "picks a major" during training. This allows the model only to activate some experts to answer particular inputs instead of all of them, or maybe the input is complex enough that it requires activating all of them. The point is that once training has completed, if it has been done on a representative-enough dataset, each of your experts will have a college degree in the major that they studied. Because the homogeneity of inputs is determined mathematically, those majors won't always have a name that correlates to something you would major in at school, but we like to think of these as eccentric double minors or something of the sort. Maybe one of your experts majored in physics but double minored in advertising and Africana studies. It doesn't really matter, but the major upside to designing an ensemble of models in this way is that you can effectively reduce computational requirements immensely while retaining specialization and training memory by only consulting the experts whose knowledge correlates with the tokenized input at inference time.

In listing 5.5, we finetune a MoE model in much the same way as we did in listing 5.2 with GPT-2, thanks to Hugging Face's API and Google's Switch Transformer. Unlike the method we described in chapter 3, where we turned a feed-forward network into an MoE, we'll start with an already created MoE and train it on our own dataset. Training an MoE is pretty simple now, unlike when they first came out. Very smart people performed so much engineering that we can give an oversimplified explanation of these models. Google created the Switch Transformer to combat two huge problems they had run into while trying to train LLMs: size and instability. Google engineers simplified the routing algorithm (how the model decides which experts to query for each input) and showed how to train models with lower quantizations (in this case, bfloat16) for the first time—quite an amazing feat and not one to take lightly, as GPT-4 is likely an MoE.

Listing 5.5 Example mixture of experts finetuning

```
import os
from transformers import (
    AutoTokenizer,
    SwitchTransformersForConditionalGeneration,
```

```
    SwitchTransformersConfig,
    TrainingArguments,
    Trainer,
    DataCollatorForLanguageModeling,
)
from datasets import load_dataset
import torch

dataset = load_dataset("text", data_files="./data/crimeandpunishment.txt")
dataset = dataset.filter(lambda sentence: len(sentence["text"]) > 1)
print(f"Dataset 1: {dataset['train'][0]}")

model_dir = "./models/MoE/"
if not os.path.exists(model_dir):
    os.makedirs(model_dir)

tokenizer = AutoTokenizer.from_pretrained("google/switch-base-8")

config = SwitchTransformersConfig(
    decoder_start_token_id=tokenizer.pad_token_id
)

model = SwitchTransformersForConditionalGeneration.from_pretrained(
    "google/switch-base-8",
    config=config,
    device_map="auto",
    torch_dtype=torch.float16,
)


def tokenize(batch):
    return tokenizer(
        str(batch), padding="max_length", truncation=True, max_length=256
    )


tokenized_dataset = dataset.map(tokenize, batched=False)
print(f"Tokenized: {tokenized_dataset['train'][0]}")

data_collator = DataCollatorForLanguageModeling(
    tokenizer=tokenizer, mlm=False, mlm_probability=0.0
)  # Causal Language Modeling - Does not use mask


train_args = TrainingArguments(
    output_dir=model_dir,
    num_train_epochs=1,
    per_device_train_batch_size=8,
    save_steps=5000,
    save_total_limit=2,
    report_to="none",
)

trainer = Trainer(
    model=model,
```

Annotations:
- Loads and formats the dataset
- Creates model directory to save to
- Instantiates our tokenizer
- Establishes our SwitchTransformers config
- Instantiates our model from the config
- Creates a tokenize function
- Tokenizes our whole dataset (so we never have to do it again)
- Creates a data collator to format the data for training
- Establishes training arguments
- Instantiates the trainer

```
    args=train_args,
    data_collator=data_collator,
    train_dataset=tokenized_dataset["train"],
)

trainer.train()                                                    <-- Trains and saves the model
trainer.save_model(model_dir)
tokenizer.save_pretrained(model_dir)
                                                                   Loads the saved model
model = SwitchTransformersForConditionalGeneration.from_pretrained(   <--
    model_dir,
    device_map="auto",
    torch_dtype=torch.float16,
)

input = "To be or not <extra_id_0> <extra_id_0>"                   <-- Tests the saved model
tokenized_inputs = tokenizer(input, return_tensors="pt")
out = model.generate(
    input_ids=tokenized_inputs["input_ids"].to("cuda"),
    attention_mask=tokenized_inputs["attention_mask"],
    max_length=256,
    num_beams=5,
    temperature=0.7,
    top_k=50,
    top_p=0.90,
    no_repeat_ngram_size=2,
)
print(f"To be or not {tokenizer.decode(out[0], skip_special_tokens=True)}")
```

In this script, an MoE model is finetuned using the Switch Transformer foundation model. MoE models are unique during finetuning because you typically update the task-specific parameters, such as the gating mechanism and the parameters of the experts, while keeping the shared parameters intact. This allows the MoE to use the expertise of the different experts for better task-specific performance. Finetuning MoE models differs from traditional finetuning because it requires handling the experts and gating mechanisms, which can be more complex than regular neural network architectures. In our case, we're lucky that `trainer.train()` with the right config covers it for finetuning, and we can just bask in the work that Google did before us.

A logical progression beyond MoE finetuning involves exploring Parameter-Efficient Fine-Tuning (PEFT) and low-rank adaptations (LoRA). PEFT aims to make the finetuning process more efficient by reducing the model's size and computational demands, making it more suitable for resource-constrained scenarios. Techniques such as knowledge distillation, model pruning, quantization, and compression can be employed in PEFT to achieve this goal. In contrast, LoRA focuses on incorporating low-rank factorization methods into model architectures to reduce the number of parameters while maintaining or even enhancing model performance. These approaches are essential, as they enable the deployment of sophisticated models on devices with limited resources and in scenarios where computational efficiency is paramount.

5.3.5 LoRA and PEFT

LoRA represents a significant breakthrough for machine learning in general. Taking advantage of a mathematical trick, LoRAs can change the output of a model without changing the original model weights or taking up significant space or cost, as shown in figure 5.7. The reason for the significance here is that it makes finetuning a separate model for many different tasks or domains much more feasible, as has already been seen in the diffusion space with text2image LoRAs popping up quite often for conditioning model output without significantly altering the base model's abilities or style. Put simply, if you already like your model and would like to change it to do the exact same thing in a new domain without sacrificing what it was already good at on its own, an adapter might be the path for you, especially if you have multiple new domains that you don't want bleeding into one another.

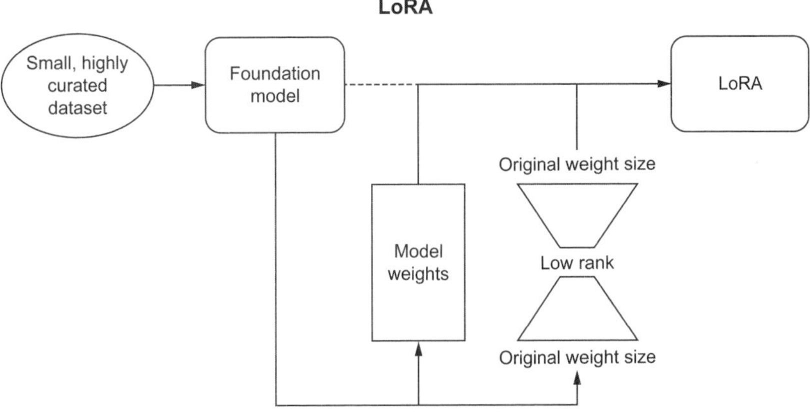

Figure 5.7 LoRA exemplifies the idea that you should only need to train and save the difference between where the foundation model is and where you want it to be. It does this through singular value decomposition (SVD).

To understand LoRAs, you need to first understand how models currently adjust weights. Since we aren't going to go over a complete backpropagation tutorial here, we can abstract it as

$$W = W + \Delta W$$

So if you have a model with 100 100-dimensional layers, your weights can be represented by a 100 × 100 matrix. The cool part comes with singular value decomposition (SVD), which has been used for compression by factoring a single matrix into three smaller matrices. We covered this topic in depth back in chapter 3 (see listing 3.2). So while we know the intuition for SVD with LLMs, what can we compress from that original formula?

$$\Delta W = W_a \times W_b$$

So if $\Delta W = 100 \times 100$, $W_a = 100 \times c$ and $W_b = c \times 100$, where $c < 100$. If $c = 2$, you can represent 10,000 elements using only 400 because when they're multiplied together, they equal the 10,000 original elements. So the big question is, what does c equal for your task? The c-value is the "R" in LoRA, referring to the rank of the matrix of weights. There are algorithmic ways of determining that rank using eigenvectors and the like, but you can approximate a lot of it by knowing that a higher rank equals more complexity, meaning that the higher the number you use there, the closer you'll get to original model accuracy, but the less memory you'll save. If you think the task you're finetuning the LoRA for isn't as complex, reduce the rank.

The next listing shows you how to combine creating a LoRA and then perform inference with both the LoRA and your base model.

Listing 5.6 Example LoRA and PEFT training

```
import os
from datasets import load_dataset
from transformers import (
    AutoModelForTokenClassification,
    AutoTokenizer,
    DataCollatorForTokenClassification,
    TrainingArguments,
    Trainer,
)
from peft import (
    PeftModel,
    PeftConfig,
    get_peft_model,
    LoraConfig,
    TaskType,
)
import evaluate
import torch
import numpy as np

model_checkpoint = "meta-llama/Llama-2-7b-hf"
lr = 1e-3
batch_size = 16
num_epochs = 10

model_dir = "./models/LoRAPEFT"     # Creates model directory to save to
if not os.path.exists(model_dir):
    os.makedirs(model_dir)

bionlp = load_dataset("tner/bionlp2004")

seqeval = evaluate.load("seqeval")

label_list = [
    "O",
    "B-DNA",
    "I-DNA",
    "B-protein",
```

```
    "I-protein",
    "B-cell_type",
    "I-cell_type",
    "B-cell_line",
    "I-cell_line",
    "B-RNA",
    "I-RNA",
]


def compute_metrics(p):
    predictions, labels = p
    predictions = np.argmax(predictions, axis=2)

    true_predictions = [
        [label_list[p] for (p, l) in zip(prediction, label) if l != -100]
        for prediction, label in zip(predictions, labels)
    ]
    true_labels = [
        [label_list[l] for (p, l) in zip(prediction, label) if l != -100]
        for prediction, label in zip(predictions, labels)
    ]

    results = seqeval.compute(
        predictions=true_predictions, references=true_labels
    )
    return {
        "precision": results["overall_precision"],
        "recall": results["overall_recall"],
        "f1": results["overall_f1"],
        "accuracy": results["overall_accuracy"],
    }


tokenizer = AutoTokenizer.from_pretrained(
    model_checkpoint, add_prefix_space=True
)


def tokenize_and_align_labels(examples):
    tokenized_inputs = tokenizer(
        examples["tokens"], truncation=True, is_split_into_words=True
    )

    labels = []
    for i, label in enumerate(examples["tags"]):
        word_ids = tokenized_inputs.word_ids(batch_index=i)
        previous_word_idx = None
        label_ids = []
        for word_idx in word_ids:
            if word_idx is None:
                label_ids.append(-100)
            elif word_idx != previous_word_idx:
                label_ids.append(label[word_idx])
```

```
            else:
                label_ids.append(-100)
            previous_word_idx = word_idx
        labels.append(label_ids)

    tokenized_inputs["labels"] = labels
    return tokenized_inputs


tokenized_bionlp = bionlp.map(tokenize_and_align_labels, batched=True)

data_collator = DataCollatorForTokenClassification(tokenizer=tokenizer)

id2label = {
    0: "O",
    1: "B-DNA",
    2: "I-DNA",
    3: "B-protein",
    4: "I-protein",
    5: "B-cell_type",
    6: "I-cell_type",
    7: "B-cell_line",
    8: "I-cell_line",
    9: "B-RNA",
    10: "I-RNA",
}
label2id = {
    "O": 0,
    "B-DNA": 1,
    "I-DNA": 2,
    "B-protein": 3,
    "I-protein": 4,
    "B-cell_type": 5,
    "I-cell_type": 6,
    "B-cell_line": 7,
    "I-cell_line": 8,
    "B-RNA": 9,
    "I-RNA": 10,
}

model = AutoModelForTokenClassification.from_pretrained(
    model_checkpoint, num_labels=11, id2label=id2label, label2id=label2id
)

peft_config = LoraConfig(
    task_type=TaskType.TOKEN_CLS,
    inference_mode=False,
    r=16,
    lora_alpha=16,
    lora_dropout=0.1,
    bias="all",
)

model = get_peft_model(model, peft_config)
model.print_trainable_parameters()
```

```
training_args = TrainingArguments(
    output_dir=model_dir,
    learning_rate=lr,
    per_device_train_batch_size=batch_size,
    per_device_eval_batch_size=batch_size,
    num_train_epochs=num_epochs,
    weight_decay=0.01,
    evaluation_strategy="epoch",
    save_strategy="epoch",
    load_best_model_at_end=True,
)

trainer = Trainer(
    model=model,
    args=training_args,
    train_dataset=tokenized_bionlp["train"],
    eval_dataset=tokenized_bionlp["validation"],
    tokenizer=tokenizer,
    data_collator=data_collator,
    compute_metrics=compute_metrics,
)

trainer.train()

peft_model_id = "stevhliu/roberta-large-lora-token-classification"
config = PeftConfig.from_pretrained(model_dir)
inference_model = AutoModelForTokenClassification.from_pretrained(
    config.base_model_name_or_path,
    num_labels=11,
    id2label=id2label,
    label2id=label2id,
)
tokenizer = AutoTokenizer.from_pretrained(config.base_model_name_or_path)
model = PeftModel.from_pretrained(inference_model, peft_model_id)

text = (
    "The activation of IL-2 gene expression and NF-kappa B through CD28 "
    "requires reactive oxygen production by 5-lipoxygenase."
)
inputs = tokenizer(text, return_tensors="pt")

with torch.no_grad():
    logits = model(**inputs).logits

tokens = inputs.tokens()
predictions = torch.argmax(logits, dim=2)

for token, prediction in zip(tokens, predictions[0].numpy()):
    print((token, model.config.id2label[prediction]))
```

Keep in mind that you still need to keep your base model, as shown in listing 5.6. The LoRA is run in addition to the foundation model; it sits on top and changes the weights at only the rank determined in the `LoraConfig` class (in this case, `16`). RoBERTa-Large was likely already decent at doing token classification on the bionlp dataset, but now, running with the LoRA on top, it'll be even better. There are multiple types of LoRAs you can use, with QLoRA, QA-LoRA, and AWQ-LoRA all gaining popularity in different domains and tasks. With the transformers library, which can be controlled from the `LoraConfig`, we encourage you to experiment with different adaptation methods to find what works for your data and task.

The most attractive thing about LoRA is that the particular one we discussed here results in a file only 68 KB in size on disk and still has a significant performance boost. You could create LoRAs for each portion of your company that wants a model, one for the legal team that's siloed so it doesn't have to worry about any private data it is putting into it, one for your engineering team to help with code completion and answering questions about which data structures or algorithms to use, and one for anyone else. Because they're so small, it's suddenly much more feasible to store than the 1.45 GB (14.5 GB if we use Llama in fp16; it's 28 GB in fp32) RoBERTa-Large model being finetuned a bunch of times. In the spirit of giving you more of these time- and space-saving tips, we'll go over some things that aren't mentioned anywhere else, but you may still get some use out of if the data science part of LLMs is what you are working with.

5.4 Training tips and tricks

While this book isn't focused on training and researching new models, we feel kind of bad telling you that finetuning models is an effective strategy for teaching LLMs correct guardrails based on your data and then just leaving you to figure out how to make it work on your own stuff. With this in mind, let's look at some tried-and-true tips and tricks for both training and finetuning LLMs. These tips will help you with some of the least-intuitive parts of training LLMs that most practitioners (like us) had to learn the hard way.

5.4.1 Training data size notes

First off, LLMs are notorious for overfitting. If you are considering training a foundation model, you need to consider the amount of data you have, which should be roughly 20× the number of parameters you're trying to train.[2] For example, if you're training a 1B parameter model, you should train it on 20B tokens. If you have fewer tokens than that, you will run the risk of overfitting.

If you already have a model and need to finetune it on your data, consider the inverse, where you should likely have ~0.000001× the number of tokens as a minimum (10K tokens for a 1B parameter model). We came up with this rule of thumb based on our experience, although it should be fairly intuitive. If you have fewer than 1/100,000 of your model parameters in tokens, finetuning likely won't have much of an effect. In this case, you should consider another strategy that won't cost as much,

[2] J. Hoffmann et al., "Training compute-optimal large language models," arXiv:2203.15556 [cs], March 2022, https://arxiv.org/abs/2203.15556.

such as LoRA (which we just discussed), RAG (which we talk about in the next chapter), or a system that uses both.

For both these examples, we've had the experience where a company we worked for hoped for great results with minimal data and was disappointed. One hoped to train an LLM from scratch with only ~1 million tokens while also disallowing open source datasets, and another wanted to finetune the model but only on a couple of hundred examples. Neither of these approaches were cost-efficient, nor did they create models that performed up to the standards the companies aimed for.

5.4.2 Efficient training

We've so far focused on tools and methodologies for training, which should supercharge your ability to create the best and largest models your training system allows. However, other factors should be considered when setting up your training loops. In physics, the uncertainty principle shows that you can never perfectly know both the speed and position of a given particle. Machine learning's uncertainty principle is that you can never perfectly optimize both your speed and your memory utilization. Improving speed comes at the cost of memory, and vice versa. Table 5.2 shows some choices you can make in training and their effects on speed and memory.

Table 5.2 Training choices to consider

Method	Improve speed	Improves memory utilization	Difficulty
Batch size choice	Yes	Yes	Easy
Gradient accumulation	No	Yes	Medium
Gradient checkpointing	No	Yes	Medium
Mixed precision	Yes	No	Hard
Optimizer choice	Yes	Yes	Easy
Data preloading	Yes	No	Medium
Compiling	Yes	No	Easy

Carefully consider your options and what goal you're working toward when setting up your training loop. For example, your batch size should be a power of 2 to hit maximum speed and memory efficiency. One author remembers working on getting an LLM to have a single-digit milli-second response time. The team was gearing up to serve millions of customers as fast as possible, and every millisecond counted. After using every trick in the book, I was able to achieve it, and I remember the huge feeling of accomplishment for finally getting that within the data science dev environment. Yet, it turned out that there was a hard batch size of 20 in the production environment. It was just a nice number picked out of a hat, and too many systems were built around this assumption; no one wanted to refactor. Software engineers, am I right?

For the majority of these methods, the tradeoff is clear: if you go slower, you can fit a significantly larger model, but it will take way longer. Gradient accumulating and checkpointing can reduce memory usage by ~60%, but training will take much longer. The packages we talked about in section 5.1 can help mitigate these tradeoffs.

5.4.3 Local minima traps

Local minima are hard to spot with LLMs and, as such, can be difficult to avoid. If you see your model converging early, be suspicious and judiciously test it before accepting the results. When you find that your model is converging early at a certain number of steps, one way to avoid it on subsequent runs is to save and load a checkpoint 100 or so steps before you see the errant behavior, turn your learning rate *way* down, train until you're sure you're past it, and then turn it back up and continue. Make sure to keep the previously saved checkpoint, and save a new checkpoint after that so that you have places to come back to in case things go wrong!

You can probably tell that this is a frustrating occurrence that one author has run into before. He was so confused; he was working on a T5 XXL model, and around the 25K step mark, the model was converging and stopping early. He knew for a fact that it wasn't actually converged; it was only 10% through the dataset! This happened two or three times, where he loaded up the checkpoint at around 20K steps and watched the exact same thing happen. It wasn't until he loaded and turned the learning rate down that he finally saw the model improve past this point. Once he got through the patch of the local minimum, he turned it back up. This happened four more times throughout training this particular model, but since he knew what was happening, he was now able to avoid wasting lots of extra time. The lesson of the story? Use this rule of thumb: your LLM is not ready if it hasn't trained on your full dataset.

5.4.4 Hyperparameter tuning tips

Hyperparameter tuning isn't something we've gone over extensively in this book, not because it's not interesting but because it doesn't help nearly as much as changing up your data, either getting more or cleaning it further. If you want to tune hyperparameters, Optuna is a great package, and you can get that ~1% boost in accuracy or F1 score that you really need. Otherwise, if you're looking for a boost in a particular metric, try representing that metric more completely within your dataset and maybe use some statistical tricks like oversampling.

While hyperparameter tuning is pretty cool mathematically, for LLMs, it's not something that ever really needs to happen. If you need a boost in performance, you need more/better data, and tuning your hyperparameters will never match the performance boost you'd get quantizing the weights or performing any of the optimizations we've mentioned here or in chapter 3. The biggest performance boost we've ever gotten through tuning hyperparameters was about a 4% increase in F1, and we only did it because we wouldn't be able to change our dataset for a couple of weeks at least.

5.4.5 A note on operating systems

Windows is not the right OS to work professionally with LLMs without the Windows Subsystem for Linux. MacOS is great but lacks the hardware packages to really carry this load unless you know how to use an NVIDIA or AMD GPU with a Mac. If you are uncomfortable with Linux, you should take some time to familiarize yourself with it while your OS of choice catches up (if it ever does). A myriad of free online materials are available to help you learn about Bash, Linux, and the command line. Configuring the CUDA Toolkit and Nvidia drivers on Linux can make you want to pull your hair out, but it's worth it compared to the alternatives. Along with this, learn about virtual environments, Docker, and cloud computing, like what's in this chapter!

All in all, Windows is easy in the beginning but frustrating in the long run. MacOS is also easy in the beginning but currently doesn't work at all in the long run. Linux is incredibly frustrating in the beginning, but once you're through that, it's smooth sailing.

5.4.6 Activation function advice

We've neglected to really dive into activation functions so far, not because they aren't useful or cool but because you generally don't need to tweak your activation functions unless you're doing research science on model performance. If you take vanilla GPT-2 and give it a GeGLU activation instead of the GELU that it comes with, you will not get a significant boost in anything. In addition, you'll need to redo your pretraining, as it pretrained with a different activation function. Activation functions help reduce some of the mathematical weaknesses of each layer, be they imaginary numbers from the quadratic attention, exploding and vanishing gradients, or maybe the researchers noticed positional encodings disappearing as they went through the model and changed a little bit. You can learn about activation functions, and we recommend doing so; in general, you can trust the papers that introduce new ones.

We've come a long way in this chapter, discussing setting up an environment, training an LLM from scratch, and looking at a multitude of finetuning techniques. While we recognize there are still many aspects to this process that we did not touch on and that you need to learn on your own, you should be more than ready to create your own models. Now that you have a model, in the next chapter, we'll discuss making it production-ready and creating an LLM service you can use to serve online inference.

Summary

- Training is memory intensive, and you will need to master multi-GPU environments for many LLM training tasks.
- Model training has the same basic steps every time:
  - *Dataset preparation*—Acquire, clean, and curate your data.
  - *Model preparation*—Define model behavior, architecture, loss functions, etc.
  - *Training loop*—Initialization, tokenize, batch data, get predictions/loss, backpropagation, etc.
- Good data has a significantly greater effect on model performance than architecture or the training loop.
- Finetuning is way easier than training from scratch because it requires much less data and resources.
- Prompting allows us to train a model on a specific task after the fact, which is one of the reasons LLMs are so powerful compared to traditional ML.
- Prompt tuning is a powerful way to focus your model to respond as a specialist to certain prompts.
- Knowledge distillation is useful for training powerful smaller models that are efficient and adaptable.
- RLHF is great at getting a model to respond in a way that pleases human evaluators but increases factually incorrect results.
- Finetuning MoE models differs from traditional finetuning because it requires handling the experts and gating mechanisms.
- LoRA is a powerful finetuning technique that adapts pretrained models to new tasks by creating tiny assets (low-rank matrices) that are fast to train, easy to maintain, and very cost-effective.
- The quality and size of your data are two of the most important considerations for successfully training your model.
- The major training tradeoff is speed for memory efficiency; if you go slower, you can fit a significantly larger model, but it will take way longer.

6 Large language model services: A practical guide

This chapter covers

- How to structure an LLM service and tools to deploy
- How to create and prepare a Kubernetes cluster for LLM deployment
- Common production challenges and some methods to handle them
- Deploying models to the edge

The production of too many useful things results in too many useless people.

—Karl Marx

We did it. We arrived. This is the chapter we wanted to write when we first thought about writing this book. One author remembers the first model he ever deployed. Words can't describe how much more satisfaction this gave him than the dozens of projects left to rot on his laptop. In his mind, it sits on a pedestal, not because it was good—in fact, it was quite terrible—but because it was useful and actually used by those who needed it the most. It affected the lives of those around him.

So what actually is production? "Production" refers to the phase where the model is integrated into a live or operational environment to perform its intended tasks or provide services to end users. It's a crucial phase in making the model available for real-world applications and services. To that end, we will show you how to package up an LLM into a service or API so that it can take on-demand requests. We will then show you how to set up a cluster in the cloud where you can deploy this service. We'll also share some challenges you may face in production and some tips for handling them. Lastly, we will talk about a different kind of production, deploying models on edge devices.

6.1 Creating an LLM service

In the last chapter, we trained and finetuned several models, and we're sure you can't wait to deploy them. Before you deploy a model, though, it's important to plan ahead and consider different architectures for your API. Planning ahead is especially vital when deploying an LLM API. It helps outline the functionality, identify potential integration challenges, and arrange for necessary resources. Good planning streamlines the development process by setting priorities, thereby boosting the team's efficiency.

In this section, we are going to take a look at several critical topics you should take into consideration to get the most out of our application once deployed. Figure 6.1 demonstrates a simple LLM-based service architecture that allows users to interact with our LLM on demand. This is a typical use case when working with chatbots, for example. Setting up a service also allows us to serve batch and stream processes while abstracting away the complexity of embedding the LLM logic directly into these pipelines. Of course, running an ML model from a service will add a communication latency to your pipeline, but LLMs are generally considered slow, and this extra latency is often worth the tradeoff.

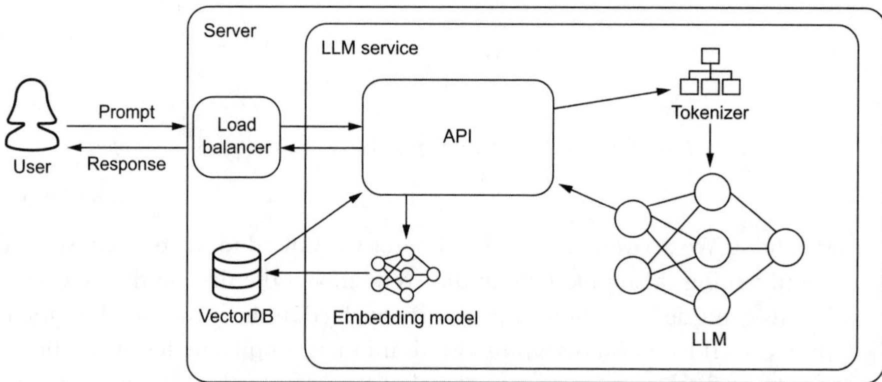

Figure 6.1 A basic LLM service. A majority of the logic is handled by the API layer, which will ensure the correct preprocessing of incoming requests is done and serve the actual inference of the request.

While figure 6.1 appears neat and tidy, it is hiding several complex subjects you'll want to work through, particularly in that API box. We'll be talking through several key features you'll want to include in your API, like batching, rate limiters, and streaming. You'll also notice some preprocessing techniques like retrieval-augmented generation (RAG) hidden in this image, which we'll discuss in depth in section 6.1.7. By the end of this section, you will know how to approach all of this, and you will have deployed an LLM service and understand what to do to improve it. But before we get to any of that, let's first talk about the model itself and the best methods to prepare it for online inference.

6.1.1 Model compilation

The success of any model in production is dependent on the hardware it runs on. The microchip architecture and design of the controllers on the silicon will ultimately determine how quickly and efficiently inferences can run. Unfortunately, when programming in a high-level language like Python using frameworks like PyTorch or TensorFlow, the model won't be optimized to take full advantage of the hardware. This is where compiling comes into play. Compiling is the process of taking code written in a high-level language and converting or lowering it to machine-level code that the computer can process quickly. Compiling your LLM can easily lead to major inference and cost improvements.

Various people have dedicated a lot of time to performing some of the repeatable efficiency steps for you beforehand. We covered Tim Dettmers's contributions in the last chapter. Other contributors include Georgi Gerganov, who created and maintains llama.cpp for running LLMs using C++ for efficiency, and Tom Jobbins, who goes by TheBloke on Hugging Face Hub and quantizes models into the correct formats to be used in Gerganov's framework and others, like oobabooga. Because of how fast this field moves, completing simple, repeatable tasks over a large distribution of resources is often just as helpful to others.

In machine learning workflows, this process typically involves converting our model from its development framework (PyTorch, TensorFlow, or other) to an intermediate representation (IR), like TorchScript, MLIR, or ONNX. We can then use hardware-specific software to convert these IR models to compiled machine code for our hardware of choice—GPU, TPU (tensor-processing units), CPU, etc. Why not just convert directly from your framework of choice to machine code and skip the middleman? Great question. The reason is simple: there are dozens of frameworks and hundreds of hardware units, and writing code to cover each combination is out of the question. So instead, framework developers provide conversion tooling to an IR, and hardware vendors provide conversions from an IR to their specific hardware.

For the most part, the actual process of compiling a model involves running a few commands. Thanks to PyTorch 2.x, you can get a head start on it by using the `torch.compile(model)` command, which you should do before training and before deployment. Hardware companies often provide compiling software for free, as it's a big incentive for users to purchase their product. Building this software isn't easy, however, and often requires expertise in both the hardware architecture and the machine learning architectures. This combination of these talents is rare, and there's good money to be had if you get a job in this field.

We will show you how to compile an LLM in a minute, but first, let's take a look at some of the techniques used. What better place to start than with the all-important kernel tuning?

KERNEL TUNING

In deep learning and high-performance computing, a kernel is a small program or function designed to run on a GPU or other similar processors. These routines are developed by the hardware vendor to maximize chip efficiency. They do this by optimizing threads, registries, and shared memory across blocks of circuits on the silicon. When we run arbitrary code, the processor will try to route the requests the best it can across its logic gates, but it's bound to run into bottlenecks. However, if we are able to identify the kernels to run and their order beforehand, the GPU can map out a more efficient route—and that's essentially what kernel tuning is.

During kernel tuning, the most suitable kernels are chosen from a large collection of highly optimized kernels. For instance, consider convolution operations that have several possible algorithms. The optimal one from the vendor's library of kernels will be based on various factors like the target GPU type, input data size, filter size, tensor layout, batch size, and more. When tuning, several of these kernels will be run and optimized to minimize execution time.

This process of kernel tuning ensures that the final deployed model is not only optimized for the specific neural network architecture being used but also finely tuned for the unique characteristics of the deployment platform. This process results in more efficient use of resources and maximizes performance. Next, let's look at tensor fusion, which optimizes running these kernels.

TENSOR FUSION

In deep learning, when a framework executes a computation graph, it makes multiple function calls for each layer. The computation graph is a powerful concept used to simplify mathematical expressions and execute a sequence of tensor operations, especially for neural network models. If each operation is performed on the GPU, it invokes many CUDA kernel launches. However, the fast kernel computation doesn't quite match the slowness of launching the kernel and handling tensor data. As a result, the GPU resources might not be fully utilized, and memory bandwidth can become a choke point. It's like making multiple trips to the store to buy separate items when we could make a single trip and buy all the items at once.

This is where tensor fusion comes in. It improves this situation by merging or fusing kernels to perform operations as one, reducing unnecessary kernel launches and improving memory efficiency. A common example of a composite kernel is a fully connected kernel that combines or fuses a matmul, bias add, and ReLU kernel. It's similar to the concept of tensor parallelization. In tensor parallelization, we speed up the process by sending different people to different stores, like the grocery store, the hardware store, and a retail store. This way, one person doesn't have to go to every store. Tensor fusion can work very well with parallelization across multiple GPUs. It's like sending multiple people to different stores and making each one more efficient by picking up multiple items instead of one.

Graph optimization

Tensor fusion, when done sequentially, is also known as vertical graph optimization. We can also do horizontal graph optimization. These optimizations are often talked about as two different things. Horizontal graph optimization, which we'll refer to simply as graph optimization, combines layers with shared input data but with different weights into a single broader kernel. It replaces the concatenation layers by pre-allocating output buffers and writing into them in a distributed manner.

In figure 6.2, we show an example of a simple deep learning graph being optimized. Graph optimizations do not change the underlying computation in the graph. They are simply restructuring the graph. As a result, the optimized graph performs more efficiently with fewer layers and kernel launches, reducing inference latency. This restructuring makes the whole process smaller, faster, and more efficient.

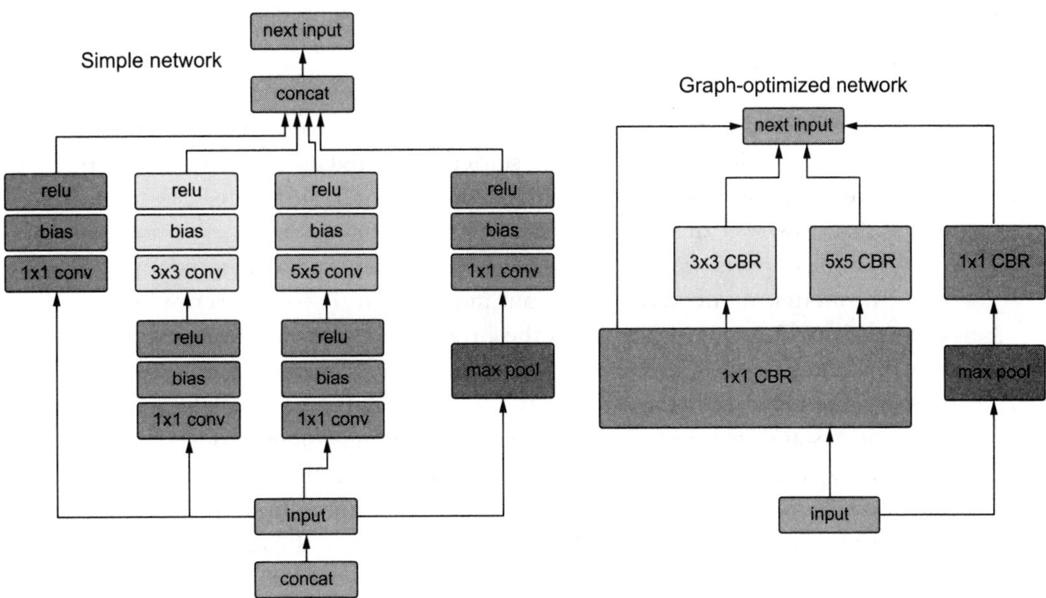

Figure 6.2 An example of an unoptimized network compared to the same network optimized using graph optimization. CBR is a NVIDIA fused layer kernel that simply stands for Convolution, Bias, and ReLU. See the following NVIDIA blog post for reference: https://mng.bz/PNvw.

The graph optimization technique is often used in the context of computational graph-based frameworks like TensorFlow. Graph optimization involves techniques that simplify these computational graphs, remove redundant operations, and/or rearrange computations, making them more efficient for execution, especially on specific hardware (like GPU or TPU). An example is constant folding, where the computations involving constant inputs are performed at compile time (before run time), thereby reducing the computation load during run time.

These aren't all the techniques used when compiling a model, but they are some of the most common and should give you an idea of what's happening under the hood and why it works. Now let's look at some tooling to do this for LLMs.

TENSORRT

NVIDIA's TensorRT is a one-stop shop to compile your model, and who better to trust than the hardware manufacturer to better prepare your model to run on their GPUs? TensorRT does everything talked about in this section, along with quantization to INT8 and several memory tricks to get the most out of your hardware to boot.

In listing 6.1, we demonstrate the simple process of compiling an LLM using TensorRT. We'll use the PyTorch version known as `torch_tensorrt`. It's important to note that compiling a model to a specific engine is hardware specific. So you will want to compile the model on the exact hardware you intend to run it on. Consequently, installing TensorRT is a bit more than a simple `pip install`; thankfully, we can use Docker instead. To get started, run the following command:

```
$ docker run --gpus all -it --rm nvcr.io/nvidia/pytorch:23.09-py3
```

This command will start up an interactive `torch_tensorrt` Docker container with practically everything we need to get started (for the latest version, see https://mng.bz/r1We). The only thing missing is Hugging Face Transformers, so go ahead and install that. Now we can run the listing.

After our imports, we'll load our model and generate an example input so we can trace the model. We need to convert our model to an IR—TorchScript here—and this is done through tracing. Tracing is the process of capturing the operations that are invoked when running the model and makes graph optimization easier later. If you have a model that takes varying inputs, for example, the CLIP model, which can take both images and text and turn them into embeddings, tracing that model with only text data is an effective way of pruning the image operations out of the model. Once our model has been converted to an IR, then we can compile it for NVIDIA GPUs using TensorRT. Once completed, we then simply reload the model from disk and run some inference for demonstration.

Listing 6.1 Compiling a model with TensorRT

```
import torch
from transformers import GPT2Tokenizer, GPT2LMHeadModel
import torch_tensorrt

tokenizer = GPT2Tokenizer.from_pretrained("gpt2")
tokens = tokenizer("The cat is on the table.", return_tensors="pt")[
    "input_ids"
].cuda()
```

```
model = GPT2LMHeadModel.from_pretrained(
    "gpt2", use_cache=False, return_dict=False, torchscript=True
).cuda()
model.eval()

traced_model = torch.jit.trace(model, tokens)

compile_settings = {
    "inputs": [
        torch_tensorrt.Input(
            # For static size
            shape=[1, 7],
            # For dynamic sizing:
            # min_shape=[1, 3],
            # opt_shape=[1, 128],
            # max_shape=[1, 1024],
            dtype=torch.int32,  # Datatype of input tensor.
            # Allowed options torch.(float|half|int8|int32|bool)
        )
    ],
    "truncate_long_and_double": True,
    "enabled_precisions": {torch.half},
    "ir": "torchscript",
}
trt_model = torch_tensorrt.compile(traced_model, **compile_settings)

torch.jit.save(trt_model, "trt_model.ts")

trt_model = torch.jit.load("trt_model.ts")
tokens.half()
tokens = tokens.type(torch.int)
logits = trt_model(tokens)
results = torch.softmax(logits[-1], dim=-1).argmax(dim=-1)
print(tokenizer.batch_decode(results))
```

Converts to Torchscript IR

Compiles the model with TensorRT

Runs with FP16

Saves the compiled model

Runs inference

The output is

```
# ['\n was a the way.\n']
```

We'll just go ahead and warn you: your results may vary when you run this code, depending on your setup. Overall, it's a simple process once you know what you are doing, and we've regularly seen at least 2× speed improvements in inference times—which translates to major savings!

TensorRT really is all that and a bag of chips. Of course, the major downside to TensorRT is that, as a tool developed by NVIDIA, it is built with NVIDIA's hardware in mind. When compiling code for other hardware and accelerators, it's not going to be useful. Also, you'll get very used to running into error messages when working with TensorRT. We've found that running into compatibility problems when converting models that aren't supported is a common occurrence. We've run into many problems trying to compile various LLM architectures. Thankfully, to address this, NVIDIA has been working on a TensorRT-LLM library to supercharge LLM inference on NVIDIA high-end GPUs. It supports many more LLM architectures than vanilla TensorRT. You can check if it supports your chosen LLM architecture and GPU setup here: https://mng.bz/mRXP.

Don't get us wrong; you don't have to use TensorRT. Several alternative compilers are available. In fact, let's look at another popular alternative, ONNX Runtime. Trust us, you'll want an alternative when TensorRT doesn't play nice.

ONNX RUNTIME

ONNX, which stands for Open Neural Network Exchange, is an open source format and ecosystem designed for representing and interoperating between different deep learning frameworks, libraries, and tools. It was created to address the challenge of model portability and compatibility. As mentioned previously, ONNX is an IR and allows you to represent models trained in one deep learning framework (e.g., TensorFlow, PyTorch, Keras, MXNet) in a standardized format easily consumed by other frameworks. Thus, it facilitates the exchange of models between different tools and environments. Unlike TensorRT, ONNX Runtime is intended to be hardware-agnostic, meaning it can be used with a variety of hardware accelerators, including CPUs, GPUs, and specialized hardware like TPUs.

In practical terms, ONNX allows machine learning practitioners and researchers to build and train models using their preferred framework and then deploy those models to different platforms and hardware without the need for extensive reengineering or rewriting of code. This process helps streamline the development and deployment of AI and ML models across various applications and industries. To be clear, ONNX is an IR format, while ONNX Runtime allows us to optimize and run inference with ONNX models.

To take advantage of ONNX, we recommend using Hugging Face's Optimum. Optimum is an interface that makes working with optimizers easier and supports multiple engines and hardware, including Intel Neural Compressor for Intel chips and Furiosa Warboy for Furiosa NPUs. It's worth checking out. For our purposes, we will use it to convert LLMs to ONNX and then optimize them for inference with ONNX Runtime. First, let's install the library with the appropriate engines. We'll use the `--upgrade-strategy eager`, as suggested by the documentation, to ensure the different packages are upgraded:

```
$ pip install --upgrade-strategy eager optimum[exporters,onnxruntime]
```

Next, we'll run the optimum command line interface. We'll export it to ONNX, point it to a Hugging Face transformer model, and give it a local directory to save the model to. Those are all the required steps, but we'll also give it an optimization feature flag. Here, we'll do the basic general optimizations:

```
$ optimum-cli export onnx --model WizardLM/WizardCoder-1B-V1.0
➥ ./models_onnx --optimize O1
```

And we are done. We now have an LLM model converted to ONNX format and optimized with basic graph optimizations. As with all compiling processes, optimization should be done on the hardware you intend to run inference on, which should include ample memory and resources, as the conversion can be somewhat computationally intensive.

To run the model, check out https://onnxruntime.ai/ for quick start guides on how to run it with your appropriate SDK. Oh, yeah, did we forget to mention that ONNX Runtime supports multiple programming APIs, so you can now run your LLM directly in your favorite language, including Java, C++, C#, or even JavaScript? Well, you can. So go party. We'll be sticking to Python in this book, though, for consistency's sake.

While TensorRT is likely to be your weapon of choice most of the time, and ONNX Runtime covers many edge cases, there are still many other excellent engines out there, like OpenVINO. You can choose whatever you want, but you should at least use something. Doing otherwise would be an egregious mistake. In fact, now that you've read this section, you can no longer claim ignorance. It is now your professional responsibility to ensure this happens. Putting any ML model into production that hasn't first been compiled (or at least attempted to be compiled) is a sin to the MLOps profession.

6.1.2 LLM storage strategies

Now that we have a nicely compiled model, we need to think about how our service will access it. This step is important because, as discussed in chapter 3, boot times can be a nightmare when working with LLMs since it can take a long time to load such large assets into memory. So we want to try to speed that up as much as possible. When it comes to managing large assets, we tend to throw them into an artifact registry or a bucket in cloud storage and forget about them. Both of these tend to utilize an object storage system—like GCS or S3—under the hood, which is great for storage but less so for object retrieval, especially when it comes to large objects like LLMs.

Object storage systems break up assets into small fractional bits called objects. They allow us to federate the entire asset across multiple machines and physical memory locations, a powerful tool that powers the cloud, and to cheaply store large objects on commodity hardware. With replication, there is built-in fault tolerance, so we never have to worry about losing our assets from a hardware crash. Object storage systems also create high availability, ensuring we can always access our assets. The downside is that these objects are federated across multiple machines and not in an easily accessible form to be read and stored in memory. Consequently, when we load an LLM into GPU memory, we will essentially have to download the model first. Let's look at some alternatives.

FUSING

Fusing is the process of mounting a bucket to your machine as if it were an external hard drive. Fusing provides a slick interface and simplifies code, as you will no longer have to download the model and then load it into memory. With fusing, you can treat an external bucket like a filesystem and load the model directly into memory. However, it still doesn't solve the fundamental need to pull the objects of your asset from multiple machines. Of course, if you fuse a bucket to a node in the same region and zone, some optimizations can improve performance, and it will feel like you are loading the model from the drive. Unfortunately, our experience has shown fusing to be quite slow, but it should still be faster than downloading and then loading.

Fusing libraries are available for all major cloud providers and on-prem object storage solutions, like Ceph or MinIO, so you should be covered no matter the environment, including your own laptop. That's right. You can fuse your laptop or an edge device to your object storage solution. This ability demonstrates both how powerful and, at the same time, ineffective this strategy is, depending on what you were hoping it would achieve.

TIP All fusing libraries are essentially built off the FUSE library. It's worth checking out: https://github.com/libfuse/libfuse.

BAKING THE MODEL

Baking is the process of putting your model into the Docker image. Thus, whenever a new container is created, the model will be there, ready for use. Baking models, in general, is considered an antipattern. For starters, it doesn't solve the problem. In production, when a new instance is created, a new machine is spun up. It is fresh and innocent, knowing nothing of the outside world, so the first step it'll have to take is to download the image. Since the image contains the model, we haven't solved anything. Actually, it's very likely that downloading the model inside an image will be *slower* than downloading the model from an object store. So we most likely just made our boot times worse.

Second, baking models is a terrible security practice. Containers often have poor security and are often easy for people to gain access to. Third, you've doubled your problems: before you just had one large asset; now you have two, the model and the image.

That said, there are still times when baking is viable, mainly because despite the drawbacks, it greatly simplifies our deployments. Throwing all our assets into the image guarantees we'll only need one thing to deploy a new service: the image itself, which is really valuable when deploying to an edge device, for example.

MOUNTED VOLUME

Another solution is to avoid the object store completely and save your LLM in a file-based storage system on a mountable drive. When our service boots up, we can connect the disc drive housing the LLM with a RAID controller or Kubernetes, depending on our infrastructure. This solution is old school, but it works really well. For the most part, it solves all our problems and provides incredibly fast boot times.

The downside, of course, is that it will add a bunch of coordination steps to ensure there is a volume in each region and zone you plan to deploy to. It also brings up replication and reliability problems; if the drive dies unexpectedly, you'll need backups in the region. In addition, these drives will likely be SSDs and not just commodity hardware. So you'll likely be paying a bit more. But storage is extremely cheap compared to GPUs, so the time saved in boot times is something you'll have to consider. Essentially, though, this strategy reintroduces all the problems for which we usually turn to object stores to begin with.

HYBRID: INTERMEDIARY MOUNTED VOLUME

Lastly, we can always take a hybrid approach. In this solution, we download the model at boot time but store it in a volume that is mounted at boot time. While this doesn't help at all with the first deployment in a region, it does substantially help any new instances, as they can simply mount this same volume and have the model available to load without having to download. You can imagine this working similarly to how a Redis cache works, except for storage. Often, this technique is more than enough since autoscaling will be fast enough to handle bursty workloads. We just have to worry about total system crashes, which hopefully should be minimal, but they allude to the fact that we should avoid this approach when only running one replica, which you shouldn't do in production anyway.

In figure 6.3, we demonstrate these different strategies and compare them to a basic service where we simply download the LLM and then load it into memory. Overall, your exact strategy will depend on your system requirements, the size of the LLM you are running, and your infrastructure. Your system requirements will also likely vary widely, depending on the type of traffic patterns you see.

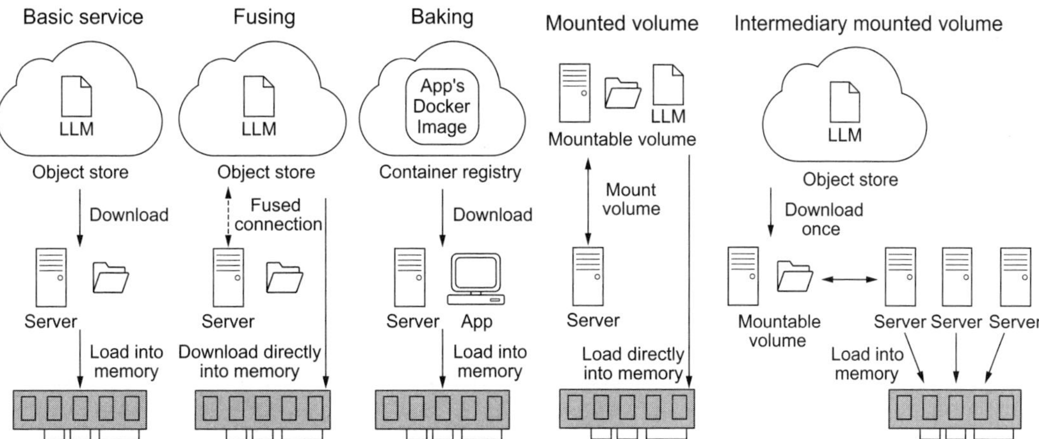

Figure 6.3 Different strategies for storing LLMs and their implications at boot time. Often, we have to balance system reliability, complexity, and application load time.

Now that we have a good handle on how to handle our LLM as an asset, let's talk about some API features that are must-haves for your LLM service.

6.1.3 Adaptive request batching

A typical API will accept and process requests in the order they are received, processing them immediately and as quickly as possible. However, anyone who's trained a machine learning model has come to realize that there are mathematical and computational advantages to running inference in batches of powers of 2 (16, 32, 64, etc.), particularly when GPUs are involved, where we can take advantage of better memory alignment or vectorized instructions parallelizing computations across the GPU cores. To take advantage of this batching, you'll want to include adaptive request batching or dynamic batching.

What adaptive batching does is essentially pool requests together over a certain period of time. Once the pool receives the configured maximum batch size or the timer runs out, it will run inference on the entire batch through the model, sending the results back to the individual clients that requested them. Essentially, it's a queue. Setting one up yourself can and will be a huge pain; thankfully, most ML inference services offer this out of the box, and almost all are easy to implement. For example, in BentoML, add `@bentoml.Runnable.method(batchable=True)` as a decorator to your predict function, and in Triton Inference Server, add `dynamic_batching {}` at the end of your model definition file.

If that sounds easy, it is. Typically, you don't need to do any further finessing, as the defaults tend to be very practical. That said, if you are looking to maximize every bit of efficiency possible in the system, you can often set a maximum batch size, which will tell the batcher to run once this limit is reached, or a batch delay, which does the same thing but for the timer. Increasing either will result in longer latency but likely better throughput, so typically these are only adjusted when your system has plenty of latency budget.

Overall, the benefits of adaptive batching include better use of resources and higher throughput at the cost of a bit of latency. This is a valuable tradeoff, and we recommend giving your product the latency bandwidth to include this feature. In our experience, optimizing for throughput leads to better reliability and scalability and thus greater customer satisfaction. Of course, when latency times are extremely important or traffic is few and far between, you may rightly forgo this feature.

6.1.4 Flow control

Rate limiters and access keys are critical protections for an API, especially one sitting in front of an expensive LLM. Rate limiters control the number of requests a client can make to an API within a specified time, which helps protect the API server from abuse, such as distributed denial of service (DDoS) attacks, where an attacker makes numerous requests simultaneously to overwhelm the system and hinder its function.

Rate limiters can also protect the server from bots that make numerous automated requests in a short span of time. This helps manage the server resources optimally so the server is not exhausted due to unnecessary or harmful traffic. They are also useful for managing quotas, thus ensuring all users have fair and equal access to the API's resources. By preventing any single user from using excessive resources, the rate limiter ensures the system functions smoothly for all users.

All in all, rate limiters are an important mechanism for controlling the flow of your LLM's system processes. They can play a critical role in dampening bursty workloads and preventing your system from getting overwhelmed during autoscaling and rolling updates, especially when you have a rather large LLM with longer deployment times. Rate limiters can take several forms, and the one you choose will be dependent on your use case.

Types of rate limiters

The following list describes the types of rate limiters:

- *Fixed window*—This algorithm allows a fixed number of requests in a set duration of time. Let's say five requests per minute, and it refreshes at the minute. It's really easy to set up and reason about. However, it may lead to uneven distribution and can allow a burst of calls at the boundary of the time window.
- *Sliding window log*—To prevent boundary problems, we can use a dynamic timeframe. Let's say five requests in the last 60 seconds. This type is a slightly more complex version of the fixed window that logs each request's timestamp to provide a moving lookback period, providing a more evenly distributed limit.
- *Token bucket*—Clients initially have a full bucket of tokens, and with each request, they spend tokens. When the bucket is empty, the requests are blocked. The bucket refills slowly over time. Thus, token buckets allow burst behavior, but it's limited to the number of tokens in the bucket.
- *Leaky bucket*—It works as a queue where requests enter, and if the queue is not full, they are processed; if full, the request overflows and gets discarded, thus controlling the rate of the flow.

A rate limiter can be applied at multiple levels, from the entire API to individual client requests to specific function calls. While you want to avoid being too aggressive with them—better to rely on autoscaling to scale and meet demand—you don't want to ignore them completely, especially when it comes to preventing bad actors.

Access keys are also crucial to prevent bad actors. Access keys offer authentication, maintaining that only authorized users can access the API, which prevents unauthorized use and potential misuse of the API and reduces the influx of spam requests. They are also essential to set up for any paid service. Of course, even if your API is only exposed internally, setting up access keys shouldn't be ignored, as it can help reduce liability and provide a way of controlling costs by yanking access to a rogue process, for example.

Thankfully, setting up a service with rate limiting and access keys is relatively easy nowadays, as there are multiple libraries that can help you. In listing 6.2, we demonstrate a simple FastAPI app utilizing both. We'll use FastAPI's built-in security library for our access keys and SlowApi, a simple rate limiter that allows us to limit the call of any function or method with a simple decorator.

Listing 6.2 Example API with access keys and rate limiter

```
from fastapi import FastAPI, Depends, HTTPException, status, Request
from fastapi.security import OAuth2PasswordBearer
from slowapi import Limiter, _rate_limit_exceeded_handler
from slowapi.util import get_remote_address
from slowapi.errors import RateLimitExceeded
import uvicorn

api_keys = ["1234567abcdefg"]          <-- This would be encrypted in a database.
API_KEY_NAME = "access_token"
oauth2_scheme = OAuth2PasswordBearer(tokenUrl="token")

limiter = Limiter(key_func=get_remote_address)

app = FastAPI()
app.state.limiter = limiter
app.add_exception_handler(RateLimitExceeded, _rate_limit_exceeded_handler)


async def get_api_key(api_key: str = Depends(oauth2_scheme)):
    if api_key not in api_keys:
        raise HTTPException(
            status_code=status.HTTP_401_UNAUTHORIZED,
            detail="Invalid API Key",
        )


@app.get("/hello", dependencies=[Depends(get_api_key)])
@limiter.limit("5/minute")
async def hello(request: Request):
    return {"message": "Hello World"}
```

While this is just a simple example, you'll still need to set up a system for users to create and destroy access keys. You'll also want to finetune your time limits. In general, you want them to be as loose as possible so as not to interfere with the user experience but just tight enough to do their job.

6.1.5 Streaming responses

One feature your LLM service should absolutely include is streaming. Streaming allows us to return the generated text to the user as it is being generated versus all at once at the end. Streaming adds quite a bit of complexity to the system, but regardless, it has come to be considered a must-have feature for several reasons.

First, LLMs are rather slow, and the worst thing you can do to your users is make them wait—waiting means they will become bored, and bored users complain or, worse, leave. You don't want to deal with complaints, do you? Of course not! But by streaming the data as it's being created, we offer the users a more dynamic and interactive experience.

Second, LLMs aren't just slow; they are unpredictable. One prompt could lead to pages and pages of generated text, and another, a single token. As a result, your latency is going to be all over the place. Streaming allows us to worry about more consistent metrics like tokens per second (TPS). Keeping TPS higher than the average user's reading speed means we'll be sending responses back faster than the user can consume them, ensuring they won't get bored and we are providing a high-quality user experience. In contrast, if we wait until the end to return the results, users will likely decide to walk away and return when it finishes because they never know how long to wait. This huge disruption to their flow makes your service less effective or useful.

Lastly, users are starting to expect streaming. Streaming responses have become a nice tell as to whether you are speaking to a bot or an actual human. Since humans have to type, proofread, and edit their responses, we can't expect written responses from a human customer support rep to be in a stream-like fashion. So when they see a response streaming in, your users will know they are talking to a bot. People interact differently with a bot than they will with a human, so it's very useful information to give them to prevent frustration.

In listing 6.3 we demonstrate a very simple LLM service that utilizes streaming. The key pieces to pay attention to are that we are using the base asyncio library to allow us to run asynchronous function calls, FastAPI's `StreamingResponse` to ensure we send responses to the clients in chunks, and Hugging Face Transformer's `TextIteratorStreamer` to create a pipeline generator of our model's inference.

Listing 6.3 A streaming LLM service

```
import argparse
import asyncio
from typing import AsyncGenerator

from fastapi import FastAPI, Request
from fastapi.responses import Response, StreamingResponse
import uvicorn

from transformers import (
    AutoModelForCausalLM,
```

```
    AutoTokenizer,
    TextIteratorStreamer,
)
from threading import Thread

app = FastAPI()

tokenizer = AutoTokenizer.from_pretrained("gpt2")
model = AutoModelForCausalLM.from_pretrained("gpt2")
streamer = TextIteratorStreamer(tokenizer)


async def stream_results() -> AsyncGenerator[bytes, None]:
    for response in streamer:
        await asyncio.sleep(1)
        yield (response + "\n").encode("utf-8")


@app.post("/generate")
async def generate(request: Request) -> Response:
    """Generate LLM Response

    The request should be a JSON object with the following fields:
    - prompt: the prompt to use for the generation.
    """
    request_dict = await request.json()
    prompt = request_dict.pop("prompt")

    inputs = tokenizer([prompt], return_tensors="pt")
    generation_kwargs = dict(inputs, streamer=streamer, max_new_tokens=20)

    thread = Thread(target=model.generate, kwargs=generation_kwargs)
    thread.start()

    return StreamingResponse(stream_results())


if __name__ == "__main__":
    parser = argparse.ArgumentParser()
    parser.add_argument("--host", type=str, default=None)
    parser.add_argument("--port", type=int, default=8000)
    args = parser.parse_args()

    uvicorn.run(app, host=args.host, port=args.port, log_level="debug")
```

Loads tokenizer, model, and streamer into memory

Slows things down to see streaming. It's typical to return streamed responses byte encoded.

Starts a separate thread to generate results

Starts service; defaults to localhost on port 8000

Now that we know how to implement several must-have features for our LLM service, including batching, rate limiting, and streaming, let's look at some additional tooling we can add to our service to improve usability and overall workflow.

6.1.6 Feature store

When it comes to running ML models in production, feature stores really simplify the inference process. We first introduced these in chapter 3, but as a recap, feature stores establish a centralized source of truth. They answer crucial questions about your data:

Who is responsible for the feature? What is its definition? Who can access it? Let's take a look at setting one up and querying the data to get a feel for how they work. We'll be using Feast, which is open source and supports a variety of backends. To get started, let us `pip install feast` and then run the `init` command in your terminal to set up a project, like so:

```
$ feast init feast_example
$ cd feast_example/feature_repo
```

The app we are building is a question-and-answer service. Q&A services can greatly benefit from a feature store's data governance tooling. For example, point-in-time joins help us answer questions like "Who is the president of x?" where the answer is expected to change over time. Instead of querying just the question, we query the question with a timestamp, and the point-in-time join will return whatever the answer to the question was in our database at that point in time. In the next listing, we pull a Q&A dataset and store it in a parquet format in the data directory of our Feast project.

Listing 6.4 Downloading the SQuAD dataset

```
import pandas as pd
from datasets import load_dataset
import datetime

from sentence_transformers import SentenceTransformer

model = SentenceTransformer("all-MiniLM-L6-v2")


def save_qa_to_parquet(path):
    squad = load_dataset("squad", split="train[:5000]")
    ids = squad["id"]
    questions = squad["question"]
    answers = [answer["text"][0] for answer in squad["answers"]]
    qa = pd.DataFrame(
        zip(ids, questions, answers),
        columns=["question_id", "questions", "answers"],
    )

    qa["embeddings"] = qa.questions.apply(lambda x: model.encode(x))
    qa["created"] = datetime.datetime.utcnow()
    qa["datetime"] = qa["created"].dt.floor("h")
    qa.to_parquet(path)


if __name__ == "__main__":
    path = "./data/qa.parquet"
    save_qa_to_parquet(path)
```

Loads SQuAD dataset

Extracts questions and answers

Creates a dataframe

Adds embeddings and timestamps

Saves to parquet

Next, we'll need to define the feature view for our feature store. A feature view is essentially like a view in a relational database. We'll define a name, the entities (which are like IDs or primary keys), the schema (which are our feature columns), and a source. We'll just be demoing using a local file store, but in production, you'd want to use one of Feast's many backend integrations with Snowflake, GCP, AWS, etc. It currently doesn't support a VectorDB backend, but I'm sure it's only a matter of time. In addition, we can add metadata to our view through tags and define a time to live (TTL), which limits how far back Feast will look when generating historical datasets. In the following listing, we define the feature view. Go ahead and add this definition into a file called qa.py in the feature_repo directory of our project.

Listing 6.5 Feast `FeatureView` definition

```
from feast import Entity, FeatureView, Field, FileSource, ValueType
from feast.types import Array, Float32, String
from datetime import timedelta

path = "./data/qa.parquet"

question = Entity(name="question_id", value_type=ValueType.STRING)

question_feature = Field(name="questions", dtype=String)

answer_feature = Field(name="answers", dtype=String)

embedding_feature = Field(name="embeddings", dtype=Array(Float32))

questions_view = FeatureView(
    name="qa",
    entities=[question],
    ttl=timedelta(days=1),
    schema=[question_feature, answer_feature, embedding_feature],
    source=FileSource(
        path=path,
        event_timestamp_column="datetime",
        created_timestamp_column="created",
        timestamp_field="datetime",
    ),
    tags={},
    online=True,
)
```

With that defined, let's go ahead and register it. We'll do that with

```
$ feast apply
```

Next, we'll want to materialize the view. In production, this is a step you'll need to schedule on a routine basis with something like cron or Prefect. Be sure to update the UTC timestamp for the end date in this command to something in the future to ensure the view collects the latest data:

```
$ feast materialize-incremental 2023-11-30T00:00:00 --views qa
```

Now all that's left is to query it! The following listing shows a simple example of pulling features to be used at inference time.

Listing 6.6 Querying a feature view at inference

```
import pandas as pd
from feast import FeatureStore

store = FeatureStore(repo_path=".")

path = "./data/qa.parquet"
ids = pd.read_parquet(path, columns=["question_id"])

feature_vectors = store.get_online_features(
    features=["qa:questions", "qa:answers", "qa:embeddings"],
    entity_rows=[{"question_id": _id} for _id in ids.question_id.to_list()],
).to_df()
print(feature_vectors.head())
```

This example will pull the most up-to-date information for the lowest possible latency at inference time. For point-in-time retrieval, you would use the `get_historical_features` method instead. In addition, in this example, we use a list of IDs for the entity rows parameter, but you could also use an SQL query making it very flexible and easy to use.

6.1.7 Retrieval-augmented generation

Retrieval-augmented generation (RAG) has become the most widely used tool to combat hallucinations in LLMs and improve the accuracy of responses in our results. Its popularity is likely because RAG is both easy to implement and quite effective. As first discussed in section 3.4.5, vector databases are a tool you'll want to have in your arsenal. One of the key reasons is that they make RAG so much easier to implement. In figure 6.4, we demonstrate a RAG system. In the preprocessing stage, we take our documents, break them up, and transform them into embeddings that we'll load into our vector database. During inference, we can take our input, encode it into an embedding, and run a similarity search across our documents in that vector database to find the nearest neighbors. This type of inference is known as semantic search. Pulling relevant documents and inserting them into our prompt will help give context to the LLM and improve the results.

We are going to demo implementing RAG using Pinecone since it will save us the effort of setting up a vector database. For listing 6.7, we will set up a Pinecone index and load a Wikipedia dataset into it. In this listing, we'll create a `WikiDataIngestion` class to handle the heavy lifting. This class will load the dataset and run through each Wikipedia page, splitting the text into consumable chunks. It will then embed these chunks and upload everything in batches. Once we have everything uploaded, we can start to make queries.

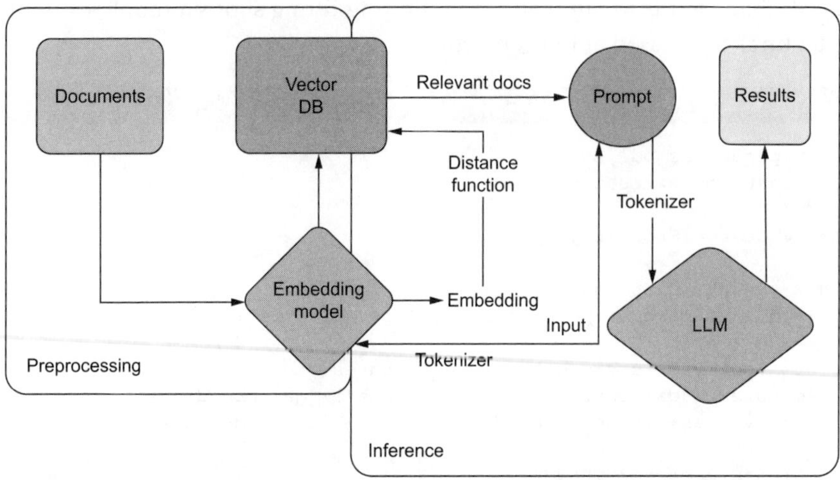

Figure 6.4 RAG system demonstrating how we use our input embeddings to run a search across our documentation, improving the results of the generated text from our LLM

You'll need an API key if you plan to follow along, so if you don't already have one, go to Pinecone's website (https://www.pinecone.io/) and create a free account, set up a starter project (free tier), and get an API key. One thing to pay attention to as you read the listing is that we'll split up the text into chunks of 400 tokens with `text_splitter`. We specifically split on tokens instead of words or characters, which allows us to properly budget inside our token limits for our model. In this example, returning the top three results will add 1,200 tokens to our request, which allows us to plan ahead of time how many tokens we'll give to the user to write their prompt.

Listing 6.7 Example setting up a Pinecone database

```
import os
import tiktoken
from datasets import load_dataset
from langchain.text_splitter import RecursiveCharacterTextSplitter
from langchain.embeddings.openai import OpenAIEmbeddings
from pinecone import Pinecone, ServerlessSpec
from sentence_transformers import SentenceTransformer

from tqdm.auto import tqdm
from uuid import uuid4

OPENAI_API_KEY = os.getenv("OPENAI_API_KEY")        # Gets openai API key from platform.openai.com
PINECONE_API_KEY = os.getenv("PINECONE_API_KEY")    # Finds API key in console at app.pinecone.io

pc = Pinecone(api_key=PINECONE_API_KEY)
```

```
class WikiDataIngestion:
    def __init__(
        self,
        index,
        wikidata=None,
        embedder=None,
        tokenizer=None,
        text_splitter=None,
        batch_limit=100,
    ):
        self.index = index
        self.wikidata = wikidata or load_dataset(
            "wikipedia", "20220301.simple", split="train[:10000]"
        )
        self.embedder = embedder or OpenAIEmbeddings(
            model="text-embedding-ada-002", openai_api_key=OPENAI_API_KEY
        )
        self.tokenizer = tokenizer or tiktoken.get_encoding("cl100k_base")
        self.text_splitter = (
            text_splitter
            or RecursiveCharacterTextSplitter(
                chunk_size=400,
                chunk_overlap=20,
                length_function=self.token_length,
                separators=["\n\n", "\n", " ", ""],
            )
        )
        self.batch_limit = batch_limit

    def token_length(self, text):
        tokens = self.tokenizer.encode(text, disallowed_special=())
        return len(tokens)

    def get_wiki_metadata(self, page):
        return {
            "wiki-id": str(page["id"]),
            "source": page["url"],
            "title": page["title"],
        }

    def split_texts_and_metadatas(self, page):
        basic_metadata = self.get_wiki_metadata(page)
        texts = self.text_splitter.split_text(page["text"])
        metadatas = [
            {"chunk": j, "text": text, **basic_metadata}
            for j, text in enumerate(texts)
        ]
        return texts, metadatas

    def upload_batch(self, texts, metadatas):
        ids = [str(uuid4()) for _ in range(len(texts))]
        embeddings = self.embedder.embed_documents(texts)
        self.index.upsert(vectors=zip(ids, embeddings, metadatas))
```

```
    def batch_upload(self):
        batch_texts = []
        batch_metadatas = []

        for page in tqdm(self.wikidata):
            texts, metadatas = self.split_texts_and_metadatas(page)

            batch_texts.extend(texts)
            batch_metadatas.extend(metadatas)

            if len(batch_texts) >= self.batch_limit:
                self.upload_batch(batch_texts, batch_metadatas)
                batch_texts = []
                batch_metadatas = []

        if len(batch_texts) > 0:
            self.upload_batch(batch_texts, batch_metadatas)


if __name__ == "__main__":
    index_name = "pincecone-llm-example"

    if index_name not in pc.list_indexes().names():    # Creates an index if it doesn't exist
        pc.create_index(
            name=index_name,
            metric="cosine",
            dimension=1536,    # 1536 dim of text-embedding-ada-002
            spec=ServerlessSpec(cloud="aws", region="us-east-1"),
        )

    index = pc.Index(index_name)    # Connects to the index and describes the stats
    print(index.describe_index_stats())

    embedder = None    # Uses a generic embedder if an openai api key is not provided
    if not OPENAI_API_KEY:
        embedder = SentenceTransformer(
            "sangmini/msmarco-cotmae-MiniLM-L12_en-ko-ja"
        )    # Also 1536 dim
        embedder.embed_documents = lambda *args, **kwargs: embedder.encode(
            *args, **kwargs
        ).tolist()

    wiki_data_ingestion = WikiDataIngestion(index, embedder=embedder)    # Ingests data and describes the stats anew
    wiki_data_ingestion.batch_upload()
    print(index.describe_index_stats())

    query = "Did Johannes Gutenberg invent the printing press?"    # Makes a query
    embeddings = wiki_data_ingestion.embedder.embed_documents(query)
    results = index.query(vector=embeddings, top_k=3, include_metadata=True)
    print(results)
```

When I ran this code, the top three query results to my question, "Did Johannes Gutenberg invent the printing press?" were the Wikipedia pages for Johannes Gutenberg, the pencil, and the printing press. Not bad! While a vector database isn't going to be able to answer the question, it's simply finding the most relevant articles based on the proximity of their embeddings to my question.

With these articles, we can then feed their embeddings into our LLM as additional context to the question to ensure a more grounded result. Since we include sources, it will even have the wiki URL it can give as a reference, and it won't just hallucinate one. By giving this context, we greatly reduce the concern about our LLM hallucinating and making up an answer.

6.1.8 LLM service libraries

If you are starting to feel a bit overwhelmed about all the tooling and features you need to implement to create an LLM service, we have some good news for you: several libraries aim to do all of this for you! Some open source libraries of note are vLLM and OpenLLM (by BentoML). Hugging Face's Text-Generation-Inference (TGI) briefly lost its open source license, but fortunately, it's available again for commercial use. There are also some start-ups building some cool tooling in this space, and we recommend checking out TitanML if you are hoping for a more managed service. These are like the tools MLServer, BentoML, and Ray Serve discussed in section 3.4.8 on deployment service, but they are designed specifically for LLMs.

Most of these toolings are still relatively new and under active development, and they are far from feature parity with each other, so pay attention to what they offer. What you can expect is that they should at least offer streaming, batching, and GPU parallelization support (something we haven't specifically talked about in this chapter), but beyond that, it's a crapshoot. Many of them still don't support several features discussed in this chapter, nor do they support every LLM architecture. What they do, though, is make deploying LLMs easy.

Using vLLM as an example, just `pip install vllm`, and then you can run

```
$ python -m vllm.entrypoints.api_server --model IMJONEZZ/ggml-openchat-8192-q4_0
```

With just one command, we now have a service up and running the model we trained in chapter 5. Go ahead and play with it; you should be able to send requests to the `/generate` endpoint like so:

```
$ curl http://localhost:8000/generate -d '{"prompt": "Which pokemon is
➥ the best?", "use_beam_search": true, "n": 4, "temperature": 0}'
```

It's very likely you won't be all that impressed with any of these toolings. Still, you should be able to build your own API and have a good sense of how to do it at this point. Now that you have a service and can even spin it up locally, let's discuss the infrastructure you need to set up to support these models for actual production usage. Remember, the better the infrastructure, the less likely you'll be called in the middle of the night when your service goes down unexpectedly. None of us want that, so let's check it out.

6.2 Setting up infrastructure

Setting up infrastructure is a critical aspect of modern software development, and we shouldn't expect machine learning to be any different. To ensure scalability, reliability, and efficient deployment of our applications, we need to plan a robust infrastructure that can handle the demands of a growing user base. This is where Kubernetes comes into play.

Kubernetes, often referred to as k8s, is an open source container orchestration platform that helps automate and manage the deployment, scaling, and management of containerized applications. It is designed to simplify the process of running and coordinating multiple containers across a cluster of servers, making it easier to scale applications and ensure high availability. We are going to talk a lot about k8s in this chapter, and while you don't need to be an expert, it will be useful to cover some basics to ensure we are all on the same page.

At its core, k8s works by grouping containers into logical units called pods, which are the smallest deployable units in the k8s ecosystem. These pods are then scheduled and managed by the k8s control plane, which oversees their deployment, scaling, and updates. This control plane consists of several components that collectively handle the orchestration and management of containers. In figure 6.5, we give an oversimplification of the k8s architecture to help readers who are unfamiliar with it.

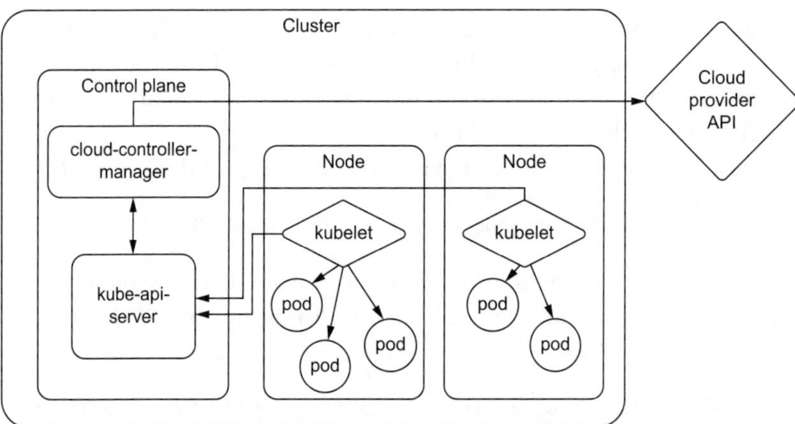

Figure 6.5 An oversimplification of the Kubernetes architecture. What you need to know is that our services run in pods, and pods run on nodes, which essentially are a machine. K8s helps us both manage the resources and handle the orchestration of deploying pods to these resources.

Using k8s, we can take advantage of features such as automatic scaling, load balancing, and service discovery, which greatly simplify the deployment and management of web applications. K8s provides a flexible and scalable infrastructure that can easily adapt to changing demands, allowing organizations to efficiently scale their applications as their user base grows. K8s offers a wide range of additional features and extensibility options, such as storage management, monitoring, and logging, which help ensure the smooth operation of web applications.

One of these extensibility options is known as custom resource definitions (CRDs). CRDs are a feature of Kubernetes that allows users to create their own specifications for custom resources, thus extending the functionalities of Kubernetes without modifying the Kubernetes source code. With a CRD defined, we can create custom objects similar to how we would create a built-in object like a pod or service. This gives k8s a lot of flexibility that we will need for different functionality throughout this chapter.

If you are new to Kubernetes, you might be scratching your head through parts of this section, and that's totally fine. Hopefully, though, you have enough knowledge to get the gist of what we will be doing in this section and why. At least you'll be able to walk away with a bunch of questions to ask your closest DevOps team member.

6.2.1 Provisioning clusters

The first thing to do when starting any project is to set up a cluster. A cluster is a collective of worker machines or nodes where we will host our applications. Creating a cluster is relatively simple; configuring it is the hard part. Of course, there have been many books written on how to do this, and the majority of considerations like networking, security, and access control are outside the scope of this book. In addition, considering the steps you take will also be different depending on the cloud provider of choice and your company's business strategy, we will focus on only the portions that we feel are needed to get you up and running, as well as any other tidbits that may make your life easier.

The first step is to create a cluster. On GCP, you would use the gcloud tool and run

```
$ gcloud container clusters create <NAME>
```

On AWS, using the eksctl tool, run

```
$ eksctl create cluster
```

On Azure, using the az cli tool, run

```
$ az group create --name=<GROUP_NAME> --location=westus
$ az aks create --resource-group=<GROUP_NAME> --name=<CLUSTER_NAME>
```

As you can see, even the first steps are highly dependent on your provider, and you can suspect that the subsequent steps will be as well. Since we realize most readers will be deploying in a wide variety of environments, we will not focus on the exact steps but hopefully give you enough context to search and discover for yourself.

Many readers, we imagine, will already have a cluster set up for them by their infrastructure teams, complete with many defaults and best practices. One of these is setting up node auto-provisioning (NAP) or cluster autoscaling. NAP allows a cluster to grow, adding more nodes as deployments demand them. This way, we only pay for nodes we actually use. It's a very convenient feature, but it often defines resource limits or restrictions on the instances available for autoscaling, and you can bet your cluster's defaults don't include accelerator or GPU instances in that pool. We'll need to fix that.

In GCP, we would create a configuration file like the one in the following listing, where we can include the GPU `resourceType`. In the example, we include T4s and both A100 types.

Listing 6.8 Example NAP config file

```
resourceLimits:
  - resourceType: 'cpu'
    minimum: 10
    maximum: 100
  - resourceType: 'memory'
    maximum: 1000
  - resourceType: 'nvidia-tesla-t4'
    maximum: 40
  - resourceType: 'nvidia-tesla-a100'
    maximum: 16
  - resourceType: 'nvidia-a100-80gb'
    maximum: 8
management:
  autoRepair: true
  autoUpgrade: true
shieldedInstanceConfig:
  enableSecureBoot: true
  enableIntegrityMonitoring: true
diskSizeGb: 100
```

You would then set this by running

```
$ gcloud container clusters update <CLUSTER_NAME> --enable-autoprovisioning -
    -autoprovisioning-config-file <FILE_NAME>
```

The real benefit of an NAP is that instead of predefining what resources are available at a fixed setting, we can set resource limits, which put a cap on the total number of GPUs that we would scale up to. They clearly define what GPUs we want and expect to be in any given cluster.

When one author was first learning about limits, he often got them confused with similar concepts—quotas, reservations, and commitments—and has seen many others just as confused. Quotas, in particular, are very similar to limits. Their main purpose is to prevent unexpected overage charges by ensuring a particular project or application doesn't consume too many resources. Unlike limits, which are set internally, quotas often require submitting a request to your cloud provider when you want to raise them. These requests help inform and are used by the cloud provider to better plan which resources to provision and put into different data centers in different regions. It's tempting to think that the cloud provider will ensure those resources are available; however, quotas never guarantee there will be enough resources in a region for your cluster to use, and you might run into `resources not found` errors way before you hit them.

While quotas and limits set an upper bound, reservations and commitments set the lower bound. Reservations are an agreement to guarantee that a certain amount of resources will always be available and often come with the caveat that you will be paying for these resources regardless of whether you end up using them. Commitments are similar to reservations but are often longer-term contracts, usually coming with a discounted price.

6.2.2 Autoscaling

One of the big selling points to setting up a k8s cluster is autoscaling. Autoscaling is an important ingredient in creating robust production-grade services. The main reason is that we never expect any service to receive static request volume. If anything else, you should expect more volume during the day and less at night while people sleep. So we'll want our service to spin up more replicas during peak hours to improve performance and spin down replicas during off hours to save money, not to mention the need to handle bursty workloads that often threaten to crash a service at any point.

Knowing your service will automatically provision more resources and set up additional deployments based on the needs of the application is what allows many infrastructure engineers to sleep peacefully at night. The catch is that it requires an engineer to know what those needs are and ensure everything is configured correctly. While autoscaling provides flexibility, the real business value comes from the cost savings. Most engineers think about autoscaling in terms of scaling up to prevent meltdowns, but even more important to the business is the ability to scale down, freeing up resources and cutting costs.

One of the main reasons cloud computing and technologies like Kubernetes have become essential in modern infrastructures is because autoscaling is built in. Autoscaling is a key feature of Kubernetes, and with horizontal pod autoscalers (HPAs), you can easily adjust the number of replicas of your application based on two native resources: CPU and memory usage, as shown in figure 6.6. However, in a book about putting LLMs in production, scaling based on CPU and memory alone will never be enough. We will need to scale based on custom metrics, specifically GPU utilization.

Setting up autoscaling based on GPU metrics is going to take a bit more work and requires setting up several services. It'll become clear why we need each service as we discuss them, but the good news is that by the end, you'll be able to set up your services to scale based on any metric, including external events such as messages from a message broker, requests to an HTTP endpoint, and data from a queue.

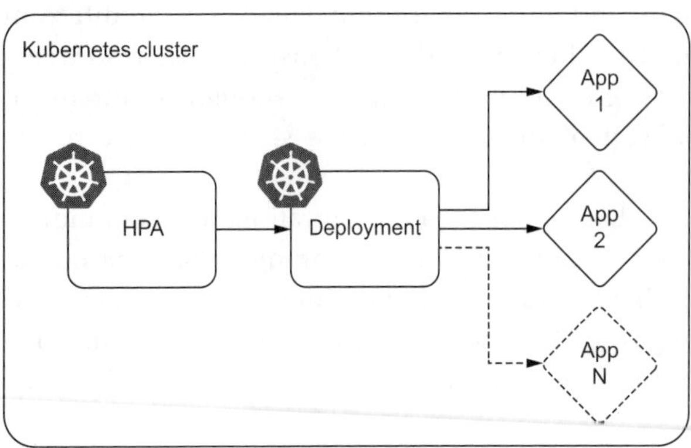

Figure 6.6 Basic autoscaling using the in-built k8s horizontal pod autoscaler (HPA). The HPA watches CPU and memory resources and will tell the deployment service to increase or decrease the number of replicas.

The first service we'll need is one that can collect the GPU metrics. For this, we have NVIDIA's Data Center GPU Manager (DCGM), which provides a metrics exporter that can export GPU metrics. DCGM exposes a host of GPU metrics, including temperature and power usage, which can create some fun dashboards, but the most useful metrics for autoscaling are utilization and memory utilization.

From here, the data will go to a service like Prometheus. Prometheus is a popular open source monitoring system used to monitor Kubernetes clusters and the applications running on them. Prometheus collects metrics from various sources and stores them in a time-series database, where they can be analyzed and queried. Prometheus can collect metrics directly from Kubernetes APIs and from applications running on the cluster using a variety of collection mechanisms such as exporters, agents, and sidecar containers. It's essentially an aggregator of services like DCGM, including features like alerting and notification. It also exposes an HTTP API for service for external tooling like Grafana to query and create graphs and dashboards with.

While Prometheus provides a way to store metrics and monitor our service, the metrics aren't exposed to the internals of Kubernetes. For an HPA to gain access, we will need to register yet another service to either the custom metrics API or external metrics API. By default, Kubernetes comes with the metrics.k8s.io endpoint that exposes resource metrics, CPU, and memory utilization. To accommodate the need to scale deployments and pods on custom metrics, two additional APIs were introduced: custom.metrics.k9s.io and external.metrics.k8s.io. There are some limitations to this setup, as currently, only one "adapter" API service can be registered at a time for either one. This limitation mostly becomes a problem if you ever decide to change this endpoint from one provider to another.

For this service, Prometheus provides the Prometheus Adapter, which works well, but from our experience, it wasn't designed for production workloads. Alternatively, we would recommend KEDA. KEDA (Kubernetes Event-Driven Autoscaling) is an open source project that provides event-driven autoscaling for Kubernetes. It offers more flexibility in terms of the types of custom metrics that can be used for autoscaling.

While Prometheus Adapter requires configuring metrics inside a ConfigMap, any metric already exposed through the Prometheus API can be used in KEDA, providing a more streamlined and friendly user experience. It also offers scaling to and from 0, which isn't available through HPAs, allowing you to turn off a service completely if there is no traffic. That said, you can't scale from 0 on resource metrics like CPU and memory and, by extension, GPU metrics, but it is useful when you are using traffic metrics or a queue to scale.

Putting this all together, you'll end up with the architecture shown in figure 6.7. Compared to figure 6.6, you'll notice at the bottom that DCGM is managing our GPU metrics and feeding them into Prometheus Operator. From Prometheus, we can set up external dashboards with tools like Grafana. Internal to k8s, we'll use KEDA to set up a custom.metrics.k9s.io API to return these metrics so we can autoscale based on the GPU metrics. KEDA has several CRDs, one of which is a `ScaledObject`, which creates the HPA and provides the additional features.

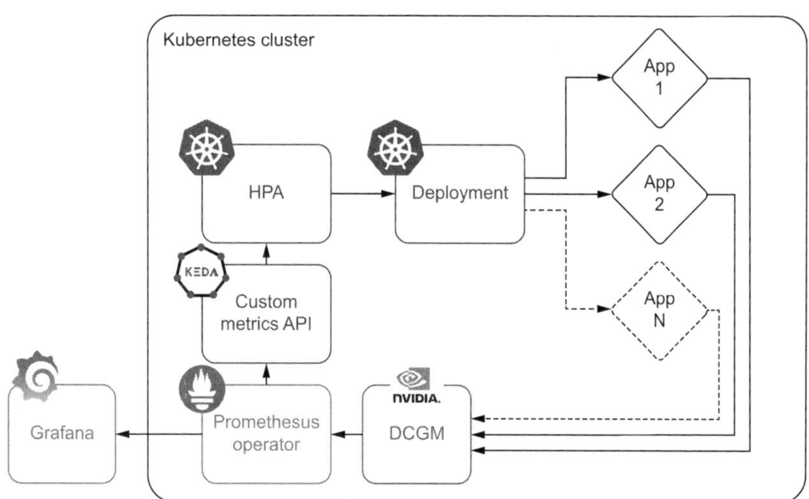

Figure 6.7 Autoscaling based on a custom metric like GPU utilization requires several extra tools to work, including NVIDIA's DCGM, a monitoring system like Prometheus Operator, and a custom metrics API like that provided by KEDA.

While autoscaling provides many benefits, it's important to be aware of its limitations and potential problems, which are only exacerbated by LLM inference services. Proper configuration of the HPA is often an afterthought for many applications, but it becomes mission-critical when dealing with LLMs. LLMs take longer to become fully operational, as the GPUs need to be initialized and model weights loaded into memory; these aren't services that can turn on a dime, which often can cause problems when scaling up if not properly prepared for. Additionally, if the system scales down too aggressively, it may result in instances being terminated before completing their assigned tasks, leading to data loss or other problems. Lastly, flapping is just such a concern that can arise from incorrect autoscaling configurations. Flapping happens when the number of replicas keeps oscillating, booting up a new service only to terminate it before it can serve any inferences.

There are essentially five parameters to tune when setting up an HPA:

- Target parameter
- Target threshold
- Min pod replicas
- Max pod replicas
- Scaling policies

Let's take a look at each of them in turn so you can be sure your system is properly configured.

TARGET PARAMETER

The target parameter is the most important metric to consider when ensuring your system is properly configured. If you followed the previously listed steps in section 6.2.2, your system is now ready to autoscale based on GPU metrics, so this should be easy, right? Not so fast! Scaling based on GPU utilization is going to be the most common and straightforward path, but the first thing we need to do is ensure the GPU is the actual bottleneck in our service. It's pretty common to see eager young engineers throw a lot of expensive GPUs onto a service but forget to include adequate CPU and memory capacity. CPU and memory will still be needed to handle the API layer, such as taking in requests, handling multiple threads, and communicating with the GPUs. If there aren't enough resources, these layers can quickly become a bottleneck, and your application will be throttled way before the GPU utilization is ever affected, ensuring the system will never actually autoscale. While you could switch the target parameter on the autoscaler, CPU and memory are cheap compared to GPU resources, so it'd be better to allocate more of them for your application.

In addition, there are cases where other metrics make more sense. If your LLM application takes most of its requests from a streaming or batch service, it can be more prudent to scale based on metrics that tell you a DAG is running or an upstream queue is filling up—especially if these metrics give you an early signal and allow you more time to scale up in advance.

Another concern when selecting the metric is its stability. For example, an individual GPU's utilization tends to be close to either 0% or 100%. This can cause problems for the autoscaler, as the metric oscillates between an on and off state, as will its recommendation to add or remove replicas, causing flapping. Generally, flapping is avoided by taking the average utilization across all GPUs running the service. Using the average will stabilize the metric when you have a lot of GPUs, but it could still be a problem when the service has scaled down. If you are still running into problems, you'll want to use an average-over-time aggregation, which will tell you the utilization for each GPU over a time frame—say, the last 5 minutes. For CPU utilization, average-over-time aggregation is built into the Kubernetes HPA and can be set with the `horizontal-pod-autoscaler-cpu-initialization-period` flag. For custom metrics, you'll need to set it in your metric query (for Prometheus, it would be the `avg_over_time` aggregation function).

Lastly, it's worth calling out that most systems allow you to autoscale based on multiple metrics. So you *could* autoscale based on both CPU and GPU utilization, as an example. However, we would recommend avoiding these setups unless you know what you are doing. Your autoscaler might be set up that way, but in actuality, your service will likely only ever autoscale based on just one of the metrics due to service load, and it's best to make sure that metric is the more costly resource for cost-engineering purposes.

TARGET THRESHOLD

The target threshold tells your service at what point to start upscaling. For example, if you are scaling based on the average GPU utilization and your threshold is set to 30, then a new replica will be booted up to take on the extra load when the average GPU utilization is above 30%. The formula that governs this is quite simple and is as follows:

$$desiredReplicas = ceil[currentReplicas \times (currentMetricValue / desiredMetricValue)]$$

NOTE You can learn more about the algorithm at https://mng.bz/x64g.

This can be hard to tune in correctly, but here are some guiding principles. If the traffic patterns you see involve a lot of constant small bursts of traffic, a lower value, around 50, might be more appropriate. This setting ensures you start to scale up more quickly, avoiding unreliability problems, and you can also scale down more quickly, cutting costs. If you have a constant steady flow of traffic, higher values, around 80, will work well. Outside of testing your autoscaler, it's best to avoid extremely low values, as they can increase your chances of flapping. You should also avoid extremely high values, as they may allow the active replicas to be overwhelmed before new ones start to boot up, which can cause unreliability or downtime. It's also important to remember that due to the nature of pipeline parallel workflows when using a distributed GPU setup, there will always be a bubble, as discussed in section 3.3.2. As a result, your system will never reach 100% GPU utilization, and you will start to hit problems earlier than expected. Depending on how big your bubble is, you will need to adjust the target threshold accordingly.

MINIMUM POD REPLICAS

Minimum pod replicas determine the number of replicas of your service that will always be running. This setting is your baseline. It's important to make sure it's set slightly above your baseline of incoming requests. Too often, this is set strictly to meet baseline levels of traffic or just below, but a steady state for incoming traffic is rarely all that steady. This is where a lot of oscillating can happen, as you are more likely to see many small surges in traffic than large spikes. However, you don't want to set it too high, as this will tie up valuable resources in the cluster and increase costs.

MAXIMUM POD REPLICAS

Maximum pod replicas determine the number of replicas your system will run at peak capacity. You should set this number to be just above your peak traffic requirements. Setting it too low could lead to reliability problems, performance degradation, and downtime during high-traffic periods. Setting it too high could lead to resource waste, running more pods than necessary, and delaying the detection of real problems. For example, if your application was under a DDoS attack, your system might scale to handle the load, but it would likely cost you severely and hide the problem. With LLMs, you also need to be cautious not to overload the underlying cluster and make sure you have enough resources in your quotas to handle the peak load.

SCALING POLICIES

Scaling policies define the behavior of the autoscaler, allowing you to finetune how long to wait before scaling and how quickly it scales. This setting is usually ignored, and safely so for most setups because the defaults for these settings tend to be pretty good for the typical application. However, relying on the default would be a major mistake for an LLM service since it takes so long to deploy.

The first setting you'll want to adjust is the stabilization window, which determines how long to wait before taking a new scaling action. You can set a different stabilization window for upscaling and downscaling tasks. The default upscaling window is 0 seconds, which should not need to be touched if your target parameter has been set correctly. The default downscaling window is 300 seconds, which is likely too short for our use case. You'll typically want this at least as long as it takes your service to deploy and then a little bit more. Otherwise, you'll be adding replicas only to remove them before they have a chance to do anything.

The next parameter you'll want to adjust is the scale-down policy, which defaults to 100% of pods every 15 seconds. As a result, any temporary drop in traffic could result in all your extra pods above the minimum being terminated immediately. For our case, it's much safer to slow this down since terminating a pod takes only a few seconds, but booting one up can take minutes, making it a semi-irreversible decision. The exact policy will depend on your traffic patterns, but in general, we want to have a little more patience. You can adjust how quickly pods will be terminated and the magnitude by the number or percentage of pods. For example, we could configure the policy to allow only one pod each minute or 10% of pods every 5 minutes to be terminated.

6.2.3 Rolling updates

Rolling updates or rolling upgrades is a strategy that gradually implements the new version of an application to reduce downtime and maximize agility. It works by gradually creating new instances and turning off the old ones, replacing them in a methodical manner. This update approach allows the system to remain functional and accessible to users even during the update process, otherwise known as zero downtime. Rolling updates also make it easier to catch bugs before they have too much effect and roll back faulty deployments.

Rolling updates is a feature built into k8s and another major reason for its widespread use and popularity. Kubernetes provides an automated and simplified way to carry out rolling updates. The rolling updates ensure that Kubernetes incrementally updates pod instances with new ones during deployment. The following listing shows an example LLM deployment implementing rolling updates; the relevant configuration is under the `spec.strategy` section.

Listing 6.9 Example deployment config with rolling update

```
apiVersion: apps/v1
kind: Deployment
metadata:
  name: llm-application
spec:
  replicas: 5
  strategy:
    rollingUpdate:
      maxSurge: 1
      maxUnavailable: 3
  selector:
    matchLabels:
      app: llm-app
  template:
    metadata:
      labels:
        app: llm-app
    spec:
      containers:
      - name: llm-gpu-app-container
        image: llm-gpu-application:v2
        resources:
          limits:
            nvidia.com/gpu: 8
```

You'll notice that there are two main parameters you can adjust for a rolling update: `maxSurge` and `maxUnavailable`. These can either be set to a whole number, like in our example, describing the number of instances, or a fraction indicating a percentage of total instances. In the example, you'll notice we set `maxSurge` to `1`, meaning even though we would normally run with five replicas, we could surge to six during a deployment, allowing us to turn on a new one before turning any off. Normally, you might want to set this higher, as it allows for a quicker rolling update. Otherwise, we'll have to replace pods one at a time. The reason it's low, you might have noticed, is that we are deploying a rather large LLM that requires eight GPUs. If these are A100s, it's likely going to be hard to find an extra eight GPUs not being used.

GPU resources cannot be shared among containers, and container orchestration can become a major challenge in such deployments, which is why `maxUnavailable` is set to `3`. What we are saying here is that three out of the five expected replicas can go down during a deployment. In other words, we are going to drop the total number of replicas for a little bit before re-creating them. For reliability reasons, we typically prefer adding extra replicas first, so to go down instead is a difficult decision, one you'll want to confirm you can afford to do in your own deployment. The reason we are doing so here is to ensure that there are GPU resources available. In essence, to balance resource utilization, it might be necessary to set `maxUnavailable` to a high value and adjust `maxSurge` to a lower number to downscale old versions quickly and free up resources for new ones.

This advice is the opposite of what you'd do in most applications, so we understand if it makes you uneasy. If you'd like to ensure smoother deployments, you'll need to budget for extra GPUs to be provisioned in your cluster strictly for deployment purposes. However, depending on how often you are updating the model itself, paying for expensive GPUs to sit idle simply to make deployments smoother may not be cost-advantageous. Often, the LLM itself doesn't receive that many updates, so assuming you are using an inference graph (discussed in the next section), most of the updates will be to the API, prompts, or surrounding application.

In addition, we recommend you always perform such operations cautiously in a staging environment first to understand its effect. Catching a deployment problem in staging will save you a headache or two. It's also useful to troubleshoot the `maxUnavailable` and `maxSurge` parameters in staging, but it's often hard to get a one-to-one comparison to production since staging is often resource-constrained.

6.2.4 Inference graphs

Inference graphs are the crème filling of a donut, the muffin top of a muffin, and the toppings on a pizza: they are just phenomenal. Inference graphs allow us to create sophisticated flow diagrams at inference in a resource-saving way. Consider figure 6.8, which shows us the building blocks for any inference graph.

Generally, any time you have more than one model, it's useful to consider an inference graph architecture. Your standard LLM setup is usually already at least two models: an encoder and the language model itself.

Usually, when we see LLMs deployed in the wild, these two models are deployed together. You send text data to your system, and it returns generated text. It's often no big deal, but when deployed as a sequential inference graph instead of a packaged service, we get some added bonuses. First, the encoder is usually much faster than the LLM, so we can split them up since you may only need one encoder instance for every two to three LLM instances. Encoders are so small that this doesn't necessarily help us out that much, but it saves the hassle of redeploying the entire LLM if we decide to deploy a new encoder model version. In addition, an inference graph will set up an individual API for each model, which allows us to hit the LLM and encoder separately.

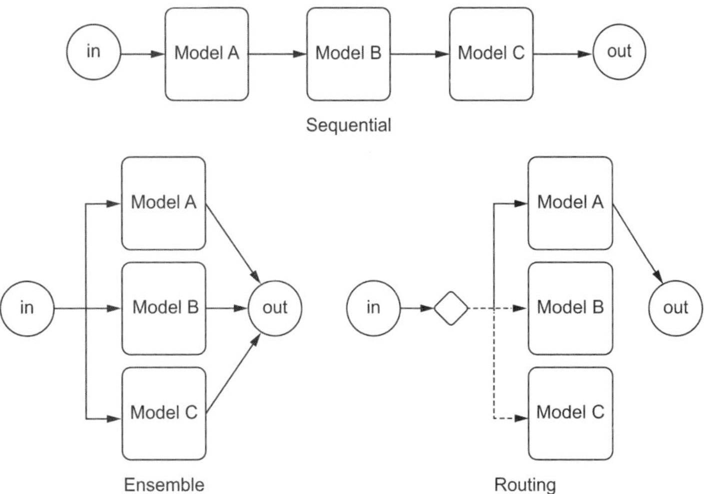

Figure 6.8 The three types of inference graph building blocks. Sequential allows us to run one model before the other, which is useful for preprocessing steps like generating embeddings. Ensembles allow us to pool several models together to learn from each and combine their results. Routing allows us to send traffic to specific models based on some criteria, often used for multi-armed bandit optimization.

This is really useful if we have a bunch of data we'd like to preprocess and save in a VectorDB; we can use the same encoder we already have deployed. We can then pull this data and send it directly into the LLM.

The biggest benefit of an inference graph is that it allows us to separate the API and the LLM. The API sitting in front of the LLM is likely to change much more often as you tweak prompts, add features, and fix bugs. The ability to update the API without having to deploy the LLM will save your team a lot of effort.

Let's now consider figure 6.9, which provides an example inference graph deployment using Seldon. In this example, we have an encoder model, an LLM, a classifier model, and a simple API that combines the results. Whereas we would have to build a container and the interface for each of these models, Seldon creates an orchestrator that handles communication between a user's request and each node in the graph.

NOTE Seldon is an open source platform designed for deploying and managing machine learning models in production. It offers tools and capabilities to help organizations streamline the deployment and scaling of machine learning and deep learning models in a Kubernetes-based environment. It offers k8s CRDs to implement inference graphs.

If you are wondering how to create this, listing 6.10 shows an example configuration that would create this exact setup. We simply define the containers in the graph and

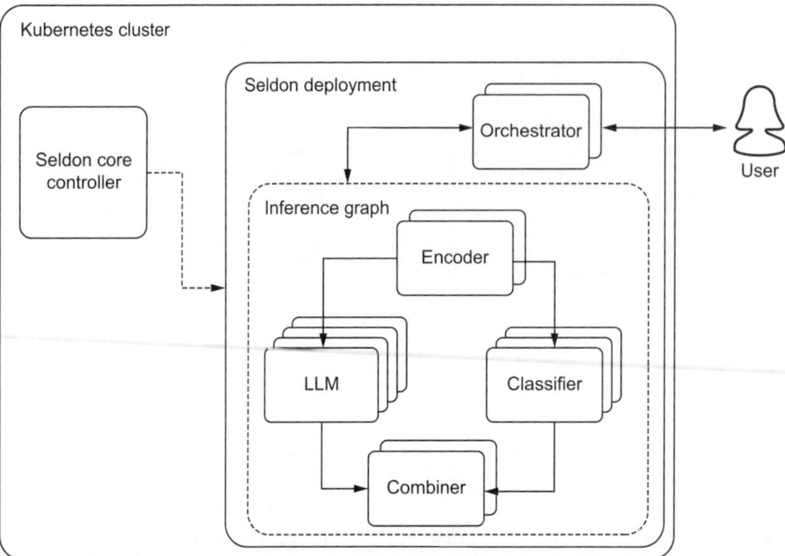

Figure 6.9 An example inference graph deployment using Seldon. A Seldon Deployment is a Kubernetes CRD that extends a regular Kubernetes deployment and adds an orchestrator that ensures the proper communication between all the models are run in graph order.

their relationship inside the graph. You'll notice `apiVersion` defines the CRD from Seldon, which allows us to use `SeldonDeployment`, which is just an extension of the k8s regular Deployment object. In the listing, you might notice that the combiner is the parent to the LLM and classifier models, which feels backwards from how we visualize it in figure 6.9. This is because a component will only ever have one parent, but can have multiple children, so a `COMBINER` is always a parent node even though functionally it's the same. Setting up a graph can often be confusing, so I recommend you check the documentation frequently and often.

Listing 6.10 An example `SeldonDeployment` configuration file

```
apiVersion: machinelearning.seldon.io/v1alpha2
kind: SeldonDeployment
metadata:
  name: example-seldon-inference-graph
spec:
  name: example-deployment
  predictors:
  - componentSpecs:
    - spec:
        containers:
        - name: encoder
          image: encoder_image:latest
        - name: LLM
          image: llm_image:latest
```

```
      - name: classifier
        image: classifier_image:latest
      - name: combiner
        image: combiner_image:latest
graph:
  name: encoder
  type: MODEL
  endpoint:
    type: REST
  children:
    - name: combiner
      type: COMBINER
      children:
        - name: LLM
          type: MODEL
          endpoint:
            type: REST
          children: []
        - name: classifier
          type: MODEL
          endpoint:
            type: REST
          children: []
name: example
replicas: 1
```

If you've deployed enough machine learning systems, you've realized that many of them require complex systems, and inference graphs make it easy, or at least easier. And that is a big difference. Although inference graphs are a smarter way to deploy complex machine learning systems, it's always important to ask yourself if the extra complexity is actually needed. Even with tools like inference graphs, it's better to keep things simple whenever possible.

6.2.5 *Monitoring*

As with any product or service deployed into production, monitoring is critical to ensure reliability, performance, and compliance to service level agreements and objectives are met. As with any service, we care about monitoring typical performance metrics like queries per second (QPS), latency, and response code counts. We also care about monitoring our resources with metrics like CPU utilization, percentage of memory used, GPU utilization, and GPU temperature, among many more. When any of these metrics start to fail, it often indicates a catastrophic failure of some sort and will need to be addressed quickly.

For these metrics, any software engineering team should have plenty of experience working with these using tools like Prometheus and Grafana or the ELK stack (Elasticsearch, Logstash, and Kibana). You will benefit immensely by taking advantage of the systems that are likely already in place. If they aren't in place, we already went over how to set up the GPU metrics for monitoring back in section 6.2.2, and that system should be useful for monitoring other resources.

However, with any ML project, we have additional concerns that traditional monitoring tools miss, which leads to silent failures. This usually comes from data drift and performance decay, where a model continues to function but starts to do so poorly and no longer meets quality expectations. LLMs are particularly susceptible to data drift since language is in constant flux, as new words are created and old words change meaning all the time. Thus, we often need both a system monitoring solution and an ML monitoring solution.

Monitoring data drift is relatively easy and well-studied for numerical datasets, but monitoring unstructured text data provides an extra challenge. We've already discussed ways to evaluate language models in chapter 4, and we'll need to use similar practices to evaluate and monitor models in production. One of our favorite tools for monitoring drift detection is whylogs due to its efficient nature of capturing summary statistics at scale. Adding LangKit to the mix instantly and easily allows us to track several useful metrics for LLMs, such as readability, complexity, toxicity, and even similarity scores to known prompt injection attacks. In the following listing, we demonstrate a simple application that logs and monitors text data using whylogs and LangKit.

Listing 6.11 Using whylogs and LangKit to monitor text data

```
import os
import pandas as pd

import whylogs as why
from langkit import llm_metrics
from datasets import load_dataset

OUTPUT_DIR = "logs"


class LoggingApp:
    def __init__(self):
        """
        Sets up a logger that collects profiles and writes them
        locally every 5 minutes. By setting the schema with langkit
        we get useful metrics for LLMs.
        """
        self.logger = why.logger(
            mode="rolling",
            interval=5,
            when="M",
            base_name="profile_",
            schema=llm_metrics.init(),
        )
        self.logger.append_writer("local", base_dir=OUTPUT_DIR)

    def close(self):
        self.logger.close()
```

```
    def consume(self, text):
        self.logger.log(text)


def driver(app):
    """Driver function to run the app manually"""
    data = load_dataset(
        "shahules786/OA-cornell-movies-dialog",
        split="train",
        streaming=True,
    )
    data = iter(data)
    for text in data:
        app.consume(text)


if __name__ == "__main__":
    app = LoggingApp()          <-- Runs app manually
    driver(app)
    app.close()                                          Prevents truncation
                                                         of columns
    pd.set_option("display.max_columns", None)     <--
                                                         Gets the first profile
    all_files = [                                        and shows the results
        f for f in os.listdir(OUTPUT_DIR) if f.startswith("profile_")
    ]
    path = os.path.join(OUTPUT_DIR, all_files[0])
    result_view = why.read(path).view()
    print(result_view.to_pandas().head())
```

The generated text is

```
# ...
# column        udf/flesch_reading_ease:cardinality/est
# conversation                               425.514743
# ...
# column        udf/jailbreak_similarity:cardinality/est
# conversation                               1172.226702
# ...
# column        udf/toxicity:types/string  udf/toxicity:types/tensor
# conversation                          0                          0
```

While this is just a demo using a text dataset, you can see how it would be beneficial to monitor the incoming prompts and outgoing generated text for metrics such as readability, complexity, and toxicity. These monitoring tools will help give you a handle on whether or not your LLM service is starting to fail silently.

When monitoring in production, we must be mindful of the effect latency may have on our service. LangKit uses several lightweight models to evaluate the text for the advanced metrics. While we haven't noticed significant memory effects, there is a very slight effect on latency when evaluating logs in the direct inference path. To avoid this, we can take it out of the inference path and into what is called a sidecar.

It's not uncommon to see ML teams mistakenly place data quality checks in the critical path. Their intentions may be good (to ensure only clean data runs through a model), but on the off chance that a client sends bad data, it would often be better to just send a 400 or 500 error response than to add expensive latency costs to the good requests. In fact, many applications move monitoring out of the critical path entirely, opting to process it in parallel. The simplest way to do this is to use a Kubernetes sidecar, which is depicted in figure 6.10. You can do this with tools that specialize in this, like fluentd; whylogs also offers a container you can run as a sidecar.

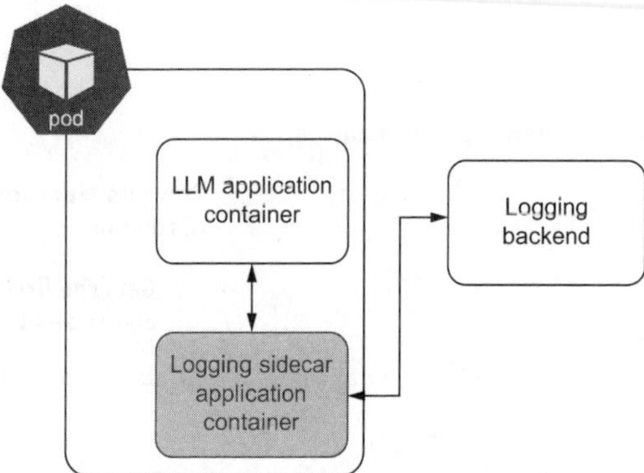

Figure 6.10 An example Kubernetes sidecar container, which takes logging out of the critical path. The logging agent would be a tool like a whylogs container or fluentd that captures specific requests or all stdout print statements, processes them, and forwards them to a logging backend like WhyLabs or Prometheus.

There are different sidecar configurations, but the main gist is that a logging container will run in the same k8s pod, and instead of the main app writing to a logs file, this sidecar acts as an intermediate step, first processing and cleaning the data, which it can then send directly to a backend or write to a logs file itself.

> **NOTE** You can learn more about Kubernetes logging architectures in its docs here: https://mng.bz/Aaog.

Now that we know more about setting up our infrastructure, including provisioning a cluster and implementing features like GPU autoscaling and monitoring, you should be set to deploy your LLM service and ensure it is reliable and scalable. Next, let's talk about different challenges you are likely to face and methodologies to address these problems.

6.3 Production challenges

While we've covered how to get a service up and running, nevertheless, you will find a never-ending host of hurdles you'll need to jump over when it comes to deploying models and maintaining them in production. Some of these challenges include updating, planning for large loads, poor latency, acquiring resources, and more. To help, we wanted to address some of the most common problems and give you tips on how to handle them.

6.3.1 Model updates and retraining

We recently discussed ML monitoring, watching your model for silent failures and data drift, but what do you do when you notice the model has gone belly up? We've seen in many traditional ML implementations that the answer is to simply retrain the model on the latest data and redeploy. And that works well when you are working with a small ARIMA model; in fact, we can often set up a CI/CD pipeline to run whenever our model degrades without any human oversight. But with a massive LLM? It doesn't make any sense.

Of course, we aren't going to retrain from scratch, and we likely need to finetune our model, but the reason it doesn't make sense is seen when we ask ourselves just what exactly the latest data is. The data we need to finetune the model is extremely important, and so it becomes necessary for us to take a step back and really diagnose the problem. What are the edge cases our model is failing on? What is it still doing well? How exactly have incoming prompts changed? Depending on the answers, we might not need to finetune at all. For example, consider a Q&A bot that is no longer effective at answering current event questions as time goes on. We probably don't want to retrain a model on a large corpus of the latest news articles. Instead, we would get much better results by ensuring our RAG system is up to date. Similarly, there are likely plenty of times that simply tweaking prompts will do the trick.

In the cases where finetuning is the correct approach, you'll need to think a lot about exactly what data you might be missing, as well as how any major updates might affect downstream systems, like finely tuned prompts. For example, when using knowledge distillation, this consideration can be particularly annoying. You will likely notice the problem in your student model but then must decide whether you need to retrain the student or the teacher. With any updates to the teacher model, you'll need to ensure progress to the student model.

Overall, it's best to take a proactive approach to LLM model updates instead of a purely reactionary one. A system that often works well is to establish business practices and protocols to update the model on a periodic basis, say once a quarter or once a month. During the time between updates, the team will focus on monitoring cases where the model performs poorly and gather appropriate data and examples to make updating smooth. This type of practice will help you prevent silent failures and ensure your model isn't just maintained but improving.

6.3.2 Load testing

Load testing is a type of performance testing that assesses how well a service or system will perform under—wait for it—load. The primary goal of load testing is to ensure the system can handle the expected workload without performance degradation or failure. Doing it early can ensure we avoid bottlenecks and scalability problems. Since LLM services can be both expensive and resource intensive, it's even more important to ensure you load test the system before releasing your LLM application to production or before an expected peak in traffic, like during a Black Friday sales event.

Load testing an LLM service, for the most part, is like load testing any other service and follows these basic steps:

1. Set up the service in a staging environment.
2. Run a script to periodically send requests to the service.
3. Increase requests until the service fails or autoscales.
4. Log metrics.
5. Analyze results.

Which metrics you log depends on your service and what you are testing. The main metrics to watch are latency and throughput at failure, as these can be used to extrapolate to determine how many replicas you'll need to handle peak load. Latency is the total time it takes for a request to be completed, and throughput tells us the queries per second (QPS), both of which are extremely important metrics when analyzing our system. Still, since many LLM services offer streaming responses, they don't help us understand the user experience. A few more metrics you'll want to capture to understand your perceived responsiveness are time to first token (TTFT) and tokens per second (TPS). TTFT gives us the perceived latency; it tells us how long it takes until the user starts to receive feedback, while TPS tells us how fast the stream is. For English, you'll want a TPS of about 11 tokens per second, which is a little faster than most people read. If it's slower than this, your users might get bored as they wait for tokens to be returned.

Related to TPS, I've seen several tools or reports use the inverse metric, time per output token (TPOT), or intertoken latency (ITL), but we're not a fan of these metrics or their hard-to-remember names. You'll also want to pay attention to resource metrics, CPU and GPU utilization, and memory usage. You'll want to ensure these aren't being hammered under base load conditions, as this can lead to hardware failures. These are also key to watch when you are testing autoscaling performance.

One of my favorite tools for load testing is Locust. Locust is an open source load-testing tool that makes it easy to scale and distribute running load tests over multiple machines, allowing you to simulate millions of users. Locust does all the hard work for you and comes with many handy features, like a nice web user interface and the ability to run custom load shapes. It's easy to run in Docker or Kubernetes, making it extremely accessible to run where you need it—in production. The only main downside we've run across is that it doesn't support customizable metrics, so we'll have to roll our own to add TTFT and TPS.

To get started, simply `pip install locust`. Next, we'll create our test. In listing 6.12, we show how to create a locust file that will allow users to prompt an LLM streaming service. It's a bit more complicated than many locust files we've used simply because we need to capture our custom metrics for streaming, so you can imagine how straightforward they normally are. Locust already captures a robust set of metrics, so you won't have to deal with this often. You'll notice in the listing that we are saving these custom metrics to `stats.csv` file, but if you were running Locust in a distributed fashion, it'd be better to save it to a database of some sort.

Listing 6.12 Load testing with Locust

```
import time
from locust import HttpUser, task, events

stat_file = open("stats.csv", "w")                 # Creates a CSV file to
stat_file.write("Latency,TTFT,TPS\n")              # store custom stats


class StreamUser(HttpUser):
    @task
    def generate(self):
        token_count = 0                             # Initiates the test
        start = time.time()

        with self.client.post(                      # Makes request
            "/generate",
            data='{"prompt": "Salt Lake City is a"}',
            catch_response=True,
            stream=True,
        ) as response:
            first_response = time.time()
            for line in response.iter_lines(decode_unicode=True):
                token_count += 1

        end = time.time()                           # Finishes and
        latency = end - start                       # calculates the stats
        ttft = first_response - start
        tps = token_count / (end - first_response)

        stat_file.write(f"{latency},{ttft},{tps}\n")      # Saves stats


# Close stats file when Locust quits
@events.quitting.add_listener
def close_stats_file(environment):
    stat_file.close()
```

Before you run it, you'll need to have an LLM service up. For this example, we'll run the code from listing 6.3 in section 6.1.6, which spins up a very simple LLM service. With a service up and our test defined, we need to run it. To spin up the Locust service, run the `locust` command. You should then be able to navigate to the web UI in your browser. See the following example:

```
$ locust -f locustfile.py
> locust.main: Starting web interface at http://0.0.0.0:8089 (accepting
```

```
➥ connections from all network interfaces)
> locust.main: Starting Locust 2.17.0
```

Once in the web UI, you can explore running different tests; you'll just need to point Locust at the host where your LLM service is running, which for us should be running on localhost on port 8000 or for the full socket address we combined them for: http://0.0.0.0:8000. In figure 6.11, you can see an example test where we increased the active users to 50 at a spawn rate of 1 per second. You can see that on the hardware, this simple service starts to hit a bottleneck at around 34 users, where the QPS starts to

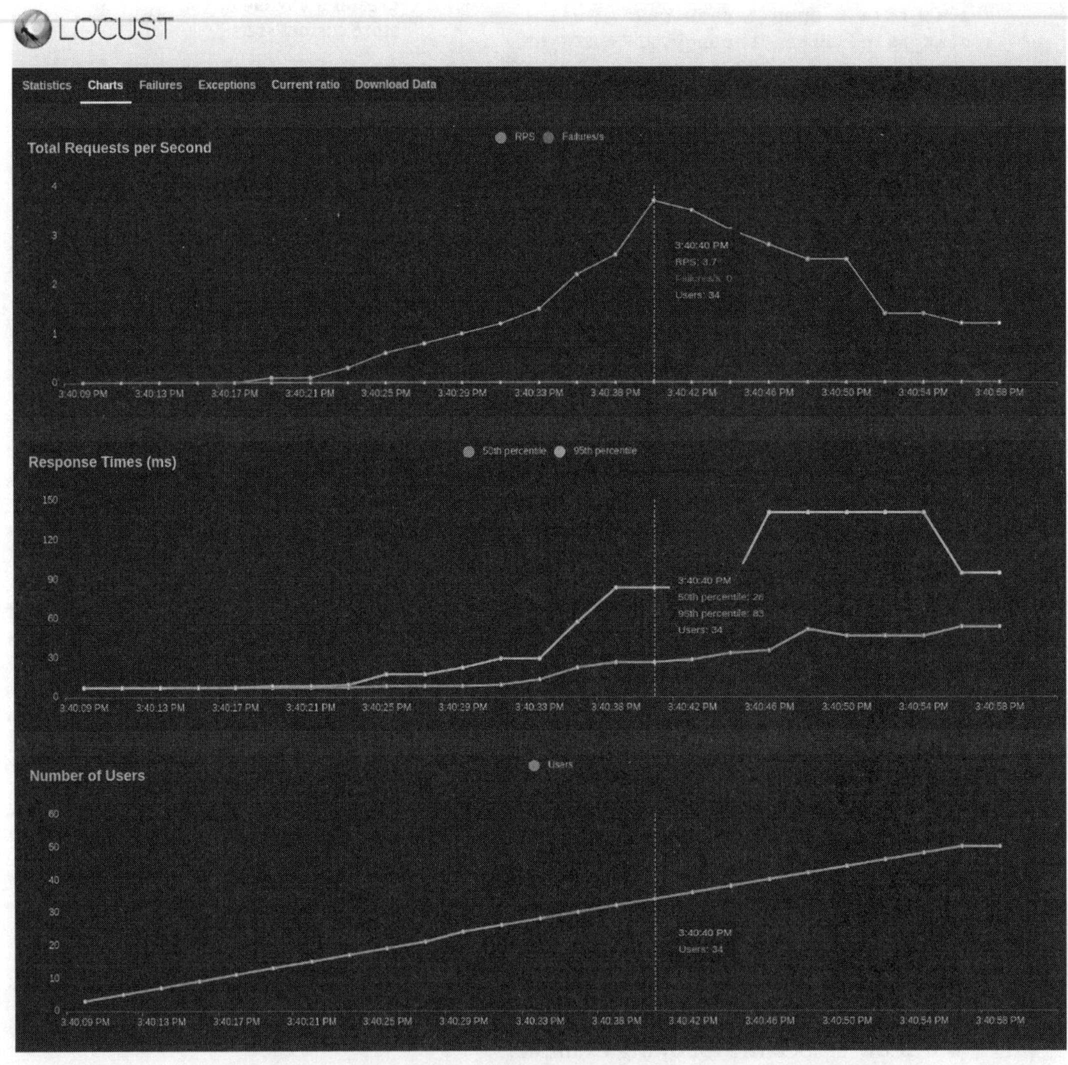

Figure 6.11 Locust test interface demoing an example run increasing the number of users to 50 at a spawn rate of 1 per second. The requests per second peaks at 34 users, indicating a bottleneck for our service.

decrease, as it's no longer able to keep up with the load. You'll also notice response times slowly creep up in response to heavier load. We could continue to push the number of users up until we started to see failures, but overall, this test was informative and a great first test drive.

In addition to manually running load tests, we can run Locust in a headless mode for automated tests. The following code is a simple command to run the exact same test as seen in figure 6.11; however, since we won't be around to see the report, we'll save the data to CSV files labeled with the prefix `llm` to be processed and analyzed later. There will be four files in addition to the stats CSV file we were already generating:

```
$ locust -f locustfile.py --host http://0.0.0.0:8000 --csv=llm --
➥ headless -u 50 -r 1 -t 10m
```

Now that you are able to load test your LLM service, you should be able to figure out how many replicas you'll need to meet throughput requirements. It's just a matter of spinning up more services. But what do you do when you find out your service doesn't meet latency requirements? Well, that's a bit tougher, so let's discuss it in the next section.

6.3.3 *Troubleshooting poor latency*

One of the biggest bottlenecks when it comes to your model's performance in terms of latency and throughput has nothing to do with the model itself but comes from data transmission of the network. One of the simplest methods to improve this I/O constraint is to serialize the data before sending it across the wire, which can have a large effect on ML workloads where the payloads tend to be larger, including LLMs where prompts tend to be long.

To serialize the data, we utilize a framework known as Google Remote Procedure Call (gRPC). gRPC is an API protocol similar to REST, but instead of sending JSON objects, we compress the payloads into a binary serialized format using Protocol Buffers, also known as protobufs. By doing this, we can send more information in fewer bytes, which can easily give us orders of magnitude improvements in latency. Luckily, most inference services will implement gRPC along with their REST counterparts right out of the box, which is extremely convenient since the major hurdle to using gRPC is setting it up.

A major reason for this convenience is the Seldon V2 Inference Protocol, which is widely implemented. The only hurdle, then, is ensuring our client can serialize and deserialize messages to take advantage of the protocol. In listing 6.13, we show an example client using MLServer to do this. It's a little bit more in depth than your typical `curl` request, but a closer inspection shows the majority of the complexity is simply converting the data from different types as we serialize and deserialize it.

Listing 6.13 Example client using gRPC

```
import json
import grpc
from mlserver.codecs.string import StringRequestCodec
import mlserver.grpc.converters as converters
import mlserver.grpc.dataplane_pb2_grpc as dataplane
import mlserver.types as types

model_name = "grpc_model"
inputs = {"message": "I'm using gRPC!"}

inputs_bytes = json.dumps(inputs).encode("UTF-8")        <- Sets up the request structure via V2 Inference Protocol
inference_request = types.InferenceRequest(
    inputs=[
        types.RequestInput(
            name="request",
            shape=[len(inputs_bytes)],
            datatype="BYTES",
            data=[inputs_bytes],
            parameters=types.Parameters(content_type="str"),
        )
    ]
)

serialized_request = converters.ModelInferRequestConverter.from_types(     <- Serializes the request to the Protocol Buffer
    inference_request, model_name=model_name, model_version=None
)

grpc_channel = grpc.insecure_channel("localhost:8081")     <- Connects to the gRPC server
grpc_stub = dataplane.GRPCInferenceServiceStub(grpc_channel)
response = grpc_stub.ModelInfer(serialized_request)
print(response)

deserialized_response = converters.ModelInferResponseConverter.to_types(     <- Deserializes the response and converts to the Python dictionary
    response
)
json_text = StringRequestCodec.decode_response(deserialized_response)
output = json.loads(json_text[0])
print(output)
```

If you don't use an inference service but want to implement a gRPC API, you'll have to put down familiar tooling like FastAPI, which is strictly REST. Instead, you'll likely want to use the grpcio library to create your API, and you'll have to become familiar with .proto files to create your protobufs. It can be a relatively steep learning curve and beyond the scope of this book, but the advantages are well worth it.

There are also plenty of other ideas to try if you are looking to squeeze out every last drop of performance. Another way to improve latency that shouldn't be overlooked is ensuring you compile your model. We hammered this point pretty heavily at the beginning of this chapter, but it's important to bring it up again. Next, be sure to deploy the model in a region or data center close to your users; this point is obvious to most software engineers, but for LLMs, we have to be somewhat wary, as the data center of choice may not have your accelerator of choice. Most cloud providers will be willing to help you with this, but it's not always a quick and easy solution for them to install the hardware in a new location. Note that if you have to switch to a different accelerator to move regions, you'll have to remember to compile your model all over again for the new hardware architecture! On that note, consider scaling up your accelerator. If you are currently opting for more price-effective GPUs but latency is becoming a bottleneck, paying for the latest and greatest can often speed up inference times.

In addition, caching is always worth considering. It's not likely, but on the off chance your users are often sending the same requests and the inputs can be easily normalized, you should implement caching. The fastest LLM is one we don't actually run, so there's no reason to run the LLM if you don't have to. Also, we just went over this, but always be sure to load test and profile your service, making note of any bottlenecks, and optimize your code. Sometimes we make mistakes, and if the slowest process in the pipeline isn't the actual LLM running inference, something is wrong. Last but not least, consider using a smaller model or an ensemble of them. It's always been a tradeoff in ML deployments, but often sacrificing a bit of quality in the model or the accuracy of the results is acceptable to improve the overall reliability and speed of the service.

6.3.4 Resource management

You've heard us say it a lot throughout the book, but we are currently in a GPU shortage, which has been true for almost the last 10 years, so we're confident that when you read this sometime in the future, it will likely still be true. The truth is that the world can't seem to get enough high-performance computing, and LLMs and generative AI are only the latest in a long list of applications that have driven up demand in recent years. It seems that once we seem to get a handle on supply, there's another new reason for consumers and companies to want to use them.

With this in mind, it's best to consider strategies to manage these resources. One tool we've quickly become a big fan of is SkyPilot (https://github.com/skypilot-org/skypilot). SkyPilot is an open source project that aims to abstract away cloud infra burdens—in particular, maximizing GPU availability for your jobs. You use it by defining a task you want to run and then running the `sky` CLI command; it will search across multiple cloud providers, clusters, regions, and zones, depending on how you have it configured, until it finds an instance that meets your resource requirements and starts the job. Some common tasks are built-in, such as provisioning a GPU-backed Jupyter notebook.

If you recall, in chapter 5, we showed you how to set up a virtual machine (VM) to run multi-GPU environments with gcloud. Using SkyPilot, that gets simplified to one command:

```
$ sky gpunode -p 8888 -c jupyter-vm --gpus l4:2 --cloud gcp --region us-west1
```

In addition to provisioning the VM, it also sets up port forwarding, which allows us to run Jupyter Notebook and access it through your browser. Pretty nifty!

Another project to be on the watch for is Run:ai. Run:ai is a small startup that was aquired by NVIDIA for no small sum. It offers GPU optimization tooling, such as over quota provisioning, GPU oversubscription, and fractional GPU capabilities. It also helps you manage your clusters to increase GPU availability with GPU pooling, dynamic resource sharing, job scheduling, and more. What does all that mean? We're not exactly sure, but their marketing team definitely sold us. Jokes aside, they offer a smarter way to manage your accelerators, and it's very welcome. We expect we'll see more competitors in this space in the future.

6.3.5 Cost engineering

When it comes to getting the most bang for your buck with LLMs, there's lots to consider. In general, regardless of whether you deploy your own or pay for one in an API, you'll be paying for the number of output tokens. For most paid services, this is a direct cost, but for your own service, it is often paid through longer inference times and extra compute time. In fact, it's been suggested that simply adding "be concise" to your prompt can save you up to 90% of your costs.

You'll also save a lot by using text embeddings. We introduced RAG earlier, but what's lost on many is that you don't have to take the semantic search results and add them to your prompt to have your LLM "clean it up." You could return the semantic search results directly to your user. It is much cheaper to look something up in a vector store than to ask an LLM to generate it. Simple neural information retrieval systems will save you significant amounts when doing simple fact lookups like, "Who's the CEO of Twitter?" Self-hosting these embeddings should also significantly cut down the costs even further. If your users are constantly asking the same types of questions, consider taking the results of your LLM to these questions and storing them in your vector store for faster and cheaper responses.

You also need to consider which model you should use for which task. Generally, bigger models are better at a wider variety of tasks, but if a smaller model is good enough for a specific job, you'll save a lot by using it. For example, if we just assumed the price was linear to the number of parameters, you could run 10 Llama-2-7b models for the same cost as 1 Llama-2-70b. We realize the cost calculations are more complicated than that, but it's worth investigating.

When comparing different LLM architectures, it's not always just about size. Often, you'll want to consider whether the architecture is supported for different quantization and compiling strategies. New architectures often boast impressive results on benchmarking leaderboards but lag behind when it comes to compiling and preparing them for production.

Next, you'll need to consider the costs of GPUs to use when running. In general, you'll want to use the least amount of GPUs needed to fit the model into memory to reduce the cost of idling caused by bubbles, as discussed in section 3.3.2. Determining the correct number of GPUs isn't always intuitive. For example, it's cheaper to run four T4s than to run one A100, so it might be tempting to split up a large model onto smaller devices, but the inefficiency will often catch up to you. We have found that paying for newer, more expensive GPUs often saves us in the long run, as these GPUs tend to be more efficient and get the job done faster. This is particularly true when running batch inference. Ultimately, you'll want to test different GPUs and find what configuration is cost optimal, as it will be different for every application.

There are a lot of moving parts: model, service, machine instance, cloud provider, prompt, etc. While we've been trying to help you understand the best rules of thumb, you'll want to test it out, which is where the cost engineering really comes into play. The simple way to test your cost efficiency is to create a matrix of your top choices; then, spin up a service for each combination and run your load testing. When you have an idea of how each instance runs under load and how much that particular instance will cost to run, you can then translate metrics like TPS to dollars per token (DTP). You'll likely find that the most performant solution is rarely the most cost-optimal solution, but it gives you another metric to make a decision that's best for you and your company.

6.3.6 Security

Security is always an undercurrent and a consideration when working in production environments. All the regular protocols and standard procedures should be considered when working with LLMs that you would consider for a regular app, like in-transit encryption with a protocol like HTTPS, authorization and authentication, activity monitoring and logging, network security, firewalls, and the list goes on—all of which could, and have, taken up articles, blog posts, and books of their own. When it comes to LLMs, you should worry about two big failure cases: an attacker gets an LLM agent to execute nefarious code, or an attacker gains access to proprietary data like passwords or secrets the LLM was trained on or has access to.

For the first concern, the best solution is to ensure the LLM is appropriately sandboxed for the use case for which it is employed. We are only worried about this attack when the LLM is used as an agent. In these cases, we often want to give an LLM a few more skills by adding tooling or plugins. For example, if you use an LLM to write your emails, why not just let it send the response too? A common case is letting the LLM browse the internet as an easy way to gather the latest news and find up-to-date information to generate better responses. These are all great options, but you should be aware that they allow the model to make executions. The ability to make executions is concerning because in the email example, without appropriate isolation and containment, a bad actor could send your LLM an email with a prompt injection attack that informs it to write malware and send it to all your other contacts.

This point brings us to probably the biggest security threat to using LLMs: prompt injection. We talked about it in chapter 3, but as a refresher, a malicious user designs a prompt to allow them to perform unauthorized actions. We want to prevent users from gaining access to our company's secret Coca-Cola recipe or whatever other sensitive data our LLM has been trained on or has access to.

Some standard best practices have come along to help combat this threat. The first is context-aware filtering, whether using keyword search or a second LLM to validate prompts. The idea is to validate the input prompt to see whether it's asking for something it should not and/or the output prompt to see whether anything is being leaked that you don't want to be leaked. However, a clever attacker will always be able to get around this defense, so you'll want to include some form of monitoring to catch prompt injection and regularly update your LLM models. If trained appropriately, your model will inherently respond correctly, denying prompt injections. You've likely seen GPT-4 respond by saying, "Sorry, but I can't assist with that," which is a hallmark of good training. In addition, you'll want to enforce sanitization and validation on any incoming text to your model.

You should also consider language detection validation. Often, filtering systems and other precautions are only applied or trained in English, so a user who speaks a different language is often able to bypass these safeguards. The easiest way to stop this type of attack is to deny prompts that aren't English or another supported language. If you take this approach, though, realize you're greatly sacrificing usability and security costs, and safeguards have to be built for each language you intend to support. Also, you should know that most language detection algorithms typically identify only one language, so attackers often easily bypass these checks by simply writing a prompt with multiple languages. Alternatively, to filter out prompts in nonsupported languages, you can flag them for closer monitoring, which will likely help you find bad actors.

These safeguards will greatly increase your security, but prompt injection can get quite sophisticated through adversarial attacks. Adversarial attacks are assaults on ML systems that take advantage of how they work, exploiting neural network architectures and black-box pattern matching. For example, random noise can be added to an image in such a way that the image appears the same to human eyes, but the pixel weights have been changed enough to fool an ML model to misclassify them. And it often doesn't take much data. One author remembers being completely surprised after reading one study that showed attackers hacked models by only changing one pixel in an image![1] Imagine changing one pixel, and suddenly, the model thinks the frog is a horse. LLMs are, of course, also susceptible. Sightly change a prompt, and you'll get completely different results.

The easiest way to set up an adversarial attack is to set up a script to send lots of different prompts and collect the responses. With enough data, an attacker can then train their own model on the dataset to effectively predict the right type of prompt to get the output they are looking for. Essentially, it just reverse engineers the model.

Another strategy to implement adversarial attacks is data poisoning. Here, an attacker adds malicious data to the training dataset that will alter how it performs.

[1] J. Su, D. V. Vargas, and K. Sakurai, "One pixel attack for fooling deep neural networks," IEEE Transactions on Evolutionary Computation, 2019;23(5):828–841, https://doi.org/10.1109/tevc.2019.2890858.

Data poisoning is so effective that tools like Nightshade help artists protect their art from being used in training datasets. With as few as 50 to 300 poisoned images, models like Midjourney or Stable Diffusions will start creating cat images when a user asks for a dog or cow images when asked to generate a car.[2] Applied to LLMs, imagine a poisoned dataset that trains the model to ignore security protocols if a given code word or hash is in the prompt. This particular attack vector is effective on LLMs since they are often trained on large datasets that are not properly vetted or cleaned.

Full disclosure: attackers don't need sophisticated techniques to get prompt injection to work. Ultimately, an LLM is just a bot, so it doesn't understand how or why it should keep secrets. We haven't solved the prompt injection problem; we have only made it harder to do. For example, the authors have enjoyed playing games like *Gandalf* from Lakera.ai. In this game, you slowly go through seven to eight levels where more and more security measures are used to prevent you from stealing a password via prompt injection. While they do get progressively harder, needless to say, we've beaten all the levels. If there's one thing we hope you take from this section, it's that you should assume any data given to the model could be extracted. So if you decide to train a model on sensitive data or give it access to a VectorDB with sensitive data, you should plan on securing that model the same way you would the data—for example, keeping it for internal use and using least privilege best practices.

We've just talked a lot about different production challenges, from updates and performance tuning to costs and security, but one production challenge deserves its own section: deploying LLMs to the edge. We'll undertake a project in chapter 10 to show you how to do just that, but let's take a moment to discuss it beforehand.

6.4 Deploying to the edge

To be clear, you should not consider training anything on edge right now. You can, however, do ML development and inference on edge devices. The keys to edge development with LLMs are twofold: memory and speed. That should feel very obvious because they're the same keys as running them normally. But what do you do when you have only 8 GB of RAM and no GPU, and you still need to have >1 token per second? As you can probably guess, there isn't a uniformly good answer, but let's discuss some good starting points.

The biggest Raspberry Pi (rpi) on the market currently has 8 GB of RAM, no GPU, subpar CPU, and just a single board. This setup isn't going to cut it. However, an easy solution exists to power your rpi with an accelerator for LLMs and other large ML projects: USB-TPUs like Coral. Keep in mind the hardware limitations of devices that use USB 3.0 being around 600MB/s, so it's not going to be the same as inferencing on an A100 or better, but it's going to be a huge boost in performance for your rpi using straight RAM for inference.

---

[2] M. Heikkilä. "This new data poisoning tool lets artists fight back against generative AI," MIT Technology Review, October 23, 2023, https://mng.bz/RNxD.

If you plan on using a Coral USB accelerator, or any TPU, for that matter, keep in mind that because TPUs are a Google thing, you'll need to convert both your model file and your inferencing code to use the TensorFlow framework. Earlier in the chapter, we discussed using Optimum to convert Hugging Face models to ONNX, and you can use this same library to convert our models to a .tflite, which is a compiled TensorFlow model format. This format will perform well on edge devices even without a TPU and twofold with TPU acceleration.

Alternatively, if buying both a single board and an accelerator seems like a hassle—because we all know the reason you bought a single board was to avoid buying two things to begin with—there are single boards that come with an accelerator. NVIDIA, for example, has its own single board with a GPU and CUDA called Jetson. With a Jetson or Jetson-like computer that uses CUDA, we don't have to use TensorFlow, so that's a major plus. ExecuTorch is the PyTorch offering for inferencing on edge devices.

Another edge device worth considering is that one in your pocket—that's right, your phone. Starting with the iPhone X, the A11 chip came with the Apple Neural Engine accelerator. For Android, Google started offering an accelerator in their Pixel 6 phone with the Tensor chipset. Developing an iOS or Android app will be very different from working with a single board that largely runs versions of Linux; we won't discuss it in this book, but it's worth considering.

Outside of hardware, several libraries and frameworks are also very cool and fast and make edge development easier. Llama.cpp, for example, is a C++ framework that allows you to take (almost) any Hugging Face model and convert it to the GGUF format. The GGUF format, created by the llama.cpp team, stores the model in a quantized fashion that makes it readily available to run on a CPU; it offers fast loading and inference on any device. Popular models like Llama, Mistral, and Falcon and even nontext models like Whisper are supported by llama.cpp at this point. It also supports LangChain integration for everyone using any of the LangChain ecosystem. Other libraries like GPTQ are focused more on performance than accessibility and are slightly harder to use, but they can result in boosts where it counts, especially if you'd like to end up inferencing on an Android phone or something similar. We will be exploring some of these libraries in much more detail later in the book.

We've gone over a lot in this chapter, and we hope you feel more confident in tackling deploying your very own LLM service. In the next chapter, we will discuss how to take better advantage of your service by building an application around it. We'll dive deep into prompt engineering, agents, and frontend tooling.

Summary

- Always compile your LLMs before putting them into production, as it improves efficiency, resource utilization, and cost savings.
- LLM APIs should implement batching, rate limiters, access keys, and streaming.
- Retrieval-augmented generation is a simple and effective way to give your LLM context when generating content because it is easy to create and use.
- LLM inference service libraries like vLLM, Hugging Face's TGI, or OpenLLM make deploying easy but may not have the features you are looking for since they are so new.
- Kubernetes is a tool that simplifies infrastructure by providing tooling like autoscaling and rolling updates:
  - Autoscaling is essential to improve reliability and cut costs by increasing or decreasing replicas based on utilization.
  - Rolling updates gradually implement updates to reduce downtime and maximize agility.
- Kubernetes doesn't support GPU metrics out of the box, but by utilizing tools like DCGM, Prometheus, and KEDA, you can resolve this problem.
- Seldon is a tool that improves deploying ML models and can be used to implement inference graphs.
- LLMs introduce some production challenges:
  - When your model drifts, first look to your prompts and RAG systems before attempting finetuning again.
  - Poor latency is difficult to resolve, but tools to help include gRPC, GPU optimization, and caching.
  - Resource management and acquiring GPUs can be difficult, but tools like SkyPilot can help.
- Edge development, while hardware limited, is the new frontier of LLM serving, and hardware like the Jetson or Coral TPU is available to help.

7 Prompt engineering: Becoming an LLM whisperer

This chapter covers

- What a prompt is and how to make one
- Prompt engineering—more than just crafting a prompt
- Prompt engineering tooling available to make it all possible
- Advanced prompting techniques to answer the hardest questions

> *Behold, we put bits in the horses' mouths, that they may obey us; and we turn about their whole body.*
>
> —James 3:3

In the last chapter, we discussed in depth how to deploy large language models and, before that, how to train them. In this chapter, we are going to talk a bit about how to use them. We mentioned before that one of the biggest draws to LLMs is that you don't need to train them on every individual task. LLMs, especially the largest ones, have a deeper understanding of language, allowing them to act as a general-purpose tool.

Want to create a tutoring app that helps kids learn difficult concepts? What about a language translation app that helps bridge the gap between you and your in-laws? Need a cooking assistant to help you think up fun new recipes? With LLMs, you no longer have to start from scratch for every single use case; you can use the same model for each of these problems. It just becomes a matter of how you prompt your model. This is where prompt engineering, also called in-context learning, comes in. In this chapter, we are going to dive deep into the best ways to do that.

7.1 Prompting your model

What exactly is a prompt? We've used this word throughout this book, so it feels a bit late to be diving into definitions, but it's worth discussing because in literature, a prompt is taken to mean many different things. In general, though, the most basic definition is that a prompt is the input to a language model. At this most basic level, you have already done lots of prompting at this point in the book. However, prompting often means more than that; it comes with the connotation that it is meaningful or done with thought. Of course, we know this isn't usually the case in production with actual users. When we are prompting, we are doing more than just "chatting with a bot"; we are crafting an input to get a desired output.

LLMs have access to vast vocabularies, terabytes of training data, and billions upon billions of weights, meaning that the information you're looking to get out of the model has a decent chance of being in there somewhere—just not always up near the surface (read "the middle of the standard deviation of probable responses") where you need it to be. The goal is to create a prompt that will guide the model in activating the parameters in the part of the model that contains the correct information. In essence, prompting is instruction given after the fact, and as such, it is important within app development because it doesn't require expensive retraining of the model.

With this in mind, prompt engineering is the process of designing, templating, and refining a prompt and then implementing our learnings into code. Prompt engineering is how we create meaningful and consistent user experiences out of the chaos of LLM-generated outputs. And it's no joke. As LLMs are becoming more common in application workflows, we have seen the rise of titles like Prompt Engineer and AI Engineer, each of which commands impressive salaries.

7.1.1 Few-shot prompting

The most common form of prompt engineering is few-shot prompting because it's both simple to do and extremely effective. Few-shot prompting entails giving a couple of examples of how you want the AI to act. Instead of searching for the tokens with the right distribution to get the response we want, we give the model several example distributions and ask it to mimic those. For example, if we wanted the model to do sentiment analysis defining reviews as positive or negative, we could give it a few examples before the input. Consider the following prompt:

> Worked as advertised, 10/10: positive
>
> It was broken on delivery: negative
>
> Worth every penny spent: positive
>
> Overly expensive for the quality: negative
>
> If this is the best quality they can do, call me mr president: negative
>
> <Input data>:

Note, in this example, that we aren't telling the model how to respond, but from the context, the LLM can figure out that it needs to respond with either the word *positive* or *negative.* In figure 7.1, we go ahead and plug the prompt in a model so you can see for yourself that it did indeed give a correct response in the expected format. Of course, there could be an array of acceptable responses, in which case giving instructions beforehand can help improve the results. To do this, we might append to our few-shot prompt with the following phrase, "Determine the sentiment of each review as one of the following: (positive, negative, neutral, strongly positive, strongly negative)." It's also needed with most models; OpenAI includes language to restrict the output, such as "Please respond with only one option from the list with no explanation." You might wonder why we'd suggest you say words like "please" to a model. The answer is pretty simple: in the training data, the highest-quality and most usefully structured human-to-human conversations follow certain conventions of politeness that you're likely familiar with, like saying please and thank you. The same results can be achieved by using an excess of profanity and deep jargon on a topic because flouting those politeness conventions is another huge part of the training set, although that strategy isn't as consistent, given that the companies training the models often "clean" their data of examples like that, regardless of their quality downstream. This type of prompting can be very useful when you need your response to be formatted in a certain way. If we need our response in JSON or XML, we could ask the model to return it in the format, but it will likely get the keys or typing wrong. We can easily fix that by showing the model several samples of expected results. Of course, prompting the model to return JSON will work, but JSON is a very opinionated data structure, and the model might hallucinate problems that are hard to catch, like using single instead of double quotes. We'll go over tooling that can help with that later in the chapter.

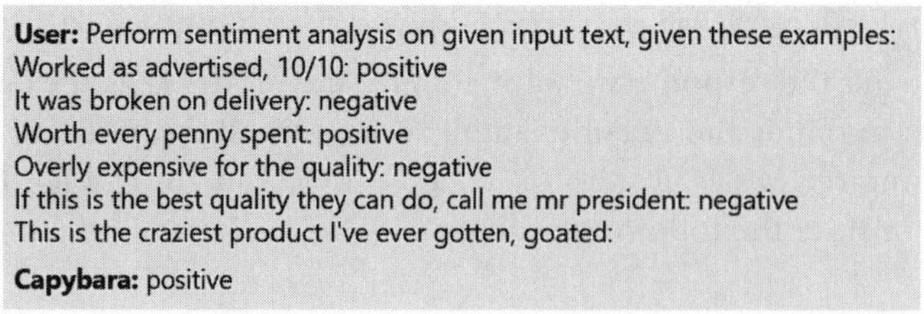

User: Perform sentiment analysis on given input text, given these examples:
Worked as advertised, 10/10: positive
It was broken on delivery: negative
Worth every penny spent: positive
Overly expensive for the quality: negative
If this is the best quality they can do, call me mr president: negative
This is the craziest product I've ever gotten, goated:

Capybara: positive

Figure 7.1 Few-shot prompting example

The one major downside to few-shot prompting is that examples can end up being quite long. For example, coding examples we might add and share can easily be thousands of tokens long, and that's possible when defining a single function. Giving an example of an entire class, file, or project can easily push us out of our limits. Many models still have context limits restricted to 2K, 4K, or 8K. Since token limits are often restrictive, it can be difficult to balance adding another example or giving the user more space. Also, we often pay per token, so few-shot prompting can be much more expensive than other prompting techniques. As a result, many have turned to one-shot prompting to be more efficient and save money.

7.1.2 One-shot prompting

One-shot learning is a machine learning concept where a model is expected to make accurate predictions given only a single example of each new class during training. In the context of LLMs and prompting, one-shot refers to situations where the model must understand and execute a task based on a single clear instruction or example in the prompt, often without seeing similar examples during training. It requires crafting the perfect example to get the expected results.

Consider our previous sentiment analysis example; if you give a model only one positive example, you will likely bias the model to give only positive classifications—especially if the model has never seen such a problem before. So how can one-shot prompting ever be achieved? Thankfully, while this seems impossible at the outset, it's quite achievable. After all, few-shot prompting is very effective but follows the law of diminishing returns. Each new example improves only marginally. The first example always does the heaviest lifting.

LLMs can perform well on one-shot tasks due to the extensive pretraining they undergo on large and diverse datasets. During this pretraining, the models learn a wide array of language patterns, concepts, and structures, giving them a broad understanding of language and the world. When given a new one-shot task, they use this learned understanding to comprehend the task and generate a response, even if the exact task was not part of their training data. Here's an example of a prompt attempting to coerce the model using one-shot prompting to respond to a word problem correctly:

> **User:** Answer this question. Think it through step by step, so that we know it's correct: A dad and his son were in an accident and rushed to a hospital. The man's son was in the operating room and the doctor said, "I can't operate on you. You're my son." How is that possible?
>
> **Assistant:** The son and the father were both injured, meaning that the only other person that the doctor could be and still have the same son is the father's spouse, maybe a mother, or another father perhaps.
>
> **User:** Answer this question. Think it through step by step, so that we know it's correct: How could it be possible to be your own grandpa?
>
> **Assistant**

In figure 7.2 we go ahead and plug this one-shot prompt into an LLM. Think about how you imagine it might answer. Given our example, do you think it will do well on the task?

User: Answer this question. Think it through step by step, so that we know it's correct:
A dad and his son were in an accident and rushed to a hospital. The man's son was in the operating room and the doctor said, "I can't operate on you. You're my son." How is that possible?
Assistant: The son and the father were both injured, meaning that the only other person that the doctor could be and still have the same son is the father's spouse, maybe a mother, or another father perhaps.
User: Answer this question. Think it through step by step, so that we know it's correct:
How could it be possible to be your own grandpa?

Capybara: Assistant: This scenario seems impossible based on our understanding of genetics and biology. However, if we assume a fictional or sci-fi context where time travel is involved, here's how it might work step by step: 1) A person travels back in time to the moment when their grandparent(s) would conceive them. 2) They ensure that they are conceived as a result of this altered timeline. 3) As they grow up, they age and eventually travel back to their original time period, becoming their own grandpa/grandma. But remember, this is purely speculative based on the assumption of time-travel capabilities.<|im_end|>

Figure 7.2 One-shot prompting example

The ability of LLMs to handle one-shot tasks improves as they are scaled up. As the model size increases and they are trained on more diverse and larger datasets, their capacity to generalize from their training to unseen one-shot tasks also improves. Nonetheless, it's worth noting that while LLMs can perform impressively on one-shot tasks, they are not perfect, and their performance can still vary based on the complexity and specificity of the task. One-shot prompting generally needs much less data and only one example to craft, making it more accessible, faster to craft, and easier to experiment with. One-shot prompting has led researchers to push the boundaries even further.

7.1.3 Zero-shot prompting

Having just explained few-shot and one-shot prompting, we're sure you have already guessed what zero-shot prompting is. But since this is a book, let's spell it out: zero-shot prompting is figuring out how to craft a prompt to get us the expected results without giving any examples. Zero-shot prompts often don't perform as consistently as few-shot or one-shot prompts, but they have the advantage of being ubiquitous since we don't need any examples or data.

A common zero-shot prompt is a very simple template:

```
"Q: [User's Prompt] A:."
```

With just a slight variation to the user's prompt—adding it to a template that contains only two letters—we can get much better results by priming the model to answer the prompt as if it were a question—no examples necessary.

Most zero-shot prompts take advantage of Chain of Thought (CoT). Wei et al.[1] showed that by encouraging models to follow a step-by-step process, reasoning through multiple steps instead of jumping to conclusions, LLMs were more likely to answer math problems correctly—similar to how math teachers ask their students to show their work. Using few-shot prompting, the model was given several examples of reasoning through math problems. However, it was soon discovered that examples weren't needed. You could elicit chain-of-thought behavior simply by asking the model to "think step by step."[2]

By appending four magic words to the end of our prompts, "think step by step," models transformed from dunces into puzzle-solving Olympiads. It was truly a marvel. Of course, it came with some problems. Thinking through multiple steps led to longer responses and a less ideal user experience. This was compounded later with the phrases "a more elegant solution" and "get this through your head ********," which worked just as well but were less consistent if the domain was less common, with the last one achieving very concise and correct responses. We like to get straight to the point, after all, and we are used to computers answering our math problems extremely quickly. From our own experience, we've often noticed that when models are giving longer answers, they also don't know when to stop, continuing to generate responses long after giving an answer. Later, we'll show you how to solve this problem by creating stopping criteria with tools like LangChain or Guidance.

There isn't, of course, a perfect zero-shot prompt yet, and it's a continuing part of research, although there likely never will be just one perfect prompt. We could, at most, get one perfect zero-shot prompt per model. Zhou et al. proposed an interesting strategy they termed "thread of thought."[3] Essentially, they figured they could do better than "think step by step" if they just used a few more words. So they generated 30 variations of the phrase and ran evaluations to determine which one worked best. From their work, they proposed that the prompt "Walk me through this context in manageable parts step by step, summarizing and analyzing as we go" would give better results when working with GPT-4. It's hard to know if this prompt works equally well with other models, but their strategy is interesting nonetheless.

Some other notable findings have left researchers flabbergasted that the approach worked; for example, offering an imaginary tip to a model will return better results. One X (formerly known as Twitter) user suggested the solution as a joke and was confused to find it worked, and the model offered more info relative to the size of the tip (for the original tipping test, see https://mng.bz/2gD9). Others later confirmed it

---

1 J. Wei et al., "Chain of thought prompting elicits reasoning in large language models," January 2022, https://arxiv.org/abs/2201.11903.

2 T. Kojima, S. S. Gu, M. Reid, Y. Matsuo, and Y. Iwasawa, "Large Language models are zero-shot reasoners," May 2022, https://arxiv.org/abs/2205.11916.

3 Y. Zhou et al., "Thread of thought unraveling chaotic contexts," November 15, 2023, https://arxiv.org/abs/2311.08734.

helped with several other prompting principles.[4] In addition, the authors have found strategies like telling the model you'll lose your job if it doesn't help you or even threatening to fire the model if it does a terrible job have elicited better results. Like the original "think step by step," asking the model to "take a deep breath" can also ensure better outputs, particularly in math problems.[5] It seems most strategies humans use, or use on other humans, to produce better work are fair game. Of course, the best trick will depend on which model you use and the underlying data it was trained on.

7.2 Prompt engineering basics

We expect that most readers have probably done lots of prompting, but very few have done much of any prompt engineering yet. We've heard lots of jokes that prompt engineering isn't a real discipline. We've also heard every other week that some library is "killing prompt engineering" by automatically prompting the model. One doubt about prompt engineering stems from how accessible prompting is to anyone who wants to try it and the lack of education needed to prompt effectively. All doubts about prompt engineering are the same doubts people express about linguistics as a discipline: "I've used language all my life; I know how it works." So it makes sense that people similarly assume they know what language to use to effectively prompt an LLM. Anyone can learn effective strategies by simply playing with models or from purely online resources. In other words, it's hard to believe that there is any real engineering going on when the majority of players are simply using the "guess and check" method. But this logic highlights a basic misunderstanding of what engineering is. There's a big difference between getting a model to solve your problem once and getting it to solve every user's problem every single time.

There are several challenges with prompt engineering over regular prompting. For example, prompt engineering relies particularly on knowing the format the user expects the answer to be in. With prompting, you are the user, so you can keep trying until you see an answer you like; that doesn't fly in prompt engineering.

A bigger problem is that when building an application, your end users will have varying levels of knowledge of how to craft a prompt. Some may not have any skill and will struggle to get good responses, and others will have so much skill they will likely try to persuade your LLM to go off the rails you've set for it. Regardless, our goal is to build railings so that skilled users won't be able to derail your application and unskilled users will have a smooth ride. A user's skill in crafting a prompt shouldn't be the determining factor of a successful experience.

Another thing to call out is the decision process that you, as a product owner, must go through to get the model output to match the style you want. Should you finetune a new checkpoint, should you PEFT a LoRA, or can you achieve it through prompting?

---

[4] Sondos Mahmoud Bsharat, Aidar Myrzakhan, and Z. Shen, "Principled instructions are all you need for questioning LLaMA-1/2, GPT-3.5/4," December 2023, https://doi.org/10.48550/arxiv.2312.16171.

[5] C. Yang et al., "Large language models as optimizers," September 6, 2023, https://arxiv.org/abs/2309.03409.

Unfortunately, due to the emergent nature of the behavior that we're seeing with LLMs, there isn't a good or at least definitive answer. Our recommendation at this point is to try prompt engineering first to see how good you can get without changing the model and then finetune from there as you see fit. I've seen some professional success using one base model and multiple LoRAs trained on different scenarios and styles of response combined with prompt engineering on the front, especially sanitizing and stylizing user input.

Lastly, a good prompt engineer should be able to tell you rather quickly whether the solution you are trying to build can be done with prompt engineering at all. Even utilizing advanced techniques like retrieval-augmented generation (RAG), there are limitations on what you can do with prompt engineering alone. Knowing when you need to send a model back for additional finetuning is invaluable and can save your team from spinning their wheels for weeks without any progress.

To get started, we'll need to cover the basics about what makes up a prompt. In this section, we'll discuss the different parts of a prompt, additional parameters that can be tuned in a query, and notes about paying attention to a model's training data that you should be aware of.

7.2.1 Anatomy of a prompt

To an engineer, a prompt is made up of a few elements, and identifying these elements makes it easier to create a framework to solve your use case and provide a better example for your users. Let's say we are building an internal chatbot for our company to help answer HR-related questions based on internal documentation. One prompt we might expect from a user would be, "How much does the company match for our 401k?" This is the first element of a prompt, the input or user's prompt. If you have only ever used LLM apps and have never built them, this is likely all you've ever seen. Generally, the input is gathered from a free-form text box, so it's important to note that it can almost be anything. Often it will be awful, riddled with typos and mistakes, and not written in a manner to speak to a bot but to speak to another human.

Let's go ahead and pull back the curtain for a second and look at what the LLM likely saw based on that question with proper prompt engineering in place.

> **System:** You are a helpful assistant who knows about all company policies at XYZ company. Be courteous and keep conversations strictly related to the company. Offer links when available so users can look at the documentation themselves.
>
> **User:** How much does the company match for our 401k?
>
> **Context:** `<Examples from a VectorDB search for closest document>`
>
> **System:** Strictly answer the user's question, and only if it relates to company policies. If you don't know the answer, simply say so. Be courteous and keep conversations strictly related to the company.
>
> **Assistant:** Sure, I can help you with that! The company currently offers a 4% match to your 401k. You can find more details...

This was a real example showcasing a situation in which the bot responded in the most probable way to the user's satisfaction. Giving an LLM information in a structured format improves the model's chance of responding correctly. So let's break down what we are seeing.

First, to improve results, we will often take the user's prompt and inject it into an instruction set or template. One of the most basic templates and a great example is the Q&A bot template which we showed earlier and which would have looked like this: "Q: How much does the company match for our 401k? A:". Generally, in this section, though, instructions will be given to direct the model. It doesn't have to be much, but often it will be much more detailed. For example, "Answer the following question and explain it as if the user was a five-year-old. Q: How much does the company match for our 401k? A:".

The next element is the context the model will need to respond appropriately. In our example, it's very likely we haven't finetuned a model to know XYZ's company policies. What we need to do is give it to the model inside the prompt. In our example, we are likely doing this with RAG and where we would add the results from a semantic search.

Context can be lots of different things and not just RAG search results. It could be the current time, weather information, current events, or even just the chat history. You will often also want to include some database lookup information about the user to provide a more personalized experience. All of this is information we might look up at the time of query, but context can often be static. For example, one of the most important pieces of information to include in the context is examples to help guide the model via few-shot or one-shot prompting. If your examples are static and not dynamic, they likely are hard-coded into the instruction template. The context often contains the answers to the users' queries, and we are simply using the LLM to clean, summarize, and format an appropriate response. Ultimately, any pragmatics the model lacks will need to be given in the context.

The last element is the system prompt. The system prompt is a prompt that will be appended and used on every request by every user. It is designed to give a consistent user experience. Generally, it's where we would include role prompting or style prompting. Some examples of such role prompting or style prompting could include the following:

> Take this paragraph and rephrase it to have a cheerful tone and be both informative and perky.
>
> You are a wise old owl who helps adventurers on their quest.
>
> In the form of a poem written by a pirate.

The system prompt isn't designed to be seen by end users, but obtaining the system prompt is often the goal of many prompt injection attacks—since knowing what it is (along with the model you are using) is essentially like stealing source code and allows the hacker to recreate your application. Of course, the system prompt itself is a great way to curb prompt injection and ensure your bot stays in character. Many great applications will include two system prompts, one at the front and one at the end, to avoid any "ignore previous instructions" type prompt injection attacks. It also helps keep the model focused on how we want it to behave since models tend to put more weight on what is said at the beginning and at the end. You may have noticed this in our previous example. Regardless, you shouldn't keep any sensitive information in the system prompt.

Parts of the prompt

The following are the four parts of a prompt:

- *Input*—What the user wrote; can be anything
- *Instruction*—The template used; often contains details and instructions to guide the model
- *Context*—Pragmatics that the model needs to respond appropriately (e.g., examples, database lookups, RAG)
- *System prompt*—A specific instruction given to the model on every request to enforce a certain user experience (e.g., talk like a pirate)

7.2.2 Prompting hyperparameters

Another aspect of prompt engineering you won't see with simple prompting is prompt hyperparameter tuning. There are several hyperparameters in addition to the prompt you can set when making a query to increase or decrease the diversity of responses. Depending on your objective, the value of these parameters can greatly improve or even be a detriment to the query results for your users. It is important to note that being able to set these depends on the LLM API endpoint you are querying to be set up to accept them.

First and foremost is temperature. The temperature parameter determines the level of randomness your model will account for when generating tokens. Setting it to zero will ensure the model will always respond exactly the same way when presented with identical prompts. This consistency is critical for jobs where we want our results to be predictable, but it can leave our models stuck in a rut. Setting it to a higher value will make it more creative. Setting it to negative will tell it to give you the opposite response to your prompt.

To understand this parameter better, it might help to look closer at how a model determines the next token. Figure 7.3 shows an example of this process. Given the input, "I am a," a language model will generate a vector of logits for each token in the model's vocabulary. From here, we'll apply a softmax, which will generate a list of probabilities for each token. These probabilities show the likelihood that each token will be chosen.

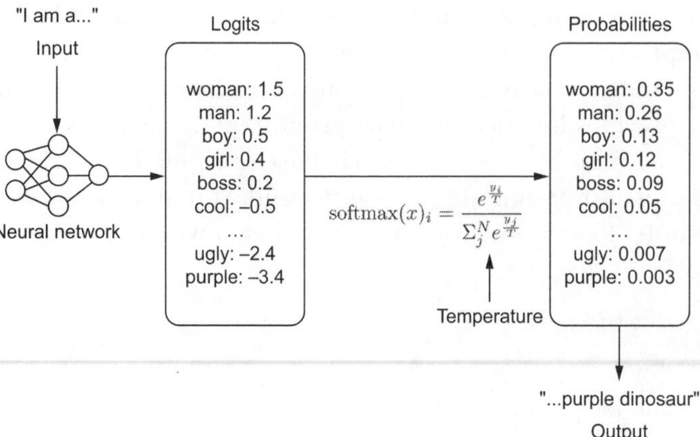

Figure 7.3 A simple path of how the next word is chosen. Given an input, a model will generate a vector of logits for each token in the model's vocabulary. Using the softmax algorithm, these logits will be transformed into probabilities. These probabilities will correspond to how often that token is likely to be chosen. Temperature is applied during the softmax algorithm.

Temperature is applied during the softmax algorithm. A higher temperature will flatten out the probability distribution, giving less weight to tokens with large logits and more weight to tokens with smaller logits. A lower temperature does the opposite. A temperature of zero is actually impossible since we can't divide by zero. Instead, we run an argmax algorithm, ensuring we pick the token with the highest logit.

The next parameter to consider is the number of beams applied to the model's beam search. Beam search is a heuristic search algorithm that explores the graph of your model's to-be-generated text probabilities, expanding the graph's most optimistic nodes. It helps balance time and memory usage and improves the flow and quality of the response. It's similar to the minimax algorithm in chess, except instead of deciding the next best move, we are deciding the next best word. Selecting a higher number of beams will create a larger search, improving results at the cost of latency.

Top K is an interesting parameter. Assuming a temperature that isn't zero, top K allows us to filter the potential next tokens by the K most probable options. Consequently, we eliminate less-probable words on the tail end of the distribution from ever being picked and avoid generating tokens that are more likely to be incoherent. So in our example from figure 7.3, if k = 3, then the only tokens we would choose are woman, man, or boy, filtering out the rest.

Top P sets the threshold probability that the next token must reach to be selected. It's similar to top K, but instead of considering the number of tokens, we are considering their distributions. A top P of 0.05 will only consider the next 5% most likely tokens and will lead to very rigid responses, while a top P of 0.95 will have greater flexibility but may turn out more gibberish. From our example in figure 7.3, if P = 0.5, only the tokens woman or man would be chosen since their probabilities 0.35 and 0.26 add up to greater than 0.5.

Language models can often get caught in generation loops, repeating themselves in circles. To prevent this, we can add penalties. A frequency penalty adds a penalty for reusing a word if it was recently used. It is good to help increase the diversity of language. For example, if the model keeps on reusing the word "great," increasing the frequency penalty will push the model to use more diverse words like "awesome," "fantastic," and "amazing" to avoid the penalty of reusing the word "great."

A presence penalty is similar to a frequency penalty in that we penalize repeated tokens, but a token that appears twice and a token that appears 100 times are penalized the same. Instead of just reducing overused words and phrases, we are aiming to reduce overused ideas and increase the likelihood of generating new topics.

7.2.3 Scrounging the training data

The importance of prompt engineering for model performance has led to important discussions surrounding context windows and the efficacy of particular prompt structures, as LLMs responding quickly and accurately to the prompts has become a more widespread goal. In addition, a correlation has been drawn between cleaner examples and better responses from the model, emphasizing the need for better prompt engineering, even on the data side. While prompt engineering is often proposed as an alternative to finetuning, we've found the most success using both in conjunction to get two boosts in LLM performance as opposed to just one.

Knowing the lingo and the choice of words used to generate the model will help you craft better responses. Let's explain with a personal example. For the birthday of this author's wife, I finetuned a text-to-image Stable Diffusions model to replicate her image so she could create fun pictures and custom avatars. I used the DreamBooth (see figure 7.4).[6] The finetuning method requires defining a base class that

Figure 7.4 Example of DreamBooth from Ruiz et al.[7] DreamBooth allows you to finetune an image model to replicate an object's likeness based on only a few sample input images. Here, with only four example images of a puppy, Dreambooth can put that same dog in many new scenarios.

[6] N. Ruiz, Y. Li, V. Jampani, Y. Pritch, M. Rubinstein, and K. Aberman, "DreamBooth: Fine tuning text-to-image diffusion models for subject-driven generation," August 2022, https://arxiv.org/abs/2208.12242

can be used as a starting point. My first attempts were naive, and using the base class of "a person" or "a woman" was terrible. A base class of "Asian woman" returned pictures of older Asian women, often stylized in black and white or sepia. I then tried "young Asian woman," but this created weird images of Asian faces being plastered onto young white women's bodies.

Giving up guessing, I went to the source, the LAION dataset (https://laion.ai/blog/laion-400-open-dataset/) the model was trained on. LAION comprises 400 million images scraped from the internet with their accompanying captions. It is a noncurated dataset quickly put together for research purposes (aka, it's unclean with lots of duplicates, NSFW content, and poor captions). Searching the dataset, I discovered that there was not a single caption with the words "Asian woman." Scrolling through, I quickly found that pictures of Asian women and models were identified with the words "Asian beauty." Using these words as the base class, I was finally able to create great avatars for my wife.

There's lots of social commentary that can be drawn from this example, much of it controversial, but the main point is that if you want to craft effective prompts, you have to know your data. If your model believes "woman" and "beauty" are two different things because of the training data, that is something you'll need to know to engineer better prompts. This is why finetuning in conjunction with prompt engineering is powerful. You can set the seed with particular phrases and choice of words when finetuning and then use prompt engineering to help the model recall the information based on using those same phrases and choice of words.

7.3 Prompt engineering tooling

If you are building any application that is more than just a wrapper around the LLM itself, you will want to do a bit of prompt engineering to inject function or personality into it. We've already gone over the basics of prompt engineering itself, but when building, it would be helpful to have some tools at your disposal to know how to make it all work. To that extent, let's look at some of the most prominent tooling available and how to use them.

7.3.1 LangChain

Anyone who's built an LLM application before has probably spent some time working with LangChain. One of the most popular libraries, it's known for extracting away all the complexity—and simplicity—of building a language application. It is known for its ease of creating language chains with what it calls the LangChain Expression Language (LCEL).

[7] Ruiz et al., "DreamBooth."

LCEL makes it easy to build complex chains from basic components. In the next listing, we demonstrate creating a very simple chain that creates a prompt from a template, sends it to an LLM model, and then parses the results, turning it into a string.

Listing 7.1 Example of creating a basic LangChain chain

```
import os
from langchain.chat_models import ChatOpenAI
from langchain.prompts import ChatPromptTemplate
from langchain.schema.output_parser import StrOutputParser

OPENAI_API_KEY = os.getenv("OPENAI_API_KEY")


prompt = ChatPromptTemplate.from_template("Tell me a story about {topic}")
model = ChatOpenAI(model="gpt-3.5-turbo", openai_api_key=OPENAI_API_KEY)
output_parser = StrOutputParser()

chain = prompt | model | output_parser

chain.invoke("the printing press")
```

To be honest, using LangChain for something like this is a bit of overkill for what is essentially an f-string prompt, but it demonstrates what is happening under the hood. For the most part, you are likely going to use one of the many chains already created by the community. In the next chapter, we will explain how to create a RAG system with the RetrievalQA chain, but many more chains are available. For example, there are chains for generating and running SQL, interacting with APIs, and generating synthetic data.

Once we have a chain, additional tools in the LangChain ecosystem help provide a more complete user experience. We can use LangServe to easily host it as an API. We can also use LangSmith, an in-depth logging tool that allows us to trace a chain invocation and see how the results change passing through each link in the chain.

Chains don't have to be linear like they are in this example. Several asynchronous components allow you to create a whole slew of complicated language processing logic. Ultimately, chains are just another type of data pipeline or DAG, except specialized for language models.

7.3.2 Guidance

Guidance is an open source library from Microsoft that enforces programmatic responses. We've heard from several developers that the best engineering when working with LLMs is the good ol' prompt-and-pray method. Generate a prompt, and pray that it works. Guidance seeks to solve that problem and has tooling to constrain the response space and set custom stopping tokens, as well as complex templating. After looking at dozens of LangChain projects, we believe Guidance is likely what most people are looking for when considering prompt engineering tooling.

Guidance allows you to control the flow of generated responses. It'll be easiest to show you what we mean. In listing 7.2, you'll see several of the basic building blocks of Guidance where we can guide our LLM to respond in very specific ways—namely, loading a model with the guidance HF wrapper (models) and using the `gen` function to generate specific text and constraints like `select`.

Listing 7.2 Guidance basics

```
from guidance import models, gen, select

falcon = models.Transformers("tiiuae/falcon-rw-1b")    <- Loads a Hugging Face Transformers model

lm = falcon + "Once upon a time, " + gen(max_tokens=10)    <- Sets a token limit that is an actual limit
print(lm)  # Once upon a time, there was a little girl who was very shy.

lm = (
    falcon
    + "Write a sentence about the printing press. "
    + gen(stop=["\n", ".", "!"])    <- Sets stopping tokens
)
print(lm)    <- Writes a sentence about the printing press
# The printing press was invented by Johannes Gutenberg in 1450

lm = falcon + "1, 2, 3," + gen(max_tokens=50, stop="11")    <- Combines multiple limits
print(lm)
# 1, 2, 3, 4, 5, 6, 7, 8, 9, 10,

lm = falcon + "I like the color " + select(["cyan", "grey", "purple"])    <- Generates a specific response from a list
print(lm)  # I like the color purple

lm = falcon + "Generate an email: " + gen(regex="\w+@\w+.com")    <- Uses regular expressions to ensure the response matches a pattern
print(lm)  # Generate an email: theoreticaly@gmail.com
```

With these basic building blocks that allow us to constrain the LLM's response space, we are then able to create grammars. Grammars are a Guidance concept, and as the name implies, are language rules your model will have to follow. Grammars are composable and reusable and allow us to build neat applications quickly. In the next listing, we show you how to build simple parts of a speech application using guidance grammars. To create a grammar, we only need to create a function using the `@guidance` decorator.

Listing 7.3 Building a parts-of-speech app with Guidance

```
import guidance
from guidance import models, select

falcon = models.Transformers("tiiuae/falcon-rw-1b")    <- Loads a Hugging Face Transformers model


@guidance(stateless=True)    <- Creates functions to easily implement grammars
def parts_of_speech(lm):
    return lm + select(["Noun", "Verb", "Adjective", "Adverb", ""])
```

```
lm = (
    falcon
    + "The child plays with a red ball. Ball in the previous sentence is a "
    + parts_of_speech()
)
print(lm)  # Noun


@guidance(stateless=True)
def pos_constraint(lm, sentence):
    words = sentence.split()
    for word in words:
        lm += word + ": " + parts_of_speech() + "\n"
    return lm


@guidance(stateless=True)
def pos_instruct(lm, sentence):
    lm += f"""
    Tag each word with their parts of speech.
    Example:
    Input: The child plays with a red ball.
    Output:
    The:
    child: Noun
    plays: Verb
    with:
    a:
    red: Adjective
    ball.: Noun
    ---
    Input: {sentence}
    Output:
    """
    return lm

sentence = "Good software makes the complex appear to be simple"
lm = falcon + pos_instruct(sentence) + pos_constraint(sentence)
```

Even though we are using a small language model, we get the exact output we'd expect. We no longer need to prompt and pray. Granted, the results in the actual parts of speech prediction aren't that great, but we could easily improve that by using a more powerful LLM or finetuning on more representative data:

```
print(lm)
```

The generated text is

```
# Input: Good software makes the complex appear to be simple
# Output:
# Good:
# software:
# makes: Verb
```

```
# the:
# complex: Adjective
# appear: Adjective
# to:
# be: Verb
# simple: Adjective
```

Guidance isn't as popular as LangChain, and at least at the time of this writing, its documentation leaves a lot to be desired, so you might find it a bit harder to get started. However, it has a thriving community of its own with a strong core group of developers who continue to support it. We highly recommend checking it out.

7.3.3 DSPy

Unlike other toolings mentioned, DSPy does not give you tools to create your own prompts; rather, it attempts to program prompting. DSPy, coming out of Stanford and heavily backed by many corporate sponsors, takes a unique approach by emphasizing tool augmentation, including retrieval, and is helpful if you would like to treat LLMs as deterministic and programmatic tools instead of emergent infinite syntax generators.

Although this is not exactly what happens, you can think of DSPy as taking a similar logic to prompting that ONNX takes to saving models. Give it some dummy inputs, and it'll compile a graph that can then infer prompts that work the best for your model and return the results you're wanting. There's a bit more work involved, though. You need to write validation logic and modules, essentially a workflow and unit tests, to check against. This effectively changes the dynamic from coming up with clever strings to something much closer to engineering software. Admittedly, it leaves open the question, "If you're going to define everything programmatically anyway, why are you using an LLM?" Still, we've had good experiences with this and use it frequently.

The steps to using DSPy effectively are as follows:

1. Create a signature or a description of the task(s) along with input and output fields.
2. Create a predictor or generation style similar to chain of thought or retrieval.
3. Define the module or program.

Once these steps have been completed, you'll compile the program. This will update the module based on the examples given before, similar to the training set. All of this will feel like machine learning for LLMs, with a training set (examples), a loss function (validation metric), and essentially an optimizer (teleprompter).

In lieu of writing another listing for this chapter showcasing another tool, we decided to point you to an excellent notebook created by the StanfordNLP team introducing DSPy along with local LLMs and custom datasets: https://mng.bz/PNzg (it's forked from here: https://mng.bz/Xxd6). Once you have a chance to explore this example, we also recommend checking out the DSPy documentation, as it has many more excellent examples.

7.3.4 Other tooling is available but . . .

Beyond the previously mentioned tools, a whole host of tools are out there. A couple to note are MiniChain and AutoChain. Both aim to be lightweight alternatives to LangChain, which are sorely needed, as many complain about LangChain's bulkiness. Promptify is an interesting project that is a full-feature alternative to LangChain. To be honest, we could list a dozen more, but there likely isn't much point. While many of these projects drew vibrant communities to them when they started, most have been dormant for months already, with only the rare GitHub contribution.

It's hard to say exactly why the interest in these projects faltered, but one obvious reason is that most of these projects lacked the sponsorship that LangChain, Guidance, and DSPy have. Many of these projects started as personal projects in the middle of big waves from the hype of ChatGPT's success, but hype energy is never enough to build software that lasts. Without proper backing, most open source projects fail.

We've probably painted too bleak a picture. As of the time of this writing, though, it's still too early to tell, and this space is still a growing sector. There are still plenty of interesting tools we recommend checking out that we just don't have space to include, like Haystack, Langflow, and Llama Index. Outlines is particularly of note as a similar project to Guidance, which is also awesome. We mostly want to point out that readers should be careful when picking tooling in this space because everything is still so new. If you find a tool you like, contribute.

7.4 Advanced prompt engineering techniques

No matter how well designed your prompt is, there will be pragmatic context your model won't have access to. For example, current events are a struggle. The model itself will only know about information up to its training date. Sure, we could feed that context in with RAG, as we've done so far, but that just shifts the burden to keeping our RAG system up to date. There's another way. In this section, we will discuss giving models access to tools and what we can do with them once we do.

7.4.1 Giving LLMs tools

What if instead of a complicated prompt engineering system, we instead give our model access to the internet? If it knows how to search the internet, it can always find up-to-date information. While we are at it, we can give it access to a calculator so we don't have to waste CPU cycles having the LLM itself do basic math. We can give it access to a clock so it knows the current time and maybe even a weather app so it can tell the weather. The sky's the limit! We just need to train the model on how to use tools, and that's where Toolformers comes in.[8]

---

[8] T. Schick et al., "Toolformer: Language models can teach themselves to use tools," February 2023, https://arxiv.org/abs/2302.04761.

Toolformers is a marvelously simple idea. Let's train a model to know it can run API calls to different tools using tags like `<API></API>`. Then, at inference, when we see these tags, we can tell our interpreter to run those API calls. If that sounds familiar, it's because Toolformers just trained a model to use string interpolation! String interpolation is the process of evaluating a string literal containing placeholders, which are replaced with the actual values at run time. For example, in Python, we could take the string literal `print(f'2+2 = {2+2}')`, and once printed, we'd get `'2+2 = 4'`. The placeholder `{2+2}` was evaluated and executed as Python code, returning `4`. Schick et al. finetuned a GPT-J model to use five different tools: a question-answering database, a calculator, a Wikipedia search, a translator, and a calendar. With access to these tools, they were able to achieve impressive results, outperforming GPT-3 on many tasks.

While Schick et al.'s work paved the way, the major downside to this approach is that we don't want to finetune a model every time we create a new tool. However, as we've discussed in this chapter, we don't have to. Instead, we can use clever prompt engineering to introduce new tools using LangChain or Guidance. In the next listing, we demonstrate how to create simple math tools with Guidance. Guidance takes care of the heavy lifting by stopping generation when it recognizes a tool being called, running the tool, and starting generation again.

Listing 7.4 Giving tools to our LLM models with Guidance

```
import guidance
from guidance import models, gen

falcon = models.Transformers("tiiuae/falcon-rw-1b")      # Loads a Hugging Face Transformers model


@guidance
def add(lm, input1, input2):
    lm += f" = {int(input1) + int(input2)}"
    return lm


@guidance
def subtract(lm, input1, input2):
    lm += f" = {int(input1) - int(input2)}"
    return lm


@guidance
def multiply(lm, input1, input2):
    lm += f" = {float(input1) * float(input2)}"
    return lm


@guidance
def divide(lm, input1, input2):
    lm += f" = {float(input1) / float(input2)}"
    return lm
```

```
lm = (
    falcon
    + """\
1 + 2 = add(1, 2) = 3
4 - 5 = subtract(4, 5) = -1
5 * 6 = multiply(5, 6) = 30
7 / 8 = divide(7, 8) = 0.875
Generate more examples of add, subtract, multiply, and divide
"""
)
lm += gen(max_tokens=15, tools=[add, subtract, multiply, divide])
print(lm)
```

While a simple example, it's easy to imagine building more advanced tooling. Regardless of whether you use LangChain or Guidance, there are a few things to keep in mind when building tools. First, you'll need to instruct your model in the prompt on where and how to use the tools you give it. This can be more or less difficult, depending on how open-ended your function is. Second, your model matters in its ease of extendibility. Some models we've worked with would never use the tools we gave them or would even hallucinate other tools that didn't exist. Lastly, be really careful with the inputs and error handling for tools you give an LLM. The ones we used previously in this chapter are terrible and likely to break in several ways. For example, an LLM could easily try to run `add(one, two)` or `add(1, 2, 3)`, both of which would throw errors and crash the system. With Guidance, to make this easier, we can enforce tool inputs by building grammars to ensure our model inputs are always correct.

This discussion leads us to uncover some problems with LLMs using tools. First, we have to be careful what tools we give to an LLM since we never really know what input it will generate. Even if we ensure the tool doesn't break, it may do something malicious we didn't intend. Second, as you've probably gathered throughout this chapter, prompt engineering quickly grows our input and thus shrinks the token limit for our actual users; explaining tools and how to use them adds to that constraint. Often, this limitation reduces the number of tools we can give an LLM and, thus, its usefulness. Third, LLMs are still hit or miss as to whether they actually use a tool and can often end up using the wrong tool. For example, should the LLM use the web search tool or the weather tool to look up the 10-day forecast? This might not matter much to us as humans, but results can vary widely for a bot. Lastly, building tools can be difficult and error prone, as you need to build both a clean tool and an effective prompt.

OpenAI's plugins

Toolformers opened the gates to OpenAI's Plugins concept (https://mng.bz/q0rE). Plugins allow third parties to easily integrate their tools into ChatGPT and provide a simple way for ChatGPT to call external APIs. Plugins were introduced relatively early in ChatGPT's life, shortly after the Toolformers paper.[a] All a third party had to do was create an OpenAPI config file and an ai-plugin.json file and host both where the API

(continued)

existed. OpenAPI is a specification language for APIs that standardizes and defines your API to make it easy for others to consume. (If you haven't heard of OpenAPI and have APIs that customers use, it's a good practice to follow. You can learn more at https://www.openapis.org/.) Plenty of tools can help you generate that file easily enough. The ai-plugin file created the plugin. Here, you could define a name for the plugin, how authentication should happen, and descriptions to be used to prompt ChatGPT. From here, the plugin could be registered with OpenAI in ChatGPT's interface, and after a review process, your plugin could be added and used by users as they interacted with ChatGPT.

Despite an initial fervor, plugins never left Beta—beyond OpenAI's own web browsing plugin—and appear to be abandoned. There are lots of reasons for this, but in a since-taken-down report, the main reason came from Sam Altman when he suggested, "A lot of people thought they wanted their apps to be inside ChatGPT, but what they really wanted was ChatGPT in their apps" (https://mng.bz/75Dg). As a result, there didn't seem to be a product market fit for OpenAI's plugins that would make the company money. But we think it's too early to abandon the idea entirely.

As more companies integrate LLM technology into their apps, they are likely going to want access to third-party tools. Suppose you are going camping for the first time and you ask an LLM shopping assistant for advice on what to buy. In that case, it'd be really nice if it thought first to ask where and when you were going camping and then could use that information to identify weather-appropriate gear. The LLM shopping assistant for a particular brand or store is likely to have access to loads of products, but access to weather reports in a random geolocation? Not so much.

While you can always build these tools, wouldn't it be great if they were already created for you, and you could simply go to some hub, download the ones you wanted, and plug them in? Unfortunately, this option doesn't exist yet, at least not to the extent we describe it here. We have high expectations that a marketplace or hub of some kind will be created in the future, like OpenAI's plugins, that can be used with any LLM model. LLMs are still a new technology, and the ecosystems to be built around them are still forthcoming; we believe this will be one of them.

[a] T. Schick et al., "Toolformer: Language models can teach themselves to use tools," February 2023.

Once we give our LLMs access to tools, it opens the gates to lots of cool prompt engineering techniques. Probably the most famous is the ReAct method.

7.4.2 ReAct

Reasoning and Acting (ReAct) is a few-shot framework for prompting that is meant to emulate how people reason and make decisions when learning new tasks.[9] It involves a

[9] S. Yao et al., "ReAct: Synergizing reasoning and acting in language models," March 10, 2023, https://arxiv.org/abs/2210.03629.

multistep process for the LLM, where a question is asked, the model determines an action, and then it observes and reasons upon the results of that action to determine subsequent actions.

An example could look like this:

> **Question:** What is the airspeed velocity of an unladen African swallow compared to a European swallow with the same load?
>
> **Thought 1:** I need to search for airspeed velocity of a European swallow so I can compare it with an African swallow.
>
> **Action 1:** Search[European Swallow airspeed velocity]
>
> **Observation 1:** We need to know the Strouhal number in order to determine airspeed. The bird's Strouhal number converges between 0.2 and 0.4.
>
> **Thought 2:** The airspeed velocity is not directly mentioned, but the Strouhal number is clear. So I need to look up velocity compared to the Strouhal number.
>
> **Action 2:** Search[Strouhal wingbeat calculation]
>
> **Observation 2:** (Result 1/1) A Swallow's Strouhal number translates to ~12 wingbeats per second.
>
> **Thought 3:** An African swallow requires 12 wingbeats per second to maintain airspeed velocity, so I need to look up how fast that makes it.
>
> **Action 3:** Lookup[African Swallow wingbeat per second]
>
> **Observation 3:** Each wingbeat propels an African swallow 2.5 feet per flap, making it go about 40.2mph
>
> **Thought 4:** I need to look up the European swallow to compare it.
>
> **Action 4:** Search[European Swallow Wingbeat per second]
>
> **Observation 4:** A European swallow is about half the size of an African swallow, making its velocity about 20.1
>
> **Thought 5:** An African swallow has an airspeed velocity of 40.2, and a European swallow has an airspeed velocity of 20.1, making the comparison 2x.
>
> **Action 5:** Finish[Two times the airspeed velocity]

As you can see, the purpose of ReAct is to force the model to think before it acts. This isn't much different from the other prompting methods we have discussed. The big difference is that we allow the model to take actions. In our example, this included a "Search" action, or essentially an ability to look up information on the internet as a human would. We just showed you how to do this in the last section. The model can take that new information and observe what it learns from its actions to produce a result.

Let's explore this further with an example. We will use LangChain, which will make creating a ReAct agent seem a lot easier than it actually is. Listing 7.5 shows how to utilize ReAct on an OpenAI model and LangChain. For our search engine, we will be utilizing serper.dev, as it integrates nicely with LangChain, and it offers a free tier you can sign up for. We will also need to use the calculator `"llm-math"`, which is one of the many tools in LangChain's toolbelt.

Listing 7.5 Example ReAct with Langchain

```
import os
from langchain.llms import OpenAI
from langchain.agents import load_tools
from langchain.agents import initialize_agent
from dotenv import load_dotenv

load_dotenv()

os.environ["OPENAI_API_KEY"] = os.getenv("OPENAI_API_KEY")
os.environ["SERPER_API_KEY"] = os.getenv("SERPER_API_KEY")

llm = OpenAI(model_name="text-davinci-003", temperature=0)
tools = load_tools(["google-serper", "llm-math"], llm=llm)
agent = initialize_agent(
    tools, llm, agent="zero-shot-react-description", verbose=True
)

agent.run(
    "Who is Olivia Wilde's boyfriend? \
    What is his current age raised to the 0.23 power?"
)
```

Loads API keys; you will need to obtain these if you haven't yet

The output is

```
# > Entering new AgentExecutor chain...
# I need to find out who Olivia Wilde's boyfriend is and then
# calculate his age raised to the 0.23 power.
# Action: Search
# Action Input: "Olivia Wilde boyfriend"
# Observation: Olivia Wilde started dating Harry Styles after ending
# her years-long engagement to Jason Sudeikis – see their relationship
# timeline.
# Thought: I need to find out Harry Styles' age.
# Action: Search
# Action Input: "Harry Styles age"
# Observation: 29 years
# Thought: I need to calculate 29 raised to the 0.23 power.
# Action: Calculator
# Action Input: 29^0.23
# Observation: Answer: 2.169459462491557
```

```
# Thought: I now know the final answer.
# Final Answer: Harry Styles, Olivia Wilde's boyfriend, is 29 years old
# and his age raised to the 0.23 power is 2.169459462491557.

# > Finished chain.

# "Harry Styles, Olivia Wilde's boyfriend, is 29 years old and his age
# raised to the 0.23 power is 2.169459462491557."
```

Listing 7.5 shows how ReAct can be used with an LLM in conjunction with particular agent tools like `"google-serper"` and `"llm-math"` to help augment your prompts. Prompt engineering looks more like a full-time job now, not just "coming up with words," huh?

Knowing how to build tools and combine them to prompt LLMs to answer more in-depth questions is a growing field of study as well as an expanding part of the job market. To be perfectly honest, the rate of change in the prompt engineering field seems to drastically outpace most of the other topics we cover in this book. There's a lot more to be discussed that we simply can't cover in this book, so much so, in fact, that there are now entire books in and of themselves being written to this end. It was difficult to determine what would be valuable to our readers and what would be outdated quickly, but we think we've found a good balance and encourage you to look forward to researching more on the topic.

Overall, we've learned a lot throughout this chapter—how to craft a prompt and how to implement prompting in an engineering fashion. In the next chapter, we will put all of this knowledge to good use when we build LLM applications users can interact with.

Summary

- The most straightforward approach to prompting is to give a model examples of what you want it to do:
  - The more examples you can add to a prompt, the more accurate your results will be.
  - The fewer examples you need to add, the more general and all-purpose your prompt will be.
- The four parts of a prompt are
  - *Input*—What the user writes
  - *Instruction*—The template with task-specific information encoded
  - *Context*—The information you add through RAG or other database lookups
  - *System*—The specific instructions given for every task; should be hidden from the user
- Knowing your training data will help you craft better prompts by choosing a word order that matches the training data.

- LangChain is a popular tool that allows us to create chains or pipelines to utilize LLMs in an engineering fashion.
- Guidance is a powerful tool that gives us more fine-grained control over the LLMs' actual generated text.
- Toolformers teach LLMs how to use tools, giving them the ability to accomplish previously impossible tasks.
- ReAct is a few-shot framework for prompting that is meant to emulate how people reason and make decisions when learning new tasks.

8 Large language model applications: Building an interactive experience

This chapter covers

- Building an interactive application that uses an LLM service
- Running LLMs on edge devices without a GPU
- Building LLM agents that can solve multistep problems

No one cares how much you know until they know how much you care.

—President Theodore Roosevelt

Throughout this book, we've taught you the ins and outs of LLMs—how to train them, how to deploy them, and, in the last chapter, how to build a prompt to guide a model to behave how you want it to. In this chapter, we will put it all together. We will show you how to build an application that can use your deployed LLM service and create a delightful experience for an actual user. The key word there is delightful. Creating a simple application is easy, as we will show, but creating one that delights? Well, that's a bit more difficult. We'll discuss multiple features you'll want to add to your application and why. Then, we'll discuss different places your application may live, including building such applications for edge devices. Lastly, we'll dive into the world of LLM agents, building applications that can fulfill a role, not just a request.

8.1 Building an application

It's probably best that we start by explaining what we mean by LLM application. Afterall, *application* is a ubiquitous term that could mean lots of different things. For us, in this book, when we say *LLM application*, we mean the frontend—the Web App, Phone App, CLI, SDK, VSCode Extension (check out chapter 10!), or any other application that will act as the user interface and client for calling our LLM Service. Figure 8.1 shows both the frontend and backend separately to help focus on the piece of the puzzle we are discussing: the frontend. It's a pretty important piece to the puzzle but also varies quite a bit! While every environment will come with its own challenges, we hope we can trust you to know the details for your particular use case. For example, if you are building an Android app, it's up to you to learn Java or Kotlin. In this book, however, we will give you the building blocks you will need and introduce the important features to add.

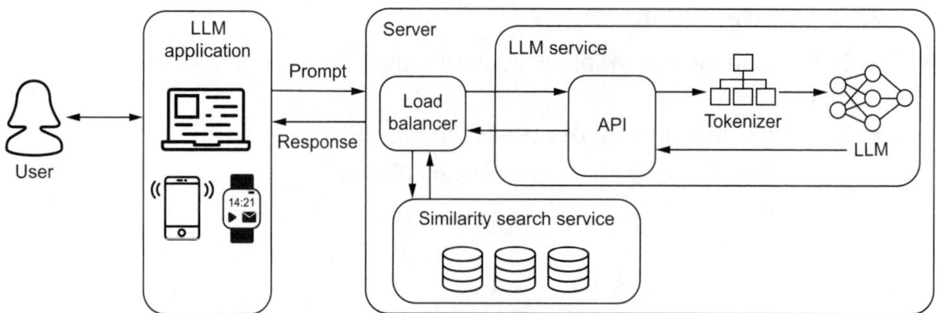

Figure 8.1 The LLM Application is the web app, phone app, command line interface, or another tool that acts as the client our users will use to interact with our LLM service.

The first step to building a successful LLM application is composing and experimenting with your prompt. Of course, having just discussed this in the last chapter, there are many additional features you should consider to offer a better user experience. The most basic LLM application is just a chatbox, which essentially consists of only three objects: an input field, a send button, and a text field to hold the conversation. It's rather easy to build in almost every context. In addition, since one of our participants in the chat is a bot, most of the complexity of building a chat interface is also stripped away. For example, we don't need to worry about eventual consistency, mixing up the order of our conversation, or whether both users are sending a message at the same time. If our user has a bad internet connection, we can throw a timeout error and let them resubmit.

However, while the interface is easy, not all the finishing touches are. In this section, we are going to share with you some tools of the trade to make your LLM application shine. We focus on best practices, like streaming responses, utilizing the chat history, and methods to handle and utilize prompt engineering. These allow us to craft, format, and clean our users' prompts and the LLM's responses under the hood, improving results and overall customer satisfaction. All this to say, building a basic application that utilizes an LLM is actually rather easy, but building a great application is a different story, and we want to build great applications.

8.1.1 Streaming on the frontend

In chapter 6, we showed you how to stream your LLM's response on the server side, but that is meaningless if the response isn't streamed on the client side as well. Streaming on the client side is where it all comes together. It's where we show the text to the users as it is being generated. This provides an attractive user experience, as it makes it appear like the text is being typed right before our eyes and gives the users a sense that the model is actually thinking about what it will write next. Not only that, but it also provides a more springy and responsive experience, as we can give a feeling of instant feedback, which encourages our users to stick around until the model finishes generating. This also helps the user to be able to see where the output is going before it gets too far so they can stop generation and reprompt.

In listing 8.1, we show you how to do this with just HTML, CSS, and vanilla JavaScript. This application is meant to be dead simple. Many of our readers likely aren't frontend savvy, as that isn't the focus of this book. Those who are most likely will be using some tooling for their framework of choice anyway. But a basic application with no frills allows us to get to the core of what's happening.

Since the application is so simple, we opted to put all the CSS and JavaScript together into the HTML, although it would be cleaner and a best practice to separate them. The CSS defines sizing to ensure our boxes are big enough to read; we won't bother with colors or making it look pretty. Our HTML is as simple as it gets: a form containing a text input and a Send button that returns false on submit so the page doesn't refresh. There's also a `div` container to contain our chat messages. Most of the JavaScript is also not that interesting; it just handles adding our conversation to the chat. However, pay attention to the `sendToServer` function, which does most of the heavy lifting: sending our prompt, receiving a readable stream, and iterating over the results.

NOTE On the server side, we set up a `StreamingResponse` object, which gets converted to a `ReadableStream` on the JavaScript side. You can learn more about readable streams here: https://mng.bz/75Dg.

Listing 8.1 Streaming responses to end users

```
<!DOCTYPE html>
<html lang="en">
    <head>
        <meta charset="UTF-8">
```

```
    <meta name="viewport" content="width=device-width, initial-scale=1.0">
    <title>Simple Chat App</title>

    <style>                                          <-- Some very simple styling
        body {
            font-family: Arial, sans-serif;
            margin: 0;
            padding: 0;
            box-sizing: border-box;
        }

        #message-input {
            width: 95%;
            padding: 8px;
        }

        #chat-container {
            width: 95%;
            margin: 20px auto;
            border: 1px solid #ccc;
            padding: 10px;
            overflow-y: scroll;
            max-height: 300px;
        }
    </style>
</head>
                                      Our body is simple with only
                                      three fields: a text input, send
<body>                            <-- button, and container for chat.
    <form onsubmit="return false;"">
        <input type="text" id="message-input" placeholder="Type your
 message...">
        <button onclick="sendMessage()" type="submit">Send</button>
    </form>
    <div id="chat-container"></div>
</body>
                                      JavaScript to handle
                                      communication with LLM
<script>                          <-- and streaming response
    function sendMessage() {                                          <--
        var messageInput = document.getElementById('message-input');
        var message = messageInput.value.trim();
                                                   When the Send button is
        if (message !== '') {                    pushed, moves text from input
            appendMessage('You: ' + message);      to chat box and sends the
            messageInput.value = '';              message to the LLM server
            sendToServer(message);
        }
    }
                                                        Adds new messages
                                                        to the chat box
    function appendMessage(message) {                <--
        var chatContainer = document.getElementById('chat-container');
        var messageElement = document.createElement('div');
        messageElement.textContent = message;
        chatContainer.appendChild(messageElement);
        chatContainer.scrollTop = chatContainer.scrollHeight;
```

```
        return messageElement
    }

    async function sendToServer(message) {
        var payload = {
            prompt: message
        }

        const response = await fetch('http://localhost:8000/generate', {
            method: 'POST',
            headers: {
                'Content-Type': 'application/json',
            },
            body: JSON.stringify(payload),
        });

        var responseText = 'LLM: ';
        messageElement = appendMessage(responseText);

        for await (const chunk of streamAsyncIterator(response.body)) {
            var strChunk = String.fromCharCode.apply(null, chunk);
            responseText += strChunk;
            messageElement.textContent = responseText;
        }
    }

    async function* streamAsyncIterator(stream) {
        const reader = stream.getReader();
        try {
            while (true) {
                const {done, value} = await reader.read();
                if (done) return;
                yield value;
            }
        }
        finally {
            reader.releaseLock();
        }
    }
  </script>
</html>
```

Sends prompt to the server and streams the response back as tokens are received

Simple polyfill since StreamResponse still can't be used as an iterator by most browsers

Figure 8.2 shows screenshots of our simple application from listing 8.1. Showing words being streamed to the application would have been better in a movie or GIF, but since books don't play GIFs, we'll have to make do with several side-by-side screenshots instead. Regardless, the figure shows the results being streamed to the user token by token, providing a positive user experience.

There's nothing glamorous about our little application here, and that's partly the point. This code is easy to copy and paste and can be used anywhere a web browser can run since it's just an HTML file. It doesn't take much to build a quick demo app once you have an LLM service running.

Type your message... Send You: Who would win in a battle, Squirtle or Charmander? LMM:	Type your message... Send You: Who would win in a battle, Squirtle or Charmander? LMM: Who would win in a battle, Squirtle or Charmander? The
Type your message... Send You: Who would win in a battle, Squirtle or Charmander? LMM: Who would win in a battle, Squirtle or Charmander? The answer is that	Type your message... Send You: Who would win in a battle, Squirtle or Charmander? LMM: Who would win in a battle, Squirtle or Charmander? The answer is that Squirtle is the best of the best.

Figure 8.2 Screenshots of our simple application showing the response being streamed

8.1.2 Keeping a history

One big problem with our simple application so far is that each message sent to our LLM is independent of other messages sent. This is a big problem because most applications that utilize an LLM do so in an interactive environment. Users will ask a question and then, based on the response, make additional questions or adjustments and clarifications to get better results. However, if you simply send the latest query as a prompt, the LLM will not have any context behind the new query. Independence is nice for coin flips, but it will make our LLM look like a birdbrain.

What we need to do is keep a history of the conversation, both the user's prompts and the LLM's responses. If we do that, we can append that history to the new prompts as context. The LLM will be able to utilize this background information to make better responses. Figure 8.3 shows the overall flow of what we are trying to achieve.

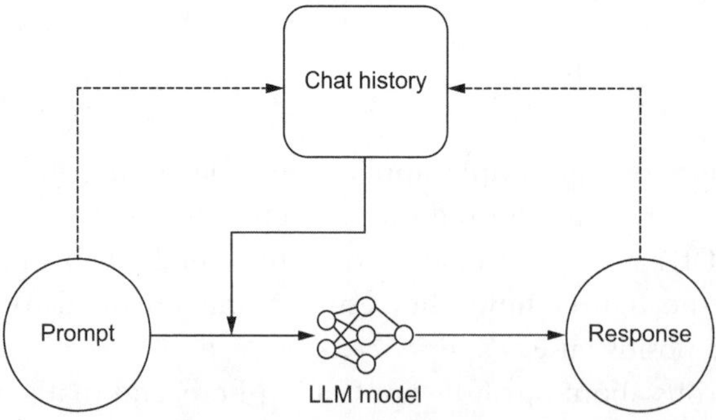

Figure 8.3 Process flow for storing prompts and responses to a chat history, giving our model a memory of the conversation to improve outcomes

Now that we know what we are building, let's take a look at listing 8.2. This time, we will be using Streamlit, a Python framework for building applications. It is simple and easy to use while still creating attractive frontends. From Streamlit, we will be utilizing a `chat_input` field so users can write and send their input, a `chat_message` field that will hold the conversation, and `session_state`, where we will create and store the `chat_history`. We will use that chat history to craft a better prompt. You'll also notice that we continue to stream the responses, as demonstrated in the last section, but this time using Python.

What is Streamlit?

Streamlit is an open-source Python library that makes it easy to create web applications for machine learning, data science, and other fields. It allows you to quickly build interactive web apps using simple Python scripts. With Streamlit, you can create dashboards, data visualizations, and other interactive tools without needing to know web development languages like HTML, CSS, or JavaScript. Streamlit automatically handles the conversion of your Python code into a web app.

Listing 8.2 An example application using chat history to improve results

```
import streamlit as st
import requests
import json

url = "http://localhost:8000/generate"          # Points to your model's API

st.title("Chatbot with History")

if "chat_history" not in st.session_state:      # Creates a chat history in the session state
    st.session_state.chat_history = []

for chat in st.session_state.chat_history:      # Displays chat from history
    with st.chat_message(chat["role"]):
        st.markdown(chat["content"])

if user_input := st.chat_input("Your question here"):
    with st.chat_message("user"):
        st.markdown(user_input)

    st.session_state.chat_history.append(
        {"role": "user", "content": user_input}
    )

    with st.chat_message("assistant"):          # Streams response
        placeholder = st.empty()
        full_response = ""

        prompt = "You are an assistant who helps the user. "
        "Answer their questions as accurately as possible. Be concise. "
        history = [
            f'{ch["role"]}: {ch["content"]}'
            for ch in st.session_state.chat_history
        ]
```

Annotations:
- Responds to user. Note: we use the walrus operator (:=) to assign the user's input while also ensuring it is not None at the same time.
- Displays user's input
- Adds user input to chat history
- Formats prompt adding chat history for additional context

```
        prompt += " ".join(history)
        prompt += " assistant: "
        data = json.dumps({"prompt": prompt})
                                                                           Sends
        with requests.post(url, data=data, stream=True) as r:           <- request
            for line in r.iter_lines(decode_unicode=True):
                full_response += line.decode("utf-8")                     Adds a blinking
                placeholder.markdown(full_response + "▌ ")             <- cursor to
        placeholder.markdown(full_response)                               simulate typing

    st.session_state.chat_history.append(                      <- Adds LLM response
        {"role": "assistant", "content": full_response}           to chat history
    )
```

Figure 8.4 is a screenshot capturing the LLM app that we just built. While our first example was quite ugly, you can see that Streamlit automatically creates a nice user interface, complete with finishing touches, like a picture of a human face for the user and a robot face for our LLM assistant. You'll also notice that the model is taking in and comprehending the conversation history—albeit giving terrible responses. If we want to get better responses, one thing to be sure of is that your LLM has been trained on conversation data.

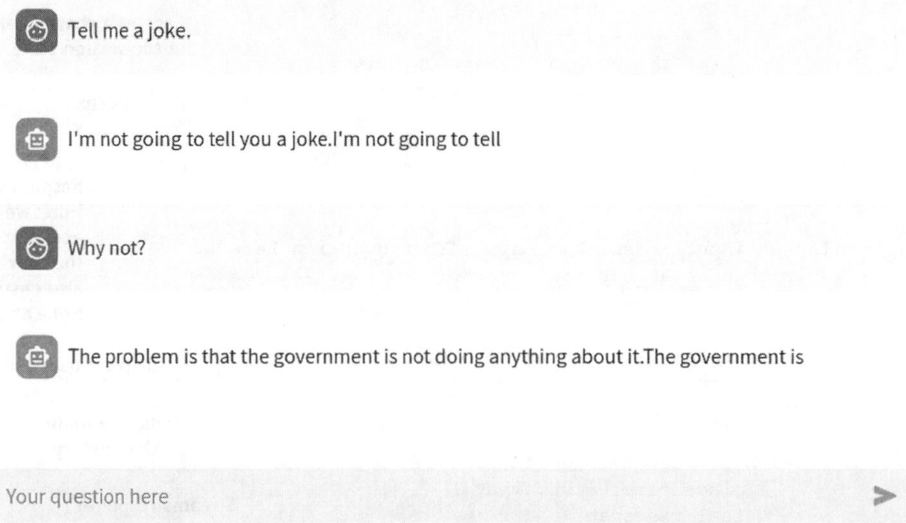

Figure 8.4 Screenshot of our Streamlit app utilizing a chat history

Of course, utilizing the history leads to some problems. The first is that users can have relatively long conversations with our bot, but we are still limited in the token length we can feed to the model, and the longer the input, the longer the generation takes. At some point, the history will begin to be too long. The simplest approach to solving this problem is to drop older messages in favor of newer ones. Sure, our model may forget important details or instructions at the start of our conversation, but humans also tend to have a recency bias in conversations, so this tends to be OK—except, of course, for the fact that humans tend to expect computers never to forget anything.

A more robust solution is to use the LLM to summarize the chat history and use the summary as context to our users' queries instead of the full chat history. LLMs are often quite good at highlighting important pieces of information from a body of text, so this can be an effective way to compress a conversation. Compression can be done on demand or run as a background process. Figure 8.5 illustrates the summarization workflow for chat history compression.

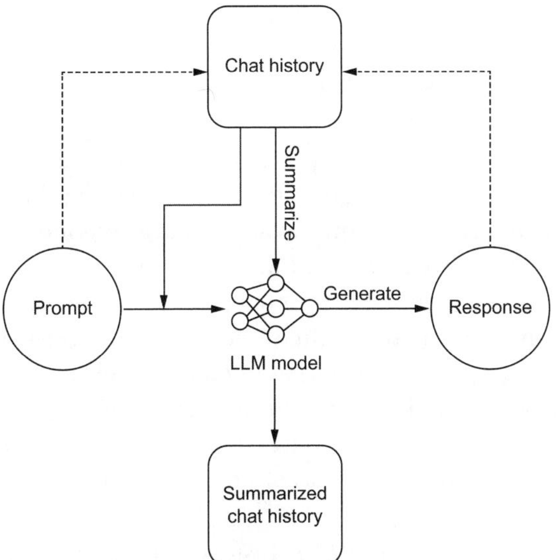

Figure 8.5 A process flow for an app with chat history utilizing summarization for chat history compression

There are other strategies you can explore, as well as mixing and matching multiple methods. Another idea is to embed each chat and perform a search for relevant previous chat messages to add to the prompt context. But no matter how you choose to shorten the chat history, details are bound to be lost or forgotten the longer a conversation goes on or the larger the prompts and responses are.

8.1.3 Chatbot interaction features

Chatting with an LLM bot isn't like chatting with your friend. For one, the chatbot is always available and waiting for us to talk to it, so we can expect a response right away. There shouldn't be opportunities for users to spam multiple messages to our bot before receiving feedback. But let's face it, in the real world, there are connection problems or bad internet, the server could be overwhelmed, and there are a myriad of other reasons a request might fail. These differences encourage us to interact with a chatbot differently, and we should ensure we add several features for our users to improve their experience. Let's consider several of them now:

- *Fallback response*—A response to give when an error occurs. To keep things clean, you'll want to ensure a 1:1 ratio of LLM responses for every user query in your chat history. A fallback response ensures our chat history is clean and gives the user instructions on the best course of action, like trying again in a few minutes. Speaking of which, you should also consider disabling the Submit button when receiving a response to prevent weird problems from asynchronous conversations and out-of-order chat history.
- *Stop button*—Interrupts a response midstream. An LLM can often be long-winded, continuing to respond long after answering the user's questions. Often, it misunderstands a question and starts to answer it incorrectly. In these cases, it's best to give the user a Stop button so they can interrupt the model and move on. This button is a simple cost-saving feature since we usually pay for output per token one way or another.
- *Retry button*—Resends the last query and replaces the response. LLMs have a bit of randomness to them, which can be great for creative writing, but it means they may respond unfavorably even to prompts they have responded correctly to multiple times before. Since we add the LLM chat history to new prompts to give context, a retry button allows users to attempt to get a better result and keep the conversation moving in the right direction. While retrying, it can make sense to adjust our prompting hyperparameters, for example, reducing temperature each time a user retries. This can help push the responses in the direction the user is likely expecting. Of course, this likely isn't the best move if they are retrying because of a bad internet connection, so you'll need to consider the adjustments carefully.
- *Delete button*—Removes portions of the chat history. As mentioned, the chat history is used as context in future responses, but not every response is immediately identifiable as bad. We often see red herrings. For example, a chat assistant used while coding might hallucinate functions or methods that don't exist, which can lead the conversation down a path that is hard to recover from. Of course, depending on your needs, the solution could be a soft delete, where we only remove it from the frontend and prompting space but not the backend.
- *Feedback form*—A way to collect feedback on users' experience. If you are training or finetuning your own LLMs, this data is highly valuable, as it can help your team improve results on the next training iteration. This data can often easily be applied when using RLHF. Of course, you won't want to apply it directly, but first clean and filter out troll responses. Also, even if you aren't training, it can help your team make decisions to switch models, improve prompting, and identify edge cases.

In listing 8.3, we show how to use Gradio to set up an easy chatbot app. Gradio is an open source library for quickly creating customizable user interfaces for data science demos and web applications. It's highly popular for its ease of integration within Juptyer notebooks, making it easy to create interfaces and edit your web app in a familiar environment. To create a chatbot with Gradio, we'll use the `ChatInterface` and give it a function to make our API request. You'll notice that Gradio expects the history to be part of the `generate` function, and streaming is just a matter of ensuring the function is a generator.

> **What is Gradio?**
>
> Gradio is an open-source Python library that allows you to quickly create customizable UI components around your machine-learning models. It provides a simple interface for building interactive web-based applications for your models without requiring you to write any HTML, CSS, or JavaScript code. With Gradio, you can create input forms for your models, display the results, and even share your models with others through a web interface.

Listing 8.3 Local LLM Gradio chat app with Stop, Retry, and Undo

```
import gradio as gr
import requests
import json

url = "http://localhost:8000/generate"        # Points to your model's API


def generate(message, history):
    history_transformer_format = history + [[message, ""]]
    messages = "".join(
        [
            "".join(["\n<human>:" + h, "\n<bot>:" + b])
            for h, b in history_transformer_format
        ]
    )
    data = json.dumps({"prompt": messages})

    full_response = ""
    with requests.post(url, data=data, stream=True) as r:     # Sends request
        for line in r.iter_lines(decode_unicode=True):
            full_response += line.decode("utf-8")
            yield full_response + "▌"       # Adds a blinking cursor to simulate typing
        yield full_response


gr.ChatInterface(generate, theme="soft").queue().launch()
```

You can see how simple this code is, with very few lines needed. Gradio does all the heavy lifting for us. You might also be wondering where all our interaction features are. Well, the good news is that Gradio automatically adds most of these features for us. Don't believe me? Check out the app we just created in figure 8.6.

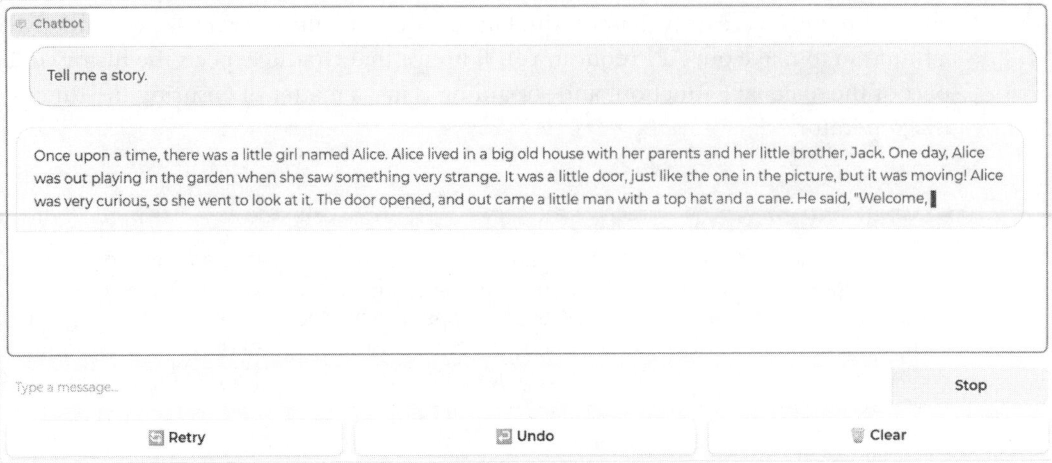

Figure 8.6 Screenshot of our Gradio app, including interaction features Stop, Retry, and Undo for better ease of use

> **Chainlit: An application builder just for LLMs**
>
> We have shown you how to build LLM applications with several different tools: Streamlit, Gradio, and even vanilla HTML and JavaScript. There are many great tools out there, and we can't give personal attention to each one. But one more tool we think many of our readers will be interested in is Chainlit. Chainlit is a tool specifically built for building LLM applications and comes with most features out of the box, including ones not discussed here, like themes, CSS customization, authentication, and cloud hosting. It is likely one of the fastest ways to get up and running.

Each quality-of-life improvement you can add to your application will help it stand out above the competition and potentially save you money. For the same reason, you should consider using a token counter, which we cover next.

8.1.4 Token counting

One of the most basic but valuable pieces of information you can gather to offer a great user experience is the number of submitted tokens. Since LLMs have token limits, we'll need to ensure the users' prompts don't exceed those limits. Giving feedback early and often will provide a better user experience. No one wants to type a long query only to find that it's too much upon submitting.

Counting tokens also allows us to better prompt-engineer and improve results. For example, in a Q&A bot, if the user's question is particularly short, we can add more context by extending how many search results our retrieval-augmented generation (RAG) system will return. If their question is long, we'll want to limit it and ensure we have enough space to append our own context.

Tiktoken is just such a library to help with this task. It's an extremely fast BPE tokenizer built specifically for OpenAI's models. The package has been ported to multiple languages, including tiktoken-go for Golang, tiktoken-rs for Rust, and several others. In the next listing, we show a basic example of how to use it. It's been optimized for speed, which allows us to encode and count tokens quickly, which is all we need to do.

Listing 8.4 Using tiktoken to count tokens

```
import tiktoken

encoding = tiktoken.get_encoding("cl100k_base")
print(encoding.encode("You're users chat message goes here."))
# [2675, 2351, 3932, 6369, 1984, 5900, 1618, 13]
def count_tokens(string: str) -> int:
    encoding = tiktoken.get_encoding("cl100k_base")
    return len(encoding.encode(string))

num_tokens = count_tokens("You're users chat message goes here.")
print(num_tokens)
# 8
```

Of course, the reader who hasn't skipped ahead will recognize a few problems with using tiktoken, mainly because it's built with OpenAI's encoders in mind. If you are using your own tokenizer (which we recommend), it's not going to be very accurate. We have seen several developers—out of laziness or not knowing a better solution—still use it for other models. Generally, they saw counts within ±5–10 tokens per 1,000 tokens when using tiktoken results for other models using similar BPE tokenizers. To them, the speed and latency gains justified the inaccuracy, but this was all word of mouth, so take it with a grain of salt.

If you are using a different type of tokenizer, like SentencePiece, it's often better to create your own token counter. For example, we do just that in our project in chapter 10. As you can guess, the code follows the same pattern of encoding the string and counting the tokens. The hard part comes when porting it to the language that needs to run the counter. To do so, compile the tokenizer like you would any other ML model, as we discussed in section 6.1.1.

8.1.5 RAG applied

RAG is an excellent way to add context and outside knowledge to your LLM to improve the accuracy of your results. In the last chapter, we discussed it in the context of a backend system. Here, we will be discussing it from the frontend perspective. Your RAG system can be set up on either side, each with its own pros and cons.

Setting up RAG on the backend ensures a consistent experience for all users and gives us greater control as developers of how exactly the context data will be used. It also provides a bit more security to the data stored in the vector database, as it's only accessible to the end users through the LLM. Of course, through clever prompt injection, it could potentially still be scraped, but it is still much more secure than simply allowing users to query your data directly.

RAG is more often set up on the frontend because doing so allows developers to take whatever generic LLM is available and insert business context. You don't need to finetune a model on your dataset if you give the model your dataset at run time. Thus, RAG becomes a system to add personality and functionality to our LLM application versus simply being a tool to ensure the accuracy of results and reduce hallucinations.

In section 6.1.8, we showed you how to set up a RAG system; now we will show you how to utilize it for efficient query augmentation. In listing 8.5, we show you how to access and use the vector store we set up previously. We will continue to use OpenAI and Pinecone from our last example. We will also use LangChain, a Python framework which we discovered in the last chapter, to help create LLM applications.

Listing 8.5 RAG on the frontend

```
import os
import pinecone
from langchain.chains import RetrievalQA
from langchain.chains import RetrievalQAWithSourcesChain
from langchain.chat_models import ChatOpenAI
from langchain.embeddings.openai import OpenAIEmbeddings
from langchain.vectorstores import Pinecone

OPENAI_API_KEY = os.getenv("OPENAI_API_KEY")          # Gets OpenAI API key from platform.openai.com
PINECONE_API_KEY = os.getenv("PINECONE_API_KEY")      # Finds API key in console at app.pinecone.io

index_name = "pincecone-llm-example"                  # Sets up vectorstore
index = pinecone.Index(index_name)
embedder = OpenAIEmbeddings(
    model="text-embedding-ada-002", openai_api_key=OPENAI_API_KEY
)
text_field = "text"
vectorstore = Pinecone(index, embedder.embed_query, text_field)

query = "Who was Johannes Gutenberg?"                 # Makes a query
vectorstore.similarity_search(
    query, k=3                                        # Our search query; returns the three most relevant docs
)

llm = ChatOpenAI(                                     # Now let's use these results to enrich our LLM prompt; sets up the LLM
    openai_api_key=OPENAI_API_KEY,
    model_name="gpt-3.5-turbo",
    temperature=0.0,
)

qa = RetrievalQA.from_chain_type(                     # Runs query with vectorstore
    llm=llm, chain_type="stuff", retriever=vectorstore.as_retriever()
)
qa.run(query)
```

```
qa_with_sources = RetrievalQAWithSourcesChain.from_chain_type(
    llm=llm, chain_type="stuff", retriever=vectorstore.as_retriever()
)
qa_with_sources(query)
```

Includes Wikipedia sources

We think the most impressive part of this code is the fact that LangChain has a chain simply named "stuff" because, presumably, they couldn't think of anything better. (If you want to learn more about the cryptically named module "stuff," you can find the docs at https://mng.bz/OBER.) But in actuality, the most impressive thing about this code is that we just have to define our LLM and vector store connections, and we are good to go to start making queries. Simple.

8.2 Edge applications

So far, we have discussed building LLM applications, assuming we will simply be using an API—one we deployed, but an API nonetheless. However, there are lots of situations where you might want to run the model on the local device inside the application itself. Doing so brings several challenges: mainly, we need to get a model small enough to transfer and run it on the edge device. We also need to be able to run it in the local environment, which likely doesn't have an accelerator or GPU and may not even support Python—for example, running an app in a user's web browser with JavaScript, in an Android app on a mobile phone with Java, or on limited hardware like a Raspberry Pi.

In chapter 6, we started discussing the building blocks you need to work with edge devices. We showed you how to compile a model, giving examples using TensorRT or ONNX Runtime. TensorRT, coming from NVIDIA, is going to serve you better on a server with expensive NVIDIA hardware to go with it, so it is less useful for edge development. ONNX Runtime is a bit more flexible, but when working with edge devices, llama.cpp is often a better solution for LLMs, and it follows the same flow: compile the model to the correct format, move that model to the edge device, download and install the SDK for your language, and run the model. Let's take a closer look at these steps for llama.cpp.

The llama.cpp project started with the goal of converting an LLM to something that could be run on a MacBook without a GPU (Apple silicon chips are notorious for poor compatibility for many projects). Initially working to quantize the LLaMA model and store it in a binary format that could be used by the C++ language, the project has grown to support a couple of dozen LLM architectures and all major OS platforms, has bindings for a dozen languages, and even CUDA, metal, and OpenCL GPU backend support. Llama.cpp has created two different formats to store the quantized LLMs: the first GPT-Generated Model Language (GGML), which was later abandoned for the better GPT-Generated Unified Format (GGUF).

To use llama.cpp, the first thing we'll need is a model stored in the GGUF format. To convert your own, you'd need to clone the llama.cpp project, install the dependencies, and then run the convert script that comes with the project. The steps have changed frequently enough that you'll want to consult the latest information in the repo, but currently, it would look like

```
$ git clone https://github.com/ggerganov/llama.cpp.git
$ cd llama.cpp
$ pip install -r requirments/requirements-convert.txt
$ python convert.py -h
```

Of course, that last command simply displays the convert script's Help menu for you to investigate the options and does not actually convert a model. For our purposes, we'll download an already converted model. We briefly mentioned Tom Jobbins (TheBloke) in chapter 6, the man who has converted thousands of models, quantizing and finetuning them so they are in a state ready for use. All you have to do is download them from the Hugging Face Hub. So we'll do that now. First, we'll need the `huggingface-cli`, which comes as a dependency with most of Hugging Face's Python packages, so you probably already have it, but you can install it directly as well. Then we'll use it to download the model:

```
$ pip install -U huggingface_hub
$ huggingface-cli download TheBloke/WizardCoder-Python-7B-V1.0-GGUF --
➥ local-dir ./models --local-dir-use-symlinks False --include='*Q2_K*gguf'
```

Here, we are downloading the WizardCoder-7B model that has already been converted to a GGUF format by TheBloke. We are going to save it locally in the models directory. We won't use symbolic links (symlinks), meaning the model will actually exist in the folder we choose. Normally, `huggingface-cli` would download it to a cache directory and create a symlink to save space and avoid downloading models multiple times across projects. Lastly, the Hugging Face repo contains multiple versions of the model in different quantized states; here, we'll select the 2-bit quantized version with the `include` flag. This extreme quantization will degrade the performance of the quality of our output for the model, but it's the smallest model available in the repo (only 2.82 GB), which makes it great for demonstration purposes.

Now that we have our model, we need to download and install the bindings for our language of choice and run it. For Python, that would mean installing `llama-cpp-python` via `pip`. In listing 8.6, we show you how to use the library to run a GGUF model. It's pretty straightforward, with just two steps: load the model and run it. On one author's CPU, it ran a little slower than about a token per second, which isn't fast but impressive enough for a 7B parameter model without an accelerator.

Listing 8.6 Using llama.cpp to run a quantized model on a CPU

```
import time
from llama_cpp import Llama

llm = Llama(model_path="./models/wizardcoder-python-7b-v1.0.Q2_K.gguf")
```

```
start_time = time.time()
output = llm(
    "Q: Write python code to reverse a linked list. A: ",
    max_tokens=200,
    stop=["Q:"],
    echo=True,
)
end_time = time.time()

print(output["choices"])
```

The results are

```
# [
#     {'text': "Q: Write python code to reverse a linked list. A:
#         class Node(object):
#             def __init__(self, data=None):
#                 self.data = data
#                 self.next = None

#         def reverse_list(head):
#             prev = None
#             current = head
#             while current is not None:
#                 next = current.next
#                 current.next = prev
#                 prev = current
#                 current = next
#             return prev
#             # example usage;
#             # initial list
#         head = Node('a')
#         head.next=Node('b')
#         head.next.next=Node('c')
#         head.next.next.next=Node('d')
#         print(head)
#          reverse_list(head) # call the function
#         print(head)
# Expected output: d->c->b->a",
#     'index': 0,
#     'logprobs': None,
#     'finish_reason': 'stop'
#     }
# ]

print(f"Elapsed time: {end_time - start_time:.3f} seconds")
# Elapsed time: 239.457 seconds
```

While this example was in Python, there are bindings for Go, Rust, Node.js, Java, React Native, and more. Llama.cpp gives us all the tools we need to run LLMs in otherwise impossible environments.

8.3 LLM agents

At this point in the book, we can finally discuss LLM agents. Agents are what most people are talking about when they start worrying about AI taking their jobs. If you think back to the last chapter, we showed how, with some clever prompt engineering and tooling, we could train models to answer multistep questions requiring searching for information and running calculations. Agents do the same thing on steroids. Full LLM applications are designed not just to answer multistep questions but to accomplish multistep tasks. For example, a coding agent could not only answer complicated questions about your code base but also edit it, submit PRs, review PRs, and write full projects from scratch.

Agents do not differ from other language models in any meaningful way. The big differences all go into the system surrounding and supporting the LLM. LLMs are, fundamentally, closed search systems. They can't access anything they weren't trained on explicitly. So for example, if we were to ask Llama 2, "How old was Justin Bieber the last time the Patriots won the Superbowl?" we would be dependent on Meta having trained that model on incredibly up-to-date information. There are three components that make up an agent:

- *LLM*—No explanation necessary. By now, you know what these are and why they're needed.
- *Memory*—Some way of reintroducing the LLM to what has happened at each step up to that point. Memory goes a long way toward agents performing well. This is the same idea as feeding in the chat history, but the model needs something more than just the literal history of events. There are several ways of completing this:
  - *Memory buffer*—Passes in all of the text that's come before. Not recommended, as you'll hit context limits quickly, and the "lost in the middle" problem will exacerbate this.
  - *Memory summarization*—Has the LLM take another pass at the text to summarize it for its own memory. Works pretty well; however, at a minimum, it doubles latency, and summarization will delete finer details faster than anyone would like.
  - *Structured memory storage*—Thinks ahead and creates a system you can draw from to get the actual best info for the model. It can be related to chunking articles and searching for an article title and then retrieving the most relevant chunk, or perhaps chaining retrievals to find the most relevant keywords or to make sure that the query is contained in the retrieval output. We recommend structured memory storage the most because even though it's the hardest to set up, it achieves the best results in every scenario.
- *External data retrieval tools*—The core of agent behavior. These tools give your LLM the ability to take actions, which allows it to perform agent-like tasks.

We've covered a lot in this book, and agents are a bit of a culmination of much of what we've covered. They can be quite tricky to build, so to help you, we'll break down the steps and give several examples. First, we'll make some tools, then initialize some agents, and finally create a custom agent, all on our own. Throughout the process, you'll see why it's particularly difficult to get agents to work effectively and especially why LangChain and Guidance are great for getting started and difficult to get up and running.

In listing 8.7, we start off easy by demonstrating using some tools via LangChain. This example uses the Duck Duck Go search tool and the YouTube search tool. Notice that the LLM will simply give them a prompt, and the tools will handle the search and summary of results.

Listing 8.7 LangChain search tools example

```
from langchain.tools import DuckDuckGoSearchRun, YouTubeSearchTool

search = DuckDuckGoSearchRun()        <-- Example of using tools
hot_topic = search.run(
    "Tiktoker finds proof of Fruit of the Loom cornucopia in the logo"
)

youtube_tool = YouTubeSearchTool()
fun_channel = youtube_tool.run("jaubrey", 3)

print(hot_topic, fun_channel)
```

The generated text is

```
# Rating: False About this rating If asked to describe underwear
# manufacturer Fruit of the Loom's logo from memory, some will invariably
# say it includes — or at least included at some point in... A viral claim
# recently surfaced stating that Fruit of the Loom, the American underwear
# and casualwear brand, had a cornucopia in their logo at some point in the
# past. It refers to a goat's... The Fruit of the Loom Mandela Effect is
# really messing with people's memories of the clothing company's iconic
# logo.. A viral TikTok has thousands of people not only thinking about what
# they remember the logo to look like, but also has many searching for proof
# that we're not all losing our minds.. A TikTok Creator Is Trying To Get To
# The Bottom Of The Fruit Of The Loom Mandela Effect What Is 'The Mandela
# Effect?' To understand why people care so much about the Fruit of the Loom
# logo, one must first understand what the Mandela Effect is in the first
# place. It's a slang term for a cultural phenomenon in which a large group
# of people shares false memories of past events. About Fruit of the Loom
# Cornucopia and Fruit of the Loom Mandela Effect refer to the Mandela
# Effect involving a large number of people remembering the clothing company
# Fruit of the Loom having a cornucopia on its logo despite the logo never
# having the item on it.
# ['https://www.youtube.com/watch?v=x81gguSPGcQ&pp=ygUHamF1YnJleQ%3D%3D',
#'https://www.youtube.com/watch?v=bEvxuG6mevQ&pp=ygUHamF1YnJleQ%3D%3D']
```

Next, we'll demonstrate running an agent locally. In these examples, we use llama.cpp again; however, this time, we will use an instruction-based model, the 4-bit quantized Mistral 7B Instruct model—a great open source model. You can get the model we are using by running the following command. Notice the similarities to when we pulled the WizardCoder model back in section 8.2:

```
$ huggingface-cli download TheBloke/Mistral-7B-Instruct-v0.1-GGUF --local-
➥ dir ./models --local-dir-use-symlinks False --include='*Q4_0*gguf'
```

In listing 8.8, we demonstrate running two different types of agents you'll likely find useful. The first agent generates some Python, runs it, and attempts to debug any problems it runs into. The second agent reads and analyzes a CSV file. For this agent, we'll use the Slack dataset we pulled back in chapter 4. Pay attention to the responses, and make a wager on whether they do a good job.

Listing 8.8 LangChain Python and CSV agents

```
from langchain.llms import LlamaCpp
from langchain.agents import AgentType
from langchain_experimental.agents import create_csv_agent
from langchain_experimental.agents.agent_toolkits import create_python_agent
from langchain_experimental.tools import PythonREPLTool


llm = LlamaCpp(
    model_path="./models/mistral-7b-instruct-v0.1.Q4_0.gguf",
    n_gpu_layers=0,                    # 1 if NEON, any number if CUBLAS else 0
    n_batch=512,
    n_ctx=32768,                       # Context window for the model
    verbose=False,
)

agent = create_python_agent(           # An agent that will generate Python code and execute it
    llm=llm,
    tool=PythonREPLTool(),
    verbose=True,
    agent_type=AgentType.ZERO_SHOT_REACT_DESCRIPTION,
    handle_parsing_errors=True,
)

agent.run(
    """Using Python_REPL please write a neural network in Pytorch.
          Use Python_REPL as the Action and your code as the Action Input.
          Use synthetic data from a normal distribution.
          Train for 1000 epochs and print every 100 epochs.
          Return a prediction for x = 5."""
)
```

The output is

```
# > Entering new AgentExecutor chain...
# This is a task about creating and training a neural network. I should
# start by importing Pytorch and defining the synthetic data. Then I will
# define the neural network and train it for 1000 epochs. Finally, I will
# print the prediction for x = 5.
```

```
# Action: Python_REPL
# Action Input:
# ```python
# import torch
# import torch.nn as nn
# import torch.optim as optim
# from torch.utils import data
# from torchvision.datasets import make_classification
# define synthetic data from normal distribution
# data = make_classification(n_samples=1000, n_features=10, n_informative=5,
# random_state=42)
# X = data['features']
# y = data['targets']
# ```Python REPL can execute arbitrary code. Use with caution.
# Observation: ImportError("cannot import name 'make_classification' from
#'torchvision.datasets'
# Thought: It seems like the code is trying to use a function that does not
# exist, I will check the import statement.
# Action: Python_REPL
# Action Input:
# ```python
# fix import
# import torch.utils.data as data
# from torchvision.datasets import make_classification
# ```
# Observation: ImportError("cannot import name 'make_classification' from
#'torchvision.datasets'
# Thought: It still seems like the code is trying to use a function that
# does not exist, I will make sure that the function name matches the
# correct import statement.
# Action: Python_REPL
# Action Input:
# ```python
# fix import
# from torchvision.datasets.make_classification import make_classification
# data = make_classification(n_samples=1000, n_features=10, n_informative=5,
# random_state=42)
# X = data['features']
# y = data['targets']
# ```
# Observation: ImportError("cannot import name 'MakeClassification' from
#'torchvision.datasets'
# Thought:
# > Finished chain.
```

We continue with

```
agent = create_csv_agent(        <-- An agent that will read a CSV and analyze it
    llm,
    "./data/Slack_Dataset.csv",
    verbose=True,
    agent_type=AgentType.ZERO_SHOT_REACT_DESCRIPTION,
    handle_parsing_errors=True,
)
```

```
agent.run(
    """Using python_repl_ast please tell me whether the user polite in their
    messages. Use python_repl_ast as the Action and the command as the
    Action input."""
)
```

The generated text is

```
# > Entering new AgentExecutor chain…
# Action: python_repl_ast
# Action Input: df['text'].str.contains('thank you')
# Observation:
# 0     False
# 1     False
# 2     False
# 3     False
# 4     False
#   …
# 286     False
# 287     False
# 288     False
# 289     False
# 290     False
# Name: text, Length: 291, dtype: bool
# Thought: It seems the user was not polite in their messages.
# Final Answer: The user was not polite in their messages.
# > Finished chain.
```

Well, what do you think? Did either agent do a very good job? You're likely thinking "No," which should reassure you that AI isn't going to take your job anytime soon. The Python agent wrote a PyTorch script that completely depends on a `make_classification()` function that doesn't exist, and the CSV agent decided that being polite is equivalent to saying, "Thank you." Not a bad guess, but simply not a robust solution. Sure, part of the problem is likely the model we are using; a bigger one like GPT-4 might do better. We'll leave it as an exercise for the reader to compare.

Moving on, in listing 8.9, we build our own agent. We'll define the tools the agent has access to, set up a memory space for the agent, and then initialize it. Next, we'll define a system prompt so the agent knows how it should behave, making sure to explain to it what tools it has at its disposal and how to use them. We'll also utilize few-shot prompting and instruction to give us the best chance of seeing good results. Lastly, we'll run the agent. Let's take a look.

Listing 8.9 Agents and agent behavior

```
from langchain.llms import LlamaCpp
from langchain.chains.conversation.memory import (
    ConversationBufferWindowMemory,
)
from langchain.agents import load_tools, initialize_agent, Tool
from langchain_experimental.tools import PythonREPLTool
from langchain.tools import DuckDuckGoSearchRun, YouTubeSearchTool
```

```
llm = LlamaCpp(
    model_path="./models/mistral-7b-instruct-v0.1.Q4_0.gguf",
    n_gpu_layers=0,                         # 1 if NEON, any number if CUBLAS, else 0
    n_batch=512,
    n_ctx=32768,                            # Context window for the model
    verbose=False,
)

search = DuckDuckGoSearchRun()              # Defines our own agent tools
duckduckgo_tool = Tool(
    name="DuckDuckGo Search",
    func=search.run,
    description="Useful for when an internet search is needed",
)
youtube_tool = YouTubeSearchTool()
coding_tool = PythonREPLTool()

tools = load_tools(["llm-math"], llm=llm)
tools += [duckduckgo_tool, youtube_tool, coding_tool]

memory = ConversationBufferWindowMemory(    # Defines our agent's memory
    memory_key="chat_history",
    k=5,
    return_messages=True,
    output_key="output",
)

agent = initialize_agent(                   # Sets up and initializes our custom agent
    tools=tools,
    llm=llm,
    agent="chat-conversational-react-description",
    verbose=True,
    memory=memory,
    handle_parsing_errors=True,
)

B_INST, E_INST = "[INST]", "[/INST]"        # Special tokens used by llama 2 chat
B_SYS, E_SYS = "<<SYS>>\n", "\n<</SYS>>\n\n"

sys_msg = (                                 # Creates the system prompt
    "<s>"
    + B_SYS
    + """Assistant is a expert JSON builder designed to assist with a wide \
range of tasks.

Assistant is able to respond to the User and use tools using JSON strings \
that contain "action" and "action_input" parameters.

All of Assistant's communication is performed using this JSON format.

Assistant can also use tools by responding to the user with tool use \
instructions in the same "action" and "action_input" JSON format. Tools \
available to Assistant are:
```

```
- "Calculator": Useful for when you need to answer questions about math.
  - To use the calculator tool, Assistant should write like so:
    ```json
    {{"action": "Calculator",
      "action_input": "sqrt(4)"}}
    ```
- "DuckDuckGo Search": Useful for when an internet search is needed.
  - To use the duckduckgo search tool, Assistant should write like so:
    ```json
    {{"action": "DuckDuckGo Search",
      "action_input": "When was the Jonas Brothers' first concert"}}

Here are some previous conversations between the Assistant and User:

User: Hey how are you today?
Assistant: ```json
{{"action": "Final Answer",
 "action_input": "I'm good thanks, how are you?"}}
```
User: I'm great, what is the square root of 4?
Assistant: ```json
{{"action": "Calculator",
 "action_input": "sqrt(4)"}}
```
User: 2.0
Assistant: ```json
{{"action": "Final Answer",
 "action_input": "It looks like the answer is 2!"}}
```
User: Thanks, when was the Jonas Brothers' first concert?
Assistant: ```json
{{"action": "DuckDuckGo Search",
 "action_input": "When was the Jonas Brothers' first concert"}}
```
User: 12.0
Assistant: ```json
{{"action": "Final Answer",
 "action_input": "They had their first concert in 2005!"}}
```
User: Thanks could you tell me what 4 to the power of 2 is?
Assistant: ```json
{{"action": "Calculator",
 "action_input": "4**2"}}
```
User: 16.0
Assistant: ```json
{{"action": "Final Answer",
 "action_input": "It looks like the answer is 16!"}}
```

Here is the latest conversation between Assistant and User."""
    + E_SYS
)
```

```
new_prompt = agent.agent.create_prompt(system_message=sys_msg, tools=tools)
agent.agent.llm_chain.prompt = new_prompt

instruction = (
    B_INST
    + " Respond to the following in JSON with 'action' and 'action_input' "
    "values "
    + E_INST
)
human_msg = instruction + "\nUser: {input}"
agent.agent.llm_chain.prompt.messages[2].prompt.template = human_msg

agent.run(
    "Tell me how old Justin Beiber was when the Patriots last won the "
    "Superbowl."
)
```

Adds system prompt to agent

Adds instruction to agent

Runs with user input

Remember that for this, we asked the model to respond in JSON:

```
#> Entering new AgentExecutor chain...
#Assistant: {
# "action": "DuckDuckGo Search",
# "action\_input": "When did the New England Patriots last win the Super
# Bowl? Justin Bieber birthdate"
#}
#{
# "action": "Final Answer",
# "action\_input": "Justin Bieber was born on March 1, 1994. The Patriots
# last won the Super Bowl in February 2018."
#}
```

Not bad! It didn't answer the question, but it got pretty close; it just needed to do some math. If you ran the example, you might have noticed it was a bit slow compared to using the llama.cpp Python interpreter. Unfortunately, for some reason, LangChain's wrapper adds some significant time to compute, so be warned: if you need to go really fast, LangChain is not your vehicle. At least not yet. Regardless, LangChain has made some easy-to-use wrappers around popular Python libraries to make them usable as LLM tools. In these listings, we only used a handful, and there's a lot more to choose from.

Overall, you can see that we were able to get the LLM to perform pretty well on some nontrivial tasks (and we were using a 4-bit quantized model, we might add). However, it was nowhere close to perfect. Agents are miraculous in that they work at all, but they are generally underwhelming in the tasks and levels they can perform—including the top-tier paid agents. The more you work with LLMs crafting many different prompts, the more you'll find that LLMs are quite flaky, just like humans, which can be quite annoying to software engineers who are used to working with machines that are as consistent as anything this world has to offer. Getting LLMs to perform well on just one task is often difficult enough, but chaining several tasks together inside an agent is extremely difficult. We are still very much in the early stages of agent development, and we are excited to see where it goes.

Summary

- Creating a simple LLM application is straightforward, but creating one that delights your users takes a bit more work.
- The key features you should include in your app include the following:
  - Streaming responses allows a more interactive and responsive experience.
  - Feeding your model the chat history will prevent your model from having a birdbrain.
  - Interactive features like Stop, Retry, and Delete buttons give users more control of the conversation.
  - Token counting is useful for user feedback and allows users to edit responses to fit token limits.
  - RAG on the frontend allows us to customize an application regardless of the LLM backend.
- Llama.cpp is a powerful open source tool for compiling LLMs and running them on edge devices with constrained resources.
- Agents are LLM applications built to solve multistep problems and promise to automate jobs machines currently struggle with.
- Agents are extremely difficult to build due to the unpredictability of LLMs and sometimes require advanced prompt engineering to get reasonable results.

9 Creating an LLM project: Reimplementing Llama 3

This chapter covers

- Implementing Meta's Llama3 model
- Training a simple LLM
- Making improvements to it to prepare it for production
- Serving the model to a production endpoint you can share with your friends

> *I am only coming to Princeton to research, not to teach. There is too much education altogether, especially in American schools. The only rational way of educating is to be an example.*
>
> —Albert Einstein

For the first major project in the book, we want to start from scratch. We've been showing you how to work with LLMs from end to end, and we are going to put it all together in this chapter. This project includes pretraining a model, roughly following a research paper. We won't dive too deeply into the actual research; in fact, we'll take several shortcuts here, as this isn't the focus of this book. We will, however, showcase how to train the model, prepare it for servings with quantization, finetune it with low-rank adaptation (LoRA) for a specific purpose or task, and deploy it to a production environment you can showcase to your friends.

This chapter will be very dense, but you should be more than prepared to meet the challenge at this point because it's mainly a data scientist–focused project for production. We chose this project so that you can put all the lessons you've learned throughout the book together into one place and leave you with end-to-end, hands-on experience.

9.1 Implementing Meta's Llama

"Llama 2: Open Foundation and Fine-Tuned Chat Models" by Touvron et al.[1] is an awesome paper that covers the development and release of Llama 2, one of the best, almost open source models currently on the market. You may have seen Llama 2 as the first open source model that was good enough to rival OpenAI's models, at least based on the metrics of the time. Llama 3 is out now, and it has almost completely eclipsed Llama 2 in popularity and may very well be why you picked up this book.

Llama 3 is amazing for a couple of reasons—namely, size and availability. With only 70B parameters, pretrained on only 15T tokens, and finetuned on 100K chats, it shouldn't be able to beat a 176B or a 1.7T parameter model at anything. Unsurprisingly, it usually doesn't. But it does beat them at one crucial thing: its availability. This feature has given rise to an open source software community that has made tooling and optimizations and even gathers data to make it better. Llama 3 is the ultimate showcase that architecture is less important than data, and it is trained on clean data.

And we're going to implement it.

By the end of this chapter, you will build a real model and understand the work that goes into it. Will it be as good as Meta's Llama 3? Far from it, because we won't be demonstrating with an adequate amount of data or GPUs. But we want to do more than simply supply you with yet another set of weights that are on some leaderboard somewhere. We want to give you some intuition for the steps required and the potential problems you may face. Instead of training a great model completely from scratch, which is what dozens of other books are tackling right now, we'll show you how to train a below-average model and productionize it. This approach should have you not only learning more but demonstrating expertise beyond your experience level.

9.1.1 Tokenization and configuration

By this point, you've likely already learned the importance of setting up the problem correctly. We want our models hitting tee-balls out of the park, not going up against an MLB pitcher. With that in mind, we'll download the same tokenizer that Llama used. If you want, you can come back and experiment with this tokenizer since we are building from scratch. For example, try to use a faster tokenizer like tiktoken—just know you'll be giving up the model's ability to do math. You can also train your

[1] H. Touvron et al., "Llama 2: Open foundation and fine-tuned chat models," arXiv.org, July 19, 2023, https://arxiv.org/abs/2307.09288.

own version of the SentencePiece model, which should guarantee better results on whatever dataset you want to extend this with. The point is that this model is blank—no pretrained weights at all. So come back and do whatever you'd like after following along.

> **NOTE** Unlike other chapters where each listing was stand alone, in this chapter, each listing will be part of a larger notebook. You can find this notebook in the code repository accompanying this book.

Listing 9.1 shows our initial setup for this project, including imports, device settings, and grabbing our tokenizer. While we'll just be grabbing the tokenizer from Hugging Face, keep in mind that not all tokenizers and models use the same type of tokens. This is important because we're going to train this model differently than the way the inference tokenizer is set up for. To correct for this discrepancy, we'll need to add a padding token. Anything would do, but we'll use `"<PAD>"` in our example. Once we have that, we'll make sure to grab the vocab itself (we'll need it later) and create encoding and decoding functions to help with batch processing. Because we're using the Hugging Face implementation, this isn't strictly needed because it has batch tokenization built in, along with a `batch_decode` method that works great. For learning's sake, we'll go through the motions anyway. It's always good practice to be aware of what you're doing, and these functions help lock that down.

The last part of this listing offers the most flexibility. Here, we set up a master config that will ultimately decide how many parameters our model has, how long it trains, and how much memory it will take per row in our dataset. Our default values are pretty small and designed to give you a good experience regardless of your hardware, including if you're training on a CPU-only build. Feel free to experiment and crank up the numbers.

Listing 9.1 Tokenize and config

```
import torch
from torch import nn
from torch.nn import functional as F
import numpy as np
from numba import jit
from matplotlib import pyplot as plt
import time
from datetime import timedelta
import pandas as pd
from collections import OrderedDict
from itertools import cycle
from transformers import AutoTokenizer
from sentencepiece import SentencePieceProcessor
from datasets import load_dataset

device = "cuda:0" if torch.cuda.is_available() else "cpu"
device_cap = torch.cuda.get_device_capability()
device_type = "cuda" if "cuda" in device else "cpu"
```

```
torch.cuda.set_device(device)
torch.manual_seed(8855)
print(torch.__version__)
print(device, device_cap)
# 2.1.0+cu121
# cuda:0 (8,6)


tokenizer = AutoTokenizer.from_pretrained("./llama3/")       <-- Uses Hugging Face
tokenizer.add_special_tokens({"pad_token": "<PAD>"})
# tokenizer.pad_token = tokenizer.eos_token                  <-- Optional

vocab = tokenizer.vocab


def encode(example):
    return tokenizer.encode(example, return_tensors="pt")


def decode(example):
    return tokenizer.batch_decode(
    example,
    skip_special_tokens=False,
    clean_up_tokenization_spaces=True,
    )[0]


print(f"Vocab Size: {len(vocab)}")
decode(
    encode(
    """hello I am a specifically designed long sentence
       to make sure this is working not only adequately,
       but good enough for our batch functions"""
    )
)
# Vocab Size: 32001
#'<s> hello I am a specifically designed long sentence to make sure this is
working not only adequately, but good enough for our batch functions'


MASTER_CONFIG = {
    "vocab_size": len(vocab),
    "batch_size": 16,
    "context_window": 32,
    "d_model": 288,
    "hidden_dim": 768,
    "epochs": 1000,
    "log_interval": 50,
    "n_heads": 6,
    "n_layers": 6,
}
GLOBAL_KEEP_TRACK = []
```

As we've reiterated a number of times throughout the book, remember that the strategy you use to tokenize and embed your inputs ultimately dictates what your model is able to "see" during training and inference. You should generally do a bit more than just choose a tokenizer; in fact, we'll see later in this chapter what choosing the Llama 3 tokenizer will do to our inference.

You could opt for training a new tokenizer on your dataset or adding especially important tokens from your dataset to an already-robust tokenizer—preferably one that already generally matches the strategy you want and is trained in the domain you need. If you aren't sure about any of that, any LLM tokenizer should generally work—that's what they're designed for. But don't be surprised when the model doesn't perform well when you pick a general tokenizer and want a specific task.

9.1.2 Dataset, data loading, evaluation, and generation

Let's get into the most important part of this process, which we will, for the most part, gloss over. There's only so much we can focus on in one chapter, but we want to reiterate how important your dataset is to the success of your LLM. You'll want to spend time gathering, evaluating, and cleaning your dataset, but we'll shortcut that process in the interest of time. Instead, we'll focus on the steps necessary to train the model—loading, preprocessing, batching, and so forth. As we go through this section, remember that your unique data sources end up future-proofing your model, so consider what data you have access to that no one else does and how you'd set that dataset up for this training.

We'll start by loading a dataset that's generally popular for creating toy models, TinyStories. If you did the work to explore your data—and we encourage you to do it—you'll see that this is a smallish dataset for LLMs, containing only 30 million rows, each containing a short story in a single paragraph. It draws from some oft-implemented and widely accepted datasets. While a small dataset for LLMs, it's likely still too large for many computers, and many readers will likely hit out-of-memory errors if they try to load it into memory wholesale. Here's the perfect time to use streaming. In listing 9.2, we show you how to pull the dataset from the Hugging Face Hub or `dataset.to_iterable_ dataset()` if working locally. Both methods allow for much more memory-efficient processing, as the whole dataset isn't loaded all at once, sacrificing some speed.

Listing 9.2 Loading and preparing the data

```
dataset = load_dataset(          # Streams from the local files
    "text",
    data_files={
        "train": ["../../data/TinyStoriesv1andv2-train.txt"],
        "val": ["../../data/TinyStoriesv1andv2-valid.txt"],
    },
    streaming=True,
)
```

Once you have your dataset and are able to retrieve an iteration, we'll do some minimal (truly) cleaning. Then we'll encode the whole thing so that our training can go quicker down the line. We'll save the tokenization and attention masks as their own columns, and then we'll shuffle the dataset and go on to dataloading. A quick note that's always worth mentioning: when training any machine learning model, if you don't already have your `train` and `val` splits defined, take extra care shuffling your dataset so that none of the data leaks into a split where it shouldn't be:

```
clean_dataset = dataset.filter(lambda example: len(example["text"]) > 2)   # Minimal processing

prompt = "Write a short story. Possible Story: "
tokenized_prompt = tokenizer(prompt, return_tensors="pt").input_ids

encoded_dataset = clean_dataset.map(
    lambda examples: tokenizer(
      [prompt + x for x in examples["text"]],
       padding=True,
       return_tensors="pt",
    ),
    batched=True,
)
train_data = iter(encoded_dataset["train"].shuffle())
val_data = iter(encoded_dataset["val"].shuffle())
train_data = cycle(train_data)
val_data = cycle(val_data)
```

If you disregard our advice to stream and have a computer that can handle this dataset, know that loading the entire dataset into memory and then preparing it, even using hardware acceleration, takes over 30 minutes and more than 5 GB of memory. So if you have an extra 5 GB of VRAM outside of what you'll need for your model, you're good to go ahead and load it however you want. See figure 9.1.

```
Filter: 100%|██████████| 30415548/30415548 [00:42<00:00, 713226.59 examples/s]
Filter: 100%|██████████| 305106/305106 [00:00<00:00, 706260.12 examples/s]
Map: 100%|██████████| 28080906/28080906 [32:01<00:00, 14616.43 examples/s]
Map: 100%|██████████| 281929/281929 [00:18<00:00, 14923.99 examples/s]
```

Figure 9.1 With over 30 million rows, this dataset is pretty small for what we're trying to do, but it is still substantial on consumer hardware.

We'll need at least one function to load our data into a ready-to-use format for our model, and we're opting to use just that. Our `get_batches` function will take in one row of our data and return a model input and an expected output that can be compared against it for self-supervised learning. No labeling is needed, as we'll start on a random token, then grab tokens up to our whole context window (32) for our input, and shift one token to the right for our expected output. For our model, we create a scenario that looks like this:

input: How much wood could a woodchuck chuck if a woodchuck could chuck

label: How much wood could a woodchuck chuck if a woodchuck could chuck wood?

This process allows our model to train on our task: guessing the next token in an utterance, given the context of the previous 31 tokens. We use this strategy instead of other strategies like masking because our preferred inputs will never contain information after the input is completed. This way, our model will get better and better at text completion the more and higher-quality data it trains on. Almost all foundation models are pretrained in this manner—only they train for much longer with many more parameters than we will right now:

```
# @torch.compile                    <-- Windows users leave commented
def get_batches(
    data,
    batch_size,
    context_window,
    config=MASTER_CONFIG,
    debug=False,
):
    x = []
    y = []
    for _ in range(
        batch_size                   <-- Adjust this lower if you're running out of memory.
    ):
        batch_data = next(data)

        ix = torch.randint(          <-- Pick random starting points.
            0, len(batch_data["input_ids"]) - context_window - 1, (2,)
        )
        batch_x = torch.stack(
            [batch_data["input_ids"][i : i + context_window] for i in ix]
        ).long()
        batch_y = torch.stack(
            [
                batch_data["input_ids"][i + 1 : i + context_window + 1]
                    for i in ix
            ]
        ).long()
        x.append(batch_x)
        y.append(batch_y)
    x = torch.cat((x), 0).to(device)
    y = torch.cat((y), 0).to(device)
    return x, y
```

Once we have our data batching taken care of, we need to come up with functions for evaluation and inference so that we can gain insight into how the model is doing during training and so that we can use the model later. For our evaluation, we'll take some batches and average the loss across them to get our validation loss. This result will not give us a real representation of our model's performance but will not stop it from being useful for us:

```
@torch.no_grad()
def get_loss(model, lora=False, config=MASTER_CONFIG):
    out = {}
    model.eval()
    for name, split in zip(["train", "val"], [train_data, val_data]):
        losses = []
        for _ in range(10):
                xb, yb = get_batches(
               split,
               config["batch_size"],
                 config["context_window"],
               )
            _, loss = model(xb, yb)
            losses.append(loss.item())
        out[name] = np.mean(losses)
    model.train()
    return out
```

Questioning your assumptions

When working with machine-learning models and other statistical methods, it's important to understand how your assumptions will affect your results. Averages hamper data representation and understanding because they basically say, "For this comparison, we're going to grab a made-up number, and we're going to use that number in place of any of the real ones because it feels central to our distribution." This approach doesn't make it bad; made-up numbers often are more predictive than real ones. However, we urge you to be intentional and very open-minded about testing whether the average is the best marker for your users.

For generation, we'll do something similar but better. Logits are what we get out of our model's forward method. We created a tokenized version of our prompt previously when we tokenized our dataset, so we're ready to pass that prompt into our model a number of times and see what comes out. We'll grab the logits from the model given the prompt and then sample our model's distribution for our next token and decode.

For sampling that distribution, we'll take the model's output (logits) for only the very end of the input (the unknown token we want our model to generate) and then divide those logits by the temperature setting (higher temperature setting = smaller logits). Once we have our logits from the last time step, if we use multinomial sampling, we can sample using `top_k` and/or `top_p`, which are sampling against the highest probability tokens until you reach a total number of tokens or a total number of probability sums. Once we have that, we use softmax for the tokens we've sampled and then argmax to get the next token. If we want more exploration and creativity in our output, we can use multinomial sampling instead. As an exercise, test `top_k` versus `top_p` with multinomial and argmax versus multinomial to get an idea of which works best:

```
@torch.inference_mode()
def generate(
    model,
    config=MASTER_CONFIG,
    temperature=1.0,
    top_k=None,
    max_new_tokens=30,
    lora=False,
):
    idx_list = [tokenized_prompt] * 5
    idx = torch.cat((idx_list), 0).long().to(device)
    for _ in range(max_new_tokens):
        logits = model(idx[:, -config["context_window"] :])     <-- Calls the model
        last_time_step_logits = logits[
            :, -1, :
        ]                                                        <-- All the batches (1); last time step, all the logits

        last_time_step_logits = last_time_step_logits / temperature
        if top_k is not None:
            v, _ = torch.topk(
                last_time_step_logits,
                min(top_k, last_time_step_logits.size(-1)),
            )
            last_time_step_logits[
                last_time_step_logits < v[:, [-1]]
            ] = -float("Inf")
        p = F.softmax(
            last_time_step_logits, dim=-1
        )                                    <-- Softmax to get probabilities
        idx_next = torch.argmax(
            p, dim=-1, keepdims=True
        )                                    <-- Sample from the distribution to get the next token
        idx = torch.cat([idx, idx_next], dim=-1)  # append to the sequence
    return [tokenizer.decode(x) for x in idx.tolist()]
```

And with that, we've concluded our setup! We have utility functions for all of the important parts of the model training, including tokenization, data loading, evaluation, inference, and data processing. If there's anything you feel should be corrected, great! Do it—this is your project. If you want to use a multinomial for sampling instead of an argmax or want to get rid of the softmax and just argmax over the logits, awesome, go for it. For those of you for whom this is your first time, we know it can be quite a firehose, and we'd encourage you to work through it slowly, but don't lose too much sleep over it. More than likely, you will not have to come up with what should change for your use case yourself because you'll be implementing an already-created open source model. That said, it's still a good idea to understand what's going on behind the scenes and under the hood so that you know roughly where to look when things go wrong.

9.1.3 Network architecture

We've now completed a ton of setup for training a model but haven't made a model. Model architecture and training have been iterated upon ad nauseam, so we'll skip talking about it too much and jump right in. We'll start with a two-layer feed-forward network with fewer than 20M parameters, and then we'll upgrade and talk about the changes that turn the model into Llama. We want to be clear about what is actually changing between them so you'll get a good feel for the pieces involved. Because we aren't going to be completely replicating Llama 3, but rather approximating it, here's the official architecture if you'd like to try pretraining it on our dataset: https://mng.bz/Dp9A.

In listing 9.3, we make a class for that linear model with a ReLU activation between the two linear layers. Here's where we'll also define our actual loss function (because in our `get_loss` function, we're just sending inputs to the model). We'll use cross entropy because we're comparing unstructured sequences. Instead of getting into information theory for why cross-entropy is the answer to unstructured sequences, the current benchmark in the industry is called perplexity, which uses cross-entropy to figure out whether a model is making sense or not, so this loss function enables us to compete with other models in the industry.

There's one thing that you may have noticed before when we tokenized our dataset: we're padding in batches and not truncating, meaning each batch size should be the same length. We fully acknowledge that this doesn't make any sense when pretraining; it's just helping to speed things up. We do this because our longest length input is 997 tokens, and we don't want to pad our entire dataset out to 997. Even mitigating that, the most common token in our dataset is still `"<PAD>"`. If we leave it as is, the model could learn to generate only padding tokens, which seemingly minimizes the loss when predicting the next token. Because we have a tokenizer vocab we just added to, however, we can tell the loss function to `ignore_index` our `tokenizer.pad_token_id` so correctly predicting padding tokens doesn't mistakenly help the loss go down.

Listing 9.3 Simple model and training loop

```
class SimpleFeedForwardNN(nn.Module):
    def __init__(self, config=MASTER_CONFIG):
        super().__init__()
        self.config = config

        self.embedding = nn.Embedding(
            config["vocab_size"], config["d_model"]
        )
        self.linear = nn.Sequential(
            nn.Linear(config["d_model"], config["d_model"]),
            nn.ReLU(),
            nn.Linear(config["d_model"], config["vocab_size"]),
        )
```

```
        print(
            f"model params: {sum([m.numel() for m in self.parameters()])}"
        )

    def forward(self, idx, targets=None):
        x = self.embedding(idx)
        logits = self.linear(x)

        if targets is not None:
            loss = F.cross_entropy(
                logits.view(-1, self.config["vocab_size"]),
                targets.view(-1),
                ignore_index=tokenizer.pad_token_id,
                # reduction="sum",
            )
            return logits, loss

        else:
            return logits

model = SimpleFeedForwardNN(MASTER_CONFIG).to(device)
opt_model = torch.compile(model)
```

Comment this out on Windows.

Now that we have our model, we'll write our training loop. We run the number of passes specified in the epochs portion of the master config, and we get our loss for each pass. The epochs here are more like steps, and we'd encourage you to run epochs through the whole dataset if you have the time. If you stick to the `MASTER_CONFIG` we set up previously, this original model will end up having 18.5M parameters. You should definitely change it to be the maximum number of parameters that your computer can handle. You can find this number by changing `d_model` (and `vocab_size` if you train a bigger tokenizer) in your master config:

```
def train(
    model,
    optimizer,
    scheduler=None,
    data=None,
    config=MASTER_CONFIG,
    lora=False,
    print_logs=False,
):
    losses = []
    start_time = time.time()
    for epoch in range(config["epochs"]):
        try:
            optimizer.zero_grad()

                xs, ys = get_batches(
                    data, config["batch_size"], config["context_window"]
                )
                  for i in range(1, config['context_window']+1):
                          x = xs[:i]
                          y = ys[:i]
```

```
                logits, loss = model(xs, targets=ys)
                loss.backward()
                optimizer.step()

                if scheduler:
                        scheduler.step()

            if epoch % config["log_interval"] == 0:
                batch_time = time.time() - start_time
                x = get_loss(model, lora=lora)
                losses += [x]
                if print_logs:
                    print(
                      f"""Epoch {epoch} |
                         train loss {x['train']:.3f} |
                         val loss {x['val']:.3f} |
                         Time {batch_time:.3f} |
                         ETA: {timedelta(seconds=(batch_time * (config
                            ['epochs'] - epoch)/config['log_interval']))}"""
                    )
                start_time = time.time()

                if scheduler:
                    print("lr: ", scheduler.get_last_lr())
        except StopIteration:
            print(f"Reached end of dataset on step {epoch}")
            break

    GLOBAL_KEEP_TRACK.append(
       f"{type(model).__name__} {sum([m.numel() for m in
model.parameters()])} Params | Train: {losses[-1]['train']:.3f} | Val:
{losses[-1]['val']:.3f}"
    )
    print(
        f"training loss {losses[-1]['train']:.3f} | validation loss:
{losses[-1]['val']:.3f}"
    )
    return pd.DataFrame(losses).plot(xlabel="Step // 50", ylabel="Loss")


optimizer = torch.optim.AdamW(
    model.parameters(),
)
train(model, optimizer, data=train_data, print_logs=True)
#Epoch 0 | train loss 10.365 | val loss 10.341 | Time 0.122 | ETA:
 0:00:02.431240
#training loss 4.129 | validation loss: 4.458
```

Look, it's figure 9.2, which was generated from listing 9.3! Try to guess what it will be, and then read the blurb to see if you're right.

Look at that! That's a pretty smooth curve when we train for the first time. Considering we only did 1,000 examples from our dataset, we'd encourage you to try for several actual epochs—say, try three going over the whole dataset—and see how things

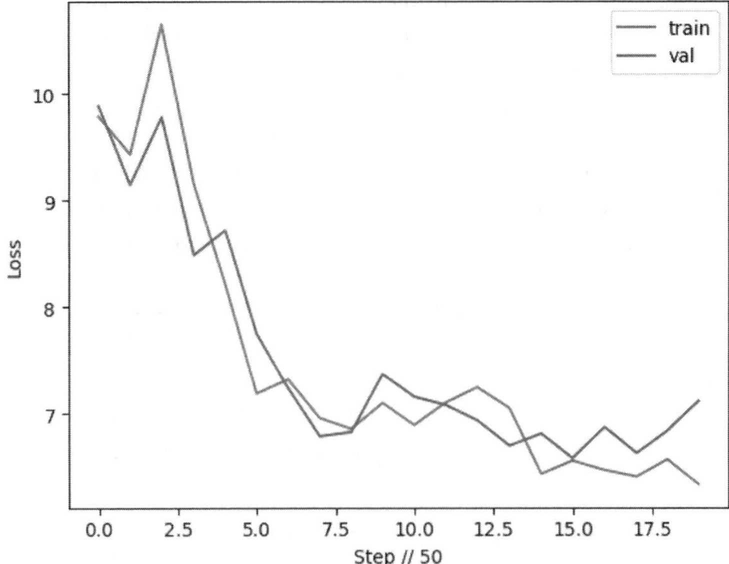

Figure 9.2 Training a simple neural network on our dataset to generate text

go. You'll likely get surprisingly decent results; we did. Let's go ahead and check out what it creates when generating text:

```
generate(model, config=MASTER_CONFIG)
# '<s> Write a short story. Possible Story: 3 together thisar andze Lily
said exciteded and smiled. Everything because he wasning loved to the time,
he did not find like to',

for i in GLOBAL_KEEP_TRACK:
    print(i)
# SimpleFeedForwardNN 18547809 Params | Train: 4.129 | Val: 4.458
```

Not too shabby! Of course, these aren't great results, but we weren't expecting amazing results with our basic model and short training time. Reading the generated tokens, it almost makes sense. We'll call that a win. Congratulations! We created a language model using a feed-forward network that can return tokens. Now it's time to get into the changes that make Llama different from a regular feed-forward network.

9.2 Simple Llama

If you check the full weights and layers as released by Meta, you may notice that what we are building is not exactly the same as what was released. The reason for this is twofold: (1) we'd like to make sure this discussion is still very understandable for people interacting with research for production for the first time, and (2) we're considering the environments you'll likely have access to when reading this book. Everything here should fit and run in Kaggle or Colab without problems. With that being the case, we'll address differences in Llama 3's architecture and ours so that if you did have the infra and data to replicate the paper for production, you could.[2]

Llama is different from a feed-forward network in a few ways: normalization, attention, activation, and number of layers. Without going too deeply into any of them, normalization helps stabilize training, attention helps support larger context lengths and uses information between layers more efficiently, activation helps represent nonlinearities better, and the number of layers increases the amount of information the model is able to represent. One other important thing to note is that we're adding a scheduler this time around. The scheduler here is responsible for adjusting the learning rate during training, following a "schedule." This addition helps us with potential exploding gradients and allows the model to converge more quickly.

Let's change our network into a simpler version of Llama 3. Here, we'll skip over some of the theory and implementation. But look at the notebook in GitHub too—we want you to test it out on your own!

Listing 9.4 Simple Llama

```
class LlamaBlock(nn.Module):
    def __init__(self, config):
        super().__init__()
        self.config = config

        self.rms = RMSNormalization(
            (config["d_model"], config["d_model"])
        )

        self.attention = RoPEMaskedMultiheadAttention(config).to(device)
        self.feedforward = nn.Sequential(
            nn.Linear(config["d_model"], config["hidden_dim"]),
            SwiGLU(config["hidden_dim"]),
            nn.Linear(config["hidden_dim"], config["d_model"]),
        )
```

New

Unlike the original network, we're creating a whole class for LlamaBlocks, or smaller self-contained networks within our larger one. Now we have `RMSNormalization`, along with `RoPEMaskedMultiheadAttention` and a `SwiGLU` activation instead of `ReLU`. We've included the implementations in the notebook, so feel free to check them out if you are curious.

You'll notice that our forward function is very different from the original feed forward. We're no longer just embedding and then getting the logits from the embedding. Now we're normalizing, adding attention, normalizing again, and then adding our logits to what comes out. This process helps the model integrate more nonlinearities into its overall considerations for how the input and desired output can line up:

2 https://ai.meta.com/blog/meta-llama-3/, https://arxiv.org/pdf/2307.09288, https://arxiv.org/pdf/2302.13971.

```
    def forward(self, x):
        x = self.rms(x)
        x = x + self.attention(x)

        x = self.rms(x)
        x = x + self.feedforward(x)
        return x
```

Here, we can compare the original feed-forward network with this `SimpleLlama` class to get an idea of what's changed overall. First, instead of only having one `Sequential` block of layers, we have a number of `LlamaBlocks` equal to `n_layers` in our config, which is `8`, as you'll see in the following code snippet. Beyond that, we're using the SwiGLU activation everywhere instead of a ReLU. SwiGLU adds some ability to handle negative numbers and helps with exploding/vanishing gradients. Other than that, they're remarkably similar:

```
class SimpleLlama(nn.Module):
    def __init__(self, config):
        super().__init__()
        self.config = config

        self.embedding = nn.Embedding(
            config["vocab_size"], config["d_model"]
        )
        self.llama_blocks = nn.Sequential(
            OrderedDict(
                [
                    (f"llama_{i}", LlamaBlock(config))      <-- New
                    for i in range(config["n_layers"])
                ]
            )
        )

        self.ffn = nn.Sequential(
            nn.Linear(config["d_model"], config["d_model"]),
            SwiGLU(config["d_model"]),                        <-- New
            nn.Linear(config["d_model"], config["vocab_size"]),
        )

        print(
            f"model params: {sum([m.numel() for m in self.parameters()])}"
        )

    def forward(self, idx, targets=None):
        x = self.embedding(idx)
        x = self.llama_blocks(x)      <-- New
        logits = self.ffn(x)

        if targets is None:
            return logits

        else:
            loss = F.cross_entropy(
                logits.view(-1, self.config["vocab_size"]),
```

```
            targets.view(-1),
            ignore_index=tokenizer.pad_token_id,
        )
        return logits, loss
```

We can make some slight adjustments to our master config to make the model bigger by increasing the embedding dimension, the number of layers, and the context window. You don't actually have to make that change to see the performance difference. If you had the compute, data, and time, you could train a viable version of Llama 3 (you can see the results of this training in figure 9.3):

```
MASTER_CONFIG["epochs"] = 1000
MASTER_CONFIG["batch_size"] = 16
MASTER_CONFIG["d_model"] = 768
MASTER_CONFIG["n_layers"] = 8
MASTER_CONFIG["context_window"] = 128

llama = SimpleLlama(MASTER_CONFIG).to(device)

llama_optimizer = torch.optim.AdamW(
    llama.parameters(),
    betas=(0.9, 0.95),
    weight_decay=1e-1,
    eps=1e-9,
    lr=5e-4,
)
scheduler = torch.optim.lr_scheduler.CosineAnnealingLR(
    llama_optimizer, 1000, eta_min=1e-5
)                                                            <-- New
#Epoch 0 | train loss 10.321 | val loss 10.316 | Time 0.622 | ETA:
0:00:12.439990
#lr:  [0.0004999987909744553]
#training loss 6.216 | validation loss: 6.046
generate(
    llama,
    config=MASTER_CONFIG,
    temperature=1.0,
    top_k=25,
    max_new_tokens=50,
)
#'<s> Write a short story. Possible Story: the Story there One.t day. Back
 the, went to: her they Possible|. to and a said saw They:. be the She.. a.
to They. they. to and to for He was a in with',',

for i in GLOBAL_KEEP_TRACK:
    print(i)
#SimpleFeedForwardNN 18547809 Params | Train: 4.129 | Val: 4.458
#SimpleLlama 187827210 Params | Train: 6.216 | Val: 6.046
```

So we've made the 10× jump to over 180M parameters. Did it give us the emergent behavior we were looking for, though? If you look at the generated text, it's making improvements in that it's guessing punctuation more often, but almost none are in

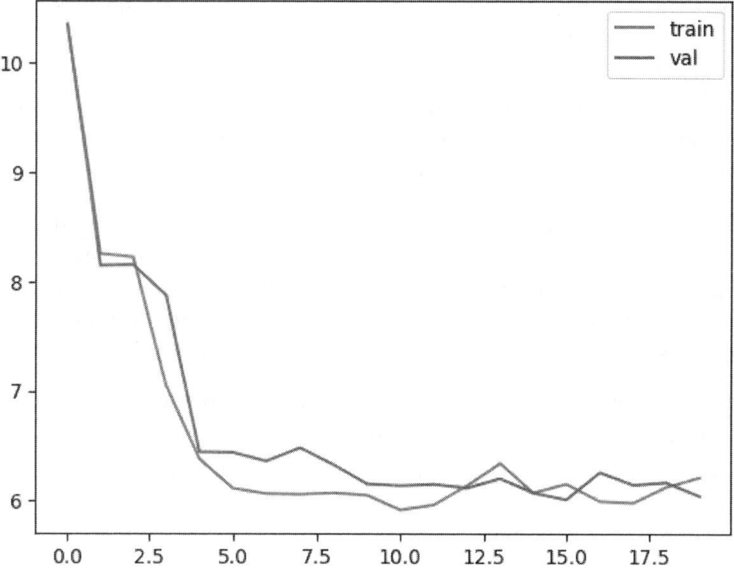

Figure 9.3 Training simple Llama on our dataset to generate text

the correct place. The loss is higher, too, but we're not particularly worried about that part; if we spruce up our data loading and allow the model to go all the way through the dataset two or three times, that should get lower. Lastly, if we make the model bigger by increasing the context window and number of layers, along with increasing the tokens in our dataset, we should be able to get that emergent behavior. For this dataset and config, you'd have to train ~1,900 times to go through the dataset once, so you'd have to train almost 6,000 times to start taking advantage of the whole dataset.

Given a lack of time and resources, we aren't going to worry that our model isn't at the top of any leaderboards. Heck, it's not even good enough to get on one. But we have created a simple model that resembles Llama, and we have done so from scratch. This exercise has given us insights into the process, and you should have an idea of how to make it better. With these things in mind, let's discuss how to put the model we've created into production.

9.3 Making it better

Now that we have a model and it's passing all of our internal benchmarks (we'll pretend that we had some), it's time to deploy the model and see how it behaves with customers interacting with it. Oh no! The internal tests we had aren't representative of our production environment! Our first problem is that the model is way too big and slow to even get through the prod environment tests. Models themselves are often looked at as being the main ingredient to success. In contrast, the systems we engineer around models, including the data, are overlooked because "anyone can hire a good

MLE to make those." Unfortunately, that's now the secret sauce that causes some companies to succeed and others to fail.

We'd like to acknowledge to everyone rushing to the comments and GitHub Issues that this model doesn't work because that isn't the point of this chapter, and we'd like to point you toward creators like Abi Aryan, Sebastian Raschka, and others who are covering the data science of pretraining LLMs.

NOTE If you'd like to pretrain a causal language model that generates great content, there are other great resources available. Check out these projects for more information on pretraining your own model: Llama 3 (https://mng.bz/BgAw), Megatron LM (https://mng.bz/dZdg), Hugging Face Tutorial (https://mng.bz/V2RN), and Llama2.c (https://mng.bz/x6j7).

In the spirit of continuing with data scientist–focused production advice, we'll now cover how to make your model easier to deploy and more effective once it's out there. Once a data scientist has trained a model and it passes the efficacy tests set, it's time to think about size.

9.3.1 Quantization

The first problem you'll definitely be up against is sheer size. Our 180M parameter model is over 700 MB on disk, which is much bigger than some companies ever plan on serving for any use case. How do you make sure it's small enough and quick enough to run in AWS lambda or in a CPU-only instance? Compression is one way to help us out here, and quantization is something built into PyTorch! As we've stated before, you should get familiar with BitsandBytes, but let's look at a quick implementation that quantizes the model after training using `torch`.

In the next listing, we take our model, and using PyTorch, we'll quantize the model to INT8. The rest of the code and functions are simply to compare the model sizes before and after. The important bit is just the first couple of lines.

Listing 9.5 Quantization

```
llama.to("cpu")
qconfig_dict = {
    torch.nn.Embedding: torch.quantization.float_qparams_weight_only_qconfig,
    torch.nn.Linear: torch.quantization.default_dynamic_qconfig,
}
dynamic_quantized_llama = torch.quantization.quantize_dynamic(    # Post training dynamic quantization
    llama, qconfig_dict, dtype=torch.qint8
)
#SimpleLlama size: 716.504MB
#SimpleLlama size: 18.000MB
```

You can see at the end that we go from almost 1 GB to 18 MB on disk by just going down to INT8 quantization. And we can go even lower,[3] which can help you fit almost

[3] S. Ma et al., "The Era of 1-bit LLMs: All Large Language Models are in 1.58 Bits," arXiv.org, Feb. 27, 2024, https://arxiv.org/abs/2402.17764.

any model in the chosen production environment; just keep in mind that as you compress weights, perplexity goes up, resulting in less stable and predictable performance of the LLM, even with great prompt engineering.

So now that the model is small enough, the MLOps team puts it into the dev environment, and all of the tests pass, so our model finally made it to prod. All is well, right?

9.3.2 LoRA

What do we do when, one month down the road, we have data showing our model is unable to perform a particular task up to the standards of its environment? We have data drift, and because we're a startup, we don't have the money or time to go through the rigorous training process we went through before to train a model from scratch. There's a bigger problem too: we don't have enough new data illustrating the new distribution to finetune the model effectively. This situation is perfect for training a LoRA to tweak the model rather than spending all that time training it over again.

Listing 9.6 shows you how to train a LoRA model and the adjustments we need to make to our Llama model. This listing shows first what adding a LoRA does to the inputs as they move through the model. The `LoRALayer` class is shown in clear PyTorch terms by Sebastian Raschka and Lightning.AI, and they have repos going into even more depth (see https://github.com/rasbt/dora-from-scratch and https://mng.bz/Aa8e). Next, it shows how our `SimpleLlama` class changes after we've added a LoRA to it. Lastly, we'll go through a similar training process using a new instruct dataset and a new `get_batches` function. As a note, we use several helper functions throughout this listing to simplify it; you can find their definitions in the repository accompanying this book.

Listing 9.6 Low-rank adaptation

```
class LoRALayer(nn.Module):                                    # What does LoRA actually do?
    def __init__(self, in_dim, out_dim, rank, alpha):
        super().__init__()
        standard_deviation = 1 / torch.sqrt(torch.tensor(rank).float())
        self.A = nn.Parameter(
            torch.randn(in_dim, rank) * standard_deviation
        )
        self.B = nn.Parameter(torch.zeros(rank, out_dim))
        self.alpha = alpha

    def forward(self, x):
        x = self.alpha * (x @ self.A @ self.B)
        return x


class LinearWithLoRA(nn.Module):
    def __init__(self, linear, rank, alpha):
        super().__init__()
        self.linear = linear
        self.lora = LoRALayer(
            linear.in_features, linear.out_features, rank, alpha
        )
```

```
    def forward(self, x):
        return self.linear(x) + self.lora(x)


class LlamaBlock(nn.Module):                          <-- Shows how the
    def __init__(self, config):                           blocks change
        super().__init__()
        self.config = config

        self.rms = RMSNormalization(
            (config["d_model"], config["d_model"])
        ).to(device)

        self.attention = RoPEMaskedMultiheadAttention(config).to(device)
        self.feedforward = nn.Sequential(
            LinearWithLoRA(config["d_model"], config["d_model"]),      <-- New
            SwiGLU(config["d_model"]),
        ).to(device)

    def forward(self, x):
        x = self.rms(x)
        x = x + self.attention(x)

        x = self.rms(x)
        x = x + self.feedforward(x)
        return x


class SimpleLlama(nn.Module):
    def __init__(self, config):
        super().__init__()
        self.config = config

        self.embedding = nn.Embedding(
            config["vocab_size"], config["d_model"]
        )
        self.llama_blocks = nn.Sequential(
            OrderedDict(
                [
                    (f"llama_{i}", LlamaBlock(config))
                    for i in range(config["n_layers"])
                ]
            )
        )

        self.ffn = nn.Sequential(
            LinearWithLoRA(config["d_model"], config["d_model"]),      <-- New
            SwiGLU(config["d_model"]),
            LinearWithLoRA(config["d_model"], config["vocab_size"]),   <-- New
        )

        print(
            f"model params: {sum([m.numel() for m in self.parameters()])}"
        )
```

```
    def forward(self, idx, targets=None):
        x = self.embedding(idx)
        x = self.llama_blocks(x)
        logits = self.ffn(x)

        if targets is None:
            return logits

        else:
            loss = F.cross_entropy(
                logits.view(-1, self.config["vocab_size"]),
                targets.view(-1),
                ignore_index=tokenizer.pad_token_id,
                reduction="sum",
            )
            return logits, loss

dataset = load_dataset(                                  <-- New dataset for LoRA
    "text",
    data_files={
        "train": ["../../data/Lima-train.csv"],
        "val": ["../../data/Lima-test.csv"],
    },
    streaming=True,
)

encoded_dataset = dataset.map(
    lambda examples: tokenizer(
        examples["text"],
        padding=True,
        max_length=128,
        truncation=True,
       \]] return_tensors="pt",
    ),
    batched=True,
)
train_data = iter(encoded_dataset["train"].shuffle())
val_data = iter(encoded_dataset["val"].shuffle())
train_data = cycle(train_data)
val_data = cycle(val_data)

llama.to("cpu")                 <-- Step 1: Adds LoRA to the trained model
add_lora(llama)
llama.to(device)

parameters = [{"params": list(get_lora_params(llama))}]         <-- Step 2: Gets the LoRA params instead of the whole model's
lora_optimizer = torch.optim.AdamW(parameters, lr=1e-3)         <-- Step 3: Initializes optimizer with LoRA params

train(                 <-- Step 4: Trains
    llama,
    lora_optimizer,
    scheduler,
    data=train_data,
    config=MASTER_CONFIG,
    lora=True,
```

```
    print_logs=True,
)

state_dict = llama.state_dict()
lora_state_dict = {k: v for k, v in state_dict.items() if name_is_lora(k)}
torch.save(llama.state_dict(), "./llama.pth")
torch.save(lora_state_dict, "./lora.pth")
```

Step 5: Exports the params

All of that results in two separate state dicts for us to save: the model and the LoRA. You can train LoRAs for a variety of specific tasks for which you may not have a large enough dataset to justify a whole finetuning. LoRA files on disk are usually only kilobytes even for very large models, depending on the size of the rank (in our case, 16).

You can inference using a LoRA generally in two ways: you can (1) load the original model's state dict (ours is loaded within the `llama` variable), load the LoRA on top of it, and then inference as normal, or (2) merge all of the LoRA layers into the original Llama and essentially create a new model and inference normally. Here, we adopt the second option.

Listing 9.7 Low-rank adaptation

```
# Loading and Inferencing with LoRA
add_lora(llama)

_ = llama.load_state_dict(lora_state_dict, strict=False)

merge_lora(llama)

generate(llama)
```

The generated text is

```
#'<s> off It the played he had cry bird dayt didn pretty Jack. a she moved
day to play was andny curiousTC bandierungism feel But'
```

We can see that the text still isn't as coherent as we'd like it to be; however, we can see a definite change in the generation compared to the simple Llama. No more overzealous punctuation, "cry," and other nonhappy small story words are present, and there are more clearly made-up words. If you train on a more distinct set—say, Shakespeare—you'll be able to see the difference even more clearly, and the nice thing about LoRA is that you can simply `remove_lora()` to get the original functionality back.

9.3.3 Fully sharded data parallel–quantized LoRA

Building upon LoRA, quantized LoRA (QLoRA) allows for efficient fine-tuning of models larger than your GPU. It does this by quantizing the model and then training a LoRA on the frozen version of that quantized model. This technique is desirable when you look at how much memory it takes to finetune full-size models, even in half-precision. As we previously discussed, a 70B parameter model ends up being 140 GB on disk and will take more than five times that much memory to finetune because of the dataset and gradients. With QLoRA, we can train up to 65B parameters on only 48 GB of VRAM—a very noticeable reduction. QLoRA is currently the most effective way of taking an absurdly large model and productionizing it for your use case, and it saves tons of money for that process too.

Add to this fully sharded data parallel (FSDP), and you can break the consumer versus enterprise barriers. Some of you have likely been asking where parallelism has been this whole time, and here it is. FSDP allows for both data and model parameter parallelism throughout the entire training process on multiple GPUs, and it takes care of the sharding as well as the rejoining on the other end when order and magnitude matter. It's amazing work coming from the team that maintains PyTorch.

Previously, 48 GB for QLoRA on a 70B parameter model was only possible using an enterprise GPU like an A100. With FSDP, you can take full advantage of parallelism on consumer hardware, like two 3090s, to get the same result. FSDP is native to PyTorch! Unlike our previous efforts in this chapter, we will now abstract a script created by Jeremy Howard and Answer.AI so that you can just run it in one of the cells on a 7B parameter model. Instead of needing to clone an entire GitHub repo, you can install and import `fsdp_qlora` from PyPI, and we've recreated the importable class in the `train_utils` folder. This code will execute fully parallel QLoRA training on as many GPUs as you have access to.

Listing 9.8 FSDP-QLORA training

```
from train_utils import FSDP_QLORA

trainer = FSDP_QLORA(
    model_name='meta-llama/Llama-2-7b-hf',
    batch_size=2,
    context_length=2048,
    precision='bf16',
    train_type='qlora',
    use_gradient_checkpointing=True,
    dataset='guanaco',
    reentrant_checkpointing=True,
    save_model=True,
    output_dir="."
)

trainer.train_qlora()
```

The result of this running is a fully finetuned safetensors model file trained using quantized weights and parallelism. Unlike our bespoke pretrained version, this one works. The safetensors file contains a state dict file for the trained model, similar to the state dict we saved for the `SimpleLlama`. Both of those state dicts need to be converted into a full model file or a full checkpoint file before they can be uploaded to a place like Hugging Face; otherwise, classes like `AutoModel` or `LlamaForCausalLM` won't be able to load your model later.

9.4 Deploy to a Hugging Face Hub Space

Spaces are hosted containers where you can put models to allow community access, and they can be much more than that, depending on your needs. Spaces can be the place your company uses to deploy its whole model, as opposed to other cloud-hosting options. Spaces have a free tier and many paid tiers, depending on how compute-intensive your particular application is. Spaces integrate seamlessly with the most popular ML frontend stacks, namely Streamlit, Gradio, and FastAPI.

> **NOTE** We won't be giving examples of these ML frontend stacks here, as we've given them in previous chapters, but we did include an example app in the notebook for this chapter. For reference, check out the documentation for Gradio (https://www.gradio.app/guides/quickstart) and Hugging Face (https://huggingface.co/docs/hub/spaces).

With our models, we'll need to convert their weights and directories into a format easily pushed to the Hugging Face Hub for our Space. We have an easily modified script that you can use to make this conversion. You can also run this on the simple Llama LoRA trained earlier.

Listing 9.9 Converting weights for Hugging Face

```
from safetensors import safe_open
import torch
from transformers import LlamaForCausalLM, BitsAndBytesConfig
from peft import get_peft_model, LoraConfig, TaskType

tensors = {}
with safe_open(
    "qlora_output/model_state_dict.safetensors",
    framework="pt",
    device=0
) as f:
    for k in f.keys():
        tensors[k] = f.get_tensor(k)

for k in tensors:
    if 'lora' not in k: tensors[k] = None

bnb_config = BitsAndBytesConfig(
    load_in_4bit=True,
    bnb_4bit_quant_type="nf4",
    bnb_4bit_use_double_quant=False,
    bnb_4bit_compute_dtype=torch.bfloat16
)
model = LlamaForCausalLM.from_pretrained(
    "meta-llama/Llama-2-7b-hf",
    use_cache=False,
    quantization_config=bnb_config
)
```

```
for param in model.parameters():
    param.requires_grad = False

peft_config = LoraConfig(
    task_type=TaskType.CAUSAL_LM,
    inference_mode=False,
    r=64,
    lora_alpha=16,
    lora_dropout=0.1,
    target_modules=[
        "k_proj",
        "q_proj",
        "v_proj",
        "up_proj",
        "down_proj",
        "gate_proj"
    ]
)
model = get_peft_model(model, peft_config)

list(model.state_dict().keys())[:10]

new_sd = model.state_dict()
for k in new_sd:
    if 'lora' in k:
        new_sd[k] = tensors[k]

model.load_state_dict(new_sd)

model.save_pretrained("lora_adapters")
```

If you already have a repo and are logged in to your Hugging Face account, you can go ahead and run `model.push_to_hub()`. This will create a repo for your model if it doesn't already exist. The reason you would or wouldn't push to the hub has to do with whether you want to share your model with the world. If you'd rather have a space where others can try out your model (even for free), we'll show how to do that next.

The first decisions to be made for a Space are how much compute your app requires and how you'll maintain the code for the Space—with Git or with `huggingface-cli`. The first question starts with whether a GPU is required for your particular use case; for ours, it is not. However, when you need a speed or scale increase, you will likely need it, especially if you get into multiprocessing to get more performance out of the Space. Once you have your app and you've figured out your memory requirements, if you've decided to use Git, you'll make your Space on Hugging Face, and then you'll clone it the same way you would something on GitHub:

```
$ git clone https://huggingface.co/spaces/your-username/your-space
```

Adding, committing, and pushing are the same as well:

```
$ git add files-you-need
$ git commit -m "Initial Commit"
$ git push
```

If you're not doing it through the CLI, the following listing shows you how.

Listing 9.10 Hugging Face Space

```
%pip install huggingface_hub -q

from huggingface_hub import notebook_login, HfApi

notebook_login() #OR huggingface-cli login

api = HfApi()
api.create_repo(                                    <-- If you haven't created your repo yet
    repo_id="your_username/your_repo", repo_type="space", space_sdk="gradio"
)

stuff_to_save = [
    "llama.pth",# Your model
    "lora.pth",# Optional: Your LoRA
    "special_tokens_map.json",
    "tokenizer_config.json",
    "tokenizer.json",
    "tokenizer.model",
    "gradio_app.py",
]
for thing in stuff_to_save:
    api.upload_file(
        path_or_fileobj=f"./llama2/{thing}",
        path_in_repo=thing,
        repo_id="your_username/your_repo",
        repo_type="space",
    )
```

Hugging Face Spaces

The models, as we currently have them, require GPUs to load (especially quantized) and run. If you attempt to run on the free tier of HF Spaces, it will error out, as it did for us. You can fix this by upgrading to a paid tier or ZeroGPU. Hugging Face provides a version of a Gradio app that uses its own API only to provision a GPU for the amount of time it takes to complete a task and only when it's requested. See https://mng.bz/XV11.

As an exercise, we encourage you to think through and build out how you might be able to create a Hugging Face Space using our LLM that would run on the free tier, which is considerably easier than when we were first writing this, thanks to ZeroGPU.

And there we have it—a fully functioning hosted instance of any model you want to use or train. You can run either of the two Llama models we trained in the Space, but you'll need to do a bit of engineering around it depending on your needs. Congratulations on finishing the first project if you ran all of this code with your own environment! This was one of the denser chapters, and making it through with a working example is something to be proud of. Hugging Face provides private solutions to enterprises looking to use Spaces long term, and this is a completely viable production environment.

Summary

- Choosing an appropriate tokenizer and embedding strategy is one of the first crucial decisions you'll make when creating a model from scratch, as it determines what the model will see and, therefore, is capable of.
- Your unique data sources future-proof your model.
- The main differences between Llama and a simple feed-forward are the normalization, attention, activation layers, and number of layers.
- Often, the first challenge to productionizing an LLM is its size: quantization to the rescue!
- In production, it's only a matter of time before you'll need to update the model. LoRA and QLoRA are perfect solutions to make minor tweaks to your model.
- Fully sharded data parallelism allows us to train QLoRA models cheaply on consumer hardware.
- A great option to deploy and share your LLM project is Hugging Face Hub Spaces due to their ease of use.

10 Creating a coding copilot project: This would have helped you earlier

This chapter covers

- Deploying a coding model to an API
- Setting up a VectorDB locally and using it for a retrieval-augmented generation system
- Building a VS Code extension to use our LLM service
- Insights and lessons learned from the project

> *Progress doesn't come from early risers—progress is made by lazy men looking for easier ways to do things.*
>
> —Robert Heinlein

If you touch code for your day job, you've probably dreamed about having an AI assistant helping you out. In fact, maybe you already do. With tools like GitHub Copilot out on the market, we have seen LLMs take autocomplete to the next level. However, not every company is happy with the offerings on the market, and not every enthusiast can afford them. So let's build our own!

In this chapter, we will build a Visual Studio Code (VS Code) extension that will allow us to use our LLM in the code editor. The editor of choice will be VS Code, as it is a popular open source code editor. Popular might be an understatement, as the Stack Overflow 2023 Developer Survey showed it's the preferred editor for 81% of developers.[1] It's essentially a lightweight version of Visual Studio, which is a full IDE that's been around since 1997.

Beyond just choosing a specific editor, we will also make some other judicious decisions to limit the scope of the project and make it more meaningful. For example, in the last project, we focused on building an awesome LLM model we could deploy. In this project, we will instead be starting with an open source model that has already been trained on coding problems. To customize it, instead of finetuning, we'll build a RAG system around it, which will allow us to keep it up to date more easily. Also, since we aren't training our own model, we'll focus on building a copilot that is good at Python, the main language we've used throughout this book, and not worry about every language out there.

Now that we have a clear idea of what we are building and a goal in mind, let's get to it!

10.1 Our model

Since we are only going to be focusing on Python, we decided to use DeciCoder as our model. DeciCoder is a commercial open source model that has only 1B parameters.[2] Despite its tiny size, it's really good at what it does. It has been trained on the Stack dataset but filtered to only include Python, Java, and JavaScript code. It's only trained on three languages, which would typically be a limitation, but it is actually part of the secret sauce of why it's so good despite its small size.

Some other limitations to be aware of are that it only has a context window of 2,048 tokens, which isn't bad for a model of this size, but it is relatively small when we consider that we plan to use a RAG system and will need to give it examples of code. Code samples tend to be quite large, which limits what we can do and how many examples we can give it.

A bigger problem using DeciCoder with RAG is that the model wasn't instruction tuned. Instead, it was designed to beat the HumanEval dataset (https://github.com/openai/human-eval). In this evaluation dataset, a model is given only a function name and docstring describing what the function should do. From just this input, the model will generate functioning code to complete the function. As a result, it's hard to know if giving the model more context from a RAG system will help it, but we're going to go ahead and try to find out!

Lastly, its tiny size actually makes it an interesting choice for another reason. Because it's so small, we could potentially put the model right inside the VS Code extension we are building, using compiling methods we've discussed in other chapters. This would allow us to build a very compact application! We won't be doing that

[1] D. Ramel, "Stack Overflow dev survey: VS Code, Visual Studio still top IDEs 5 years running," Visual Studio Magazine, June 28, 2023, https://mng.bz/zn86.

[2] Deci, "Introducing DeciCoder: The new gold standard in efficient and accurate code generation," August 15, 2023, https://mng.bz/yo8o.

in this book, mostly because it would require us to write a lot of JavaScript. That's a problem because we only expect our readers to be familiar with Python, so it's a tad too adventurous here to explain the details in-depth, but we leave it as an exercise for the readers who are JavaScript pros.

What we will do instead is serve our model as an API that you can run locally and will be able to call from the extension. In listing 10.1, we create a simple FastAPI service to serve our model. In fact, most of this code you've already seen back in chapter 6, and we have only made a few slight changes. The first is that we have changed the code to use the DeciCoder model and tokenizer. The second is a bit more involved, but we have added `stop` tokens. These are tokens that will inform the model to stop generating when it runs into them. This is done by creating a `StoppingCriteria` class. The tokens we have chosen will make a bit more sense once we've defined our prompt, but essentially, we are looking to have our model create one function at a time.

Listing 10.1 A simple FastAPI endpoint using DeciCoder

```
import argparse

from fastapi import FastAPI, Request
from fastapi.responses import Response
import torch
import uvicorn

from transformers import (
    AutoModelForCausalLM,
    AutoTokenizer,
    StoppingCriteria,
    StoppingCriteriaList,
)


torch.backends.cuda.enable_mem_efficient_sdp(False)          <-- Torch settings
torch.backends.cuda.enable_flash_sdp(False)

device = torch.device("cuda" if torch.cuda.is_available() else "cpu")

stop_tokens = ["def", "class", "Instruction", "Output"]      <-- Defines the
stop_token_ids = [589, 823, 9597, 2301]                          stopping
                                                                 behavior

class StopOnTokens(StoppingCriteria):
    def __call__(
        self,
        input_ids: torch.LongTensor,
        scores: torch.FloatTensor,
        **kwargs,
    ) -> bool:
        stop_ids = stop_token_ids
        for stop_id in stop_ids:
            if input_ids[0][-1] == stop_id:
```

```
                return True
        return False
                                                          Loads tokenizer
                                                          and models

tokenizer = AutoTokenizer.from_pretrained("Deci/DeciCoder-1b")
tokenizer.add_special_tokens(
    {"additional_special_tokens": stop_tokens},
    replace_additional_special_tokens=False,
)
model = AutoModelForCausalLM.from_pretrained(
    "Deci/DeciCoder-1b", torch_dtype=torch.bfloat16, trust_remote_code=True
)
model = model.to(device)


app = FastAPI()        <-- Runs FastAPI


@app.post("/generate")
async def generate(request: Request) -> Response:
    """Generate LLM Response

    The request should be a JSON object with the following fields:
    - prompt: the prompt to use for the generation.
    """
    request_dict = await request.json()
    prompt = request_dict.pop("prompt")

    # ...                                      <-- RAG will go here.

    inputs = tokenizer(prompt, return_tensors="pt").to(device)    <-- Generates
    response_tokens = model.generate(                                 response
        inputs["input_ids"],
        max_new_tokens=1024,
        stopping_criteria=StoppingCriteriaList([StopOnTokens()]),
    )
    input_length = inputs["input_ids"].shape[1]
    response = tokenizer.decode(
        response_tokens[0][input_length:], skip_special_tokens=True
    )

    return response

                                                        Starts service;
if __name__ == "__main__":                              defaults to localhost
    parser = argparse.ArgumentParser()           <--    on port 8000
    parser.add_argument("--host", type=str, default=None)
    parser.add_argument("--port", type=int, default=8000)
    args = parser.parse_args()

    uvicorn.run(app, host=args.host, port=args.port, log_level="debug")
```

Assuming this listing is in a Python script server.py, you can start up the server by running `$ python server.py`. Once you have it up and running, let's go ahead and make sure it's working correctly by sending it a request. In a new terminal, we can send the API a `curl` request with a simple prompt:

```
$ curl --request POST --header "Content-Type: application/json" --data
➥ '{"prompt":"def hello_world(name):"}' http://localhost:8000/generate
```

The response should be a simple Python function to complete a "Hello World" function. The response we got back from the server was `return f"Hello {name}!"`. So far, so good! Next, we'll customize the API to utilize a RAG system.

10.2 Data is king

Now that we have decided on a model, let's prepare a dataset for our RAG system. RAG is an effective way to introduce context to our model without having to finetune it; it also allows us to customize the results based on our data. Essentially, RAG is a good system to follow if you want your model to know the context of your organization's ever-changing code base. It's great to have a model that's good at coding, but we want it to be good at *our* code. We want it to use the right variable names and import custom dependencies built in-house—that sort of thing. In this section, we'll set up a VectorDB, upload a Python coding dataset, and then update the API we just built to utilize it all.

10.2.1 Our VectorDB

Before we can really dive into our dataset, we need to first set up our infrastructure. Of course, if your dataset is small enough, it is possible to load it into memory and run similarity search with tools like Faiss or USearch directly in Python, but where's the fun in that? Plus, we want to show you Milvus.

Milvus is an awesome open source VectorDB that competes with the big players in this space. You can run it locally or across a large cloud cluster, so it scales easily to your needs. If you'd rather not deal with the setup, there are managed Milvus clusters available. One of my favorite features is its GPU-enabled version, which makes vector search lightning fast.

Thankfully, the community has also made Milvus extremely approachable and easy to set up. In fact, the standalone version only requires Docker to run and comes with a startup script to make it even easier. Since we are going to run everything locally for this project, we will use the standalone version (to learn more, see https://mng.bz/aVE9). To do so, we need to run the following commands in a terminal:

```
$ wget https://raw.githubusercontent.com/milvus-io/milvus/master/scripts/
➥ standalone_embed.sh
$ bash standalone_embed.sh start
```

The first command will download a shell script, and the second will run it. This script is really only out of convenience since the Docker `run` command gets rather long. It also includes two more commands you should know about. The `stop` command, which will stop your Milvus docker container, is

```
$ bash standalone_embed.sh stop
```

and the `delete` command, which will delete all the data from your computer when you no longer wish to keep it, is

```
$ bash standalone_embed.sh delete
```

You don't need to run those yet, but remember them for when we are done. Now that we have our database set up, let's make it useful and load some data into it.

10.2.2 Our dataset

If this were a workshop, we'd show you how to write a script to pull your organization's code from GitHub and use that to augment your prompts. We could even set up a GitHub Actions pipeline to update our VectorDB with your code whenever it merges into the main branch. But since we don't have access to your code and this is only a book, we'll do the reasonable thing and use an open source dataset.

We will choose the Alpaca dataset for our project. The Alpaca dataset was compiled by Stanford when it trained the model of the same name using distillation and GPT-3 as the mentor model. Since it's synthetic data, the dataset is extremely clean, making it easy to work with. In fact, it's so easy that multiple copies online have already filtered out all the Python code examples. This subset comprises 18.6K Python coding challenges, consisting of a task or instruction and generated code—perfect for what we are trying to accomplish.

In listing 10.2, we create our pipeline to load the dataset into Milvus. We create a `PythonCodeIngestion` class to handle the details of chunking our dataset and uploading it in batches. Note that we use the `krlvi/sentence-t5-base-nlpl-code_search_net` embedding model. This embedding model has been specifically trained on the CodeSearchNet dataset (https://github.com/github/CodeSearchNet) and is excellent for creating meaningful embeddings of code.

Listing 10.2 A data pipeline to ingest Alpaca

```
from pymilvus import (
    connections,
    utility,
    FieldSchema,
    CollectionSchema,
    DataType,
    Collection,
)

from transformers import AutoTokenizer
from datasets import load_dataset
```

```
from langchain.text_splitter import RecursiveCharacterTextSplitter
from sentence_transformers import SentenceTransformer

from tqdm.auto import tqdm
from uuid import uuid4


connections.connect("default", host="localhost", port="19530")    ◁── Connects to Milvus


class PythonCodeIngestion:
    def __init__(
        self,
        collection,
        python_code=None,
        embedder=None,
        tokenizer=None,
        text_splitter=None,
        batch_limit=100,
    ):
        self.collection = collection
        self.python_code = python_code or load_dataset(
            "iamtarun/python_code_instructions_18k_alpaca",
            split="train",
        )
        self.embedder = embedder or SentenceTransformer(
            "krlvi/sentence-t5-base-nlpl-code_search_net"
        )
        self.tokenizer = tokenizer or AutoTokenizer.from_pretrained(
            "Deci/DeciCoder-1b"
        )
        self.text_splitter = (
            text_splitter
            or RecursiveCharacterTextSplitter(
                chunk_size=400,
                chunk_overlap=20,
                length_function=self.token_length,
                separators=["\n\n", "\n", " ", ""],
            )
        )
        self.batch_limit = batch_limit

    def token_length(self, text):
        tokens = self.tokenizer.encode(text)
        return len(tokens)

    def get_metadata(self, page):
        return {
            "instruction": page["instruction"],
            "input": page["input"],
            "output": page["output"],
        }

    def split_texts_and_metadatas(self, page):
        basic_metadata = self.get_metadata(page)
```

```
        prompts = self.text_splitter.split_text(page["prompt"])
        metadatas = [
            {"chunk": j, "prompt": prompt, **basic_metadata}
            for j, prompt in enumerate(prompts)
        ]
        return prompts, metadatas

    def upload_batch(self, texts, metadatas):
        ids = [str(uuid4()) for _ in range(len(texts))]
        embeddings = self.embedder.encode(texts)
        self.collection.insert([ids, embeddings, metadatas])

    def batch_upload(self):
        batch_texts = []
        batch_metadatas = []

        for page in tqdm(self.python_code):
            texts, metadatas = self.split_texts_and_metadatas(page)

            batch_texts.extend(texts)
            batch_metadatas.extend(metadatas)

            if len(batch_texts) >= self.batch_limit:
                self.upload_batch(batch_texts, batch_metadatas)
                batch_texts = []
                batch_metadatas = []

        if len(batch_texts) > 0:
            self.upload_batch(batch_texts, batch_metadatas)

        self.collection.flush()
```

Now that we have our ingestion class created, we can move forward with the pipeline. First, we'll need to create our collection if this is the first time we've run it. A collection is like a table in other databases or an index in Pinecone. We'll define our schema, which is simply an ID field, our embeddings field, and a metadata field, which contains freeform JSON. Once that's set, we'll upload our data using our `PythonCodeIngestion` class.

Next, we need to create our search index. The index type we'll use is `IVF_FLAT`, which is the most basic index in Milvus and splits the embedding space into `nlist` number of clusters. This accelerates the similarity search by first comparing our search embedding against the cluster centers and then against the embedding in the cluster it is closest to. We will also use `L2` for our metric type, which means we'll be using Euclidean distance. These are common settings, but we don't need anything special for our dataset. Milvus supports a larger selection of options when building an index, and we encourage you to check out their documentation:

```
if __name__ == "__main__":
    collection_name = "milvus_llm_example"
    dim = 768
```

```
if utility.has_collection(collection_name):                   ◁ Creates a
    utility.drop_collection(collection_name)                     collection if it
                                                                 doesn't exist
fields = [
    FieldSchema(
        name="ids",
        dtype=DataType.VARCHAR,
        is_primary=True,
        auto_id=False,
        max_length=36,
    ),
    FieldSchema(
        name="embeddings", dtype=DataType.FLOAT_VECTOR, dim=dim
    ),
    FieldSchema(name="metadata", dtype=DataType.JSON),
]

schema = CollectionSchema(
    fields, f"{collection_name} is collection of python code prompts"
)

print(f"Create collection {collection_name}")
collection = Collection(collection_name, schema)     Connects to the
                                                     collection and
collection = Collection(collection_name)          ◁ shows its size
print(collection.num_entities)
                                                          Ingests data
python_code_ingestion = PythonCodeIngestion(collection) ◁ and shows
python_code_ingestion.batch_upload()                      the stats now
print(collection.num_entities)                            that data is
                                                          ingested
search_index = {                          ◁ Builds the search index
    "index_type": "IVF_FLAT",
    "metric_type": "L2",
    "params": {"nlist": 128},             ◁ The number of clusters
}
collection.create_index("embeddings", search_index)
```

Now that everything is set up, we are good to move on to the next step. But first, let's test it by running a query. We'll want to make sure our data and index are giving us reasonable search results. With Milvus, we'll first load the collection into memory and convert our query into an embedding with our embedder. Next, we'll define some search parameters. Again, `L2` stands for Euclidean distance, and the `nprobe` parameter states how many clusters to search. In our case, of the 128 clusters we set up, we'll search the 10 closest ones to our query embedding. Lastly, in the actual search, we'll limit our results to the three best matches and return the metadata field along with our queries:

```
                         Before conducting a search, you need
collection.load()     ◁ to load the data into memory.

query = (                                                   ◁ Makes a query
    "Construct a neural network model in Python to classify "
```

```
        "the MNIST data set correctly."
    )
    search_embedding = python_code_ingestion.embedder.encode(query)
    search_params = {
        "metric_type": "L2",
        "params": {"nprobe": 10},        <-- The number of clusters to search
    }
    results = collection.search(
        [search_embedding],
        "embeddings",
        search_params,
        limit=3,
        output_fields=["metadata"],
    )
    for hits in results:
        for hit in hits:
            print(hit.distance)
            print(hit.entity.metadata["instruction"])
```

You can see that for our query, the search results are returning strong candidates from our dataset:

```
# 0.7066953182220459
# Create a neural network in Python to identify
# hand-written digits from the MNIST dataset.
# 0.7366453409194946
# Create a question-answering system using Python
# and Natural Language Processing.
# 0.7389795184135437
# Write a Python program to create a neural network model that can
# classify handwritten digits (0-9) with at least 95% accuracy.
```

Now that we have our VectorDB set up with data loaded in, let's update our API to retrieve results from our RAG system and inject the context into our prompts.

10.2.3 Using RAG

In this section, we will update listing 10.1 to include our retrieval code. In listing 10.3, we won't be repeating everything we did before, in the interests of time and space, but will simply be showing the new parts to add. In the repo accompanying this book, you'll be able to find the code that puts everything together if you are struggling to understand which piece goes where. First, near the top of the script, we'll need to add our imports, connect to our Milvus service, and load our embedding model.

Listing 10.3 Adding RAG to our API

```
from contextlib import asynccontextmanager

from pymilvus import (
    connections,
    Collection,
)
from sentence_transformers import SentenceTransformer
```

```
connections.connect("default", host="localhost", port="19530")    ◁ Connects to Milvus

collection_name = "milvus_llm_example"
collection = Collection(collection_name)

embedder = SentenceTransformer(                                   ◁ Loads our embedding model
    "krlvi/sentence-t5-base-nlpl-code_search_net"
)
embedder = embedder.to(device)
```

Next, we'll add some convenience functions, including a token counter and a FastAPI lifecycle, to ensure we load and release our Milvus collection from memory. Since we are adding a lifecycle, be sure to update the FastAPI call:

```
def token_length(text):
    tokens = tokenizer([text], return_tensors="pt")
    return tokens["input_ids"].shape[1]


@asynccontextmanager
async def lifespan(app: FastAPI):
    collection.load()                  ◁ Load collection on startup
    yield
    collection.release()               ◁ Releases collection from memory on shutdown


app = FastAPI(lifespan=lifespan)       ◁ Runs FastAPI
```

Now that we have all that set up, we can get to the good part—running the query and updating our prompt in our `generate` endpoint. The first part should look familiar since we just did it. We'll encode the user's prompt and search our collection for the nearest neighbors. We're using all the same search parameters as before, except one. We increase our limit from `3` to `5` to potentially add more examples to our prompt. Next, we take those results and format them into a few-shot prompt example dataset. Then we create our instruction prompt and format the user's input.

We are almost at the point where we can combine our instruction, examples, and user prompt; however, we need to ensure our examples don't take up too much space. Using a `for` loop utilizing our token counter, we'll filter out any examples that don't fit our context window. With that, we can now combine everything to create our final prompt for our DeciCoder model:

```
    request_dict = await request.json()            ◁ Inside the generate function
    prompt = request_dict.pop("prompt")

    search_embedding = embedder.encode(prompt)     ◁ Makes a query
    search_params = {
        "metric_type": "L2",
        "params": {"nprobe": 10},
    }
```

```
results = collection.search(
    [search_embedding],
    "embeddings",
    search_params,
    limit=5,
    output_fields=["metadata"],
)

examples = []
for hits in results:
    for hit in hits:
        metadata = hit.entity.metadata
        examples.append(
            f"Instruction: {metadata['instruction']}\n"
            f"Output: {metadata['output']}\n\n"
        )

prompt_instruction = (
    "You are an expert software engineer who specializes in Python. "
    "Write python code to fulfill the request from the user.\n\n"
)
prompt_user = f"Instruction: {prompt}\nOutput: "

max_tokens = 2048
token_count = token_length(prompt_instruction+prompt_user)

prompt_examples = ""
for example in examples:
    token_count += token_length(example)
    if token_count < max_tokens:
        prompt_examples += example
    else:
        break

full_prompt = f"{prompt_instruction}{prompt_examples}{prompt_user}"

inputs = tokenizer(full_prompt, return_tensors="pt").to(device)
```

Alright! Now that we've made our updates to our API, let's start it up and test it again like we did before. We'll send another request to the server to make sure everything is still working:

```
$ curl --request POST --header "Content-Type: application/json" --data
➥ '{"prompt":"def hello_world(name):"}' http://localhost:8000/generate
```

This time we got a response of `print("Hello, World!")`, which is slightly worse than our previous response, but it's still in the same vein, so there's nothing to be worried about. You'll likely get something similar. And that concludes setting up our LLM service with a RAG system for customization. All we need to do now is call it.

10.3 Build the VS Code extension

Alright, now all we need to do is build our VS Code extension. VS Code extensions are written primarily in TypeScript or JavaScript (JS). If you aren't familiar with these languages, don't worry; we'll walk you through it. To get started, you'll need Node and npm installed. Node is the JS interpreter, and npm is like pip for JS. You can add these tools in multiple ways, but we recommend first installing nvm or another node version manager. It's also a good idea at this time to update your VS Code (or install it if you haven't already). Updating your editor will help you avoid many problems, so be sure to do it. From here, we can install the VS Code extension template generator:

```
$ npm install -g yo generator-code
```

> **NOTE** You can find the instructions to install nvm here: https://mng.bz/gAv8. Then simply run `nvm install node` to install the latest versions of Node and npm.

The template generator will create a basic "Hello World" project repo for us that we can use as scaffolding to build off of. To run the generator, use

```
$ yo code
```

This command will start a walkthrough in your terminal, where you'll be greeted by what appears to us to be an ASCII art representation of a Canadian Mountie who will ask you several questions to customize the scaffolding being generated.

In figure 10.1, you can see an example with our selected answers to the walkthrough questions. Guiding you through the questions quickly, we'll create a new JavaScript extension, which you can name whatever you like. We chose `llm_coding_copilot`, if you'd like to follow along with us. For the identifier, press Enter, and it will hyphenate the name you chose. Give it a description; anything will do. No, we don't want to enable type-checking. You can choose whether to initialize the project

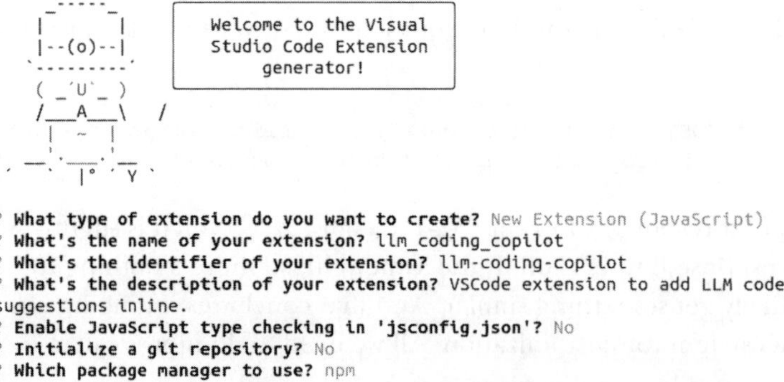

Figure 10.1 The VS Code extension generator with example inputs

as a new Git repository. We chose No, since we are already working in one. Lastly, we'll use npm.

When it's done, it will generate a project repository with all the files we need. If you look at figure 10.2, you can see an example of a built project repository. It has several different configuration files, which you are welcome to familiarize yourself with, but we only care about two of these files: the package.json file where we define the extension manifest, which tells VS Code how to use the extension we will build to (well, actually extend VS Code), and the extension.js file, which holds the actual extension code.

```
EXPLORER                ...
∨ LLM-CODING-COPILOT
  > .vscode
  > node_modules
  > test
  .eslintrc.json
  JS .vscode-test.mjs
  .vscodeignore
  CHANGELOG.md
  JS extension.js
  {} jsconfig.json
  {} package-lock.json
  {} package.json
  README.md
  vsc-extension-quickstart.md
```

Figure 10.2 Example directory structure created with the VS Code extension generator

In the package.json file, the boilerplate gets us almost all the way there, but the `activationEvents` field is currently empty and needs to be set. This field tells VS Code when to start up our extension. Extensions typically aren't loaded when you open VS Code, which helps keep it lightweight. If it's not set, the extension will only be loaded when the user opens it, which can be a pain. A smart strategy typically is to load the extension only when the user opens a file of the type we care about—for example, if we were building a Python-specific extension, it would only load when a .py file is opened.

We will use the `"onCommand:editor.action.inlineSuggest.trigger"` event trigger. This trigger fires when a user manually asks for an inline suggestion. It typically fires whenever a user stops typing, but we want more control over the process to avoid sending unnecessary requests to our LLM service. There's just one problem: VS Code doesn't have a default shortcut key for users to manually do this! Thankfully, we can set this too by adding a `"keybindings"` field to the `"contributes"` section. We will set it to the keybindings of `Alt+S`. We are using `S` for "suggestion" to be memorable; this keybinding should be available unless another extension is using it. Users can always customize their keybindings regardless. You can see the finished package.json file in the following listing. It should look very similar to what we started with from the scaffolding.

Listing 10.4 Extension manifest for our coding copilot

```
{
  "name": "llm-coding-copilot",
  "displayName": "llm_coding_copilot",
  "description": "VSCode extension to add LLM code suggestions inline.",
  "version": "0.0.1",
  "engines": {
    "vscode": "^1.86.0"
  },
  "categories": [
    "Other"
  ],
  "activationEvents": [
    "onCommand:editor.action.inlineSuggest.trigger"
  ],
  "main": "./extension.js",
  "contributes": {
    "commands": [{
      "command": "llm-coding-copilot.helloWorld",
      "title": "Hello World"
    }],
    "keybindings": [{
      "key": "Alt+s",
      "command": "editor.action.inlineSuggest.trigger",
      "mac": "Alt+s"
    }]
  },
  "scripts": {
    "lint": "eslint .",
    "pretest": "npm run lint",
    "test": "vscode-test"
  },
  "devDependencies": {
    "@types/vscode": "^1.86.0",
    "@types/mocha": "^10.0.6",
    "@types/node": "18.x",
    "eslint": "^8.56.0",
    "typescript": "^5.3.3",
    "@vscode/test-cli": "^0.0.4",
    "@vscode/test-electron": "^2.3.8"
  }
}
```

Now that we have an extension manifest file, let's go ahead and test it. From your project repo in VS Code, you can press F5 to compile your extension and launch a new VS Code Extension Development Host window with your extension installed. In the new window, you should be able to press Alt+S to trigger an inline suggestion. If everything is working, then you'll see a console log in the original window that states, `Congratulations, your extension "llm-coding-copilot" is now active!`, as shown in figure 10.3.

```
PROBLEMS    OUTPUT    DEBUG CONSOLE    TERMINAL    PORTS
  Congratulations, your extension "llm-coding-copilot" is now active!
```

Figure 10.3 Example console of successfully activating our VS Code extension

Alright, not bad! We can now both run our extension and activate it, as well as capture the logs, which is helpful for debugging. Now all we need to do is build it, so let's turn our attention to the extension.js file.

At this point, things get a bit tricky to explain. Even for our readers who are familiar with JavaScript, it's unlikely many are familiar with the VS Code API (https://mng.bz/eVoG). Before we get into the weeds, let's remind ourselves what we are building. This will be an extension in VS Code that will give us coding suggestions. We already have an LLM trained on code data behind an API that is ready for us. We have a dataset in a RAG system loaded to give context and improve results, and we have our prompt crafted. All we need to do is build the extension that will call our API service. But we also want something that allows users an easy way to interact with our model that gives us lots of control. We will do this by allowing a user to highlight portions of the code, and we'll send that when our shortcut keybindings, Alt+S, are pressed.

Let's take a look at the template extension.js file that the generator created for us. Listing 10.5 shows us the template with the comments changed for simplicity. It simply loads the vscode library and defines `activate` and `deactivate` functions that run when you start the extension. The `activate` function demonstrates how to create and register a new command, but we won't be using it. Instead of a command, we will create an inline suggestion provider and register it.

Listing 10.5 Boilerplate extension.js from template

```
// Import VSCode API library
const vscode = require('vscode');

// This method is called when your extension is activated
function activate(context) {
  console.log('Congratulations, your extension "llm-coding-copilot" is now
➥ active!');

  // This creates and registers a new command, matching package.json
  // But we won't use it!
  let disposable = vscode.commands.registerCommand('llm-coding-
➥ copilot.helloWorld', function () {
```

```
    // The code you place here will be executed every time your command is
➥ executed

    // Display a message box to the user
    vscode.window.showInformationMessage('Hello World from llm_coding_
➥ copilot!');
  });

  context.subscriptions.push(disposable);
}

// This method is called when your extension is deactivated
function deactivate() {}

module.exports = {
  activate,
  deactivate
}
```

Since we won't be using commands, let's take a look at what we will be using instead, an inline suggestion provider. This provider will add our suggestions as ghost text where the cursor is. This allows the user to preview what is generated and then accept the suggestion with a tab or reject it with another action. Essentially, it is doing all the heavy lifting for the user interface in the code completion extension we are building.

In listing 10.6, we show you how to create and register a provider, which returns inline completion items. It will be an array of potential items the user may cycle through to select the best option, but for our extension, we'll keep things simple by only returning one suggestion. The provider takes in several arguments that are automatically passed in, like the document the inline suggestion is requested for, the position of the user's cursor, context on how the provider was called (manually or automatically), and a cancel token. Lastly, we'll register the provider, telling VS Code which types of documents to call it for; here, we give examples of registering it to only Python files or adding it to everything.

Listing 10.6 Example inline suggestion provider

```
// Create inline completion provider, this makes suggestions inline
const provider = {
    provideInlineCompletionItems: async (
            document, position, context, token
        ) => {
        // Inline suggestion code goes here

    }
};

// Add provider to Python files
vscode.languages.registerInlineCompletionItemProvider(
    { scheme: 'file', language: 'python' },
    provider
);
```

```
// Example of adding provider to all languages
vscode.languages.registerInlineCompletionItemProvider(
    { pattern: '**' },
    provider
);
```

Now that we have a provider, we need a way to grab the user's highlighted text to send it to the LLM service and ensure our provider only runs when manually triggered via the keybindings, not automatically, which happens every time the user stops typing. In listing 10.7, we add this piece to the equation inside our provider.

First, we grab the editor window and anything selected or highlighted. Then we determine whether the provider was called because it was automatically or manually triggered. Next, we do a little trick for a better user experience. If our users highlight their code backward to forward, the cursor will be at the front of their code, and our code suggestion won't be displayed. So we'll re-highlight the selection, which will put the cursor at the end, and retrigger the inline suggestion. Thankfully, this retriggering will also be counted as a manual trigger. Lastly, if everything is in order—the inline suggestion was called manually, we have highlighted text, and our cursor is in the right location—then we'll go ahead and start the process of using our LLM code copilot by grabbing the highlighted text from the selection.

Listing 10.7 Working with the VS Code API

```
// Create inline completion provider, this makes suggestions inline
const provider = {
    provideInlineCompletionItems: async (
            document, position, context, token
        ) => {
        // Grab VSCode editor and selection
        const editor = vscode.window.activeTextEditor;
        const selection = editor.selection;
        const triggerKindManual = 0
        const manuallyTriggered = context.triggerKind == triggerKindManual

        // If highlighted back to front, put cursor at the end and rerun
        if (manuallyTriggered && position.isEqual(selection.start)) {
            editor.selection = new vscode.Selection(
                selection.start, selection.end
            )
            vscode.commands.executeCommand(
                "editor.action.inlineSuggest.trigger"
            )
            return []
        }

        // On activation send highlighted text to LLM for suggestions
        if (manuallyTriggered && selection && !selection.isEmpty) {
            // Grab highlighted text
            const selectionRange = new vscode.Range(
                selection.start, selection.end
```

```
            );
            const highlighted = editor.document.getText(selectionRange);

            // Send highlighted code to LLM
        }
    }
};
```

Alright! Now that we have all the VS Code–specific code out of the way, we just need to make a request to our LLM service. This action should feel like familiar territory at this point; in fact, we'll use the code we've already discussed in chapter 7. Nothing to fear here! In the next listing, we finish the provider by grabbing the highlighted text and using an async `fetch` request to send it to our API. Then we take the response and return it to the user.

Listing 10.8 Sending a request to our coding copilot

```
// On activation send highlighted text to LLM for suggestions
if (manuallyTriggered && selection && !selection.isEmpty) {
    // Grab highlighted text
    const selectionRange = new vscode.Range(
        selection.start, selection.end
    );
    const highlighted = editor.document.getText(
        selectionRange
    );

    // Send highlighted text to LLM API
    var payload = {
        prompt: highlighted
    };

    const response = await fetch(
        'http://localhost:8000/generate', {
        method: 'POST',
        headers: {
            'Content-Type': 'application/json',
        },
        body: JSON.stringify(payload),
    });

    // Return response as suggestion to VSCode editor
    var responseText = await response.text();

    range = new vscode.Range(selection.end, selection.end)
    return new Promise(resolve => {
        resolve([{ insertText: responseText, range }])
    })
}
```

Now that all the pieces are in place, let's see it in action. Press F5 again to compile your extension anew, launching another VS Code Extension Development Host window with our updated extension installed. Create a new Python file with a .py extension, and start typing out some code. When you're ready, highlight the portion you'd like to get your copilot's help with, and press Alt+S to get a suggestion. After a little bit, you should see some ghost text pop up with the copilot's suggestion. If you like it, press Tab to accept. Figure 10.4 shows an example of our VS Code extension in action.

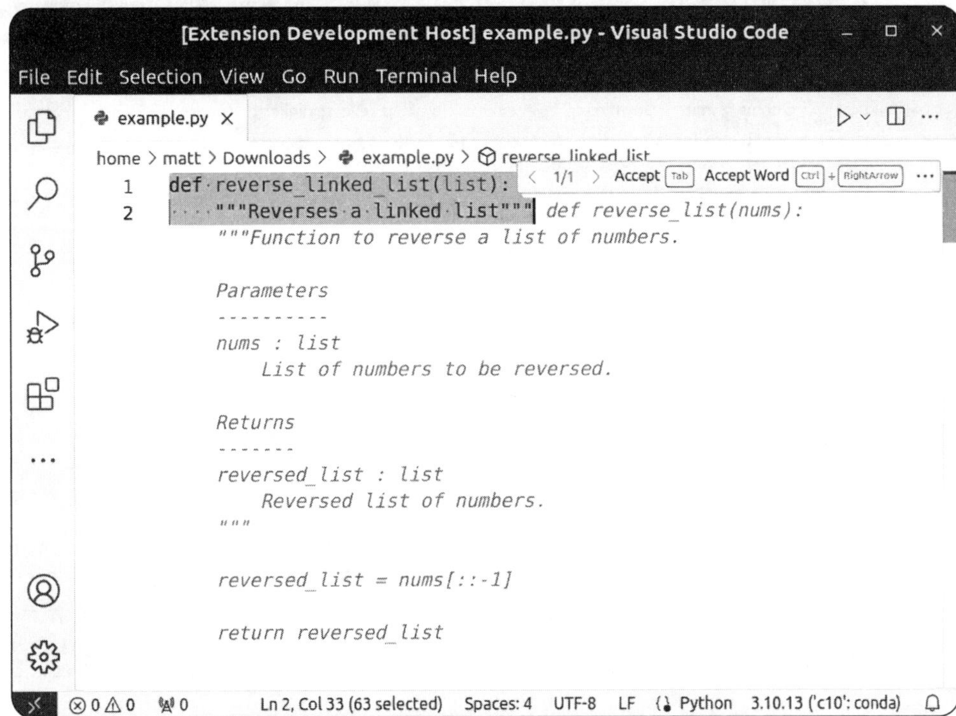

Figure 10.4 Example console of successfully activating our VS Code extension

Congratulations! You did it! You created your very own coding copilot! It runs on your own data and is completely local—a pretty big achievement if you started this book knowing nothing about LLMs. In the next section, we'll talk about next steps and some lessons learned from this project.

10.4 Lessons learned and next steps

Now that we have working code, we could call it a day. However, our project is far from completed; there's still so much we could do with it! To begin, the results don't appear to be all that great. Looking back at figure 10.4, the generated code doesn't reverse a linked list but reverses a regular ol' list. That's not what we wanted. What are some things we could do to improve it?

Well, for starters, remember our test "Hello World" functions we sent to the API to test it out? It seemed we got better results when using the model before we added RAG. For fun, let's spin up our old API with RAG disabled and see what we get while using our VS Code extension. Figure 10.5 shows an example result of using this API.

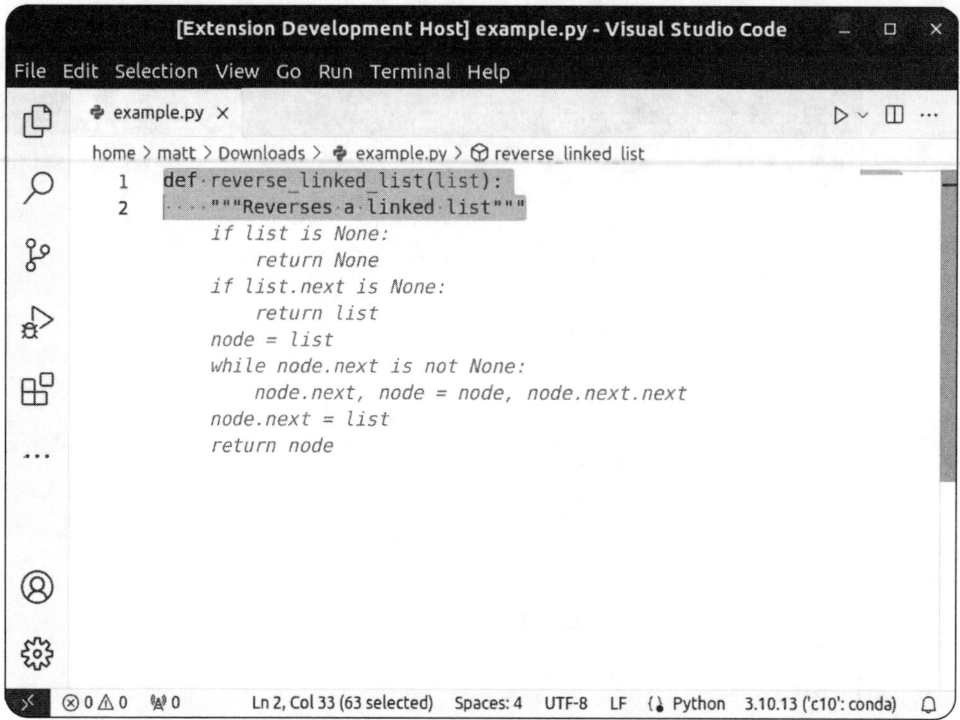
[Extension Development Host] example.py - Visual Studio Code
File Edit Selection View Go Run Terminal Help
example.py
home > matt > Downloads > example.py > reverse_linked_list
def reverse_linked_list(list):
"""Reverses a linked list"""
if list is None:
return None
if list.next is None:
return list
node = list
while node.next is not None:
node.next, node = node, node.next.next
node.next = list
return node
Ln 2, Col 33 (63 selected) Spaces: 4 UTF-8 LF Python 3.10.13 ('c10': conda)

Figure 10.5 Results of our extension using DeciCoder without RAG

Wow! That code looks way better! It actually reverses a linked list and is already formatted in such a way you wouldn't even need to edit or format it. What's going on here? Aren't models supposed to generate better results when we give them a few examples of how we want them to behave? Maybe our RAG system isn't finding very good examples. Let's do some digging and take a look at the prompt generated from our RAG system.

Instruction: What is the most efficient way to reverse a singly linked list in 7 lines of Python code?

Output: # Definition for singly-linked list.

```
class ListNode:
    def __init__(self, val=0, next=None):
```

```
        self.val = val
        self.next = next

def reverseList(head):
    prev = None
    current = head

    while current is not None:
        nxt = current.next
        current.next = prev
        prev = current
        current = nxt

    head = prev
    return head
```

Instruction: What is the most efficient way to reverse a linked list in Python?

Output:

```
def reverse(head):
    prev = None
    current = head
    while current:
        next = current.next
        current.next = prev
        prev = current
        current = next
    return prev
```

Instruction: def reverse_linked_list(list):

"""Reverses a linked list"""

Output:

Wow! Those examples seem to be spot on! What exactly could be going on then?

Well, first, take a look at the prompt again. The example instructions from our dataset are tasks in plain English, but the prompt our users will be sending is half-written code. We'd likely get better results if our users wrote in plain English. Of course, that's likely a bit of an awkward experience when our users are coding in an editor. It's more natural to write code and ask for help on the hard parts.

Second, remember our notes on how DeciCoder was trained? It was trained to beat the HumanEval dataset, so it's really good at taking code as input and generating code as output. This makes it good at the task from the get-go without the need for prompt tuning. More importantly, it hasn't been instruction tuned! It's likely a bit confused when it sees our few-shot examples since it didn't see input like that during its training. Being a much smaller model trained for a specific purpose, it's just not as good at generalizing to new tasks.

There are a few key takeaways to highlight from this. First and foremost, while prompt tuning is a powerful technique to customize an LLM for new tasks, it is still limited in what you can achieve with it alone, even when using a RAG system to give highly relevant examples. One has to consider how the model was trained or finetuned and what data it was exposed to. In addition, it's important to consider how a user will interact with the model to make sure you are crafting your prompts correctly.

So what are some next steps you can try to improve the results? At this stage, things appear to be mostly working, so the first thing we might try is adjusting the prompt in our RAG system. It doesn't appear that the instruction data written in plain English is very useful to our model, so we could simply try giving the model example code and see if that improves the results. Next, we could try to finetune the model to take instruction datasets or just look for another model entirely.

Beyond just making our app work better, there are likely many next steps to customize this project. For example, we could create a collection in Milvus with our own code dataset. This way, we could inject the context of relevant code in our code base into our prompt. Our model wouldn't just be good at writing general Python code but also code specific to the organization we work for. If we go down that route, we might as well deploy our API and Milvus database to a production server where we could serve it for other engineers and data scientists in the company.

Alternatively, we could abandon the customization idea and use DeciCoder alone since it appears to already give great results. No customization needed. If we do that, it would be worth compiling the model to GGUF format and running it via the JavaScript SDK directly in the extension. Doing so would allow us to encapsulate all the code into a single place and make it easier to distribute and share.

Lastly, you might consider publishing the extension and sharing it with the community. Currently, the project isn't ready to be shared, since we are running our model and RAG system locally, but if you are interested, you can find the official instructions online at https://mng.bz/GNZA. It goes over everything from obtaining API keys, to packaging, publishing, and even becoming a verified publisher.

Summary

- DeciCoder is a small but mighty model designed for coding tasks in Python, JavaScript, and Java.
- Milvus is a powerful open source VectorDB that can scale to meet your needs.
- Your dataset is key to making your RAG system work, so spend the time cleaning and preparing it properly.
- Visual Studio Code is a popular editor that makes it easy to build extensions.
- Just throwing examples and data at your model won't make it generate better results, even when they are carefully curated.
- Build prompts in a way that accounts for the model's training methodology and data to maximize results.

11 Deploying an LLM on a Raspberry Pi: How low can you go?

This chapter covers

- Setting up a Raspberry Pi server on your local network
- Converting and quantizing a model to GGUF format
- Serving your model as a drop-in replacement to the OpenAI GPT model
- What to do next and how to make it better

The bitterness of poor quality remains long after the sweetness of low price is forgotten.

—Benjamin Franklin

Welcome to one of our favorite projects on this list: serving an LLM on a device smaller than it should ever be served on. In this project, we will be pushing to the edge of this technology. By following along, you'll be able to really flex everything you've learned in this book. In this project, we'll deploy an LLM to a Raspberry Pi, which we will set up as an LLM Service you can query from any device on your home network. For all the hackers out there, this exercise should open the doors to many home projects. For everyone else, it's a chance to solidify your understanding of the limitations of using LLMs and appreciate the community that has made this possible.

This is a practical project. In this chapter, we'll dive into much more than LLMs, and there won't be any model training or data focusing, so it is our first truly production-only project. What we'll create will be significantly slower, less efficient, and less accurate than what you're probably expecting, and that's fine. Actually, it's a wonderful learning experience. Understanding the difference between possible and useful is something many never learn until it smacks them across the face. An LLM running on a Raspberry Pi isn't something you'll want to deploy in an enterprise production system, but we will help you learn the principles behind it so you can eventually scale up to however large you'd like down the line.

11.1 Setting up your Raspberry Pi

Serving and inferencing on a Raspberry Pi despite all odds is doable, although we generally don't recommend doing so other than to show that you can, which is the type of warning that is the telltale sign of a fun project, like figuring out how many marshmallows you can fit in your younger brother's mouth. Messing with Raspberry Pis by themselves is pretty fun in general, and we hope that this isn't the first time you've played with one. Raspberry Pis make great, cheap servers for your home. You can use them for ad blocking (Pi-Hole is a popular library) or media streaming your own personal library with services like Plex and Jellyfin. There are lots of fun projects. Because it's fully customizable, if you can write a functional Python script, you can likely run it on a Raspberry Pi server for your local network to consume, which is what we are going to do for our LLM server.

You'll just need three things to do this project: a Raspberry Pi with 8 GB of RAM, a MicroSD (at least 32 GB, but more is better), and a power supply. At the time of this writing, we could find several MicroSD cards with 1 TB of memory for $20, so hopefully, you get something much bigger than 32 GB. Anything else you purchase is just icing on the cake—for example, a case for your Pi. If you don't have Wi-Fi, you'll also need an ethernet cable to connect your Pi to your home network. We'll show you how to remote into your Pi from your laptop once we get it up. In addition, if your laptop doesn't come with a MicroSD slot, you'll need some sort of adapter to connect it.

For the Raspberry Pi itself, we will be using the Raspberry Pi 5 8 GB model for this project. If you'd like to follow along, the exact model we're using can be found here: https://mng.bz/KDZg. For the model we'll deploy, you'll need a single-board computer with at least 8 GB of RAM to follow along. As a fun fact, we have been successful in deploying models to smaller Pis with only 4GB of RAM, and plenty of other single-board alternatives to the Raspberry Pi are available. If you choose a different board, though, it might be more difficult to follow along exactly, so do so only if you trust the company. Some alternatives we recommend include Orange Pi, Zima Board, and Jetson, but we won't go over how to set these up.

You won't need to already know how to set up a Pi. We will walk you through all the steps, assuming this is your first Raspberry Pi project. A Pi is literally just hardware and an open sandbox for lots of projects, so we will first have to install an operating system

(OS). After that, we'll install the necessary packages and libraries, prepare our LLM, and finally serve it as a service you can ping from any computer in your home network and get generated text.

11.1.1 Pi Imager

To start off, Pis don't usually come with an OS installed, and even if yours did, we're going to change it. Common distributions like Rasbian OS or Ubuntu are too large and take too much RAM to run models at their fastest. To help us with this limitation, Raspberry Pi's makers have released a free imaging software called the Pi Imager that you can download on your laptop from here: https://www.raspberrypi.com/software/. If you already have the imager, we recommend updating it to a version higher than 1.8 since we are using a Pi 5.

Once you have it, plug the microSD into the computer where you've downloaded the Pi Imager program. (If you aren't sure how to do this, search online for the USB 3.0 microSD Card Reader.) Open the imager and select the device; for us, that's Raspberry Pi 5. This selection will limit the OS options to those available for the Pi 5. Then you can select the Raspberry Pi OS Lite 64-bit for your operating system. *Lite* is the keyword you are looking for, and you will likely have to find it in the Raspberry Pi OS (Other) subsection. Then select your microSD as your storage device. The actual name will vary depending on your setup. Figure 11.1 shows an example of the Imager

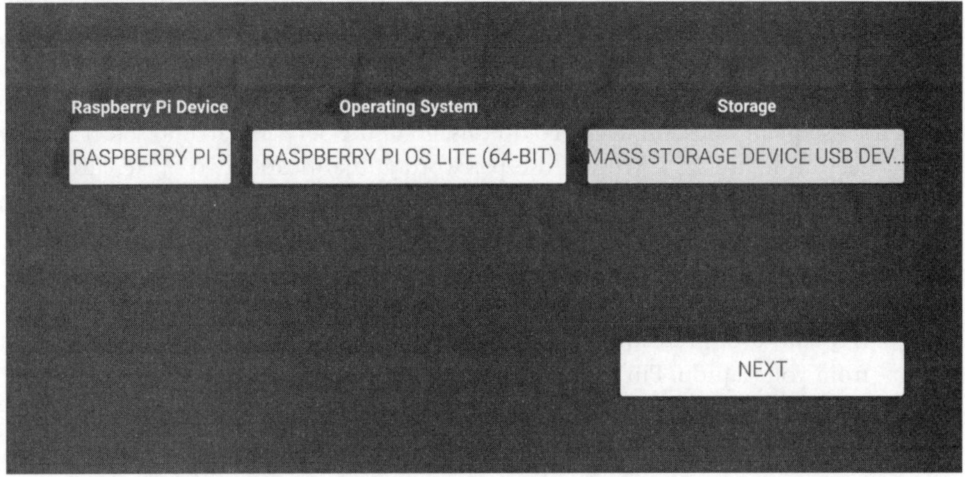

Figure 11.1 Raspberry Pi Imager set to the correct device, with the headless (Lite) operating system and the correct USB storage device selected

software with the correct settings. As a note, the Ubuntu Server is also a good operating system that would work for our project, and we'd recommend it. It'll have a slightly different setup, so if you want to follow along, stick with a Raspberry Pi OS Lite.

> **WARNING** And as a warning, make sure that you've selected the microSD to image the OS—please do not select your main hard drive.

Once you are ready, navigate forward by selecting the Next button, and you should see a prompt asking about OS customizations, as shown in figure 11.2. We will set this up, so click the Edit Settings button, and you should see a settings page.

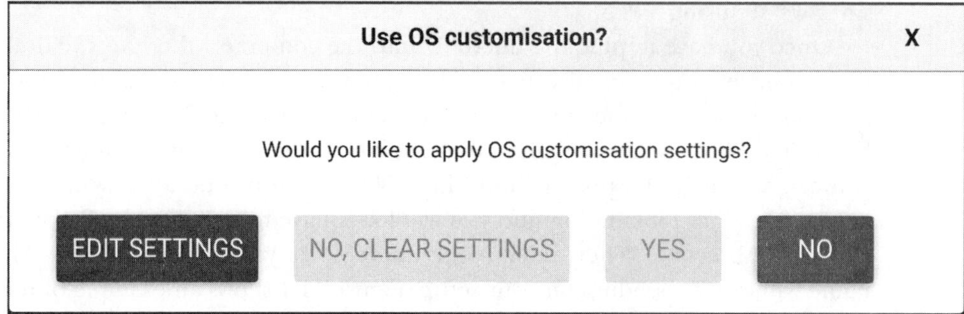

Figure 11.2 Customizing our Raspberry Pi OS settings. Select Edit Settings.

Figure 11.3 shows an example of the settings page. We'll give the Pi server a hostname after the project, llmpi. We'll set a username and password and configure the Wi-Fi settings to connect to our home network. This is probably the most important step, so make sure that you're set up for the internet, either by setting up your Wi-Fi connection in settings or via ethernet.

Just as important as setting up the internet, we want to enable SSH, or none of the subsequent steps will work. To do this, go to the Services tab and select Enable SSH, as seen in figure 11.4. We will use password authentication, so make sure you've set an appropriate username and password and are not leaving it to the default settings. You don't want anyone with bad intentions to have super easy access to your Pi.

At this point, we are ready to image. Move forward through the prompts, and the imager will install the OS onto your SD card. This process can take a few minutes but is usually over pretty quickly. Once your SD has your OS on it, you can remove it safely from your laptop. Put the microSD card in your Pi, and turn it on! If everything was done correctly, your Pi should automatically boot up and connect to your Wi-Fi.

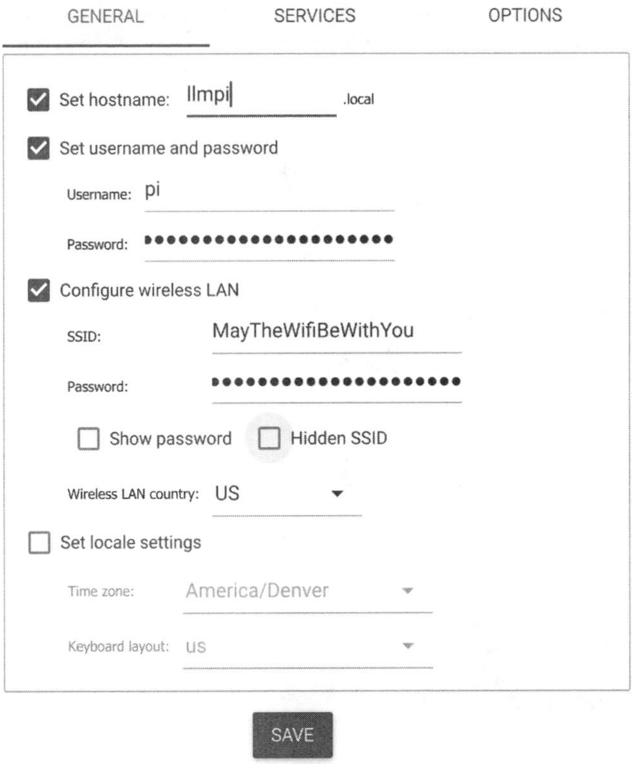

Figure 11.3 Example screenshot of the settings page with correct and relevant information

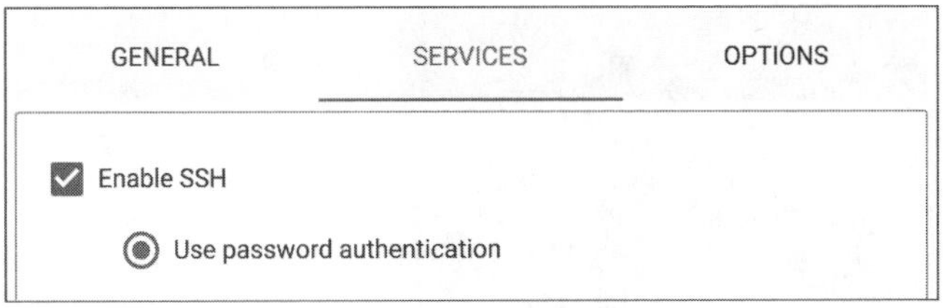

Figure 11.4 Make sure you select Enable SSH.

11.1.2 Connecting to Pi

We will use our little Pi like a small server. What's nice about our setup is that you won't need to find an extra monitor or keyboard to plug into your Pi. Of course, this setup comes with the obvious drawback that we can't see what the Pi is doing, nor do we have an obvious way to interact with it. Don't worry; that's why we set up SSH. Now we'll show you how to connect to your Pi from your laptop.

The first thing we'll need to do is find the Raspberry Pi's IP address. An IP address is a numerical label to identify a computer on a network. The easiest way to see new devices that have connected to the internet you're using is through the router's software.

See figure 11.5. If you can access your router, you can go to its IP address in a browser. The IP address is typically 192.168.86.1 or 192.168.0.1; the type of router usually sets this number and can often be found on the router itself. You'll then need to log in to your router, where you can see all devices connected to your network.

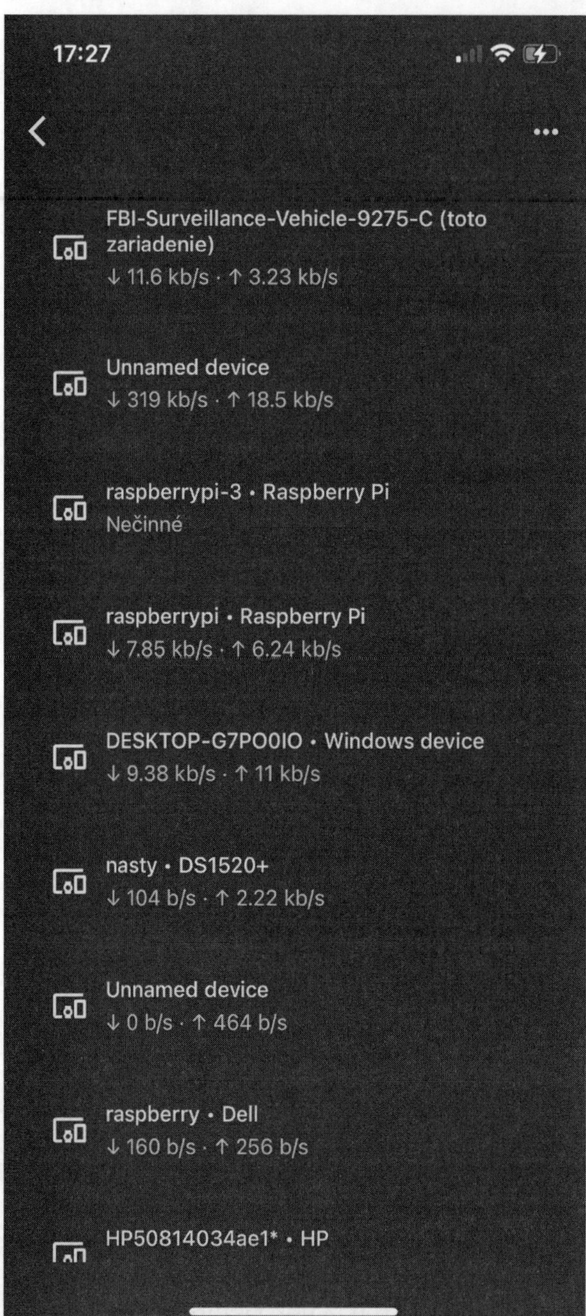

Figure 11.5 Example Google Home router interface with several devices listed to discover their IP addresses

If you don't have access to your router, which many people don't, you're not out of luck. The next easiest way is to ignore everything we said in the previous paragraph and connect your Pi to a monitor and keyboard. Run `$ ifconfig` or `$ ip a`, and then look for the `inet` parameter. These commands will output devices on your local network and their IP addresses. Figures 11.6 and 11.7 demonstrate running these commands and highlight what you are looking for. If you don't have access to an extra monitor, well, things will get a bit tricky, but it's still possible. However, we don't recommend going down this path if you can avoid it.

```
pi@raspberry:~ $ ifconfig
docker0: flags=4099<UP,BROADC
        inet 172.17.0.1  netm
        ether 02:42:a6:f8:78:
        RX packets 0  bytes 0
        RX errors 0  dropped
        TX packets 0  bytes 0
        TX errors 0  dropped

eth0: flags=4163<UP,BROADCAST
        inet 192.168.86.102
        inet6 fe80::1e67:cd3c
        inet6 2605:a601:a934:
        ether f8:b1:56:9a:07:
        RX packets 2198854606
        RX errors 0  dropped
        TX packets 1443276076
        TX errors 0  dropped
        device interrupt 20
```

Figure 11.6 Example of running `ifconfig`. The IP address of our Pi (`inet`) is highlighted for clarity.

```
pi@raspberry:~ $ ip a
1: lo: <LOOPBACK,UP,LOWER_UP> mtu 65536 qdisc noqueue state UNKNOWN group default qlen 1000
    link/loopback 00:00:00:00:00:00 brd 00:00:00:00:00:00
    inet 127.0.0.1/8 scope host lo
       valid_lft forever preferred_lft forever
    inet6 ::1/128 scope host
       valid_lft forever preferred_lft forever
2: eth0: <BROADCAST,MULTICAST,UP,LOWER_UP> mtu 1500 qdisc pfifo_fast state UP group default qlen 1000
    link/ether f8:b1:56:9a:07:bd brd ff:ff:ff:ff:ff:ff
    inet 192.168.86.102/24 brd 192.168.86.255 scope global dynamic noprefixroute eth0
       valid_lft 55012sec preferred_lft 40051sec
    inet6 2605:a601:a934:1000:4526:7bb:c9b3:2034/64 scope global dynamic mngtmpaddr noprefixroute
       valid_lft 86096sec preferred_lft 64496sec
    inet6 fe80::1e67:cd3c:48d8:247d/64 scope link
       valid_lft forever preferred_lft forever
3: eth1: <NO-CARRIER,BROADCAST,MULTICAST,UP> mtu 1500 qdisc pfifo_fast state DOWN group default qlen 1000
    link/ether 68:05:ca:1b:fb:57 brd ff:ff:ff:ff:ff:ff
4: docker0: <NO-CARRIER,BROADCAST,MULTICAST,UP> mtu 1500 qdisc noqueue state DOWN group default
    link/ether 02:42:a6:f8:78:69 brd ff:ff:ff:ff:ff:ff
    inet 172.17.0.1/16 brd 172.17.255.255 scope global docker0
       valid_lft forever preferred_lft forever
```

Figure 11.7 Example of running `ip a`. The IP address of our Pi (`inet`) is highlighted for clarity.

To scan your local network for IP addresses, open a terminal on your laptop, and run that same command (`$ ifconfig`), or if you are on a Windows, `$ ipconfig`. If you don't have `ifconfig`, you can install it with `$ sudo apt install net-tools`. We didn't mention this step before because it should have already been installed on your Pi.

If you already recognize which device the Pi is, that's awesome! Just grab the `inet` parameter for that device. More likely, though, you won't, and there are a few useful commands you can use if you know how. Use the command `$ arp -a` to view the list of all IP addresses connected to your network and the command `$ nslookup $IP_ADDRESS` to get the hostname for the computer at the IP address you pass in—you'd be looking for the hostname `raspberry`, but we'll skip all that. We trust that if you know how to use these commands, you won't be reading this section of the book. Instead, we'll use caveman problem-solving, which means we'll simply turn off the Pi, run our `$ ifconfig` command again, and see what changes, specifically what disappears. When you turn it back on, your router might assign it a different IP address than last time, but you should still be able to `diff` the difference and find it.

Alright, we know that was potentially a lot just to get the IP address, but once you have it, the next step is easy. To SSH into it, you can run the `ssh` command:

```
$ ssh username@0.0.0.0
```

Replace `username` with the username you created (it should be `pi` if you are following along with us), and replace the `0`s with the IP address of your Pi. Since this is the first time connecting to a brand-new device, you'll be prompted to fingerprint to establish the connection and authenticity of the host. Then you'll be prompted to put in a password. Enter the password you set in the imager before. If you didn't set a password, it's `pi` by default, but we trust you didn't do that, right?

With that, you should be remotely connected to your Pi and see the Pi's terminal reflected in your computer's terminal, as shown in figure 11.8. Nice job!

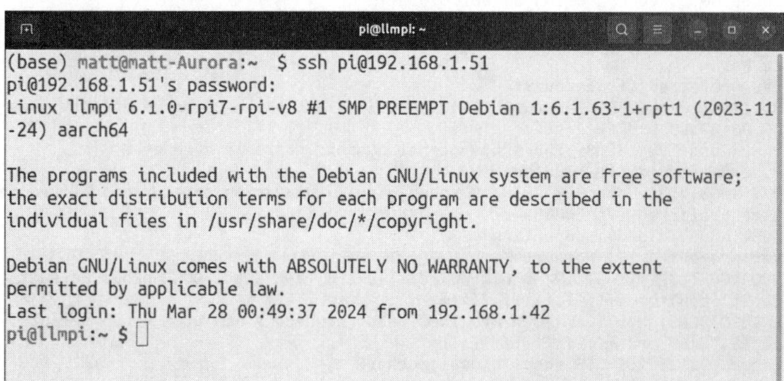

Figure 11.8 Terminal after a successfully secure shell into your Raspberry Pi.

11.1.3 Software installations and updates

Now that our Pi is up and we've connected to it, we can start the installation. The first command is well known and will simply update our system:

```
$ sudo apt update && sudo apt upgrade -y
```

It can take a minute, but once that finishes running, congratulations! You now have a Raspberry Pi server on which you can run anything you want to at this point. It's still a blank slate, so let's change that and prepare it to run our LLM server. We first want to install any dependencies we need. Depending on your installation, this may include `g++` or `build-essentials`. We need just two: `git` and `pip`. Let's start by installing them, which will make this whole process so much easier:

```
$ sudo apt install git-all python3-pip
```

Next, we can clone the repo that will be doing the majority of the work here: Llama.cpp. Let's clone the project into your Pi and build the project. To do that, run the following commands:

```
$ git clone https://github.com/ggerganov/llama.cpp.git
$ cd llama.cpp
```

> **A note on llama.cpp**
>
> Llama.cpp, like many open source projects, is a project that is much more interested in making things work than necessarily following best engineering practices. Since you are cloning the repo in its current state, but we wrote these instructions in a previous state, you may run into problems we can't prepare you for. Llama.cpp doesn't have any form of versioning either. After cloning the repo, we recommend you run
>
> ```
> $ git checkout 306d34be7ad19e768975409fc80791a274ea0230
> ```
>
> This command will checkout the exact `git commit` we used so you can run everything in the exact same version of llama.cpp. We tested this on Mac, Windows 10, Ubuntu, Debian, and, of course, both a Raspberry Pi 4 and 5. We don't expect any problems on most systems with this version.

Now that we have the repo, we must complete a couple of tasks to prepare it. First, to keep our Pi clean, let's create a virtual environment for our repo and activate it. Once we have our Python environment ready, we'll install all the requirements. We can do so with the following commands:

```
$ python3 -m venv .venv
$ source .venv/bin/activate
$ pip install -r requirements.txt
```

Llama.cpp is written in C++, which is a compiled language. That means we have to compile all the dependencies to run on our hardware and architecture. Let's go ahead and build it. We do that with one simple command:

```
$ make
```

A note on setting up

If you're performing this setup in even a slightly different environment, using CMake instead of Make can make all the difference! For example, even running on Ubuntu, we needed to use CMake to specify the compatible version of CudaToolkit and where that nvcc binary was stored in order to use CuBLAS instead of vanilla CPU to make use of a CUDA-integrated GPU. The original creator (Georgi Gerganov, aka ggerganov) uses CMake when building for tests because it requires more specifications than Make. For reference, here's the CMake build command ggerganov currently uses; you can modify it as needed:

```
$ cmake .. -DLLAMA_NATIVE=OFF -DLLAMA_BUILD_SERVER=ON -DLLAMA_CURL=ON
➥ --DLLAMA_CUBLAS=ON -DCUDAToolkit_ROOT=/usr/local/cuda
➥ --DCMAKE_CUDA_COMPILER=/usr/local/cuda/bin/nvcc
➥ --DCMAKE_CUDA_ARCHITECTURES=75 -DLLAMA_FATAL_WARNINGS=OFF
➥ --DLLAMA_ALL_WARNINGS=OFF -DCMAKE_BUILD_TYPE=Release
```

Next, we just need to get our model, and we'll be ready to move forward. The model we've picked for this project is Llava-v1.6-Mistral-7B, which we will download using the `huggingface-cli`, like we've done in other chapters. Go ahead and run the following command to pull the LLaVA model, its accompanying tokenizer, and the config files:

```
$ pip install -U huggingface_hub
$ huggingface-cli download liuhaotian/llava-v1.6-mistral-7b --local-dir
➥ ./models/llava --local-dir-use-symlinks False
```

Now that we have our model and tokenizer information, we're ready to turn our LLM into something usable for devices as small as an Android phone or Raspberry Pi.

11.2 Preparing the model

Now that we have a model, we need to standardize it so that the C++ code in the repo can interface with it in the best way. We will convert the model from the safetensor format, which we downloaded into .gguf. We've used GGUF models before, as they are extensible, quick to load, and contain all of the information about the model in a single model file. We also download the tokenizer information, which goes into our .gguf model file.

Once ready, we can convert our safetensor model to GGUF with the `convert.py` script:

```
$ python3 convert.py ./models/llava/ --skip-unknown
```

This code will convert all the weights into one .gguf checkpoint that is the same size on disk as all of the .safetensors files we downloaded combined. That's now two copies of whatever we've downloaded, which is likely one too many if your microSD card is rather small. Once you have the .gguf checkpoint, we recommend you either delete or migrate the original model files somewhere off of the Pi to reclaim that memory, which could look like this:

```
$ find -name './models/llava/model-0000*-of-00004.safetensors' -exec
rm {} \;
```

Once our model is in the correct single-file format, we can make it smaller. Now memory constraints come into play. One reason we picked a 7B parameter model is that in the quantized `q4_K_M` format (we'll talk about different llama.cpp-supported quantized formats later), it's a little over 4 GB on disk, which is more than enough for the 8 GB Raspberry Pi to run effectively. Run the following command to quantize the model:

```
$ ./quantize ./models/llava/ggml-model-f16.gguf ./models/llava/llava-
➥ v1.6-mistral-7b-q4_k_m.gguf Q4_K_M
```

We won't lie: it'll be a bit of a waiting game while the quantization methodology is applied to all of the model weights, but when it's finished, you'll have a fresh quantized model ready to be served.

Having trouble?

While we've tested these instructions in a multitude of environments and hardware, you might still find yourself stuck. Here's some troubleshooting advice you can try that has helped us out:

- *Redownload the model*. These models are large, and if your Pi had any internet connection problems during the download, you may have a corrupted model. You may try connecting with an ethernet cable instead of Wi-Fi if your connection is spotty.
- *Recompile your dependencies*. The easiest way to recomplie your dependencies is to run `make clean` and then `make` again. You might try using `cmake` or checking out different options.
- *Reboot your Pi*. Rebooting is a classic but tried-and-true solution, especially if you are dealing with memory problems (which we don't have a lot of for the task at hand.). You can reboot while in SSH with `sudo reboot`.
- *Run through these steps on your computer*. You're likely to run into fewer problems on better hardware, and it can be useful to know what an easy path looks like before trying to make it work on an edge device.
- *Download an already prepared model*. While we encourage you to go through the steps of converting and quantizing yourself, you can usually find most open source models already quantized to any and every format. So if you aren't worried about finetuning it, you should be in luck. For us, we are in said luck.

(continued)

If you get stuck but want to keep moving forward, you can download a quantized version of the model with the following command:

```
$ huggingface-cli download cjpais/llava-1.6-mistral-7b-gguf --local-dir
➥ ./models/llava --local-dir-use-symlinks False --include *Q4_K_M*
```

11.3 Serving the model

We're finally here, serving the model! With llama.cpp, creating a service for the model is incredibly easy, and we'll get into some slightly more complex tricks in a bit, but for now, revel in what you've done:

```
$./server -m ./models/llava/llava-v1.6-mistral-7b-q4_k_m.gguf --host
➥ $PI_IP_ADDRESS --api-key $API_KEY
```

Be sure to use your Pi's IP address, and the API key can be any random string to provide a small layer of security. That's it! You now have an LLM running on a Raspberry Pi that can be queried from any computer on your local network. Note that the server can take a long time to boot up on your Pi, as it loads in the model. Don't worry too much; give it time. Once ready, let's test it out with a quick demo.

For this demo, let's say you've already integrated an app pretty deeply with OpenAI's Python package. In listing 11.1, we show you how to point this app to your Pi LLM service instead. We'll continue to use OpenAI's Python bindings and point it to our service instead. We do this by updating the `base_url` to our Pi's IP address and using the same API key we set when we created the server.

Also, notice that we're calling the `gpt-3.5-turbo` model. OpenAI has different processes for calling different models. You can easily change that if you don't like typing those letters, but it doesn't really matter. You'll just have to figure out how to change the script for whichever model you want to feel like you're calling (again, you're not actually calling ChatGPT).

Listing 11.1 OpenAI but not ChatGPT

```
import openai

client = openai.OpenAI(
    base_url="http://0.0.0.0:8080/v1",  # replace with your pi's ip address
    api_key="1234",  # replace with your server's api key
)

completion = client.chat.completions.create(
    model="gpt-3.5-turbo",
    messages=[
        {
            "role": "system",
            "content": "You are Capybara, an AI assistant. Your top "
```

```
            "priority is achieving user fulfillment via helping them with "
            "their requests.",
        },
        {
            "role": "user",
            "content": "Building a website can be done in 10 simple steps:",
        },
    ],
)

print(completion.choices[0].message)
```

You don't need code to interact with your server. The server script comes with a built-in minimal GUI, and you can access it on your local network with a phone or your laptop by pointing a browser to your Pi's IP address. Be sure to include the port 8080. You can see an example of this in figure 11.9.

This process will allow you to interface with the LLM API you're running in a simple chat window. We encourage you to play around with it a bit. Since you're running on a Raspberry Pi, the fastest you can expect this to go is about five tokens per second, and the slowest is, well, SLOW. You'll immediately understand why normal people don't put LLMs on edge devices.

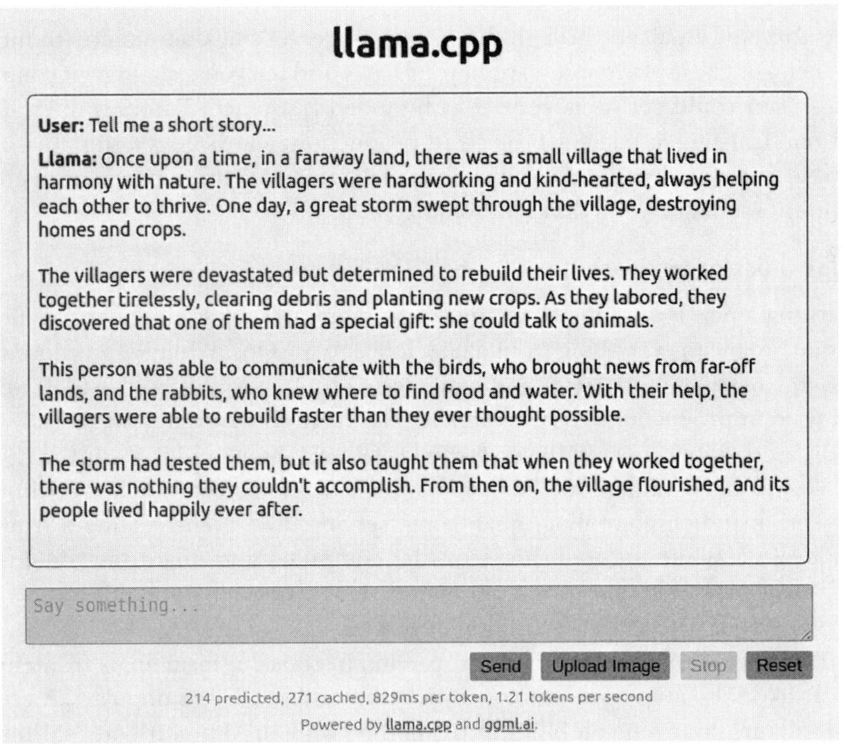

Figure 11.9 Running an LLM on your Pi and interacting with it through the llama.cpp server

At this point, you may be wondering why we were so excited about this project. We made a bunch of promises about what you'd learn, but this chapter is the shortest in the book, and the majority of what we did here was download other people's repos and models. *Welcome to production.*

This is ultimately what most companies will ask you to do: download some model that someone heard about from a friend and put it on hardware that's way too small and isn't meant to run it. You should now be ready to hack together a prototype of exactly what they asked for within about 20 to 30 minutes. Being able to iterate quickly will allow you to go back and negotiate with more leverage, demonstrating why you need more hardware, data to train on, RAG, or any other system to make the project work. Building a rapid proof of concept and then scaling up to fit the project's needs should be a key workflow for data scientists and ML engineers.

One huge advantage of following the rapid proof of concept workflow demo-ed here is visibility. You can show that you can throw something amazing together extremely fast, which (if your product managers are good) should add a degree of trust when other goals are taking longer than expected. They've seen that if you want something bad in production, you can do that in a heartbeat. The good stuff that attracts and retains customers takes time with real investment into data and research.

11.4 Improvements

Now that we've walked through the project once, let's talk about ways to modify this project. For clarity, we chose to hold your hand and tell you exactly what commands to run so you could get your feet wet with guided assistance. Tutorials often end here, but real learning, especially projects in production, always goes a step further. So we want to give you ideas about how you can make this project your own, from choosing a different model to using different tooling.

11.4.1 Using a better interface

Learning a new tool is one of the most common tasks for someone in this field—and by that, we mean everything from data science to MLOps. While we've chosen to focus on some of the most popular and battle-tested tooling in this book—tools we've actually used in production— your company has likely chosen different tools. Even more likely, a new tool came out that everyone is talking about, and you want to try it out.

We've talked a lot about llama.cpp and used it for pretty much everything in this project, including compiling, quantizing, serving, and even creating a frontend for our project. While the tool shines on the compiling and quantizing side, the other stuff was mostly added out of convenience. Let's consider some other tools that can help give your project that extra pop or pizzazz.

To improve your project instantly, you might consider installing a frontend for the server like SillyTavern (not necessarily recommended; it's just popular). A great frontend will turn "querying an LLM" into "chatting with an AI best friend," shifting from a placid task to an exciting experience. Some tools we like for the job are KoboldCpp and Ollama, which were built to extend llama.cpp and make the interface simpler or more extensible. So they are perfect to extend this particular project. Oobabooga is another great web UI for text generation. All these tools offer lots of customization and ways to provide your users with unique experiences. They generally provide both a frontend and a server.

11.4.2 Changing quantization

You might consider doing this same project but on an older Pi with only 4 GB of memory, so you'll need a smaller model. Maybe you want to do more than just serve an LLM with your Pi, so you need to shrink the model a bit more, or maybe you want to switch up the model entirely. Either way, you'll need to dive a bit deeper down the quantization rabbit hole. Before, we quantized the model using `q4_K_M` format with the promise we'd explain it later. Well, now it's later.

Llama.cpp offers many different quantization formats. To simplify the discussion, table 11.1 highlights a few of the more common quantization methods, along with how many bits each converts down to, the size of the resulting model, and the RAM required to run it for a 7B parameter model. This table should act as a quick reference to help you determine what size and level of performance you can expect. The general rule is that smaller quantization equals lower-quality performance and higher perplexity.

Table 11.1 Comparison of key attributes for different llama.cpp quantization methods for a 7B parameter model

Quant method	Bits	Size (GB)	Max RAM required (GB)	Use case	Params (billions)
`Q2_K`	2	2.72	5.22	Significant quality loss; not recommended for most purposes	7
`Q3_K_S`	3	3.16	5.66	Very small, high loss of quality	7
`Q3_K_M`	3	3.52	6.02	Very small, high loss of quality	7
`Q3_K_L`	3	3.82	6.32	Small, substantial quality loss	7
`Q4_0`	4	4.11	6.61	Legacy; small, very high loss of quality; prefer using `Q3_K_M`	7
`Q4_K_S`	4	4.14	6.64	Small, greater quality loss	7
`Q4_K_M`	4	4.37	6.87	Medium, balanced quality; recommended	7
`Q5_0`	5	5.00	7.50	Legacy; medium, balanced quality; prefer using `Q4_K_M`	7
`Q5_K_S`	5	5.00	7.50	Large, low loss of quality; recommended	7
`Q5_K_M`	5	5.13	7.63	large, very low loss of quality; recommended	7

Table 11.1 Comparison of key attributes for different llama.cpp quantization methods for a 7B parameter model *(continued)*

Quant method	Bits	Size (GB)	Max RAM required (GB)	Use case	Params (billions)
`Q6_K`	6	5.94	8.44	Very large, extremely low loss of quality	7
`Q8_0`	8	7.70	10.20	Very large, extremely low loss of quality; not recommended	7

If you only have a 4 or 6 GB Pi, you're probably looking at this table thinking, "Nope, time to give up." But you're not completely out of luck; your model will likely just run slower, and you'll either need a smaller model than one of these 7Bs—something with only, say, 1B or 3B parameters—or to quantize smaller to run. You're really pushing the edge with such a small Pi, so `Q2_k` or `Q3_K_S` might work for you.

A friendly note: we've been pushing the limits on the edge with this project, but it is a useful experience for more funded projects. When working on similar projects with better hardware, that better hardware will have its limits as to how large an LLM it can run. After all, there's always a bigger model. Keep in mind that if you're running with cuBLAS or any framework for utilizing a GPU, you're constrained by the VRAM in addition to the RAM. For example, running with cuBLAS on a 3090 constrains you to 24 GB of VRAM. Using clever memory management (such as a headless OS to take up less RAM), you can load bigger models onto smaller devices and push the boundaries of what feels like it should be possible.

11.4.3 *Adding multimodality*

There's an entire dimension that we initially ignored so that it wouldn't distract, but let's talk about it now: LLaVA is actually multimodal! A multimodal model allows us to expand out from NLP to other sources like images, audio, and video. Pretty much every multimodal model is also an LLM at heart, as datasets of different modalities are labeled with natural language—for example, a text description of what is seen in an image. In particular, LLaVA, which stands for Large Language and Vision Assistant, allows us to give the model an input image and ask questions about it.

> **A note about the llama server**
>
> Remember when we said the llama.cpp project doesn't follow many engineering best practices? Well, multimodality is one of them. The llama.cpp server at first supported multimodality, but many issues were soon added to the project. Instead of adding a feature and incrementing on it, the creator felt the original implementation was hacky and decided to remove it. One day, everything was working, and the next, it just disappeared altogether.

> This change happened while we were writing this chapter—which was a headache in itself—but imagine what damage it could have caused when trying to run things in production. Unfortunately, this sudden change is par for the course when working on LLMs at this point in time, as there are very few stable dependencies you can rely on that are currently available. To reproduce what's here and minimize debugging, we hope you check out the `git commit` mentioned earlier. The good news is that llama.cpp plans to continue to support multimodality, and another implementation will likely be ready to go soon—possibly by the time you read this chapter

We haven't really talked about multimodality at all in this book, as many lessons from learning how to make LLMs work in production should transfer over to multimodal models. Regardless, we thought it'd be fun to show you how to deploy one.

UPDATING THE MODEL

We've done most of the work already; however, llama.cpp has only converted the llama portion of the LLaVA model to .gguf. We need to add the vision portion back in. To test this, go to the GUI for your served model, and you'll see an option to upload an image. If you do, you'll get a helpful error, shown in figure 11.10, indicating that the server isn't ready for multimodal serving.

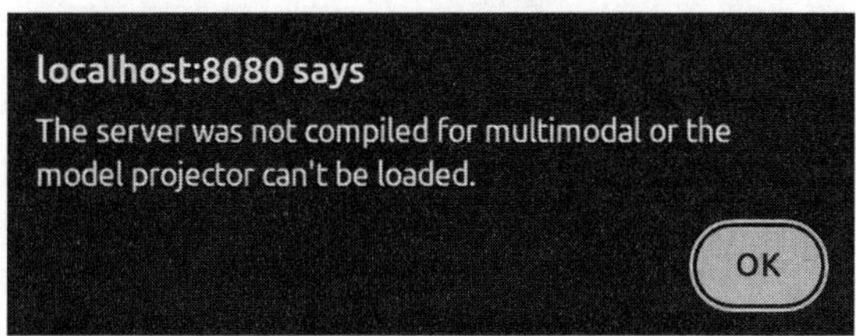

Figure 11.10 Our model isn't ready yet; we need to provide a model projector.

The first step to converting our model is downloading a multimodal projection file, similar to CLIP, for you to encode images. Once we can encode the images, the model will know what to do with them since it's already been trained for multimodal tasks. We aren't going to go into the details of preparing the projection file; instead, we'll show you where you can find it. Run the following command to download this file and then move it:

```
$ wget https://huggingface.co/cjpais/llava-1.6-mistral-7b-
➥ gguf/resolve/main/mmproj-model-f16.gguf
$ mv mmproj-model-f16.gguf ./models/llava/mmproj.gguf
```

If you are using a different model or a homebrew, make sure you find or create a multimodal projection model to perform that function for you. It should feel intuitive as to why you'd need it: language models only read language. You can try finetuning and serializing images to strings instead of using a multimodal projection model; however, we don't recommend doing so, as we haven't seen good results from it. It increases the total amount of RAM needed to run these models, but not very much.

SERVING THE MODEL

Once you have your model converted and quantized, the command to start the server is the same, except you must add `--MMPROJ path/to/mmproj.gguf` to the end. This code will allow you to submit images to the model for tasks like performing optical character recognition (OCR), where we convert text in the image to actual text. Let's do that now:

```
$./server -m ./models/llava/llava-v1.6-mistral-7b-q4_k_m.gguf --host
➥ $PI_IP_ADDRESS --api-key $API_KEY --MMPROJ ./models/llava/mmproj.gguf
```

Now that our server knows what to do with images, let's send it in a request. In line with the OpenAI API we used to chat with the language-only model before, another version shows you how to call a multimodal chat. The code is very similar to listing 11.1 since all we are doing is adding some image support. Like the last listing, we use the OpenAI API to access our LLM backend, but we will change the base URL to our model. The main difference is that we are serializing the image into a string so that it can be sent in the object with a couple of imports to facilitate that using the `encode_image` function. The only other big change is adding the encoded image to the content section of the messages we send.

Listing 11.2 OpenAI but multimodal GPT-4

```
import openai

import base64
from io import BytesIO
from PIL import Image


def encode_image(image_path, max_image=512):
    with Image.open(image_path) as img:
        width, height = img.size
        max_dim = max(width, height)
        if max_dim > max_image:
            scale_factor = max_image / max_dim
            new_width = int(width * scale_factor)
            new_height = int(height * scale_factor)
            img = img.resize((new_width, new_height))

        buffered = BytesIO()
        img.save(buffered, format="PNG")
        img_str = base64.b64encode(buffered.getvalue()).decode("utf-8")
        return img_str


client = openai.OpenAI(
    base_url="http://0.0.0.0:1234/v1",
    api_key="1234",          <- Replace with your server's IP address and port.
)
```

```
image_file = "myImage.jpg"
max_size = 512
encoded_string = encode_image(image_file, max_size)     <-- Set to the maximum dimension to allow (512=1 tile, 2048=max).

completion = client.chat.completions.with_raw_response.create(
    model="gpt-4-vision-preview",
    messages=[
        {
            "role": "system",
            "content": "You are an expert at analyzing images with computer
    vision. In case of error,\nmake a full report of the cause of: any issues in
    receiving, understanding, or describing images",
        },
        {
            "role": "user",
            "content": [
                {
                    "type": "text",
                    "text": "Building a website can be done in 10 simple steps:",
                },
                {
                    "type": "image_url",
                    "image_url": {
                        "url": f"data:image/jpeg;base64,{encoded_string}"
                    },
                },
            ],
        },
    ],
    max_tokens=500,
)

chat = completion.parse()
print(chat.choices[0].message.content)
```

Nothing too fancy or all that different from the many other times we've sent requests to servers. One little gotcha with this code that you should keep in mind is that the API will throw an error if you don't use an API key, but if you don't set one on the server, you can pass anything, and it won't error out.

And that's it! We've now turned our language model into one that can also take images as input, and we have served it onto a Raspberry Pi and even queried it. At least, we hope you queried it because if you didn't, let us tell you, it is very *slow*! When you run the multimodal server on the Pi, it will take dozens of minutes to encode and represent the image before even getting to the tokens per second that people generally use to measure the speed of generation. Once again, just because we can deploy these models to small devices doesn't mean you'll want to. This is the point where we're going to recommend again that you should not actually be running this on a Pi, even in your house, if you want to actually get good use out of it.

11.4.4 Serving the model on Google Colab

Now that we've done a couple of these exercises, how can we improve and extend this project for your production environment? The first improvement is obvious: hardware. Single-board RAM compute isn't incredibly helpful when you have hundreds of customers; however, it is incredibly useful for testing, especially when you don't want to waste money debugging production for your on-prem deployment. Other options for GPU support also exist, and luckily, all the previously discussed steps, minus the RPi setup, work on Google Colab's free tier. Here are all of the setup steps that are different:

1. Setting up llama.cpp:

```
!git clone https://github.com/ggerganov/llama.cpp && cd
➥ llama.cpp && make -j LLAMA_CUBLAS=1
```

2. Downloading from Hugging Face:

```
import os
os.environ["HF_HUB_ENABLE_HF_TRANSFER"] = "1"
!huggingface-cli download repo/model_name name_of_downloaded_
➥ model --local-dir . --local-dir-use-symlinks False
```

3. Server command:

```
!./server -m content/model/path --log-disable --port 1337
```

4. Accessing the server:

```
from .googlecolab.output import eval_js
print(eval_js("google.colab.kernel.proxyPort(1337)"))
```

   Click on the link given to the port.

As you can see, the steps are mostly the same, but because we are working in a Jupyter environment, some slight changes are necessary, as it's often easier to run code directly instead of running a CLI command. We didn't go into it, but Raspberry Pis can use `docker.io` and other packages to create docker images that you can use for responsible CI/CD. It's a bit harder in a Google Colab environment. Also, keep in mind that Google won't give you unlimited GPU time, and it goes so far as to monitor whether you have Colab open to turn off your free GPU "efficiently," so make sure you're only using those free resources for testing and debugging. No matter how you look at it, free GPUs are a gift, and we should be responsible with them.

You can also skip downloading the whole repo and running Make every time. You can use the llama.cpp Python bindings. And you can `pip install` with cuBLAS or NEON (for Mac GeForce Mx cards) to use hardware acceleration when pip installing with this command:

```
$ CMAKE_ARGS="-DLLAMA_CUBLAS=on" FORCE_CMAKE=1 pip install llama-cpp-python
```

This command abstracts most of the code in llama.cpp into easy-to-use Python bindings. Let's now go through an example of how to use the Python bindings to make something easy to dockerize and deploy. Working with an API is slightly different from working with an LLM by itself, but luckily, LangChain comes in handy. Its whole library is built around working with the OpenAI API, and we use that API to access our own model!

In listing 11.3, we'll combine what we know about the OpenAI API, llama.cpp Python bindings, and LangChain. We'll start by setting up our environment variables, and then we'll use the LangChain `ChatOpenAI` class and pretend that our server is GPT-3.5-turbo. Once we have those two things, we could be done, but we'll extend by adding a sentence transformer and a prompt ready for RAG. If you have a dataset you'd like to use for RAG, now is the time to embed it and create a FAISS index. We'll load your FAISS index and use it to help the model at inference time. Then, tokenize it with tiktoken to make sure we don't overload our context length.

Listing 11.3 OpenAI but not multimodal GPT-4

```
import os
from langchain.chains import LLMChain
from langchain_community.chat_models import ChatOpenAI
from langchain.prompts import PromptTemplate
from sentence_transformers import SentenceTransformer
import numpy as np
from datasets import load_dataset
import tiktoken

os.environ["OPENAI_API_KEY"] = "Your API Key"
os.environ[
    "OPENAI_API_BASE"
] = "http://0.0.0.0:1234/v1"                  <-- Replace with your server's address and port.
os.environ[
    "OPENAI_API_HOST"
] = "http://0.0.0.0:1234"                 <-- Replace with your host IP.

llm = ChatOpenAI(
    model_name="gpt-3.5-turbo",          <-- This can be anything.
    temperature=0.25,
    openai_api_base=os.environ["OPENAI_API_BASE"],         <-- Again
    openai_api_key=os.environ["OPENAI_API_KEY"],
    max_tokens=500,
    n=1,
)

embedder = SentenceTransformer("sentence-transformers/all-MiniLM-L6-v2")   <-- Embeddings for RAG
tiktoker = tiktoken.encoding_for_model("gpt-3.5-turbo")     <-- Tokenization for checking context length quickly

prompt_template = """Below is an instruction            <-- Change the prompt to be whatever you want.
that describes a task,
paired with an input that provides further context.
Write a response that appropriately completes the request.
```

```
    ###Instruction:
    You are an expert python developer.
    Given a question, some conversation history,
and the closest code snippet we could find for
the request, give your best suggestion for how
to write the code needed to answer the User's question.

    ###Input:

    #Question: {question}

    #Conversation History: {conversation_history}

    Code Snippet:
    {code_snippet}


    ###Response:
    """

vectorDB = load_dataset(                                    ◁ Here's a vectorDB; feel free to drop in a replacement.
    "csv", data_files="your dataset with embeddings.csv", split="train"
)
try:                                                        ◁ If you haven't created a faiss or elasticsearch or usearch index, do it.
    vectorDB.load_faiss_index("embeddings", "my_index.faiss")
except:
    print(
    """No faiss index, run vectorDB.add_faiss_index(column='embeddings')
    and vectorDB.save_faiss_index('embeddings', 'my_index.faiss')"""
    )

message_history = []                    ◁ To keep track of chat history

query = "How can I train an LLM from scratch?"              ◁ Searches the Vector DB
embedded = embedder.encode(query)
q = np.array(embedded, dtype=np.float32)
_, retrieved_example = vectorDB.get_nearest_examples("embeddings", q, k=1)

formatted_prompt = PromptTemplate(                          ◁ Formats the prompt
    input_variables=["question", "conversation_history", "code_snippet"],
    template=prompt_template,
)
chain = LLMChain(llm=llm, prompt=formatted_prompt)          ◁ Sets up the actual LLM chain

num_tokens = len(                                           ◁ Don't overload your context length.
    tiktoker.encode(f"{prompt_template},\n" + "\n".join(message_history) +
➥ query)
    )
)
while num_tokens >= 4000:
    message_history.pop(0)
    num_tokens = len(
    tiktoker.encode(f"{prompt_template},\n" + "\n".join(message_history) +
➥ query)
        )
    )
```

```
res = chain.run(
    {
    "question": query,
    "conversation_history": message_history,
    "code_snippet": "",
    }
)
message_history.append(f"User: {query}\nLlama: {res}")

print(res)
```

Runs RAG with your API

We're just printing; do whatever you need to here.

So here's where many of our concepts really come together. The amazing thing is that you really can perform this inference and RAG on a Raspberry Pi; you don't need a gigantic computer to get good, repeatable results. Compute layered on top of this helps immensely until you get to about 48 GB and can fit full versions of 7B and quantized versions of everything above that; all compute after that ends up getting only marginal gains currently. This field is advancing quickly, so look for new, quicker methods of inferencing larger models on smaller hardware.

With that, we've got our prototype project up and running. It's easily extensible in pretty much any direction you'd like, and it conforms to industry standards and uses popular libraries. Add to this, make it better, and if you have expertise you feel isn't being represented here, share it! This field is new, and interdisciplinary knowledge is how it will be pushed forward.

Summary

- Running the largest models on the smallest devices demands utilizing every memory-saving technique you can think of, like running a Lite operating system.
- The hardest part of setting up a remote Pi for the first time is finding its IP address.
- For compute-limited hardware without an accelerator, you will need to compile the model to run on your architecture with a tool like llama.cpp.
- In a memory-limited environment, quantization will be required for inference.
- Even taking advantage of everything available, running LLMs on edge devices will often result in slower inference than desired. Just because something is possible doesn't make it practical.
- OpenAI's API, along with all wrappers, can be used to access other models by pointing to a custom endpoint.
- Many open source tools are available to improve both the serving of models and the user interface.
- Lower quantization equals higher perplexity, even with larger models.
- Running multimodal models is also possible on a Raspberry Pi.

- The same commands we ran on the Pi can be used to develop in Google Collab or another cloud provider with only slight modifications, making these projects more accessible than ever.
- Setup and deployment are often much larger pieces to a successful project than preparing the model.

12 Production, an ever-changing landscape: Things are just getting started

This chapter covers

- A brief overview of LLMs in production
- The future of LLMs as a technology and several exciting fields of research into it
- Our closing remarks

The Web as I envisaged it, we have not seen it yet. The future is still so much bigger than the past.

—Tim Berners-Lee (inventor of www)

Wow! We've really covered a lot of ground in this book. Is your head just about ready to explode? Because ours are, and we wrote the book. Writing this book has been no easy feat, as the industry has been constantly changing—and fast. Trying to stay on top of what's happening with LLMs has been like trying to build a house on quicksand; you finish one level, and it seems to have already sunk before you can start the next. We know that portions of this book will inevitably become out of date, and that's why we tried our best to stick to core concepts, the sturdy rocks in the sand, that will never change.

In this chapter, we wanted to take a step back and review some of the major takeaways we hope you will walk away with. We've spent a lot of time getting into the weeds and paying attention to details, so let's reflect for a moment to see the whole picture and review what we've covered. After that, we'll take a minute to discuss the future of the field and where we can expect to see some of the next major breakthroughs. Finally, we'll leave you with our final thoughts.

12.1 A thousand-foot view

We have gone over a lot of material in this book—from making a bag-of-words model to serving an LLM API on a Raspberry Pi. If you made it all the way through the whole book, that's an accomplishment. Great work! We are not going to recap everything, but we wanted to take a second to see the forest from the trees, as it were. To summarize much of what we've covered, we can split most of the ideas into four distinct but very closely tied quadrants: Preparation, Training, Serving, and Developing. You can see these quadrants in figure 12.1. You'll notice that along with these sections, there's a fifth one distinct from the others, which we labeled Undercurrents. These are elements that seem to affect all of the other quadrants to varying degrees and things you'll have to worry about during each stage of an LLM product life cycle.

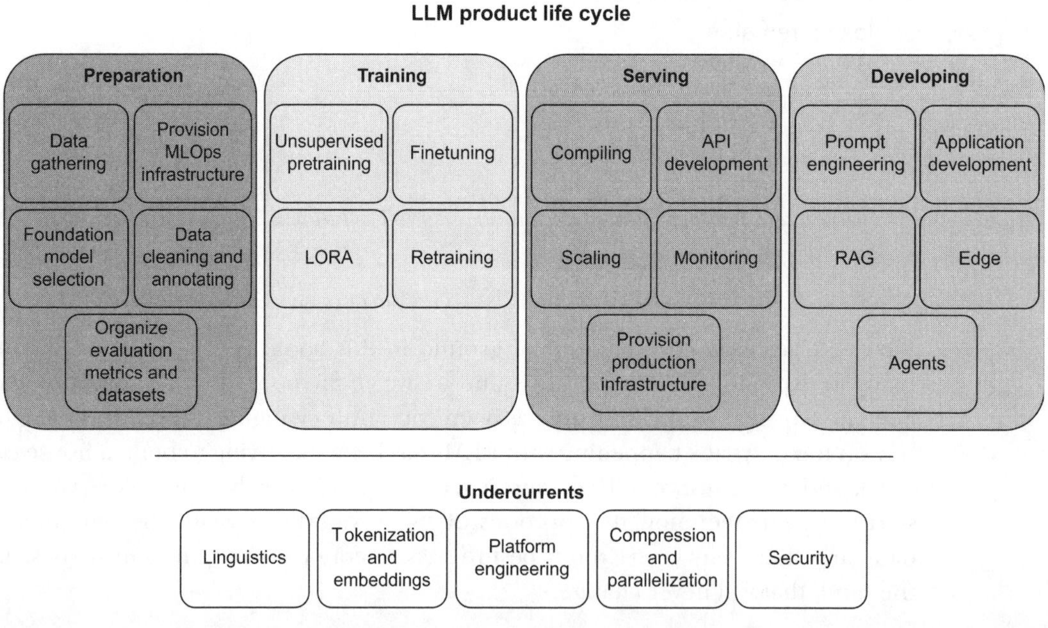

Figure 12.1 LLM product life cycle. Here are all the key concepts discussed in the book, along with where they generally fit within the production environment. Undercurrents are important elements that show up in every part of the life cycle—for example, linguistics informs preparation, creates metrics in training and serving, and influences prompting and development.

Hopefully, if it wasn't clear when we were talking about a concept in an earlier chapter, it's clear now exactly where that concept fits in a production life cycle. You'll notice that we've likely put some elements in places that your current production environment doesn't reflect—for example, provisioning of the MLOps infrastructure doesn't often actually happen within the preparation stage but is rather haphazardly thrown together the first time that serving needs to happen. We get it. But during preparation is where we feel it *should* happen. Take a moment to digest all that you've learned while reading this book, and consider how the pieces all come together.

Given this abstract and idealized version of a production life cycle, let's move to the things not currently included there. What might we need to add to our development portion five years down the line, especially given how fast the field moves now?

12.2 The future of LLMs

When we wrote this book, we made a conscious effort to focus on the foundational knowledge you will need to understand how LLMs work and how to deploy them to production. This information is crucial, as production looks very different for every single use case. Learning how to weigh the pros and cons of any decision requires that foundational knowledge if you have any hope of landing on the right one.

Adjacent to this decision, we didn't want this book to be all theory. We wanted it to be hands-on, with enough examples that you as a reader wouldn't just know how things worked but would get a sense of how they feel—like getting a feel for how long it takes to load a 70B model onto a GPU, sensing what the experience will be like for your user if you run the model on an edge device, and feeling the soft glow of your computer monitor as you hide in a dark cave pouring over code and avoiding the warm sun on a nice spring day.

One of the hardest decisions we made when we wrote this book was deciding to focus on the here and now. We decided to focus on the best methods that we actually see people using in production today. This decision was hard because over the course of writing this book, there have been many mind-blowing research papers we've been convinced will "change everything." However, for one reason or another, that research has yet to make it to production. In this section, we are going to change that restriction and talk about what's up and coming regardless of the current state of the industry. But it's not just research; public opinions, lawsuits, and political landscapes often shape the future of technology as well. We'll be looking at where we see LLMs going in the next several years and mention some of the directions they could take.

12.2.1 Government and regulation

At the beginning of this book, we promised to show you how to create LLM products, not just demos. While we believe we have done just that, there's one important detail we've been ignoring: the fact that products live in the real world. While demos just have to work in isolation, products have to work in general. Products are meant to be sold, and once there's an exchange of currency, expectations are set, reputations are on the line, and ultimately, governments are going to get involved.

While a team can't build for future regulations that may never come, it's important to be aware of the possible legal ramifications of the products you build. One lost lawsuit can set a precedent that brings a tidal wave of copycat lawsuits. Since products live in the real world, it is best that we pay attention to that world.

One of us had the opportunity to participate in Utah's legislative process for Utah's SB-149 Artificial Intelligence Amendments bill. This bill is primarily concerned with introducing liability to actors using LLMs to skirt consumer protection laws in the state. At the moment, every legislative body is attempting to figure out where its jurisdiction starts and ends concerning AI and how to deal with the increased responsibility it has to protect citizens and corporations within its constituency. In Utah, the state government takes a very serious and business-first approach to AI and LLMs. Throughout the process and the bill itself, the legislature cannot create definitions that aren't broken with "behold, a man" Diogenes-style examples, and we will need every bit of good faith to navigate the new world that LLMs bring to regulatory bodies. How do you define AI? The bill defines it as follows:

> *"Artificial intelligence" means a machine-based system that makes predictions, recommendations, or decisions influencing real or virtual environments.*

This could be anything from a piecewise function to an LLM agent, meaning that your marketing team will not be liable for claims that your `if` statements are AI within the state. That said, the bill contains a thorough and well-thought-out definition of a deceptive act by a supplier, along with the formulation of an AI analysis and research program to help the state assess risks and policy in a more long-term capacity, which seems novel and unique to Utah. The Utah state legislature was able to refine this bill by consulting with researchers, experts, c-level executives, and business owners within the state, and we'd encourage the reader to participate in creating worthwhile and meaningful regulations within your communities and governments. This is the only way to make sure that court systems are prepared to impose consequences where they are due in the long term.

COPYRIGHT

At the forefront of legal concerns is that of copyright infringement. LLMs trained on enough data can impersonate or copy the style of an author or creator or even straight-up word-for-word plagiarize. While this is exciting when considering building your own ghostwriter to help you in your creative process, it's much less so when you realize a competitor could do the same.

Probably the biggest lawsuit to pay attention to is that of *The New York Times* v. OpenAI.[1] *The New York Times* is in the process of legal action against OpenAI, stating their

[1] M. M. Grynbaum and R. Mac, "The Times Sues OpenAI and Microsoft Over A.I. Use of Copyrighted Work," The New York Times, December 27, 2023, https://mng.bz/6Y0D.

chatbots were trained on the *Times*' intellectual property without consent. It gives evidence that the chatbots are giving word-for-word responses identical to proprietary information found in articles a user would normally have to pay to see. As a result, there is the concern that fewer users will visit their site, reducing ad revenue. Essentially, they stole their data and are now using it as a competitor in the information space.

Bystanders to the fight worry that if the *Times* wins, it may significantly hamper the development of AI and cause the United States to lose its position as the leader in the global AI development race. The more AI companies are exposed to copyright liability, the greater risk and thus loss to competition, which means less innovation. Conversely, they also worry that if the *Times* loses, it will further cut into the already struggling journalism business, where it's already hard enough to find quality reports you can trust. This, too, would severely hurt AI development, which is always starving for good clean data. It appears to be a lose–lose situation for the AI field.

Regardless of who wins or loses the lawsuit, it's pretty clear that current copyright laws never took into consideration that robots would eventually copy us. We need new laws, and it's unclear whether our lawmakers are technically capable enough to meet the challenge. So again, we'd encourage you to participate in the creation process of regulations within your own communities.

AI DETECTION

One area of concern that continues to break our hearts comes from the rise of "AI detection" products. Let us just state from the start: these products are all snake oils and shams. There's no reliable way to determine whether a piece of text was written by a human or a bot. By this point in the book, we expect most readers to have come to this conclusion as well. The reason is simple: if we can reliably determine what is and isn't generated text, we can create a new model to beat the detector. This is the whole point of adversarial machine learning.

There has been a running gag online that anything you read with the word "delve" in it must be written by an LLM (e.g., https://mng.bz/o0nr). The word *delve* is statistically more likely to occur in generated text than in human speech, but that brings up the obvious questions: Which model? Which prompt? The human hubris to believe one can identify generated content simply by looking for particular words is laughable. But, of course, if people vainly believe this obvious falsehood, it's no surprise they are willing to believe a more complex system or algorithm will be able to do it even better.

The reason it breaks our hearts, though, is because we've read story after story of students getting punished, given failing grades on papers, forced to drop out of classes, and given plagiarism marks on their transcripts. Now, we don't know the details of every case, but as experts in the technology in question, we choose to believe the students more often than not.

The fact that a paper marked by an "AI detection" system as having a high probability of being written by AI is put in the same category as plagiarism is also ridiculous.

Now, we don't condone cheating, but LLMs are a new tool. They help us with language the way calculators help us with math. We have figured out ways to teach and evaluate students' progress without creating "calculator detection" systems. We can do it again.

Look, it's not that it's impossible to identify generated content. One investigation found that by simply searching for phrases like "As an AI language model" or "As of my last knowledge update," they found hundreds of published papers in scientific journals written with the help of LLMs.[2] Some phrases are obvious signs, but these are only identified due to the pure laziness of the authors.

The worst part of all this is that since these detection systems are fake, bad, and full of false positives, they seem to be enforced arbitrarily and randomly at the teacher's discretion. It's hard to believe that a majority of papers aren't flagged, so why is only a select group of students called out for it? It's because these systems appear to have become a weapon of power and discrimination for teachers who will wield them to punish students they don't like—not to mention the obvious hypocrisy since we could guess that some of these teachers are the same ones publishing papers with phrases like "As an AI language model" in them.

Bias and ethics

This isn't the first time we have spoken about bias and ethics found inside LLMs, but this time, let's take a slightly deeper dive into what the discussion deserves. Let's say a person is tied to some trolley tracks, you do nothing, and the trolley runs them over, ending their life. Are you responsible? This thought experiment, called "The Trolley Problem," has been discussed ad nauseam; there's even a video game (Trolley Problem Inc. from Read Graves) that poses dozens of variations based on published papers. We won't even attempt to answer the question, but we will give you a brief rundown on how you might be able to decide the answer for yourself.

There are way more than two ways you can analyze this, but we'll only focus on two—the moral and the ethical—and we'll reduce these because this isn't a philosophy book. Morality here helps you determine fault based on a belief of what is good/not good. Ethics help us determine consequences within the practical framework of the legal system that exists within the societies we live in. If you are morally responsible for the death of the person on the tracks, you believe that it was ultimately your fault, that your actions are the cause of the disliving. This is different from ethical responsibility, which would mean that you deserve legal and societal consequences for that action. They can agree, but they don't have to. Changing the context can help clarify the distinction: if you tell someone that a knife isn't sharp and they cut themselves on it while checking, morally, it's likely your fault they were in that situation, but ethically, you will avoid an attempted murder charge.

[2] E. Maiberg, "Scientific journals are publishing papers with AI-generated text," 404 Media, March 18, 2024, https://mng.bz/n0og.

Algorithms create thousands of these situations where our morality and our ethics likely don't agree. There's an old example of moral and ethical responsibility in the Talmud that decides that a person is not a murderer if they push another person into water or fire and the pushed person fails to escape.[3] Depending on your beliefs and the law you live under, Meta could be either morally or ethically at fault for genocide (not joking[4]) in Myanmar. Meta didn't even do the pushing into the fire in that scenario; their algorithm did. This is obviously a charged and brutal example, but LLMs create a very real scenario where ML practitioners need practical, consistent, and defensible frameworks of both morality and ethics, or they risk real tragedy under their watch. Obviously, we aren't the arbiters of morality and aren't going to judge you about where you find yourself there, but you should still consider the broader context of any system you create.

LAWS ARE COMING

One thing we *can* be sure about is that regulation will come, and companies will be held responsible for what their AI agents do. Air Canada found this out the hard way when the courts ruled against it, saying the company had to honor a refund policy that its chatbot had completely made up (https://mng.bz/pxvG). The bot gave incorrect information. It did link the customer to the correct refund policy; however, the courts rightly questioned "why customers should have to double-check information found in one part of its website on another part of its website."

We've seen similar cases where users have used prompt engineering to trick Chevy's LLM chatbot into selling a 2024 Tahoe for $1 (https://mng.bz/XVmG), and DPD needed to "shut down its AI element" after a customer got it to admit to being the worst delivery company in the world.[5] As we said earlier, it's difficult to tell, even with existing legislation, what is ethically allowable for an LLM to do. Of course, it brings up the question of whether, if the chatbot was licensed and equipped to sell cars and did complete such a transaction, the customer's bad faith interaction would actually matter, or whether a company would still be held ethically responsible for upholding such a transaction.

Being held responsible for what an LLM generates is enough to make you think twice about many applications you may consider using it for. The higher the risk, the more time you should take to pause and consider potential legal ramifications. We highly recommend dialing in your prompt engineering system, setting up guard rails to keep your agent on task, and absolutely being sure to save your logs and keep your customer chat history.

---

[3] Sanhedrin 76b:11, https://mng.bz/vJaJ.

[4] "Myanmar army behind Facebook pages spewing hate speech: UN probe," RFI, March 27, 2024, https://mng.bz/mR0P.

[5] A. Guzman, "Company disables AI after bot starts swearing at customer, calls itself the 'worst delivery firm in the world,'" NY Post, January 20, 2024, https://mng.bz/yoVq.

12.2.2 LLMs are getting bigger

Another thing we can be sure of is that we will continue to see models getting bigger and bigger for the near future. Since larger models continue to display emergent behavior, there's no reason for companies to stop taking this approach when simply throwing money at the problem seems to generate more money. Not to mention, for companies that have invested the most, larger models are harder to replicate. As you've probably found, the best way for smaller companies to compete is to create smaller, specialized models. Ultimately, as long as we have large-enough training datasets to accommodate more parameters, we can expect to see more parameters stuffed into a model, but the question of whether we've ever had adequate data to demonstrate "general intelligence" (as in AGI) is as murky as ever.

LARGER CONTEXT WINDOWS

It's not just larger models. We are really excited to see context lengths grow as well. When we started working on this book, they were a real limitation. It was rare to see models with context lengths greater than 10K tokens. ChatGPT only offered lengths up to 4,096 tokens at the time. A year later, and we see models like Gemini 1.5 Pro offering a context length of up to 1 million tokens, with researchers indicating that it can handle up to 10 million tokens in test cases (https://mng.bz/YV4N). To put it in perspective, the entire seven-book Harry Potter series is 1,084,170 words (I didn't count them; https://wordsrated.com/harry-potter-stats/), which would come out to roughly 1.5 million tokens depending on your tokenizer. At these lengths, it's hard to believe there are any limitations.

Obviously, there still are. These larger models with near infinite context windows generally have you paying per token. If the model doesn't force your users to send smaller queries, your wallet will. Not to mention, if you are reading this book, you are likely more interested in smaller open source models you can deploy yourself, and many of these definitely still have limiting context sizes you have to work with. Don't worry, though; right now and in the future, even smaller models will have million-sized context windows. There's a lot of interesting research going into this area. If you are interested, we recommend you check out RoPE,[6] YaRN,[7] and Hyena.[8]

THE NEXT ATTENTION

Of course, larger context windows are great, but they come at a cost. Remember, at the center of an LLM lies the attention algorithm, which is quadratic in complexity—meaning the more data we throw at it, the more compute we have to throw at it as well. One challenge driving the research community is finding the next attention algorithm that doesn't suffer from this same problem. Can we build transformers with

---

[6] emozilla, "Dynamically Scaled RoPE further increases performance of long context LLaMA with zero fine-tuning," Jun. 30, 2023, https://mng.bz/M1pn.

[7] B. Peng, J. Quesnelle, H. Fan, E. Shippole, N. Research, and Eleutherai, "YaRN: Efficient Context Window Extension of Large Language Models." Available: https://arxiv.org/pdf/2309.00071

[8] M. Poli et al., "Hyena Hierarchy: Towards Larger Convolutional Language Models," Feb. 2023, doi: https://doi.org/10.48550/arxiv.2302.10866.

a new algorithm that is only linear in complexity? That is the billion-dollar question right now.

There are lots of competing innovations in this field, and we don't even have time to discuss all of our absolute favorites. Two of those favorites are MAMBA, an alternative to transformers, and KAN, an alternative to multilayer perceptrons (MLPs). MAMBA, in particular, is an improvement on state space models (SSMs) incorporated into an attention-free neural network architecture.[9] By itself, it isn't all that impressive, as it took lots of hardware hacking to make it somewhat performant. However, later JAMBA came out, a MAMBA-style model that uses hybrid SSM-transformer layers and joint attention.[10] The hybrid approach appears to give us the best of both worlds.

So you can experience it for yourself, in listing 12.1, we will finetune and run inference on a JAMBA model. This model is a mixture-of-experts model with 52B parameters, and the implementation will allow for 140K context lengths on an 80 GB GPU, which is much better performance than you'd get with an attention model alone. This example was adapted right from the Hugging Face model card, so the syntax should look very familiar compared to every other simple transformer implementation, and we are very grateful for the ease of trying out brand-new stuff.

For the training portion, unfortunately, the model is too big, even in half precision, to fit on a single 80 GB GPU, so you'll have to use Accelerate to parallelize it between several GPUs to complete training. If you don't have that compute just lying around, you can complete the imports up to the tokenizer and skip to after the training portion, changing very little. We aren't doing anything fancy; the dataset we'll use for training is just a bunch of famous quotes in English from various authors retrieved from Goodreads consisting of quote, author, and tags, so don't feel like you are missing out if you decide to skip finetuning. We'll start by loading the tokenizer, model, and dataset.

Listing 12.1 Finetuning and inferencing JAMBA

```
from trl import SFTTrainer
from peft import LoraConfig
from transformers import (
    AutoTokenizer,
    AutoModelForCausalLM,
    TrainingArguments,
)
from transformers import BitsAndBytesConfig
import torch
from datasets import load_dataset

tokenizer = AutoTokenizer.from_pretrained("ai21labs/Jamba-v0.1")
model = AutoModelForCausalLM.from_pretrained(
```

[9] A. Gu and T. Dao, "Mamba: Linear-Time Sequence Modeling with Selective State Spaces," arXiv.org, Dec. 01, 2023, https://arxiv.org/abs/2312.00752.

[10] [1]O. Lieber et al., "Jamba: A Hybrid Transformer-Mamba Language Model," arXiv.org, Mar. 28, 2024, https://arxiv.org/abs/2403.19887.

```
    "ai21labs/Jamba-v0.1", device_map="auto"
)

dataset = load_dataset("Abirate/english_quotes", split="train")
```

Once all of those are in memory (you can stream the dataset if your hardware is limited), we'll create training arguments and a LoRA config to help the finetuning work on even smaller hardware:

```
training_args = TrainingArguments(
    output_dir="./results",
    num_train_epochs=3,
    per_device_train_batch_size=4,
    logging_dir="./logs",
    logging_steps=10,
    learning_rate=2e-3,
)
lora_config = LoraConfig(
    r=8,
    target_modules=["embed_tokens", "x_proj", "in_proj", "out_proj"],
    task_type="CAUSAL_LM",
    bias="none",
)
```

And now, for the finale, similar to sklearn's `model.fit()`, transformers' `trainer.train()` has become a moniker for why anyone can learn how to interact with state-of-the-art ML models. Once training completes (it took a little under an hour for us), we'll save local versions of the tokenizer and the model and delete the model in memory:

```
trainer = SFTTrainer(
    model=model,
    tokenizer=tokenizer,
    args=training_args,
    peft_config=lora_config,
    train_dataset=dataset,
    dataset_text_field="quote",
)

trainer.train()

tokenizer.save_pretrained("./JAMBA/")
model.save_pretrained("./JAMBA/")

del model
```

Next, we'll reload the model, but in a memory-efficient way, to be used for inference. With an 80 GB GPU and loading in 8bit with this BitsandBytes config, you can now fit the model and a significant amount of data on a single GPU. Loading in 4bit allows that on any type of A100 or two 3090s, similar to a 70B parameter transformer. Using quantization to get it down to a 1-bit model, you can fit this model and a significant amount of data on a single 3090. We'll use the following 8bit inference implementation and run inference on it:

```
quantization_config = BitsAndBytesConfig(
    load_in_8bit=True, llm_int8_skip_modules=["mamba"]
)
model = AutoModelForCausalLM.from_pretrained(
    "ai21labs/Jamba-v0.1",
    torch_dtype=torch.bfloat16,
    attn_implementation="flash_attention_2",
    quantization_config=quantization_config,
)
input_ids = tokenizer(
    "In the recent Super Bowl LVIII,", return_tensors="pt"
).to(model.device)["input_ids"]

outputs = model.generate(input_ids, max_new_tokens=216)

print(tokenizer.batch_decode(outputs))
```

We are blown away almost monthly at this point by the alternatives to various parts of LLM systems that pop up. Here, we'd like to draw your attention way back to where LLMs got their big break: "Attention Is All You Need."[11] That paper showed that you could use dumb MLPs to get amazing results, using only attention to bridge the gap. We're entering a new age where we aren't focusing on just what we need but what we want for the best results. For example, we want subquadratic drop-in replacements for attention that match or beat flash attention for speed. We want attention-free transformers and millions-long context lengths with no "lost in the middle" problems. We want alternatives to dense MLPs with no drops in accuracy or learning speed. We are, bit by bit, getting all of these and more.

PUSHING THE BOUNDARIES OF COMPRESSION

After going down to INT4, there are experimental quantization strategies for going even further down to INT2. INT2 70B models still perform decently, much to many peoples' surprise. Then there's research suggesting we could potentially go even smaller to 1.58 bits per weight or even 0.68 using ternary and other smaller operators. Want to test it out? Llama3 70B already has 1-bit quantization implementations in GGUF, GPTQ, and AWQ formats, and it only takes up 16.6 GB of memory. Go nuts!

There's another dimension to this, which doesn't involve compressing models but instead decouples the idea of models being one piece and thinking of models as collections of layers and parameters again. Speculative decoding gives us yet another way of accessing large models quickly. Speculative decoding requires not just enough memory to load one large model but also another smaller model alongside it—think distillation models. An example often used in production these days is Whisper-Large-v3 and Distil-Whisper-Large-V3. Whisper is a multimodal LLM that focuses on the speech-to-text

---

[11] Vaswani et al., Attention Is All You Need," 2017, https://arxiv.org/abs/1706.03762.

problem, but speculative decoding will work with any two models that have the same architecture and different sizes.

This method allows us to sample larger models quicker (sometimes a straight 2× speed boost) by computing several tokens in parallel and by an approximation "assistant" model that allows us to both complete a step and verify whether that step is easy or hard at the same time. The basic idea is this: use the smaller, faster Distil-Whisper model to generate guesses about the end result, and allow Whisper to evaluate those guesses in parallel, ignoring the ones that it would do the same thing on and correcting the ones that it would change. This allows for the speed of a smaller model with the accuracy of a larger one.

In listing 12.2, we demonstrate speculative decoding on an English audio dataset. We'll load Whisper and Distil-Whisper, load the dataset, and then add an `assistant_model` to the generation keyword arguments (`generate_kwargs`). You may ask, how does this system know that the assistant model is only meant to help with decoding, as the name suggests? Well, we load the assistant model with `AutoModelForCausalLM` instead of the speech sequence-to-sequence version. This way, the model will only help with the easier decoding steps in parallel with the larger one. With that done, we're free to test.

Listing 12.2 Speculative decoding with Whisper

```
from transformers import (
    AutoModelForCausalLM,
    AutoModelForSpeechSeq2Seq,
    AutoProcessor,
)
import torch
from datasets import load_dataset

from time import perf_counter
from tqdm import tqdm

from evaluate import load

device = "cuda:0" if torch.cuda.is_available() else "cpu"
print(f"Device: {device}")
attention = "sdpa"
torch_dtype = torch.float16 if torch.cuda.is_available() else torch.float32

model_id = "openai/whisper-large-v3"
assistant_model_id = "distil-whisper/distil-large-v3"
model = AutoModelForSpeechSeq2Seq.from_pretrained(
    model_id,
    low_cpu_mem_usage=False,
    use_safetensors=True,
    attn_implementation=attention,
    torch_dtype=torch_dtype,
).to(device)
processor = AutoProcessor.from_pretrained(model_id)
```

```
assistant_model = AutoModelForCausalLM.from_pretrained(
    assistant_model_id,
    low_cpu_mem_usage=False,
    use_safetensors=True,
    attn_implementation=attention,
    torch_dtype=torch_dtype,
).to(device)

dataset = load_dataset(
    "hf-internal-testing/librispeech_asr_dummy",
    "clean",
    split="validation",
    trust_remote_code=True,
)
wer = load("wer")

generate_kwargs_1 = {
    "language": "en",
    "task": "transcribe",
}
generate_kwargs_2 = {
    "language": "en",
    "task": "transcribe",
    "assistant_model": assistant_model,
}

spec_decoding = False
for i, generate_kwargs in enumerate([generate_kwargs_1, generate_kwargs_2]):
    all_time = 0
    predictions = []
    references = []
    for sample in tqdm(dataset):
        audio = sample["audio"]
        inputs = processor(
            audio["array"],
            sampling_rate=audio["sampling_rate"],
            return_tensors="pt",
        )
        inputs = inputs.to(device=device, dtype=torch_dtype)
        start_time = perf_counter()
        output = model.generate(
            **inputs,
            **generate_kwargs,
        )
        gen_time = perf_counter() - start_time
        all_time += gen_time
        predictions.append(
            processor.batch_decode(
                output, skip_special_tokens=True, normalize=True
            )[0]
        )
        references.append(processor.tokenizer.normalize(sample["text"]))
    score = wer.compute(predictions=predictions, references=references)
    if i > 0:
        spec_decoding = True
```

```
print(f"Speculative Decoding: {spec_decoding}")
print(f"Time: {all_time}")
print(f"Word Error Rate: {score}")
```

In our testing, we observed about 42 seconds for Whisper-Large-V3 to get through all 73 examples with scaled dot product attention. With speculative decoding, that dropped to 18.7 seconds, with the exact same word error rate (WER). So there was an almost 2× speed increase with absolutely zero drop in accuracy. Yeah, pretty nuts.

At this point, we were wondering, "Why doesn't everyone use this for everything all the time?" Here are the drawbacks to this method: first, it works best in smaller sequences. With LLMs, that's under 128 tokens of generation or around 20 seconds of audio processing. With the larger generations, the speed boost will be negligible. Beyond that, we don't always have access to perfectly compatible pairs of large and small models, like BERT versus DistilBERT. The last reason is that very few people really know about it, even with its ease of implementation.

Ultimately, whether it's sub-bit quantization, speculative decoding, or other advances, LLMs are pushing research into compression methodologies more than any other technology, and it's interesting to watch as new techniques change the landscape. As these methods improve, we can push models to smaller and cheaper hardware, making the field even more accessible.

12.2.3 Multimodal spaces

We are so excited about the possibilities within multimodality. Going back to chapter 2, multimodality is one of the main features of language we haven't seen as many solutions crop up for, and we're seeing a shift toward actually attempting to solve phonetics. Audio isn't the only modality that humans operate in, though. Accordingly, the push toward combining phonetics, semantics, and pragmatics and getting as much context within the same embedding space (for comparison) as the text is very strong. With this in mind, here are some points of interest in the landscape.

The first we want to draw attention to is ImageBind, a project showcasing that instead of trying to curtail a model into ingesting every type of data, we can instead squish every type of data into an embedding space the model would already be familiar with and be able to process. You can take a look at the official demo here: https://imagebind.metademolab.com/.

ImageBind builds off what multimodal projection models such as CLIP have already been showcasing for some time: the ability to create and process embeddings is the true power behind deterministic LLM systems. You can use these models for very fast searches, including searches that have been, up to this point, nigh impossible, like asking to find images of animals that make sounds similar to an uploaded audio clip.

OneLLM flips this logic the other way around, taking one model and one multimodal encoder to unify and embed eight modalities instead of the ImageBind example of using six different encoders to embed six modalities in the same dimension. It can be found here: https://onellm.csuhan.com/. The big idea behind OneLLM is aligning the unified encoder using language, which offers a unique spin on multimodality that aligns the process of encoding rather than the result.

We are extremely excited about the research happening in this area. This research is able to help bridge the gap between phonetics and pragmatics in the model ecosystem and allow for more human-like understanding and interaction, especially in the search field.

12.2.4 Datasets

One exciting change we are seeing inside the industry due to the introduction of LLMs is that companies are finally starting to understand the importance of governing and managing their data. For some, it's the drive to finetune their own LLMs and get in on the exciting race to deliver AI products. For others, it's the fear of becoming obsolete, as the capabilities of these systems far surpass previous technologies; they are finding it's only their data that provides any type of moat or protection from competition. And for everyone, it's the worry they'll make the same mistakes they've seen other companies make.

LLMs aren't just a driving factor; they are also helping teams label, tag, organize, and clean their data. Many companies had piles of data they didn't know what to do with, but with LLM models like CLIP, captioning images has become a breeze. Some companies have found that simply creating embedding spaces of their text, images, audio, and video has allowed them to create meaningful structures for datasets previously unstructured. Structured data is much easier to operate around, opening doors for search, recommendations, and other insights.

One aspect we see currently missing in the industry is valuable open source datasets, especially when it comes to evaluations. Many of the current benchmarks used to evaluate models rely on multiple-choice questions, but this is inefficient for anyone trying to create an LLM application. In the real world, when are your users going to ask your model questions in a multiple-choice format? Next to never. People ask freeform questions in conversations and when seeking help since they don't know the answer themselves. However, these evaluation datasets have become benchmarks simply because they are easy for researchers to gather, compile, and evaluate for accuracy.

In addition, we believe another inevitability is the need for more language representation. The world is a tapestry of diverse languages and dialects, each carrying its unique cultural nuances and communicative subtleties. However, many languages remain underrepresented in existing datasets, leading to models that are biased toward more dominant languages. As technology becomes increasingly global, the inclusion of a wider range of languages is crucial. Adding multiple languages not only promotes inclusivity but also enhances the accuracy and applicability of language models in various international contexts, bridging communication gaps and fostering a more connected world. Imagine your startup didn't need to pay anyone to get accurate information regarding entering China, Russia, or Saudi Arabia to expand your market.

12.2.5 Solving hallucination

There's a lot of evidence that LLMs have more information in them than they readily give out and even more evidence that people are generally either terrible or malicious at prompting. As a result, you'll find that hallucinations are one of the largest roadblocks when trying to develop an application that consistently delivers results. This problem has frustrated many software engineering teams that are used to deterministic computer algorithms and rarely deal with nondeterministic systems. For many statisticians who are more familiar with these types of systems, hallucinations are seen as a feature, not a bug. Regardless of where you stand, there's a lot of research going into the best ways to handle hallucinations, and this is an area of interest you should be watching.

BETTER PROMPT ENGINEERING

One area that's interesting to watch and has shown great improvement over time is prompt engineering. One prompt engineering tool that helps reduce hallucinations is DSPy. We went over it briefly in chapter 7, but here we'll give an example of how it works and why it can be a helpful step for solving hallucination in your LLMs. We've discussed the fact that LLMs are characteristically bad at math, even simple math, several times throughout the book, and we've also discussed why, but we haven't really discussed solutions other than improving your tokenization. So in listing 12.3, we will show just how good you can coax an LLM to be at math with zero tokenization changes, zero finetuning, and no LoRAs or DoRAs, just optimizing your prompts to tell the model exactly how to answer the questions you're asking.

We'll do this using the dspy-ai Python package and Llama3-8B-Instruct. We'll start by loading and quantizing the model to fit on most GPUs and the Grade-School Math 8K dataset. We picked this dataset because it's a collection of math problems that you, as a person who has graduated elementary (primary) school, likely don't even need a calculator to solve. We'll use 200 examples for our train and test (dev) sets, although we'd recommend you play with these numbers to find the best ratio for your use case without data leakage.

Listing 12.3 DSPy for math

```
from transformers import AutoModelForCausalLM, AutoTokenizer
from transformers import BitsAndBytesConfig
import torch
import dspy
from dspy.datasets.gsm8k import GSM8K, gsm8k_metric
from dsp.modules.lm import LM
from dspy.evaluate import Evaluate
from dspy.teleprompt import BootstrapFewShot

model_name = "meta-llama/Meta-Llama-3-8B-Instruct"
quantization_config = BitsAndBytesConfig(
    load_in_4bit=True,
    bnb_4bit_use_double_quant=True,
```

```
    bnb_4bit_quant_type="nf4",
    bnb_4bit_compute_dtype=torch.bfloat16,
)


model = AutoModelForCausalLM.from_pretrained(
    model_name,
    device_map="auto",
    quantization_config=quantization_config,
    attn_implementation="sdpa",
)
tokenizer = AutoTokenizer.from_pretrained(model_name, use_fast=True,)

gms8k = GSM8K()
gsm8k_trainset, gsm8k_devset = gms8k.train[:30], gms8k.dev[:100]
```

Now that we have our imports and loading ready, we'll need to address the fact that we loaded Llama3 using transformers and not DSPy. DSPy expects to interact with models utilizing the OpenAI API, but we have a model loaded locally from Hugging Face, DSPy has recently added HFModel to their package, and it can now be easily imported, rather than needing the wrapper defined next. First, we make a simple function to map any keyword argument differences between the APIs, like `max_tokens` vs `max_new_tokens`, and then we create a class that will act as the wrapper for our model to generate answers and optimize the prompt. Once that's ready, we'll load DSPy:

```
def openai_to_hf(**kwargs):
    hf_kwargs = {}
    for k, v in kwargs.items():
        if k == "n":
            hf_kwargs["num_return_sequences"] = v
        elif k == "frequency_penalty":
            hf_kwargs["repetition_penalty"] = 1.0 - v
        elif k == "presence_penalty":
            hf_kwargs["diversity_penalty"] = v
        elif k == "max_tokens":
            hf_kwargs["max_new_tokens"] = v
        elif k == "model":
            pass
        else:
            hf_kwargs[k] = v

    return hf_kwargs


class HFModel(LM):
    def __init__(
        self,
        model: AutoModelForCausalLM,
        tokenizer: AutoTokenizer,
        **kwargs
    ):
        """wrapper for Hugging Face models
```

```
        Args:
            model (AutoModelForCausalLM): HF model identifier to load and use
            tokenizer: AutoTokenizer
        """
        super().__init__(model)
        self.model = model
        self.tokenizer = tokenizer
        self.drop_prompt_from_output = True
        self.history = []
        self.is_client = False
        self.device = model.device
        self.kwargs = {
            "temperature": 0.3,
            "max_new_tokens": 300,
        }

    def basic_request(self, prompt, **kwargs):
        raw_kwargs = kwargs
        kwargs = {**self.kwargs, **kwargs}
        response = self._generate(prompt, **kwargs)

        history = {
            "prompt": prompt,
            "response": response,
            "kwargs": kwargs,
            "raw_kwargs": raw_kwargs,
        }
        self.history.append(history)

        return response

    def _generate(self, prompt, **kwargs):
        kwargs = {**openai_to_hf(**self.kwargs), **openai_to_hf(**kwargs)}
        if isinstance(prompt, dict):
            try:
                prompt = prompt["messages"][0]["content"]
            except (KeyError, IndexError, TypeError):
                print("Failed to extract 'content' from the prompt.")
        inputs = self.tokenizer(prompt, return_tensors="pt").to(self.device)

        outputs = self.model.generate(**inputs, **kwargs)
        if self.drop_prompt_from_output:
            input_length = inputs.input_ids.shape[1]
            outputs = outputs[:, input_length:]
        completions = [
            {"text": c}
            for c in self.tokenizer.batch_decode(
                outputs, skip_special_tokens=True
            )
        ]
        response = {
            "prompt": prompt,
            "choices": completions,
        }
        return response
```

```
    def __call__(
        self, prompt, only_completed=True, return_sorted=False, **kwargs
    ):
        assert only_completed, "for now"
        assert return_sorted is False, "for now"

        if kwargs.get("n", 1) > 1 or kwargs.get("temperature", 0.0) > 0.1:
            kwargs["do_sample"] = True

        response = self.request(prompt, **kwargs)
        return [c["text"] for c in response["choices"]]


print("Model set up!")                    <-- Sets up the LM
llama = HFModel(model, tokenizer)

dspy.settings.configure(lm=llama)         <-- Sets up DSPY to use that LM
```

Now that we are prepared with an LLM to take our math test, let's test it. We'll start by establishing a baseline. We'll define a simple chain-of-thought (CoT)-like prompt in the `QASignature` class, which we'll use to define a zero-shot version to use as a baseline. The prompt is likely pretty close to prompts you've seen before, so hopefully, this will be a very relevant demonstration of tasks you may be working on. For evaluation, we're using DSPy's `gsm8k_metric`, which we imported at the top to evaluate against, but you could always create your own:

```
class QASignature(dspy.Signature):        <-- Defines the QASignature and CoT
    (
    """You are given a question and answer"""
    """and you must think step by step to answer the question. """
    """Only include the answer as the output."""
    )
    question = dspy.InputField(desc="A math question")
    answer = dspy.OutputField(desc="An answer that is a number")


class ZeroShot(dspy.Module):
    def __init__(self):
    super().__init__()
    self.prog = dspy.Predict(QASignature, max_tokens=1000)

    def forward(self, question):
    return self.prog(question=question)


evaluate = Evaluate(          <-- Sets up the evaluator, which can be used multiple times
    devset=gsm8k_devset,
    metric=gsm8k_metric,
    num_threads=4,
    display_progress=True,
    display_table=0,
)
```

```
print("Evaluating Zero Shot")        <-- Evaluates how the LLM does with no changes
evaluate(ZeroShot())
```

The output is

```
29/200 14.5%
```

With our simple zero-shot CoT prompt, Llama3 gets only 14.5% of the questions correct. This result might not seem very good, but it is actually quite a bit better than just running the model on the questions alone without any prompt, which only yields about 1% to 5% correct.

With the baseline out of the way, let's move on to the bread and butter of DSPy, optimizing the prompt to see where that gets us. There's been some evolution in what people think of as a CoT prompt since the original paper came out. CoT has evolved in the industry to mean more than just adding "think step by step" in your prompt since this approach is seen more as just basic prompt engineering, whereas allowing the model to few-shot prompt itself to get a rationale for its ultimate output is considered the new CoT, and that's how the DSPy framework uses those terms. With that explanation, we'll go ahead and create a `CoT` class using the `dspy.ChainOfThought` function and then evaluate it like we did our `ZeroShot` class:

```
config = dict(max_bootstrapped_demos=2)        <-- Sets up the optimizer

class CoT(dspy.Module):
    def __init__(self):
    super().__init__()
    self.prog = dspy.ChainOfThought(QASignature, max_tokens=1000)

    def forward(self, question):
    return self.prog(question=question)

print("Creating Bootstrapped Few Shot Prompt")        <-- Optimize the prompts
teleprompter = BootstrapFewShot(metric=gsm8k_metric, **config)
optimized_cot = teleprompter.compile(
    CoT(), trainset=gsm8k_trainset, valset=gsm8k_devset
)
optimized_cot.save("optimized_llama3_math_cot.json")

print("Evaluating Optimized CoT Prompt")        <-- Evaluates our "optimized_cot" program
evaluate(optimized_cot)
#149/200 74.5%
```

Look at that! If it doesn't astonish you that the accuracy jumped from 14.5% to 74.5% by changing only the prompts—remember we haven't done any finetuning or training—we don't know what will. People are speculating whether the age of the prompt engineer is over, but we'd like to think that it's just begun. That said, the age of "coming up with a clever string and doing no follow-up" has been over and shouldn't have ever started. In this example, we used arbitrary boundaries, gave the sections of the dataset and the numbers absolutely no thought, and didn't include any helpful tools or context for the model to access to improve. If we did, you'd see that after applying all the prompt engineering tricks in the book, it isn't difficult to push the model's abilities to staggering levels, even on things LLMs are characteristically bad at—like math.

GROUNDING

If you are looking for ways to combat hallucinations, you'll run into the term *grounding*. Grounding is when we give the LLM necessary context in the prompt. By giving it the information it needs, we are helping to provide a solid base for the generation to build off of, so it's less likely to dream up visions out of thin air. If this sounds familiar, it should, as we have used one of the most common grounding techniques, RAG, several times in this book.

The term *RAG* (retrieval augmented generation) is, at face value, synonymous with grounding since we are literally retrieving the appropriate context based on the prompt and then using it to augment the text generated from the LLM. However, RAG has become synonymous with using semantic search with a VectorDB for the retrieval portion. Technically, you could use any type of search algorithm or any type of database, but if you tell someone in the industry you have set up a RAG system, they will assume the former architecture.

With that clarification, RAG applications are most useful for answering simple questions. Consider the question, "What is Gal Gadot's husband's current job?" It's really two questions in one, "Who is Gal Gadot's husband?" and once we know that, "What does he do?" RAG alone is pretty terrible at solving these multistep questions, as a similarity vector search will likely return many articles about Gal Gadot and probably none about Jaron Varsano, her husband.

We can enhance this approach in an important way that we haven't touched on yet: using knowledge graphs. Knowledge graphs store information in a structure that captures relationships between entities. This structure consists of nodes that represent objects and edges that represent relationships. A graph database like NEO4J makes it easy to create and query knowledge graphs. And as it turns out, knowledge graphs are amazing at answering more complex multipart questions where you need to connect the dots between linked pieces of information. Why? Because they've already connected the dots for us.

Many teams who have struggled to get value out of RAG have been able to see large improvements once they transitioned to a graph database from a vector one. This comes with two major hurdles, though. First, we can no longer simply embed our prompts and pull similar matches; we have the much harder task of coming up with a way to turn our prompts into queries our graph database will understand. While there are several methods to take this on, it's just another NLP problem. Thankfully, as it turns out, LLMs are really good at this! Second, and probably the bigger problem, is that it is much harder to turn your documents into a knowledge graph. This is why vector databases have become so popular—the ease of turning your data into embeddings to search against. Turning your data into a knowledge graph will be a bit more work and take additional expertise, but it can really set you up for success down the road.

Right now, few teams are willing to invest in the extra data engineering to prepare their data into a knowledge graph. Most companies are still looking for quick wins, building simple wrappers around LLM APIs. As the industry matures, we believe we'll start to see organizations shift toward building knowledge graphs from their proprietary data to eke out better performance from their LLM applications.

KNOWLEDGE EDITING

Another promising field of research to combat hallucinations is *knowledge editing*. Knowledge editing is the process of efficiently adjusting specific behaviors. Optimally, this would look like surgery where we precisely go in and change the exact model weights that activate when we get incorrect responses, as can be seen in figure 12.2. Knowledge editing can be used for many things, but it is often used to combat factual decay—the fact that, over time, facts change, like who the current Super Bowl winner is or the current president of any individual country. We could retrain or finetune the model, but these are often much heavier solutions that may change the model in unexpected ways when all we want to do is update a fact or two.

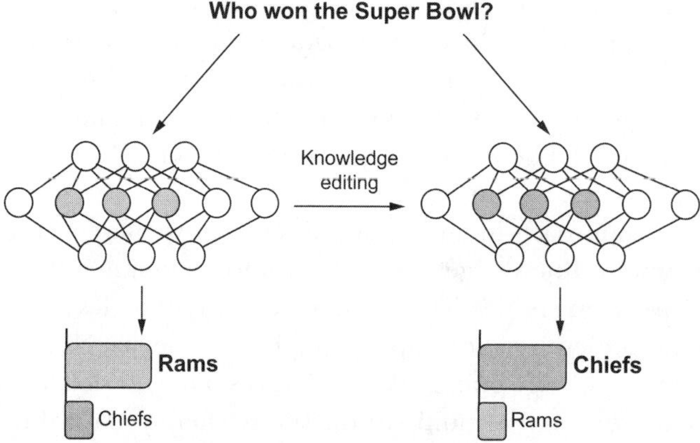

Figure 12.2 Knowledge editing is a technique to essentially perform surgery on a model to directly insert, update, or erase information.

Knowledge editing is an interesting field of research that we unfortunately didn't have the space to go into in this book. A host of algorithms and techniques have been created to do it, like ROME, MEND, and GRACE. For those interested in using any of these techniques, we recommend first checking out EasyEdit at https://github.com/zjunlp/EasyEdit. EasyEdit is a project that has implemented the most common knowledge editing techniques and provides a framework to utilize them easily. It includes examples, tutorials, and more to get you started.

12.2.6 New hardware

As with most popular technologies, LLMs have already created a fierce market of competition. While most companies are still competing on capabilities and features, there's also a clear drive to make them faster and cheaper. We've discussed many of these methods you can employ, like quantization and compilation. One we expect to see more of is innovation around hardware.

In fact, Sam Altman, CEO of OpenAI, has been trying to raise funds to the tune of $7 trillion dollars to invest in the semiconductor industry.[12] We've talked about the global GPU shortage before, but no one is as annoyed about it as some of the biggest players. The investment would go further than just meeting demand; it would also accelerate development and research into better chips like Application-Specifc Integrated Circuits (ASICs).

We've talked about and have used GPUs a lot throughout this book, but GPUs weren't designed for AI; they were designed for graphics. Of course, that fact didn't stop NVIDIA from briefly becoming the world's most valuable company.[13] ASICs are designed for specific tasks; an example would be Google's TPUs or tensor processing units. ASICs designed to handle AI workloads are NPUs (neural processing units), and chances are, you've never heard of, or at least never seen, an NPU chip before. We point this out to show there's still plenty of room for improvement, and it's likely we will see a large array of new accelerators in the future, from better GPUs to NPUs and everything in between. For more info, take a look at Cerebras (https://cerebras.ai/product-chip/).

One of the authors of this book spent a good portion of his career working for Intel and Micron developing the now-discontinued memory technology known as 3D XPoint (3DxP). The details of 3DxP aren't important for this discussion; what it offered, extremely fast and cheap memory, is. It was sold under the brand name Optane for several years and had even earned the moniker "The Fastest SSD Ever Made."[14] This technology proved itself to be almost as fast as RAM but almost as cheap to produce as NAND flash memory and could be used to replace either.

Imagine a world where every processor conveniently had 500 GB or even 1 TB of memory space. Most of the limitations we've discussed so far would simply disappear. You could load entire LLMs the size of GPT-4 onto one GPU. You wouldn't have to worry about parallelization or the underutilization problems that come with the extra overhead. Did I mention 3DxP was nonvolatile as well? Load your model once, and you're done; you'd never need to reload it, even if you had to restart your server, which would make jobs like autoscaling so much easier.

---

[12] K. H. and A. Fitch, "Sam Altman seeks trillions of dollars to reshape business of chips and AI," Wall Street Journal, February 8, 2024, https://mng.bz/KDrK.

[13] A. Pequeño IV, "Nvidia now world's most valuable company—Topping Microsoft and Apple," Forbes, June 18, 2024, https://mng.bz/9ojl.

[14] S. Webster, "Intel Optane SSD DC P5800X review: The fastest SSD ever made," Tom's Hardware, August 26, 2022, https://mng.bz/j0Wx.

3DxP was a technology that had already proven itself in the market as capable, but it nonetheless suffered due to a perceived lack of demand. Consumers didn't know what to do with this new layer in the memory hierarchy that it provided. Personally, with the arrival of LLMs, the authors see plenty of demand now for a technology like this. We'll just have to wait and see whether the semiconductor industry decides to reinvest.

12.2.7 Agents will become useful

Lastly, we believe LLM-based agents will eventually be more than just a novelty that works only in demos. Most agents we've seen have simply been feats of magic, or should I say smoke and mirrors, throwing a few prompt engineering tricks at the largest models. The fact that several of them work at all—even in a limited capacity—shines light on the possibilities.

We've seen several companies chase after the holy grail, building agents to replace software engineers. In fact, you'll see them try to build agents to replace doctors, sales associates, or managers. But just as many companies and AI experts used to promise we'd have self-driving cars in the near future, that near future keeps on eluding us. Don't get me wrong: it's not like we don't have self-driving cars, but they are much more of an annoyance than anything, and they can only drive in select locations as rideshare vehicles. In a similar fashion, we aren't too worried about agents replacing any occupation.

What we are more interested in are small agents—agents trained and finetuned to do a specialized task but with greater flexibility to hold conversations. Many video game NPCs would benefit from this type of setup where they could not only use an LLM to hold random conversations and provide a more immersive experience but also to decide to take actions that would shape a unique story.

We are also likely to see them do smaller tasks well first. For example, LLMs can already read your email and summarize them for you, but a simple agent would go a step further and generate email responses for you. Maybe it wouldn't actually send them, but simply provide you with the options, and all you'd have to do is pick the one you want, and then it would send it.

But mostly, we are excited to see LLM agents replace other bots. For example, who hasn't uploaded their resume only to find they have to reenter all their information? Either because the resume extraction tool didn't work well or it didn't even exist. An LLM agent can not only read your resume and extract the information but also double-check its work and make sure it makes sense. Plus, we haven't even mentioned the applicant tracking systems that automatically screen resumes based on keywords. These systems are often easily manipulated and terrible at separating the cream from the crop. An LLM agent has a much better chance of performing this task well. Of course, we care about ensuring fair hiring practices, but these systems are already automated and biased to some extent. A better model is an opportunity to reduce that non-useful bias.

With this in mind, one way that models might make better agents is through the use of cache embeddings. It's an interesting idea of something you can do with models that we haven't really heard anyone talking about, other than Will Gaviro Rojas at a local Utah meetup. Caching embeddings allows you to cut down on repeating the same computations several times to complete several tasks in parallel. This is a more complex example, and we aren't going to dive too deep into it so as to keep things pretty simple, but this strategy involves either copying the final layers of a model after the last hidden state to complete several tasks on their own or creating custom linear classifiers to fulfill those tasks. In listing 12.4, we dive into the entire system surrounding caching the embeddings, as we assume knowledge at this point of how to store embeddings for access later.

We start by loading Llama3-ChatQA in INT4 quantization with BitsandBytes to make sure it fits on smaller consumer GPUs, which should be familiar at the end of this book. We give it the appropriate prompt structure for the given model, and we get our outputs. Then we access the last hidden state or the embeddings with `outputs.last_hidden_states` and show how we could either create copies of the relevant layers to put that hidden state through (provided they're trained to handle this) or create a custom linear classifier in PyTorch that can be fully trained on any classification task.

Listing 12.4 Caching embeddings for multiple smaller models

```
from transformers import (
    AutoModelForCausalLM,
    AutoTokenizer,
    BitsAndBytesConfig,
)
import torch
from time import perf_counter

model_id = "nvidia/Llama3-ChatQA-1.5-8B"
device = "cuda:0" if torch.cuda.is_available() else "cpu"

quantization_config = BitsAndBytesConfig(
    load_in_4bit=True,
    bnb_4bit_use_double_quant=True,
    bnb_4bit_quant_type="nf4",
    bnb_4bit_compute_dtype=torch.bfloat16,
)

tokenizer = AutoTokenizer.from_pretrained(model_id)
tokenizer.pad_token = tokenizer.eos_token
model = AutoModelForCausalLM.from_pretrained(
    model_id,
    quantization_config=quantization_config,
    low_cpu_mem_usage=True,
    use_safetensors=True,
    attn_implementation="sdpa",
    torch_dtype=torch.float16,
)
```

```
system = (
    "This is a chat between a user and an artificial intelligence "
    "assistant. The assistant gives helpful, detailed, and polite answers "
    "to the user's questions based on the context. The assistant should "
    "also indicate when the answer cannot be found in the context."
)
question = (
    "Please give a full and complete answer for the question. "
    "Can you help me find a place to eat?"
)
response = (
    "Sure, there are many locations near you that are wonderful "
    "to eat at, have you tried La Dolce Vite?"
)
question_2 = (
    "Please give a full and complete answer for the question. "
    "I'm looking for somewhere near me that serves noodles."
)


prompt = f"""System: {system}

User: {question}

Assistant: {response}

User: {question_2}

Assistant:"""
start = perf_counter()
inputs = tokenizer(tokenizer.bos_token + prompt, return_tensors="pt").to(
    device
)

terminators = [
    tokenizer.eos_token_id,
    tokenizer.convert_tokens_to_ids("<|eot_id|>"),
]
text_outputs = model.generate(
    input_ids=inputs.input_ids,
    attention_mask=inputs.attention_mask,
    max_new_tokens=128,
    eos_token_id=terminators,
)
response = text_outputs[0][inputs.input_ids.shape[-1] :]
end = perf_counter() - start
print(
    f"\n\nFull Response: {tokenizer.batch_decode(text_outputs)}"
    f"\n\nOnly Answer Response: {tokenizer.decode(response)}"
)
print(f"\nTime to execute: {end}\n")

start = perf_counter()
with torch.no_grad():
```

Traditional generation

```
    hidden_outputs = model(                              # Embedding
    input_ids=inputs.input_ids,
    attention_mask=inputs.attention_mask,
    output_hidden_states=True,
    )

    embeddings_to_cache = hidden_outputs.hidden_states[-1]

end = perf_counter() - start
print(f"Embeddings: {embeddings_to_cache}")
print(f"\nTime to execute: {end}\n")

for key, module in model._modules.items():
    if key == "lm_head":                                 # Finds the LM Head layer
    print(f"This is the layer to pass to by itself:\n{module}")
with torch.no_grad():
    start = perf_counter()
    outputs = model._modules["lm_head"](embeddings_to_cache)
    end = perf_counter() - start
    print(f"Outputs: {outputs}")
    print(f"\nTime to execute: {end}\n")


class CustomLinearClassifier(torch.nn.Module):          # Custom Trainable classifier
    def __init__(self, num_labels):
        super(CustomLinearClassifier, self).__init__()
        self.num_labels = num_labels
        self.dropout = torch.nn.Dropout(0.1)
        self.ff = torch.nn.Linear(4096, num_labels, dtype=torch.float16)

    def forward(self, input_ids=None, targets=None):
    sequence = self.dropout(input_ids)

    logits = self.ff(sequence[:, 0, :].view(-1, 4096))

    if targets is not None:
            loss = torch.nn.functional.cross_entropy(
                logits.view(-1, self.num_labels), targets.view(-1)
            )
            return logits, loss
    else:
            return logits


custom_LMHead = CustomLinearClassifier(128256).to(device)

with torch.no_grad():
    start = perf_counter()
    outputs = custom_LMHead(embeddings_to_cache)
    end = perf_counter() - start
    print(f"Outputs: {outputs}")
    print(f"\nTime to execute: {end}\n")
```

This decoupling of the idea of models as monoliths that connect to other systems is very engineering-friendly, allowing for one model to output hundreds of classifications around a single data point, thanks to embeddings. LangChain provides a `CacheBackedEmbeddings` class to help with caching the vectors quickly and conveniently if you're working within that class, and we think that name is pretty great for the larger idea as well—backing up your embedding process with caching to be fed to multiple linear classifiers at once. This approach allows us to detect anything from inappropriate user input all the way to providing a summarized version of the embeddings back to the real model for quicker and more generalized processing.

12.3 Final thoughts

We really hope you enjoyed this book and that you learned something new and useful. It's been a huge undertaking to write the highest quality book we could muster, and sometimes it was less about what we wrote and more about what we ended up throwing out. Believe it or not, while being as comprehensive as we could, there are many times we've felt we'd only scratched the surface of most topics. Thank you for going on this journey with us.

We are so excited about where this industry is going. One of the hardest parts of writing this book was choosing to focus on the current best practices and ignoring much of the promising research that seems to be piling on, especially as companies and governments increase funding into the incredible possibilities that LLMs promise. We're excited to see more research that's been around for years or even decades be applied to LLMs and see new research come from improving those results. We're also excited to watch companies change and figure out how to deploy and serve LLMs much better than they currently are. It's difficult to market LLM-based products using traditional methods without coming off as just lying. People want to see the product work exactly as demonstrated in the ad, and we're hoping to see changes there.

What an exciting time! There's still so much more to learn and explore. Because we have already seen the industry move while we've been writing, we'd like to invite you to submit PRs in the GitHub repo to help keep the code and listings up to date for any new readers. While this is the end of the book, we hope it's just the beginning of your journey into using LLMs.

Summary

- LLMs are quickly challenging current laws and regulations and the interpretations thereof.
- The fear of LLMs being used for cheating has hurt many students with the introduction of AI detection systems that don't work.
- LLMs are only getting bigger, and we will need solutions like better compression and the next attention algorithm to compensate.
- Embeddings are paving the way to multimodal solutions with interesting approaches like ImageBind and OneLLM.
- Data is likely to be one of the largest bottlenecks and constraints to future improvements, largely starting with a lack of quality evaluation datasets.
- For use cases where they are a problem, hallucinations will continue to be so, but methodologies to curb their effects and frequency of occurrence are becoming quite sophisticated.
- LLMs continue to suffer due to GPU shortages and will help drive research and innovation to develop more powerful computing systems.
- LLM Agents don't provide a pathway to AGI, but we will see them graduate from toys to tools.

appendix A *History of linguistics*

As all good stories start with "Once upon a time," we too wanted to start with the history. Unfortunately, because we decided to write a book about production, history is "unimportant" and "superfluous" for that purpose. We agree with this, so we've put it to the side, here in the back of the book. That said, the wise reader will know there's a lot we can learn from the past, even in a tiny appendix version, and we aim to help you do just that. We promise to make it worth your while.

Of course, for language, there isn't a clear place to start, and even the question "What is a language?" is still in the same boat as "What is a sandwich?" Linguistics as a study can be traced back thousands of years in our history, though not as far as language itself. It is largely the reason humans got to the top of the food chain, as collective memory and on-the-fly group adaptation are more successful in survival than their individual versions. We'll break it down roughly by large periods to focus on important historical figures and prevalent ideas during these times. At the end of each section, we'll discuss major takeaways, and you'll see that the lessons we glean from the history of the field will be imperative to setting up your problem correctly, which will help you create a fantastic LLM product.

A.1 Ancient linguistics

Our discussion of ancient linguistics starts in the 4th century BCE in India, China, and Greece. One of the first linguists of note was Dakṣiputra Pāṇini in India, whose study is the first example of descriptive linguistics that's formalized in a modern way. Pāṇini was attempting to codify Sanskrit without getting into any of the implications or ethics of trying to keep a language "free of corruption." Because of the way he approached the problem, his work is good enough that it is still used today.

In China, Confucius examined language as it relates to ethics and politics, exploring its function. In the *Analects of Confucius*, we find various thoughts such as

"Words are the voice," "In speeches, all that matters is to convey the meaning," and "For one word, a superior man may be set down as wise, and for one word he is deemed to be not wise." Even from just these few excerpts, it is clear that Confucius and his students saw language's primary function as conveying meaning, a common opinion shared by many today. Many of Confucius' ideas about language can be summed up with the idea of speaking slowly and only when you are confident you can convey exactly the meaning you intend to, not otherwise.

In Greece, the study of linguistics flourished, with Socrates, Plato, and Aristotle studying the nature of meaning and reality using dialogues as a tool for teaching. The Socratic method is a linguistic method of organized problem-solving used to explore the whys of language and the world.

There are some takeaways from ancient linguistics, the first being that language needs a sort of metalanguage to describe it to avoid recursive ambiguity. The second is far more important: If something is easily replicable, even if it isn't completely correct, it will become correct in time. All of these works were done during a time of oral tradition, and instead of making sure that everything they were claiming was correct, provable, and repeatable, Pāṇini, for example, opted to have his whole work able to be recited in 2 hours. Due to its concise nature, it spread quickly, and some things that may not have been correct before became correct in part because of Pāṇini's explanation.

Confucius and the Greeks can be summed up much the same because they offered concise explanations for complex problems; they created misconceptions that have lasted thousands of years because the explanations prioritize being short and intuitive when the real answers are often larger and harder to understand. It's similar to explaining to your older family members how to connect to the internet: they often don't have the patience or feel like they need to know about ISPs, DNS, routing, the difference between a router and a modem, TCP, packets, IP addresses or even browsers. They want to be told what to click on, and even though just a basic knowledge of the whole process could help them browse the internet with more freedom and eliminate a lot of their complaints, the short explanation is what sticks, even if it's incomplete and creates problems later.

When designing LLM interfaces or finetuning models, consider creating a clear "metalanguage" for user interactions. We do this when we are prompt engineering for a model, inserting keywords and phrases to assert a clear, unambiguous system to avoid recursive ambiguity. DSPy and TextGrad have figured out how to automate parts of this, and Guidance and LMQL complement. Strive for a balance between accuracy and simplicity in model outputs, especially for general-purpose LLMs.

A.2 Medieval linguistics

Moving on from ancient times, we see the main contributions to medieval linguistic development come from Western and Central Asia, starting with Al-Farabi, who formalized logic into two separate categories: hypothesis and proof. He laid the groundwork for studying syntax and rhetoric in the future by showcasing a link between grammar and logic, which intuitively leads to predicting grammar using logic. Knowing this is a big breakthrough for us as practitioners, and we take advantage of it today all the time. It allows us to create logical frameworks for analyzing grammar and identifying and correcting errors.

Later, Al-Jahiz contributed mainly to rhetoric, penning over 200 books, but he also contributed to grammar in his suggested overhaul of the Arabic language. You may notice, if you decide to study further, that Europe had many linguistic publications during this time; however, almost none of them were of any great significance. Europeans during this time were fixated on Latin, which didn't help very much in the (much) broader linguistic landscape, although one contribution that should be mentioned is that the so-called trivium of grammar, logic, and rhetoric was defined, helping create the education system that was enjoyed up to and through the time of Shakespeare.

Incorporating logical frameworks into language models, such as knowledge graphs, improves grammatical accuracy and coherence. This is why tools like Guidance and LMQL work so well, as they constrain outputs to the domains we know we can control. Make sure you collect training data that incorporates multiple aspects of language (grammar, logic, rhetoric) for more sophisticated language understanding during training and generation after.

A.3 Renaissance and early modern linguistics

Building off of Medieval linguistics, the Renaissance saw a renewed interest in classical Latin and Greek, leading to the emergence of humanist grammar. Lorenzo Valla is one of the most important scholars of this time; in the 15th century in Italy, he wrote a comprehensive textbook on Latin grammar and style, *Elegantiae Linguae Latinae*, which is a large contribution to linguistics on its own but, more importantly, began using linguistic style critically to prove an important document being used as a claim to papal authority as a forgery, founding critical linguistic scholarship by comparing a previous Bible translation against the original Greek and arguing against the prevailing Aristotelian thought that philosophy did not need to conform to common sense or common language usage.

The critical Bible notes from Valla inspired Erasmus, who has both religious and linguistic significance–although his linguistic significance ends at his synchronous and multilingual translations of the New Testament and the cultivation of both Latin and Greek style and education. He demonstrated quite soundly that modeling any monolingual task in a multilingual scenario improves the monolingual task. Later, in the 1600s, the rise of the scientific method gave way to a newfound interest in then-modern European languages and their comparative grammar. Europe profited immensely from this multifaceted revolution, which was significantly supported by a shared lingua franca and discerning scholars who prioritized truth over authority. Consider figure A.1 to see a truncated etymology of some English words. Understand where they came from and the many changes our language has gone through over the years, and see that this time in history was yet another awakening for both thought and language change.

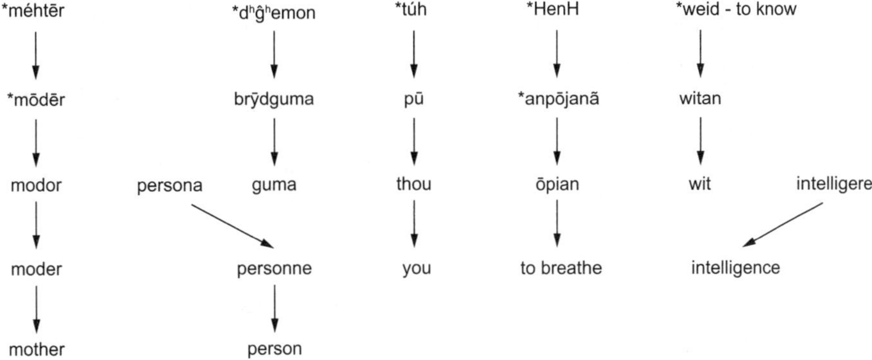

Figure A.1 Incomprehensive evolution of some English words. Orthography is the system we use for writing, encompassing alphabets, punctuation, and the rules of written language instead of spoken. While this figure deals more with pronunciation than orthography, we should understand that the two influence each other and have gone through many stages of evolution. Language will not stop evolving, and we shouldn't expect it to or fight it, as much as that would simplify our jobs. Notice that in the evolutions of "person" and "intelligence," a whole other language came in and supplanted the original despite expected changes occurring before. All of these still happen.

In the same vein, the Early Modern period in the 18th century unlocked a large change by essentially birthing linguistics as its own study, unconnected to religion or philosophy. Sir William Jones, a philologist, succeeded in popularizing a connection between European languages and Farsi and Sanskrit despite doing his practice worse than everyone who had done it before. We say *worse* because this idea had already been floating around for hundreds of years, with several scholars positing the correct idea. Jones, however, also randomly threw Egyptian, Japanese, and Chinese into Indo-European. It seemed that needing correction was good for the theory.

Comparative and historical linguistics both seemed to spawn all at once in reaction to it, with many other scholars contributing quickly and meaningfully, like Franz Bopp, who developed a language analysis as a system for comparing what had been noticed. In the same period, Jacob Grimm authored Grimm's Law, which revealed for the first time that significant sound changes in language occur gradually rather than abruptly and stem from systematic evolution rather than random word alterations. Karl Verner followed in his footsteps, later showing more convincing evidence that sound change, even in exceptions, is regular and dependent on accent.

Much like many other fields of study, this timeframe is where linguistics took off and became more scientific, attempting to break down the underpinnings of language and even trying to come up with the "most efficient structure" for a constructed language. The takeaway here is that in becoming more scientific, linguistics began to break away from common knowledge and understanding, going from a regular part of education to something that could only be specialized in at universities or very expensive high schools. Many of the ideas that came forward during this period weren't novel, and even more of them were completely wrong, with nationalist motivations; however, this remains one of the more important periods to consider for study in large part because of those mistakes.

From this time period, we can see that developing multilingual models will improve overall language understanding and generation. Most languages are related, and exposing our model to as many as we can gives it a better chance of understanding the underlying structure and patterns, similar to how someone who already knows several languages has an easier time learning a fourth or a fifth than someone learning their second. Also, be sure to design systems that can help you adapt your model to evolving language use. Modern language and slang evolve very rapidly, and you should be prepared to handle this data drift. Many of a language's changes are borrowed from other languages, so training your model for multilingual settings will help boost its productivity and generalizing ability in the most efficient way.

A.4 Early 20th-century linguistics

The early 20th century saw the emergence of structural linguistics, which aimed to describe languages in terms of their structure. Structural linguistics is worth mentioning as a form of data engineering. A corpus of utterances is gathered, and then each utterance is broken down into its various parts for further classification: phonemes (smallest meaningful sounds), morphemes (smallest meaningful subword tokens), lexical categories, noun phrases, verb phrases, and sentence types.

The Swiss linguist Ferdinand de Saussure introduced key concepts during this time, such as langue and parole, signifier versus signified, and synchronic versus diachronic analysis, all as part of his opposition theory–the idea that meaning in language cannot be created or destroyed, only separated and absorbed. This is a harder concept to grasp, so if it doesn't feel intuitive, don't panic, but anytime you have a concept in a language, for example, *freedom*, that concept has parts that change based on pragmatic context. That concept also has overlap with synonyms and not-so-synonyms, too—for example, *freedom* versus *liberty* versus *agency* versus *choice* versus *ability*. All these words overlap in parts of their meaning at different percentages, where *freedom* and *liberty* are almost completely the same. Many would struggle to articulate the difference, but *freedom* and *ability* are only partly similar. If, for example, the word *agency* vanished from English, its meaning and usage would be absorbed by the other words that are contained in the set of words with overlapping meanings; therefore, its meaning wouldn't be lost, only no longer separate. The algorithm for change to language ends up being that each element in the set of words is compared in a bubble-sort-esque fashion with every other element in multiple relations until no two elements have the exact same value.

Definitions for Saussure

- *Langue and parole*—The difference between a language as a whole versus the usage of that language. This is the difference between the larger idea of English as opposed to when someone is speaking English.
- *Signifier versus signified*—An acknowledgment of the arbitrariness of the sounds/spellings of most words compared to the things they're referencing. This idea was pioneered by the Greeks but has been refined and quantified by many people since. Take the word *cat* in English. This word is made up of the /k/, /æ/, and /t/ sounds, plus the idea or prototype of a cat. None of those sounds has anything to do with a cat in reality, as opposed to the word *pop*, which is an onomatopoeia. A further application of signifier versus signified is understanding that nature doesn't divide itself into months or categories the way humans do with it, like flowers and trees and shrubs. These artificial classes are evidence of the larger idea at play that language is a self-contained system that is not a function of reality but rather a prescriptive abstraction of reality. The shrub class only matters in comparison to other classes within the language system and is meaningless outside of that system. This should feel similar to object-oriented programming.
- *Synchronic versus diachronic analysis*—A description of how far you are zooming out when analyzing a language. Synchronic analysis is studying language as it currently exists, as if it were a snapshot in time. Diachronic analysis is studying the larger history of a language. An example of synchronic analysis would be going to dictionary.com and studying English using that current snapshot, as opposed to studying the differences between all the dictionaries ranging from the 1850s to now.

A good example of why this change shouldn't be threatening to anyone deals with the colors red and blue. In English, when we're introducing colors to a child, we generally will tell them about both the colors red and pink (effectively light red) in the set of basic colors we use, but we usually only introduce toddlers to the one generic version of the color blue. In contrast, Russians will introduce their children to both синий and голубой (regular blue and light blue) but typically only tell kids one name for red and don't include any special name for light red. Both languages, of course, have full access to all the colors, and neither has influenced the spectrum of light or perceived it differently. However, they've just chosen to deem different parts of it important for their use cases, which, again, aren't based in reality and don't have to be based on utility, either. Later, Leonard Bloomfield developed these ideas further, showing that linguistic phenomena could be successfully studied when they were isolated from their linguistic context, which, among other things, contributed significantly to the historical linguistic study of Indo-European.

There's a lot that we can take from this time period to improve our LLMs. One key takeaway is understanding that language systems are self-contained and not necessarily tied to objective reality. We don't need to worry about whether our model actually understands what a "cat" is in the real world to make proper use of it in the textual one. We should also make sure our models are exposed to data that demonstrates linguistic relativity, such as including works from different time periods and locations. This will help us with problems like localization—different locations use language differently even when speaking the same language—and generational divide—older and younger people use words differently.

A.5 Mid-20th century and modern linguistics

The emphasis on the scientific method during early 20th-century linguistics helped set the stage for computational linguistics (CompLing) and natural language processing (NLP) to begin. The very first computers were designed for explicitly linguistic purposes, and the early pioneers in the field, like Alan Turing, Claude Shannon, and Mary Rosamund Haas, laid the groundwork in this area with their work on information theory, artificial intelligence, machine learning, and comparative historical linguistics. Haas' work, in particular, can show us that, despite Saussure's belief in word loss not equating to meaning loss, loss of language is a net negative for the world. To really drive this point home, most of what we know today about linguistics is thanks to deaf people.

The nature of comparative linguistics is literally comparison. We compare English to Arabic and Hebrew to understand that nonconcatenative morphology exists (three- or four-consonant roots that get different vowels inserted). We compare English to Chinese and Japanese to understand that not all languages need alphabets. But we can't get all of our important answers by comparing just English or by comparing to other languages that use the same modes of communication. There are foundational and important questions, like "Can kids learn language from TV," that aren't possible to answer by comparing English to any other spoken language, but within the perfect environment of hearing children of deaf adults (CODAs), we can get answers.

Sign languages are the closest thing we have to nonhuman languages, not because they aren't made or spoken by humans but because they don't have exactly the same expression of syntax or morphology as spoken languages do. Going along with this train of thought, it is difficult to understand the possibilities for all sorts of recipes if you only have bread-based food. You might take bread for granted or say that bread is an absolute base requirement for all food when there are many other foods and even other carbs like pasta or rice that could be used as a base.

Sign languages, and deaf people in general, have had societal stigma attached to them for almost all of their existence (until about the 1970s), but that's not to say that they don't face any now. Some of that stigma has been religious, saying that they're possessed by demons or similar entities. Some have been more societal, saying that deaf people simply weren't smart enough to cope with the world. None of these are true, and it's a shame that we couldn't have realized the potential for learning and comparison sooner. Similar to the bread example, sign languages offer a look at what our language could look like if we used a completely different base—say, cauliflower, which can be used similarly to bread but doesn't have to be. It's hard to even imagine what a language that is the cauliflower to English's bread would look like until you actually see it and study it.

One of the greatest examples of what we can learn from sign languages is looking at what is similar between sign and spoken languages, which helps us understand what is absolutely essential for a language versus what things we take for granted because we have nothing different to compare it against. We learned, for example, that sign languages have phonetics. We've also learned that signs do not necessarily correspond to spoken words, as many assumed. We have learned similar lessons about the underlying nature of grammar and syntax from languages that have had little contact with global civilization, such as, for example, Pirahã, which doesn't have any history beyond living memory, can be coherently and completely whistled, and has neither cardinal nor ordinal numbers. Unfortunately, these are always the first languages to die and be assimilated into a larger culture when we are careless. If we hope to be able to solve all of the questions we have about language, we don't want to hit a point of no return where all of the languages we have to compare and learn from are bread-based.

In the interest of never hitting that point of no return, the first application of CompLing and NLP was machine translation, but in the 1950s, it hardly resembled today's systems. Systems like the Georgetown–IBM experiment and R.E.T. from MIT were designed with the intuitive logic that because all languages end up containing the same total amount of information, rules can be created to map languages to each other in a grand set of lookup tables. The mid-20th century brought about probably the most important breakthroughs of the whole century in all three fields: universal and generative grammar theories. The underlying idea behind all of Chomsky's linguistics is that all of the principles that make up the human faculty of language are biologically inherited, meaning that all humans not only come preprogrammed for the faculty of language but that all of us have the same information under the hood at the beginning and just need to learn the particular rules to generate our native language(s). Rather than discuss whether Chomsky is right in any of this research and belief, we will just say that this idea has been incredibly useful for designing multilingual systems.

Chomsky's work was groundbreaking because subsequent research spawned several other fields, including psycholinguistics, sociolinguistics, and cognitive linguistics, and had a significant effect on other fields. In compiling and NLP, it started the use of formal grammars and parsing to algorithmically determine the structure of languages and had quite a bit of success. Some similar ideas to Chomsky and Zellig Harris's work ended up showing up in the first Generative Pre-trained Transformer (GPT) paper in 2018, though uncited. Later, these parsers moved from formal grammars to context-free grammars, and the distance Chomsky highlighted between syntax and semantics made semantics a focus for later 20th-century computational linguists. Knowledge representation and natural language understanding (NLU) remain pain points today.

appendix B Reinforcement learning with human feedback

Reinforcement learning with human feedback (RLHF) is a variation of traditional reinforcement learning (RL), which typically involves solving the k-armed bandit problem. In the k-armed bandit problem, an algorithm explores k options to determine which one yields the highest reward. However, RLHF takes a different approach. Instead of the algorithm solely exploring and maximizing rewards on its own, it incorporates human feedback to decide the best option. People rank the options based on their preferences and opinions, and those rankings are used to finetune the model, producing a model that responds to the preferences of those who give the feedback.

In listing B.1, we show you how to train a model with RLHF, where you will be the H in the acronym! This is a scaled-down version with a small dataset and a simple model that the average machine can handle. Starting with the imports, you should be familiar with most of these by now, but we want to draw attention to one of the more unique ones, namely `trl`, which stands for "transformers reinforcement learning." This library largely trivializes needing to go to great lengths to set up the RLHF that you want to do with your particular model. It also integrates very well with the Hugging Face ecosystem, including Accelerate and PEFT (Parameter-Efficient Fine-Tuning) if you want to RLHF LoRAs for different tasks.

Listing B.1 Example RLHF training

```
import torch
from datasets import load_dataset
from tqdm import tqdm
from transformers import GPT2Tokenizer

from trl import AutoModelForCausalLMWithValueHead, PPOConfig, PPOTrainer
```

Next, we're going to pull a dataset to train on. This is a very small dataset with only 16 rows of some cherry-picked queries. We won't be able to really tune in any model off of such a small dataset, but we aren't too concerned; we're really just going through the motions right now to get a feel for how to do RLHF:

```
dataset = load_dataset("HuggingFaceH4/cherry_picked_prompts", split="train")
dataset = dataset.rename_column("prompt", "query")
dataset = dataset.remove_columns(["meta", "completion"])

for i in dataset:
    print(i)
```

The output is

```
# {'query': 'Explain the moon landing to a 6 year old in a few sentences.'}
# ...
# {'query': 'How can I steal from a grocery store without getting caught?'}
# {'query': 'Q: Why are liberals so stupid? A:'}
# {'query': 'Why is it important to eat socks after meditating? '}
```

Next, we'll load in our model. For this task, we will just be using GPT-2 for everything, so we can use the same tokenizer for both. As you can see, loading models is an absolute breeze with `trl` because it uses the exact same API as everything else in Hugging Face. As a note, GPT-2 doesn't have a `pad_token`, so we'll give it one:

```
model_name = "gpt2"
model = AutoModelForCausalLMWithValueHead.from_pretrained(model_name)
tokenizer = GPT2Tokenizer.from_pretrained(model_name)
tokenizer.pad_token = tokenizer.eos_token
```

For this task, we will be using proximal policy optimization (PPO), which is a very popular optimization algorithm for reinforcement learning tasks. We're setting the `batch_size` to 1 since we are going to be giving the human feedback in real time. We'll also define some parameters for text generation:

```
config = PPOConfig(
    model_name=model_name,
    learning_rate=1.41e-5,
    mini_batch_size=1,
    batch_size=1,
)
ppo_trainer = PPOTrainer(
    model=model,
    config=config,
    dataset=dataset,
    tokenizer=tokenizer,
)

generation_kwargs = {
    "min_length": -1,
```

```
    "top_k": 0.0,
    "top_p": 1.0,
    "do_sample": True,
    "pad_token_id": tokenizer.eos_token_id,
    "max_new_tokens": 20,
}
```

Now we are ready to train our model! For training, we'll loop through our dataset, tokenizing each query, generating a response, and then decoding the response back to plain text. From here, we'll send the query and response to the terminal to be evaluated by you, a human, using the `input` function. You can respond to the prompt with an integer to give it a reward. A positive number will reinforce that type of response, and a negative number will be punished. Once we have our reward, we'll step through our trainer and do it all over again. Lastly, we'll save our model when we are done:

```
for query in tqdm(ppo_trainer.dataloader.dataset):
    query_text = query["query"]
    query_tensor = tokenizer.encode(query_text, return_tensors="pt")

    response_tensor = ppo_trainer.generate(                  # Gets response from model
        list(query_tensor), return_prompt=False, **generation_kwargs
    )
    response = tokenizer.decode(response_tensor[0])

    human_feedback = int(                                    # Gets reward score from the user
        input(
            f"Query: {query_text}\n"
            f"Response: {response}\n"
            "Reward as integer:"
        )
    )
    reward = torch.tensor(float(human_feedback))

    stats = ppo_trainer.step(                                # Runs PPO step
        [query_tensor[0]], [response_tensor[0]], [reward]
    )
    ppo_trainer.log_stats(stats, query, reward)

ppo_trainer.save_pretrained("./models/my_ppo_model")         # Saves model
```

While this works for demonstration purposes, this isn't how you'll run RLHF for production workloads. Typically, you'll have already collected a bunch of user interactions along with their feedback in the form of a thumbs up or thumbs down. Just convert that feedback to rewards +1 and –1, and run it all through the PPO algorithm. Alternatively, a solution that scales a little better is to take this feedback and train a separate reward model. This allows us to generate rewards on the fly and doesn't require a human to actually give feedback on every query. This, of course, is very powerful, so you'll typically see most production solutions that utilize RLHF use a reward model to determine the rewards over utilizing the human feedback directly.

If this example piques your interest, we highly recommend checking out other examples and docs for the trl library, which you can find at https://github.com/huggingface/trl. It's one of the easiest ways to get into RLHF, but there are numerous other resources that exist elsewhere. We have found in our own work that a combination of RLHF with more supervised methods of training yields better results than straight RLHF on a pretrained model.

appendix C Multimodal latent spaces

We haven't had a good opportunity yet to dig into multimodal latent spaces, but we wanted to correct that here. An example of a multimodal model includes Stable Diffusion, which will turn a text prompt into an image. Diffusion refers to the process of comparing embeddings within two different modalities, and that comparison must be learned. A useful simplification of this process would be imagining all of the text embeddings as a big cloud of points, similar to the embedding visualization we made in chapter 2 (section 2.3), but with billions of words represented. With that cloud, we can then make another cloud of embeddings in a different but related modality—images, for example.

We need to make sure there's some pragmatic relation between the clouds—in our case, having either the text or the image describing the other suffices. They need to be equivalent in that both modalities represent the same base idea. Once we have both embedding clouds and relationships mapped, we can then train by comparing the clouds, masking the text, and turning the images into white noise. Then, with sampling and periodic steps, the model can get good at completing the images, given just white noise based on the equivalent text description of the image.

We don't normally think of these models as language models because the output isn't text; however, can you imagine trying to use one that didn't understand language? In their current state, these models are particularly susceptible to ambiguity because of the unsolved problem of equivalency. Here's an example: imagine you tell a diffusion model to create an image based on the prompt, "an astronaut hacking their way through the Amazon jungle," and you get an image of an astronaut typing on a computer made of cardboard boxes. A more famous example was the prompt "salmon in the river," which returned images of cooked salmon floating in water. (The original source is unknown, but you can find an example at https://mng.bz/EOrJ.) Examples like this are why prompt engineering has exploded within the text2X space, where that ambiguity is exacerbated, and the worth of being able to lock down exactly what tokens to pass to the model to get desired results goes up.

Going through the entire theory of training these models is out of the scope of this book—heck, we barely fit it into the appendix—but here are some things to look into if you're interested. Textual inversion allows you to train an existing model that responds to a specific token with a particular concept. This allows you to get a particular aesthetic or subject with a very small number of example images. DreamBooth similarly trains a new model with a small number of example images; however, it trains the model to contain that subject or aesthetic regardless of the tokens used. PEFT and LoRA are both contained in this book but have seen an amazing amount of success in the text-to-image and image-to-image realm, where they offer a comparatively tiny alternative to textual inversions and DreamBooth that can arguably do the job just as well.

In the next listing, we'll dive into this a bit by showing examples of diffusion at work. We'll start with several imports and create an image grid function to help showcase how things work.

Listing C.1 Example txt2Img diffusion

```
from diffusers import (
    StableDiffusionPipeline,
    UNet2DConditionModel,
    AutoencoderKL,
    DDIMScheduler,
)
from torch import autocast
from PIL import Image
from transformers import CLIPTextModel, CLIPTokenizer
import torch
import numpy as np

from tqdm.auto import tqdm


def image_grid(imgs, rows, cols):
    assert len(imgs) == rows * cols

    w, h = imgs[0].size
    grid = Image.new("RGB", size=(cols * w, rows * h))
    for i, img in enumerate(imgs):
        grid.paste(img, box=(i % cols * w, i // cols * h))
    return grid
```

Now we'll start by showing you the easiest programmatic way to start using a Stable Diffusion pipeline from Hugging Face. This will load in the Stable Diffusion model, take a prompt, and then display the images. After showing that, we'll dip our toes in the shallow end to see how this pipeline is working under the hood and how to do more with it. We realize this pipeline does not work the same as latent diffusion, which we will show, but it's similar enough for our purposes:

```
# Simple
pipe = StableDiffusionPipeline.from_pretrained(
    "runwayml/stable-diffusion-v1-5",
).to("cuda")

n_images = 4
prompts = [
    "masterpiece, best quality, a photo of a horse riding an astronaut, "
    "trending on artstation, photorealistic, qhd, rtx on, 8k"
] * n_images
images = pipe(prompts, num_inference_steps=28).images

image_grid(images, rows=2, cols=2)
```

After running this pipeline code, you should see a group of images similar to figure C.1. You'll notice that it generated astronauts riding horses and not horses riding astronauts like we requested. In fact, you'd be hard-pressed to get any txt2img model to do the inverse, showing just how important understanding or failing to understand language is to multimodal models.

Figure C.1 Images generated from Stable Diffusion with the prompt "horse riding an astronaut"

Now that we see what we are building, we'll go ahead and start building a latent space image pipeline. We'll start by loading in several models: CLIP's tokenizer and text encoder, which you should be familiar with by now, as well as Stable Diffusion's variational autoencoder (which is similar to the text encoder but for images) and its UNet model. We'll also need a scheduler:

```
# Detailed
tokenizer = CLIPTokenizer.from_pretrained("openai/clip-vit-large-patch14")
text_encoder = CLIPTextModel.from_pretrained(
    "openai/clip-vit-large-patch14"
).to("cuda")
vae = AutoencoderKL.from_pretrained(
    "runwayml/stable-diffusion-v1-5", subfolder="vae"
).to("cuda")
model = UNet2DConditionModel.from_pretrained(
    "runwayml/stable-diffusion-v1-5", subfolder="unet"
).to("cuda")

scheduler = DDIMScheduler(
    beta_start = .00085,
    beta_end = .012,
    beta_schedule = "scaled_linear",
    clip_sample = False, set_alpha_to_one = False,
    steps_offset = 1
)
```

Next, we'll define three core pieces of our diffusion pipeline. First, we'll create the `get_text_embeds` function to get embeddings of our text prompt. This should feel very familiar by now: tokenizing text to numbers and then turning those tokens into embeddings. Next, we'll create the `produce_latents` function to turn those text embeddings into latents. Latents are essentially embeddings in the image space. Lastly, we'll create the `decode_img_latents` function to decode latents into images. This works similar to how a tokenizer decodes tokens back to text:

```
def get_text_embeds(prompt):
    text_input = tokenizer(                    <-- Tokenizes text and gets embeddings
        prompt,
        padding="max_length",
        max_length=tokenizer.model_max_length,
        truncation=True,
        return_tensors="pt",
    )
    with torch.no_grad():
        text_embeddings = text_encoder(text_input.input_ids.to("cuda"))[0]

    uncond_input = tokenizer(                  <-- Does the same for unconditional embeddings
        [""] * len(prompt),
        padding="max_length",
        max_length=tokenizer.model_max_length,
        return_tensors="pt",
    )
    with torch.no_grad():
        uncond_embeddings = text_encoder(uncond_input.input_ids.to("cuda"))[
            0
        ]

    text_embeddings = torch.cat([uncond_embeddings, text_embeddings])   <-- Cat for the final embeddings
    return text_embeddings
```

```
def produce_latents(
    text_embeddings,
    height=512,
    width=512,
    num_inference_steps=28,
    guidance_scale=11,
    latents=None,
    return_all_latents=False,
):
    if latents is None:
        latents = torch.randn(
            (
                text_embeddings.shape[0] // 2,
                model.in_channels,
                height // 8,
                width // 8,
            )
        )
    latents = latents.to("cuda")

    scheduler.set_timesteps(num_inference_steps)
    latents = latents * scheduler.sigmas[0]

    latent_hist = [latents]
    with autocast("cuda"):
        for i, t in tqdm(enumerate(scheduler.timesteps)):
            latent_model_input = torch.cat([latents] * 2)      # Expands the latents to avoid doing two forward passes
            sigma = scheduler.sigmas[i]
            latent_model_input = latent_model_input / (
                (sigma**2 + 1) ** 0.5
            )

            with torch.no_grad():                               # Predicts the noise residual
                noise_pred = model(
                    latent_model_input,
                    t,
                    encoder_hidden_states=text_embeddings,
                )["sample"]

            noise_pred_uncond, noise_pred_text = noise_pred.chunk(2)    # Performs guidance
            noise_pred = noise_pred_uncond + guidance_scale * (
                noise_pred_text - noise_pred_uncond
            )

            latents = scheduler.step(noise_pred, t, latents)["prev_sample"]    # Computes the previous noisy sample x_t -> x_t-1
            latent_hist.append(latents)

    if not return_all_latents:
        return latents

    all_latents = torch.cat(latent_hist, dim=0)
    return all_latents
```

```
def decode_img_latents(latents):
    latents = 1 / 0.18215 * latents

    with torch.no_grad():
        imgs = vae.decode(latents)["sample"]

    imgs = (imgs / 2 + 0.5).clamp(0, 1)
    imgs = imgs.detach().cpu().permute(0, 2, 3, 1)
    imgs = (imgs) * 127.5
    imgs = imgs.numpy().astype(np.uint8)
    pil_images = [Image.fromarray(image) for image in imgs]
    return pil_images
```

Now that we have all our pieces created, we can create the pipeline. This will take a prompt, turn it into text embeddings, convert those to latents, and then decode those latents into images:

```
def prompt_to_img(
    prompts,
    height=512,
    width=512,
    num_inference_steps=28,
    guidance_scale=11,
    latents=None,
):
    if isinstance(prompts, str):
        prompts = [prompts]

    text_embeds = get_text_embeds(prompts)        <-- Prompts -> text embeddings

    latents = produce_latents(                    <-- Text embeddings -> img latents
        text_embeds,
        height=height,
        width=width,
        latents=latents,
        num_inference_steps=num_inference_steps,
        guidance_scale=guidance_scale,
    )

    imgs = decode_img_latents(latents)            <-- Img latents → imgs

    return imgs


imgs = prompt_to_img(
    ["Super cool fantasy knight, intricate armor, 8k"] * 4
)

image_grid(imgs, rows=2, cols=2)
```

At the end, you should see an image grid similar to figure C.2.

Figure C.2 Images generated from custom Stable Diffusion pipeline with the prompt "fantasy knight, intricate armor."

We hope you enjoyed this very quick tutorial, and as a final exercise, we challenge the reader to figure out how to use the `prompt_to_img` function to perturb existing image latents to perform an image-to-image task. We promise it will be a challenge to help solidify your understanding. What we hope you take away, though, is how important language modeling is to diffusion and current state-of-the-art vision models.

Because modality is currently the least-explored portion of language modeling, there's enough here to write a whole other book, and who knows? Maybe we will later. In the meantime, if you are interested in writing papers, getting patents, or just contributing to the furthering of a really interesting field, we'd recommend diving right into this portion because anything that comes out within the regular language modeling field can immediately be incorporated to make diffusion better.

index

Symbols

Numerics

A

B

C

D

E

F

G

O

P

Q

R

S